The *Essential* Handbook of Treatment and Prevention of Alcohol Problems

The *Essential* Handbook of Treatment and Prevention of Alcohol Problems

Edited by

Nick Heather

School of Psychology and Sport Sciences
Northumbria University, UK

and

Tim Stockwell

National Drug Research Institute
Curtin University of Technology, Australia

John Wiley & Sons, Ltd

This publication is designed to provide accurate and authoritative information in regard to the subject
matter covered. It is sold on the understanding that the Publisher is not engaged in rendering professional
services. If professional advice or other expert assistance is required, the services of a competent
professional should be sought.

Other Wiley Editorial Offices

John Wiley & Sons Inc., 111 River Street, Hoboken, NJ 07030, USA

Jossey-Bass, 989 Market Street, San Francisco, CA 94103-1741, USA

Wiley-VCH Verlag GmbH, Boschstr. 12, D-69469 Weinheim, Germany

John Wiley & Sons Australia Ltd, 33 Park Road, Milton, Queensland 4064, Australia

John Wiley & Sons (Asia) Pte Ltd, 2 Clementi Loop #02-01, Jin Xing Distripark, Singapore 129809

John Wiley & Sons Canada Ltd, 22 Worcester Road, Etobicoke, Ontario, Canada M9W 1L1

Wiley also publishes its books in a variety of electronic formats. Some content that appears in print may
not be available in electronic books.

Library of Congress Cataloging-in-Publication Data
International handbook of alcohol dependence and problems. Selections.
 The essential handbook of treatment and prevention of alcohol problems / edited by Nick Heather and
Tim Stockwell.
     p.   cm.
Includes bibliographical references and indexes.
  ISBN 0-470-86296-3
  1. Alcoholism–Treatment–Handbooks, manuals, etc.   2. Alcoholism–Prevention–Handbooks, manuals,
etc.   I. Heather, Nick.   II. Stockwell, Tim.   III. Title.
  RC565.I53425 2004
  616.86′1–dc22
                                                                                        2003014723

British Library Cataloguing in Publication Data
A catalogue record for this book is available from the British Library

ISBN 0-470-86296-3

Typeset in 9^1/$_2$/11pt Times by SNP Best-set Typesetter Ltd., Hong Kong
Printed and bound in Great Britain by TJ International Ltd, Padstow, Cornwall
This book is printed on acid-free paper responsibly manufactured from sustainable forestry
in which at least two trees are planted for each one used for paper production.

Contents

About the Editors

Nick Heather

After working for ten years as a clinical psychologist in the UK National Health Service, in 1979 Nick Heather developed and led the Addictive Behaviours Research Group at the University of Dundee. In 1987 he became founding Director of the National Drug and Alcohol Research Centre at the University of New South Wales, Australia. He returned to the UK at the beginning of 1994 and is now Emeritus Professor of Alcohol and Other Drug Studies at Northumbria University. He has published many scientific articles, books, book chapters and other publications, mostly in the area of addictions and with an emphasis on the treatment of alcohol problems.

Tim Stockwell

Tim Stockwell has been Director of the National Drug Research Institute, Curtin University, Western Australia (formerly the National Centre for Research into the Prevention of Drug Abuse) since June 1996 and served as Deputy Director for seven years prior to that. He studied Psychology and Philosophy at Oxford University, obtained a PhD at the Institute of Psychiatry, University of London, and is a qualified clinical psychologist. He served as Regional Editor for Australasia of the journal *Addiction* for 6 years and has published over 140 research papers, book chapters and monographs, plus several books on prevention and treatment issues. His current interests include alcohol taxation, liquor licensing legislation and the assessment of alcohol consumption and related problems at the community, regional and national levels. He has worked as a consultant to the World Health Organization and the United Nations Drug Control Program.

List of Contributors

Jeff Allison, *Jeff Allison Training Consultancy, 3 Comiston Gardens, Edinburgh EH10 5QH, UK*

Britt K. Anderson, *Portland DBT Program, 5125 SW Macadam Ave., Ste. 145, Portland, OR 97239, USA*

Kevin Boots, *WA Country Health Service, 189 Royal Street, East Perth, WA 6004, Australia*

Janice M. Brown, *RTI International, Research Triangle Park, NC 27709-2194, USA*

Russell Carvolth, *Policy and Projects, Alcohol Tobacco and Other Drug Services, Public Health Services Branch, Queensland Health, GPO Box 48, Brisbane 4000, Australia*

Sally Casswell, *Centre for Social and Health Outcomes Research and Evaluation (SHORE), Massey University, PO Box 6137, Wellesley Street, Auckland, New Zealand*

Jonathan Chick, *Alcohol Problems Clinic, Royal Edinburgh Hospital, 35 Morningside Park, Edinburgh EH10 5HD, UK*

Chad Emrick, *University of Colorado Health Sciences Center, 3525 South Tamatac Drive, Suite 360, Denver, CO 80237, USA*

Paul Gruenewald, *Prevention Research Center, Pacific Institute for Research & Evaluation, 2150 Shattuck Avenue, Suite 900, Berkeley, CA 94704, USA*

Nick Heather, *School of Psychology and Sport Sciences, Northumbria University, Newcastle upon Tyne NE1 8ST, UK*

Linda Hill, *C/- New Zealand Drug Foundation, PO Box 3082, Wellington, New Zealand*

Harold D. Holder, *Prevention Research Center, Pacific Institute for Research & Evaluation, 2150 Shattuck Avenue, Suite 900, Berkeley, CA 94704, USA*

Ross Homel, *School of Criminology and Criminal Justice, Griffith University, West Approach Drive, Nathan, Brisbane, Queensland 4111, Australia*

David Kavanagh, *Department of Psychiatry, University of Queensland, Brisbane, Queensland 4072, Australia*

Harald K.-H. Klingemann, *University of Applied Sciences, School of Social Work, Berne, Switzerland*

G. Alan Marlatt, *Addictive Behaviors Research Center, Department of Psychology, University of Washington, Seattle, WA 98195, USA*

Nyanda McBride, *National Drug Research Institute, Curtin University of Technology, GPO Box U1987, Perth 6845, Western Australia*

Gillian McIlwain, *School of Criminology and Criminial Justice, Griffith University, West Approach Drive, Nathan, Brisbane, Queensland 4111, Australia*

A. James McKnight, *78 Farragut Road, Annapolis, MD 21403, USA*

Richard Midford, *National Drug Research Institute, Curtin University of Technology, GPO Box U1987, Perth 6845, Western Australia*

Kim T. Mueser, *Dartmouth Medical School, Dartmouth Psychiatric Research Center, Main Building, 105 Pleasant Street, Hanover, NH 03301, USA*

Esa Österberg, *Social Research Unit for Alcohol, Studies STAKES, National Research and Development Centre for Welfare and Health, Siltasaarenkatu 18, PO BOX 220, FIN-00531 Helsinki, Finland*

George A. Parks, *Department of Psychology, University of Washington, 2611 NE 125th Street, Suite 201, Seattle, WA 98195-4357, USA*

Duncan Raistrick, *Leeds Addiction Unit, 19 Springfield Mount, Leeds LS2 9NG, UK*

Stephen Rollnick, *Department of General Practice, University of Wales College of Medicine, PO Box 68, Cardiff CF1 3XA, UK*

Harvey Skinner, *Department of Public Health Sciences, Faculty of Medicine, University of Toronto, McMurrich Building, Toronto, Ontario M5S 1A8, Canada*

Tim Stockwell, *National Drug Research Institute, Curtin University of Technology, GPO BOX U1987, Perth, WA 6845, Australia*

Andrew J. Treno, *Prevention Research Center, 2150 Shattuck Avenue, Suite 900, Berkeley, CA 94704, USA*

Robert B. Voas, *Public Services Research Institute, Pacific Institute for Research and Evaluation, Calverton, MD, USA*

Malissa Yang, *Faculty of Health Sciences, McMaster University Medical School, 1200 Main Street W, Hamilton, Ontario L8N 3Z5, Canada*

Preface

Alcohol has been the most widely used mood-altering substance from earliest recorded history. The idea that alcohol consumption sometimes causes medical, personal, social and other harms is as old as the manufacture and consumption of alcohol itself. Today more alcohol is consumed than ever before and the World Health Organization (2002) estimates that globally alcohol misuse caused 1.8 million deaths in the year 2000, compared with only 0.2 million from the use of illicit drugs. Alcohol was the third leading cause of preventable death and disability globally (after smoking and high blood pressure) and in some developing regions of the world alcohol is the leading cause of preventable death and disability (WHO, 2002). Alcohol misuse is also implicated in serious social, economic and legal problems, placing a substantial burden on economically developed and developing countries alike.

In counterpoint to these depressing statistics, the last three decades have also seen an explosion of social, psychological and clinical research to identify effective strategies to prevent and treat alcohol-related problems. This book contains an updated selection of reviews of "what works" in the treatment and prevention of alcohol problems drawn from the critically acclaimed *International Handbook of Alcohol Dependence and Problems* (Heather et al., 2001). These reviews provide authoritative summaries for health and other professionals concerned to provide effective responses to alcohol-related problems.

The *International Handbook of Alcohol Dependence and Problems* was intended to provide a high-level, comprehensive coverage of the entire field of alcohol studies. It contained six sections, 42 chapters and 892 pages, and was aimed primarily at a library market. The substantial text was very favourably reviewed but the book was inevitably expensive and, in fact, priced outside the purchasing range of many practitioners in the area of alcohol problems treatment and prevention, the very people with whom we were most concerned to communicate.

It was therefore decided to produce a slimmed-down and more affordable version of the handbook and this has resulted in the present volume. The problem of which chapters to leave out and which to keep was easily solved; since the new book was aimed mainly at practitioners in the field, we decided that it was the chapters in the last two parts of the *International Handbook* on the treatment and the prevention of alcohol problems that would have most practical relevance to our intended readership and which it was therefore *essential* to retain. It should immediately be noted that this *Essential Handbook of Treatment and Prevention of Alcohol Problems* is not a new edition of the retained chapters from the *International Handbook* but rather an updated reprint of them. We asked authors to restrict themselves to a few, minor changes—mainly to updates on factual information, new references and the correction of typographical and other small errors, as would normally be done in a reprint of an existing book.

In the original handbook our contributors, who included many internationally recognized experts on their chosen topics, were asked to write authoritative, science-based reviews of knowledge in their areas of special interest. They were asked not to attempt a theoretical or research "cutting edge" of their topics, since these may be found elsewhere in more narrowly focussed works or peer-reviewed journals. Rather, they were requested to compile a general, up-to-date summary of knowledge in their respective areas, making decisions about what was of primary importance to include in such a summary. With this remit in mind, we also requested that referencing should be selective, with an emphasis on key hypotheses and the most prominent research findings.

There were several features of the original handbook that have proved successful and which we have kept here. These are the short synopsis at the beginning of each chapter that aims to summarize its contents in accessible language, the list of Key Works and Suggestions for Further Reading at the conclusion of each chapter and the Editor's Introduction preceding each Part of the book, with the aim of describing the wider context of the subject matter in the chapters of the section and of preparing the ground so that the reader can obtain maximum benefit from them.

Despite the omission of the four major sections that led up to the parts on treatment and prevention, it is obvious that those earlier parts are still relevant to a full understanding of the background to the material in this *Essential Handbook*. Thus, for example, the six chapters in the original Part III on "Antecedents of Drinking, Alcohol Problems and Dependence" all bear on the forms taken by the modern approaches to treatment that are described in the present Part I on treatment and recovery. Similarly, the five chapters in the original Part IV on "Drinking Patterns and Types of Alcohol Problem" make clear connections with the chapters in the present Part II on prevention. We would be delighted if interested readers found this to be sufficient motivation to invest in a copy of the *International Handbook* but, failing that, we encourage them to consult a library copy.

Many thanks are due to Laura Reynolds for help in the compilation of the indexes. On behalf of the contributors to the *Essential Handbook*, we are grateful to Vivien Ward of John Wiley and Sons for first suggesting the idea of this book and to Lesley Valerio, Deborah Egleton and other staff at Wiley for their help in producing it.

Nick Heather
Tim Stockwell
May 2003

REFERENCES

Heather, N., Peters, T.J. & Stockwell, T. (Eds) (2001). *International Handbook of Alcohol Dependence and Problems*. Chichester: John Wiley and Sons.

World Health Organization (2002). *World Health Report 2002: Reducing Risks, Promoting Healthy Life*. Geneva: World Health Organization.

Part I

Treatment and Recovery

Edited by Nick Heather
*School of Psychology and Sport Sciences, Northumbia University,
Newcastle upon Tyne, UK*

EDITOR'S INTRODUCTION

This is a very exciting time in the science of treatment for alcohol dependence and problems, a time of uncertainty but also of great promise. It should always be remembered that
the scientific study of treatment in this field is a relatively recent phenomenon, with very
few outcome studies or controlled trials appearing before the end of World War II. In the
years since then, the volume of scientific work has steadily grown from a trickle to a veri-
table flood and we are now confronted with a massive number of relevant publications in
the scientific literature. More important than quantity, the quality of research, too, has
greatly increased over this period; sample sizes, levels of methodological and statistical
sophistication, and standards of scientific reporting have all shown marked improvements.
We are now seeing a growing tendency towards multicentre and cross-cultural research and
this can only increase the amount of secure knowledge in the field. The closing years of the
twentieth century witnessed the publication of results from the largest and most expensive
randomized controlled trial ever mounted, not only of treatment of alcohol problems but
of any kind of psychosocial treatment for any type of disorder (Project MATCH Research
Group, 1997a,b, 1998). Any evaluation of the "state of the art" of alcohol treatment research
must use this study as its starting point.

Ironically, it is the results of Project MATCH that have been partly responsible for the
present uncertainty in the field. There was a time during the late 1970s and early 1980s
when, following the classic publications by Emrick (1975) and Edwards et al. (1977), the
question was seriously asked whether treatment for alcohol problems could be said to work
at all (see Chapter 8, this volume). During the 1980s, the great hope for an improvement
in success rates was perceived to lie in the potential for client–treatment matching (Institute of Medicine, 1990), i.e. the simple idea, commonplace in many areas of health care,
that certain types of client need certain types of treatment to show maximum benefit.
It was this matching hypothesis that Project MATCH was designed to test. While four clinically useful matching effects were identified in the project (see Project MATCH Research
Group, 1997a,b, 1998), the more general hypothesis, that careful matching would improve
overall success rates, was not confirmed. While this result does not completely invalidate
the potential usefulness of client–treatment matching, since several possible forms of
matching were not investigated by Project MATCH (see Heather, 1999), it is clearly disappointing to those who believed that matching represented the best prospect for a radical
improvement in the effectiveness of treatment for alcohol problems.

Another unsettling finding from Project MATCH was that, irrespective of any
client–treatment matches that did or did not appear, the overall effectiveness of the three
treatments studied—Cognitive-behavioural Coping Skills Therapy (CBT), Motivational
Enhancement Therapy (MET) and Twelve-step Facilitation Therapy (TSF)—was about the
same. This pattern did not change throughout a 3 year follow-up period (Project MATCH
Research Group, 1998). This certainly does not mean that the treatments studied were ineffective; on the contrary, although the design did not include a "no treatment" control group,
the absolute success and improvement rates of all three treatment modalities were impressive—higher than reported in most other studies and clearly higher than those typically
found among routine treatment services. This encourages the idea that, if routine treatment
were carried out to the high standards of therapist training and quality control of treatment delivery shown in Project MATCH, the effectiveness of everyday service provision
could be significantly increased; in short, Project MATCH showed that treatment *can* be
highly effective if delivered in the right way.

Nevertheless, the lack of statistical and clinically relevant differences between the three
MATCH treatments is disappointing to those who had hoped for unambiguous answers
to crucial questions regarding the possible superiority of one form of treatment over

others—in other words, to the clear identification of a main "treatment of choice" for alcohol problems. From the most pessimistic point of view, the conclusion from the MATCH findings might be that it does not matter what kind of treatment one gives problem drinkers, they will show the same degree of improvement from all of them. While this is obviously to overstate the case, views of this kind are often heard and suggest that variables other than treatment type—perhaps client motivation to change, level of therapist skill or empathy, or a combination of both—are mainly responsible for variations in treatment outcome.

How can all this be reconciled with the main conclusion of Janice M. Brown's overview of the treatment effectiveness literature in Chapter 1—the conclusion that there are clear and large differences in the effectiveness of different types of treatment for alcohol problems? In fact, the difficulty is more apparent than real. In the first place, two of the MATCH treatments, CBT and MET, are among those listed by Brown as effective treatments; many of the components of CBT, such as social skills training and relapse prevention methods, are well supported by research evidence; and the effectiveness of MET is consistent with evidence that motivational interviewing receives "overwhelming support" (Chapter 1, p. 11) from the literature. Although most of the studies supporting motivational interviewing targeted the non-treatment population of heavy drinkers (see Chapter 8), the evidence at least shows that this is an effective way of persuading people to change their drinking behaviour. TSF, the other treatment modality included in Project MATCH, had not previously been examined in a controlled trial and it has not been possible, for obvious reasons, to conduct a randomized controlled trial of the effectiveness of Alcoholics Anonymous (see Chapter 11, this volume). Thus the literature prior to Project MATCH provides no evidence either way on the effectiveness of Twelve-step approaches.

There is still the difficulty that, with a few exceptions, Project MATCH gave no grounds for the encouragement of client–treatment matching and, while a number of effective treatments are listed in Chapter 1, there is little clear guidance available on which types of client should be offered each of them. However, the MATCH findings apply only to *systematic* client–treatment matching, i.e. to a formal treatment system with rules to channel clients into specific types of therapeutic approach; they have little or no bearing on the traditional clinical skill of tailoring treatment to the unique needs, goals and characteristics of a particular client in the individual case. Thus, the evidence shows that treatment providers have available to them a range of effective treatments from which to select the approach that appears, on clinical grounds, to give the client the best chances of improvement—in the words of Miller et al. (1998), a "wealth of alternatives" from which to choose.

Another valuable conclusion from Chapter 1 is that there is a range of treatments for which there is no evidence of effectiveness. This does not mean that there has been no research on these treatments but that there has been research, in some cases extensive, that has failed to provide any grounds for confidence in these treatments. From her own national perspective, Brown remarks that all these ineffective approaches are typically offered in US treatment programmes and, combined with the fact that the effective treatments are typically not used (Miller & Hester, 1986), this is one of the most outstanding examples one could find of the oft-lamented gap between research evidence and clinical practice. Although this situation might not be so bad in some other countries, there is probably no national treatment service to which it does not apply to some extent.

Yet another useful aspect of Chapter 1 is the focus on the economic aspects of treatment delivery. It cannot be repeated often enough that, even in the richest countries of the world, demand for health care provision will always exceed supply. Thus, the recent emphasis in research on the cost–benefits and cost–effectiveness of treatment for alcohol problems should not be seen as an attempt to palm off problem drinkers with second-best treatment but, on the contrary, as a rational response to the situation of ever-increasing demands for treatment in the face of limited health care resources, with the aim of ensuring that alcohol treatments retain their place in the panoply of treatment services on offer. This issue is especially relevant to an evaluation of brief intervention and is explored further in Chapter 8.

However potentially effective a treatment might be, it is essential that it is appropriate to the client's needs and circumstances, and also that there is a solid basis for deciding whether or not it has been successful and to what degree. This is the area of assessment and is the topic of Chapter 2 by Yang & Skinner. The authors include both brief intervention and specialized treatment within the remit of their chapter and make a useful practical distinction between two forms of assessment—alcohol problem identification and comprehensive assessment. It is often said that assessment, rather than being a quite separate process from treatment proper, is the first step in a competent and effective treatment programme, and this emerges clearly from Chapter 2.

In many ways, detoxification is the least controversial aspect of treatment for alcohol problems and the one where there is most agreement among practitioners and researchers alike. In Chapter 3, Duncan Raistrick describes the alcohol withdrawal syndrome in detail before stating that detoxification is usually a very straightforward procedure. However, the exceptions to this rule are sufficiently serious in their consequences that clinicians are advised to maintain vigilance throughout the detoxification procedure. The indications for and uses of a number of drug treatments and adjunctive therapies are described, while the need for accurate measurement of withdrawal severity and the outcome of detoxification is stressed. What may be found controversial is Raistrick's view that "dependence should be seen as a purely psychological phenomenon to which withdrawal makes some, quite limited contribution" (p. 36). This well-argued case deserves serious consideration.

Pharmacological agents are, of course, the main method of treatment for the alcohol withdrawal syndrome. However, Chapter 4 by Jonathan Chick is not concerned with this use of therapeutic drugs but with the effort to change harmful drinking behaviour and, in particular, with ways to prevent relapse (see also Chapter 6). The last decade has seen major developments in this area, most notably research and implementation in practice of acamprosate, naltrexone and other opioid antagonists, and serotonin-enhancing drugs such as fluoxetine (Prozac). These drugs are described in Chapter 4, as well as more traditional agents used in the treatment of alcohol problems, such as disulfiram and other deterrent drugs. In a useful review, Chick provides information on mode of action, evidence of efficacy, characteristics of responders, interaction with other therapies, unwanted effects, use in practice and what to tell patients. An important conclusion of this chapter is that evidence favours the use of these drugs in combination with some form of psychosocial therapy and that, at best, they "are only an aid to establishing a change in lifestyle" (p. 64).

Part I then proceeds with chapters written by the same team of authors (Parks, Marlatt & Anderson) on two related treatment approaches. However, the extensive research evidence on them and their importance in the spectrum of currently available treatment modalities justifies the inclusion of separate chapters in the book. Both chapters form part of a cognitive-behavioural approach to problem drinking, but Chapter 5 deals with assessment and intervention procedures designed to facilitate an initial change in behaviour, whereas Chapter 6 is concerned with the attempt to ensure that initial gains are maintained over time. With regard to the latter, the work of G. Alan Marlatt and his colleagues in the late 1970s and early 1980s, summarized in the book by Marlatt & Gordon (1985), ushered in a revolutionary change in thinking about and treating alcohol use disorders. While others may have observed before that alcohol dependence and other addictive behaviours were essentially relapsing conditions, the implications of this simple observation had not previously been logically explored, rigorously investigated and developed into a highly practical approach to treatment. As a consequence, relapse prevention therapy came to exert a profound influence on research and practice in the addictions field throughout the world. With regard to the more general cognitive-behavioural perspective, it is fair to say that, as a body of treatment principles, methods and procedures, it is the approach to treatment of alcohol problems best supported by research evidence of any yet devised. These secure scientific foundations, together with the flexibility and usefulness of the approach, are well illustrated in Chapters 5 and 6.

The approach to treatment that could be considered in the last decade to have rivalled or even surpassed cognitive-behavioural therapy in popularity among professionals in the alcohol field is motivational interviewing, and this is the topic of Chapter 7 by Rollnick & Allison. Beginning with a classic article by W.R. Miller in 1983, the principles and methods of motivational interviewing have exerted a profound and lasting influence on therapeutic interactions with problem drinkers all over the world, an influence that was reinforced with the publication of a widely-read text by Miller and one of the authors of Chapter 7 (Miller & Rollnick, 1991, 2002). The very popularity of this approach means that it must have struck a chord in the experience of many people working to help problem drinkers. The chapter outlines the practice of motivational interviewing, and the key principles and core skill areas of the method. The relevant research evidence is briefly reviewed and the main opportunities and limitations of motivational interviewing are discussed.

The chapters in this section described so far include a number of important and relatively recent changes in the treatment of alcohol problems. Yet another of these crucial developments is what has become known as the "broadening of the base" of treatment, i.e. the move away from an almost exclusive preoccupation in the disease theory of alcoholism with the relatively few severely dependent individuals in society to a wider focus on the total range of alcohol-related harm, as represented by the many levels and varieties of harm that exist. This expansion of concern, which can best be seen as part of a public health perspective on alcohol problems, was first evident in the late 1970s (see Heather & Robertson, 1981) but was well summarized by a book by the Institute of Medicine in the USA in 1990. In practical terms, the chief component of this broadening of the base of treatment is the advent of "brief interventions" and this is the subject matter of Chapter 8 by Nick Heather. However, the chapter begins by making a clear distinction between two different classes of activity that have been called brief interventions—brief treatment and opportunistic brief intervention—and the need for this distinction, for the purposes of clarity and progress in the field, is explained. The chapter goes on to consider the origins of interest in both classes of brief interventions, the evidence bearing on their effectiveness, the range of applications associated with them and their potential benefits for the effort to reduce alcohol-related harm on a widespread scale. Both classes of intervention have important implications for the cost-effectiveness of services which are also described in the chapter.

The most recent issue to have captured the attention of treatment providers is the difficulty in providing adequate help to people who suffer from both addictive disorders and other psychiatric disturbances. This difficulty has been long recognized in the literature but it is only within the last decade or so that research and practice have given serious attention to ways it might be solved. Certainly, no book claiming to cover the current treatment of alcohol problems could be considered complete without separate attention to the area of comorbidity with psychiatric disorder. In Chapter 9, Mueser & Kavanagh begin by reviewing research on the prevalence of various types of comorbidity before describing the main principles and methods underlying treatment. The authors make a strong case for an integrated and systematic approach to the treatment of comorbidity and for the need to provide specialized approaches to particular psychiatric disorders among those with alcohol use disorders.

Despite justified optimism about the actual and potential effectiveness of treatment for alcohol problems, it is always salutary to remind ourselves that many people recover from alcohol dependence and problems, sometimes of a severe kind, without any professional help. Apart from any other consideration, it is obvious that treatment providers, theorists and researchers alike can learn a great deal from the study of such people. The two main ways in which recovery is accomplished without professional assistance are described in the remaining chapters of the section. In Chapter 10, Harald K.-H. Klingemann discusses natural recovery from alcohol problems by placing it within the context of recovery from addictive disorders in general, arguing that the nature of "self-change" demands revisions to standard conceptions of addiction itself. In reviewing research evidence in this area, Klingemann highlights the methodological problems this research faces. The chapter concludes with a discussion of the implications of the evidence on self-change for both treatment and policy regarding addictive disorders.

In the second chapter concerned with recovery without professional help, and the last in Part I, Chad Emrick describes and discusses the Fellowship of Alcoholics Anonymous (AA) and other mutual-aid groups in Chapter 11. In modern times, AA affiliates were the first to offer any kind of organized help to people suffering from alcohol dependence and problems in the 1930s and did so, moreover, in the face of professional and scientific indifference; there is no doubt that the Fellowship has saved the lives of hundreds of thousands of people since that time. It must also be recognized that there has often been a conflict of beliefs, perspectives and priorities between AA and the formal treatment and scientific community interested in alcohol problems, a conflict summarized some time ago as that between the "craftsman" and the "professional" (Kalb & Propper, 1976; Cook, 1985). More recently, however, there are signs that a form of *rapprochement* has been reached between the two sides, especially since the abatement of the so-called "controlled drinking controversy" (see Heather & Robertson, 1981; Roizen, 1987). One mark of this is the publication of a volume on research approaches to AA (McCrady & Miller, 1993). Another is that the primary purpose of Chapter 11 is "to inform health care workers and other interested readers about Alcoholics Anonymous" (p. 178). In addition to this advice and several other useful kinds of information, Emrick describes a range of mutual-aid groups from around the world that are not based on the AA Twelve Steps. The significance of these groups, and especially of the newer ones such as Rational Recovery, Secular Organizations for Sobriety and Women for Sobriety, is that they may be able to retain the considerable benefits of mutual aid without also insisting on the spiritual content of AA which, while many find it essential to their recovery, others find unacceptable.

REFERENCES

Cook, D.R. (1985). Craftsman vs. professional: analysis of the controlled drinking controversy. *Journal of Studies on Alcohol,* **46**, 433–442.

Edwards, G., Orford, J., Egert, S., Guthrie, S., Hawker, A., Hensman, C., Mitcheson, M., Oppenheimer, E. & Taylor, C. (1977). Alcoholism: a controlled study of "treatment" and "advice". *Journal of Studies on Alcohol,* **38**, 1004–1031.

Emrick, C.D. (1975). A review of psychologically oriented treatment of alcoholism: II. The relative effectiveness of different treatment approaches and the effectiveness of treatment vs. no treatment. *Quarterly Journal of Studies on Alcohol,* **36**, 88–108.

Heather, N. (1999). Some common methodological criticisms of Project MATCH: are they justified? *Addiction,* **94**, 36–39.

Heather, N. & Robertson, I. (1981). *Controlled Drinking.* London: Methuen.

Institute of Medicine (1990). *Broadening the Base of Treatment for Alcohol Problems.* Washington, DC: National Academy Press.

Kalb, M. & Propper, M.S. (1976). The future of alcohology: craft or science? *American Journal of Psychiatry*, **133**, 641–645.

McCrady, B.S. & Miller, W.R. (Eds) (1993). *Research on Alcoholics Anonymous: Opportunities and Alternatives*. New Brunswick, NJ: Rutgers Center of Alcohol Studies.

Marlatt, G.A. & Gordon, J.R. (1985). *Relapse Prevention: Maintenance Strategies in the Treatment of Addictive Behaviors*. New York: Guilford.

Miller, W.R. (1983). Motivational interviewing with problem drinkers. *Behavioural Psychotherapy*, **1**, 147–172.

Miller, W.R. & Hester, R.K. (1986). The effectiveness of alcoholism treatment: what research reveals. In W.R. Miller & N. Heather (Eds), *Treating Addictive Behaviors: Processes of Change* (pp. 121–174). New York: Plenum.

Miller, W.R. & Rollnick, S. (1991). *Motivational Interviewing: Preparing People to Change Addictive Behavior*. New York: Guilford.

Miller, W.R. & Rollnick, S. (2002). *Motivational Interviewing: Preparing People for Change* (2nd edition). New York: Guilford.

Miller, W.R., Andrews, N.R., Wilbourne, P. & Bennett, M.E. (1998). A wealth of alternatives: effective treatments for alcohol problems. In W.R. Miller & N. Heather (Eds), *Treating Addictive Behaviors*, 2nd edn (pp. 203–216). New York: Plenum.

Project MATCH Research Group (1997a). Matching alcoholism treatments to client heterogeneity: Project MATCH posttreatment drinking outcomes. *Journal of Studies on Alcohol*, **58**, 7–29.

Project MATCH Research Group (1997b). Project MATCH secondary *a priori* hypotheses. *Addiction*, **92**, 1655–1682.

Project MATCH Research Group (1998). Matching alcoholism treatments to client heterogeneity: Project MATCH three-year drinking outcomes. *Alcoholism: Experimental & Clinical Research*, **22**, 1300–1311.

Roizen, R. (1987). The great controlled-drinking controversy. In M. Galanter (Ed.), *Recent Developments in Alcoholism*, Vol. 5 (pp. 245–279). New York: Plenum.

Chapter 1

The Effectiveness of Treatment

Janice M. Brown
RTI International, Research Triangle Park, NC, USA

Synopsis

Over the past decade, the treatment outcome research has consistently shown that there are effective treatment approaches for alcohol problems. These approaches include brief interventions and motivational interviewing, social skills training, community reinforcement, behavior contracting, relapse prevention and some aversion therapies. The commonality among these treatment approaches is the focus on actively engaging the client in the processes of suppressing use and teaching alternative coping skills. Research has also indicated that some of the more typical US treatment components are not effective and often show no improvement or worse outcomes when compared to well-articulated interventions.

Pharmacologic agents that suppress the desire to drink have shown promise in reducing alcohol consumption. Naltrexone, an opiate receptor antagonist, has demonstrated effectiveness in several well-controlled studies. Withdrawal medications, psychiatric agents, and disulfiram show more limited effectiveness in US populations.

There are a number of additional factors to consider when determining treatment effectiveness. Comorbidity of psychiatric diagnoses often complicates the picture and calls for a broader focus. Factors such as therapist characteristics and treatment setting frequently interact with treatment type. Research indicates that, in general, an empathic approach, in which one demonstrates respect and support of patients, appears to be most effective. The ongoing issue of inpatient vs. outpatient treatment remains equivocal. However, recent concerns over containment of health care costs supports a growing trend to favor outpatient approaches.

The total economic costs of substance abuse remain high. Cost–benefit analyses show that the dollars invested in treatment serve to reduce overall health and social costs. The data indicate that including substance abuse treatment in a comprehensive health care plan can have a significant impact on savings.

The Essential Handbook of Treatment and Prevention of Alcohol Problems. Edited by N. Heather and T. Stockwell.
© 2004 John Wiley & Sons Ltd. ISBN 0-470-86296-3.

A growing body of literature points to the differential effectiveness of treatment approaches for alcohol problems (Finney & Monahan, 1996; Holder et al., 1991; McCaul & Furst, 1994; Miller et al., 1995, 1998). The increased emphasis on accountability in addictions treatment and the current efforts to contain health-care costs have resulted in demands for proof of efficacy for the various approaches. Treatment outcome research is used by practitioners and policy makers to determine the impact of specific treatments, with a particular emphasis on effectiveness and cost-offset. Effectiveness concerns whether specific improvements (e.g. family relationships, general functioning, emotional/physical health) have resulted from the application of a particular modality. Cost-offset refers to whether addictions treatment "pays" for itself by reducing subsequent expenses (e.g. reduced accidents, improvements in work performance).

Over the past 40 years, treatments for alcohol problems have included insight psychotherapy, brief interventions and motivational approaches, psychosurgery, psychotropic and psychedelic medications, drug agonists and antagonists, electric shock, behavior contracting, marital and family therapy, acupuncture, controlled use, self-help groups, hospitalization, social skills training, hypnosis, outpatient counseling, nausea aversion, relaxation therapy, bibliotherapy, cognitive therapy and surgical implants. With such a diversity of approaches, an important issue is to determine efficacy while at the same time keeping client characteristics and cost-effectiveness at the forefront. This chapter provides a summary of treatment approaches with documented effectiveness as well as those with limited or no treatment efficacy. An economic evaluation of treatment approaches and predictors of treatment outcome are also included.

TREATMENT EFFECTIVENESS

Research indicates that the majority of individuals drink less frequently and consume less alcohol when they do drink following alcoholism treatment (McKay & Maisto, 1993; Moos, Finney & Cronkite, 1990), although short-term outcomes (e.g. 3 months) are more favorable than those from studies with at least a year follow-up. Positive outcomes yield benefits for alcoholics and their families, as well as leading to savings to society in terms of decreased costs for medical, social and criminal justice services. Reviews of treatment outcome for alcohol problems have developed from early efforts to summarize findings (Bowman & Jellinek, 1941), to reports which derived outcome statistics (Emrick, 1974), to more recent publications examining efficacy in controlled studies with data on cost-effectiveness (Finney & Monahan, 1996; Holder et al., 1991; Miller et al., 1995). Clearly, the literature suggests that a variety of approaches can be effective, some more than others because of the nature of the treatment and the intensity of the approach.

Treatment Approaches with Documented Effectiveness

There are a number of treatment protocols for which controlled research has consistently found positive results, with more recent treatment outcome studies taking into account methodological quality (Miller et al., 1995) and cost-effectiveness (Finney & Monahan, 1996; Holder et al., 1991). Research continues to clarify the mechanisms for successful treatment outcome and provided here is a summary of interventions receiving strong support.

Brief Interventions and Motivational Interviewing

Brief interventions (see also Chapter 8, this volume) vary in length from a few minutes to one to three sessions of assessment and feedback. The goals of brief interventions include problem recognition, commitment to change, reduced alcohol consumption and brief skills training. In a review of 32 controlled studies using brief interventions, Bien et al. (1993) reported that brief interventions were more effective than no treatment and often as effective as more extensive treatment. Individuals whose alcohol consumption is high, but who are not necessarily alcohol-dependent, are the primary targets for brief interventions. These approaches have several common components, including providing feedback, encouraging client responsibility for change, offering advice, providing a menu of alternatives, using an empathic approach and reinforcing the client. Brief interventions have also proved effective in reducing tobacco use and other drug use (Heather, 1998). In an atmosphere that promotes harm reduction, brief interventions offer an exciting alternative to more extensive treatment approaches.

Motivational interviewing strategies (see also Chapter 7, this volume) seek to initiate a client's intrinsic motivation to change (Miller & Rollnick, 1991). The approaches are based on the philosophy that ultimately it is the client who holds the key to successful recovery, once a commitment has been established. Understanding ambivalence as a central feature of a client's hesitance to change and using encouragement and empathy to discover what makes it worthwhile to change are central. Tapping into values and providing feedback of risk and harm appear to strengthen clients' commitment. A recent review of motivational treatment approaches offered overwhelming support for the use of these strategies in the early treatment of heavy drinkers in a variety of settings (Miller et al., 1998).

Social Skills Training

Social skills training (see also Chapter 5, this volume) is usually incorporated into a more comprehensive "broad spectrum" approach and includes a focus on communication skills, such as assertiveness, for social relations. In general, the underlying assumption has been that drinking problems arise because the individual lacks specific coping skills for sober living. These deficits can include inability to cope with interpersonal situations as well as deficits in environmental (i.e. work) situations. The competent therapist will investigate the underlying sources of an individual's vulnerability that can precipitate problem drinking. Research suggests that there are a number of domains for skills training: (a) interpersonal skills; (b) emotional coping for mood regulation; (c) coping skills for dealing with life stressors, and (d) coping with substance cues (Monti et al., 1995). The research evidence for the efficacy of social skills training in a comprehensive treatment package is strong and the core elements can be found in many other approaches. Compared with other approaches, social skills training yielded efficacy scores second only to brief interventions and motivational interviewing (Miller et al., 1998). Social skills training can be delivered individually or in group interactions and appears to be particularly appropriate for more severely dependent individuals who are more likely to experience serious psychopathology.

Community Reinforcement

The community reinforcement approach (CRA) attempts to increase clients' access to positive activities and makes involvement in these activities contingent on abstinence (Azrin et al., 1982) (see also Chapter 5). This approach combines many of the components of other behavioral approaches, including monitored disulfiram, behavior contracting, behavioral marital therapy, social skills training, motivational counseling and mood management. Some of the largest treatment effects in the literature have been associated with the community reinforcement approach (Miller et al., 1995). Compared to more traditional treatment approaches, the CRA has been shown to be more successful in helping inpatient or outpatient alcoholics remain sober and employed. Although community reinforcement is a more intense treatment approach, it is consistent with the basic philosophy of several other effective approaches. The ability to establish rewarding relationships, to focus on changing the social environment so that positive reinforcement is available, and to reduce reinforcement for drinking are emphasized with the community reinforcement and other approaches. The key appears to be helping the client to find and become involved in activities that are more rewarding than drinking.

Behavior Contracting

Behavior contracting approaches are drawn from operant conditioning principles (Bigelow, 2001) and are used to establish a contingent relation between specific treatment goals (e.g. attending AA meetings) and a desired reinforcer. Written behavioral contracts are a way of actively engaging the client in treatment. Drinking goals are made explicit and specific behaviors to achieve these goals are outlined. Behavioral contracts are also useful for providing alternative behaviors to drinking. When evaluated either as an individual treatment approach or as part of marital therapy, behavior contracting consistently yielded positive results (Miller et al., 1995).

Aversion Therapies

The primary goal of aversion therapies is to produce an aversive reaction to alcohol by establishing a conditioned response to cues associated with drinking (Drobes et al., 2001). The conditioning can be accomplished by using electric shock, apneic paralysis, chemical agents or imaginal techniques. Overall, results indicate that aversion therapies are effective in the short term with respect to a reduction in alcohol consumption (Miller et al., 1995). However, there appears to be a differential effect for the various forms of aversion. Nausea aversion therapy, in which a drug is administered so that nausea and emesis occur immediately following sipping and swallowing alcoholic beverages, has demonstrated a positive outcome in a number of studies and covert sensitization, which uses imaginal techniques to induce a conditioned aversion, has also shown promising findings, while apneic paralysis and electric shock have shown less encouraging results (Holder et al., 1991; Miller et al., 1995). In general, studies that have carefully defined procedures and which have documented the occurrence of classical conditioning have shown the strongest results.

Relapse Prevention

Relapse prevention constitutes a behavioral approach with the goal of reducing the cues that precipitate relapse to alcohol (see also Chapter 6). Relapse can be triggered by stress, emotional states, craving or environmental stressors, and strategies that teach individuals how to cope with these events have demonstrated success in preventing relapse (Monti et al., 1995). Early approaches to treatment focused on initiating change, but paid little attention to strategies designed to maintain behavior change, with the result that relapse to drinking was the most common outcome of alcohol treatment. Subsequent research on the study of the determinants of relapse led to the development of interventions to increase self-efficacy and coping skills.

Evaluations of the efficacy of relapse prevention efforts have yielded mixed results (Miller et al., 1995), but evidence suggests that interventions focusing on modifying cognitions related to failure and teaching individuals to quickly recover from lapses can be successful (Weingardt & Marlatt, 1998). A number of studies have demonstrated an interaction between self-efficacy and aftercare participation. Individuals with high self-efficacy who also participated more frequently in aftercare sessions had significantly better outcomes than all other groups, but aftercare participation improved treatment outcomes for those initially low in self-efficacy (Rychtarik et al., 1992). Similar results were found in a randomized trial of aftercare participation (McKay, Maisto & O'Farrell, 1993). Additional research has indicated that relapse prevention may be more effective for certain subtypes of alcoholics, and compliance may be indicative of a type of motivation for sustaining change (Donovan, 1998). From a harm-reduction perspective, relapse prevention efforts may serve to lessen the severity of relapse and minimize the harm associated with continuing alcohol use.

Summary

Effective treatments appear to have several common strategies: suppressing use, eliciting motivation for change, and teaching alternative coping skills. Treatment approaches which actively engage the client in the treatment process appear to produce more positive outcomes. Furthermore, studies yielding positive outcomes may provide insight into both the etiology and mechanisms for resolution of alcohol problems.

Treatment Approaches with Limited Evidence of Effectiveness

There are also a number of commonly used treatment approaches that do not show any evidence of effectiveness. These approaches comprise the largest number of treatment studies and are summarized below.

Insight Psychotherapy

Psychotherapy seeks to uncover unconscious causes for a person's alcohol problems. The goal is insight and psychotherapy is frequently studied as an adjunctive component to alcohol treatment. In general, studies do not reveal consistent positive results; in fact, the trend favors patients who did not receive psychotherapy (Miller et al., 1995).

Confrontational Counseling

Confrontational interventions seek to break down defenses, particularly denial. Historically, confrontation has been considered an essential component of alcohol treatment, yet no studies have shown positive findings for approaches using confrontation (Finney & Monahan, 1996; Holder et al., 1991; Miller et al., 1995). In a controlled evaluation of therapist styles, Miller and colleagues (1993) found that confrontation yielded significantly more resistance and predicted poorer outcomes 1 year after a brief intervention. Miller & Rollnick (1991) suggested that confrontation is a *goal* rather than a procedure and that the occurrence of client resistance during a session should serve as immediate feedback for altering the therapeutic approach.

Relaxation Training

The use of relaxation training or other stress reduction techniques has intuitive appeal but there is no scientific evidence to support their use (Miller et al., 1998). The impact of these findings supports the growing doubts that individuals drink to relieve stress.

General Alcoholism Counseling

This type of counseling is usually directive and supportive but not specifically confrontational. One of the difficulties in evaluating general strategies is that they are frequently poorly defined and contrasted with additive components. However, the results of controlled evaluations indicate that alcoholism counseling is ineffective.

Education

Education is without question one of the most common components of standard alcohol treatment programs. The intent is to convey information to help the person change drinking problems. Controlled studies of the use of educational lectures and films have consistently revealed negative findings (Finney & Monahan, 1996; Miller et al., 1998). There is no research support for the notion that alcohol problems result from a lack of knowledge and thus, no impact on outcome from providing the "missing" knowledge.

Milieu Therapy

Implicit in the use of milieu therapy is the idea that recovery is aided by the *place* in which therapy occurs. The therapeutic atmosphere is itself thought to be beneficial. This idea is commonly associated with inpatient or residential programs which seek to promote an atmosphere of healing. Results of controlled research do not provide evidence to support residential/milieu therapy over less costly outpatient treatment and in fact, milieu therapy most frequently yields a less positive outcome when compared to a brief intervention (Miller et al., 1995, 1998).

Summary

It is surprising that virtually all of the ineffective treatment approaches are precisely those offered in the typical US treatment program. Historically, the treatment of alcohol problems has been regularly followed by relapse; thus, one could assume that the "standard" treatment is ineffective. One common theme among ineffective approaches is their vague and imprecise description and, as Miller et al. (1995) have pointed out, well-articulated studies serve to promote treatment effectiveness.

Pharmacologic Approaches

Pharmacological agents for the treatment of alcohol disorders (see also Chapter 4, this volume) have a long history and can be classified according to several major categories: (a) intoxication agents that reverse the effects of alcohol; (b) withdrawal agents; (c) psychiatric comorbidity agents, and (d) desire and compulsion agents. Much has been written about the effectiveness of disulfiram, and treatment outcome reviews generally agree that its effectiveness is limited. Likewise, withdrawal and psychiatric medications appear to be appropriate only for select populations of alcoholics, although this may not be applicable to countries other than the USA.

The current research interest appears to be in medications that target the desire for alcohol. A potential area for study is the opioid system, which has been implicated in alcohol's rewarding effects. Several studies have examined the effectiveness of naltrexone (ReVia), an opiate receptor antagonist, for decreasing alcohol consumption (O'Malley et al., 1992; Weinrieb & O'Brien, 1997). These studies have provided evidence of naltrexone's effectiveness in decreasing alcohol craving and drinking days. Among patients who did return to drinking, those taking naltrexone and who received coping skills training were least likely to return to heavy drinking but the cumulative rate of abstinence was highest for patients who received naltrexone and supportive therapy.

Naltrexone appears to be well-tolerated and effective in helping to stop resumption of binge drinking. There are presently more than a dozen studies examining the various aspects of using naltrexone as an adjunct to alcohol treatment. Future studies will need to determine more specific doses, the optimal duration of treatment, and whether subtypes of alcoholics would benefit from using naltrexone.

PATIENT–TREATMENT MATCHING

An emerging trend in the early 1990s was to look beyond the issues of whether alcohol treatment worked or which treatment was most effective to the possibility that matching individuals to treatment based on individual characteristics would improve treatment outcomes. The idea of matching individuals to treatment was not new to the alcohol field and a review of matching studies indicated that some treatment approaches were, in fact, more effective than others for patients with certain characteristics (Mattson et al., 1994). In order to more clearly make recommendations about patient–treatment matching, the National Institute on Alcohol Abuse and Alcoholism initiated a multisite clinical trial entitled Project MATCH (Matching Alcoholism Treatment to Client Heterogeneity). The goal was to determine whether different types of alcoholics respond selectively to particular treatment approaches. For example, cognitive-behavioral therapy was hypothesized to be more effective for patients with higher alcohol involvement, cognitive impairment and sociopathy. Twelve-step facilitation therapy was hypothesized to be useful for individuals with greater alcohol involvement and meaning seeking. Motivational enhancement therapy was hypothesized to be more effective for clients with high conceptual levels and low readiness to change (Project MATCH Research Group, 1997).

Unfortunately, the results from Project MATCH challenged the view that patient–treatment matching would yield more positive outcomes. That is, there were few differences in outcomes when patients were randomly assigned to three distinctly different treatment approaches (Project MATCH Research Group, 1997). These results should be interpreted cautiously. Clearly, support for various treatment approaches does not mean that all clients will benefit from those approaches, or that no client ever benefits from less effective approaches. The trial demonstrated that regardless of treatment, patients had a greater number of abstinent days and a significant decrease in the number of drinks on drinking days. The results are further complicated by the nature of the study. This was the largest clinical trial ever conducted and each of the treatment approaches was manualized. The careful monitoring of treatment delivery, limiting attrition and delivering an adequate amount of treatment, may have served to make the modalities more similar than different with respect to therapist involvement.

PREDICTORS OF TREATMENT OUTCOME

Treatment modality is not the only criterion that influences treatment outcome. The existence of other psychopathology, the specifics of treatment setting, and therapists' effects all interact to determine treatment effectiveness. These additional variables are gaining interest in the alcohol treatment field and serve to guide treatment decisions.

Cormorbidity

It is only within the last decade that dual-diagnosis patients have received research attention (see also Chapter 9, this volume). The rates of concurrent psychiatric disorders are high and a summary of recent research findings indicated that individuals with comorbid psychiatric diagnoses have poorer alcohol treatment outcomes (McKay & Maisto, 1993). This research takes on significance with respect to matching patients to more appropriate (e.g. psychotherapy) treatments. For example, Longabaugh et al. (1994) reported that alcoholics with antisocial personality disorder (ASP) had better outcomes with a cognitive-behavioral approach when compared to a relationship enhancement approach, and a second study indicated that alcoholics with ASP showed significant improvement in several drinking measures when treated with nortriptyline (Powell et al., 1995). Relatedly, recent studies have examined the effectiveness of treatment for individuals with comorbid drug dependence and reported an increased rate of relapse to both substances (Brower et al., 1994; Brown, Seraganian & Tremblay, 1993). Two of the challenges in treating dual-diagnosed patients are the differences in the nature of their problems and variability in their degree of motivation. Clearly there is a need for longitudinal studies of dual-diagnosis patients. Such research may identify the most effective treatment, provide insight into the temporal order of symptoms in those with anxiety or depressive disorders, and help to provide a theoretical base from which to develop appropriate treatment approaches.

Therapist Effects

Therapist effects can have a significant impact on treatment outcome, yet few studies have controlled for them. The primary characteristics appear to be empathy and respect for patients (Najavits & Weiss, 1994). Given the variability in therapist's styles, the alcohol treatment field has placed more of an emphasis on manualized treatment. Manual-driven treatment controls for variability and attempts to maximize the effects of successful therapist styles. Importantly, the success of brief interventions and motivational interviewing may well be due to the focus placed on empathy and support from the therapist. In fact, several studies identify therapist empathy as the pivotal factor in clients' long-term treatment outcomes (Miller et al., 1998).

Treatment Setting and Treatment Type

Alcohol treatment services are delivered in two primary settings: inpatient and outpatient. Inpatient services typically consist of short-term residential care and are often used for acute detoxification (Brown & Baumann, 1998). Inpatient care also provides intensive, highly structured treatment. Outpatient settings provide more long-term maintenance and can be either intensive, which have been modeled after day treatment programs, or typical, which usually include weekly group therapy sessions. Because of concern over rising health care costs, more emphasis is being placed on outpatient care for all phases of treatment (McCaul & Furst, 1994). Evidence from controlled clinical efficacy studies on the advantages of inpatient vs. outpatient treatment suggests little difference in effectiveness (Institute of Medicine, 1989; Miller et al., 1995). Other treatment variables, such as modality, duration of treatment and therapist characteristics, appear to have a more direct impact on treatment outcome.

There is some evidence that comprehensive treatments are more effective than less intensive approaches (McKay & Maisto, 1993). However, these findings appear to be based on studies of more severe or dual-diagnosed alcoholics. In general, the data do not support intense inpatient treatment for all alcoholics, particularly those with uncomplicated alcohol dependence, but research is lacking on the role of these settings for individuals with additional diagnoses (McCrady & Langenbucher, 1996). With respect to treatment type, a number of approaches have been used, including 12-Step-based approaches, psycho-dynamic therapy and cognitive-behavioral interventions. Holder et al. (1991) concluded that brief interventions and cognitive-behavioral approaches appear to be more effective overall.

COST-EFFECTIVENESS

Costs Associated with Treatment

Whether alcohol treatment services are cost-effective is a fundamental question in this era of cost containment. The issue is one of determining which alcohol treatment modalities are the most effective for the least cost. The results of a meta-analysis of 33 treatment modalities suggested that brief interventions are the most cost-effective treatment and residential-milieu therapies are the least cost-effective (Holder et al., 1991). More recent research differs from these original findings in both cost and effectiveness determinations and points to the need to consider patient subgroups (Finney & Monahan, 1996). Nonethe-less, both studies agreed that the more effective modalities consistently were in the medium-low to low cost range, and modalities with poor evidence were associated with higher costs. An important caveat to these findings is that none of the comparisons were done with individuals who were matched to treatment. It is likely that more expensive, intensive treatments may be necessary and cost-effective for more severe patients.

Cost-offset

Cost-offset has as it fundamental objective cost savings and alone may not be a realistic social policy goal. Decisions not to fund more expensive treatments in an effort to contain costs may have important implications, because if the substance abuse problem worsens, the eventual result will be much higher costs (Fox et al., 1995). Estimates of the extent of alcohol-related hospital utilization are typically based on reviews of medical records and studies indicate that alcohol-related admissions have a significant impact on the cost of inpatient care (Gordis, 1987). In general, the cost-offset literature has focused on the health care costs following treatment and one study demonstrated 24% lower health-related costs for treated vs. untreated alcoholics over a 14 year follow-up period (Holder & Blose, 1992). Other researchers have found that treated alcoholics' use of medical care decreased by 61% in the first year after treatment (Hoffman, De Hart & Fulkerson, 1993), absenteeism and medical claims were reduced (McDonnell Douglas Corporation, 1989) and arrests and incarcerations were decreased (Finigan, 1996). Holder (1998) summarized his review of the research on cost effectiveness with three major points: (1) untreated alcoholics use health care and incur costs at a rate about twice that of their non-alcoholic peers, (2) total health care utilization and costs begin to drop once treatment begins, and (3) there are no appar-ent gender differences in the utilization and associated costs before and after treatment initiation.

SUMMARY

The past 40 years have brought with them a wealth of information about the treatment of alcohol problems. We have convincing evidence for the effectiveness of treatment and are at the frontier of developing new medications to reduce craving and relapse. Typically, in alcoholism treatment, lower cost treatments are at least as effective as more expensive ones and successful treatment is associated with lowered health care costs. Clearly, no one treatment will work for everyone. Perhaps encouraging professionals to adopt a comprehensive treatment program with a variety of approaches will allow more individuals to seek treatment. Encouraging individuals to understand that they have options and that they can be active participants in recovery represents a more sensitive approach to treatment.

KEY WORKS AND SUGGESTIONS FOR FURTHER READING

Hester, R.K. & Miller, W.R. (1995). *Handbook of Alcoholism Treatment Approaches: Effective Alternatives*, 2nd edn. Needham Heights, MA: Allyn and Bacon.

This handbook describes a variety of alternative treatment methods for helping those with alcohol problems. The book is written for practitioners and chapters have been contributed by some of the leading researchers in the field. Each clinical chapter includes an overview of the technique, special clinical considerations and guidelines for clinical applications.

Miller, W.R. & Heather, N. (1998). *Treating Addictive Behaviors*, 2nd edn. New York: Plenum.

Written from the perspective of the transtheoretical model of change, this edited book is a compilation of works by authors who base their writing on the latest research in the addictions field. Sections focus on understanding change, preparing for and facilitating change, and sustaining change in individuals who present with addictive behaviors. The book represents a collaboration between basic and applied research.

Miller, W.R. & Rollnick, S. (2002). *Motivational Interviewing: Preparing People for Change, 2nd edn.* New York: Guilford.

This volume is a must for clinicians working with individuals who are ambivalent about changing. This clearly written and immensely useful book outlines the steps to working with challenging clients. Motivational interviewing is detailed and practice exercises are included.

Project MATCH Research Group (1997). Matching alcoholism treatments to client heterogeneity: Project MATCH post-treatment drinking outcomes. *Journal of Studies on Alcohol*, **58**, 7–29.

This article represents an excellent overview of Project MATCH, including methodological details, research hypotheses, and directions for future research. The authors discuss the benefits of matching clients to treatment and provide a useful set of references for treatment delivery.

REFERENCES

Azrin, N.H., Sisson, R.W., Meyers, R. & Godley, M. (1982). Alcoholism treatment by disulfiram and community reinforcement therapy. *Behavior Research and Therapy*, **14**, 339–348.

Bien, T.H., Miller, W.R. & Tonigan, J.S. (1993). Brief interventions for alcohol problems: a review. *Addiction*, **88**, 315–336.

Bigelow, G.E. (2001). An operant behavioral perspective on alcohol abuse and dependence. In N. Heather, T.J. Peters & T. Stockwell (Eds), *International Handbook of Alcohol Dependence and Problems* (pp. 299–315). Chichester, UK: John Wiley & Sons.

Bowman, K.M. & Jellinek, E.M. (1941). Alcohol addiction and its treatment. *Quarterly Journal of Studies on Alcohol*, **2**, 98–176.

Brower, K.J., Blow, F.C., Hill, E.M. & Mudd, S.A. (1994). Treatment outcome of alcoholics with and without cocaine disorders. *Alcoholism: Clinical and Experimental Research*, **18**, 734–739.

Brown, J.M. & Baumann, B.D. (1998). Recent advances in assessment and treatment of alcohol abuse and dependence. In L. Vandecreek, S. Knapp & T.L. Jackson (Eds), *Innovations in Clinical Practice: A Sourcebook*, Vol. 16 (pp. 81–93). Sarasota, FL: Professional Resources Press.

Brown, T.G., Seraganian, P. & Tremblay, J. (1993). Alcohol and cocaine abusers 6 months after traditional treatment: do they fare as well as problem drinkers? *Journal of Substance Abuse Treatment*, **10**, 545–552.

Donovan, D.M. (1998). Continuing care: promoting the maintenance of change. In W.R. Miller & N. Heather (Eds), *Treating Addictive Behaviors*, 2nd edn (pp. 317–336). New York: Plenum.

Drobes, D.J., Saladin, M.E. & Tiffany, S.T. (2001). Classical conditioning mechanisms in alcohol dependence. In N. Heather, T.J. Peters & T. Stockwell (Eds), *International Handbook of Alcohol Dependence and Problems* (pp. 281–297). Chichester, UK: John Wiley & Sons.

Emrick, C.D. (1974). A review of psychologically oriented treatment of alcoholism: I. The use and interrelationships of outcome criteria and drinking behavior following treatment. *Quarterly Journal of Studies on Alcohol*, **35**, 523–549.

Finigan, M. (1996). Societal outcomes and cost savings of drug and alcohol treatment in the state of Oregon. Prepared for the Office of Alcohol and Drug Abuse Programs, Oregon Department of Human Resource, and Governor's Council on Alcohol and Drug Abuse Programs, Salem, OR.

Finney, J.W. & Monahan, S.C. (1996). The cost-effectiveness of treatment for alcoholism: a second approximation. *Journal of Studies on Alcohol*, **57**, 229–243.

Fox, K., Merrill, J.C., Chang, H.H. & Califano, J.A. Jr (1995). Estimating the costs of substance abuse to the Medicaid hospital care program. *American Journal of Public Health*, **85**, 48–54.

Gordis, E. (1987). Accessible and affordable health care for alcoholism and related problems: strategy for cost containment. *Journal of Studies on Alcohol*, **48**, 579–585.

Heather, N. (1998). Using brief opportunities for change in medical settings. In W.R. Miller & N. Heather (Eds), *Treating Addictive Behaviors*, 2nd edn (pp. 133–147). New York: Plenum.

Hoffman, N.G., De Hart, S.S. & Fulkerson, J.A. (1993). Medical care utilization as a function of recovery status following chemical addictions treatment. *Journal of Addictive Disease*, **12**, 97–108.

Holder, H.D. (1998). Cost benefits of substance abuse treatment: An overview of results from alcohol and drug abuse. *Journal of Mental Health Policy and Economics*, **1**, 23–29.

Holder, H.D. & Blose, J.O. (1992). The reduction of health care costs associated with alcoholism treatment: a 14-year longitudinal study. *Journal of Studies on Alcohol*, **53**, 293–302.

Holder, H.D., Longabaugh, R., Miller, W.R. & Rubonis, A.V. (1991). The cost-effectiveness of treatment for alcoholism: a first approximation. *Journal of Studies on Alcohol*, **52**, 517–540.

Institute of Medicine (1989). *Prevention and Treatment of Alcohol Problems: Research Opportunities*. Washington, DC: Institute of Medicine.

Longabaugh, R., Rubin, A., Malloy, P., Beattie, M., Clifford, P.R. & Noel, N. (1994). Drinking outcomes of alcohol abusers diagnosed with antisocial personality disorder. *Alcoholism: Clinical and Experimental Research*, **18**, 778–785.

Mattson, M.E., Allen, J.P., Longabaugh, R., Nickless, C.J., Connors, G.J. & Kadden, R.M. (1994). A chronological review of empirical studies matching alcoholic clients to treatment. *Journal of Studies on Alcohol*, **12**(Suppl.), 16–29.

McCaul, M.E. & Furst, J. (1994). Alcoholism treatment in the United States. *Alcohol Health and Research World*, **18**, 253–260.

McCrady, B.S. & Langenbucher, J.W. (1996). Alcohol treatment and health care system reform. *Archives of General Psychiatry*, **53**, 737–746.

McDonnell Douglas Corporation & Alexander Consulting Group (1989). *Employee assistance program financial offset study, 1985–1988*. Washington DC: McDonnell Douglas Corporation.

McKay, J.R. & Maisto, S.A. (1993). An overview and critique of advances in the treatment of alcohol use disorders. *Drugs & Society*, **8**, 1–29.

McKay, J.R., Maisto, S.A. & O'Farrell, T.J. (1993).   End-of-treatment self-efficacy, aftercare and drinking outcomes of alcoholic men. *Alcoholism: Clinical and Experimental Research*, **17**, 1078–1083.

Miller, W.R., Andrews, N.R., Wilbourne, P. & Bennett, M.E. (1998).   A wealth of alternatives: effective treatments for alcohol problems. In W.R. Miller & N. Heather (Eds), *Treating Addictive Behaviors*, 2nd edn (pp. 203–216). New York: Plenum.

Miller, W.R., Benefield, R.G. & Tonigan, J.S. (1993).   Enhancing motivation for change in problem drinking: a controlled comparison of two therapist styles. *Journal of Consulting and Clinical Psychology*, **61**, 455–461.

Miller, W.R., Brown, J.M., Simpson, T.L., Handmaker, N.S., Bien, T.H., Luckie, L.F., Montgomery, H.A., Hester, R.K. & Tonigan, J.S. (1995).   What works? A methodological analysis of the alcohol treatment outcome literature. In R.K. Hester & W.R. Miller (Eds), *Handbook of Alcoholism Treatment Approaches: Effective Alternatives*, 2nd edn (pp. 12–44). Needham Heights, MA: Allyn and Bacon.

Miller, W.R. & Rollnick, S. (1991).   *Motivational Interviewing: Preparing People to Change Addictive Behavior.* New York: Guilford.

Miller, W.R. & Rollnick, S. (2002).   *Motivational Interviewing: Preparing People for Change* (2nd edn). New York: Guilford.

Monti, P.M., Rohsenow, D.J., Colby, S.M. & Abrams, D.B. (1995).   Coping and social skills training. In R.K. Hester & W.R. Miller (Eds), *Handbook of Alcoholism Treatment Approaches: Effective Alternatives*, 2nd edn (pp. 221–241). Needham Heights, MA: Allyn and Bacon.

Moos, R.H., Finney, J.W. & Cronkite, R.C. (1990).   *Alcoholism Treatment: Context, Process, and Outcome.* New York: Oxford University Press.

Najavits, L.M. & Weiss, R.D. (1994).   Variations in therapist effectiveness in the treatment of patients with substance use disorders: an empirical review. *Addiction*, **89**, 679–688.

O'Malley, S.S., Jaffe, A.J., Chang, G., Schottenfeld, R.S., Meyer, R.E. & Roundsaville, B. (1992).   Naltrexone and coping skills therapy for alcohol dependence: a controlled study. *Archives of General Psychiatry*, **49**, 881–887.

Powell, B.J., Campbell, J.L., Landon, J.F., Liskow, B.I., Thomas, H.M., Nickel, E.J., Dale, T.M., Penick, E.C., Samuelson, S.D. & Lacoursiere, R.B. (1995).   A double-blind, placebo-controlled study of nortriptyline and bromocriptine in male alcoholics subtyped by comorbid psychiatric disorders. *Alcoholism: Clinical and Experimental Research*, **19**, 462–468.

Project MATCH Research Group (1997).   Matching alcoholism treatments to client heterogeneity: Project MATCH posttreatment drinking outcomes. *Journal of Studies on Alcohol*, **58**, 7–29.

Rychtarik, R.G., Prue, D.M., Rapp, S.R. & King, A.C. (1992).   Self-efficacy, aftercare and relapse in a treatment program for alcoholic. *Journal of Studies on Alcohol*, **53**, 435–440.

Weingardt, K.R. & Marlatt, G.A. (1998).   Sustaining change: helping those who are still using. In W.R. Miller & N. Heather (Eds), *Treating Addictive Behaviors*, 2nd edn (pp. 337–351). New York: Plenum.

Weinrieb, R.M. & O'Brien, C.P. (1997).   Naltrexone in the treatment of alcoholism. *Annual Review in Medicine*, **48**, 477–487.

Chapter 2

Assessment for Brief Intervention and Treatment

Malissa Yang
McMaster University Medical School, Hamilton, Ontario, Canada
and
Harvey Skinner
Department of Public Health Sciences, University of Toronto, Toronto, Ontario, Canada

Synopsis

Our understanding of alcohol problems has evolved such that they are viewed as multifactorial and existing on a continuum ranging from milder forms of problem drinking to severe alcohol dependence. Clinicians need practical tools for screening and assessment that encompass the social, behavioral and biological factors influencing a client's alcohol use and life functioning. The chapter describes a two-stage process, including alcohol problem identification (screening, case finding) followed by comprehensive assessment.

The identification stage addresses the basic questions of whether an alcohol problem is present and further action is necessary. This may take place in a range of community and primary care settings. The aim is to detect individuals with alcohol problems and either provide brief intervention (advice, counseling) or refer for further assessment and specialized treatment. There is good evidence that identifying individuals with early-stage or less severe alcohol problems and providing brief intervention is effective in reducing alcohol consumption and related problems.

The comprehensive assessment stage is essential for characterizing the specific nature and severity of the client's alcohol problems, as well as for providing a basis for intervention planning. Ongoing assessment throughout treatment and follow-up is crucial for adjusting the treatment plan and for giving feedback on goal attainment to the client (outcomes). Moreover, assessment functions well beyond information gathering. The process of assessment and

The Essential *Handbook of Treatment and Prevention of Alcohol Problems.* Edited by N. Heather and T. Stockwell.
© 2004 John Wiley & Sons Ltd. ISBN 0-470-86296-3.

personalized feedback are vital components in behavior change. Clinicians can provide assessment feedback in supportive ways to built readiness and motivation for change, using the principles of motivational interviewing. For example, assessment results can be used to highlight a discrepancy between the client's drinking and a related goal (e.g. improve relationships with family).

The identification and assessment of alcohol problems is a challenge because no single assessment method or instrument has been found to give a complete picture of the nature and severity of problems. Therefore, convergence of information gathered across several assessment modalities, including standardized instruments, collateral sources (e.g. family), medical examinations and biological tests, is important for getting an accurate picture of the client's level of alcohol consumption and related problems. The selection of assessment procedures will be guided by the specific purposes of assessment and practical constraints of the clinical setting.

In brief, assessment is essential for assisting the client and clinician in developing a "shared" treatment plan, fine-tuning the intervention process and monitoring progress toward goal attainment. The basics are: (a) to think clearly through the particular need and role of assessment in a given setting; (b) to incorporate a sequential, comprehensive regimen that fits the constraints of everyday clinical practice; and (c) to ensure that accurate and timely information is provided for motivation enhancement, clinical decision making and outcome evaluation.

In the past 25 years, important strides have been made in understanding alcohol problems and diverse intervention approaches have been developed. Alcohol problems are no longer viewed as a unitary, "all-or-nothing" clinical entity (e.g. "alcoholism") for which there is a single best treatment. Rather, alcohol problems are now broadly conceptualized as disorders that range from mild forms to very severe manifestations, with treatment considerations varying in accordance with the severity and unique characteristics of the individual's problem and situation (Tucker, Donovan & Marlatt, 1999; Institute of Medicine, 1990; Skinner, 1990).

Before the clinician and client begin the treatment process, a comprehensive assessment is essential. The primary aims are two-fold: (a) to assess the severity of problems related to drinking and degree of alcohol dependence (i.e. none, mild, moderate, severe); and (b) to determine which intervention approach and level of treatment (e.g. brief vs. intensive) is most appropriate for this client. A clear picture is needed of the physiological, social and behavioral antecedents and consequences of alcohol problems. However, alcohol use and problems must also be understood and interventions applied considering the environment in which the individual is embedded.

Assessment is not just a discrete step occurring prior to treatment. Rather, it is a systematic, continuous process which elucidates the initial clinical impression of the individual and alcohol problem, aids in the formulation of a treatment plan, helps match the client to an appropriate intervention, provides feedback on the course of treatment and evaluates treatment outcome. This chapter examines these purposes and stages of assessment in alcohol problems, reviews current assessment methods and highlights issues regarding assessment in special populations.

CHARACTERIZING THE PROBLEM AND THE INDIVIDUAL

The severity and specific manifestations of alcohol problems can differ widely between individuals. During the assessment, the clinician's goal is to gain knowledge about the particular kind of alcohol problem an individual is experiencing and to understand the evolution of the individual's alcohol problem over time. The domains of interest include the client's physical or medical condition, the environment in which the drinking occurs, the frequency of drinking and amount of alcohol consumed, the drinking history, the consequences of alcohol use, and past treatment history. Individual clients will vary greatly along these domains and gathering specific information about these assessment variables allows the clinician to define and prioritize issues for intervention.

Using a variety of assessment modalities, the clinician seeks to determine the individual client's characteristics and his/her life situation, which ultimately influence treatment decisions and contribute to treatment outcome (Allen & Columbus, 1995). Although assessment allows the clinician to characterize the individual and the nature of the alcohol problem, it also yields clinical benefits. For example, giving individualized feedback based on assessment results can enhance motivation for and commitment to behavior change and can help clients formulate personal goals for improvement (Skinner et al., 1985).

SEQUENTIAL AND MULTIDIMENSIONAL ASSESSMENT

Although it is important to implement systematic procedures for alcohol assessment, the extent to which an individual client is assessed and the manner in which the assessment takes place will depend on the unique characteristics of the client and the particular community or clinical setting. The process of assessment can be considered in stages, each of which may or may not lead to the next stage. The *first stage* in alcohol assessment begins with identification (screening or case finding), where the basic question is whether an alcohol problem is present and whether further assessment is necessary (Connors, 1995). The objective is to detect individuals with alcohol problems and to set the stage for further assessment and intervention, as warranted. Increasingly, evidence indicates that identifying individuals with early-stage, less severe alcohol abuse and providing brief intervention (advice or counselling) is effective in reducing alcohol consumption and related problems (Zweben & Fleming, 1999; Heather, 1996; Bien et al., 1993).

Identification is mostly performed in primary health care settings where individuals generally present for health concerns that are not related to alcohol abuse. A number of well-studied screening instruments, such as the CAGE and AUDIT, can aid in the identification of alcohol problems among ambulatory populations (Allen et al., 1995). Clinicians should select a screening measure based on test acceptability to clients and providers, whether there are adequate resources (i.e. time, financial, personnel) and whether it is logistically possible to incorporate reliable screening procedures into routine clinical practice. Screening should have responsive procedures for feedback to clients and appropriate referrals for further evaluation.

Once a screen alerts the clinician to the presence of an alcohol problem, further assessment is needed to diagnose an alcohol disorder. The *second stage* in alcohol assessment involves using a variety of modalities, including standardized psychometric instruments or questionnaires, diagnostic interviews, medical examinations, physiological measures, or some combination thereof, to describe as fully as possible the extent and nature of the problem(s) experienced by the individual who is drinking. At this stage, the clinician should aim to learn as much as possible about the client's use of alcohol, signs and symptoms of alcohol abuse and dependence, and the consequences of alcohol use (Skinner, 1984). Although there is a tendency for clinicians, particularly those not involved specifically in treating alcohol problems, to rely solely on alcohol consumption (i.e. quantity of use) in diagnosing alcohol abuse or dependence, a comprehensive assessment should elicit information along a variety of important dimensions. An individual's level of alcohol use alone does not fully characterize his/her alcohol problems.

One crucial dimension that requires extensive assessment is the individual's drinking history. In addition to quantity and frequency of alcohol use, the clinician must obtain a clear and detailed description of variables such as drinking style (i.e. continuous vs. binge), typical drinking situations and antecedents of drinking (Sobell & Sobell, 1995). Knowledge about the duration of the individual's alcohol abuse and previous attempts to stop drinking helps the clinician to deduce which treatment methods may or may not work. A second dimension that must be explored during the assessment is the extent of the individual's dependence on alcohol, including the degree of impairment of control over drinking, physical tolerance to alcohol (i.e. a decrease in response to alcohol that occurs with continued use), withdrawal symptoms (i.e. tremor, nausea and vomiting, insomnia, delirium, anxiety, restlessness, fatigue, etc.) and compulsivity of drinking (Davidson, 1987; Skinner & Allen, 1982)

The third dimension incorporates biomedical and psychosocial problems related to the client's alcohol abuse. These may include medical conditions resulting from prolonged abuse of alcohol, problems with family members or other social relationships, legal or vocational problems, intellectual or cognitive impairment and anxiety or depression. Clinicians are also advised to explore for the presence of psychiatric conditions, which often accompany alcohol problems and can play a role in its etiology, development and treatment (Miller & Ries, 1991; Nathan, 1997).

Yet another important dimension to assess is the client's motivation and readiness to change drinking behavior, a factor which is key in deciding the next appropriate treatment step (Donovan & Rosengren, 1999; Miller & Rollnick, 1991). Finally, collecting additional information regarding use of other psychoactive substances, demographic data, family structure and circumstances, family history of alcohol use, social stability and personality ensures that an assessment is comprehensive. Convergence of detailed information along multiple dimensions will give the clinician a clear picture of the severity of the alcohol problem experienced by a given individual and guide the direction of the treatment process.

PLANNING AND GUIDING THE TREATMENT PROCESS

Using various assessment modalities (e.g. standardized assessment instruments, medical history, physiological measures, collateral sources), the clinician aims to combine the characterization of a given individual with knowledge of intervention options in order to provide appropriate and effective treatment. For example, clients exhibiting signs of more severe alcohol dependence are generally referred for intensive treatment at specialized addiction clinics. On the other hand, individuals in the early stages of alcohol problems may not manifest classic signs and symptoms and may show resistance to change. Clinicians must rely on assessment indicators, such as marital or job problems, relationship conflicts and mood disorders, to identify the presence of an alcohol problem and build motivation for treatment alternatives, such as brief counseling (Donovan & Rosengren,1999; Zweben & Fleming, 1999). Optimally, assessment and treatment should be continuous and reciprocal, so that initial assessment guides treatment goals and interventions, and subsequent assessment throughout the course of treatment provides feedback to clinician and patient as well as indicating new or ongoing problem areas to pursue. Assessment should be regarded as an ongoing activity that supports clinical decision making throughout the course of treatment.

ASSESSMENT MODALITIES

Standardized Instruments

Screening is used to identify individuals who have alcohol-related problems or who are at risk for such problems. A number of standardized instruments are available to help the clinician screen for alcohol problems. The CAGE, MAST, TWEAK, and AUDIT are commonly used for adults and are considered to be acceptably reliable and valid in a variety of situations (Connors, 1995; Crowe et al., 1997; Allen et al., 1995). Preference for screening measures will vary between individual clinicians and different settings. Decisions should be based on the kind of population being assessed, amount of time and resources available, clinical or community setting and goals of screening. Providing personal and non-confrontational feedback to clients regarding screening results can be a significant component of brief intervention.

When a screening result alerts the clinician to a potential alcohol problem, a more exhaustive assessment is in order. This gives a greater understanding of how much drinking is taking place and how drinking fits into the client's activities, resources and relationships. A myriad of psychometric instruments have been designed to aid the clinician in this endeavor. Structured diagnostic interview instruments are designed to help clinicians formally diagnose alcohol dependence and alcohol abuse according to the categorical DSM-IV (Structured Clinical Interview for DSM-IV; First et al., 1995) and ICD (Composite International Diagnostic Interview, Robins et al., 1988) systems. Before selecting and using a diagnostic measure, clinicians must be clear about what constructs are to be measured and what the purpose of measurement is. Individual cases may call for different assessment instruments or measures (Maisto & McKay, 1995).

Whether the assessment is for clinical or research purposes will influence the choice of the diagnostic instrument. The clinician, whose main priority is to develop an appropriate treatment strategy for the individual client, will be primarily interested in using an instrument that identifies the unique needs of the client and guides treatment planning. Standardized instruments, particularly those that are brief, less structured and easy to administer, can be very useful for the busy clinician (e.g. Alcohol Dependence Scale: Skinner & Horn, 1984; Drinking Inventory of Consequences: Miller, Tonigan & Longabaugh, 1995). In contrast, researchers tend to explore a wider range of variables related to alcohol problems. Lengthier and more detailed questionnaires may be more appropriate for research purposes. For example, formal diagnostic interviews require resources, including trained personnel, money to pay for a measure and time for administration, which may not be available in clinical settings, particularly busy primary care facilities.

The choice of instrument will also vary between clinical settings. Formal diagnostic interviews may be warranted in specialized alcohol treatment settings, while more concise questionnaires may be more appropriate in community or primary health centers. Several measures designed to assess multiple dimensions of alcohol problems may also be effective (e.g. Addiction Severity Index: McLellan et al., 1992; Alcohol Use Inventory: Horn et al., 1987). An important consideration is the availability of psychometric evidence for a particular measure. Validity and reliability are the two primary psychometric characteristics to consider in an assessment instrument. Other things being equal, stronger psychometric characteristics will make one measure preferable to another (Maisto & McKay, 1995).

Instruments are also available to assess various other factors, including readiness to change (Readiness to Change Questionnaire: Rollnick et al., 1992) and self-efficacy (Inventory of Drinking Situations: Annis et al., 1987), which may be of interest to the clinician. The extent to which information is gathered for these variables and the extent to which these issues require exploration will vary between individuals and should be undertaken as needed (Institute of Medicine, 1990).

Additional issues to address when choosing an alcohol assessment instrument include the assessment time-frame (i.e. period of client functioning that is of interest), administrative options (i.e. self-administered vs. structured interview), training required for administration, and scoring and fee for use. It is recommended that, in selecting a suitable instrument, clinicians who are assessing clients for treatment should seek a measure (or a combination of measures) which balances the need to obtain extensive information regarding the client's alcohol use and life functioning with the need to be efficient and parsimonious, given the wide array of possible areas that could be assessed. At present, there is no universally accepted gold standard for the assessment of alcohol problems. Treatment of alcohol problems can be enhanced by the judicious use of standardized psychometric instruments to characterize clients during the course of treatment. Clinicians should be aware of the strengths and weaknesses of alternative psychometric instruments that can assist them in the assessment process.

Whether an individual's self-report of alcohol use and related problems can be trusted is an issue of ongoing debate. The balance of the scientific literature suggests that alcohol abusers' self-reports are relatively accurate and can be used with confidence if the assessment takes place under appropriate conditions (for reviews, see Babor et al., 1990; Maisto et al., 1990; Sobell & Sobell, 1995; Skinner, 1984). In many circumstances, self-report instruments are significantly more accurate than other assessment modalities, including physical examination and laboratory findings. It should be noted that, with the exception of self-monitoring, all measures of alcohol use and alcohol-related problems rely on retrospective self-reporting, and some amount of error is to be expected. Self-reports should not be considered inherently valid or invalid. Rather, whether confidence can be placed on individuals' self-reported alcohol use and related problems will depend on the individual client, the context in which assessment takes place, the specific information that is elicited and the purposes for which assessment is undertaken. Conditions that enhance truthful self-reporting include individuals being sober and alcohol-free during assessment, assurance of confidentiality, a comfortable, non-threatening clinical environment, and clear, understandable questions.

Medical History

A medical history and examination may accompany routine screening for alcohol problems, be undertaken when a screening measure indicates that an alcohol problem potentially exists, or be incorporated into a comprehensive assessment of an individual with an identified alcohol problem (Skinner & Holt, 1987). Primary care physicians are in an optimal position to perform such examinations. Clinical signs and symptoms associated with alcoholism can range from subtle and relatively benign to more severe and dramatic. Common physical indicators to look for include skin vascularization, hand or tongue tremor, modest hypertension, stigmata of accidents or trauma, history of gastrointestinal problems, gastric or duodenal ulcers and cognitive deficits (Saunders & Conigrave, 1990; Skinner et al., 1986). A history of alcohol problems in the family raises the index of suspicion that a patient might be at increased risk. Signs of neuropsychological and cognitive impairment are also indicators of hazardous alcohol consumption.

While medical conditions such as liver cirrhosis usually confirm alcohol dependence, the absence of alcohol-related medical problems does not rule out the diagnosis. Furthermore, no distinct symptom or test result can clearly establish a diagnosis of alcohol abuse or dependence. Clinicians should keep in mind that the most readily recognized symptoms of alcohol problems generally arise only in later stages of alcohol dependence, after years of heavy drinking. A complete history must probe for earlier, more subtle signs and patterns of alcohol abuse, including job-related problems, marital discord and/or domestic violence, difficulties in sleeping, chronic relationship difficulties, financial trouble, depression and anxiety, and so on. Structured or semi-structured interviewing, with the use of standardized questions, is preferred over free-form interviewing, which can be inconsistent in collecting essential kinds of assessment information.

Biological Measures

Accurate information on alcohol consumption during the pretreatment assessment is important for diagnosis and treatment outcome evaluation. Several biological measures demonstrate strong reliability for indicating an individual's alcohol use in the past 24 hour period. The breathalyser, which measures the presence of alcohol in the breath, is an efficient method to determine whether an individual has consumed alcohol in the immediate past. Simple laboratory testing of blood, urine and sweat can also accurately indicate recent alcohol intake. These markers are direct measures of alcohol in bodily fluids and are considered to be sensitive, specific, inexpensive and easy to administer (Anton, Litten & Allen, 1995). (See also Whitfield, 2001)

Detection of alcohol use over longer periods through physiological testing is more challenging and relies on measuring the effects of alcohol on the body rather than directly measuring the presence of alcohol (Anton, Litten & Allen, 1995). Abnormalities in γ-glutamyltransferase (GGT), mean corpuscular volume (MCV), aspartate aminotransferase (AST) or alanine aminotransferase (ALT) are indicators of chronic alcohol consumption. These markers of heavy and sustained alcohol use are well studied, routinely used, relatively cost-efficient and widely available. However, the results must be interpreted with caution because they generally lack sufficient sensitivity and specificity (Leigh & Skinner, 1988). Furthermore, conventional biological markers are insensitive to early-stage problem drinking (Saunders & Conigrave, 1990). High-density lipoproteins, 5-hydroxytryptophol, β-hexosaminidase, carbohydrate-deficient transferrin (CDT), alcohol congeners, and blood acetaldehyde adducts (AA) are newer biological measures under investigation.

In choosing a biological test, clinicians will want to consider the window of assessment (i.e. the amount of time that a marker will remain positive following drinking), the nature of the population (i.e. ambulatory vs. alcoholics), and the sensitivity and specificity of the particular test. While physiological tests are often considered to be the most "objective" measure of alcohol abuse, no single test can definitively identify or give a comprehensive assessment for this complex condition. The only true indicator of alcohol consumption is the detection of alcohol or one of its metabolites in body fluids. No laboratory test possesses both high sensitivity and specificity for detecting alcohol use outside of the previous 24 hours.

Clinicians are also advised to consider alternative factors that may be causing abnormal laboratory results. Individuals from an ambulatory population who drink excessively but are otherwise relatively healthy will have normal test results but may still require intervention for alcohol problems. The level of "abnormal" intake will vary from person to person (e.g. male vs. female). Furthermore, not all clients with hazardous alcohol use or dependence will demonstrate abnormalities in laboratory tests. Thus, standard laboratory tests are not sufficiently sensitive to be used as the primary basis of screening and assessment. The most valuable role for a physiological test is the detection of hazardous levels of alcohol intake. Biological measures are also useful for monitoring treatment progress by corroborating self-reported alcohol use and comparing subsequent tests with baseline levels. It is recommended that laboratory tests alone should not be relied upon to identify alcohol problems and should always be used in combination with data from other assessment modalities.

Other Modalities

In light of concerns regarding the accuracy of clients' self-reports, clinicians may explore collateral sources to gather further assessment information. Such sources may include clients' spouses, family members or employers (Nathan, 1997). However, it should not be assumed that collateral observers give unbiased, accurate and detailed reports. For clients who lack social supports there may not be any suitable individuals who can consistently observe and report their behavior. Friends and co-workers may be fairly accurate in reporting frequency of drinking but can generally only provide a gross estimate of the actual quantity of alcohol consumed or of the presence of alcohol dependence symptoms (Sobell & Sobell, 1995; Skinner, 1984). Examining court documents, police and employment records may also give a clearer picture of the client's previous alcohol problems.

Self-monitoring is an assessment technique that involves having an individual record the occurrences of alcohol as well as the conditions that precede, accompany and follow drinking. The client is requested to keep a daily log of the number and types of drinks consumed and the particular situations and times when drinking occurred. This method is ideal because it does not depend on retrospective self-reporting and can increase motivation to reduce the drinking behavior. Self-monitoring procedures are especially useful for assessing alcohol consumption and problems after treatment initiation and during follow-up. Both the clinician and the client can use self-monitoring information as a relatively objective and continuous record with which to evaluate progress and setbacks.

Self-monitoring is also valuable for providing information surrounding relapse episodes. Recording urges to drink or thoughts and actions related to alcohol may aid in identifying situations or events that place the client at risk for relapse and in modifying treatment goals. Having the client play an active role in the assessment and treatment process can also enhance motivation to reduce or quit drinking. However, client compliance in keeping a consistent record may be problematic, particularly among chronic alcohol abusers who may lack motivation, organizational skills and social supports. Also, clinicians must decide the level of confidence they have that clients are reporting alcohol use and related problems honestly and accurately.

Clinicians may wish to combine different assessment tools. Composite indices of alcohol problems can be derived both within and across assessment modalities. For example, a composite of medical history and laboratory tests can substantially increase diagnostic accuracy (Skinner et al., 1986, Skinner & Holt, 1987). A battery of questionnaires, incorporating various standardized scales, may also elucidate the extent of alcohol-related problems experienced by the client. Combining a physical examination for signs and symptoms of excessive alcohol use with brief questionnaires and laboratory tests may also improve assessment. Indeed, a most valuable use of laboratory tests is to corroborate clients' self-reports of alcohol consumption during treatment and follow-up. The choice of measures or components that make up the composite index can also be modified to suit the stage of treatment.

Collecting assessment information from multiple modalities will enhance the degree of confidence that clinicians can have in clients' self-reports regarding alcohol use and in the overall characterization of the alcohol problem. Ultimately, selection of the components of a comprehensive clinical assessment will be at the discretion of the clinician. In choosing any modality for alcohol assessment, the limitations of particular tests and the unique situational needs must be kept in mind. Ultimately, confidence in the accuracy of assessments is enhanced by convergence among a variety of alternative measurement modalities.

SPECIAL POPULATIONS

Adolescents

A comprehensive assessment plays an equally important role in the identification and treatment of alcohol problems among adolescents. From a preventive perspective, the negative consequences of excessive drinking may be curtailed if problems are identified and treated in earlier, less serious stages. The diagnostic criteria for alcohol abuse and dependence have largely been developed from research with adult populations. However, withdrawal symptoms, tolerance and medical problems present differently in adolescents than in adults. Clinicians should be aware that adolescents with alcohol problems demonstrate very heterogeneous patterns of symptoms, which are mainly psychosocial rather than physical (Alexander, 1991; Martin et al., 1995). Physical examination and laboratory testing are not as helpful for identifying alcohol problems as a comprehensive interview and full appreciation of the more subtle signs in this population (Alderman, Schonberg & Cohen, 1992).

Adolescents' patterns of alcohol and other drug use can vary considerably over time according to variables over which they may not have much control, including availability of money, the opportunity to use and the influence of peers. Multiple drug use and coexisting psychiatric problems can make assessment among adolescents particularly challenging (Upfold, 1997). Routine screening for alcohol problems in primary care settings is particularly important in the adolescent population in order to prevent the development of more serious and health-threatening alcohol abuse and dependence.

It is crucial for the clinician to develop a sense of trust and rapport with the adolescent in order to gather accurate and complete assessment information and, ultimately, to achieve positive treatment outcomes. Clinicians are encouraged to develop and use innovative methods of assessment, which may be more helpful than conventional assessment tools in eliciting accurate information from adolescent clients (Leccese & Waldron, 1994). The adolescent should be assessed separately and then, if possible, the family can be assessed as a unit.

Several assessment procedures have been designed specifically for adolescents for whom detection and diagnosis may be tricky (Connors, 1995). Available assessment instruments include the Adolescent Drinking Index (ADI), the Personal Experience Inventory (PEI: Winters & Henly, 1989), the Adolescent Alcohol Expectancy Questionnaire (AEQ-A: Brown, Christianson & Goldman, 1987), the Adolescent Drug Abuse Diagnosis (ADAD: Friedman & Utada, 1989), the Personal Experience Screening Questionnaire (PESQ) and the Substance Abuse Screening Test (SAST) (Nathan, 1997; Rogers, Speraw & Ozbek, 1995). As with adults, the use of composite indices that combine assessment modalities will enhance assessment of adolescent clients. Although treatment programs have been developed for adolescents, better assessment procedures to determine the most appropriate course of treatment for individual adolescents are needed.

Populations with Coexisting Psychiatric Conditions

In both clinical and community contexts, alcohol problems are commonly accompanied by coexisting psychiatric conditions (Miller & Ries, 1991). Estimates vary on the prevalence of comorbidity. However, as many as half to two-thirds of clinical samples of patients with alcohol dependence are likely to have a lifetime diagnosis of another psychiatric disorder (Davidson & Ritson, 1993). The psychiatric syndromes that most often coexist with alcohol disorders are anxiety disorders, personality disorders and abuse of other psychoactive substances. Accurate assessment of coexisting psychiatric disorders in alcoholic clients is crucial to treatment planning and outcome (Nathan, 1997). Failure to detect other psychiatric problems can deprive clients of potentially helpful treatments. Prescription of medication must proceed with care to avoid the development of further substance dependence. (See also Chapter 9, this volume.)

Early research proposed that psychiatric clients used alcohol as a way to reduce tension, stress and anxiety. However, this "tension reduction" hypothesis has been challenged and does not appear to adequately explain the etiology or maintenance of alcohol abuse. Anxiety is a frequently found condition in patients with alcohol dependence. It appears that in most cases, anxiety is a consequence rather than a cause of heavy drinking (Allan, 1995). Generally, most depressive and anxiety symptoms recede once the alcoholic client is detoxified and has been abstinent from alcohol for a period of time (Allan, 1995; Davidson & Ritson, 1993). However, it should not be assumed that one disorder which preceded another necessarily caused the second condition. As in all clients with alcohol problems, it is recommended that clinicians take a broad and comprehensive approach to assessment and attempt to look at the alcohol use in the life context. This approach will aid in meeting the distinct assessment and treatment needs of the client.

A particular challenge in assessing and treating clients with both alcohol problems and psychiatric disorders is to determine the relative importance of each condition. Also, the intoxication and withdrawal from alcohol can produce psychiatric symptoms that characterize psychiatric disorders. Structured clinical interviews, such as the Composite International Diagnostic Interview (CIDI), the Schedules for Clinical Assessment in Neuropsychiatry (SCAN) and the Structured Clinical Interview for DSM-IV (SCID), will be most helpful in assessing cases where comorbidity is suspected (Albanese et al., 1994). Such in-depth evaluation allows the clinician to probe the severity of both the alcohol abuse and the psychiatric symptoms, their history and the context surrounding their occurrence, in order to arrive at proper diagnoses. Before a comprehensive assessment can take place, the clinician must ensure that clients are not intoxicated or experiencing alcohol withdrawal at the time of the assessment. Physiological testing may be appropriate for this determination.

Clinicians should be aware that comorbid psychiatric conditions can play a role in the etiology of alcohol dependence and make treatment more difficult. Alcohol dependence and co-occurring morbidity must both be assessed and treated, often by different means. Having an additional psychiatric disorder can alter the course of alcohol dependence in various ways, including hastening the development of dependence on alcohol, exhibition of impulsivity, aggression and risky behavior by the client, and poorer prognosis.

CONCLUSION

There is no shortage of tools to aid the clinician in the identification and assessment of alcohol problems. The key is: (a) to think clearly through the particular need and role of assessment in a given setting; (b) to incorporate a sequential, comprehensive regimen that fits the constraints of everyday clinical practice; and (c) to ensure that accurate and timely information is provided for motivation enhancement, clinical decision making and outcome evaluation. Ultimately, the purpose of assessment is to assist the client and clinician in developing a "shared" treatment plan, adjusting or fine-tuning the intervention and monitoring progress toward goal attainment.

KEY WORKS AND SUGGESTIONS FOR FURTHER READING

Allen J.P. & Columbus M. (1995).   *Assessing Alcohol Problems: A Guide for Clinicians and Researchers.* National Institute on Alcohol Abuse and Alcoholism Treatment Handbook Series 4. Bethesda, MD: US Department of Health and Human Services, Public Health Service, National Institutes of Health, National Institute on Alcohol Abuse and Alcoholism.

Provides a very practical review of assessment approaches and instruments.

Institute of Medicine (1990).   *Broadening the Base of Treatment for Alcohol Problems.* Washington, DC: National Academy Press.

Provides the most comprehensive yet readable discussion of key concepts and methods for identification of alcohol problems in the community (Chapter 9), assessment (Chapter 10), client–treatment matching (Chapter 11) and treatment outcome (Chapter 12).

Tucker J.A., Donovan D.M. & Marlatt G.A. (1999).   *Changing Addictive Behavior: Bridging Clinical and Public Health Strategies.* New York: Guilford.

Provides an excellent overview of latest thinking regarding the integration of clinical and public health approaches to addictions. Of particular note for assessment are chapters on motivation (Chapter 5), stages of change (Chapter 6), brief interventions (Chapter 9) and stepped care (Chapter 12).

REFERENCES

Adger, H. Jr (1991).   Problems of alcohol and other drug use and abuse in adolescents. *Journal of Adolescent Health,* **12**, 606–613.

Albanese, M.J., Bartel, R.L., Bruno, R.F., Morgenbesser, M.W. & Schatzberg, A.F. (1994).   Comparison of measures used to determine substance abuse in an inpatient psychiatric population. *American Journal of Psychiatry,* **151**, 1077–1078.

Alderman, E.M., Schonberg, S.K. & Cohen, M.I. (1992).   The pediatrician's role in the diagnosis and treatment of substance abuse. *Pediatrics in Review,* **13**, 314–318.

Alexander, B. (1991).   Alcohol abuse in adolescents. *American Family Physician,* **43**, 527–532.

Allan, C.A. (1995).   Alcohol problems and anxiety disorders—a critical review. *Alcohol & Alcoholism,* **30**, 145–151.

Allen, J.P., Maisto, S.A. & Connors, G.J. (1995).   Self-report screening tests for alcohol problems in primary care. *Archives of Internal Medicine,* **155**, 1726–1730.

Allen, J.P., & Columbus, M. (1995).   *Assessing Alcohol Problems: A Guide for Clinicians and Researchers.* National Institute on Alcohol Abuse and Alcoholism Treatment Handbook Series, 4. Bethesda, MD: US Department of Health and Human Services, Public Health Service, National Institutes of Health, National Institute on Alcohol Abuse and Alcoholism.

Annis, H.M., Graham, J.M. & Davis, C.S. (1987). *Inventory of Drinking Situations (IDS) User's Guide*. Toronto: Addiction Research Foundation.

Anton, R.F., Litten, R.Z. & Allen, J.P. (1995). Biological assessment of alcohol consumption. In J.P. Allen & M. Columbus (Eds), *Assessing Alcohol Problems: A Guide for Clinicians and Researchers* (pp. 31–39). National Institute on Alcohol Abuse and Alcoholism Treatment Handbook Series, 4. Bethesda, MD: US Department of Health and Human Services, Public Health Service, National Institutes of Health, National Instate on Alcohol Abuse and Alcoholism.

Babor, T.F., Brown, J. & Del Boca, F.K. (1990). Validity of self-reports in applied research on addictive behaviors: fact or fiction? *Addictive Behaviors*, **12**, 5–32.

Bien, T., Miller, W. & Tonigan, J. (1993). Brief interventions for alcohol problems: a review. *Addiction*, **88**, 315–336.

Brown, J. Kranzler, H.R. & Del Boca, F.K. (1992). Self-reports by alcohol and drug abuse inpatients: factors affecting reliability and validity. *British Journal of Addiction*, **87**, 1013–1024.

Brown, S.A., Christiansen, B.A. & Goldman, M.S. (1987). The Alcohol Expectancy Questionnaire: an instrument for the assessment of adolescent and adult alcohol expectancies. *Journal of Studies in Alcohol*, **48**, 483–491.

Connors, G.J. (1995). Screening for alcohol problems. In J.P. Allen & M. Columbus (Eds), *Assessing Alcohol Problems: A Guide for Clinicians and Researchers* (pp. 17–29). National Institute on Alcohol Abuse and Alcoholism Treatment Handbook Series, 4. Bethesda, MD: US Department of Health and Human Services, Public Health Service, National Institutes of Health, National Institute on Alcohol Abuse and Alcoholism.

Crowe, R.R., Kramer, J.R., Hesselbrock, V., Manos, G. & Bucholz, K.K. (1997). The utility of the Brief MAST and the CAGE in identifying alcohol problems: results from national high-risk and community samples. *Archives of Family Medicine*, **6**(5), 477–483.

Davidson, K.M. & Ritson, E.B. (1993). The relationship between alcohol dependence and depression. *Alcohol & Alcoholism*, **28**(2), 147–155.

Davidson, R. (1987). Assessment of the alcohol dependence syndrome: a review of self-report screening questionnaires. *British Journal of Clinical Psychology*, **26**, 243–255.

Donovan, D.M. (1995). Assessments to aid in the treatment planning process. In J.P. Allen & M. Columbus (Eds), *Assessing Alcohol Problems: A Guide for Clinicians and Researchers* (pp. 75–122). National Institute on Alcohol Abuse and Alcoholism Treatment Handbook Series, 4. Department of Health and Human Services, Public Health Service, National Institutes of Health, National Institute on Alcohol Abuse and Alcoholism.

Donovan, D.M. & Rosengren, D.B. (1999). Motivation for behavior change and treatment among substance abusers. In J.A. Tucker, D.M. Donovan & G.A. Marlatt (Eds), *Changing Addictive Behavior: Bridging Clinical and Public Health Strategies*. New York: Guilford.

First, M.G., Spitzer, R.L., Gibbon, M. & Williams, J.B.W. (1995). *Structured Clinical Interview for SDM-IV—Patient Version*. New York: Biometrics Department, New York State Psychiatric Institute.

Friedman, A.S. & Utada, A. (1989). A method for diagnosing and planning the treatment of adolescent drug abusers: the Adolescent Drug Abuse Diagnosis (ADAD) instrument. *Journal of Drug Education*, **19**, 285–312.

Heather, N. (1996). The public health and brief interventions for excessive alcohol consumption: the British experience. *Addictive Behaviors*, **21**, 857–863.

Horn, J.L., Wanberg, K.W. & Foster, F.M. (1987). *Guide to the Alcohol Use Inventory*. Minneapolis, MN: National Computer Systems.

Institute of Medicine (1990). *Broadening the Base of Treatment for Alcohol Problems*. Washington, DC: National Academy Press.

Kaminer, Y., Bukstein, O.G. & Tarter, R.E. (1991). The Teen Addiction Severity Index: rationale and reliability. *International Journal of Addiction*, **26**, 219–226.

Leccese, M. & Waldron, H.B. (1994). Assessing adolescent substance use: a critique of current measurement instruments. *Journal of Substance Abuse Treatment*, **11**(6), 553–563.

Leigh, G. & Skinner, H.A. (1988). Physiological assessment. In D.M. Donovan & G.A. Marlatt (Eds), *Assessment of Addictive Behaviors* (pp. 112–136). New York: Guilford.

Liftik, J. (1995). Assessment. In S. Brown (Ed.), *Treating Alcoholism* (pp. 57–93). San Francisco, CA: Jossey-Bass.

Maisto, S.A. & McKay, J.R. (1995).   Diagnosis. In J.P. Allen & M. Columbus (Eds), *Assessing Alcohol Problems: A Guide for Clinicians and Researchers* (pp. 41–54). National Institute on Alcohol Abuse and Alcoholism Treatment Handbook Series, 4. Bethesda, MD: US Department of Health and Human Services, Public Health Service, National Institutes of Health, National Instate on Alcohol Abuse and Alcoholism.

Maisto, S.A., McKay, J.R. & Connor, G.J. (1990).   Self-report issues in substance abuse: state of the art and future directions. *Behavioral Assessment*, **12**, 117–134.

Martin, C.S., Kaczynski, N.A., Maisto, S.A., Bukstein, O.M. & Moss, H.B. (1995).   Patterns of DSM-IV alcohol abuse and dependence symptoms in adolescent drinkers. *Journal of Studies on Alcohol*, **56**(6), 672–680.

McLellan, A.T., Kushner, H., Metzger, D., Peters, R., Smith, I., Grissom, G., Pettinati, H. & Argeriou, M. (1992).   The fifth edition of the Addiction Severity Index. *Journal of Substance Abuse Treatment*, **9**, 199–213.

Miller, N.S. & Ries, R.K. (1991).   Drug and alcohol dependence and psychiatric populations: the need for diagnosis, intervention, and training. *Comprehensive Psychiatry*, **32**(3), 268–276.

Miller, W. & Rollnick, S. (1991).   *Motivational Interviewing: Preparing People to Change Addictive Behavior.* New York: Guilford.

Miller, W.R., Tonigan, J.S. & Longabaugh, R. (1995).   *The Drinker Inventory of Consequences (DrInC): An Instrument for Assessing Adverse Consequences of Alcohol Abuse.* Test Manual. Project MATCH Monograph Series. Rockville, MD: US Department of Health and Human Services.

Nathan, P.E. (1997).   Assessing substance abusers. In L.L. Murphy & J.C. Impara (Eds), *Assessment of Substance Abuse* (pp. xvii–xxix). Lincoln, NE: University of Nebraska.

Robins, L.N., Wing, A.U. & Wittchen, R. *et al.* (1988).   The Composite International Diagnostic Interview. *Archives of Genered Psychiatry*, **45**, 1069–1077.

Rogers, P.D., Speraw, S.R. & Ozbek, I. (1995).   The assessment of the identified substance abusing adolescent. *Pediatric Clinics of North America*, **42**(2), 351–369.

Rollnick, S., Heather, N., Gold, R. & Hall, W. (1992).   Development of a short "Readiness to Change Questionnaire" for use in brief, opportunistic interventions among excessive drinkers. *British Journal of Addiction*, **87**, 743–754.

Samet, J.H., Rollnick, S. & Barnes, H. (1996).   Beyond CAGE: A brief clinical approach after detection of substance abuse. *Archives of Internal Medicine*, **156**, 2287–2293.

Saunders, J.B. & Conigrave, K.M. (1990).   Early identification of alcohol problems. *Canadian Medical Association Journal*, **143**, 1060–1068.

Schorling, J.B. & Buchsbaum, D.G. (1997).   Screening for alcohol and drug abuse. *Alcohol & Other Substance Abuse*, **81**, 845–865.

Skinner, H.A. (1984).   Assessing alcohol use by patients in treatment. In R.C. Smart, H. Cappell, F.B. Glaser, Y. Israel, H. Kalant, W. Schmidt & E.M. Sellers (Eds), *Research Advances in Alcohol & Drug Problems*, Volume 8 (pp. 183–207). New York: Plenum.

Skinner, H.A. (1990). Spectrum of drinkers and intervention opportunities. *Canadian Medical Association Journal*, **143**, 1054–1059.

Skinner, H.A. & Allen, B.A. (1982).   Alcohol dependence syndrome: measurement and validation. *Journal of Abnormal Psychology*, **91**, 199–209.

Skinner, H.A. & Horn, J.L. (1984).   *Alcohol Dependence Scale: Users' Guide.* Toronto: Addiction Research Foundation.

Skinner, H.A. & Holt, S. (1987).   *The Alcohol Clinical Index: Strategies for Identifying Patients with Alcohol Problems.* Toronto: Addiction Research Foundation.

Skinner, H., McIntosh, M. & Palmer, W. (1985).   Lifestyle assessment: just asking makes a difference. *British Medical Journal*, **290**, 214–216.

Skinner, H.A., Holt, S., Sheu, W.J. & Israel, Y. (1986).   Clinical versus laboratory detection of alcohol abuse: the Alcohol Clinical Index. *British Medical Journal*, **292**, 1703–1708.

Sobell, L.C. & Sobell, M.B. (1995).   Alcohol consumption measures. In J.P. Allen & M. Columbus (Eds), *Assessing Alcohol Problems: A Guide for Clinicians and Researchers* (pp. 55–73). National Institute on Alcohol Abuse and Alcoholism Treatment Handbook Series, 4. Bethesda, MD: US Department of Health and Human Services, Public Health Service, National Institutes of Health, National Instate on Alcohol Abuse and Alcoholism.

Upfold, D.N. (1997). Assessment and outpatient counselling for adolescents and young adults. In S. Harrison & V. Carver (Eds), *Alcohol & Drug Problems: A Practical Guide for Counsellors* (pp. 319–339). Toronto: Addiction Research Foundation.

Tucker, J.A., Donovan, D.M. & Marlatt, G.A. (1999). *Changing Addictive Behavior: Bridging Clinical and Public Health Strategies*. New York: Guilford.

Whitfield, J.B. (2001). Diagnostic and monitoring investigations. In N. Heather, T.J. Peters & T. Stockwell (Eds), *International Handbook of Alcohol Dependence and Problems*. (pp. 227–250). Chickester, UK.: John Wiley & Sons.

Winters, K.C. & Henly, G.A. (1989). *Personal Experience Inventory (PEI) Test and Manual*. Los Angeles, CA: Western Psychological Services.

Zweben, A. & Fleming, M.F. (1999). Brief interventions for alcohol and drug problems. In J.A. Tucker, D.M. Donovan & G.A. Marlatt. *Changing Addictive Behavior: Bridging Clinical and Public Health Strategies* (pp. 251–282). New York: Guilford.

Chapter 3

Alcohol Withdrawal and Detoxification

Duncan Raistrick
Leeds Addiction Unit, Leeds, UK

Synopsis

The characteristics of alcohol withdrawal are well known. Under experimental conditions anyone can be made tolerant to the effects of alcohol and experience withdrawal symptoms on abrupt withdrawal or marked reduction of intake; in vivo it is usually after several years of regular drinking that a person begins to experience withdrawal symptoms. The severity of withdrawal can be seen to exist along a continuum ranging from the mild tremulous state through seizures and on to alcoholic delirium. It is probable that this continuum is, in reality, made up of different symptom clusters which are associated with different neurochemical systems. All of these systems are under the influence of g-aminobutyric acid (GABA) and hence the rationale for using benzodiazepines and other central nervous system depressants for the treatment of withdrawal.

Detoxification is usually a very straightforward procedure. When complications do happen they are often serious and it is, therefore, important that clinicians maintain vigilance throughout all detoxification procedures. There are a number of standardized scales to measure the severity of alcohol withdrawal and use of these scales has been shown to be helpful in the early identification of complications during detoxification and in minimizing the dose of sedative medication used to control withdrawal. There is evidence to support the use of chlordiazepoxide as the drug of first choice for the management of alcohol withdrawal; chlordiazepoxide is relatively safe, even in combination with alcohol, has a low addictive potential and can be uniquely identified on toxicology screening. Chlormethiazole is, however, superior where there is a risk of seizures or delirium but it has a lower safety profile. Potentially dangerous medical conditions are frequently associated with the more severe withdrawal states, indicating the need for full medical work-up in these cases. The setting in which detoxi-

The Essential *Handbook of Treatment and Prevention of Alcohol Problems.* Edited by N. Heather and T. Stockwell.
© 2004 John Wiley & Sons Ltd. ISBN 0-470-86296-3.

fication should take place needs to be judged on the basis of the expected severity of withdrawal and the social support available to an individual. Home or inpatient detoxifications are costly compared to other options and can normally be offered only in circumstances where there is clinical or social need.

The relationship between withdrawal symptomatology and alcohol dependence has long been controversial. There is no doubt that relief drinking is powerfully reinforced when it occurs but this is insufficient to justify the dominance of withdrawal over other drinking cues that feed into the learning processes, underpinning dependence. Dependence should be seen as a purely psychological phenomenon to which withdrawal makes some, quite limited, contribution. Tolerance and withdrawal can be subsumed under the umbrella of "neuro-adaptation" rather than using the more confusing terminology of "physical dependence".

KEY ISSUES OF UNDERSTANDING

Detoxification services are generally seen to be an important component of any alcohol treatment system. The purpose of detoxification is to minimize the severity of the withdrawal symptoms that occur when alcohol consumption is abruptly stopped or markedly reduced. Detoxification is not as straightforward or mundane a procedure as it may appear at first sight; however, it is not so much the management of withdrawal that has excited controversy but, rather, the meaning of withdrawal in understanding dependence—for example, Stockwell (1994) argues that alcohol withdrawal symptoms are of little practical importance and Tober (1992) argues that withdrawal symptoms have no place in the definition of dependence. After nearly 50 years of scientific investigation, the understanding of alcohol tolerance and withdrawal has reached a maturity, so that their final resting place in the whole spectrum of alcohol problems and problem drinking is closer to being settled.

Alcohol Withdrawal

There have been descriptions throughout history of symptoms and signs that would now be recognized as belonging to an alcohol withdrawal syndrome. The Edinburgh physician Thomas Sutton is credited with describing delirium tremens in 1813 and attributing the condition to alcohol withdrawal. Confirmation of the connection between drinking, stopping drinking and the experience of withdrawal is, however, relatively recent. In the classic study by Isbell et al. (1955), 10 ex-morphine addicts received daily dosing with alcohol for periods of up to 12 weeks. On abrupt withdrawal of alcohol, the subjects experienced significant symptoms, including tremor, sweating, vomiting, diarrhoea, hyper-reflexia, fever, raised blood pressure and insomnia; two subjects experienced convulsions and four subjects experienced hallucinations or delirium. The work of Isbell and colleagues left questions unanswered but was a sufficient basis for proceeding with further elucidation of the nature of withdrawal by the use of laboratory-style experimentation in human beings. In a selective review of this research, Gross (1977) concluded that the severity of the alcohol withdrawal syndrome would relate to alcohol intake modified by the contribution of residual effects of previous drinking and the abruptness of withdrawal. He went on to describe a factor structure of withdrawal: *Factor 1—hallucinogenic* consists of nausea, tinitus, visual disturbance, pruritis, parasthesiae, muscle pain, agitation, sleep disturbance, tactile hallucinations, and hallucinations which are auditory or visual or both: *Factor 2—affective and physiological* consists of anxiety, depression, tremor and sweats: *Factor 3—delirium* consists

Table 3.1 The 10 most common and the 10 most specific symptoms of alcohol withdrawal

	Most common symptoms	Most specific symptoms
1	Depression	Whole body shakes
2	Anxiety	Facial tremulousness
3	Irritability	Hand and finger shakes
4	Tiredness	Cannot face the day
5	Craving	Panicky
6	Restlessness	Guilty
7	Insomnia	Nausea
8	Confusion	Visual hallucinations
9	Sweating	Weakness
10	Weakness	Depression

Source: adapted from Hershon (1977).

of clouding of the sensorium, impairment of consciousness and impairment of contact with the observer. Factors 1 and 2 were seen as existing along a continuum of severity, whereas factor 3 appeared more complex, since it increased both during drinking and on withdrawal.

In a sophisticated analysis of alcohol withdrawal symptoms, Hershon (1977) reasoned that symptoms of withdrawal should (a) be absent during periods of light drinking, (b) be present during periods of heavy drinking, (c) disappear after 10 days of abstinence, (d) be present first thing in the morning, and (e) be relieved by further drinking—he applied these criteria as a series of filters to symptoms reported by 100 male drinkers in the previous month, so that he was able to separate those symptoms most specific to alcohol withdrawal from symptoms that happen to be commonly present during withdrawal (see Table 3.1). The implications of these data are that commonly occurring symptoms, perhaps the result of minor stress or the consequence of accumulated alcohol-related problems, may incorrectly be attributed to alcohol withdrawal and may lead to inaccurate assessment and inappropriate pharmacotherapy as part of a detoxification programme.

Edwards (1990) concludes that the evidence from animal and human research suggests that anyone can develop tolerance and withdrawal symptoms within a short space of time, days or weeks, provided that a sufficiently high and regular dose of alcohol is taken. Whether or when withdrawal symptoms occur is largely a function of dose and frequency scheduling, or in other words an individual's drinking pattern; typically, but not necessarily, persistent withdrawal symptoms are a feature of the later stages of a drinking career. Once withdrawal symptoms have occurred, then subsequent manifestations in terms of both frequency and severity will depend upon a complex interaction of factors, but above all blood alcohol level seems to be important. Vinson & Menezes (1991), for example, found significant but low-order correlations between blood alcohol on admission to rehabilitation services and severity of withdrawal symptoms. Alcohol affects several different neurochemical systems which probably accounts for the variable picture of alcohol withdrawal.

It appears to be the case that the more severe withdrawal states are associated with additional and multiple risk factors, although high blood alcohol levels remain an important element within the aetiology. Schuckit et al. (1995) report on a cohort of 1648 alcohol-dependent men and women where 12.8% of subjects had experienced at least one episode of alcoholic delirium or convulsions during withdrawal. The most powerful discriminating variables between those with histories of more and less severe withdrawal were the maximum number of drinks per day and the total number of withdrawal episodes; the use of non-prescribed depressant drugs and a greater number of medical problems were also significant. In a cohort of 72 "alcoholics" hospitalized for detoxification, Essardas et al. (1994) report that 46% of subjects had convulsions and 25% developed alcoholic delirium. In contrast, Mayo-Smith & Bernard (1995) report on a cohort of 1044 subjects admitted for inpatient detoxification and given unlimited oxazepam titrated against severity of alcohol withdrawal: only 1.1% of subjects experienced seizures, with peak incidence occurring 12–48 hours after the last oxazepam dose, and without progression to alcoholic delirium. Tsuang et al. (1994) found that 9% of 532 subjects attending a day programme had a diagnosis of alcoholic hallucinosis; compared to those without a history of hallucinations, these subjects had an earlier onset of alcohol problems, consumed more alcohol per occasion and were more likely to experiment with a variety of illicit drugs.

It is not possible to say with any degree of precision what withdrawal symptomatology will be associated with what kind of drinking pattern in what kind of person. In broad brush terms, alcohol withdrawal can be seen as existing along a continuum from mild tremulousness, with or without affective change, through to seizures, hallucinations, and delirium. Whether or not this is truly a continuum or, more likely, different symptom clusters (see Hershon, 1977; Gross, 1977; Stockwell et al., 1979), reflecting withdrawal responses by different neurochemical mechanisms, is unclear. Alcoholic delirium is in some ways an exception to this general proposition. Kramp et al. (1979) compared 20 subjects with tremor and hallucinations against 20 patients with tremor, hallucinations and delirium. The main difference between subjects was that the delirium group had embarked on a drinking binge prior to the onset of symptoms and continued drinking in spite of symptoms. However, both groups required the same amount of sedation, which was carefully titrated to achieve the end-point of inducing sleep. It was therefore concluded that delirium may be qualitatively different to the simple hallucinatory state and, once triggered, have a natural history of its own. The data on the latency from abstinence or marked reduction of intake to the manifestation of different withdrawal elements are inconsistent; nonetheless there is a clear ordering of symptoms. It is plausible to think in terms of a hierarchy of neurochemical systems, each requiring greater biochemical disturbance to launch different aspects of the withdrawal syndrome. It may be that kindling and the long elimination time from high blood alcohol concentrations combine to produce this effect.

Withdrawal Symptoms and Dependence

The International Classification of Diseases (World Health Organization, 1992) defines alcohol dependence as a psychobiological state based on the provisional description of alcohol dependence by Edwards & Gross (1976). The important advance here is that dependence is seen as a unitary concept and the old distinction between psychological and physical dependence is dispensed with. Physical dependence was almost synonymous with what is now referred to as neuro-adaptation, that is, tolerance to the effects of alcohol and withdrawal symptoms, but implicit in the use of the word "dependence" was a notion that neuro-adaptation of itself was driving an individual's drinking. The centrality to dependence of withdrawal symptoms continues to excite debate.

Edwards (1990) has argued that withdrawal symptoms should be seen as a special case drinking cue which is integral to the concept of dependence. He has proposed some kind of "watershed", a threshold beyond which individuals experience withdrawal, which thereafter becomes the dominant drinking cue; this is at odds with ideas about continua of severity. While acknowledging that the scientific evidence in support of this view is weak,

Edwards (p. 458) asserts that the clinical evidence is strong: "science is not science . . . until it is tested against what our . . . patients have to tell us". The veracity of this position will continue to be debated; one difficulty of the clinicians' viewpoint is that clinicians usually see a rather small segment of the drinking population and what is really needed is research that spans the whole range of drinkers. The preferred synthesis is that the mix of cues for current drinking start out as predominantly social but are then progressively replaced by pharmacological and then physiological cues. Progression is not inevitable and a mix of all three categories of drinking cue can usually be found, even in circumstances where withdrawal has come to be a preoccupation.

Hershon (1977) looked specifically at the question of which withdrawal symptoms provoked drinking and which were then relieved by drinking, or in other words whether the drinking behaviour was then reinforced. The three most commonly reported symptoms in the Hershon study—depression, anxiety and irritability—were said to have provoked drinking by 83%, 85% and 66% of subjects, respectively, and drinking was 70%, 82% and 66% successful at relieving the symptoms. One interpretation of these data is that negative mood states, whether or not part of physiological withdrawal, are commonly associated with withdrawal and are likely to provoke relief drinking. This is consistent with other evidence that negative mood states are powerful triggers of drinking (see Marlatt, 1985, pp. 37–44). As dependence increases, so drinking becomes a response triggered by ever more cues and cue complexes; for example, Rankin et al. (1982) present evidence that subjects who experience more withdrawal symptoms at one and the same time experience more drinking cues. In a strict sense, detoxification is intended to ameliorate the severity of withdrawal symptoms and thereby eliminate the negative reinforcement of relief drinking. In practice, a broad spectrum of drinking cues are diminished as the process of detoxification progresses.

Raistrick et al. (1994) have conceptualized dependence as a purely psychological phenomenon which is best understood in terms of classical and operant conditioning mechanisms. At a day-to-day clinical practice level, dependence can be thought of as an over-learned collection of thoughts and behaviours related to drinking that are the product of repeated episodes of positive and negative reinforcement: examples of positive reinforcement might be *increased sociability* or *desire for intoxication*, examples of negative reinforcement might be *avoidance of withdrawal* or *relief of depressed mood*. In short, withdrawal symptoms are seen as one among many sources of reinforcement which contribute to dependence in any individual.

The purely psychological formulation of dependence takes account of withdrawal symptoms which, however important and self-generating as drinking cues, need to be taken in the wider context. For example, Tabakoff (1990) has argued that if relief drinking were solely to do with alleviating withdrawal symptomatology, then a single "dose" of alcohol would normally be sufficient for several hours' relief. In practice, early morning drinking often becomes continuous, as if to recapture an alcohol effect: this can be seen as an example of impaired control. Giving undue emphasis to substance specific withdrawal has two further problems: first, it does not take account of the transferability of dependence from one substance to another; second, it does not allow for the measurement of dependence in people who have achieved abstinence, which will have important implications for future treatment. Raistrick et al. (1994) have developed an instrument, the Leeds Dependence Questionnaire, which balances cognitive and behavioural markers of psychological dependence. It is to be expected that this instrument will correlate highly with measures of dependence that emphasize withdrawal symptoms, provided that dependence is being measured during a heavy drinking phase, in people who experience withdrawal, and provided that dependence remains focused on one substance. In short, the psychological view of dependence is a theoretically more satisfactory account of dependence than the psychobiological model.

THE MANAGEMENT OF DETOXIFICATION

Carroll (1997) argues that it is unhelpful for psychosocial therapies and pharmaco-therapies to develop separately; rather, it is the integration of therapies that will deliver the most cost-effective outcomes and should, therefore, be the basis of good practice. Broadly speaking, pharmacotherapies are targeted at a narrow-spectrum of symptoms of psychiatric disorder, in this case withdrawal, and stand in contrast to broader-spectrum psychosocial treatments. Detoxification is, however, something of an exception to the general rule of integrating therapies in that it is largely a stand-alone procedure, which can be used in or out of a therapy programme as circumstances demand but with the caveat that detoxification should always be seen as a therapy opportunity.

Timing of Detoxification

The Transtheoretical Stages of Change Model described by Prochaska & DiClemente (1984) has become a popular clinical tool in the addiction field. Notwithstanding the "trans-theoretical" label, the model has much to do with motivation to change. The Model has been criticized for lacking empirical support and for attempting to define change in stages, rather than along a continuum (see Davidson, 1992). More importantly the five stages of change described in the Model have proved resistant to accurate identification, either by means of clinical assessment or by self-completion questionnaire. The Model predicts that detoxification is an intervention matched to the "action stage", albeit that there are good reasons for detoxification at other stages. Detoxification is commonly misprescribed: first, because practitioners are likely to want their problem drinkers to be at the "action stage" where people are seen to be moving out of addictive behaviour; second, problem drinkers themselves put forward the seductive argument, "If I can go away and detox, then every-thing will be alright"; and third, doctors find it easy to prescribe medication when they have no other appropriate response to make. The problem with careless prescribing is that a failed detoxification risks lowering a patient's self-efficacy and increasing therapist pessimism.

The key to a successful, planned detoxification is preparation. Before proceeding with detoxification, it is the job of the therapist to bring the problem drinker through to the point of readiness to change; this is not to do with transient thoughts about wanting to stop drinking or even actual changes in drinking when these have been occasioned by short-term negative consequences of drinking. The hallmark features of readiness to change are having a positive outcome expectancy or, in other words, a well-considered belief that life will be better without drinking, and self-efficacy or, in other words, a belief that a change in drinking can be achieved. Repeated failure at detoxification will make it more difficult to build self-efficacy in the future. It is a crucial part of the preparation work to identify a supportive other person, to plan activities for the detoxification period and the week imme-diately following, and to check that any practical arrangements, such as childcare or time off from work or travel, are planned in advance.

For opiate users, Phillips et al. (1986) found that a general neuroticism factor and the degree of expected distress during withdrawal were related to subsequent severity of symp-toms. Detoxification is likely to be more problematic where individuals are frightened of what might happen to them and it follows that allaying anxiety is an important part of preparation. Green & Gossop (1988) have shown that simple information giving can be effective at reducing the severity and duration of withdrawal symptoms. Johnston et al. (1991) found that patients with a DSM-III-R diagnosis of anxiety disorder and alcohol dependence experienced significantly greater levels of anxiety throughout detoxification as

compared to alcohol dependence only patients. Milby et al. (1986) identified a pathologi-
cal fear of detoxification in 22–32% of patients attending different methadone maintenance
programmes. This detoxification phobia was found in people with longer drug using histories; the phobias seem to have been acquired during treatment with methadone and can
therefore be seen as iatrogenic. There is no direct counterpart in heavy drinkers but there
is every reason to suppose that the general principle of involving patients in their detoxification will ameliorate anxieties and improve outcome. Coexisting anxiety disorder may
require concurrent therapy.

While it is ideal to plan detoxification with people who have reached the stage of wanting
to change their drinking, there are other occasions when detoxification is indicated. First,
it may be expedient to detoxify someone experiencing withdrawal symptoms after an
enforced abstinence, such as admission to hospital or imprisonment. Second, it is standard
practice to detoxify prior to treatment in a residential programme. Whether it makes sense
routinely to detoxify prior to outpatient therapy is less certain, unless someone's drinking
is so out of control that there is no prospect of any psychosocial therapy succeeding without
prior detoxification. Third, the person who has relapsed after securing a period of abstinence may require detoxification to restabilize.

The Setting for Detoxification

Alcohol treatment has been in rapid evolution over the last 20 years; the treatment population has been extended from the severe "alcoholic" to include people with a relatively
mild alcohol problem and the variety of therapists has been extended to include psychol-
ogists, counsellors, nurses and doctors, among others. Detoxification programmes have also
evolved to take advantage of the range of professional skills available and to respond to
the changing needs of problem drinkers who have come forward for treatment. The aims
of a detoxification programme are to monitor the severity of withdrawal, identify any
complications of withdrawal in order to ensure safety, and to manage withdrawal with a
minimum of discomfort for the patient.

Community-based detoxification can be delivered in the home, on an outpatient or day-
patient basis or within a supported residential facility. Home detoxification is relatively
expensive and should be reserved for people unable to travel to an outpatient unit, for
example, people who have child care problems, disabled people, the elderly. In rural areas
it is likely to be the case that home detoxification is more convenient and no more costly
than the outpatient option. The model of home detoxification developed by Stockwell
et al. (1990) involves daily visits from a psychiatric nurse trained to assess withdrawal and
monitor for complications; any prescribing or medical care is provided by a consultant-led
team or on a shared care basis with a general practitioner. Successful home detoxification
also requires supportive and sensible friends or relatives to stay with the patient during the
detoxification. For people without a home or without the support of friends or relatives, a
community-based facility is a safe alternative to inpatient care. For example, in a recent
study of 1629 admissions to a detoxification centre staffed by care workers, only four people
required transfer to psychiatric care and 17 to a general hospital (Mortimer & Edwards,
1994). The homeless tend to drink relatively modest quantities of alcohol, spread throughout the day, and usually do not experience marked withdrawal problems. The management
of uncomplicated alcohol withdrawal in whatever setting may or may not include the use
of medication. Whitfield et al. (1978) describe the safe detoxification of 1024 people who
presented to non-drug detoxification centres with a variety of medical complications and
severities of withdrawal. The success of these centres depends upon training staff to feel
confident about monitoring withdrawal in order to identify those clients who are in need

of medical help, and training that enables staff quickly to form a helping alliance with clients.

Consideration should always be given to home or residential detoxification for elderly people. Comparing a small group of elderly residents, mean age 69 years, with a younger group, mean age 30 years, who had been admitted for alcohol withdrawal, Brower et al. (1994) found the elderly group experienced significantly more withdrawal symptoms for a longer duration, even though the medication regimes were similar. The elderly group were more likely to show cognitive impairment, day-time sleepiness, weakness and raised blood pressure and were therefore at greater risk.

Standard Pharmacotherapy

The rationale for the pharmacotherapy of alcohol withdrawal is based on the capacity of alcohol to enhance the inhibitory effects of the neurotransmitter γ-aminobutyric acid (GABA) and to diminish the activity of the excitatory N-methyl-D-aspartate, NMDA, receptors. Glue & Nutt (1990) have suggested that the clinical symptoms of withdrawal can be explained by overactivity of the dopaminergic (hallucinations), NMDA (seizures) and noradrenergic (sympathetic activity) systems: each of these systems is under the influence of GABA.

The incidence of withdrawal symptoms requiring pharmacotherapy will vary markedly, depending upon the population of drinkers attending a particular service. Factors that will predict severe withdrawal are: (a) recent high levels of alcohol consumption; (b) previous history of severe withdrawal; (c) previous history of seizures or delirium; (d) concomitant use of psychoactive drugs; (e) poor physical health; and (f) high levels of anxiety and other psychiatric disorder. There is an evidence base to support the good practice of detoxification but the apparently forgiving nature of withdrawal management can lead clinicians into being complacent and unsafe.

For the majority of patients, withdrawal symptoms begin to emerge after some 6–8 hours and peak within the next 24 hours—only rarely do major symptoms persist beyond 5 days. The risk of seizures is small after 2 days and delirium is unlikely to emerge anew in patients who have been adequately treated. In untreated patients, status epilepticus may be the presenting problem (see Alldredge & Lowenstein, 1993). Delirium may be the presenting problem in patients who are still drinking but have markedly reduced their alcohol intake (Kramp & Hemmingsen, 1979), although the incidence is more usually seen to peak at around 4 days post-abstinence. It follows from these time scales that the general aim of pharmacotherapy is rapidly to achieve therapeutic levels of medication and to taper the dose after 48 hours.

The most effective treatments for withdrawal are all GABA-enhancing. The first-line drugs are all sedatives and, to a lesser or greater extent, have the problem that they may cause undue sedation, particularly if taken in the presence of alcohol or other central nervous system depressants. Aside from the medical treatment of alcoholic delirium, there are three basic protocols for detoxification, each of which suits different circumstances:

- *Fixed dose regimen*. In this regimen patients are assessed according to some rather crude measure of withdrawal severity and assigned to a starting point on a predetermined reduction programme. This kind of regime is clinically questionable but may be a satisfactory approach for patients with less severe withdrawal problems or as an expedience where nursing and medical resources are limited.
- *Variable dose regime*. This is probably the most widely used approach and well suited to outpatient or home detoxification. The aim is to prescribe a sufficient but minimal dose of sedative according to a clinical rating of withdrawal severity; ratings should be

made using one of the standardized measurement scales that are discussed below. This approach requires the regular availability of medical, nursing and pharmacy staff.

- *Loading dose regime.* This approach is best suited to inpatient or possibly home detoxification. The principle is that a loading dose of a long-acting sedative is given incrementally to achieve an end-point of light sleep. No further medication is given and detoxification depends on the slow elimination of the drug. This can be a cost-effective approach but skilled supervision and monitoring are required in the initial stages.

In a review of drug treatments for alcohol withdrawal, Williams & McBride (1998) evaluate 14 randomized, double-blind placebo-controlled and 22 randomized, double-blind controlled trials. They highlight serious methodological problems in most of the studies reviewed but, in overview, conclude that benzodiazepines and chlormethiazole are superior to placebo and of similar effectiveness to each other in treating withdrawal, including preventing seizures and delirium. Shaw (1995) concurs with this general conclusion but also concludes that the different pharmacokinetics of benzodiazepines may be used to advantage. A further consideration in favour of benzodiazepines is the availability of the benzodiazepine antagonist flumazenil in the event of overdose. The differences between chlordiazepoxide, diazepam, lorazepam and chlormethiazole as first-line treatments for alcohol withdrawal are marginal, and so it is sensible that clinicians select one or possibly two drugs and become totally familiar with their characteristics.

Chlordiazepoxide

Chlordiazepoxide is long-acting, half-life 5–15 hours, and has active metabolites with half-lives up to 100 hours; there is therefore a risk of an accumulation of active drug leading to unwanted sedation and confusion, especially in the elderly. Chlordiazepoxide has a low addictive potential and a high margin of safety when taken with alcohol. The metabolites of chlordiazepoxide are unique and can, therefore, be separately identified on urine toxicology screening. There is a strong argument for using chlordiazepoxide as the first-line drug in non-residential settings using fixed or variable protocols (see Duncan & Taylor, 1996). A typical reduction regime is presented in Table 3.2.

Diazepam

Diazepam is long-acting, half-life 10–30 hours, and has active metabolites with half-lives up to 100 hours. Accumulation problems are the same as for chlordiazepoxide. Diazepam is more rapidly absorbed than chlordiazepoxide, which gives it a greater addictive potential

Table 3.2 Fixed protocol for chlordiazepoxide withdrawal regimen

	Morning (mg)	Midday (mg)	Evening (mg)	Night (mg)	Total daily dose (mg)
Day 1	30	30	30	30	120
Day 2	30	20	20	30	100
Day 3	20	20	20	20	80
Day 4	20	10	10	20	60
Day 5	10	10	10	10	40
Day 6	10	10	0	10	30
Day 7	10	0	0	10	20

For moderate severity of withdrawal start at day 3, and for mild severity day 5.

but also makes it more suitable for a loading regime. Ritson & Chick (1986) have favoured diazepam, noting its smooth action and its effect on relieving anxiety and depression. Salloum et al. (1995) found that of 37 patients requiring pharmacotherapy and given a loading dose regime, 15 required a single 20 mg dose, 14 required 40–100 mg and 8 required 120–220 mg. They reported no complications related to this treatment.

Lorazepam

Lorazepam is short-acting, half-life 10–20 hours, and has no active metabolites. Lorazepam is well absorbed intramuscularly and can be seen as suited to loading regimes, particularly in patients presenting with more severe symptoms, the elderly and patients with markedly impaired liver function. The short half-life increases the addictive potential of lorazepam and also increases the potential for seizures if the drug is tapered without due caution. Hosein et al. (1978) report on the treatment of 21 patients with incipient alcoholic delirium who were successfully treated with an initial injection of lorazepam 5 mg followed by a tapering dose of oral lorazepam.

Chlormethiazole

Chlormethiazole is short acting, half-life 3–6 hours. The potency of chlormethiazole and its short half-life confer a high addictive potential. It is more likely than benzodiazepines to complicate respiratory insufficiency and to be lethal in combination with alcohol. On the other hand, chlormethiazole is consistently found to be superior to benzodiazepines in preventing seizures and delirium, suggesting that it is the drug of choice for more severe withdrawal and use on an inpatient basis only. Morgan (1995) advises that severe withdrawal symptoms are best controlled by an intravenous infusion of 0.8% chlormethiazole; this should only occur in a general medical setting where there are skilled staff to monitor fluid balance and so forth. She recommends an initial drip rate of 3.0–7.5 ml/minute to induce shallow sleep and thereafter reducing the infusion rate to 0.5–1.0 ml/minute with regular checks to ensure that the patient can be roused.

If hallucinations are a feature of withdrawal, then haloperidol is the treatment of choice and regimens should reflect standard psychiatric practice. Shaw (1995) has estimated that regularly drinking more than 24 units of alcohol on heavy days increases the risk of severe withdrawal, which includes hallucinations in 7.3–32%. Anticipation of severe withdrawal should provoke a full medical work-up, to include examination for Wernicke's encephalopathy, hepatic failure, subdural haematoma, checks for hypoglycaemia, electrolyte balance (including magnesium) and toxicology screen. Where an individual has neglected his/her diet or is scoring in the high risk area of a standard rating scale, then there is strong evidence in favour of giving multivitamin supplements, which should contain at least thiamine 300 mg daily and magnesium supplements. There is an argument for giving vitamin supplements on a routine basis, given that the potential benefits are so great and the cost so small (Cook & Thompson, 1997).

Williams & McBride (1998) concluded that carbamazepine may be an alternative first-line drug to benzodiazepines. Carbamazepine has the advantage of being effective in severe alcohol withdrawal, including alcoholic delirium. It does not interact with alcohol, it is not contraindicated for patients with liver damage and it is thought to prevent the kindling process, which has been implicated in the genesis of seizures and delirium. Carbamazepine is somewhat more expensive than benzodiazepines and there is a risk of serious haematological side effects.

Given the complexity of alcohol effects on neurotransmitter systems, a logical approach to alcohol withdrawal is to use ethanol itself as a pharmacological agent. This is usually not practical because of the problems of dispensing pharmaceutical ethanol and the problem of blood alcohol being a major cue for loss of control over further drinking. However, one setting in which ethanol substitution can be convenient is the intensive care unit. Wilkens et al. (1998) successfully treated 11 postoperative patients for alcohol withdrawal by means of ethanol infusion. They found ethanol elimination rates of 18–50 mg/100 ml/hour, which is rather higher than the widely assumed elimination rate of 15 mg/100 ml/hour.

Adjunctive Therapies

Much of the alcohol withdrawal syndrome is due to adrenergic overactivity. It follows that in cases where either benzodiazepines are deemed unsuitable or where autonomic over-activity is marked, then both α-2-adrenergic agonists, such as lofexidine, and β-adrenergic blockers, such as atenolol, may be beneficial. These drugs can be used either alone or in combination with benzodiazepines (see Brewer, 1995). Neither of these groups of drugs have any effect on preventing seizures or delirium, nor are they expected to have an impact on mood or sleep disturbance. Among other drugs that have found a rationale in the treatment of alcohol withdrawal, Williams & McBride (1998) found insufficient evidence to recommend the use of lithium, bromocriptine or γ-hydroxybutyric acid.

The use of non-pharmaceutical, non-specific "feel-good" therapies has become increasingly popular. These treatments, which include acupuncture, aromatherapy, massage and homeopathy, can be used either on a stand-alone basis for patients with mild withdrawal symptoms or as an adjunctive to pharmacotherapy. Auricular acupuncture has particular appeal, in that it is easy to organize in a variety of settings, it can be done on an individual or group basis, it is inexpensive and there is limited evidence supporting efficacy beyond a generalized "feel-good effect" (Bullock et al., 1989).

Aftercare

In an ideal situation, detoxification will be part of a therapy programme and so aftercare will be planned in advance. The need for post-detoxification treatment will vary enormously from one person to another, depending upon their social circumstances, their psychological well-being and previous levels of dependence. Whatever the long-term drinking goal, a period of total abstinence is usually desirable post-detoxification. Whether or not the detoxification service should offer disulfiram as an aid to abstinence or anti-craving drugs, at least in the period between finishing detoxification and the follow-up key worker appointment, is a policy issue for clinical teams.

If there was any suggestion of mental illness in the pre-detoxification assessment, then the service should also make a full psychiatric assessment post-detoxification. As many as 80% of problem drinkers entering treatment experience psychological symptoms, often as a mixed picture of dysphoria, anxiety, depression, panic and insomnia; in severe cases, ideas of self-harm and hopelessness may be cause for concern. Usually these symptoms fall short of a psychiatric disorder and melt away after a period of abstinence. For example, Driessen et al. (1996) found that for inpatients, who are expected to have high rates of comorbidity, the prevalence of psychiatric disorders 2 weeks post-detoxification was 3% schizophrenia, 13% affective disorder, 22% phobic disorders and 2% generalized anxiety. Brown & Irwin (1991) demonstrated a week-on-week fall in anxiety scores post-detoxification, which continued through to 3 months follow-up. Psychiatric disorder can complicate the management of detoxification; however, Araujo et al. (1996) found no differential effect on drop-out rates between those with and those without disorder. It follows that any treatment for psychiatric disorder should be delayed, preferably for as long as 4 weeks post-detoxification (see Raimo & Schuckit, 1998).

MEASURING WITHDRAWAL AND AUDIT OF DETOXIFICATION

It is usual to use a rating scale to measure the severity of alcohol withdrawal for the dual purpose of determining the dose of medication prescribed to attenuate withdrawal symptomatology and to identify any complications of detoxification. The commonly used scales are all derived from a 20-item scale developed by Gross et al. (1971), who themselves went on to develop a shortened *Selected Severity Assessment Scale* (Gross et al., 1973, pp. 365–376). The original instrument developed by Gross and colleagues had good inter-rater reliability, except on the item "quality of contact". "Visual disturbances" were differentiated from "visual illusions" or "visual hallucinations"; "visual disturbances" were thought to be toxic in origin and consist of phenomena such as flashes of light or moving coloured spots. In addition to the 20 items, the scale is supplemented by charting temperature, pulse and number of seizures should any occur.

Shaw et al. (1981) developed a reliable and validated 15 item scale, the Clinical Institute Withdrawal Assessment for Alcohol (CIWA-A), which was designed for hourly administration. Sullivan et al. (1989) have revised this scale and produced the CIWA-Ar, which has only 10 items. Competent nurses can complete an evaluation in less than 2 minutes. The scale excludes seizures on the grounds that these are rare events which can be noted in the clinical assessment. Equally, pulse and blood pressure, which were not found to correlate with severity of withdrawal, are recorded as indicators of the whole clinical picture. The authors recommend that pharmacological treatment is not indicated for scores less than 10 and clinical judgement should determine the use of pharmacotherapy for scores between 10 and 20.

Metcalfe et al. (1995) also developed a 10 item modification of the CIWA-A but reached rather different clinical judgements to the previous authors. In contrast to the CIWA-Ar, they retained the seizures, "quality of contact" and "thought disturbance" items from the parent instrument. In this case, seizures were included on the grounds that they are relatively common (5–15% of problem drinkers referred for detoxification) and for the reason that around one-third of cases of alcoholic delirium are preceded by one or more seizures. "Quality of contact" and "thought disturbance" items were judged to provide early warning of more severe withdrawal. Thus, the Windsor Clinic Alcohol Withdrawal Assessment Scale (WCAWAS) was designed to be clinically more relevant than CIWA-Ar and the items chosen were seen to be objective. Of the 142 patients in their validation study, 8% developed complicated withdrawals: five developed visual hallucinations, one alcoholic delirium and five had grand mal seizures.

Wetterling et al. (1997) have also devised a scale which seeks to improve upon the CIWA-Ar. As with the CIWA-Ar, the Alcohol Withdrawal Syndrome Scale (AWSS) was derived from a statistical analysis of CIWA-A; seizures were eliminated on the grounds of rarity and irrelevance as a clinical predictor. In their validation study of 256 subjects referred for detoxification, 10.5% developed alcoholic delirium. The authors recommend that scores of five or less be considered mild withdrawal, requiring no medication, and scores 10 or greater be considered severe withdrawal and high risk for complications. The three shorter rating scales, CIWA-Ar, WCAWAS and AWSS, can each be seen as a suitable instrument for monitoring the clinical progress of detoxification. In choosing a particular scale, clinicians will apply their own preferences and intuition; a key issue is whether or

Table 3.3 Scoring systems for different alcohol withdrawal scales

	DCCRS Gross et al. (1971)	CIWA-A Shaw et al. (1981)	CIWA-Ar Sullivan et al. (1989)	WCAWAS Metcalfe et al. (1995)	AWSS Wetterling et al. (1997)
Pulse rate					0–3
Blood pressure					0–3
Temperature					0–3
Respiration rate					0–3
Sweating	0–7	0–7	0–7		0–3
Anxiety	0–7	0–7	0–7	0–4	0–2
Tremor	0–7	0–7	0–7	0–8	0–3
Depression	0–7				
Agitation	0–7	0–7	0–7	0–8	0–4
Snout reflex	0–2				
Hallucinations	0–4	0–3			0–4
Tactile		0–6	0–7		
Auditory		0–6	0–7	0–8	
Visual		0–6	0–7	0–10	
Nausea and vomiting	0–7	0–7	0–7	0–6	
Pruritus	0–7				
Muscle pain	0–7				
Sleep disturbance	0–7				
Nightmares	0–7				
Tinitus	0–7				
Headache		0–7	0–7		
Eating disturbed	0–7				
Thought disturbance		0–3		0–6	
Orientation	0–4	0–4	0–4	0–10	0–3
Impaired consciousness	0–7				
Quality of contact	0–7	0–7		0–6	0–3
Impaired gait	0–7				
Visual disturbance	0–7				
Flushing of the face		0–2			
Insight	0–7				
Seizures		0 or 7		0 or 10	
Max. Score	129	86	67	76	34

not to include withdrawal seizures. The scoring system for different scales is presented in Table 3.3.

Measuring the effectiveness of treatment at minimizing the severity of withdrawal and at preventing complications is one valid indicator of outcome. Equally, detoxification has the clear aim of achieving an alcohol-free state and so, logically, outcome could be assessed on this basis. However, these limited goals lack conviction as outcome measures, and another solution is to tailor outcomes to include more of a feel for the local clinicians' views of success. For example, it may be useful to report the percentage of patients prescribed disulfiram or anti-craving drugs, the percentage of patients attending their therapist post-detoxification or the percentage that continue to take prescribed medication. As well as following the clinical course of detoxification, there is also a need to audit the process of detoxification. First, audit should show evidence of preparation—has the patient been given adequate information? Has a supportive other person been involved? Has a plan of daily activities been worked out? Second, there should be monitoring of the clinical ratings of withdrawal against prescribing practice and complications of withdrawal. Third, there should be some measure of engagement in ongoing therapy where this is appropriate.

There are two things that are important to remember about detoxification. First, improved case management has reduced the mortality rate for the most severe withdrawal state, alcoholic delirium, from in excess of 15% 20 years ago to under 5% today: death is usually caused by cardiovascular collapse, concurrent infection, irreversible hypoglycaemia or malignant hyperthermia. Good case management of withdrawal, whether mild or severe, requires constant vigilance to detect complications. Second, detoxification is an opportunity to help people change. Good therapy can steer the learning experience in the desired direction. A colleague relates the clinical anecdote of two cases which did not have the benefit of addiction therapy during detoxification. One, a film director in his 40s, the other a retired builder, were referred to her clinic during the same month following inpatient admissions for reasons quite unrelated to alcohol dependence. During both inpatient stays, alcoholic delirium was the consequence of the abrupt and unreported cessation of alcohol consumption. At their first consultation, both patients related their frightening experiences, the one concluding "I must never start drinking again", the other concluding "I must never stop drinking again".

KEY WORKS AND SUGGESTIONS FOR FURTHER READING

Edwards, G., Gross, M.M., Keller, M., Moser, J. & Room, R. (Eds) (1977). *Alcohol-related Disabilities*. Geneva: World Health Organization.

This publications gives a good account of the thinking that separated alcohol dependence from alcohol-related problems. There are useful definitions and reference to some of the classic studies of alcohol withdrawal problems.

Stahl, S.M. (1996). *Essential Pharmacology: Neuroscientific Basis and Practical Applications*. Cambridge: Cambridge University Press.

This is a richly illustrated book which offers a very understandable account of neurochemical mechanisms. The book is not specific to alcohol but rather gives an excellent overview of the principal neurochemical pathways and the mechanisms of pharmacotherapies for mental illness problems.

Heather, N. & Robertson, I. (1997). *Problem Drinking*, 3rd edn. Oxford: Oxford University Press.

This easy to read book summarizes the evidence which supports the view that problem drinking is primarily a learned behaviour. An understanding of these arguments is necessary in order to set the management of withdrawal symptoms in the broader treatment context.

Institute of Medicine (1990). *Broadening the Base of Treatment for Alcohol Problems*. Washington, DC: National Academy Press.

This book contains some interesting analysis of key issues that have challenged the expanding alcohol treatment field. Detoxification services are mentioned in several sections but it is the introduction to needs analysis and cost benefits that may be of particular interest.

REFERENCES

Alldredge, B.K. & Lowenstein, D.H. (1993). Status epilepticus related to alcohol abuse. *Epilepsia*, **34**, 1033–1037.

Araujo, L., Goldberg, P., Eyma, J., Madhusoodanan, S., Buff, D.D., Shamim, K. & Brenner, R. (1996). The effect of anxiety and depression on completion/withdrawal status in patients admitted to substance abuse detoxification program. *Journal of Substance Abuse Treatment*, **13**, 61–66.

Brewer, C. (1995). Second-line and "alternative" treatments for alcohol withdrawal: α-agonists, β-blockers, anticonvulsants, acupuncture and neuro-electric therapy. *Alcohol and Alcoholism*, **30**, 799–803.

Brower, K.J., Mudd, S., Blow, F.C., Young, J.P. & Hill, E.M. (1994). Severity and treatment of alcohol withdrawal in elderly versus younger patients. *Alcoholism: Clinical and Experimental Research*, **18**, 196–201.

Brown, S.A. & Irwin, M. (1991). Changes in anxiety among abstinent male alcoholics. *Journal of Studies on Alcohol*, **52**, 55–61.

Bullock, M.L., Culliton, P.D. & Olander, R.T. (1989). Controlled trial of acupuncture for severe recidivist alcoholism. *Lancet*, **1**, 1435–1438.

Carroll, K.M. (1997). Integrating psychotherapy and pharmacotherapy to improve drug abuse outcomes. *Addictive Behaviours*, **22**, 233–245.

Cook, C.H. & Thomson, A.D. (1997). B-complex vitamins in the prophylaxis and treatment of Wernicke–Korsakoff syndrome. *British Journal of Hospital Medicine*, **57**, 461–465.

Davidson, R. (1992). The Prochaska and DiClemente model: reply to the debate. *British Journal of Addiction*, **87**, 833–835.

Driessen, M., Arolt, V., John, U., Veltrup, C. & Dilling, H. (1996). Psychiatric comorbidity in hospitalized alcoholics after detoxification treatment. *European Addiction Research*, **2**, 17–23.

Duncan, D. & Taylor, D. (1996). Chlormethiazole or chlordiazepoxide in alcohol detoxification. *Psychiatric Bulletin*, **20**, 599–601.

Edwards, G. (1990). Withdrawal symptoms and alcohol dependence: fruitful mysteries. *British Journal of Addiction*, **85**, 447–461.

Edwards, G. & Gross, M.M. (1976). Alcohol dependence: provisional description of a clinical syndrome. *British Medical Journal*, **1**, 1058–1061.

Essardas, D.H., Santolaria, F.J., Reimers, G.E., Jorge, J.A., Lopez, B.N., Hernandez, M.F. et al. (1994). Alcohol withdrawal syndrome and seizures. *Alcohol and Alcoholism*, **29**, 323–328.

Glue, P. & Nutt, D. (1990). Overexcitement and disinhibition: dynamic neurotransmitter interactions in alcohol withdrawal. *British Journal of Psychiatry*, **157**, 491–499.

Green, L. & Gossop, M. (1988). Effects of information on the opiate withdrawal syndrome. *British Journal of Addiction*, **83**, 305–309.

Gross, M.M., Rosenblatt, S.M., Chartoff, S., Hermann, A., Schachter, M., Sheinkin, D. & Broman, M. (1971). Evaluation of acute alcoholic psychoses and related states. *Quarterly Journal of Studies on Alcohol*, **32**, 611–619.

Gross, M.M., Lewis, E. & Nagarajan, M. (1973). An improved quantitative system for assessing the acute alcoholic psychoses and related states (TSA and SSA). In M.M. Gross (Ed.), *Advances in Experimental Medicine and Biology, Vol 35. Alcohol Intoxication and Withdrawal: Experimental Studies*. New York: Plenum.

Gross, M.M. (1977). Psychobiological contributions to the alcohol dependence syndrome: a selective review of recent research. In G. Edwards, M.M. Gross, M. Keller, J. Moser & R. Room (Eds), *Alcohol-related Disabilities*. WHO Offset Publication No. 32. Geneva: World Health Organization.

Hershon, H.I. (1977). Alcohol withdrawal symptoms and drinking behavior. *Journal of Studies on Alcohol*, **38**, 953–971.

Hosein, I.N., de Freitas, R. & Beaubrun, M.H. (1978). Intramuscular/oral lorazepam in acute alcohol withdrawal and incipient delirium tremens. *Current Medical Research and Opinion*, **5**, 632–636.

Isbell, H., Fraser, H.F., Wikler, A., Belleville, M.A. & Eisenman, A.J. (1955). An experimental study of the etiology of "rum fits" and delirium tremens. *Quarterly Journal on Studies of Alcohol*, **16**, 1–33.

Johnston, A.L., Thevos, A.K., Randall, C.L. & Anton, R.F. (1991). Increased severity of alcohol with-drawal in inpatient alcoholics with a coexisting anxiety diagnosis. *British Journal of Addiction*, **86**, 719–725.

Kramp, P. & Hemmingsen, R. (1979). Delirium tremens: some clinical features, Part I. *Acta Psychiatrica Scandinavica*, **60**, 393–404.

Kramp, P., Hemmingsen, R. & Rafaelsen, O.J. (1979). Delirium tremens: some clinical features, Part II. *Acta Psychiatrica Scandinavica*, **60**, 405–422.

Marlatt, G.A. (1985). Relapse prevention: theoretical rationale and overview of the model. In A. Marlatt & J. Gordon (Eds), *Relapse Prevention*. London: Guilford.

Mayo-Smith, M.F. & Bernard, D. (1995). Late-onset seizures in alcohol withdrawal. *Alcoholism: Clinical and Experimental Research*, **19**, 656–659.

Metcalfe, P., Sobers, M. & Dewey, M. (1995). The Windsor Clinical Alcohol Withdrawal Assessment Scale (WCAWAS): investigation of factors associated with complicated withdrawals. *Alcohol and Alcoholism*, **30**, 367–372.

Milby, J.B., Gurwitch, R.H., Wiebe, D.J., Ling, W., McLellan, T. & Woody, G.E. (1986). Prevalence and diagnostic reliability of methadone maintenance detoxification fear. *American Journal of Psychiatry*, **143**, 739–743.

Morgan, M.Y. (1995). The management of alcohol withdrawal using chlormethiazole. *Alcohol and Alcoholism*, **30**, 771–774.

Mortimer, R. & Edwards, J.G. (1994). Detoxification in a community-based alcohol recovery unit and psychiatric department of a general hospital. A comparative study. *Psychiatric Bulletin*, **18**, 218–220.

Phillips, G.T., Gossop, M. & Bradley, B. (1986). The influence of psychological factors on the opiate withdrawal syndrome. *British Journal of Psychiatry*, **149**, 235–238.

Prochaska, J.O. & DiClemente, C.C. (1984). *The Transtheoretical Approach: Crossing the Traditional Boundaries of Therapy*. Homewood: Dow Jones/Irwin.

Raimo, E.B. & Schuckit, M.A. (1998). Alcohol dependence and mood disorders. *Addictive Behaviours*, **23**, 933–946.

Raistrick, D., Bradshaw, J., Tober, G., Weiner, J., Allison, J. & Healey, C. (1994). Development of the Leeds Dependence Questionnaire. *Addiction*, **89**, 563–572.

Rankin, H., Stockwell, T. & Hodgson, R. (1982). Cues for drinking and degrees of alcohol dependence. *British Journal of Addiction*, **77**, 287–296.

Ritson, B. & Chick, J. (1986). Comparison of two benzodiazepines in the treatment of alcohol withdrawal: effects on symptoms and cognitive recovery. *Drug and Alcohol Dependence*, **18**, 329–334.

Salloum, I.M., Cornelius, J.R., Daley, D.C. & Thase, M.E. (1995). The utility of diazepam loading in the treatment of alcohol withdrawal among psychiatric inpatients. *Psychopharmacology Bulletin*, **31**, 305–310.

Schuckit, M.A., Tipp, J.E., Reich, T., Hesselbrock, V.M. & Bucholz, K.K. (1995). The histories of withdrawal convulsions and delirium tremens in 1648 alcohol dependent subjects. *Addiction*, **90**, 1335–1347.

Shaw, J.M., Sellers, G.S., Kaplan, H.L. & Sandor, P. (1981). Development of optimal treatment tactics for alcohol withdrawal. I. Assessment and effectiveness of supportive care. *Journal of Clinical Psychopharmacology*, **1**, 382–388.

Shaw, G.K. (1995). Detoxification: the use of benzodiazepines. *Alcohol and Alcoholism*, **30**, 765–770.

Stockwell, T., Hodgson, R., Edwards, G., Taylor, C. & Rankin, H. (1979). The development of a questionnaire to measure severity of alcohol dependence. *British Journal of Addiction*, **74**, 79–87.

Stockwell, T., Bolt, L., Milner, I., Pugh, P. & Young, I. (1990). Home detoxification for problem drinkers: acceptability to clients, relatives, general practitioners and outcome after 60 days. *British Journal of Addiction*, **85**, 61–70.

Stockwell, T. (1994). Alcohol withdrawal: an adaptation to heavy drinking of no practical significance? *Addiction*, **89**, 1447–1453.

Sullivan, J.T., Sykora, K., Schneiderman, J., Naranjo, C.A. & Sellers, E.M. (1989). Assessment of alcohol withdrawal: the revised clinical institute withdrawal assessment for alcohol scale (CIWA-Ar). *British Journal of Addiction*, **84**, 1353–1357.

Tabakoff, B. (1990).   One man's craving is another man's dependence. *British Journal of Addiction*, **85**, 1253–1254.
Tober, G. (1992).   What is dependence and why is it important? *Clinical Psychology Forum*, **41**, 14–16.
Tsaung, J.W., Irwin, M.R., Smith, T.L. & Schuckit, M.A. (1994).   Characteristics of men with alcoholic hallucinosis. *Addiction*, **89**, 73–78.
Vinson, D.C. & Menezes, M. (1991).   Admission alcohol level: a predictor of the course of alcohol withdrawal. *Journal of Family Practice*, **33**, 161–167.
Wetterling, T., Kanitz, R., Besters, B., Fischer, D., Zerfass, B., John, U. et al. (1997).   A new rating scale for the assessment of the alcohol-withdrawal syndrome (AWS scale). *Alcohol and Alcoholism*, **32**, 753–760.
Whitfield, C.L., Thompson, G., Lamb, A., Spencer, V., Pfeifer, M. & Browning-Ferrando, M. (1978).   Detoxification of 1024 alcoholic patients without psychoactive drugs. *Journal of the American Medical Association*, **239**, 1409–1410.
Wilkens, L., Ruschulte, H., Ruckoldt, H., Hecker, H., Scroder, D., Piepenbrock, S. & Leuwer, M. (1998).   Standard calculation of ethanol elimination rate is to sufficient to provide ethanol substitution therapy in the postoperative course of alcohol-dependent patients. *Intensive Care Medicine*, **24**, 459–463.
Williams, D. & McBride, A.J. (1998).   The drug treatment of alcohol withdrawal symptoms: a systematic review. *Alcohol and Alcoholism*, **33**, 103–115.
World Health Organization (1992).   *The ICD-10 Classification of Mental and Behavioural Disorders: Clinical Descriptions and Diagnostic Guidelines*. Geneva: WHO.

Chapter 4

Pharmacological Treatments

Jonathan Chick
Alcohol Problems Clinic, Royal Edinburgh Hospital, Edinburgh, UK

Synopsis

For years, the only medications that could help prevent relapse in alcohol dependence were the deterrent drugs such as disulfiram, and even those appeared only to be effective when taken under supervision. Based on research into the neurochemical pathways involved in animal models of alcohol preference and dependence, three types of drugs have been developed which are safe in humans and have been found to reduce relapse rates in alcohol dependence, at least under certain conditions: acamprosate, opioid antagonists and some serotonin-enhancing drugs. The use in practice of these medications, as well as that of disulfiram, is described in this chapter, together with a summary of their proposed mode of action, their effectiveness, their unwanted effects, the characteristics of patients most likely to respond (although information here is often lacking) and their interaction with other therapies. Another chapter deals with the use of medication in treating alcohol withdrawal.

Treating an addiction with another drug sometimes alarms sufferers, their families and therapists. Is it not substituting one addiction with another? The drug therapies tested to reduce relapse during outpatient treatment, to be described in the main section of this chapter, have not been shown to be abused for their psychotropic effects, and do not prolong a dependent state because of cross-tolerance with alcohol, as occurs with benzodiazepines. Neither do they worsen the psychomotor retardation caused by ethanol if the person drinks. Evidence about their mode of action, safety and efficacy will be presented.

The Essential *Handbook of Treatment and Prevention of Alcohol Problems.* Edited by N. Heather and T. Stockwell.
© 2004 John Wiley & Sons Ltd. ISBN 0-470-86296-3.

DETERRENT MEDICATION

Mode of Action

Disulfiram, if taken regularly in a sufficient dose, causes an unpleasant reaction 15–20 minutes after alcohol enters the body. The reaction is due to accumulation of the intermediate metabolite of ethanol, acetaldehyde. The patient flushes, experiences headache, pounding in the chest or head, tightness in breathing, nausea and perhaps vomits. Hypotension can be dangerous, but deaths have been exceedingly rare, with documented cases usually being individuals who had received large doses and/or had pre-existing heart disease. The efficacy of disulfiram depends on deterring the patient from drinking because of fear or distaste for the reaction.

In the typical dose of 200 or 250 mg/day, some individuals will have only a mild reaction if they drink alcohol. Probably some patients, at varying frequency and without declaring it to the therapist or without it being obvious, consume small amounts of alcohol. This was the likely explanation for the finding that the urinary marker of recent ethanol consumption, 5-hydroxytryptophol, can sometimes signal positive for ethanol in patients taking disulfiram, but normalizes if the dose of disulfiram is increased (Helander, 1998).

In the past, surgical implantation of disulfiram tablets under the skin was sometimes used as a longer-term deterrent. This is seldom used now, partly because the active drug was often not detectable in blood after about 2 weeks. However, when patients were told that there was a risk of a reaction for several months after the implant was inserted, many patients had long periods of abstinence, especially if they had tested it out and had a reaction in the early weeks. Local skin reactions occurred in some patients.

The antimicrobial drug metronidazole causes a disulfiram-like interaction with ethanol and has been used in treating alcohol dependence, as a deterrent. However, it has several, albeit infrequent, toxic effects and is not a drug to prescribe lightly. Calcium carbimide is a drug with similar properties to disulfiram, but it is out of production.

Evidence of Efficacy

Hughes & Cook (1997) and Wright & Moore (1990) reviewed published efficacy studies. It is only when compliance with the medication has been improved by supervision that randomized controlled studies show with consistency that disulfiram is associated with a better outcome on drinking measures than placebo. In some patients, it is the belief that if they drink while taking the tablet they will be ill that enhances abstinence. Thus, in the randomized controlled study analysed by Fuller & Williford (1980), there was no difference at the end of 1 year between groups who had received 1 mg disulfiram (insufficient to cause an ethanol reaction) and 250 mg.

Many patients do not test out the reaction. However, a difficulty in placebo-controlled studies is that telling subjects they may be prescribed a dummy may lead to a greater number of subjects testing it out. Of those who test it out, a proportion will not get much reaction, even on a dose of 200 mg or 250 mg. For those, the drug loses its effect. Thus, for the research subject and the investigator to remain blind to the treatment could be seen as preventing a test of one of the features of the disulfiram treatment package, namely, the instillation of fear to drink. This could be part of the explanation for the failure to show an effect of disulfiram in the all-patient analysis in the largest reported trial ($n = 605$) of unsupervised disulfiram (Fuller et al., 1986). Nevertheless, Fuller et al. found that amongst patients who attended all appointments (thus, a compliant group), such that there were sufficient detailed data on patterns of drinking, disulfiram 250 mg daily was associated with significantly fewer drinking days than disulfiram 1 mg or placebo.

There seems to be a tendency in some patients for disulfiram treatment to become less effective over time. For example, Chick et al. (1992) compared supervised disulfiram to vitamin C. The "blind" assessor rated more abstinent days and less total consumption in the 6 months of the trial in the disulfiram group. However, in the last month of the study the groups' mean consumption did not differ. This may be due to diminishing compliance, or a waning of the fear of the reaction.

Characteristics of Responders

The literature is contradictory in specifying who benefits from being offered disulfiram (Hughes & Cook, 1997). Having a partner or supervisor to aid compliance, and some incentive, would seem to be important. In a randomized trial comparing disulfiram vs. no medication in patients dependent on both cocaine and alcohol, patients allocated to disulfiram had longer periods of abstinence from alcohol and longer periods of abstinence from cocaine (Carroll et al., 1998). The authors speculated that the patients had the incentive to receive help to get off cocaine. When a methadone prescription is the incentive in methadone maintenance clinics, patients with coexisting opiate and alcohol dependence do better if they take disulfiram as a condition of their prescription (Liebson et al., 1978).

Interaction with Other Therapies

Trials have not applied randomized methods to compare whether disulfiram is more effective when combined with some psychosocial treatments rather than others. The largest treatment effect size in the disulfiram literature (although in a small sample of 42 patients) was seen by Azrin (1976) in a study in which supervised disulfiram was added to community reinforcement therapy (see Bigelow, 2001 and Chapter 1, this volume.) and marital behavioural therapy. Azrin found almost 100% abstinence over 2 years in the 20 disulfiram patients. In the studies of Azrin and colleagues (Azrin, 1976; Azrin et al., 1982), when disulfiram was shown to produce an added advantage, it had been part of a contract and ingestion was supervised.

Duckert & Johnsen (1987) studied the use of disulfiram combined with a behaviour therapy approach which permitted patients to choose their own goals, including "controlled drinking". Some patients used the disulfiram intermittently, and interspersed this with drinking; some patients used it to deal with high-risk situations they had identified in the psychological therapy. Compared to non-users of disulfiram, users consumed significantly less alcohol by the end of the study.

Disulfiram has been used with apparent success with acamprosate (see below), in a study where random allocation was made to either acamprosate or placebo, and some patients also chose to take disulfiram. The longest time to relapse was seen in patients taking both drugs (Besson et al., 1998).

Unwanted Effects

One or more unwanted effects, including drowsiness, headache or, less commonly, bad breath or skin rash, occurs in about every tenth patient.

Very rare but potentially fatal liver hypersensitivity has been reported. This type of liver reaction is reported in a number of other medications in common use over many years, e.g. chlorpromazine (Largactil). For disulfiram, death due to liver hypersensitivity is estimated to occur in 1 in 25,000 patients treated per year (Chick, 1999). Most cases have developed in the first 3 months of treatment. Overall, disulfiram is associated with improvement in liver function tests compared to control groups rather than worsening—presumably due to reduction of drinking (Chick et al., 1992).

Controlled studies have not found that there are more complaints of sexual dysfunction in patients taking disulfiram than in control groups. Peripheral neuropathy (almost always reversible) has been reported in rare cases following some months of treatment at doses of over 250 mg. There are a few reports of psychosis induced by disulfiram and a history of psychotic illness has been a contraindication in the licensing in some countries. The risk is so low and the need to help schizophrenic patients with alcohol problems is sometimes so pressing that in other countries that contraindication is changed to a "caution". There are many documented cases where improvement due to abstaining from alcohol has occurred in psychotic patients while taking disulfiram, and in a dose of up to 250 mg/day there are no problems from unwanted effects or interactions with medication for the psychiatric illness (Larson et al., 1992).

Disulfiram slows the breakdown of a number of commonly prescribed medications, including some antidepressants such as amitryptiline and imipramine, and this can be therapeutic rather than harmful. However, with other affected compounds, such as anticonvulsants (e.g. phenytoin) and warfarin, there are risks of toxic effects and the combination should be avoided or extra plasma monitoring put in place. Unwanted effects of disulfiram have been reviewed in detail by Chick (1999).

Use in Practice

Disulfiram should not be given to patients with active or recent heart disease. Great caution must be used if prescribing to patients taking medication to lower blood pressure, when the hypotension resulting if the patient drank alcohol having been taking disulfiram would be exaggerated and extremely dangerous. Like many drugs metabolized in the liver, it should not be given in advanced liver disease. There is no consensus as to whether or not it should be given to people with mild or moderately abnormal liver enzyme tests. If it aids sobriety, then the liver damaged by alcohol can improve.

Disulfiram enables the individual to get used to life without alcohol and allows time for confidence to resume in the family and at work. It only works if taken consistently. It is suggested to patients that they recruit someone to help them remember to take it and see them take it, such as their partner, or a nurse or welfare officer at work, a high street pharmacist, or a nurse at the clinic or a Health Centre. This can be either daily or three times a week in a larger dose, so that at least 1400 mg/week is taken. The tablet can be taken dispersed in water so that it can be seen to be swallowed.

It is common to prescribe disulfiram for 6 months, but many patients and their families ask to continue the method much longer. There are sometimes slips, even after long periods of abstinence when the disulfiram is ceased, and many patients keep a supply to use when they are at risk of drinking, for example, on a business trip away or at a social event.

Some clinics regard disulfiram as "a last ditch". Indeed, after numerous admissions and relapses, clinics may make further treatment conditional on supervised disulfiram. This was documented as successful in a controlled study by Sereny et al. (1986).

Sometimes an employer is prepared to reinstate an employee suspended because of an alcohol-related infringement if the employer knows that supervised disulfiram is being taken. When employees on their final warning were offered supervised disulfiram, they reduced their annual absenteeism rate from 10% to 2%. However, after the year's disciplinary period ended and some stopped the disulfiram, annual absenteeism of these employees rose again, towards but not reaching the previous level (Robichaud et al., 1979). While ethically repugnant to some physicians, supervised disulfiram can be effective as part of probation or when there is a deferral of sentence while the Court waits to see if good behaviour is maintained (Chick, 1998).

There is no consensus on whether or not blood tests to monitor liver function should be repeated at intervals. The very rare disulfiram-induced hepatitis mentioned above seems to commence very suddenly. It has been argued that even monthly blood tests cannot guarantee early detection of the reaction and that the rarity of the condition therefore does not justify frequent testing (Chick, 1999)

It is recognized practice to increase the dose of disulfiram, for example to 400 mg/day, if the patient finds the deterrent method useful in principle, but has tested out the alcohol reaction and the reaction has not been severe enough to act as a deterrent.

What to Tell Patients

Patients should be informed about the risks of the reaction, the need to avoid ethanol in foods or some medicines, and of the unwanted effects.

Patients may object that it is weakness to take a deterrent pill, instead of using "will-power". But they may agree that will-power is not always there when most needed. With the pills, a decision to drink or not still has to be made, but only once a day. An analogy can be made with recovery after a fracture—a splint permits stability to allow the fracture to heal.

THE OPIOID ANTAGONISTS

Mode of Action

The brain's own opiate transmitters, endorphins, are involved in the release of dopamine in the nucleus accumbens, which is believed to be part of the brain substrate of reward and addiction (see Lingford-Hughes & Nutt, 2001). There are drugs which antagonize endorphin transmission. Of these drugs, naltrexone and nalmefene reach the brain after having been taken by mouth and act for some 24 hours, making them potentially relevant for the clinical situation. Stimulating endorphin transmission is one of many acute actions of ethanol on the limbic system.

Naltrexone reduces ethanol-seeking in dependent animals. Several strains of alcohol-consuming animals show "catch-up drinking" after periods of imposed abstinence, much like the human reinstatement phenomenon. Naltrexone reduces catch-up drinking. Reid et al. (1996) have studied the durability of naltrexone's effects in alcohol-consuming rats. They found that the naltrexone-induced inhibition of ethanol drinking did not diminish when naltrexone was continued over some days. But when naltrexone was replaced by placebo, drinking immediately resumed at the level of the control rats. There was no carry-over of its effect. Part of naltrexone's action may be to reduce the positive, rewarding effects of ethanol, and studies of its effect on non-dependent drinking in humans, and its subjective correlates, have tended to support this (for a recent study and review, see Davidson et al., 1999). It could be that some alcohol-dependent individuals have a particularly pronounced endorphin response to alcohol (Gianoulakis et al., 1996) and by blocking this, naltrexone can help prevent relapse in susceptible individuals after the first drink is taken.

Sinclair (1998) proposes that when drinking is repeated while positive effects of ethanol are blocked by the opioid antagonist, drinking behaviour will gradually be extinguished, as in a classical conditioning paradigm (see Chapter 14). Thus, naltrexone's action in reducing drinking will only appear if the subject consumes some ethanol on a number of occasions while premedicated with naltrexone.

A related hypothesis is that, as well as reducing positive experiences of drinking, naltrexone may also reduce the strength of conditioned positive associations of drinking, including positive thoughts about drinking and the intensity of positive cue-triggered urges to drink (O'Brien et al., 1998). But a test of this in the laboratory by Modesto-Lowe et al. (1997) found that 1 week of pre-treatment with naltrexone did not reduce the desire to take alcohol expressed by patients with coexisting alcohol and cocaine dependence after watching a film about drinking.

In the follow-up studies of naltrexone in the treatment of alcohol dependence, subjects who lapse have been asked about their experiences after a drink is taken. In the study of O'Malley et al. (1992), amongst those who took at least one drink during the 3 month outpatient treatment period, subjects who were prescribed daily naltrexone reported lower levels of craving for alcohol compared to subjects who received placebo, and were more likely to give reasons for terminating drinking that were consistent with decreased incentive to drink (O'Malley et al., 1996a). Some patients who resume drinking while taking naltrexone report that they felt less of the ethanol "high". Perhaps they then experience less impulse to carry on drinking (Volpicelli et al., 1995).

Evidence of Efficacy

Three double-blind randomized controlled studies of naltrexone in detoxified patients taking part in an outpatient treatment programme have been published at the time of writing. They mostly show a reduced risk of relapse [defined as more than five US standard drinks (65 g ethanol) in a day], over a 3 month study duration. The same result was found for nalmefene (Mason et al., 1999).

In the two earliest studies that had the most unequivocal results, the effect size of naltrexone treatment in reducing the percentage of days drinking was 0.42 (Volpicelli et al., 1992) and 0.60 (O'Malley et al., 1992; for review, see Volpicelli et al., 1995). An effect size of 1.0 means success in all patients and 0.0 in none. For comparison, the mean effect size in reducing depressive symptoms in meta-analyses of studies of fluoxetine in the treatment of depression is around 0.4. In the first Veterans Administration hospital study of Volpicelli et al. (1992), naltrexone treatment was associated with greater reduction in craving than placebo, but not with a significantly greater rate of total abstinence. The effect in reducing relapse (defined as more than 5 drinks per day) was greatest when the subsample of those who had taken at least one drink during the study was examined. However, in the O'Malley study there was an advantage to naltrexone in the numbers of patients who reported achieving total abstinence as well as a reduction of drinking overall.

The marker of drinking, serum aspartate aminotransferase (AST) level, was significantly lower at 3 months in the naltrexone group compared to the placebo group for O'Malley et al. (1992), with a similar but non-significant trend for the less specific marker alanine aminotransferase. There was a non-significant trend in the study of Volpicelli et al. (1992) for lower serum AST and serum γ-glutamyl transferase (GGT) levels in the naltrexone group compared to the placebo group.

Subsequent analyses and further studies have found that compliance is critical. O'Brien et al. (1996) showed that the naltrexone treatment effect in the study of Volpicelli et al. (1992) was higher among those who complied with medication than among less compliant patients. In a later 3 month outpatient study at the same centre, the overall advantage of naltrexone treatment was only modest, with 35% of the naltrexone group relapsing over 3 months compared to 53% in the placebo group. However, among those who completed treatment, relapse occurred in only 25% of naltrexone-treated subjects compared to 53% of placebo subjects (Volpicelli et al., 1997).

Some clinicians have wondered whether, unlike the animal results of Reid et al. (1996; see above), the efficacy of naltrexone might wane with longer use. This has not yet been answered. Relating to appropriate length of treatment are the findings of O'Malley (1996b), who followed patients from the study quoted above (O'Malley, 1992) for 6 months after withdrawal of medication. Although there was no sudden peak of relapse, there was a tendency for the previous naltrexone-treated patients to relapse, so that after 6 months there was no statistically significant difference between the groups. While there are no controlled studies of longer than 3 months duration, it might nevertheless be appropriate in some patients to continue prescribing it for longer.

Characteristics of Responders

Peterson et al. (1996) compared response to drinking alcohol in young non-alcoholic men at high genetic risk of alcohol dependence with that in controls. They had a greater increase in heart rate after drinking, and peak production of plasma β-endorphin correlated with increased heart rate. They proposed that a subset of those at high risk for alcoholism might be characterized by heightened heart-rate response to ethanol mediated by endorphin production, and that these persons might differentially benefit from naltrexone treatment. Volpicelli et al. (1995) found that beneficial response to naltrexone in their original study was greater in those who initially had reported high levels of craving for alcohol and higher levels of somatic symptoms.

Jaffe et al. (1996), in a post-hoc analysis of the results of the naltrexone/placebo trial of O'Malley et al. (1992), found that naltrexone had additionally benefited patients who at intake to the study had high craving, poor learning ability and more severe dependence.

Interaction with Other Therapies

In their study of random allocation to naltrexone or placebo, O'Malley et al. (1992) found that there was a greater advantage of naltrexone to placebo in patients who, in the psychotherapy arm of the trial, had been randomly allocated to cognitive-behavioural therapy rather than to supportive therapy. Balldin et al. (1998) designed a similar study, and found a response to naltrexone *only* in those allocated to cognitive-behavioural therapy, and no effect in those in the "treatment-as-usual" group.

Unwanted Effects

Early speculation that opiate antagonists might cause dysphoria seemed to be supported by statements from heroin addicts given naltrexone, even when they were apparently some weeks free of heroin. Placebo-controlled studies in alcohol-dependent patients have consistently only revealed one unwanted effect that is commoner in naltrexone-treated patients—nausea. Headache, dizziness and weight loss have also been found to be commoner in naltrexone-treated than placebo groups. Neither depression nor inability to feel pleasure are associated with the use of naltrexone by alcohol-dependent patients. There are only anecdotal reports of alterations (increase and decrease) in sexual performance or desire. Data have been systematically collected on patients who have taken naltrexone for up to a year, and no cumulative harm has been detected (Croop et al., 1997).

Use in Practice

Naltrexone is prescribed as one 50 mg tablet each morning. To reduce the risk of early side-effects, a half tablet is usually given for the first 3 or 4 days. Naltrexone is to aid those who are striving to remain completely abstinent. Despite the data from the studies quoted above showing that its effect was greatest in those who had had a lapse, at the time of writing there is no published controlled study showing naltrexone as an aid to moderating drinking. If patients drink while taking naltrexone, they are advised to continue the drug but also put into play all methods they can to terminate the lapse and regain abstinence. Because regular compliance is necessary if an overall effect of naltrexone is to be seen, a sustained-release injection is being developed (Kranzler et al., 1998). Naltrexone is metabolized in the liver and should not be used when there is hepatic decompensation.

ACAMPROSATE (CALCIUM ACETYL HOMOTAURINATE)

Mode of Action

The inhibitory neurotransmitter γ-aminobutyric acid (GABA) and the excitatory transmitter glutamate are known to be important in alcohol dependence (see Lingford-Hughes & Nutt, 2001). Acamprosate acts in a dose-dependent way to reduce glutamate transmission by acting at the NMDA receptor complex. It may also reduce activity of the voltage-operated calcium channels, which are over-active after alcohol withdrawal (Littleton, 1995). It does this without any benzodiazepine-like tranquillizing action.

Indicators of excessive brain glutamate activity can be detected in the cerebrospinal fluid of alcohol-dependent patients at least a month following withdrawal from alcohol (Tsai et al., 1998), and this may contribute to what Begleiter & Porjesz (1979) proposed might be a "sub-acute withdrawal syndrome". They referred to the psychological and physiological parameters (e.g. irritability, anxiety, depression, sleep EEG, temperature control, cortisol response to stressors and electrophysiological signs of nervous system hyperexcitability) which are abnormal during withdrawal and still abnormal up to 4 months later.

Acamprosate reduces drinking in alcohol-dependent animals, and reduces the reinstatement of drinking behaviour and withdrawal symptoms in animals re-exposed to alcohol after a period of abstinence. It does not substitute for ethanol or benzodiazepines in animals in the sense that they will seek out acamprosate; that is, it is not in itself rewarding (reviewed by Littleton, 1995). Although acamprosate has been called an anti-craving medication, that conscious experience of craving is not felt by many drinkers who relapse. It may be more accurate to say that acamprosate may reduce drinking by altering the sub-acute withdrawal state, and perhaps drinking triggered by priming doses of alcohol and cues to drinking that have been conditioned via the GABA–glutamate system.

Evidence of Efficacy

The first randomized controlled study of acamprosate in recently detoxified patients found that 33% of acamprosate-treated patients relapsed during the 3 month outpatient period, compared to 66% of placebo patients (Lhuintre et al., 1985). The effect was subsequently seen to be dose-related in a larger 12 month study (Paille et al., 1995). The dose-related effect was also shown by Pelc et al. (1997). Other large randomized controlled studies, each in at least 200 alcohol-dependent newly abstinent patients, have shown acamprosate's efficacy, typically enhancing complete abstinence by some 20% above the rate achieved in the placebo group (i.e. approximately doubling the proportion of complete abstainers) for up to 1 year (e.g. Whitworth et al., 1996; Sass et al., 1996; Poldrugo, 1997). These studies also found that the cumulative total of days of abstinence was significantly greater in the acamprosate-treated patients. Some of these studies (e.g. Whitworth et al., 1996) followed patients into the year after medication was withdrawn, without evidence of sudden relapse. Whereas the Swiss study by Besson et al. (1998) of 110 patients found that the advantage of acamprosate over placebo persisted until the end of a 12 month period, the smaller, earlier Swiss study (Ladewig et al., 1993) had found that a significant trend to advantage was detected only in the first 3 months.

With regard to objective markers of alcohol consumption, Paille et al. (1995) found the self-report data showing acamprosate-treated patients drank less overall was corroborated by significantly lower GGT levels during the 1 year follow-up compared to placebo-treated patients. Corroboration by significantly greater improvement in GGT was found in the Italian study (Poldrugo, 1997) and the Swiss study of Besson et al. (1998).

The large UK multicentre study (Chick et al., 2000) is the only study known to the author in which acamprosate was not associated with statistically significantly better outcome than placebo. Another large study (Lhuintre et al., 1990) was less clear in terms of self-reported abstinence than the other studies quoted above, but nevertheless found an advantage to acamprosate in terms of serum GGT.

Characteristics of Responders

Data in the efficacy studies just quoted have been analysed to tease out which type of patient is most likely to benefit from acamprosate. None has been revealed. Lesch & Walter (1996) have proposed the more "pure" alcohol-dependent patients without psychiatric disorders or evidence of early childhood behaviour disorder related to brain injury.

Interaction with Other Therapies

No interaction with type of outpatient therapy has been found. Acamprosate has been used safely while patients are prescribed antidepressants. In the study of Besson et al. (1998), patients who requested it were permitted to also take disulfiram. Those patients who were randomly allocated to acamprosate and also took disulfiram did better than those who were not also taking disulfiram. Although it could be that those who chose to take disulfiram as well as the study medication were specially well-motivated, it may be that the drug effects are important: taking acamprosate may reduce the need to drink, and disulfiram reinforces the conscious determination to avoid alcohol.

Unwanted Effects

Diarrhoea and abdominal discomfort are the only common (approximately 10%) unwanted effects reported, and this is usually mild. Acamprosate is excreted via the kidney without being metabolized in the liver. Thus, in mild to moderate liver disease (before kidney function is affected), it is safe. It has no abuse potential and does not interact harmfully with alcohol.

Use in Practice

In the studies showing efficacy of acamprosate, patients met criteria for alcohol dependence, expressed a goal of abstinence and commenced the drug within a week or two after the last drink. Its advantage over placebo emerges in the first 2 months after withdrawal. It has not been tested as a stand-alone treatment, although in some of the above studies the psychosocial treatment offered was not intensive. Until more precise information is available, these points should guide its use.

SEROTONERGIC AND NORADRENERGIC MEDICATIONS (ANTIDEPRESSANTS)

Mode of Action

Numerous animal studies have implicated serotonin (5-HT) transmission in alcohol preference and dependence (Le et al., 1996; see Lingford-Hughes & Nutt, 2001). Specific 5-HT-reuptake inhibitors (SSRIs) reduce volitional drinking in animals, but their effect in reducing drinking in non-depressed alcohol-dependent patients is equivocal, is more predictable in non-dependent drinkers, and tends to be short-lived (reviewed by Lejoyeux, 1996; Pettinati, 1996). In particular, no effect of fluoxetine was seen in the large, well-designed and analysed controlled study of Kranzler et al. (1995).

For citalopram, the results are more positive, and Angelone et al. (1998) found that citalopram and fluvoxamine were associated with 52% and 56%, respectively, of complete abstinence compared to placebo of 30% over 16 weeks (reanalysed here to the intention to treat sample).

When depressive symptoms are present in the newly detoxified patients, SSRIs and other antidepressants have been found to help more consistently. Imipramine helped depressive symptoms in alcoholics with a primary depressive illness, and if depression lifted, drinking was seen to improve (McGrath et al., 1996). Cornelius et al. (1997) found severely depressed patients recovered more from their depression, drank less and had more abstinent days if they took fluoxetine in a 3 month study, although rates of attaining complete abstinence were not significantly different statistically; however, there was a trend: fluoxetine 28%, placebo 15%. Desipramine, a tricyclic antidepressant that enhances transmission via noradrenaline more than via serotonin, reduced relapse in alcohol-dependent patients who also had major depression, but not if they did not meet major depression criteria (Mason et al., 1994). Powell et al. (1995), in a group of male alcoholics followed for 6 months, found that nortryptiline, another noradrenergic antidepressant, was associated with reduction of drinking greater than placebo, not in depressives but in those with antisocial personality disorder, who tended, if they were in the placebo group, to have the worst outcome (antisocial personality disorder is closer to Type II than Type I; see Epstein, 2001). Buspirone, the 5-HT_{1A} partial agonist, is a treatment for anxiety disorders, and it also reduces ethanol drinking in rats who have been regularly taking ethanol for many weeks independent of the anxiolytic effect of the drug. Kranzler et al. (1994) found that buspirone, started in a low dose with gradual increase to a full dose to avoid initial unwanted effects, reduced drinking as well as anxiety in anxious alcohol-dependent patients. Subsequent studies led to the conclusion that buspirone is only indicated if patients have significant anxiety.

Lithium is not a treatment for alcohol dependence itself, but is effective if there is primary manic-depressive disorder.

Characteristics of Responders

As discussed above, psychiatric disorders such as depression or anxiety disorder predict response to serotonin drugs. There is evidence that post-traumatic stress disorder responds to these drugs, and there are patients whose alcohol dependence is linked to this disorder. An argument has been put forward that impulsive, socially disorganized, early onset patients ("Type B" or "Type I", see Epstein, 2001) would be those who would respond to serotonin-enhancing drugs, but there has been little clinical support so far. If anything, the opposite is emerging. Kranzler et al. (1996) found type B alcoholics drank more when taking fluoxetine than placebo, and Pettinati et al. (2000) found that the SSRI sertraline slightly improved the outcome for Type A alcoholics (later onset, more socially stable, less severe) but did not do so in Type B.

Interactions with Other Therapies

Kranzler et al. (1996), in a controlled study of fluoxetine, found an association between poorer response to cognitive therapy and taking fluoxetine in Type B patients. Such associations may occur by chance and require replication in specifically designed studies.

Unwanted Effects

Tihonen et al. (1996) reported an advantage to citalopram in self-report, relatives' report and GGT after 3 months treatment, with a higher drop-out rate in the placebo group than the citalopram group. They only presented data on patients who had taken a full week of drug therapy, which may have excluded some of those who had unwanted effects from the drug (numbers excluded were not published). Initial side-effects of SSRIs (nausea, agitation, insomnia) cause people to stop treatment. One reason why fluoxetine may have emerged as more effective than placebo in the small placebo-controlled study of fluoxetine of Janiri et al. (1996) is because small doses of benzodiazepine were allowed.

OTHER COMPOUNDS INVESTIGATED

Benzodiazepine tranquillizers substitute partly for alcohol. When alcohol dependence is related to severe chronic anxiety persisting some weeks into abstinence, a long-acting benzodiazepine, such as chlordiazepoxide or diazepam, may permit a better quality of life and reduce the risk of relapse to drinking. However, dependence on the benzodiazepine is likely and the anxiety condition may remain chronic. Benzodiazepines should be avoided in impulsive individuals or those with a history of drug misuse, since abuse may develop, and should be avoided in persons with a history of aggression. The medication is best used as an occasional aid, rather than a regular prescription, e.g. to enable a severely phobic patient to travel by bus or train. The occasions when specialists in alcohol dependence recommend long-term benzodiazepines are rare (see review by Lejoyeux et al., 1998).

Tiapride is a selective D2 dopamine antagonist which was shown in outpatient samples of anxious/depressed alcoholic patients to be associated with better outcome after 6 months (see Shaw et al., 1994). It is licensed for this in some countries. However, two larger, more methodologically sound studies showed no evidence of efficacy. These have been reported at meetings but are not yet published.

Carbamazepine, chiefly known as an anticonvulsant but with mood-stabilizing properties too, was found to lengthen the time to first drink in small placebo-controlled study (Mueller et al., 1997).

GHB (γ-ydroxybutyric acid) is a sedative that can be habit-forming. It has been shown to reduce relapse rates in studies lasting 6 months (Gallimberti et al., 1992). Its abuse potential may limit its acceptance as a treatment for alcohol dependence (Addolorato et al., 1996).

Animal models have found that preparations from the plant St John's Wort (*Hypericum*), which is prescribed in some countries for mild depression, reduces ethanol-seeking behaviour and consumption in laboratory animals, but there are no published controlled studies of its use in alcohol-dependent patients.

SUMMARY

New medications are beginning to find their place in preventing relapse in alcohol dependence, but have only been tested where psychological therapy is also offered. In time, whether or not they might have a place in primary care, with minimal psychological therapy, will be tested. At best, these treatments are only an aid to establishing a change in lifestyle. A medication to enable an individual to regain control of drinking, so that thereafter alcohol can be enjoyed in moderation, has not yet been identified. However, if the erratic nature of the journey to an acceptance of abstinence and adjustment to that way of life can be smoothed by taking specific medications, then their place is assured.

KEY WORKS AND SUGGESTIONS FOR FURTHER READING

O'Brien, C.P. & McLellan, A.T. (1996).   Myths about the treatment of addiction. *Lancet*, **347**, 237–240.

A challenging argument for viewing addictions as diseases meriting investigation of their biological causes and biological treatments.

Kranzler, H. (2000).   Pharmacotherapy of alcoholism: gaps in knowledge and opportunities for research. *Alcohol and Alcoholism*, **35**, 537–547.

Raimo, E.B. & Schuckit, M. (1998).   Alcohol dependence and mood disorders. *Addictive Behaviours*, **23**, 933–946.

An exploration of the complex relationship between alcohol dependence and mood disorders, with implications for treatment.

REFERENCES

Addolorato, G., Castelli, E., Stefanini, G.F., Casella, G., Caputo, F., Marsigli, L., Bernardi, M., Gasbarrini, G. & the GHB Study Group (1996).   An open multicentric study evaluating 4-hydroxybutyric acid sodium salt in the medium-term treatment of 179 alcohol-dependent subjects. *Alcohol and Alcoholism*, **31**, 341–345.

Angelone, S.M., Bellini, L., Di Bella, D. & Catalano, M. (1998). Effects of fluvoxamine and citalopram in maintaining abstinence in a sample of Italian detoxified alcoholics. *Alcohol and Alcoholism*, **33**, 151–156.

Azrin, N.H. (1976). Improvements in the community reinforcement approach. *Behaviour Research and Therapy*, **14**, 339–348.

Azrin, N.H., Sisson, R.W., Meyers, R. & Godley, M. (1982). Alcoholism treatment by disulfiram and community reinforcement therapy. *Journal of Behaviour Therapy and Experimental Psychiatry*, **13**, 105–112.

Balldin, J., Berglund, M. & Borg, S. (1998). The Swedish naltrexone study, present results. *European Psychiatry*, **14**(Suppl. l4), 154s (Abstract).

Begleiter, H., Porjesz, B. (1979). Persistence of a subacute withdrawal syndrome following chronic alcohol intake. *Drug and Alcohol Dependence*, **4**, 353–357.

Besson, J., Aeby, F., Kasas, A., Lehert, P. & Potgieter, A. (1998). Combined efficacy of acamprosate and disulfiram in the treatment of alcoholism: a controlled study. *Alcoholism: Clinical and Experimental Research*, **22**, 573–579.

Bigelow, G.E. (2001). An operant perspective on alcohol abuse and dependence. In N. Heather, T.J. Peters & T. Stockwell (Eds), *International Handbook of Alcohol Dependence and Problems*. (pp. 299–315). Chichester, U.K.: John Wiley & Sons.

Carroll, K.M., Nich, C., Ball, S.A., McCance, E. & Rounsaville, B.J. (1998). Treatment of cocaine and alcohol dependence with psychotherapy and disulfiram. *Addiction*, **93**, 713–728.

Chick, J., Gough, K., Falkowski, W. et al. (1992). Disulfiram treatment of alcoholism. *British Journal of Psychiatry*, **161**, 84–89.

Chick, J. (1999). Safety issues concerning the use of disulfiram in treating alcohol dependence. *Drug Safety*, **20**, 427–435.

Chick, J. (1998). Treatment of alcoholic violent offenders—ethics and efficacy. *Alcohol and Alcoholism*, **33**, 20–25.

Chick, J., Howlett, H., Morgan, M.Y. & Ritson, B. (2000). United Kingdom Multicentre Acamprosate Study (UKMAS): a 6 month prospective study of acamprosate versus placebo in preventing relapse after withdrawal from alcohol. *Alcohol and Alcoholism*, **35**, 176–187.

Cornelius, J.R., Salloun, I.M., Ehler, J.G. et al. (1997). Fluoxetine reduced depressive symptoms and alcohol consumption in patients with comorbid major depression and alcohol dependence. *Archives of General Psychiatry*, **54**, 700–705.

Croop, R., Faulkner, E.B. & Labriola, D.F. (1997). The safety profile of naltrexone in the treatment of alcoholism—results from a multicentre usage study. *Archives of General Psychiatry*, **54**, 1130–1135.

Davidson, D., Palfai, Y., Bird, C. & Swift, R. (1999). Effects of naltrexone on alcohol self-administration in heavy drinkers. *Alcoholism: Clinical and Experimental Research*, **23**, 195–203.

Duckert, F. & Johnsen, J. (1987). Behavioural use of disulfiram in the treatment of problem drinking. *International Journal of the Addictions*, **22**, 445–454.

Epstein, E.E. (2001). Classification of alcohol-related problems and dependence. In N. Heather, T.J. Peters & T. Stockwell (Eds), *International Handbook of Alcohol Dependence and Problems*. (pp. 47–70). Chichester, U.K.: John Wiley & Sons.

Fuller, R.K. & Williford, W.O. (1980). Life-table analysis of abstinence in a study evaluating the efficacy of disulfiram. *Alcoholism: Clinical and Experimental Research*, **4**, 298–301.

Fuller, R.K., Branchey, L., Brightwell, D.R. et al. (1986). Disulfiram in the treatment of alcoholism: a Veterans Administration cooperative study. *Journal of the American Medical Association*, **256**, 1449–1455.

Gallimberti, L., Ferri, M., Ferrara, S.D., Fadda, F. & Gessa, G.L. (1992). γ-Hydroxybutyric acid in the treatment of alcohol dependence: a double blind study. *Alcoholism: Clinical and Experimental Research*, **16**, 673–676.

Gianoulakis, C., Krishnan, B. & Thavundayil, J. (1996). Enhanced sensitivity to pituitary β-endorphin to ethanol in subjects at high risk of alcoholism. *Archives of General Psychiatry*, **53**, 250–257.

Helander, A. (1998). Monitoring relapse drinking during disulfiram therapy by assay of urinary 5-hydroxytryptophol. *Alcoholism: Clinical and Experimental Research*, **22**, 111–114.

Hughes, J.C. & Cook, C. (1997). The efficacy of disulfiram—a review of outcome studies. *Addiction*, **92**, 381–396.

Jaffe, A.J., Rounsaville, B., Chang, G., Schottenfield, R.S., Meyer, R.F. & O'Malley, S.S. (1996). Naltrexone, relapse prevention and supportive therapy with alcoholics: an analysis of patient treatment matching. *Journal of Consulting and Clinical Psychology*, **64**, 1044–1063.

Janiri, L., Gobbi, G., Manelli, P., Pozzi, G., Serretti, A. & Tempesta, E. (1996). Effects of fluoxetine at antidepressant doses on short-term outcome of detoxified alcoholics. *International Journal of Clinical Psychopharmacology*, **11**, 109–117.

Kranzler, H.R., Burleson, J.A., Boca, F.K., Babor, T.F., Korner, P., Brown, P. & Bohn, M.J. (1994). Buspirone treatment of anxious alcoholics. *Archives of General Psychiatry*, **51**, 720–731.

Kranzler, H.R., Burleson, J.A., Korner, P., del Boca, F.K., Bohn, M.J., Brow, J. & Liebowitz, N. (1995). Placebo-controlled trial of fluoxetine as an adjunct to relapse prevention in alcoholics. *American Journal of Psychiatry*, **152**, 391–397.

Kranzler, H.R., Burleson, J.A., Brown, J. & Babor, T.F. (1996). Fluoxetine treatment seems to reduce the beneficial effect of cognitive-behavioural therapy in Type B alcoholics. *Alcoholism: Clinical and Experimental Research*, **20**, 1534–1541.

Kranzler, H.R., Modesto-Lowe, V. & Nuwayser, E.S. (1998). Sustained-release naltrexone for alcoholism treatment: a preliminary study *Alcoholism: Clinical and Experimental Research*, **22**, 1074–1079.

Ladewig, D., Knecht, T., Lehert, P. & Fend, A. (1993). Acamprosat—ein Stabilisierungsfaktor in der Langzeitentwohnung von Alkoholabhangigen. *Therapeutische Umschau*, **50**, 182–187.

Larson, E.W., Lincy, A., Rommans, T.A. & Morse, R.M. (1992). Disulfiram treatment of patients with both alcohol dependence and other psychiatric disorders: a review. *Alcoholism: Clinical and Experimental Research*, **16**, 125–136.

Lê, A.D., Tomkins, D.M. & Sellers, E.M. (1996). Use of serotonin (5-HT) and opiate-based drugs in the pharmacotherapy of alcohol dependence: an overview of the preclinical data *Alcohol and Alcoholism*, **31**(Suppl. 1), 27–32.

Lejoyeux, M. (1996). Use of serotonin (5-hydroxytryptamine) reuptake inhibitors in the treatment of alcoholism. *Alcohol and Alcoholism*, **31**(Suppl. 1), 69–76.

Lejoyeux, M., Solomon, J. & Ades, J. (1998). Benzodiazepine treatment for alcohol-dependent patients. *Alcohol and Alcoholism*, **33**, 563–575.

Lesch, O.M. & Walter, H. (1996). Subtypes of alcoholism and their role in therapy. *Alcohol and Alcoholism*, **31**(Suppl. 1), 59–62.

Liebson, I., Tommasello, A. & Bigelow, L.G. (1978). A behavioural treatment of alcoholic methadone patients. *Annals of Internal Medicine*, **89**, 342–344.

Lingford-Hughes, A. & Nutt, D. (2001). Neuropharmacology of ethanol and alcohol dependence. In N. Heather, T.J. Peters & T. Stockwell (Eds), *International Handbook of Alcohol Dependence and Problems*. (pp. 103–127). Chichester, U.K.: John Wiley & Sons.

Littleton, J. (1995). Acamprosate in alcohol dependence: how does it work? *Addiction*, **90**, 1179–1188.

Lhuintre, J.P., Moore, N.D., Saligaut, C. et al. (1985). Ability of calcium bis-acetyl homotaurinate, a GABA agonist, to prevent relapse in weaned alcoholics. *Lancet*, **1**, 1015–1016.

Lhuintre, J.P., Moore, N., Tran, G. et al. (1990). Acamprosate appears to decrease alcohol intake in weaned alcoholics. *Alcohol and Alcoholism*, **25**, 613–622.

Mason, B.J., Ritvo, E.C., Morgan, R.O., Salvato, F.R., Goldberg, G., Welch, B. & Mantero-Atienza, E. (1994). A double-blind, placebo-controlled pilot study to evaluate the efficacy and safety of oral nalmefene HCL for alcohol dependence. *Journal of the American Medical Association*, **18**, 1162–1167.

Mason, B.J., Kocsis, J.H., Ritvo, E.C. & Cutler, R.B. (1996). A double-blind, placebo-controlled trial of desimpramine for primary alcohol dependence stratified for the presence or absence of major depression. *Journal of the American Medical Association*, **275**, 761–767.

McGrath, P.J., Nunes, E.V., Stewart, J.W. et al. (1996). Imipramine treatment of alcoholics with primary depression: a placebo-controlled clinical trial. *Archives of General Psychiatry*, **53**, 232–240.

Mason, B.J., Salvato, F.R., Williams, L.D., Ritro, E.C. & Cutler, R.V. (1999). A double-blind, placebo-controlled study of oral nalmefene for alcohol dependence. *Archives of General Psychiatry*, **56**, 719–724.

Modesto-Lowe, V., Burleson, J.A., Hersh, D., Bauer, L.O. & Kranzler, H.R. (1997). Effects of naltrexone on cue-elcitied craving for alcohol and cocaine. *Drug and Alcohol Dependence*, **49**, 9–16.

Muellet, T.I., Stout, R.L., Rudden, S., Brown, R.A., Gordon, A., Solomon, D.A. & Recupero, P.R. (1997). A double-blind placebo-controlled pilot study of carbamazepine for the treatment of alcohol dependence. *Alcoholism: Clinical and Experimental Research*, **21**, 86–92.

O'Brien, C.P., Volpicelli, L.A. & Volpicelli, J.R. (1996). Naltrexone in the treatment of alcoholism: a clinical review. *Alcohol*, **13**: 35–39.

O'Malley, S.S., Jaffe, A.J., Chang, G., Schottenfeld, R.S., Meyer, R.E. & Rounsaville, B. (1992). Naltrexone and coping skills therapy for alcohol dependence, a controlled study. *Archives of General Psychiatry*, **49**, 881–887.

O'Malley, S.S., Jaffe, A.J., Rode, S. & Rounsaville, B.J. (1996a). Experience of a "slip" among alcoholics treated with naltrexone. *American Journal of Psychiatry*, **153**, 281–283.

O'Malley, S.S. (1996b). Six month follow-up of naltrexone and psychotherapy for alcohol dependence. *Archives of General Psychiatry*, **53**, 217–224.

Paille, F.M., Guelfi, J.D., Perkins, A.C., Royer, R.J., Steru, L. & Perot, P. (1995). Randomised multicentre trial of acamprosate in a maintenance programme of abstinence after alcohol detoxification. *Alcohol and Alcoholism*, **30**, 239–247.

Pelc, I., Verbanck, P., Le, Bon., M., Gavrilovic, M., Lion, K. & Lehert P. (1997). Efficacy and safety of acamprosate in the treatment of detoxified alcohol-dependent patients: a 90-day dose finding study. *British Journal of Psychiatry*, **171**, 73–77.

Peterson, J.B., Pihl, R.O., Gianoulakis, C., Conrod, P., Finn, P.R., Stewart, S.H., LeMarquand, D.G. & Bruce, K.R. (1996). Ethanol-induced change in cardiac and endogenous opiate function and risk for alcoholism. *Alcoholism: Clinical and Experimental Research*, **20**, 1542–1552.

Pettinati, H.M. (1996). Use of serotonin selective pharmacotherapy in the treatment of alcohol dependence. *Alcoholism: Clinical and Experimental Research*, **20**, 23–29.

Pettinati, H.M., Volpicelli, J.R., Kranzler, H.R., Luck, G., Rubstalis, M.R. & Cnaan, A. (2000). Sertraline treatment for alcohol dependence: interactive of medication and alcoholic subtype. *Alcoholism: Clinical and Experimental Research*, **24**, 1041–1049.

Poldrugo, F. (1997). Acamprosate treatment in a long-term community based alcohol rehabilitation programme. *Addiction*, **92**, 1537–1547.

Powell, B.J., Campbell, J.L., Landon, J.F. et al. (1995). A double-blind placebo-controlled study of nortryptiline and bromocriptine in male alcoholics subtyped by comorbid psychiatric disorders. *Alcohol: Clinical and Experimental Research*, **19**, 462–468.

Reid, L.D., Gardell, L.R., Chattopadhyay, S. & Hubbell, C.L. (1996). Periodic naltrexone and propensity to take alcoholic beverage. *Alcohol: Clinical and Experimental*, **20**, 1329–1334.

Robichaud, C., Strickland, D., Bigelow, G. et al. (1979). Disulfiram maintenance employee alcoholism treatment: a three phase evaluation. *Behaviour Research and Therapy*, **17**, 618–621.

Sass, H., Soyka, M., Mann, K. & Ziegelgansberger, W. (1996). Relapse prevention by acamprosate: results from a placebo controlled study in alcohol dependence. *Archives of General Psychiatry*, **53**, 673–680.

Sereny, G., Sharma, V., Holt, S. & Gordis, E. (1986). Mandatory supervised Antabuse therapy in an out-patient alcoholism program: a pilot study. *Alcoholism: Clinical and Experimental Research*, **10**, 290–292.

Sinclair, J.D. (1998). New treatment options for substance abuse from a public health standpoint. *Annals of Medicine*, **30**, 406–411.

Shaw, G.K., Waller, S., Majumdar, S.K., Alberts, J.L., Latham, C.J. & Dunn, G. (1994). Tiapride in the prevention of relapse in recently detoxified alcoholics. *British Journal of Psychiatry*, **165**, 515–523.

Tihonen, J., Ryynänen, O.-P., Kauhanen, J., Hakola, H.P.A. & Salaspuro, M. (1996). Citalopram in the treatment of alcoholism: a double-blind placebo controlled study. *Pharmacopsychiatry*, **29**, 27–29.

Tsai, G.E., Ragan, P., Chang, R., Chen, S., Linnoila, M.I. & Coyle, J.T. (1998). Increased glutamatergic neurotransmission and oxidative stress after alcohol withdrawal. *American Journal of Psychiatry*, **155**, 726–732.

Volpicelli, J.R., Alterman, A.I., Hayashida, M. & O'Brien, C.P. (1992). Naltrexone in the treatment of alcohol dependence. *Archives of General Psychiatry*, **49**, 876–880.

Volpicelli, J.R., Volpicelli, L.A. & O'Brien, C.P. (1995). Medical management of alcohol dependence: clinical use and limitations of naltrexone treatment. *Alcohol and Alcoholism*, **30**, 789–798.

Volpicelli, J.R., Rhines, K.C., Rines, J.S., Volpicelli, L.A., Alterman, A.I. & O'Brien, C.P. (1997). Naltrexone and alcohol dependence: role of subject compliance. *Archives of General Psychiatry*, **54**, 737–742.

Whitworth, A.B., Fischer, F., Lesch, O., Nimmerrichter, A., Oberauer, H., Platz, A., Walter, H. & Fleischhacker, W.W. (1996). Comparison of acamprosate and placebo in long-term treatment of alcohol dependence. *Lancet*, **347**, 1438–1442.

Wright, C. & Moore, R.D. (1990). Disulfiram treatment of alcoholism. *American Journal of Medicine*, **88**, 647–655.

Chapter 5

Cognitive-behavioral Alcohol Treatment

George A. Parks
G. Alan Marlatt
and
Britt K. Anderson
Addictive Behaviors Research Center, University of Washington, Seattle, WA, USA

Synopsis

What follows is the first of two chapters devoted to a cognitive-behavioral approach to the treatment of alcohol abuse and dependence. The goal of this chapter is to provide a state-of-the-art overview of this therapeutic approach to alcohol treatment, about which more detailed discussions are available elsewhere (Mackay et al., 1991; Kadden, 1994). The next chapter in this two-part series will present a cognitive-behavioral model of Relapse Prevention Therapy (RPT). The present chapter begins by placing cognitive-behavioral approaches to alcohol treatment within the context of various conceptual models of addictive behaviors. The four primary models include the moral *model, the* disease *or* medical *model, the* spiritual *or* enlightenment *model, and the* compensatory *model, which differ in their determination of responsibility for the development and resolution of addictive behaviors. Stages in the acquisition and change of alcohol-related problems are then presented. Alcohol problems and related consequences lie on a continuum and can range from mild difficulties to more severe dependency. It is important that treatment be appropriate for both the level of dependency and degree of motivation that exists for each individual. The basic principles of cognitive-behavioral alcohol treatment are also discussed. Based on social learning theory, alcohol dependence is conceptualized as a learned behavior that represents a maladaptive coping mechanism for life's stressors. Practice guidelines for a*

The Essential *Handbook of Treatment and Prevention of Alcohol Problems.* Edited by N. Heather and T. Stockwell.
© 2004 John Wiley & Sons Ltd. ISBN 0-470-86296-3.

cognitive-behavioral approach with clients and the scope, duration, and aims of cognitive-behavioral alcohol treatment are explained. This approach necessitates an objective and non-judgmental therapeutic style that allows for collaboration and flexibility between therapist and client. Additionally, assessment and goal setting are ongoing activities during the course of therapy and guide the overall process. The next section summarizes behavioral therapy *and* cognitive therapy *assessment and intervention strategies, both of which constitute the ingredients of this approach. Behavioral assessment involves a functional analysis of the drinking behavior, which evaluates the situational antecedents, the intensity and frequency of the drinking behavior itself and the consequences that may be reinforcing the problematic behavior. Behavioral treatment techniques include aversive approaches designed to reduce the reinforcing aspects of alcohol through electric shock, nausea-inducing drugs or imagery, cue exposure therapy, relaxation training, contingency management, which involves restructuring one's environment, and coping skills training. In contrast, cognitive assessment focuses on the manner in which behavior is mediated by thoughts and internal events. Clients are asked to self-monitor and record their thoughts and expectancies related to drinking, so that faulty beliefs can be challenged. Cognitive treatment techniques include teaching appraisal of situations that represent a risk for heavy drinking, problem-solving training to cope with life's demands, and cognitive restructuring to confront negative thoughts. Both behavioral and cognitive techniques rely heavily on the use of role-plays, modeling, homework and feedback to facilitate the learning process. A contemporary cognitive-behavioral alcohol therapy protocol developed by Monti and colleagues (Kadden et al., 1995; Monti et al., 1989) is briefly described. Finally, the chapter concludes with a discussion of the potential benefits of cognitive-behavioral alcohol treatment and a brief review of empirical support for the efficacy of alcohol treatments based on this theoretical approach.*

CONCEPTUAL MODELS OF ADDICTIVE BEHAVIORS

In order to highlight the unique contribution to alcohol treatment that a cognitive-behavioral approach can provide, a brief discussion of various conceptualizations of the etiology and treatment of alcohol dependence follows. Each of these models of addictive behavior makes different predictions about the nature, course and outcome of alcohol treatment. These predictions influence not only therapist behaviors, but also the clients' beliefs about treatment entry, staying in treatment, treatment success and relapse (Marlatt et al., 1997; Miller et al., 1996).

A model of helping and coping created by Brickman et al. (1982) helps to clarify four divergent conceptual approaches to the development and modification of addictive behaviors in general and alcohol dependence in particular. In their presentation, Brickman and his associates asked the following two questions: (a) to what extent is an individual considered personally responsible for the initial development of the addictive behavior problem?; and (b) to what extent is the person responsible for and capable of changing the behavior problem on his/her own, without treatment? Based on answers to these two questions, four general models of helping and coping were formulated which can readily be applied to addictive behaviors, including alcohol dependence (Marlatt, 1992).

These four models consist of: the *moral* model, in which a person is held responsible for both acquiring and changing his/her alcohol problem; the *disease* or *medical* model, where a person is held responsible for neither the acquisition nor the change of his/her alcohol problem; the *spiritual* or *enlightenment* model, where a person is held responsible for the development of his/her alcohol problem but is not responsible for changing it; and finally, the *compensatory* model, where a person is not held responsible for the development of his/her alcohol problem but is seen as responsible for changing their problem and considered capable of doing so.

The *disease* model of alcohol dependence, or "alcoholism", remains the dominant conceptual model or paradigm of both alcohol and drug treatment, especially in the USA. However, this situation is changing in response to empirical evidence, managed care cost containment policies and greater pressures to demonstrate treatment efficacy and effectiveness (Miller & Hester, 1986). Therapies based on a cognitive-behavioral approach have recently been developed and tested as alternatives treatments or as adjuncts to more traditional alcohol and drug treatment programs based on the disease model (Cook, 1988a, b).

A COGNITIVE-BEHAVIORAL APPROACH TO ALCOHOL TREATMENT

The moral, disease and spiritual models of addictive behaviors represent three alternative approaches to alcohol treatment. It is within the fourth and final model in Brickman's typology, the *compensatory* model, that we place cognitive-behavioral approaches to alcohol treatment. This perspective is called the compensatory model because, while an individual is not considered responsible for the development of alcohol abuse or dependence, he/she is believed to be capable of compensating for it. Both self-change and change through the assistance of others are seen as valid alternatives. Cognitive-behavioral approaches to alcohol dependence are based largely on the principles of social learning theory, as elaborated by Bandura (1969, 1986, 1997). The major assumption of the cognitive-behavioral model is that addictive behaviors, including alcohol dependence, are learned, maladaptive habit patterns acquired through the interactive processes of classical conditioning, instrumental learning and cognitive mediation (see Gorman, 2001). From this point of view, addictive behaviors are maladaptive coping responses when they become the central means individuals use to cope with the stress of life's demands.

Strong reinforcers that reward alcohol use with immediate consequences, such as euphoric feelings of pleasure (positive reinforcement) or the reduction or elimination of negative states, such as anxiety and pain (negative reinforcement), maintain these excessive behaviors or addictive habits. The alcohol dependence syndrome is characterized by both the presence of immediate gratification and the experience of delayed negative consequences. The reinforcement dynamics of this biphasic effect of drinking contribute to an individual's overgeneralized use of alcohol and interfere with his/her efforts to abstain from drinking or to engage in controlled or moderate consumption.

Defining alcohol dependence as a maladaptive *habit* rather than as alcoholism, a disease-based addiction, does not diminish the disorder's intensity or resistance to change. Indeed, over-learned habits, such as the excessive drinking characteristic of alcohol dependence, can become nearly or completely involuntary. The drinker may perform them with little conscious awareness or attention. Because alcohol use is effective in increasing pleasure and decreasing pain, attempts to abstain in the absence of viable alternative coping behaviors will lead to increased stress and distress. An individual's ongoing stress and unmet needs may then motivate the resumption of excessive drinking and the reinstatement of alcohol dependence, despite the predictably severe negative consequences of this behavior.

In this model of addictive behaviors, the development of alcohol abuse or dependence is seen as a result of the interaction of biological, psychological and sociocultural forces. In this *biopsychosocial* model, biological factors, such as genetic vulnerability and substance-induced physiological changes; psychological factors, such as expectancies, attributions and coping skills; and sociocultural factors, such as family history, peer influences, cultural and ethnic background, advertising and the media, all influence the development of addictive behaviors (Donovan, 1988). This biopsychosocial model of addictive behaviors describes alcohol dependence as a complex disorder with multiple determinants in systematic inter-action during its development, maintenance and treatment. Therefore, cognitive-behavioral alcohol treatments must be designed to effectively address the interaction of these multi-ple factors as they influence alcohol dependence at different stages of its development and amelioration.

In addition to having biological and sociocultural causes and consequences, addictive behaviors, such the excessive drinking characteristic of alcohol abuse or dependence, are temporarily effective, yet ultimately maladaptive, coping mechanisms. Cognitive-behavioral alcohol treatment views therapy as a habit change process during which clients gradually replace addictive behaviors with new and more adaptive coping skills. The overall goal of cognitive-behavioral approaches to treatment is to help clients meet life's demands without resorting to the excessive use of alcohol and its associated problems. In this model, relapse is defined as a mistake or error in a process of new learning. It may also be thought of as a temporary setback in the journey from being controlled by alcohol dependence to the recovery of life-style balance, self-control and personal freedom that characterize health and well-being. (A more thorough discussion of cognitive-behavioral Relapse Prevention Therapy follows in Chapter 6.)

MOTIVATION AND STAGES OF CHANGE

Effective cognitive-behavioral alcohol treatment requires that both therapist and client understand the stages that occur when one acquires an abusive or dependent pattern of drinking and the stages that occur when drinking behavior changes to a moderate level of consumption or is eliminated entirely. Cognitive-behavioral therapy is based on an empiri-cal, developmental model of alcohol use disorders, which attempts to delineate the natural history of excessive drinking and alcohol-related problems. As therapist and client refine this understanding, they collaborate to generate an effective treatment plan for either indi-vidual or group therapy formats. This developmental approach to alcohol treatment takes advantage of research examining drinking behavior, the development of alcohol problems, and variability in current patterns of drinking from a longitudinal perspective (Marlatt et al., 1988; Vaillant, 1995).

The potential development of alcohol dependence or other alcohol-related problems begins with exposure and experimentation with alcohol, often during childhood or adoles-cence. Whether an alcohol-related problem of any type develops depends on a variety of biopsychosocial factors including genetic vulnerability, family dynamics, peer relations, conduct problems, media depictions of drinking, and access to alcohol. Most individuals who drink do so with little or no problem; some individuals experience occasional mild to moderate alcohol-related problems; and a few unfortunate others progress to the devel-opment of alcohol abuse or dependence disorders (IOM, 1990; Marlatt, 1992). Therefore, rather than the overly simplistic notion of either having or not having the disease of alco-holism, the cognitive-behavioral developmental perspective views alcohol use and alcohol-related problems as existing on a continuum of use and severity of consequences. This analysis is consistent with the notion of a spectrum of alcohol-related problems, each of which is best addressed by a different level of treatment, ranging from prevention and brief intervention to more intensive treatment (IOM, 1990).

Just as the development of alcohol-use disorders occurs in stages, it also seems that indi-viduals go through as series of predictable *stages of change* when trying to alter their drink-ing behavior. In our previous work on relapse prevention (Marlatt & Gordon, 1985; Marlatt

& Parks, 1982), we proposed that habit change is a *journey* that occurs in three stages. These stages consist of *preparation* for the journey, involving motivation and commitment; *departure*, involving cessation or quitting the addictive behavior; and finally, the *maintenance* stage, involving coping with the challenges one will encounter to resume excessive drinking. It is during the maintenance stage that clients must work the hardest to maintain their motivation and commitment over the long term and avoid the problem of relapse (see Chapter 6).

A related stages of change model, first applied to smokers and later to other addictive behaviors, has been developed and refined by Prochaska & DiClemente (1992). An important point illustrated by both stages of change models is that therapeutic interventions, to be maximally effective, should be relevant to the stage of change a client is experiencing. Cognitive-behavioral alcohol treatment includes ongoing assessment of a client's motivation at various stages of change, and strategically integrates motivational enhancement interventions throughout the course of therapy (Baer et al., 1999; Miller & Rollnick, 1991; also see Chapter 7). Cognitive and behavioral assessment and intervention strategies designed specifically for the action, maintenance, and relapse stages are gradually introduced as client motivation increases during the preparation or determination stage of change (Prochaska & DiClemente, 1992; also see Chapter 6).

PRINCIPLES OF COGNITIVE-BEHAVIORAL ALCOHOL TREATMENT

As stated earlier, the theoretical heritage of cognitive-behavioral alcohol treatment derives from the social learning approach to understanding human behavior, more recently referred to as social cognitive theory (Bandura, 1969, 1986, 1997). Based on a tradition of empirical studies and theoretical hypothesis testing, the social cognitive approach has evolved within psychology from earlier behavioral theories but departs from a strictly behavioral approach to human problems by incorporating the principles of reciprocal determinism, observational learning, social cognition and self-regulation. Cognitive-behavioral alcohol treatment combines behavioral and cognitive interventions in an overall approach that emphasizes self-management and rejects labeling clients with traits like "alcoholic" or "drug addict", which are often promoted by moral and disease models of addiction. The psycho-educational philosophy of this approach focuses on enhancing client motivation, providing new knowledge about drinking and its consequences, and fostering coping skills to empower a person to maintain long-term freedom from excessive and problematic alcohol use.

The first principle of cognitive-behavioral alcohol treatment is that the excessive drinking characteristic of alcohol abuse and dependence disorders is conceptualized as a set of socially learned behaviors with multiple determinants. These determinants include genetic factors, past learning, situational antecedents, cognitive processes and immediate positive and delayed negative consequences. This treatment approach focuses on: (a) situational antecedents of excessive drinking, such as time of day, place, people, activities; (b) internal states, such as anxiety, depression or other unpleasant emotions or painful sensations that may increase the likelihood of excessive drinking; (c) cognitive processes, such as expectancies about the rewarding effects of alcohol and attributions infusing alcohol with the power of a magic elixir to transform moods; and (d) the reinforcing consequences that serve to maintain drinking behavior at an excessive level. Cognitive-behavioral alcohol treatment integrates classical conditioning mechanisms (see Drobes et al., 2001), instrumental learning (see Bigelow, 2001), and social-cognitive processes (see Collins & Bradizza, 2001) in the understanding of the etiology of excessive drinking and its therapeutic techniques of treatment. Consistent with a social learning analysis of excessive drinking, alcohol dependence can be treated most effectively by a combination of both behavioral and cognitive techniques.

A second basic principle of this treatment approach is that alcohol abuse or dependence and other addictive behaviors are viewed as maladaptive mechanisms for coping with stress. This *adaptive orientation* views stress as resulting from an imbalance between environmental demands (stressors) and an individual's coping resources. The client's level of stress, vulnerability to stress and repertoire of coping responses that reduce or eliminate the need for excessive drinking as a coping mechanism are essential factors in cognitive-behavioral alcohol treatment. As an individual faces the demands of stressful living, an increasing imbalance may occur that taxes or exceeds his/her ability to adapt to, master or at least tolerate these circumstances without resorting to excessive drinking. To the extent that effective cognitive or behavioral coping skills are not possessed or implemented, excessive alcohol use may be seen as an effective short-term coping strategy, even at the expense of long-term negative consequences.

The third basic principle of a cognitive-behavioral alcohol treatment is that drinking behavior can be understood as existing on a continuum of use and severity of consequences which may not always be perfectly correlated. This continuum ranges from abstinence with no alcohol-related problems, at one extreme, to alcohol dependence with many alcohol-related problems at the other extreme, with many intermediate locations on the continuum between these two endpoints. This principle contrasts with the traditional model of alcoholism as a progressive disease, which assumes the potential for addiction to be present or absent and, if present, to intensify in severity as time goes on. From a cognitive-behavioral point of view, alcohol consumption is viewed as a learned behavior, determined by the same processes regardless of where an individual's drinking falls on the continuum of use and severity of consequences. The learning processes involved in alcohol consumption, including important biopsychosocial factors, determine drinking at all levels of the continuum and are no different from the learning processes that govern the acquisition and change of other non-addictive behaviors. This continuity of learning processes in human behavior allows the cognitive-behavioral therapist to help clients replace the habit of excessive drinking with the cognitive and behavioral skills to cope with the stress of life's demands.

CLINICAL PRACTICE GUIDELINES

The essence of cognitive-behavioral alcohol treatment is the movement from a *disease model* of deficits, powerlessness and loss of control to a *competence model* based on enhanced motivation, increased awareness, skill acquisition and social support (Marlatt & Parks, 1999). Traditional approaches to the treatment of alcoholism initiate therapy by using confrontational techniques designed to "break through the denial system" and force clients into accepting a diagnostic label such as "alcoholic". In contrast, a cognitive-behavioral approach attempts to foster a sense of objectivity or detachment in the way individuals approach their alcohol-related problems (see Chapter 7). By relating to the client as a colleague or co-therapist, cognitive-behavioral therapists hope to encourage a sense of cooperation and openness during the therapy process. Using this approach helps clients learn to perceive their excessive drinking as something they *do*, rather than as an indication of someone they *are*. By adopting this objective and detached approach, clients may be able to free themselves from any guilt and defensiveness that would otherwise bias their view of their alcohol-related problem and their ability to change their excessive drinking behavior.

Cognitive-behavioral therapists encourage clients to take an active role in treatment planning and decision-making processes throughout the course of treatment and to assume progressively more personal responsibility for their treatment at every stage of the therapy program. Within-session exercises and between-session homework assignments, such as bibiliotherapy and self-monitoring, are carefully explained and demonstrated by the therapist so that the client understands their rationale and importance. Over time, the client becomes his/her own therapist as he/she gains new knowledge and masters new skills. Self-control or self-management is the ultimate goal of treatment and, after termination of the therapy proper, the client is in charge of aftercare planning and the implementation of an individually tailored relapse prevention program (see Chapter 6). The overall goals of cognitive-behavioral alcohol treatment are: (a) to increase and maintain motivation for change; (b) to enhance awareness and choice concerning drinking behavior; and (c) to develop coping skills and self-control capacities.

SCOPE, DURATION AND AIMS OF COGNITIVE-BEHAVIORAL ALCOHOL TREATMENT

Cognitive-behavioral alcohol treatment begins with a thorough biopsychosocial assessment of the client. Utilizing a multivariate, biopsychosocial model in treatment requires a comprehensive and integrated assessment of the client, focusing on social and medical history, level of alcohol dependence, alcohol-related problems, drinking behaviors, coping skills deficits, psychiatric comorbidity and social support. A comprehensive pre-treatment assessment involves the multiple systems of physiological, cognitive, psychological, behavioral, and social factors. While begun prior to treatment, assessment is an ongoing interactive process between therapist and client that contributes to the development of a treatment plan matching the person to an appropriate type and intensity of cognitive-behavioral treatment. Assessment includes continuous monitoring of the client's progress throughout therapy and frequent feedback about currently achieved and anticipated treatment outcomes.

Cognitive-behavioral alcohol treatment employs a public health approach that matches clients to levels of care, depending on the severity of alcohol abuse or dependence and on factors such as psychiatric comorbidity, other drug use, cognitive or neurological impairment and criminal conduct. A stepped-care approach offers interventions ranging in intensity and duration, from psycho-educational programs and brief interventions (see Chapter 8) to intensive outpatient treatment or on to medically supervised inpatient alcohol treatment. Initial matching of clients to treatments is determined by comprehensive assessment results. Ongoing assessment of clients determines whether a specific course of treatment should be continued and whether a client should be moved backward or forward in terms of the intensity and duration of treatment needed (see Chapters 1, 2).

Cognitive-behavioral alcohol treatment also allows for some flexibility with regard to the ultimate goal of therapy. Considerable controversy has existed concerning the appropriateness of "controlled drinking" as a goal for alcoholics or alcohol-dependent individuals (Marlatt et al., 1993; Heather & Robertson, 1983). However, in clinical practice the goals of abstinence or moderation are often determined more by program policy or consumer choice than by objective assessment or research findings (Marlatt et al., 1997). Obviously, alcohol treatment will not work unless the person begins and continues therapy. Insisting on a goal of abstinence may create a high threshold for treatment entry and continuation. Harm reduction approaches to alcohol treatment (Marlatt, 1998) and motivational interviewing (Miller & Rollnick, 1991; see also Chapter 8) attempt to provide consumers with low-threshold access to treatment services. While the harm reduction approach includes abstinence as the ideal goal for alcohol-dependent individuals, consistent with the stages of change model, any progress toward abstinence is viewed as therapeutic progress. From a cognitive-behavioral point of view, abstinence, moderation or even attenuated drinking can be appropriate goals of alcohol treatment for clients, depending on their unique characteristics and life circumstances (Jarvis et al., 1995).

Although clients may not initially choose or accept abstinence as their treatment goal, over time they may decide that it is in their best interest not to drink. They will often then begin to ask their therapist for interventions aimed at drinking cessation, rather that moderation or attenuation. The ultimate therapeutic objective is to help clients create those outcomes that are desirable to the client, that reduce harm and that are safe and attainable. Jarvis, Tebbutt & Mattick (1995) suggest the following factors as guidelines for choosing appropriate goals for alcohol treatment: medical complications, alcohol-induced organic brain damage, cognitive impairment, psychiatric comorbidity, physical withdrawal, severity of alcohol dependence, drinking history, social support and partner preference (see also Heather & Robertson, 1989).

BEHAVIORAL ASSESSMENT

Cognitive-behavioral alcohol treatment utilizes assessment techniques and clinical interventions that integrate traditional behavioral therapy strategies with cognitive therapy interventions. Early behavioral therapy approaches to alcohol treatment focused primarily on the clinical application of the principles of classical conditioning and instrumental learning. While this approach has since been viewed as overly simplistic, it has served a useful heuristic purpose and several key aspects of behavioral therapy continue to be central to the contemporary and more mediational cognitive-behavioral approach to alcohol treatment.

The cornerstone of assessment in behavioral therapy is the functional analysis of behavior. This assessment method continues to be fundamental in the practice of effective cognitive-behavioral alcohol treatment. Functional analysis is a behavioral assessment procedure which involves observing and measuring the *antecedents* of drinking behavior, the rate and pattern of alcohol consumption *behavior* itself, and the *consequences* of alcohol use that reinforce drinking. The first step in the functional analysis of alcohol consumption is to determine and help the client understand the most frequent and potent antecedents for his/her drinking behavior. This is done while teaching the client that selective attention, subjective interpretations and expectancies are cognitive factors that determine the choice and meaning of drinking situations. A second step in the functional analysis of alcohol consumption is to instruct clients in observing and measuring the frequency, quantity, duration and intensity of drinking behavior and its associated temporal and situational patterns. Finally, consequences that serve to maintain drinking behavior are assessed and discussed, including positive physiological consequences such as increased pleasure and decreased pain, emotional consequences such as tension reduction and greater emotional expressiveness, and social consequences such as peer approval and acceptance.

Useful behavioral assessment techniques include self-monitoring of drinking behavior, as well as questionnaires and structured interviews like the Comprehensive Drinking Profile, the Brief Drinking Profile, and the Timeline Follow-back Method (Donovan & Marlatt, 1988; Sobell & Sobell, 1993). A cognitive-behavioral approach to alcohol treatment also requires the assessment of level of alcohol dependence and the nature and severity of any alcohol-related problems (Allen & Columbus, 1995; Donovan & Marlatt, 1988).

BEHAVIORAL THERAPY INTERVENTIONS

Aversive Therapies

Aversive therapies are designed to reduce the reinforcing properties of drinking by changing the valence of drinking-related cues from positive to negative through counter-conditioning procedures. In this technique, an aversive unconditioned stimulus is paired with a reinforcing conditioned stimulus, such as alcohol use. The goal of this classical conditioning procedure is for the client to experience an aversive conditioned response to alcohol and to avoid drinking after the conditioning has occurred. Two forms of aversive stimuli that have been shown to reduce a person's desire to drink are electric shock and nausea-inducing drugs, such as disulfiram (Antabuse) and calcium carbimide. Nausea-inducing drugs are more effective than electric shock, although both of these aversive techniques pose both ethical and procedural problems (Chapter 4).

A more cognitive-behavioral version of aversive therapy involves imaginal pairing of unpleasant events with alcohol, rather than actual *in vivo* pairing. This procedure, called covert sensitization, includes three phases (Rimmele et al., 1989). In the first phase, the client is guided through positive imagery of drinking and then an aversive response such as vomiting. In the second phase, the aversive imagery is paired with suggestions of non-drinking alternatives, allowing the client to escape the negative consequences if he/she chooses not to continue drinking. Finally, in phase three, non-drinking alternatives are given prior to the experience of any aversive consequences, allowing the client to avoid them if he/she chooses not to drink in the first place. Despite their promise and empirical support, aversion therapies may be useful only for initial abstinence and have not been utilized very heavily by alcohol treatment providers.

Cue Exposure

Classical conditioning approaches to behavioral therapy suggest that alcohol-dependent drinkers may develop conditioned craving responses to drinking-related antecedent stimuli because of their drinking history (Drobes et al., 2001). This suggests that cue reactivity must be addressed during treatment in order for dependent drinkers to learn to anticipate and cope with cravings for alcohol and urges to drink without a return to excessive consumption. Traditional treatment programs usually do everything they can to minimize or eliminate all tempting stimuli from the protected environment of the therapeutic setting. Clients are discouraged from ever mentioning the possibility of encountering temptations to drink excessively. Without preparation or warning, exposure to cues associated with past heavy drinking can be an overwhelming and discouraging experience that is often interpreted by clients as an indication that the treatment has failed or that treatment effects have worn off. The presence of alcohol cues may disrupt the coping responses of dependent drinkers, with those who are more dependent showing greater impairment in their coping behaviors.

Cue exposure may be most effective when paired with response prevention and coping skills training designed to prepare clients for the temptations they will encounter in the course of their everyday lives (Monti et al., 1989; Marlatt, 1990). Extensive research is currently under way assessing the efficacy of incorporating cue exposure therapy into cognitive-behavioral skills training, in order to improve the effectiveness of treatment outcome (Rohsenow et al., 1994, Drummond et al., 1995).

Relaxation Training

To the degree that stress causes unpleasant physical sensations and associated dysphoric moods, it is a high-risk situation for excessive alcohol use. An important coping skill for clients to learn is how to use the physical and emotional signs of stress as cues to "stop, look and listen" and to try something to cope besides heavy drinking. Relaxation training is a fundamental coping skill in the repertoire of a person trying to avoid excessive drinking. It can help clients to reduce their anxiety and tension when facing stressful situations and minimize their typical levels of motor and psychological tension. Relaxation training can also assist a person to remain calm and to think clearly in circumstances that require effective problem solving and fast action. Many individuals believe in the tension-reducing properties of alcohol, whether or not they are true, and, without an alternative means to relax, excessive drinking may be a person's only means of coping with painful sensations and unpleasant emotions. Relaxation training fosters general stress-reduction and can be taught to clients using various techniques that either reduce muscle tension, develop deep breathing skills or focus on the use of pleasant imagery (Monti et al., 1989). In addition to relaxation training, both meditation and exercise have been shown to have similar stress-reducing properties.

Contingency Management

Contingency management procedures assist clients to re-structure their environment to decrease the rewards associated with alcohol use and increase the costs of excessive drinking. The principles of contingency management are based on operant or instrumental learning approaches to human behavior (see Bigelow, 2001). Contingency management techniques include providing incentives for compliance with alcohol treatment and positive reinforcement from spouses or friends for sobriety. This approach is combined with punishment, in the form of withdrawal of attention and approval contingent on the resumption of excessive drinking, and provisions for social support, recreational activities and vocational counseling.

The Community Reinforcement Approach to alcohol treatment is a contingency management intervention strategy that has demonstrated its effectiveness in both inpatient and outpatient settings (Hunt & Azrin, 1973; Smith & Meyers, 1995). It is compatible with either moderation or abstinence treatment goals. The program involves a functional analysis of drinking behavior, basic skills training, problem-solving training, drinking refusal training, and social, recreational and vocational counseling, including marital therapy where indicated.

Skills Training

Behavioral and cognitive skills training techniques, sometimes called coping skills training, form the cornerstone of cognitive-behavioral alcohol treatment. Monti et al. (1989) have categorized these coping skills as either *intra*personal or *inter*personal and have developed a session-by-session manual for skills training in their treatment protocol. Individuals with a history of heavy drinking may be deficient in coping skills, such as rational thinking, problem solving, assertiveness or effective conflict resolution. A functional analysis of drinking identifies deficits in those skills the client needs to learn and practice in order to regain abstinence or maintain moderate use in situations previously associated with excessive drinking.

A series of behavioral skills, such as blood alcohol discrimination, pacing of drinking, drinking refusal and setting moderation goals, have been used in behavioral self-control training to help clients whose goal is moderation rather than abstinence. In addition, clients whose goals are moderation or abstinence can benefit from social skills acquisition, such as communications training, assertiveness training, creating and maintaining social support networks and vocational training. Interpersonal skills training is often necessary because many individuals lacking in social skills use alcohol excessively as a way of coping with stressful situations involving others, especially interpersonal conflict (Marlatt & Parks, 1982).

Monti et al. (1989) provide modules on a number of specific interpersonal skills, as well as guidelines for how to conduct skills training sessions. In this regard, verbal instructions introducing skills are followed by modeling, role-playing and active practice by clients until mastery in analog therapy situations is achieved. Homework assignments provide clients with practice of new social skills in real-life situations where excessive drinking is a definite risk. Success and failure in coping with these situations is debriefed in individual or group therapy sessions, allowing for both a review of previously taught skills and feedback to the client on his/her efforts. Interpersonal skills are also important to the acquisition and maintenance of social support during the process of acquiring greater mastery of social skills.

COGNITIVE ASSESSMENT

A major strength of cognitive-behavioral alcohol treatment lies in the integrated combination of behavioral and cognitive intervention strategies. An initial step in the conduct of cognitive assessment and intervention is to persuade clients of the important role that thoughts and other internal events play in excessive drinking. While behavioral assessment involves the functional analysis of antecedents, behavior and consequences, cognitive assessment involves a focusing of attention on the mediation of behavior by internal events, such as self-talk and mental images.

One way to get the idea of cognitive mediation across to clients is to use the notion popularized by rational-emotive behavioral therapy, that "people are disturbed not by things, but by the views which they take of them" (Ellis et al., 1988). Most clients readily understand that their drinking-related attitudes, beliefs and expectations are important contributors to their excessive drinking when a few examples are analyzed using the ABCs of rational-emotive behavioral therapy. This involves identifying the activating event (A), exploring the client's interpretation of the event by discussing his/her beliefs, expectations, automatic thoughts and self-talk (B), and demonstrating how these beliefs and expectations take the form of internal dialogue or self-talk and contribute to the consequence of excessive drinking (C).

Once the rationale for cognitive assessment and intervention has been firmly established, clients are asked to begin self-monitoring their thoughts and other internal events in those situations that have in the past been related to excessive drinking. Clients are also taught about the importance of assessing and changing their cognitive appraisal of events. They are encouraged to examine and challenge their beliefs and expectancies about the transforming effects of alcohol and to develop greater self-efficacy expectations for mastery of life events without heavy drinking. Cognitive assessment falls within the intrapersonal skills domain of Monti et al. (1989), which includes a number of specific training modules to be briefly reviewed below. The Daily Thought Record and the Daily Record of Cravings are cognitive therapy techniques designed to help clients self-monitor their drinking-related thoughts (Beck et al., 1993). In addition, a number of questionnaires and interview methods have been devised to help therapist and client assess cognitive factors related to alcohol dependence, including alcohol outcome and self-efficacy expectancies (Allen & Columbus, 1995).

COGNITIVE THERAPY INTERVENTIONS

Appraisal

An initial cognitive intervention strategy is to assess the client's characteristic manner of evaluating whether various situations pose a risk for excessive drinking and, if they do, why they do. This strategy is consistent with the notion that people respond not to the *actual* situation, but to the situation as they *perceive* it to be. The importance of the appraisal process in understanding and treating alcohol problems is based on the work of Lazarus et al. (1974) and, more specifically, on the work of Sanchez-Craig et al. (1987). In this model, two types of appraisal are important to assess. *Primary* appraisal is the process by which a situation is judged beneficial, harmful, or irrelevant to the task of avoiding excessive drinking. *Secondary* appraisal refers to one's ability to identify and implement behavioral alternatives to coping with stress without drinking.

Based on this analysis of the relevance of appraisal for effective coping, Sanchez-Craig et al. (1987) suggest performing a functional analysis of the client's beliefs, expectations and attributions regarding drinking and their relationship to the emotions and behavioral intentions the client experiences. Given this information on the appraisal process, clients are taught new, more adaptive ways to appraise situations and are encouraged to reconsider attributions made about their appraisal of past negative events. The reappraisal process follows the basic formula of all cognitive-behavioral interventions. That is, clients first become aware of their thoughts and related behaviors by learning to identify situations in which they are likely to drink excessively. Additionally, they are taught how their primary and secondary appraisals influence this process. Then clients are taught to generate new, more effective cognitive strategies and to rehearse these strategies in both treatment and real life until mastery is achieved. This approach to reappraisal is consistent with both rational-emotive behavioral therapy (Ellis et al., 1988) and with the use of overt verbal instructions to modify the self-statements of clients used in Meichenbaum's (1977) stress inoculation training approach to control impulsivity and schizophrenic behavior.

Problem-solving Training

Cognitive and behavioral coping skills training focuses on specific thoughts or situations related to the likelihood of excessive drinking. In addition to this situation-specific strategy, cognitive-behavioral alcohol treatment combines training in general problem solving with specific skills training that focuses on the client's unique challenges and resources regarding his/her drinking. Adopting a problem-solving orientation to these situations (D'Zurilla & Goldfried, 1971) gives clients greater flexibility and adaptability in new stressful situations, rather than having to rely solely on the rote learning of a number of discrete coping skills that may or may not generalize across various settings and situations. In this sense, maintaining abstinence from alcohol or moderating drinking may be largely dependent on the ability of clients to use problem solving to cope effectively with the demands of those life situations previously associated with excessive drinking.

D'Zurilla & Goldfried (1971) describe five general stages that focus on key cognitive processes that have been seen as a prescription for effective problem solving in situations involving the risk of excessive drinking. In real life, problem solving may not take place in such a sequential manner. There might be substantial overlap between the stages; a client may jump back and forth from stage to stage or even work on different stages simultaneously. Nevertheless, the stages listed below can be seen as a method for effective problem solving and are usually helpful in the education of clients who have problem-solving deficits.

D'Zurilla & Goldfried (1971) recommend five steps for effective problem solving: (a) identifying a client's style of approaching problems and helping him/her to improve a maladaptive general orientation to problems is vital for effective problem solving; (b) assisting a client in the skill of problem definition allows him/her to formulate a problem in a clear, simple and unambiguous form, thereby facilitating a solution; (c) teaching a client the skill of generating alternative solutions to the problem is a vital step and is often facilitated by teaching the technique of brainstorming; (d) helping a client to weigh the consequences of various alternative solutions with the assistance of a decision matrix or decision balance sheet; and (e) verification, where the client and therapist evaluate the outcome of the client's problem-solving effort, allowing for feedback and correction if needed. Eventually, it is assumed that the client will select a viable solution and the verification of its effectiveness should result in increased self-efficacy for mastering life events without excessive drinking.

Cognitive Restructuring

Problem-solving training helps clients to better identify and resolve the everyday challenges they face in their efforts to achieve their therapeutic and life goals. Cognitive or "thought" restructuring gives clients a cognitive skill that focuses their awareness on identifying those beliefs, patterns of thinking, attributions and expectations that are related to excessive drinking and alcohol-related problems. During this procedure, clients engage in ongoing self-monitoring and written recording of internal states, such as inner dialogue or self-talk related to excessive drinking. Through this process of client self-assessment, client and therapist try to create a functional analysis of the antecedent events, beliefs and consequences that form a client's typical pattern of excessive drinking. Client handouts and recording forms are often used to assist clients in making a systematic analysis of the relationship between their thinking and their problematic drinking.

Awareness of internal states and the relationships between certain ways of thinking and excessive alcohol use lays the foundation for cognitive restructuring. The next step is teaching clients how to "restructure" or alter their thinking by first interrupting a sequence of "negative" thoughts and then by challenging those thoughts, eventually leading to new, more adaptive ways of thinking. Clients are taught to "stop, look and listen" for thoughts leading to excessive drinking, especially as they face situations and circumstances where heavy alcohol consumption used to occur. Strategies to identify negative thinking are combined with in-session and/or in-group practice in discussing these beliefs, expectations and attributions and challenging them. Negative thinking is challenged, based either on the rationality of its content, on the evidence supporting it or on the presence of distortion or errors in thinking (Ellis et al., 1988; Beck et al., 1993).

A CONTEMPORARY COGNITIVE-BEHAVIORAL ALCOHOL TREATMENT PROTOCOL

Monti et al. have developed a cognitive-behavioral coping skills therapy protocol that systematically combines the cognitive and behavioral assessment and intervention elements previously described into treatment manuals for practitioners (Kadden et al., 1995; Monti et al., 1989). These manuals guide therapists engaged in the treatment of individuals with alcohol abuse and dependence disorders to an understanding of a social learning approach to alcohol consumption, an appreciation of the rationale for coping skills training, and the creation of a session-by-session treatment program, including both assessment and intervention procedures. They divide their coping skills training program into interpersonal and intrapersonal components, which roughly correspond to behavioral and cognitive therapy interventions. This cognitive-behavioral alcohol treatment protocol has been applied in both inpatient and outpatient settings, using both individual and group therapy formats. A version of this protocol was chosen as the cognitive-behavioral intervention in the Project MATCH study (Kadden et al., 1995).

POTENTIAL BENEFITS OF COGNITIVE-BEHAVIORAL ALCOHOL TREATMENT

Cognitive-behavioral alcohol treatment avoids the stigma and shame of labeling clients as "alcoholic" because clients are instead viewed as individuals with drinking behavior problems, or bad habits, that are not their fault but that can be changed with knowledge, effort and support. This approach to treatment creates a low threshold for treatment entry, fosters openness and cooperation in clients, and increases the likelihood of continued treatment compliance. Another benefit of this science-based approach to alcohol treatment is that specific, yet flexible, treatment goals can be derived and modified, depending on the nature and severity of a client's alcohol dependence and his/her stage in the habit change process. This is true in part because assessment of the nature and severity of the alcohol-related problem and feedback to the client occur at the onset of treatment and are an ongoing process during therapy. Since therapeutic goals are made explicit and agreed upon by therapist and client in advance, it is readily apparent to both the therapist and the client whether a treatment intervention is effective in achieving its desired results as therapy progresses. Finally, because cognitive-behavioral alcohol treatment is an empirically-derived approach and endeavors to evolve and improve as new evidence accumulates from efficacy and effectiveness studies, the intervention components and protocols of cognitive-behavioral alcohol treatment are designed to be evaluated and modified by the results of ongoing clinical research trials and the outcome effectiveness of active treatment programs.

EMPIRICAL SUPPORT FOR COGNITIVE-BEHAVIORAL ALCOHOL TREATMENT

Cognitive-behavioral therapies are often recommended as "what works" best for the treatment of a number of mental and medical disorders, including substance use disorders such as alcohol abuse and dependence, because these science-based protocols have been supported by outcome research testing their efficacy through randomized controlled experimental designs (Nathan & Gorman, 1998; Chambless & Hollon, 1998). Specifically, empirical support for the efficacy of cognitive-behavioral therapies as preferred treatments for drug abuse (Carroll, 1996) and for alcohol use disorders (Miller & Hester, 1986; Hester & Miller, 1995; Nathan & Gorman, 1998) is very strong. For example, Hester & Miller (1995), in their comprehensive review of alcohol treatment outcome studies, listed the following six cognitive-behavioral therapy techniques among their top 10 interventions with the strongest empirical evidence: social skills training, community reinforcement approach, behavioral contracting, aversion therapy (nausea), relapse prevention, and cognitive therapy. There is substantial evidence that constituent ingredients or components of a more integrated cognitive-behavioral alcohol treatment program are effective when applied to drug and alcohol problems. This evidence will be reviewed in Chapter 6 on Relapse Prevention Therapy (Marlatt & Parks, 1999; Carroll, 1996; Irvin et al., 1999). For the purposes of this chapter, let us end with the following statement of endorsement for this therapeutic approach by Monti and colleagues as they discuss the efficacy of cognitive-behavioral treatment for both substance and alcohol use disorders:

> Since the essential core elements in CSST (Coping and Social Skills Training) have a strong theoretical base as well as solid empirical support from research treatment outcome studies, they should be an integral part of any state-of-the-art intervention for clients with addictive behaviors in general, and of alcohol prevention and treatment in particular (Monti et al., 1995).

KEY WORKS AND SUGGESTIONS FOR FURTHER READING

Broadening the Base of Treatment for Alcohol Problems. Institute of Medicine (1990). Washington, DC: National Academy Press.

This report highlights the continuum of alcohol-related problems and disorders that can range from mild difficulties to severe dependency. The importance of matching treatment intensity to problem intensity is emphasized.

Kadden, R. et al. (1995). *Cognitive-behavioral Coping Skills Therapy Manual: A Clinical Research Guide for Therapists Treating Individuals with Alcohol Abuse and Dependence.* National Institute on Alcohol Abuse and Alcoholism Project MATCH Monograph Series. Bethesda, MD: US Department of Health and Human Services.

This manual was developed for Project MATCH and is a modified version of the treatment approach developed by Monti and his colleagues. The manual provides guidelines for 22 cognitive-behavioral therapy sessions that can be combined in an individualized manner.

Sobell, M.B. & Sobell, L.C. (1993). *Problem Drinkers: Guided Self-change Treatment.* New York: Guilford.

The Sobells describe the nature and scope of problem drinking and provide a detailed description of a guided self-change treatment approach.

Monti, P.M. et al. (1989). *Treating Alcohol Dependence.* New York: Guilford.

This book presents 27 cognitive-behavioral treatment sessions for alcohol-dependent clients. It formed the basis of the Project MATCH CBT manual. This treatment approach is geared towards a group setting and incorporates the development of both interpersonal and intrapersonal coping skills.

Jarvis, T.J., Tebbutt, J. & Mattick, R.P. (1995). *Treatment Approaches for Alcohol and Drug Dependence: An Introductory Guide.* Chichester: Wiley.

This book describes basic treatment approaches without going into the detail of specific session-by-session instructions. It addresses general topics such as assessment, motivational enhancement and goal setting, as well as more specific techniques.

REFERENCES

Allen, J.P. & Columbus, M. (1995). *Assessing Alcohol Problems: A Guide for Clinicians and Researchers*. National Institute on Alcohol Abuse and Alcoholism Treatment Handbook, Series 4, Bethesda, MD: US Department of Health and Human Services.

Baer, J.S., Kivlahan, D.R. & Donovan, D.M. (1999). Integrating skills training and motivational therapies: implications for the treatment of substance dependence. *Journal of Substance Abuse Treatment*, **17**(1–2), 15–24.

Bandura, A. (1969). *Principles of Behavior Modification*. New York: Holt, Rinehart & Winston.

Bandura, A. (1997). *Self-efficacy: The Exercise of Control*. San Francisco, CA: W.H. Freeman.

Bandura, A. (1986). *Social Foundations of Thought and Action: A Social Cognitive Theory*. Englewood Cliffs, NJ: Prentice Hall.

Beck, A.T., Wright, F.D., Newman, C.F. & Liese, B.S. (1993). *Cognitive Therapy of Substance Abuse*. New York: Guilford.

Bigelow, G.E. (2001). An operant behavioral perspective on alcohol abuse and dependence. In N. Heather, T.J. Peters & T. Stockwell (Eds), *International Handbook of Alcohol Dependence and Problems* (pp. 281–298). Chichester, UK: John Wiley & Sons.

Brickman, P., Rabinowitz, V.C., Karuza, J., Coates, D., Cohn, E. & Kidder, L. (1982). Models of helping and coping. *American Psychologist*, **37**(4), 368–384.

Carroll, K.M. (1996). Relapse prevention as a psychosocial treatment: a review of controlled clinical trials. *Experimental and Clinical Psychopharmacology*, **4**(1), 46–54.

Chambless, D.L. & Hollon, S.D. (1998). Defining empirically supported therapies. *Journal of Consulting and Clinical Psychology*, **66**, 7–19.

Collins, R.L. & Bradizza, C.M. (2001). Social and cognitive learning processes. In N. Heather, T.J. Peters & T. Stockwell (Eds), *International Handbook of Alcohol Dependence and Problems* (pp. 299–316). Chichester, U.K.: John Wiley & Sons.

Cook, C.C.H. (1988a). The Minnesota model in the management of drug and alcohol dependency: miracle method or myth? Part I: The philosophy and the programme. *British Journal of Addiction*, **83**, 625–634.

Cook, C.C.H. (1988b). The Minnesota model in the management of drug and alcohol dependency: miracle method or myth?: Part II: evidence and conclusions. *British Journal of Addiction*, **83**, 735–748.

Donovan, D.M. (1988). Assessment of addictive behaviors: implications of an emerging biopsychosocial model. In D.M. Donovan & G.A. Marlatt (Eds), *Assessment of Addictive Behaviors* (pp. 3–50). New York: Guilford.

Donovan, D.M. & Marlatt, G.A. (1988). *Assessment of Addictive Behaviors*. New York: Guilford.

Drobes, D.J., Saladin, M.E. & Tiffany, S.T. (2001). Classical conditioning mechanisms in alcohol dependence. In N. Heather, T.J. Peters & T. Stockwell (Eds), *International Handbook of Alcohol Dependence and Problems* (pp. 257–280). Chichester, U.K.: John Wiley & Sons.

Drummond, D.C., Tiffany, S.T., Glautier, S. & Remington, B. (Eds) (1995). *Addictive Behavior: Cue Exposure Theory and Practice*. Chichester: Wiley.

D'Zurilla, T.J. & Goldfried, M.R. (1971). Problem solving and behavior modification. *Journal of Abnormal Psychology*, **78**, 107–126.

Ellis, A., McInerney, J.F., DiGiuseppe, R. & Yeager, R.R. (1988). *Rational-emotive Therapy with Alcoholics and Substance Abusers*. Boston, MA: Allyn and Bacon.

Gorman, D.M. (2001). Developmental processes. In N. Heather, T.J. Peters & T. Stockwell (Eds), *International Handbook of Alcohol Dependence and Problems* (pp. 339–356). Chichester, U.K.: John Wiley & Sons.

Heather, N. & Robertson, I. (1989). *Problem Drinking*, 2nd edn. Oxford: Oxford University Press.

Heather, N. & Robertson, I. (1983). *Controlled Drinking*, revised edn. New York: Methuen.

Hester, R.K. & Miller, W.R. (Eds) (1995). *Handbook of Alcoholism Treatment Approaches: Effective Alternatives*, 3rd edn. Boston MA: Allyn & Bacon.

Hunt, G.M. & Azrin, N.H. (1973). A community-reinforcement approach to alcoholism. *Behaviour Research and Therapy*, **11**, 91–104.

Institute of Medicine (IOM) (1990). *Broadening the Base of Treatment for Alcohol Problems.* Washington, DC: National Academy Press.

Irvin, J.E., Bowers, C.A., Dunn, M.E. & Wang, M.C. (1999). Efficacy of relapse prevention: a meta-analytic review. *Journal of Consulting and Clinical Psychology*, **67**(4), 563–570.

Jarvis, T.J., Tebbutt, J. & Mattick, R.P. (1995). *Treatment Approaches for Alcohol Aand Drug Dependence: An Introductory Guide.* Chichester: Wiley.

Kadden, R.M. (1994). Cognitive-behavioral approaches to alcoholism treatment. *Alcohol Health and Research World*, **18**(4), 279–286.

Kadden, R., Carroll, K., Donovan, D., Conney, N., Monti, P., Abrams, D., Litt, M. & Hester, R. (1995). *Cognitive-behavioral Coping Skills Therapy Manual: A Clinical Research Guide for Therapists Treating Individuals with Alcohol Abuse and Dependence.* National Institute on Alcohol Abuse and Alcoholism, Project MATCH Monograph Series. Bethesda, MD: US Department of Health and Human Services.

Lazarus, R.S., Averill, J.R. & Opton, E.M. (1974). The psychology of coping: issues of research and assessment. In G.V. Coelbo, D.A. Hamburg & J.E. Adams (Eds), *Coping and Adaption* (pp. 249–315). New York: Basic Books.

Mackay, P.W., Donovan, D.M. & Marlatt, G.A. (1991). Cognitive and behavioral approaches to alcohol abuse. In R.J. Frances & S.I. Miller (Eds), *Clinical Textbook of Addictive Disorders* (pp. 452–481). New York: Guilford.

Marlatt, G.A. (Ed.) (1998). *Harm Reduction: Pragmatic Strategies for Managing High-risk Behaviors.* New York: Guilford.

Marlatt, G.A. (1992). Substance abuse: implications of a biopsychosocial model for prevention, treatment, and relapse prevention. In J. Grabowski & G.R. VandenBos (Eds), *Psychopharmacology: Basic Mechanisms and Applied Interventions* (pp. 131–162). Washington, DC: America Psychological Association.

Marlatt, G.A. (1990). Cue exposure and relapse prevention in the treatment of addictive behaviors. *Addictive Behaviors*, **15**, 395–399.

Marlatt, G.A., Larimer, M.E., Baer, J.S. & Quigley, L.A. (1993). Harm reduction for alcohol problems: moving beyond the controlled drinking controversy. *Behavior Therapy*, **24**, 461–504.

Marlatt, G.A., Baer, J.S., Donovan, D.M. & Kivlahan, D.R. (1988). Addictive behaviors: etiology and treatment. In M.K. Roszenweig & L.W. Porter (Eds), *Annual Review of Psychology*, Vol. 39 (pp. 223–252). Palo Alto, CA: Annual Reviews Inc.

Marlatt, G.A. & Gordon, J.R. (Ed.) (1985). *Relapse Prevention: Maintenance Strategies in the Treatment of Addictive Behaviors.* New York: Guilford.

Marlatt, G.A. & Parks, G.A. (1982). Self-management of addictive behaviors. In F.H. Kanfer & P. Karoly (Eds), *Self-management of Behavior Change: From Theory to Practice* (pp. 443–488). New York: Pergamon.

Marlatt, G.A. & Parks, G.A. (1999). Keeping "what works" working: cognitive-behavioral relapse prevention therapy with substance abusing offenders. In E.J. Latessa (Ed.), *Strategic Solutions: The International Community Corrections Association Examines Substance Abuse* (pp. 161–233). Lanham, MD: American Correctional Association.

Marlatt, G.A., Tucker, J.A., Donovan, D.M. & Vuchinich, R.E. (1997). Help-seeking by substance abusers: the role of harm reduction and behavioral-economic approaches to facilitate treatment entry and retention. In L.S. Onken, J.D. Blaine & J.J. Boren (Eds), *Beyond the Therapeutic Alliance: Keeping the Drug-dependent Individual in Treatment.* National Institute on Drug Abuse Research Monograph 165, 44–84. Rockville, MD: US Department of Health and Human Services.

Meichenbaum, D.H. (1977). *Cognitive-behavioral Modification.* New York: Plenum.

Miller, W.R. & Hester, R.K. (1986). The effectiveness of alcoholism treatment. What research reveals. In W.R. Miller & N. Heather (Eds), *Treating Addictive Behaviors: Processes of Change* (pp. 175–203). New York: Plenum.

Miller, W.R. & Rollnick, S. (1991). *Motivational Interviewing: Preparing People to Change Addictive Behaviors.* New York: Guilford.

Miller, W.R., Westerberg, V.S., Harris, R.J. & Tonigan, J.S. (1996). What predicts relapse? Prospective testing of antecedent models. *Addiction*, **91**(Suppl.).

Monti, P.M., Abrams, D.B., Kadden, R.M. & Conney, N.L. (1989). *Treating Alcohol Dependence.* New York: Guilford.

Monti, P.M., Rohsenow, D.J., Colby, S.M. & Abrams, D.B. (1995). Coping and social skills training. In R.K. Hester & W.R. Miller (Eds), *Handbook of Alcoholism Treatment Approaches: Effective Alternatives*, 2nd edn (pp. 221–241). Boston, MA: Allyn and Bacon.

Nathan, P.E. & Gorman, J.M. (1998). *A Guide to Treatments that Work*. New York: Oxford University Press.

Prochaska, J.O. & DiClemente, C.C. (1992). In search of how people change: applications to addictive behaviors. *American Psychologist*, **47**, 1102–1114.

Rimmele, C.T., Miller, W.R. & Dougher, M.J. (1989). Aversion therapies. In R.K. Hester & W.R. Miller (Eds), *Handbook of Alcoholism Treatment Approaches* (pp. 128–140). New York: Pergamon.

Rohsenow, D.J., Monti, P.M., Rubonis, A.V., Sirota, A.D., Niaura, R.S., Colby, S.M., Wunschel, S.M. & Abrams, D.B. (1994). Cue reactivity as a predictor of drinking among male alcoholics. *Journal of Consulting and Clinical Psychology*, **62**, 620–626.

Sanchez-Craig, M., Wilkinson, D.A. & Walker, K. (1987). Theory and methods for secondary prevention of alcohol problems: a cognitively based approach. In W.M. Cox (Eds), *Treatment and Prevention of Alcohol Problems* (pp. 287–331). Orlando, FL: Academic Press.

Sobell, M.B. & Sobell, L.C. (1993). *Problem Drinkers: Guided Self-change Treatment*. New York: Guilford.

Smith, J.E. & Meyers, R.J. (1995). The Community Reinforcement Approach. In R.K. Hester & W.R. Miller (Eds), *Handbook of Alcoholism Treatment Approaches: Effective Alternatives*; 2nd edn. Boston, MA: Allyn & Bacon.

Vaillant, G.E. (1995). *The Natural History of Alcoholism* (revised edn). Cambridge: Harvard University Press.

Chapter 6

Relapse Prevention Therapy

George A. Parks
Britt K. Anderson
and
G. Alan Marlatt
*Addictive Behaviors Research Center, University of Washington,
Seattle, WA, USA*

Synopsis

What follows is the second of two chapters devoted to a cognitive-behavioral approach to the treatment of alcohol abuse and dependence. In Chapter 5, we provided an overview of this therapeutic approach by placing it within a typology of conceptual models, summarizing the main principles of cognitive-behavioral alcohol treatment and reviewing both cognitive and behavioral assessment and intervention techniques that are the constituent ingredients of this empirically-supported form of therapy. The goal of this chapter is to present an overview of a cognitive-behavioral approach to the problem of relapse, Relapse Prevention Therapy (RPT).

The chapter begins by introducing a conceptual model of relapse prevention and discussing the cyclical nature of long-term behavioral change. From this perspective, relapse is a natural part of the process of change and does not represent failure. Rather, lapses or relapses represent opportunities for clients to gain a greater understanding of their unique challenges in changing drinking behavior and to learn new skills to better cope in the future. High-risk situations represent difficult circumstances in which goals of abstinence or moderation may be tested. Common across a range of addictive behaviors, they can be broadly described as interpersonal or intrapersonal situations in which one's sense of control is threatened. The process of relapse, from the experience of high-risk situations to an initial lapse, is then presented. Positive outcome expectancies regarding the effects of alcohol, degree of self-efficacy and the acquisition of effective coping skills all play a role in this process. Additionally, when a lapse occurs there is often an abstinence violation effect, composed of guilty feelings and a sense of inherent powerlessness, which can interact with these other factors and

The Essential Handbook of Treatment and Prevention of Alcohol Problems. Edited by N. Heather and T. Stockwell.
© 2004 John Wiley & Sons Ltd. ISBN 0-470-86296-3.

trigger a relapse. A client may unknowingly contribute to a relapse through several covert antecedents that lead him/her to a high-risk situation. For example, the desire for the pleasurable effects of alcohol, a lack of life-style balance, the experience of urges and craving, and cognitive factors such as rationalization, denial and apparently irrelevant decisions, all may represent links in the chain leading up to a relapse. A thorough analysis of a relapse experience will reveal these steps and contribute to a greater understanding of the relapse process.

RPT intervention strategies are then discussed. Specific RPT strategies are designed to address the immediate precursors of relapse and include assessment of high-risk situations and coping skills, training of new coping skills, challenging positive outcome expectancies associated with alcohol use, and coping with lapses and the abstinence violation effect. Global RPT strategies are focused on broader issues of life-style balance and awareness of covert determinants of relapse. These include an assessment and emphasis on life-style balance, coping with the desire for indulgence through substitute indulgences, coping with cravings for alcohol and urges to drink, and coping with cognitive distortions to minimize the likelihood of relapse. Finally, two empirical reviews of RPT are discussed. Both support the use of RPT as an effective treatment for alcohol problems.

THE NATURE OF RELAPSE

What is the best way to conceptualize the *maintenance stage* of habit change? One approach is to consider the maintenance stage as a period following treatment and successful abstinence or moderation, during which therapeutic effects wear off over time. In this theory of treatment decay, one would expect the risk of relapse to increase over time as treatment effects wear off. Therefore, booster sessions of alcohol treatment are typically recommended to bolster the lagging effects of the initial therapy. Relapse Prevention Therapy (RPT) provides an alternative view of the maintenance stage of habit change as an opportunity for new learning to occur. Since drinking is a learned behavior from a cognitive-behavioral point of view, the maintenance stage can be conceptualized as a time to practice "unlearning" old drinking behaviors and replacing these previously dominant responses by experimenting with new learning. Using this theoretical model, one would expect the risk of relapse to decrease over time as clients learn to avoid errors and to acquire and more firmly establish new responses related to alcohol.

In RPT, quitting drinking or exerting control over alcohol consumption is like embarking on an extended journey, with the act of departure (quitting or moderating) only the first of many steps (see discussion of stages of change in Chapter 5). If clients and therapists believe that habit change is successful once drinking has ceased or is moderated, little attention and effort will be placed on the demands of the perilous journey of maintaining change ahead. From a stages of change perspective, after a client has made a successful change in drinking behavior, usually through a series of advances and setbacks, the focus shifts to the stability of the changes achieved. In the maintenance stage, therapeutic gains from the action stage will be consolidated and clients will attempt to identify and implement strategies to avoid relapse. During the first 90 days, when risk of relapse is highest, a client must work hard to maintain his/her motivation and commitment to the ultimate goal of abstinence or sustained moderation. Research has demonstrated that most of the variance in long-term treatment outcome can be attributed to events that occur *after* the action stage, or *after* treatment has been completed (Cronkite & Moos, 1980). This research underscores the need for RPT during both the action and maintenance stages of change and the need for aftercare and social support following the termination of alcohol treatment.

Failure to maintain the changes achieved during the *action stage* of change may lead the client to the *relapse stage*. Although traditionally viewed an indication of treatment failure or the gradual extinction of treatment effects, a cognitive-behavioral view of relapse conceptualizes it as a fluid and dynamic process that is best understood as a natural transition in the habit change process. Relapse prevention and relapse management strategies are necessary at the action, maintenance and relapse stages in order for habit change to be successful in the long run. Cognitive-behavioral *relapse prevention strategies* are designed to cope with the high-risk situations that precede a slip or lapse and *relapse management strategies* are designed to prevent a slip or lapse from becoming a full-blown relapse.

Since change is a cyclical process, most clients will not be completely successful on their first attempt to alter their drinking behavior. Therefore, RPT is also designed to teach clients not to be demoralized or to view relapse as a failure, but to re-ignite their motivation and commitment to change and to risk beginning the journey again. The lessons learned from each lapse or even relapse may bring clients closer to stable maintenance if they are viewed as opportunities to learn, rather than failures, dead ends, or an indication that the disease of alcoholism is incurable.

HIGH-RISK SITUATIONS FOR RELAPSE

After a client completes treatment, he/she experiences a sense of perceived control while maintaining abstinence from drinking or a moderated level of alcohol consumption. The longer the period of successful abstinence or moderation, the greater the individual's perception of control and self-efficacy is likely to be. Abstinence or moderation will usually continue until the person encounters a *high-risk situation* or *relapse trigger*. A high-risk situation is defined as any internal or external event or factor that poses a threat to the individual's sense of perceived control or ability to cope with the immediate situation or its subjective consequences (e.g. elicitation of negative emotions).

In an analysis of 311 initial relapse episodes obtained from clients with a variety of addictive behavior problems (alcohol, smoking, heroin addiction, compulsive gambling and overeating), three high-risk situations were identified that were associated with almost three-quarters of all the relapses reported: negative emotional states, interpersonal conflict, and social pressure (Cummings et al., 1980). Overall, these high-risk factors can be more specifically divided into *intrapersonal* and *interpersonal* determinants. *Intra*personal determinants refer to those precipitating factors that do not require the presence of another person and include negative emotional states, negative physical states, positive emotional states, testing personal control and urges and temptations. *Inter*personal determinants refer to those precipitating factors that require the current or recent presence of another person and include interpersonal conflict, direct and indirect social pressure, and positive emotional states experienced in social settings.

THE RELAPSE PROCESS: THE PATH FROM HIGH-RISK SITUATIONS TO RELAPSE

If a client has learned and can implement an effective coping response to deal with a high-risk situation (e.g. assertiveness in response to direct social pressure, or relaxation to reduce anxiety and tension), the probability of relapse may decrease significantly (see Figure 6.1). The RPT model proposes that when a person copes effectively with a high-risk situation, he/she is likely to experience an increased sense of mastery and a perception of self-control or self-efficacy. The concept of *self-efficacy* (Bandura, 1977, 1997)

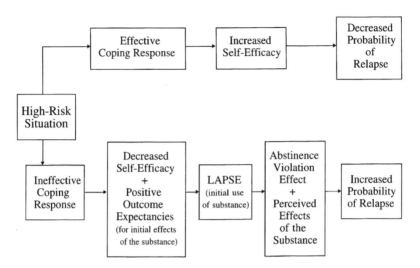

Figure 6.1 A cognitive-behavioral model of the relapse process

refers to an individual's expectation concerning his/her capacity to cope effectively with a specific situation or a particular task. As the duration of abstinence or moderation increases, clients have the experience of coping effectively with one high-risk situation after another. However, what happens if a client has not learned or cannot execute an effective coping response when exposed to a high-risk situation? The RPT model predicts that failure to effectively cope with a high-risk situation is likely to create decreased self-efficacy and possibly engender a sense of helplessness and powerlessness to cope with other life demands.

As self-efficacy decreases, clients are likely to focus more narrowly on the anticipated immediate positive effects of drinking, especially if they recall that alcohol helped them cope in the past. Attraction to the immediate gratification of excessive drinking becomes dominant in a person's mind and the reality of the delayed negative effects of drinking fades. Research has demonstrated that positive outcome expectancies for the effects of alcohol are potent determinants of excessive use (Marlatt & Rohsenow, 1980). The combination of being unable or unwilling to cope effectively with a high-risk situation, combined with positive outcome expectancies for the effects of drinking, greatly increases the probability of an initial lapse or slip.

After a lapse has been experienced, many clients may experience a further decrease in self-efficacy coupled with the tendency to give up trying to cope and give in to further temptations to continue to drink. To account for this reaction to the transgression of an absolute rule, we have proposed a mechanism called the *abstinence violation effect* (AVE) which is termed the *rule violation effect* (RVE) when applied more broadly to moderation as a goal (Marlatt & Gordon, 1985). The AVE is characterized by two key factors: *cognitive dissonance* (a discrepancy between one's identity as an abstainer and one's current drinking behavior) and an *attribution* of the cause of the lapse to *internal uncontrollable factors* (blaming oneself for lack of willpower). The final factor to be considered concerning the immediate determinants of relapse is the initial intoxicating effects of drinking alcohol experienced by the person following the lapse or slip. It is likely that the immediate outcome of drinking will be a "high" or euphoric state (positive reinforcement) or perhaps a reduction in any negative emotional or physical states (negative reinforcement). These initial effects of the lapse interact with the AVE to further increase the probability of relapse by priming the person to continue engaging in excessive drinking.

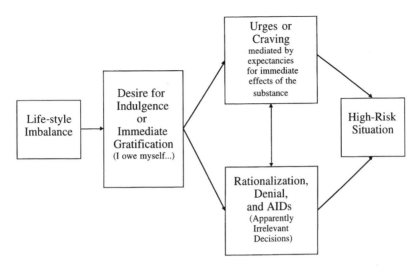

Figure 6.2   Relapse set-ups: covert antecedents of relapse situations

RELAPSE SET-UPS: COVERT ANTECEDENTS OF RELAPSE

In many, perhaps most, relapse episodes, clients report they were not expecting a high-risk situation to occur or were not well prepared to cope effectively with it when it did occur. Usually, after extensive debriefing and analysis of relapse episodes, the lapse or subsequent relapse appears to be the last link in a chain of events that preceded exposure to the high-risk situation itself. It seems as if, perhaps unknowingly, even paradoxically, the client has set him/herself up for relapse (see Figure 6.2).

Why would a person set him/herself up for relapse? The immediate gratification of drinking is a welcome relief from the relative deprivation of abstinence or the restraints of moderation and the individual may believe that it is difficult to cope with life's demands without excessive drinking. For many clients, the instant gratification of excessive drinking may outweigh the cost of any anticipated future negative consequences. Cognitive distortions, such as denial and rationalization, make it easier to set up one's own relapse episode with the added benefit of not having to take responsibility for it.

Research studies and clinical experience suggest that the degree of balance in a person's daily life has a significant impact on the desire for indulgence and immediate gratification. *Life-style imbalance* is the first covert antecedent in a chain of events that can lead to a relapse set-up. A key aspect of life-style balance is the number of daily activities perceived as required by external demands, or *shoulds*, and those activities perceived as engaged in for enjoyment and pleasure, or *wants*. If shoulds are much greater that wants, a client may experience a sense of relative self-deprivation and a corresponding *desire for indulgence* or immediate gratification. More broadly conceived, life-style balance refers to the amount of stress in a person's daily life compared with stress-reducing activities, such as social support, exercise or meditation.

Relapse set-ups are also caused by affective and cognitive processes that mask a client's actual intentions and move the client closer to a high-risk situation. Affectively, the desire for indulgence may be experienced as an urge or craving for alcohol. An urge is defined as the relatively sudden impulse to engage in a pleasurable act. Craving is defined as the subjective desire to experience the expected effects of a given behaviour. While the disease model of alcoholism views craving as a result of acute withdrawal or an internal physiological need for alcohol, the RPT model recognizes that both craving and urges may also be elicited by conditioned environmental cues associated with withdrawal or past alcohol use and that urges and cravings are mediated by the expectation of immediate pleasure or reduced pain associated with drinking (Rohsenow et al., 1994).

In addition to affective processes, covert antecedents of a relapse episode are influenced by three cognitive factors: rationalization, denial, and apparently irrelevant decisions (AIDs), which are associated with the chain of events preceding exposure to a high-risk situation. A *rationalization* is an explanation or an seemingly legitimate excuse to engage in drinking behaviour. *Denial* is a similar defense mechanism in which an individual will deny the existence of any motive to engage in drinking and may also deny awareness of the delayed negative consequences of resuming excessive drinking. Both rationalization and denial are cognitive distortions that occur with little awareness and may promote a client's covert planning of exposure to a high-risk situation. AIDs stand for a number of mini-decisions made over time, each of which seems innocent or irrelevant to relapsing in and of itself (e.g. a man decides to visit his old friends at the neighborhood bar) but in combination bring the client closer to exposure to a relapse triggering high-risk situation. One of the primary goals of RPT is to train clients to recognize *early warning signs* that precede exposure to a high-risk situation, and to execute intervention strategies before it is too late to do anything and the temptations in the high-risk situation become too compelling to resist.

RPT INTERVENTION STRATEGIES

RPT intervention strategies represent a menu of treatment alternatives aimed at both the immediate and covert aspects of relapse that can be individually tailored to various clinical populations, to particular addictive behaviors including alcohol dependence, and to different treatment settings. These strategies can be grouped into three categories: coping skills training, cognitive therapy and life-style modification. *Coping skills training strategies* include behavioral and cognitive techniques to effectively cope with high-risk situations and to enhance self-efficacy. *Cognitive therapy* procedures are designed to provide clients with ways of reframing the habit change process (i.e. to view it as a learning process and as a journey), to correcting cognitive distortions and to introduce coping imagery to deal with urges and craving. Finally, *life-style modification* strategies (e.g. meditation, exercise, spiritual practices) are designed to strengthen the client's global coping capacity and to reduce the frequency and intensity of the desire for indulgence and the experience of urges and craving.

Initially, RPT assessment and intervention strategies are designed to teach clients to anticipate and cope with the possibility of relapse. Clients are taught to recognize and cope with high-risk situations that may precipitate a lapse and to modify cognitions and other reactions to prevent a single lapse from developing into a full-blown relapse. Because these procedures are focused on the immediate precipitants of the relapse process, they are referred to collectively as *specific intervention strategies* (Figure 6.3). As clients master these techniques, clinical practice extends beyond a microanalysis of the relapse process and the initial lapse and involves strategies designed to modify the client's life-style and to identify and cope with covert determinants of relapse (early warning signals, cognitive distortions and relapse set-ups). As a group, these procedures are called *global intervention strategies.*

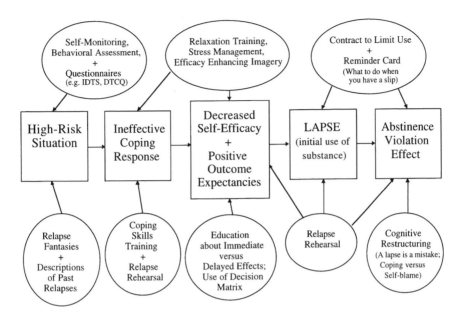

Figure 6.3 Specific relapse prevention therapy intervention strategies

SPECIFIC RPT INTERVENTION STRATEGIES

Assessment of High-risk Situations

Autobiographies

One of the first homework assignments in RPT is for clients to write a brief autobiography describing the history and development of their alcohol problem. Clients are asked to focus on their subjective image of themselves as they progressed through the stages of habit acquisition leading to alcohol abuse or dependence. The following points are emphasized: a description of parental and extended family alcohol and drug use habits, a description of the first episode of drinking to drunkenness, the role of alcohol and drugs in the client's adult life up to the present, factors associated with any increases in the severity of the client's drinking problem, the self-image of the client as a drinker, and any previous attempts to quit or moderate on one's own or with the assistance of treatment. The purpose of this technique is to identify high-risk situations and to get a baseline assessment of the client's self-image while engaging in excessive drinking. Clients are also asked to write a brief essay describing their future as an ex-drinker or a moderate drinker.

Past Relapses

Most clients in treatment will have tried either on their own or in previous treatment to abstain from alcohol or moderate their use. Asking clients to describe past relapses may provide important clues to future high-risk situations and deficits in coping skills. The therapist and the client can classify the descriptions of past relapses into the categories previously presented in order to determine the situational or personal factors that had the greatest impact. It is also useful to determine the client's attitude toward these past "failures" to remain abstinent or to drink moderately, because many clients develop negative attitudes toward future change attempts, based on attributions that they have a deficit in willpower or self-control. *Cognitive reframing* of past relapses will be necessary to reduce the client's fear of the prospect of yet another failure. The therapist can encourage the client to attribute past relapses as due to a lack of skill or effort, not to immutable internal factors.

Relapse Fantasies

This guided imagery technique involves asking the client to imagine as vividly as possible what it would take to resume drinking. Clients are asked to repeat this technique either in a therapy session or on his/her own as homework for as many possible relapse scenarios as he/she can envision. If a client denies that relapse is a possibility or has difficulty using his/her imagination, the therapist and client can brainstorm together, perhaps using any past relapses as a guide. Questionnaire techniques to be described below can also be used to gain a better understanding of a client's unique profile of high-risk situations.

Self-Monitoring

When clients who are still drinking alcohol or using drugs enter therapy, prior to quitting they are asked to self-monitor their use on a daily basis by keeping track of drinking, the situational context in which it occurs, and the immediate consequences of the behaviour. In most cases, RPT programs are initiated after abstinence or moderation has been achieved by some means. In this situation, self-monitoring of tempting high-risk situations for excessive drinking is a useful technique. Clients are asked to keep track of exposure to situations or personal factors that cause them to have urges or craving to resume drinking excessively.

Questionnaires for Assessing High-risk Situations

The *Inventory of Drug-Taking Situations (IDTS)* developed by Annis, Turner & Sklar (1997b) is a 50-item self-report questionnaire which provides a profile of a client's high-risk situations by measuring those circumstances in which a client has used alcohol heavily in the past year. Clients are asked to indicate their frequency of heavy drinking in each of 50 specific situations. The eight high-risk categories previously described are divided into three areas: *negative situations* (unpleasant emotions, physical discomfort, conflict with others), *positive situations* (pleasant times with others, pleasant emotions), and *temptation situations* (urges and temptations, social pressure to use, testing personal control). Research has documented the utility of the IDTS as a reliable and valid instrument for helping therapists and clients recognize situations in which the client has had alcohol problems in the past and to begin working on acquiring coping skills specific to those situations.

Another excellent tool for assessing a client's specific high-risk situations and coping deficits is the *Substance Abuse Relapse Assessment* (SARA) (Schonfeld, Peters & Dolente, 1993). This structured interview technique based on the RPT model yields the frequency and pattern of substance use for the 30 days preceding the last use of the substance; has the client describe the antecedents of substance abuse including places, activities and companions; assesses coping skills; identifies the most problematic substance in the client's lifetime; identifies the consequences of substance use; and, in a final section, describes the client's responses to previous slips or lapses. SARA also provides the client and therapist with instructions on how to develop an individualized substance abuse behavior chain.

Assessing Coping Skills

The Situational Competency Test (SCT)

The SCT is a role-play technique developed by Chaney, O'Leary & Marlatt (1978) requiring clients to give a verbal response to a series of high-risk situations presented by a narrator on audio tape. The client is presented with a series of high-risk scenarios drawn from the categories of high-risk situations previously described. In the initial use of the SCT, four scoring measures were used: *latency, duration, compliance* and *specification of new behavior*. *Latency* is defined as the elapsed time from the termination of the recorded situation to the beginning of the subject's verbal response. *Response duration* is taken as the frequency of words in the response. *Compliance* is a dichotomous score indicating whether or not the subject gave in to the situation without attempting to engage in an alternative coping response.

Specification of new behavior is also a dichotomous score indicating whether the description of the problem-solving behavior or coping response was given in enough detail for someone else to be able to use the description as a guide to perform the behavior. This technique is a good way to assess coping skills deficits and to begin the process of coping skills training.

Coping Skills Training

Stimulus Control

This behavioral technique is particularly important in the early phase of the maintenance stage of habit change, before self-efficacy has increased and before new, more effective coping skills for handling high-risk situations have been learned. The situational cues previously associated with drinking are likely to create craving, urges and temptations to resume the old pattern of excessive alcohol consumption. Several stimulus control strategies can be easily learned and applied while more extensive coping skills training is under way. The first option is *avoidance* of those high-risk situations that have been identified in the assessment as having the highest problem potential. While this may not be practical in all cases, there are many situations that can be avoided with some forethought and vigilance. Where avoidance is not possible, or when a high-risk situation appears to occur unexpectedly, *escape* is the next best option. Some preparation may be necessary to prepare a client with escape plans for the most probable high-risk situations. Finally, if neither avoidance or escape is possible, *delay* of action may be a final stop-gap measure to buy time until escape is possible.

Coping Skills

Once the high-risk situations have been identified, the client can then be taught to respond to these situational cues as discriminative stimuli ("highway signs") for behavior change. The cornerstone of the RPT approach to maintaining behavior change is *coping skills training* (e.g. Chaney, O'Leary & Marlatt, 1978). For clients whose coping responses are blocked by fear or anxiety, the therapist should attempt to disinhibit the behavior through an appropriate anxiety-reduction procedure, such as systematic desensitization or general relaxation training. For clients who show deficiencies in their coping skills repertoire, however, the therapist attempts to teach them new coping skills, using a systematic and structured approach. The RPT approach combines training in general problem-solving ability with specific skill training focused on the client's unique challenges and resources. Adopting a problem-solving orientation to stressful situations (D'Zurilla & Goldfried, 1971) gives clients greater flexibility and adaptability in new problem situations, rather than having to rely solely on the rote learning of a number of discrete skills that may or may not generalize across various settings and situations. Coping skills training methods incorporate components of direct instruction, modeling, behavioral rehearsal, therapist coaching and feedback from the therapist.

Relapse Rehearsal

Sometimes a therapist and a client can do coping skills training *in vivo*, in which the therapist accompanies the client while he/she is exposed to high-risk situations in real-life settings. However, the therapist can also make use of imagery or role-plays to represent the high-risk situation. This procedure, called *relapse rehearsal*, is similar to the relapse fantasy technique mentioned earlier. In the relapse rehearsal procedure, the therapist goes beyond the imagined scenario of relapse to include scenes in which the client can imagine or practice engaging in appropriate coping responses. This behavioral procedure, known as covert modeling, can also be used to help clients cope with their reactions to a lapse. Relapse rehearsal can be extended into a role-playing procedure, either in individual therapy or in the context of RPT group work.

Stress Management

In addition to teaching the clients to respond effectively when confronted with specific high-risk situations, there are a number of additional relaxation training and stress management procedures the therapist can draw upon to increase the client's overall capacity to cope. Relaxation training may provide the client with an increased perception of control overall, thereby reducing the stress "load" that any given situation may pose for the individual. Such procedures as progressive muscle relaxation training, meditation, exercise and various stress management techniques are extremely useful in aiding the client to cope more effectively with the hassles and demands of daily life.

Assessing Self-efficacy

The *Drug-Taking Confidence Questionnaire* (DTCQ) (Annis, Sklar & Turner, 1997a) is available to measure a client's confidence in avoiding heavy drinking or drug use across the same eight high-risk categories and 50 specific risk situations included in the IDTS. Clients using the DTCQ are asked to imagine themselves in each of the 50 risky situations and to indicate on an accompanying scale how confident they are that they would be able to resist the urge to drink heavily or use a specific drug. Studies of clients' confidence in coping with risky situations have found that clients are less likely to relapse in situations where they have a high level of confidence in their ability to cope. The DTCQ allows therapists to gauge a client's self-efficacy in coping with high-risk situations at different stages in the treatment process, providing a measure of the client's progress.

Enhancing Self-efficacy

In terms of the relapse prevention model, *self-efficacy* refers to the judgments or expectations about one's capacity to cope with specific high-risk situations. Until a high-risk situation is encountered, there is little threat to this perception of control, since urges and temptations are minimal or absent. If a coping response is successfully performed, the individual's judgment of efficacy will be strengthened for coping with similar situations as they arise on subsequent occasions. Guided imagery can be used to enhance efficacy in a manner similar to relapse rehearsal. In this procedure, the therapist gently guides the client who is experiencing anxiety or having trouble generating successful coping strategies with subtle prompts that can later be internalized by the client. Efficacy-enhancing imagery is used to augment coping skills training and to assess the client's current level of self-efficacy and coping skills mastery.

Challenging Positive Outcome Expectancies

Positive outcome expectancies for the immediate effects of alcohol play an influential role in the relapse process. As a reminder of its potent effects, this phenomenon is called the *problem of immediate gratification* or *PIG*. The image of a hungry and insatiable PIG provides clients with a vivid reminder of the costs of impulsive consumption. Education about both the immediate and delayed effects of alcohol use may help offset the tendency to exaggerate the positive effects of drinking and to minimize its negative effects. A decision matrix can be an important resource to reduce the PIG phenomenon and the myopia of having outcome expectancies that focus only on the immediate positive effects of drinking. The decision matrix cells concerning both immediate and long-term effects of drinking or not drinking can serve as a potent reminder that alcohol use has its costs.

Coping with Lapses and the AVE

The occurrence of a lapse, while not a catastrophe, cannot be viewed as a totally harmless event. It is a moment of crisis that combines both danger and opportunity, with the most dangerous period immediately following the slip. There are several recommended strategies, or *relapse emergency procedures*, to employ whenever a lapse occurs. These can be presented to clients in summary form by the use of a *reminder card* that should be kept handy in the event that a lapse occurs. Since specific coping strategies will vary from client to client, therapists may wish to help a particular client prepare an individualized reminder card that fits that person's unique set of vulnerabilities and resources.

The following strategies for coping with lapse and the AVE are adapted from *Relapse Prevention* (Marlatt & Gordon, 1985):

1. *Stop, look and listen.* The first thing to do when a lapse occurs is to *stop* the ongoing flow of events and to *look* and *listen* to what is happening. The lapse is a warning signal indicating that you are in danger.
2. *Keep calm.* The first reaction to a lapse may be one of feeling guilty and blaming oneself for what has happened. This is a normal reaction and is to be expected. Give yourself enough time to allow this reaction to arise and to pass away, just like an ocean wave that builds in strength, peaks at a crest, and then ebbs away.
3. *Renew your commitment.* After a lapse, the most difficult problem to deal with is motivation. You may feel like giving up. Think back over the reasons why you decided to change your behavior in the first place. Renew your commitment.
4. *Review the situation leading up to the lapse.* Don't yield to the tendency to blame yourself for what happened. Instead, look at the slip as a specific unique event. Ask yourself the following questions. What events led up to the slip? Were there any early

warning signals that preceded the lapse? What was the nature of the high-risk situation that triggered the slip?

5. *Implement your plan for recovery.* After a slip, you must turn your renewed commitment into a plan of action to be carried out immediately. First, get rid of all alcohol or other stimuli associated with drinking. Second, remove yourself from the high-risk situation if at all possible. If necessary, find an alternative means of gratifying your need for satisfactions.

6. *Ask for help.* Make it easier on yourself if you find that you need help: ask for it! Ask your friends who are present to help in any way they can. If you are alone, call your therapist or AA sponsor and seek out their assistance and support. If you know about a crisis center, give them a call for assistance.

After the lapse has occurred, the client should be reassured that the therapist or RPT group will not censure or blame him/her for the mistake, as often occurs in traditional programs. Instead, clients should receive compassion and understanding, along with encouragement to learn everything possible about how to cope with similar situations in the future through a thorough debriefing of the lapse and its consequences. Clients are taught to review the details of the events and thoughts that led to the high-risk situation, to develop and practice new coping responses that are likely to be more effective in future situations, and to reframe their reactions to the slip as an error that is correctable with effort on their part and not as a sign of failure or moral weakness.

GLOBAL RPT INTERVENTION STRATEGIES

Providing clients with behavioral coping skills training and cognitive strategies to effectively cope with high-risk situations and lapses is vital to the success of any relapse prevention program. However, simply teaching clients to cope with one high-risk situation after another is not enough for long-term success in habit change. Even if every situation could be identified, teaching the client to cope effectively with each situation is likely to be time consuming and inefficient. In addition, the coping skills training and cognitive therapy procedures previously described are, by necessity, specific to the situations encountered and their unique cognitive and emotional consequences. In order to develop a more comprehensive and effective program of habit change, it is necessary to: (a) help the clients develop a more balanced life-style in order to increase their overall capacity to cope with stress, as well as incrementally to increase self-efficacy; and (b) teach clients how to identify and anticipate the early warning signals that preceded exposure to high-risk situations and to implement coping strategies designed to reduce the probability of a lapse or a relapse (Figure 6.4).

Assessment of Life-style Balance

As stated earlier, the degree of balance or imbalance in a person's daily life has a significant impact on the desire for indulgence and immediate gratification. The first step in applying global RPT intervention strategies is to assess the client's quality of life with a focus on areas of life-style imbalance. A good place to start assessing life-style balance is by paying attention to the areas of life previously mentioned by the client. Areas to explore include, but are not limited to: physical health, including chronic illness; exercise and nutrition; psychological health, including co-occurring psychological conditions, such as DSM-IV Axis I disorders and DSM-IV Axis II disorders; interpersonal factors, including family

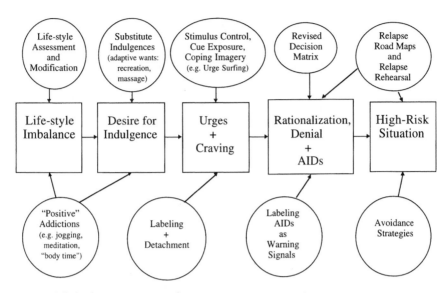

Figure 6.4   Global relapse prevention therapy intervention strategies

dynamics and the extent and quality of other social support; employment, including job satisfaction and security; the client's current financial situation, including savings and debt; and the client's spiritual beliefs and practices. In addition to clinical interviews, two life-style questionnaires designed for use in substance abuse treatment are available: *The Health and Daily Living Form* and the *Lifestyle Assessment Questionnaire* (Murphy & Impara, 1996). Both instruments can be used as therapist-administered structured interviews or as self-report questionnaires.

Increasing Life-style Balance

Once life-style imbalance has been assessed and its implications have been thoroughly discussed with the client, a comprehensive self-management program to improve the client's overall life-style and to increase his/her capacity to cope with the experience of more pervasive stress factors is begun. Life-style modification procedures are designed to identify and circumvent the covert antecedents of relapse that set up exposure to high-risk situations and to promote life-long habit change to create greater mental, emotional, physical and spiritual well-being.

The specific life-style modifications recommended in the RPT approach depend on the client's unique needs and abilities. A program of exercise, meditation, enhanced social activities, or weekly massages to reduce muscle tension are among the many possibilities. Some clients are simply encouraged to create some time and space in their daily routine for discretionary activities to reduce stress and enhance pleasure.

Coping with the Desire for Indulgence: Substitute Indulgences

As life-style imbalance is likely to create a desire for indulgence, one effective strategy is to search for activities that might be *substitute indulgences* that are not harmful or addictive. In this regard, Glasser (1974) has described behaviors such as excessive drinking and drug abuse as negative addictions that initially feel good, but produce long-term harm. Conversely, Glasser describes "positive addictions" (e.g. running, meditation, hiking, hobbies) as producing short-term discomfort or even pain while creating long-term benefits to physical health and to psychological well-being. Positive addictions often become wants as clients begin to gain mastery and look forward to engaging in these activities as a source of pleasure. An added benefit of positive addictions is that they often involve developing new skills and social relationships, which may increase a person's self-efficacy and create social networks with peers who model and support a healthy life-style.

Coping with Craving for Alcohol and Urges to Drink

Stimulus Control

Despite one's best attempts to modify life-style and to learn and practice positive addictions and substitute indulgences, occasional urges and cravings do arise. Quite often, urges and craving are conditioned responses triggered by external cues, such as the sight of others engaged in drinking. The frequency of these externally triggered urges and craving can be reduced by using *stimulus control techniques* designed to minimize exposure to these cues. In some circumstances, simply avoiding the situation is the best strategy. Using a highway metaphor for habit change, avoidance strategies can serve as an *emergency detour* allowing the client to escape exposure by a last-minute defensive maneuver. Later, when coping skills are better learned and more effective, it may be less dangerous to venture down that high-risk road. In any case, viable avoidance strategies may serve a person well for a time and enhance his/her sense of self-efficacy and personal choice while more sophisticated coping strategies are being learned.

Cue Exposure

Stimulus control techniques such as avoidance are at best short-term solutions to the challenges posed by urges and craving. Eventually, the client will have to learn and master effective techniques to cope with these tempting situations. One approach in this regard is *cue exposure* (Drummond et al., 1995). Traditional treatment programs do everything they can to minimize or eliminate all tempting stimuli from the protected environment of the therapeutic setting. Without preparation or warning, exposure to cues associated with addictive behaviors can be an overwhelming and discouraging experience and is often interpreted by the client as an indication that the treatment has failed or that treatment effects have worn off. Cue exposure treatments administered in either analog situations or *in vivo* can assist clients to avoid lapse when they cannot avoid drinking cues.

Coping Imagery

In addition to contemporary approaches, such as cue exposure, it is often helpful when teaching clients to cope with urges and craving to emphasize that the discomfort and agitation associated with these conditioned internal sensations is expected and natural. Most people have the mistaken idea that once an urge or craving begins, it will increase in intensity until drinking occurs. In helping clients to cope with the seemingly overwhelming power of growing urges and craving, it is helpful to teach them that these conditioned responses will rise in intensity, reach a peak, and then subside. In this respect, urges and craving can be compared to waves on the ocean; they rise, they crest, and then they fall, in a repeated cycle. *Urge surfing* uses the wave metaphor to help clients gain control over these seemingly unmanageable events. The client is taught to label these urges or craving as an ocean wave that reaches a peak, crests, and then subsides. Clients visualize learning to "ride the wave" through the peak experience of craving to its eventual decline. Clients are initially taught the urge surfing technique through guided imagery and then encouraged to try it on their own whenever they are exposed to alcohol cues.

Self-monitoring

Another way to foster detachment and disidentification with urges and craving is to have clients use *self-monitoring procedures* to keep track of these experiences. The *craving diary* is a technique used in a number of RPT programs to gain information and to help cope with craving. The client is asked to keep track of the internal and external cues that stimulated a craving, his/her mood, the strength of the craving, how long it lasted, coping skills used, and how successful or unsuccessful these coping strategies were.

Craving Cards

Just as a reminder card is used to automate the client's emergency response to a lapse, *craving cards* are designed to help clients cope with intense urges and cravings at a time when they may have trouble generating adaptive thoughts and behavioral coping skills. These cards include both general and specific suggestions for how the client can survive an urge and craving emergency without a lapse. A sample card might include tips on recognizing and labeling cravings, brief instructions for relaxation techniques, positive self-statements that encourage continued abstinence, tips on how to use distraction and incompatible responses, an abbreviated decision balance sheet, and emergency escape directions, including phone numbers of individuals willing to offer social support.

Coping with Cognitive Distortions

Urges and cravings usually do not operate at a conscious level, but are likely to be masked by the cognitive distortions and defense mechanisms described in the discussion of covert antecedents of high-risk situations. As such, these dimly perceived sensations and strong emotions fueled with forbidden desires set up the possibility of relapse by allowing for *apparently irrelevant decisions* (AIDs) to bring the person closer to exposure to a high-risk situation. Teaching clients to become vigilant for these early warning signals and to engage in explicit self-talk that questions their motivations and intentions can help them to recognize and acknowledge the direct relevance of these AIDs to the increased risk of relapse. By acknowledging to oneself that these mini-decisions actually represent urges and craving to return to excessive drinking, one is better able to recognize them as early warning signals on the road to relapse. Deliberately labeling the true nature of urges and craving before they motivate apparently irrelevant decisions is a good way to foster detachment and a stronger sense of self-efficacy.

EMPIRICAL SUPPORT FOR RELAPSE PREVENTION THERAPY

In this section, we will described two reviews which provide evidence for the therapeutic efficacy of treatments derived from the RPT model in their ability to effectively help clients overcome alcohol dependence and other addictive behavioral problems.

Carroll (1996) reviewed more than 24 randomized controlled trials evaluating the effectiveness of RPT as a psychosocial treatment for substance abuse. Her selection criteria included "only those randomized controlled trials that evaluated a treatment approach defined as *relapse prevention* or evaluated a coping skills approach that explicitly invoked the work of Marlatt" (Carroll, 1996, p. 46). After reviewing these studies, Carroll concluded:

> Across different substances of abuse, there is evidence for the effectiveness on substance use outcomes for relapse prevention over no-treatment control conditions, mixed findings when compared with attention and discussion control conditions, and findings that relapse prevention appears comparable, but not better than, other active treatments. (Carroll, 1996, p. 51).

In her review, Carroll (1996) discusses three areas that emerged as having particular promise for the effective application of RPT. First, Carroll notes that while RPT may not always prevent relapse better than other active treatments, several investigations suggest that RPT is more effective than available alternatives in relapse management (i.e. reducing the intensity of lapse episodes if they do occur). Second, numerous studies, especially those comparing RPT to other psychotherapies, have found RPT to be particularly effective at maintaining treatment effects over long-term follow-up measurement. In addition, Carroll's review suggests the presence of what she calls "delayed emergence of effects for relapse prevention", in which clients actually improve in coping ability over time (Carroll, 1996, p. 52). Finally, Carroll (1996) suggests that relapse prevention may be most effective "for more impaired substance abusers, including those with more severe levels of substance abuse, greater levels of negative affect, and greater perceived deficits in coping skills" (Carroll, 1996, p. 52).

Narrative reviews of substance abuse treatment studies, such as the one by Carroll (1996), serve a useful purpose for both researchers and clinicians, but conclusions from descriptive analysis are not readily quantified and may be subject to various interpretations. On the other hand, *meta-analytic reviews* of treatment outcome studies use statistical techniques to measure and quantify treatment effects, allowing more precise comparisons and conclusions regarding the relative effectiveness of different treatment alternatives (Lipsey & Wilson, 1993). A meta-analytic review of the efficacy of Relapse Prevention Therapy has been recently completed and will be summarized below.

Irvin, Bowers, Dunn & Wang (1999) selected 17 controlled studies with 72 hypotheses in order to evaluate the overall effectiveness of RPT as a substance abuse treatment and to identify moderator variables that may reliably impact the outcome of treatment. Six moderator variables were studied: treatment modality; theoretical orientation of prior therapy delivered before relapse prevention; treatment setting; type of outcome measure used to determine effectiveness; medication as an adjunct to relapse prevention; and finally, type of substance use disorder treated by the RPT interventions.

In their discussion of the results of the meta-analytic review of RPT outcome studies, Irvin et al. (1999) conclude that "relapse prevention is highly effective for both alcohol-use and substance-use disorders". They go on to say that the effect size for this finding was significant and the available evidence indicates the overall effectiveness of RPT as a substance abuse treatment for both habit cessation and maintenance. Additionally, relapse prevention appears to be most effective when applied to alcohol or poly-substance use disorders, combined with adjunctive use of medications, and when evaluated immediately following treatment using uncontrolled pre–post tests (Irvin et al., 1999). These two treatment outcome reviews provide encouraging evidence on the effectiveness of RPT as a treatment for alcohol problems. Overall, RPT appears to be a promising intervention for use in alcohol and substance abuse treatment.

KEY WORKS AND SUGGESTIONS FOR FURTHER READING

Marlatt, G.A. & Gordon, J.R. (1985). *Relapse Prevention: Maintenance Strategies in the Treatment of Addictive Behaviors.* New York: Guilford.

Part I of this book presents a detailed exposition of the relapse prevention model that forms the basis of RPT. Part II presents application of RPT with specific addictive behaviors such as alcohol, smoking, and weight control. This is still the most complete presentation of RPT in print.

Wanigaratne, S., Wallace, W., Pullin, J., Keaney, F. & Farmer R. (1990). *Relapse Prevention for Addictive Behaviors: A Manual for Therapists.*

This manual is a practical introductory guide to conducting RPT with any type of addictive behavior. Written in a clear and engaging style, it presents an overview of the relapse prevention model as well as descriptions of how to implement both specific and global RPT interventions for individuals or groups.

Annis, H.M., Herie, M.A. & Watkin-Merek, L. (1996). *Structured Relapse Prevention: An Outpatient Counselling Approach.* Toronto: Addiction Research Foundation of Ontario.

A treatment manual and videotape developed by Helen Annis and her colleagues at the Addiction Research Foundation that presents a systematic protocol for use in outpatient settings. The five major components of SRP include assessment, motivational interviewing, treatment planning, initiation of change and maintenance of change.

Annis, H.M., Turner, N.E. & Sklar, S.M. (1997). *IDTS: Inventory of Drug-Taking Situations.* Toronto: Addiction Research Foundation of Ontario.

This manual provides guidelines for using the IDTS, which assesses a client's most problematic triggers for relapse based on the taxonomy of high-risk situations developed by Marlatt. The IDTS is available as a paper and pencil questionnaire or as computerized software.

Swanson, J. & Cooper, A. (1994). *The Complete Relapse Prevention Skills Program.*

This program based on the RPT model offers clinicians and clients a package of user-friendly yet sophisticated tools to prevent and manage relapse. The program includes an integrated set of clinician's guides as well as client pamphlets, workbooks and videotapes.

Roberts, L.J., Shaner, A. & Eckman, T. (1999). *Overcoming Addictions: Skills Training for People with Schizophrenia.*

A therapist manual with accompanying video offering a step-by-step approach to RPT with clients presenting with co-occurring substance use and mental disorders. The best resource currently available for RPT coping skills training.

REFERENCES

Annis, H.M., Sklar, S.M. & Turner, N.E. (1997a). *DTCQ—Drug-Taking Confidence Questionnaire.* Toronto: Addiction Research Foundation of Ontario.
Annis, H.M., Turner, N.E. & Sklar, S.M. (1997b). *IDTS—Inventory of Drug-Taking Situations.* Toronto: Addiction Research Foundation of Ontario.

Bandura, A. (1977). Self-efficacy: toward a unifying theory of behavioral change. *Psychological Review*, **84**, 191–215.

Bandura, A. (1997). *Self-Efficacy: The Exercise of Control*. San Francisco, CA: W.H. Freeman.

Carroll, K.M. (1996). Relapse prevention as a psychosocial treatment: a review of controlled clinical trials. *Experimental and Clinical Psychopharmacology*, **4**(1), 46–54.

Chaney, E.F., O'Leary, M.R. & Marlatt, G.A. (1978). Skill training with alcoholics. *Journal of Consulting and Clinical Psychology*, **46**, 1092–1104.

Cronkite, R. & Moos, R. (1980). The determinants of post-treatment functioning of alcoholic patients: a conceptual framework. *Journal of Consulting and Clinical Psychology*, **48**, 305–316.

Cummings, C., Gordon, J.R. & Marlatt, G.A. (1980). Relapse: strategies of prevention and prediction. In W.R. Miller (Ed.), *The Addictive Behaviors*, Oxford: Pergamon.

Drummond, D.C., Tiffany, S.T., Glautier, S. & Remington, B. (1995). *Addictive Behaviour: Cue Exposure Theory and Practice*. Chichecter: Wiley.

D'Zurilla, T.J. & Goldfried, M.R. (1971). Problem solving and behavior modification. *Journal of Abnormal Psychology*, **78**, 107–126.

Glasser, W. (1974). *Positive Addictions*. New York: Harper and Row.

Irvine, J.E., Bowers, C.A., Dunn, M.E. & Wang, M.C. (1999). Efficacy of relapse prevention: a meta-analytic reviews. *Journal of Consulting and Clinical Psychology*, **67**(4), 563–570.

Lipsey, M. & Wilson, D.B. (1993). The efficacy of psychological, educational, and behavioral treatment: confirmation from meta-analysis. *American Psychologist*, **48**(12), 1181–1209.

Marlatt, G.A. (1978). Craving for alcohol, loss of control, and relapse: a cognitive-behavioral analysis. In P.E. Nathan, G.A. Marlatt & T. Loberg (Ed.), *Alcoholism: New Directions in Behavioral Research and Treatment*. New York: Plenum.

Marlatt, G.A. & Gordon, J.R. (Ed.) (1985). *Relapse Prevention: Maintenance Strategies in the Treatment of Addictive Behaviors*. New York: Guilford.

Marlatt, G.A. & Parks, G.A. (1982). Self-Management of addictive behaviors. In F.H. Kanfer & P. Karoly (Ed.), *Self-Management of Behavior Change: From Theory to Practice* (pp. 443–488). New York: Pergamon.

Marlatt, G.A. & Rohsenow, D.J. (1980). Cognitive processes in alcohol use: expectancy and the balanced placebo design. In N.K. Mello (Ed.), *Advances in Substance Abuse*, Vol. 1. Greenwich, CT: JAI Press.

Murphy, L.L. & Impara, J.C. (1996). *Buros Desk Reference to Assessment of Substance Abuse*. Lincoln, NE: University of Nebraska Press.

Rohsenow, D.J., Monti, P.M., Rubonis, A.V., Sirota, A.D., Niaura, R.S., Colby, S.M., Wunschel, S.M. & Abrams, D.B. (1994). Cue reactivity as a predictor of drinking among male alcoholics. *Journal of Consulting and Clinical Psychology*, **62**, 620–626.

Schonfeld, L., Peters, R.H. & Dolente, A.S. (1993). *SARA—Substance Abuse Relapse Assessment*. Odessa, FL: Psychological Assessment Resources Inc.

Chapter 7

Motivational Interviewing

Stephen Rollnick
*Department of General Practice, University of Wales College
of Medicine, Cardiff, UK*
and
Jeff Allison
Jeff Allison Training Consultancy, Edinburgh, UK

Synopsis

This chapter begins with the context in which motivational interviewing was developed: the often conflict-ridden encounters in alcohol counselling in which poor motivation, denial and resistance were viewed as ingrained qualities of clients themselves. A psychologist trained in client-centred counselling, William R. Miller, developed the hypothesis that the way clients were spoken to could either enhance or minimize motivation to change. The method that emerged provided counsellors with the skills to reduce resistance and explore the uncertainty about change (ambivalence) so common among problem drinkers. It is guided by the notion that motivation to change should not be imposed from without, in the form of counsellor arguments for change, but elicited from within the client. This chapter outlines the practice of motivational interviewing, starting with three central concepts—readiness, ambivalence and resistance. It then turns to the principles and three core skill areas—empathic listening, eliciting self-motivating statements and responding to resistance. The chapter concludes with a brief review of research evidence and a discussion of the opportunities and limitations of motivational interviewing.

Every therapist knows that motivation is a vital element of change. Nowhere is this clearer than in the treatment of addictive behaviours, which are, if one thinks about it, fundamentally motivational problems. Addictive behaviours are by definition highly motivated, in that they persist against an accumulating tide of aversive consequences. When one continues to act despite great

The Essential *Handbook of Treatment and Prevention of Alcohol Problems.* Edited by N. Heather and T. Stockwell.
© 2004 John Wiley & Sons Ltd. ISBN 0-470-86296-3.

personal risk and cost, something is overriding common sense. In the context of war, we call it bravery or heroism. In the context of pleasure, we call it addiction (Miller, 1998).

It is a common experience for alcohol counsellors to sigh at the inability of clients to change their lives. Conversations about them abound with frustration—about the hardships they face in the outside world and about difficult encounters in the consulting room. Traditionally, lack of progress in alcohol treatment has been attributed to client failings, with lack of motivation often seen as the main culprit. The counsellor, often with a clear sense of where the client is going wrong, tries to steer the person in the right direction. The response is often passivity, disagreement or outright denial.

Motivational interviewing presents the counsellor with a quite different perspective: low motivation is not just a client problem but a shifting state that is very sensitive to the behaviour of the counsellor. Progress in counselling is more likely to occur if the client is given room to breathe, if motivation to change is not imposed from without, but elicited from within in an atmosphere free of conflict. How these tasks are achieved is the subject of this chapter, the principal aims of which are to describe the origins and content of motivational interviewing and to briefly consider some new directions for practice and research.

THE ORIGINS OF MOTIVATIONAL INTERVIEWING

When a client says, ". . . you don't seem to understand, it's not just the alcohol, it's my marriage as well . . .", how should a counsellor respond? How might the counsellor influence the course of the conversation to the satisfaction of both parties?

It was questions like these that were asked by a group of clinicians in the early 1980s in seminars with William R. Miller in Bergen, Norway. The answers pointed to something which was quite different to everyday practice in addiction treatment at the time, particularly in North America: instead of attributing client resistance and poor motivation to the client, Miller, a client-centred psychotherapist, suggested that a confrontational interviewing style could enhance and reinforce these problems. Stated positively, *the counsellor could use empathic listening to minimize resistance and increase motivation for change.* What emerged was an outline of motivational interviewing (Miller, 1983) which must have struck a chord in the field. Ten to 15 years later, this variant of client-centred counselling had become one of the most popular approaches to the treatment of alcohol problems. The method was subsequently revised and enlarged (Miller & Rollnick, 1991), a research base emerged, and attempts were made to adapt the method to other client groups and settings. There are numerous unanswered questions about the effective ingredients of motivational interviewing and its relation to other treatment approaches. Nevertheless, its central principle, that motivation to change should be elicited from people, not somehow imposed on them, has clearly proved useful in a treatment culture with a history of sometimes coercive solutions to the problem of the unmotivated problem drinker.

THE DEFINITION AND SPIRIT OF MOTIVATIONAL INTERVIEWING

Motivational interviewing has been described as a counselling *style* (Rollnick & Miller, 1995). Matters of technique have thus been rendered secondary to an *atmosphere of constructive conversation about behaviour change*, in which the counsellor uses empathic listening initially to understand the client's perspective and minimize resistance. Upon this foundation of respectful collaboration, strategies and techniques are used to explore the person's values and goals and their relation to the addictive problem, and to elicit motivation for change from the client. The method, however, *is* confrontational. Whereas in traditional alcohol counselling the confrontation often was overt, in motivational interviewing the confrontation is intended to arise *within* the client, not between the parties to the conversation. Such discomfiture increases the probability of change, providing certain other conditions support change.

This activity is not viewed as equivalent to non-directive counselling; it also involves being directive. Counsellors need to provide clear structure to the session. They frequently also have a clear view about what direction they would like the client to take. Typically this involves gently coaching the client to explore the conflicts and contradictions so prevalent in addiction problems. By summarizing these for the client, and giving the person room to reflect, it is assumed that motivation to change is more likely to be enhanced. The definition of motivational interviewing provided by Rollnick & Miller (1995) is: *a directive, client-centred counselling style for eliciting behaviour change by helping clients explore and resolve ambivalence.* Before turning to the more technical "how to" aspects of motivational interviewing, the use of this counselling style will be illustrated with reference to three concepts that have guided the development of the method. Awareness of them ensures that the method is viewed, not as a set of techniques, but as a skilful listening task in the first instance.

Three Useful Concepts

Readiness

One useful way to view motivation is as a state of readiness to change, which fluctuates and can be influenced by others (Miller & Rollnick, 1991). The stages of change model (DiClemente & Prochaska, 1998), which emerged almost simultaneously with motivational interviewing, provided a construct, readiness to change, which proved useful for the understanding and conduct of a motivational interviewing session. There are a number of ways of conceptualizing readiness. One is to think in terms of stages of change, as Prochaska & DiClemente (1998) have done. Despite debates about its measurement and scientific status (see Davidson, 1998), this stage-based framework has been a source of inspiration to counsellors because it indicates that people have different needs, depending on their stage of change, and that simply moving stages during counselling might be beneficial. Another way of conceptualizing readiness is to view it as a continuum (Rollnick, 1998). Although obviously oversimplified, with no reference being made to a circular process, the notion of a continuum of readiness highlights the need to maintain *congruence* with the client's readiness on an ongoing basis in counselling (Rollnick et al., 1999). Moreover, jump ahead of the client and resistance will be the outcome.

Counsellor awareness of shifting readiness is invaluable for the skilful use of motivational interviewing. The therapist's role is to keep in step with the client. In this difficult terrain, either party, with equal ease and suddenness, might lose his/her footing. Debates on the purpose of the counselling, the route to be taken, doubts about the importance of the goal and one's capacity to reach it, all serve to make the task ever more fraught. Not only is the client usually cautious but the counsellor, often with limited time for the journey, may run ahead of the client's readiness, shouting encouragement and entreaties backwards across an ever-broadening gulf. If the gulf becomes too great, the conversation, in all but name, is ended, and it is not uncommon for both parties to blame the other for failure and wasting time. It is sensitivity to readiness that enables the so-called resistance behaviours of the client to be kept to a minimum and for rapport to be sustained through difficult passages. In motivational interviewing, the counsellor always walks beside the client, in step with his/her readiness to change.

Ambivalence

This concept was placed at the centre of the description of motivational interviewing (Miller & Rollnick, 1991) because it provided counsellors with a conceptual anchor for dealing with the uncertainty about behaviour change that pervades so many counselling sessions. If change is a process, and if all change is preceded by some degree of ambivalence, then ambivalence is a normal and defining state endured by all in degrees. It is doubtless the case that change is not made without inconvenience, even from worse to better. Such inconvenience may be hard to comprehend from the perspective of the outsider, especially when the behaviour is perceived by others as problematic and therefore surely troublesome to the individual. But for the person with the "problematic" behaviour, change may be effortful and enervating, not least because it may demand a reconfiguration of beliefs concerning the particular role that the behaviour fulfils and its attendant value. As Miller has noted in conversation with an "ambivalent client", ". . . it's almost like giving up a part of yourself, in a way, to think about changing . . . it's offensive to think about that because it's like sacrificing part of who you've become . . . (it's) . . . a letting go of something that (is) dear to you . . ." (Miller, Rollnick & Moyers, 1998). It is the *inter-relationship of ambivalence about change and the client's goals and core values* that is the substance of motivational interviewing.

Where problematic alcohol use is the focus of discussion, many conversations about change demand a period of discomforting ambivalence wherein the client may feel a range of emotions perhaps hitherto unrecognized and inexperienced. To feel, at once, that, "I don't want to and I want to!" is both the source of immobilization and mobilization. It is the problem and the solution; it is the explanation of inaction and the seed of action. To increase the probability of change—the client's readiness—the counsellor's task is to encourage the client to change the balance of "weights" from one clause, "I don't want to . . ." to the other, "I want to . . ."; to shift commitment from one posture to the other. In motivational interviewing the shift is attempted by harnessing the client's own motivation, by gentle coaching, not by using a clever argument or therapeutic technique. It is the client who is encouraged to express a recognition of problems and express concern about these problems, who talks with determination to make changes and with hope and optimism in his/her own ability to achieve his/her goals; these are the cognitive, affective and behavioural domains of motivation for change. Clients hear themselves articulating a desire for change—not the counsellor's words, but theirs. In traditional alcohol counselling, many a counsellor has fallen into the trap of overtly taking sides, of trying to persuade an ambivalent client about the advantages of change or about the dangers of continued drinking. The outcome is often a more entrenched client who defends the "no change" position with even greater authority. Motivational interviewing provides a counselling style that avoids this problem of postural confrontation and helps, first, the counsellor to avoid eliciting defensiveness whilst maintaining direction and, second, the client to explore his/her ambivalence about change without experiencing the process as hostile and insensitive.

For many clients, the experience of hearing themselves exploring personal discrepancies out loud provokes strong emotions; for some, such turmoil is so disturbing and painful that a strong desire to quickly re-establish a sense of internal continuity results in attempts to "fight back", using the counsellor as a foil. During this period of heightened ambivalence, the counsellor's overarching need is, in one sense, to remove him/herself from the debate, to distance him/herself from the client's competing voices. The role and tasks of a "chair" are most apt here. Particularly through the skilful employment of reflection, the counsellor moderates the articulated "voices" of the client, acknowledging the many divergent viewpoints.

Resistance

The connection between expressions of ambivalence and resistance can be illustrated thus; the client says, "I'd like to do it, but I can't"; to which the counsellor responds, "But if you succeeded for a month last time, maybe you can do better this time?"; to which the clients replies, "Yes, but I can't because . . .". The conversation then continues, *ad nauseam*, in a spiral of wills, the two combatants locked as wrestlers until one party is exhausted and submits. Such activity has little connection with effective addiction counselling and certainly no similarity in style with motivational interviewing.

What is resistance? In the description of motivational interviewing, resistance is viewed as observable behaviour that arises when the counsellor loses demonstrable congruence with the client (Miller & Rollnick, 1991). In short, in its most active form, it is often a consequence of counsellor behaviour and therefore amenable to change—provided that the counsellor understands the dynamic process in which he/she is engaged. Resistance may be conceived of as a general reluctance to make progress, or as opposition to the counsellor or what the counsellor thinks is best, or as the client's expectations as to the posture of the agency the counsellor represents, or even, more traditionally, as "denial". Conceived of another way—from the position and perspective of the client—resistance might be viewed as we might view resistance movements in war: as an heroic defence and counteraction to a perceived or quite palpable threat. What might the client be defending or maintaining? His/her self-esteem, personal values or the articulating of a particularly important opinion—one, perhaps, that expresses a core belief held dear by the client. Most commonly, the threat is an injunction, not always expressly stated but felt nonetheless, "Think differently, act differently!" Such injunctions rarely elicit the response, "Of course, whatever you say. You're absolutely right". Responding constructively to rapport damaged by miscommunication and confusion is particularly important in the early stages of counselling. This skill is at the heart of motivational interviewing.

THE PRACTICE OF MOTIVATIONAL INTERVIEWING

Principles

Express Empathy

Empathic listening is the fundamental principle that ensures that the counsellor remains in step with the needs and aspirations of the client. Its practice, enhanced considerably by the use of reflective listening, involves both simple summary statements, designed to ensure parity with the client, and more complex statements that enable the skilled counsellor to gently but directively highlight elements of the client's dilemma that might encourage resolution of ambivalence.

Roll with Resistance

This principle highlights the need to avoid non-constructive conversations, which resemble a battle of wills. Guidance is provided in the outline of motivational interviewing about how to achieve greater harmony in the counselling session.

Support Self-efficacy

There is strong research support for the importance of self-efficacy as a predictor of success in changing behaviour (Miller & Rollnick, 1991). Put simply, developing a sense that, "I can cope in this situation" and "I will do this in that difficult situation" will be of benefit to clients. In a motivational interviewing session, emphasis is placed on eliciting this inner conviction, rather than imposing it from without. This does not mean that the counsellor cannot make suggestions. Rather, suggestions are made and specific problems discussed in the context of a brainstorming session in which the client is encouraged to take charge of decision making.

Develop Discrepancy

In the exploration of the client's personal values and aspirations for the future, a particular state of discomfort, termed discrepancy, can arise from the contrast between what the person wants from life and the self-destructive nature of the addiction problem. "I like the drink but it's getting me nowhere and tearing my life apart. I have no future", is a common expression from the exasperated client in addiction counselling. In motivational interviewing this kind of discomforting realization is not viewed as a problem to be avoided, but as something that can be a catalyst for change. The development of the discrepancy principle is not a pointer to the use of clever technique for creating discomfort, but to the value of allowing clients to see how the problem might be at odds with what is dear to them and their hopes for the future. Its practice requires a sensitivity and ability to empathize that is critical for avoiding the ethical challenge that therapy should not be making clients feel uncomfortable. A useful protective guideline can be phrased thus: the more discrepancy is deployed, the deeper should be the quality of empathic listening.

The Method

Empathic Listening Skills

These skills form the basis of motivational interviewing. Definitions of open questions, affirmation, summarizing and reflective listening can be found in Miller & Rollnick (1991). Reflective listening is the principal vehicle for conveying empathy with the client and the most amenable to skilful use. Discussion about ambivalence, decision-making and behaviour change can be fraught with tension, both between and within the two parties involved. The use of simple reflective listening can ensure that the client feels understood in the often confusing discussion that takes place. A guideline suggested by practitioners is that one should aim to increase the proportion and accuracy of reflective listening statements and decrease the proportion of questions. The more thoughtful and understanding is the practitioner, the more likely the patient is to become contemplative and, in doing so, to make new connections. Disentangling conflicting motives is part of the task for both parties.

In the example below, a client is engaged in talking about ambivalence. The counsellor's task is not to jump ahead to any other topic but merely to allow the client to explore this conflict. Simple reflective listening statements are used to do this.

COUNSELLOR: So what have you noticed about the effect of alcohol on your mood?
CLIENT: It's like my saviour, because you see it is sometimes the only time I really feel at peace with myself, like really relaxed.
COUNSELLOR: It comes over you and you feel so different.

CLIENT: Yes, and this goes on for a long time. There can be all hell breaking loose around me and I won't let it touch me.

COUNSELLOR: It protects you from all sorts of troubles.

CLIENT: For a while and then it's like my punishment is not far away, like the time will come when I feel upset, little things, and I get upset and even angry.

COUNSELLOR: You get this lovely lift and you also get these darker moments.

CLIENT: Exactly, but they don't just last for a moment. You should see what I am like the next day, I feel really down, like my life is a roller coaster of highs and lows, and the drink is my master. I don't like that.

Eliciting Self-motivating Statements (Change Talk)

This complex sounding task is really quite simple: instead of presenting arguments for change to the client, the counsellor elicits these from the client. This is not a technical matter of eliciting these statements and ignoring arguments for not changing, but of giving the client time to express ambivalence free of distraction in an atmosphere in which the counsellor's main task is to listen and understand. In the dialogue noted above, reflective listening was used to do just this, and the last statement from the client is a self-motivating statement and an expression of concern about drinking.

More complex reflective listening statements (see Miller & Rollnick, 1991) have been identified that assist the counsellor to extend, highlight or even redirect the focus of discussion. Thus, new meanings can be added to reflective statements, which amount to subtle interpretations. Particularly useful is the double-sided reflection, where the counsellor looks for contrasting feelings and captures them in a single brief statement; e.g. "So you feel like it's killing you sometimes, and it also gives you so much pleasure".

It is in using these more complex reflections that an element of directiveness is added to the encounter. One can, for example, highlight certain issues and not others, thus obliging the client to respond accordingly. How and when reflections are used in this way depends on the specific circumstances and quality of the rapport between the parties. Some counsellors argue that it is best to use simple reflections in the early part of a counselling session and turn to more complex interpretations only when the rapport is strong enough. In any event, a useful guideline is not to try to be clever in using artful reflections but to track very carefully what the client is saying. Self-motivational statements usually emerge quite naturally from this process.

Responding to Resistance

Responding constructively to resistance, which can be viewed as damaged rapport, is particularly important in the early stages of an encounter, when the possibilities for miscommunication are so common. Being frank about the counsellor's role and motives, and then focusing on the client's agenda using reflective listening statements, can do a great deal to diffuse tension and misunderstanding. One of the most common mistakes made by counsellors is to assume greater readiness to change than is felt by the client. Resistance will be the outcome. Similar, and very common in the alcohol field, is the tendency to focus on alcohol at all costs, when the client is equally or more concerned about something else. The outcome will be damaged rapport and disengagement.

Responding to resistance is not merely a technical matter. The counsellor's attitude should reflect acknowledgement of the client's need to maintain dignity, self-respect and to be heard and acknowledged. Upon this basis of respect, the counsellor responds to resistance by coming alongside the client, thereby undermining the oppositional nature of the interaction. Reflective listening is the most useful way of doing this. In the example below, the counsellor focuses on "an alcohol problem" to begin with, elicits defensiveness from an angry client in response and then repairs the damage using reflective listening.

COUNSELLOR: I understand that you have come to see me about your drinking, is that correct?

CLIENT: No it's not. I thought that would happen here, like you go on just like my wife—drinking, drinking, drinking, as if it's all due to drinking. I tell you, if all you want to do is talk about drinking, I may as well go home. It's just a waste of my time. (*A single misdirected closed question has earned the counsellor the reward of a battle. In the dialogue that follows, the counsellor resists the temptation to argue back, and uses reflective listening to come alongside the client and diffuse the tension.*)

COUNSELLOR: For you, there's a much bigger picture. It's not just the alcohol that's bothering you.

CLIENT: That's right, because time and time again I get told that my drinking is a problem, like it's the only thing that matters.

COUNSELLOR: Other things also matter and you don't want them to be sidelined in our meeting today.

CLIENT: No that's exactly right, I want to talk about other things as well.

COUNSELLOR: Tell me, taking your time, about these other things.

Summary

There is more technical depth to the practice of motivational interviewing than described above. However, at its heart is an attempt to have a quiet and constructive discussion about change in which the client drives the process as much as possible. The counsellor will actively look for opportunities to explore ambivalence about drinking and will try to understand what broader values and issues are important to the client. How the client's aspirations coexist or conflict with the drinking problem will often provide the fuel for decision-making and change.

THE RESEARCH BASE

Research on motivational interviewing initially focused on the use of this counselling style when feeding back the results of a "Drinker's Check-Up" assessment (Bien et al., 1993; Brown & Miller, 1993; Miller et al., 1998). The generally positive results that emerged have since been supplemented by other studies in other settings, e.g. among heroin users (Saunders et al., 1995), heavy drinkers in a hospital setting (Heather et al., 1996) and smokers in primary care (Butler et al., 1999). In Project MATCH, a brief four-session version of motivational interviewing turned out to be as effective as more intensive treatments for problem drinkers (Project MATCH Research Group, 1997), although this study was largely unable to establish how to match individual clients to different treatments. Studies outside the addictions field, e.g. among patients with diabetes (Smith et al., 1997), have also emerged.

The question, "Is motivational interviewing effective?" can be answered in different ways. The Project MATCH findings clearly suggest that it is comparable in effectiveness to two other standard approaches to treatment (cognitive-behavioural therapy and a twelve-step facilitation approach; see also Chapter 1, this volume). Fewer studies have compared it to no treatment. In general health care settings, two studies have noted a tendency for motivational interviewing to be effective among those designated as less ready to change (Heather et al., 1996; Butler et al., 1999). However, little is known about what elements of the method are particularly effective. One study suggests that an effective element is the absence of confrontational statements from the counsellor which elicit resistance and lead to poorer client outcome (Miller, Benefield & Tonigan, 1993). Much of the uncertainty about effective mechanisms and counsellor behaviour can be resolved by studying session content as well as outcome. To this end, a number of attempts have been made to provide researchers, clinicians and trainers with coding instruments for analysing recorded interviews. During the last few years, the MISC (Motivational Interviewing Skill Coding) and more recently MISC 2.0, together with the 1-PASS Coding System, are revealing the significant motivational features of conversations about change. Of perhaps greatest importance, psycholinguistics may well prove to be the critical framework, through the study of client commitment language and its evocation, for developing more effective practice (for details, see the MINT website).

OPPORTUNITIES AND LIMITATIONS

Despite the positive outcome of controlled trials and the apparent popularity of motivational interviewing, the commitment of counsellors to developing and extending their empathic listening skills will be critical to its survival. Without this commitment, motivational interviewing could be mistakenly viewed or practised as a set of simple techniques applied on or to clients. This approach is unlikely to be of enduring benefit to the field, since it involves discarding the use of the one element of motivational interviewing, empathic listening, which has stood the test of numerous research efforts. Until the acquisition of these listening skills is placed at the centre of pre-qualification training for counsellors and emphasized throughout their professional development, motivational interviewing will have a limited role in the field of alcohol counselling.

Counsellors are usually taught different methods as relatively distinct entities, then left to integrate them in everyday practice. Whether this is the most productive training strategy is an open question. It might be tempting to take the results of Project MATCH and argue that, since there was little difference in effectiveness across treatments, there is a case for integrating different methods into a single broad model of addiction counselling. The findings of the UK Alcohol Treatment Trial (see Chapter 8, this volume) will certainly contribute to this debate. If there were to be a move towards integrating treatment approaches, which is compatible with developments like the *transtheoretical* stages of change model (Miller & Heather, 1998), motivational interviewing might serve as a useful base for such a method.

Consultations and conversations about whether or not to change behaviour are obviously not unique to the addictions field. Interest has been shown in using motivational interviewing to grapple with motivation challenges among, for example, patients with diabetes, eating disorders, heart disease and clients in criminal justice and psychiatric settings. Often however, consultation time is shorter in these settings, and practitioners have less experience of using empathic listening skills and less time to learn them. Attempts have therefore been made to simplify motivational interviewing while retaining its essential client-centred foundation (see e.g. Rollnick et al., 1999).

CONCLUSION

If motivational interviewing has made a contribution to the alcohol field, it has been the realization that empathic listening can become a highly sophisticated skill, capable of helping client and counsellor manoeuvre through the sometimes entangled jungle of mixed emotions, motivations and conflicts that lie at the heart of so many drinking problems. Helping clients to find out what they really want and value, and how alcohol fits in, requires a deftness of touch in the consulting room that motivational interviewing has attempted to harness.

KEY WORKS AND SUGGESTIONS FOR FURTHER READING

Last year, the second edition of the original and principal text on motivational interviewing was published (see Miller & Rollnick, 2002). This contains both a necessary reflection by the originators on the previous ten years—in which a variety of developments are discussed and adjustments to the "model" suggested—and contributions from thirty–five clinicians, trainers and researchers from around the world on developments in the practice and theory of MI. The text also contains a major review of the research literature.

The reader may also wish to examine the following:

Davies, P. (1979). Motivation, responsibility and sickness in the psychiatric treatment of alcoholism. *British Journal of Psychiatry*, **134**, 449–458.

Davies, P. (1981). Expectations and therapeutic practices in outpatient clinics for alcohol problems. *British Journal of Addiction*, **76**, 159–173.

These two papers by Davies provide a vivid account of what went on in traditional alcoholism treatment. They provided some of the impetus for developing motivational interviewing.

Miller, W.R. & Heather, N. (Eds) (1998). *Treating Addictive Behaviours*, 2nd edn. New York: Plenum.

This edited volume contains many useful reviews and critiques, including a detailed examination of the stages of change model, a chapter on motivation by William R. Miller and one on common processes across treatments by Stephen Rollnick.

Orford, J. (1985). *Excessive Appetites: A Psychological View of Addictions*. New York: Wiley.

An interesting account of different behaviours to which people can become excessively attached, with the concept of ambivalence close to the heart of the book.

www.motivationalinterview.org

A website produced by the International Motivational Interviewing Network of Trainers (MINT), which contains updates on research, bibliography, news of training events and a trainer's newsletter.

REFERENCES

Bien, T., Miller, W. & Boroughs, J. (1993). Motivational interviewing with alcohol outpatients. *Behavioural & Cognitive Psychotherapy*, **21**, 347–356.

Brown, J. & Miller, W. (1993). Impact of motivational interviewing on participation in residential alcoholism treatment. *Psychology of Addictive Behaviours*, **7**, 211–218.

Butler, C., Rollnick, S., Cohen, D., Russell, I., Bachmann, M. & Stott, N. (1999). Motivational consulting versus brief advice for smokers in general practice: a randomized trial. *British Journal of General Practice*, **49**, 611–616.

DiClemente, C.C. & Prochaska, J. (1998). Toward a comprehensive, transtheoretical model of change: stages of change and addictive behaviours. In W.R. Miller & N. Heather (Eds), *Treating Addictive Behaviours*, 2nd edn. New York: Plenum.

Davidson, R. (1998). The transtheoretical model: a critical overview. In W.R. Miller & N. Heather (Eds), *Treating Addictive Behaviours*, 2nd edn. New York: Plenum.

Egan, G. (1994). *The Skilled Helper: A Problem Management Approach to Helping*. Pacific Grove, CA: Brooks/Cole.

Heather, N., Rollnick, S., Bell, A. & Richmond, R. (1996). Effects of brief counselling among male heavy drinkers identified on general hospital wards. *Drug & Alcohol Review*, **15**, 29–38.

Miller, W.R. (1983). Motivational interviewing with problem drinkers. *Behavioural Psychotherapy*, **1**, 147–172.

Miller, W.R. & Heather, N. (Eds) (1998). *Treating Addictive Behaviours*, 2nd edn. New York: Plenum.

Miller, W.R. & Rollnick, S. (1991). *Motivational Interviewing: Preparing People to Change Addictive Behaviour*. New York: Guilford.

Miller, W.R. & Rollnick, S. (2002). *Motivational Interviewing: Preparing People for Change* (2nd edition). New York: Guilford.

Miller, W.R., Benefield, R.G. & Tonigan, J.S. (1993). Enhancing motivation for change in problem drinking: a controlled comparison of two therapist styles. *Journal of Consulting and Clinical Psychology*, **61**, 455–461.

Miller, W., Sovereign, G. & Krege, B. (1988). Motivational interviewing with problem drinkers: II. The drinker's check-up as a preventative intervention. *Behavioural Psychotherapy*, **16**, 251–268.

Miller, W.R., Rollnick S. & Moyers, T. (1998). *Motivational Inteviewing*. Professional Training Videotape Series. Albuquerque, NM: University of New Mexico.

Miller, W.R. (1998). Enhancing motivation for change. In W.R. Miller & N. Heather (Eds), *Treating Addictive Behaviours*, 2nd edn. New York: Plenum.

Prochaska, J. & DiClemente, C. (1998). Comments, criteria and creating better models: in response to Davidson. In W.R. Miller & N. Heather (Eds), *Treating Addictive Behaviours*, 2nd edn. New York: Plenum.

Project MATCH Research Group (1997). Matching alcohol treatment to client heterogeneity: Project MATCH posttreatment drinking outcomes. *Journal of Studies on Alcohol*, **58**, 7–29.

Rollnick, S. (1998). Readiness, importance and confidence: critical conditions of change in treatment. In W.R. Miller & N. Heather (Eds), *Treating Addictive Behaviour*, 2nd edn. New York: Plenum.

Rollnick, S. & Miller W.R. (1995). What is motivational interviewing? *Behavioural & Cognitive Psychotherapy*, **23**, 325–334.

Rollnick, S., Mason, P. & Butler, C. (1999). *Health Behavior Change: A Guide for Practitioners*. Edinburgh: Churchill Livingstone.

Saunders, W., Wilkinson, C. & Phillips, M. (1995). The impact of a brief motivational intervention with opiate users attending a methadone programme. *Addiction*, **90**, 415–422.

Smith, D.E., Heckemeyer, C.M., Kratt, P.P. & Mason, D.E. (1997). Motivational interviewing to improve adherence to a behavioral weight-control program for older obese women with NIDDM: a pilot study. *Diabetes Care*, **20**, 53–54.

Truax, C.B. & Carkhuff, R.R. (1967). *Toward Effective Counseling & Psychotherapy*. Chicago, IL: Aldine.

Chapter 8

Brief Interventions

Nick Heather
*School of Psychology and Sports Sciences, Northumbria University,
Newcastle upon Tyne, UK*

Synopsis

Brief interventions are not merely a passing fancy in the alcohol problems field but a crucial and permanent addition to the range of strategies used to combat alcohol-related harm. It is important to distinguish between two classes of brief intervention—brief treatment and opportunistic brief intervention. Brief treatment is offered to people who are seeking help for an alcohol problem and is delivered in specialist treatment centres; opportunistic brief intervention is delivered among their other duties by generalist workers and is aimed at people who must be identified as excessive drinkers in settings where they have attended for reasons other than to seek help for an alcohol problem. Brief treatment is usually longer than opportunistic brief intervention, is aimed at problem drinkers with relatively more severe problems and derives from an evidence base quite different from that applying to opportunistic brief intervention. The latter is best seen as part of a public health approach to alcohol-related harm.

Interest in brief treatment originated from trials of treatment for alcohol problems beginning in the 1970s, showing no differences in outcome between briefer and more intensive modalities. Evidence in favour of brief treatment was greatly strengthened by the findings of Project MATCH, which reported no clinically significant differences in overall outcome between a four-session treatment (Motivational Enhancement Therapy: MET) and two more intensive, 12-session treatments. Project MATCH did report some client–treatment matches that favoured the use of either MET or more intensive approaches. Questions relating to the relative effectiveness and cost-effectiveness of brief and more intensive treatment are currently being investigated in the UK Alcohol Treatment Trial. Perhaps the main potential of brief treatment is its ability to deliver more cost-effective treatment programmes in times of limited resources for health care funding and competition for these limited resources from different branches of health care.

The Essential *Handbook of Treatment and Prevention of Alcohol Problems.* Edited by N. Heather and T. Stockwell.
© 2004 John Wiley & Sons Ltd. ISBN 0-470-86296-3.

The impetus for interest in opportunistic brief interventions against excessive drinking comes partly from a trial reported in 1979 of brief advice on smoking cessation by general medical practitioners (GPs). This showed that, if brief advice were routinely implemented by GPs throughout the UK, the gains to public health would be enormous. A similar logic underpinned a series of trials of alcohol opportunistic brief intervention in primary health care and has also been applied to other generalist settings, such as general hospital wards, accident and emergency departments, social services, educational institutions, criminal justice settings and the workplace. A number of reviews and meta-analyses of opportunistic brief intervention have reached positive conclusions but several important research and practical issues remain to be addressed. In particular, efforts to achieve widespread implementation of opportunistic brief interventions by the medical and nursing professions have so far been largely unsuccessful, but research on this implementation process is proceeding. It is argued in this chapter that, especially given the reluctance by governments to introduce preventive control measures against excessive drinking, the widespread, routine and enduring implementation of opportunistic brief intervention by the medical and other professions represents the best chance of achieving a significant reduction in alcohol-related harm among the population at large.

The term "brief interventions" is much in vogue in alcohol treatment circles these days. Research on brief interventions and applications in practice attract attention in many countries of the world and among international organizations in the alcohol field. Some may conclude that brief interventions are merely a current fad in alcohol treatment, a passing fashion like others before it that will be superseded in time by some other popular idea. This chapter will argue that this is not the case—that brief interventions have an indispensable and crucial role to play in the response to alcohol problems and should be regarded as a permanent addition to the range of methods used to counter alcohol-related harm.

The chapter will review the origins of interest in brief interventions and the various justifications for their use. Obstacles that have been encountered in disseminating and implementing brief interventions—in other words, in translating research findings into practice—will be discussed. However, the chapter will be mostly focused on reviewing research evidence on the effectiveness and cost-effectiveness of brief interventions. Readers interested in clinical descriptions of brief interventions and how-to-do-it guides should look elsewhere (Bien, Miller & Tonigan, 1993; Heather, 1995a; NIAAA, 1995; Rollnick, Mason & Butler, 1999).

TWO DOMAINS OF BRIEF INTERVENTION

Before proceeding, it is necessary to clarify one outstanding issue. Despite their popularity, there is still much confusion about the precise nature of brief interventions and their aims. The main source of confusion is a failure to make a clear distinction between two different forms of activity that have been called brief interventions: the distinction between their use with people who are actively seeking help for an alcohol problem and with those who are not. As argued in more detail elsewhere (Heather, 1995b), although the two types of intervention may in some senses be seen as lying along a single continuum, there are dangers in confusing the evidence relating to these domains, not least the danger that evidence in favour of brief interventions in non-specialist settings like general medical practice will be interpreted as evidence that more intensive interventions in specialist alcohol treatment settings are unnecessary.

To avoid adding to this confusion, this chapter will employ different terms to describe these two sorts of brief intervention activity—opportunistic brief interventions and brief treatment. Opportunistic brief interventions (OBIs) are those that take place in community settings and are delivered by non-specialist personnel, such as general medical practitioners and other primary health care staff, hospital physicians and nurses, social workers, probation officers and other generalist professions. They need consist of only a few minutes advice and encouragement but may also take somewhat longer than this. They are directed almost exclusively at excessive drinkers who are not complaining about or seeking help for an alcohol problem, and who therefore have to be identified by opportunistic screening or some other identification process. These drinkers will normally show only mild alcohol dependence and relatively low levels of alcohol problems. As we shall see, reasons for interest in OBIs, the forms they take, the evidence underlying their application in practice and their role in the treatment and prevention of alcohol problems are quite different from those applying to the other domain of brief interventions.

As the name suggests, brief treatment (BT) consists of relatively briefer forms of treatment delivered by therapists or counsellors working in alcohol or addiction specialist agencies to those who are seeking, or have been mandated or persuaded to seek, help for their alcohol problems. Although described as brief, these treatments are normally longer and more intensive than OBIs. Since clients are self-selected by their attendance at specialist alcohol treatment agencies, screening and identification are unnecessary. Clients offered BT will usually show higher levels of dependence and alcohol-related impairment than those typically offered OBI in generalist settings, although not as high as other clients of specialist treatment centres. Another difference is that evidence supporting the use of BT comes mainly from studies that find no differences in effectiveness between briefer and more intensive, conventional forms of treatment, whereas evidence in favour of OBIs comes from studies that compare their effects with those of no intervention or, at least, even more minimal intervention. Thus, the task of judging the strength of the evidence is crucially different in each case.

BRIEF TREATMENT

Origins of Interest in Brief Treatment

The key event in stimulating interest in BT among alcohol treatment specialists was the publication in 1976–1977 of the results of a treatment trial carried out at the Maudsley Hospital in London (Edwards et al., 1977). Following a comprehensive 3 hour assessment, 100 married, male, problem drinkers were randomly allocated to receive either conventional inpatient or outpatient treatment, complete with the full panoply of services available at a leading psychiatric institution and lasting several months, or to a single counselling session with a psychiatrist involving the client and his wife and delivered "in constructive and sympathetic terms". At follow-up 1 and 2 years later, no statistically significant differences were found between these two groups in drinking behaviour, alcohol-related problems, social adjustment or any other outcome measure. This lack of difference in outcome between BT and intensive treatment was repeated in a follow-up of this cohort 12 years after entry to treatment (Edwards et al., 1983).

The results of this study shocked many people involved in providing alcohol problems treatment, leading to pessimism about the benefits of conventional treatment and whether it could be said to work at all (see e.g. Heather, Robertson & Davies, 1985). While such a nihilistic reaction to the findings of the Maudsley study has generally been abandoned, several subsequent studies, as we shall see, have supported its main implication that brief, inexpensive treatment can often be as beneficial as a full, conventional treatment programme and have led to a major re-evaluation of the necessary requirements for effective treatment of alcohol problems.

Studies of Intensive vs. Briefer Treatment

Following Edwards et al.'s (1977) report, their study was criticized on several grounds. Tuchfeld (1977) suggested that the overall finding of no differences between groups might disguise an interaction in the outcome data, such that those with more severe dependence might do relatively better with more intensive treatment. This appeared to be borne out in the second year follow-up data from the Maudsley study (Orford & Edwards, 1977) in which "gamma alcoholics" with severe dependence benefited more from intensive treatment and non-gamma alcoholics seemed to do better with brief advice. While this hypothesis was not confirmed in a retrospective analysis of level of dependence and outcome in the original sample by Edwards & Taylor (1994), the idea that briefer treatment is more suited to clients with lower degrees of dependence, while more intensive treatment is still necessary for those with more severe dependence, has been a durable principle among treatment practitioners. Unfortunately, although it may be consistent with common sense, there is little research evidence to support this principle.

A related criticism of the Maudsley study was that, as shown by their intact marriages, the clients were relatively socially stable and, moreover, showed little evidence of psychiatric disturbance. Both these factors are known to be associated with a good prognosis from treatment (Gibbs & Flanagan, 1977; McLellan et al., 1983). Thus, it may be that these clients would have responded well to any kind of intervention, including brief advice. If the trial had been conducted among clients of lower social stability and/or with significant psychiatric problems, who often comprise a substantial proportion of clients in routine treatment programmes, differences between the effects of intensive and briefer treatment may have been greater (Kissin, 1977). Another obvious point is that, since the study was confined to men, the findings could not be applied to female problem drinkers.

These alleged deficiencies of the Maudsley study were addressed in a further comparison of intensive and brief treatment by Chick et al. (1988), which included women and unmarried clients. Following assessment, 152 attenders at an alcohol problems clinic in Edinburgh were randomly allocated to extended inpatient or outpatient treatment or to one of two forms of brief intervention—"simple advice", consisting of no more than 5 minutes standardized advice to stop drinking, or "amplified advice", in which a psychiatrist was given 30–60 minutes to increase the client's motivation to make a radical change in drinking behaviour. At follow-up 2 years later, those who had received extended treatment did not show a higher rate of abstinence, which was nearly always the explicit goal of treatment, than those given the briefer interventions, or any greater improvement in employment or relationship status. However, the extended treatment group was functioning better in that clients had accumulated less harm from their drinking during the follow-up period. Remarkably, no differences were apparent between the simple and amplified advice groups.

Also at the Maudsley Hospital, Drummond et al. (1990) gave 40 clients of an alcohol problems clinic a thorough assessment followed by brief advice. Clients were then randomized to receive outpatient counselling at the clinic or referral back to their general medical practitioners for medical monitoring. At a 6-month follow-up, both groups showed substantial improvements on a range of relevant measures and no significant differences in outcome were detected.

In another study of intensive vs. BT among clients of specialist alcohol treatment services in New Zealand, Chapman & Huygens (1988) reported no differences in effectiveness between a single session of advice and either 6 weeks of inpatient treatment or 6 weeks of twice-weekly outpatient treatment. However, this study and those of Edwards et al. (1977) and Chick et al. (1988) have been criticized by Mattick & Jarvis (1994) on the grounds that the treatments under investigation were not delivered as they were intended. Thus, a substantial proportion of clients in the BT groups in fact received additional treatment, either because they were deemed to need it or sought it themselves, while some of those in the intensive groups received only brief help because they dropped out of regular treatment. Mattick & Jarvis argued that these factors would tend to obscure potential differences between intensive and brief treatment.

Studies of Moderation-orientated Treatment

In addition to comparisons of brief and intensive treatment among those referred to specialist alcohol problems clinics, there is another set of studies that compare the effects of different intensities of treatment aimed at a moderation goal among problem drinkers with less severe impairment. These studies are included here under the heading of BT because clients are seeking help but are channelled into treatment by unconventional means, often by self-referral through media advertisements.

A series of studies by William R. Miller and his colleagues from the University of New Mexico (Miller & Taylor, 1980; Miller, Taylor & West, 1980; Miller, Gribskov & Mortell, 1981) compared the effects of a self-help manual based on cognitive-behavioural principles and accompanied by minimal therapist contact with various types of cognitive-behavioural therapy, delivered on an outpatient basis in either individual or group formats. None of these studies showed any advantage for conventional behavioural treatment. Rates of improvement for both minimal and intensive approaches were high (60–70%) and stable at a 2 year follow-up (Miller & Baca, 1983). Other studies (e.g. Carpenter, Lyons & Miller, 1985; Skutle & Berg, 1987; Sannibale, 1988) have reported comparable findings among various populations of problem drinkers in different countries. Following these earlier studies, Miller and his colleagues developed a brief motivational intervention aimed at media-recruited heavy drinkers (the *Drinker's Check-up)* and reported some evidence for its effectiveness (Miller, Sovereign & Krege, 1988). In a study of conjoint therapy among moderately severe problem drinkers, using both moderation and abstinence goals, Zweben, Pearlman & Lee (1988) found no differences in outcome at an 18-month follow-up between a single conjoint session of advice and the provision of eight conjoint sessions. Neither this study nor those of Drummond et al. (1990) and Miller & Baca (1983) found any relationship between severity of dependence and the relative effectiveness of brief vs. intensive treatment.

It must be pointed out that sample sizes in the studies reviewed so far in this section were typically small, so that the conclusion of equivalence between treatments becomes hazardous because of low statistical power to detect real differences in effectiveness. If widespread implementation of a form of treatment in a health care system is envisaged, even a small superiority of one treatment over another becomes important, especially if considerations of cost-effectiveness are introduced into the argument. It may need very large samples to detect these small effect sizes.

Project MATCH

The hypothesis that BT is generally as effective as more intensive treatment has gained considerable support from the results of Project MATCH, the largest study of the effects of treatment for alcohol problems ever carried out (Project MATCH Research Group, 1997a,b, 1998). The project involved 10 treatment sites in the USA and a total of 1726 clients, divided into two parallel but independent clinical trials—an outpatient arm (n = 952) and an aftercare arm (n = 774). It was designed to assess the benefits of matching clients showing alcohol dependence or abuse to three different treatments with respect to a variety of client attributes. Clients within each arm of the study were randomly assigned to three 12-week, manual-guided interventions: Twelve-step Facilitation Therapy (TSF), an approach following the principles of Alcoholics Anonymous and founded on the idea that alcoholism is a spiritual and medical disease; Cognitive-behavioural Coping Skills Therapy (CBT), an approach based on social learning theory; and Motivational Enhancement Therapy (MET), a less intensive form of therapy based on the principles of motivational psychology. Each of these modalities was delivered by trained therapists on a one-to-one basis. CBT and TSF consisted of 12 weekly sessions, while MET consisted of four sessions spread over 12 weeks.

Project MATCH was primarily concerned with client–treatment matches (i.e. interactions between the effects of treatments and characteristics of clients) and the main effects of treatment were not the focus of the study. However, these main effects are of great interest for present purposes. The overall conclusion was that there were no clinically meaningful differences in success rates among the three treatments studied. This basic finding, which was undoubtedly surprising to many in the field, has the important implication that a briefer treatment, MET, was no less effective than two more intensive treatments, CBT and TSF. This applied across the entire range of clients in the sample and not only to those of lower dependence or problem severity. This is an important point because, as we have seen, the consensus on the effectiveness of BTs before Project MATCH was that they should be confined to clients with lower levels of dependence and problems.

Equally important, since MET consisted of only one-third the number of sessions available in the two more intensive treatments, it would seem at first sight that it was the more cost-effective treatment. In times of limited funding for health care services in all countries of the world and of fierce competition for these limited resources among different areas of health care, the cost-effectiveness of treatment becomes a matter of paramount concern for service delivery. If two or more treatments do not differ in effectiveness, it is obviously a rational strategy to prefer the cheaper treatment. In fact, Cisler et al. (1998) showed that MET was somewhat more than one-third as expensive to deliver as the other treatments, but nevertheless concluded that it was clearly the most cost-effective option.

We have noted that there were no interactions between the relative effectiveness of MATCH treatments and level of alcohol dependence. But were there any other indications of what types of client might be especially suited to either briefer or more intensive forms of treatment? A few matching effects discovered by the project are relevant to this issue:

1. *Network support for drinking.* In the outpatient arm only, those individuals with a social network supportive of drinking (i.e. those with lots of heavy-drinking friends) did better with TSF than MET. Interestingly, this effect did not emerge until the 3 year follow-up (Project MATCH Research Group, 1988), implying that it took time for the behavioural changes in question to come about, but when it did emerge it was the largest matching effect identified in the trial. An analysis of the data by Longabaugh et al. (1998) showed that this effect was mediated by involvement with *Alcoholics Anonymous*. The clear implication here is that outpatients with social networks supportive of drinking will benefit especially from a Twelve-step programme, because that is the most effective means of eliminating heavy-drinking friends and acquaintances from the social network.

2. *Client anger.*   Also specific to the outpatient arm, the finding here was that clients initially high in anger reported more days of abstinence and fewer drinks per drinking day if they had received MET than if they had received CBT (Project MATCH Research Group, 1997b). This effect persisted from the 1 year to the 3 year follow-up point (Project MATCH Research Group, 1998). This can be understood as a consequence of the deliberately non-confrontational nature of MET, and high client anger at initial assessment is clearly a positive indicator for the offer of MET.

3. *Readiness to change.*   Perhaps the chief matching hypothesis relevant to the effects of MET was that clients with lower "readiness to change" in terms of Prochaska & DiClemente's (1992) stages of change model would do better with MET than with CBT, whereas the reverse would apply to those who had reached the action stage of change. This was because the motivational content of MET was thought to be more helpful to clients who were still ambivalent about changing their drinking behaviour but less relevant to those who had already decided to make this change. There was some evidence to support this hypothesis from the outpatient arm of the trial but the matching effect in question was "time-dependent", i.e. it did not meet the MATCH investigators' stringent criterion that a matching effect should be robust over time throughout the follow-up period (Project MATCH Research Group, 1997a). Nevertheless, it is worth observing that, at the follow-up one year after the end of treatment, the hypothesis was supported by the data; if the investigators had carried out only one follow-up, as is often the case in treatment trials, and restricted analysis to clients' drinking status at that time, the readiness to change matching hypothesis would have been regarded as confirmed.

Returning to treatment main effects, note that the two major criticisms made of previous work on brief vs. intensive treatment (see above) cannot be applied to Project MATCH. First, the great majority of clients received a substantial "dose" of treatment, there was no switching between modalities and the number of sessions received by CBT and TSF clients was substantially greater than that received by MET clients. Second, because of the very large sample sizes in the two arms of the study, needed to test specific matching hypotheses, there is very little possibility of insufficient statistical power to detect genuine main effects of treatment, even very minor effects.

Nevertheless, there are some difficulties in interpreting the MATCH findings as unequivocally supportive of the effectiveness of BT for the normal run of clients attending specialist alcohol services. First, a commonly-voiced criticism of the trial is that various factors—including the intensive 8 hour pre-treatment assessment, the five follow-up visits during the first year after the end of treatment, the exclusion of clients with polydrug dependence or low social stability, the additional treatment obtained by many clients outside the trial, the high levels of therapist qualifications and training, and the rigorous quality control over treatment delivery—could have blunted any potential differences between the outcomes of the treatments studied (see Heather, 1999). Differences between treatments that were obscured by the conditions of a rigorous research trial, so the argument runs, might well exist in the "real world" of day-to-day treatment delivery and, especially, to differences between briefer and intensive treatment. While there are reasons for believing that some of the grounds for this criticism are misplaced or exaggerated (Heather, 1999), they must be carefully considered in evaluating the evidence in favour of BT.

Second, deductions from research findings from one country to another must always be accompanied by considerable caution. This is because of different treatment systems as well as wider cultural influences affecting drinking behaviour and attitudes to alcohol. Ideally, implications for practice of the MATCH findings should explored in research within the treatment systems of other countries before they are considered relevant to practical applications. As one illustration of this point, MATCH findings have little bearing on the outcome of clients in moderation-orientated programmes since, although abstinence may have been urged with different degrees of emphasis in the three treatments, moderation was never an explicit goal of any of them. This particular limitation must be borne in mind when thinking about the implications of the findings in countries like the UK, Australia and some others, where the moderation goal is offered to a sizeable minority of clients in treatment for alcohol problems.

Finally, it should be emphasized that MATCH was a pragmatic trial aimed primarily at decision-making rather than theoretical advance. It was also aimed explicitly at discovering treatment–client matches, not at evaluating the comparative effectiveness of different treatment modalities. For these reasons, the factors of treatment type and treatment intensity were deliberately confounded in the design. Thus, accepting for the moment that the results show MET to be as effective as the two more intensive treatments, we cannot be sure whether this was because of the specifically motivational nature of MET or whether it would apply to BT, of roughly the same intensity as MET, in general. To decide this issue, another trial would be necessary which added to the MATCH design either an intensive form of MET or briefer forms of CBT and TSF. All we can conclude from the MATCH results is that, given the qualifications and reservations expressed above, a briefer treatment in the form of MET is as effective as more intensive treatments represented by CBT and TSF.

The UK Alcohol Treatment Trial

Implications of MATCH findings for treatment of alcohol problems in the UK are currently being explored in a trial funded by the Medical Research Council—the United Kingdom Alcohol Treatment Trial (UKATT). The starting point for UKATT is the finding from Project MATCH that has been the focus of the preceding section of this chapter—that a briefer treatment in the form of MET was as effective in reducing harmful drinking as two more intensive treatments. Thus, the general hypothesis it was aimed to test was that, in the UK treatment system, MET would be as effective as more intensive treatment. Another hypothesis flows from this: in the UK treatment system, MET will be more cost-effective than more intensive treatment.

According to Popper (1959), good science proceeds by the attempt to *falsify* hypotheses. In other words, researchers should subject their hypotheses to the most stringent test possible by inventing experiments where the hypothesis is thought least likely to be confirmed. How does this apply to the hypothesis that MET is as effective as, and therefore more cost-effective than, more intensive treatment? An obvious response to this question is the view that MET should be tested against the most effective form of intensive treatment available or, in other words, the form that is best supported by the research literature.

The conclusion reached by UKATT investigators from recent reviews of the literature (Holder et al., 1991; Thom et al., 1994; Miller et al., 1995; Finney & Monahan, 1996) was that, among relatively intensive treatment modalities, those with the most favourable results tend to contain a strong social or, at least, interpersonal element (see UKATT Research Team, 2001). In the light of this evidence and based on feasibility work, a treatment modality called *social behaviour and network therapy* (SBNT) was developed by integrating a number of strategies used previously in other approaches reported in the literature. These strategies, which are all focused on the central aim of helping the client to build positive social support for a change in drinking, were drawn from network therapy (Galanter, 1993), behavioural marital therapy (e.g. McCrady et al., 1991), unilateral family therapy (e.g.

Thomas & Ager, 1993), social aspects of the community reinforcement approach (e.g. Sisson & Azrin, 1989), relapse prevention (e.g. Chaney, O'Leary & Marlatt, 1978) and social skills training (e.g. Oei & Jackson, 1980). However, SBNT represents the first treatment modality in which these various methods and treatment principles have been brought together within a unified social treatment with theoretical coherence.

In the UKATT, SBNT is carried out over eight sessions, combining core and elective topics, and lasting 50 minutes each. This is compared with a version of MET scheduled for three 50-minute sessions in weeks 1, 2 and 8 of the treatment period. The UKATT version of MET is a modified form of that used in Project MATCH (Miller et al., 1992), with changes designed to make MET more relevant to the UK treatment context and to the requirements of UKATT (see UKATT Research Team, 2001).

There are a few other characteristics of UKATT that are relevant to the issue of brief vs. intensive treatment and to an exploration of the implications of Project MATCH findings. First, without sacrificing internal validity, the investigators have made very effort to increase the external validity of the trial (i.e. its relevance to routine treatment provision in the UK). This has been done by reducing the pre-treatment assessment as far as possible, by scheduling only two follow-up assessments during the first year post-treatment, by limiting exclusion criteria to include as many clients as possible who would normally receive treatment at UK specialist centres, and by selecting therapists from treatment personnel employed by the treatment services in which the research is taking place. Screening and identification of potential clients for the trial is carried out by non-UKATT clinical staff in conjunction with routine assessment procedures in place in the participating treatment centres.

Second, despite the emphasis on the main effects of treatment in UKATT, it is possible that interactions in the data will be found indicating which types of client are more likely to benefit from SBNT than from MET and which do as well or better with the briefer as with the more intensive treatment. The discovery of some relevant matching effects in Project MATCH suggests this possibility. Thus, specific matching hypotheses will be tested in UKATT and follow-up data will also be inspected for possible matching effects that were not predicted and could be further examined in another study. The interactions investigated will also include therapist–treatment matches, i.e. the possibility that some therapist characteristics are associated with better outcomes with MET and some others with SBNT.

Finally, since the issue of the relative cost-effectiveness of a briefer and a more intensive treatment is of prime importance in UKATT, an economic evaluation has been built into the design of the trial and relevant data from clinical sites and clients is being gathered concurrently with all other data. It is very unlikely that the results of the UKATT will be the "last word" on the issue of brief vs. intensive specialist treatment for alcohol problems, but the investigators hope that these results, when they begin to appear in 2004, can be used to improve the effectiveness and efficiency of treatment services.

Conclusions Regarding Brief Treatment

In considering the conclusions that may be drawn from this short review of evidence on the relative effectiveness of brief and intensive treatment for alcohol problems, it cannot be emphasized too strongly that the cost-effectiveness of treatment should already be a matter of paramount concern to treatment providers and will remain so in future. It is often pointed out that the total availability of health care resources is diminishing because of developments in expensive medical technology and of demographic changes due to the greater longevity of the population. Even in wealthy industrialized societies and in times of economic prosperity, there will never be enough resources to meet all society's demands for health care. Increasingly, those responsible for funding treatment services will expect to see evidence, not only that services are effective in helping people recover from alcohol-related disabilities, but that resources devoted to the treatment of alcohol problems would not be more beneficially diverted to other areas of health care. If we can bring about equivalent gains in health and adjustment for lower costs, there can surely be no rational objection in principle to implementing briefer forms of treatment.

From a clinical viewpoint, the very least that can be concluded from the evidence is that many clients do not need protracted and relatively expensive treatment programmes to show marked improvements in drinking behaviour. If we can clearly identify these clients, precious resources can be released for the treatment of those who do need more intensive help. The weight of accumulated evidence supports the offer of briefer forms of moderation-orientated treatment with clients who have comparatively less severe alcohol problems and levels of dependence (cf. Mattick & Jarvis, 1993, 1994). Brief treatment of this kind may be especially suited to problem drinkers who refer themselves for help, rather than those who have been coerced or persuaded by others to attend a treatment service.

If, despite the evidence, such a policy is regarded as risky because there may be some less severely-affected individuals who nevertheless need a more intensive and/or abstinence-based approach to improve or avoid further deterioration, BT could be implemented as the first step in a *stepped care* model of treatment (Sobell & Sobell, 1993; Breslin et al., 1997). This is an approach in which clients are systematically followed-up after treatment and those who have not benefited are offered successively more intensive treatments. Clients with characteristics for which there is clear evidence that more intensive approaches will be needed can be immediately assigned to higher steps in the sequence, and experience gained from outcomes of the stepped care programme can be used gradually to improve the efficiency of the treatment model. It will be seen that the stepped care model contains within it a built-in mechanism for the cost-effective use of resources. Outcome research on this model is urgently needed.

With regard to the treatment of those with more severe levels of dependence and/or more serious alcohol problems, conclusions from the evidence are less certain. Project MATCH (see above) produced evidence that clients with high levels of anger and resentment at intake to treatment benefit more from a briefer, motivational approach (MET) than from cognitive-behavioural therapy or a 12-step approach. On the other hand, clients with heavy-drinking social networks seem to fare better with a more intensive approach, like TSF, that seeks, among other things, to modify the social network. The intuitively-appealing idea that clients who are less ready to change drinking behaviour will benefit more from MET than from more intensive treatment needs further support before it can be regarded as secure. Beyond this, and despite the findings of Project MATCH on the overall equivalence of brief and intensive treatment outcome, the evidence does not yet justify the offer of MET as the standard treatment for alcohol problems. It is hoped that the results of UKATT will help to clarify this issue, at least as far as treatment in the UK is concerned.

OPPORTUNISTIC BRIEF INTERVENTIONS

Origins of Interest in Opportunistic Brief Interventions

Although several influences have conspired to create an interest in opportunistic brief interventions (OBIs) against excessive drinking, a key event was the publication of a paper in the smoking cessation field. Russell et al. (1979) allocated 2138 smokers attending their general practitioners (GPs) in London to one of four groups: (1) a non-intervention control; (2) a questionnaire-only group; (3) a group given simple advice by the GP to stop smoking; and (4) a group advised to stop smoking, given a leaflet to assist them and warned that they would be followed-up. The proportion of smokers in group 4 who stopped smoking during the first month and were still not smoking 1 year later was 5.1%, and this was significantly greater than the corresponding proportions in the other groups. From a clinical point of view, this success rate seems unacceptably low. However, as Russell and colleagues pointed out, over 90% of people in Britain visit their GP at least once in 5 years and the average number of attendances, by smokers and non-smokers alike, is over three per year. Figures from other countries are likely to be similar. Thus, if the simple routine given in group 4 of this study were consistently applied by all GPs in the UK, the yield would exceed half a million ex-smokers per year, a figure that could not be matched by increasing the number of specialist withdrawal clinics in the country from about 50 to 10,000.

This scenario provides the main justification for OBI in the smoking field and is applicable in principle to any area of heath care in which a change in behaviour is targeted, including excessive drinking. Stimulated by the Russell et al. (1979) findings, during the 1980s researchers in the alcohol field began to apply the same logic to OBI by GPs designed to reduce the alcohol consumption of heavy-drinking patients to "safe" or low-risk levels (i.e. under levels recommended by medical authorities.) The first study of this kind, carried out in Scotland by Heather and colleagues (1987), failed to find a clear effect of GP advice to cut down drinking, but this study probably had insufficient statistical power to detect such an effect. However, in a much larger study, Wallace, Cutler & Haines (1988) used 47 group practices throughout the UK. Excessive drinkers in the intervention group received an assessment interview about alcohol consumption, problems and dependence, and were then given advice and information about how to cut down drinking plus a drinking diary. Up to five repeat consultations were scheduled. Patients in the control group received assessment and usual care. At 1 year follow-up, the proportion of men with excessive alcohol consumption had fallen by 44% in the treatment group compared with 26% in the controls, with corresponding proportions among women of 48% and 29%. The public health potential of OBIs was highlighted by Wallace et al. (1988) when they calculated that consistent implementation of their intervention programme by GPs throughout the UK would result in a reduction from excessive to low-risk levels of the drinking of 250,000 men and 67,500 women each year.

Aims and Characteristics

The crucial aims and characteristics of OBIs, and the ways in which these differ from those of brief treatment, should now be apparent. First, the main aim is a reduction in hazardous and harmful drinking in the population at large; the justification for OBIs in practice rests, not on an impressively high success rate among the individuals who receive them, but on a relatively low success rate with a high *impact* through widespread implementation in a primary health care system. For this reason, OBI is best described as part of the public health approach to alcohol-related harm (Heather, 1996). It can easily be demonstrated that, because their numbers are so large, reducing drinking among people with comparatively mild problems and dependence results in a much greater reduction in the total sum of alcohol-related harm in a society than reducing problems among severely dependent and seriously affected individuals. Once more to use the UK as an example, the *General Household Survey* in 1996 (Office of National Statistics, 1998) showed that 28% of adult (16+) males and 13% of adult females reported drinking over the limits recommended by the Royal College of Physicians (1987). Among young (16–24) men and women, the figures rose to 35% and 21%, respectively. There are reasons for believing that even these figures may be underestimates but they nevertheless reveal the enormous extent of excessive drinking in the UK general population and the gains to public health and welfare if the drinking of a substantial proportion of these excessive drinkers could be reduced. This does not mean, of course, that the problems of the more severely dependent should be ignored, but merely that interventions to curtail alcohol-related harm should be widened to embrace the much larger group of low-dependence drinkers (Institute of Medicine, 1990).

Second, although the main impact of OBIs is on public health, it is obviously expected that individual excessive drinkers will derive benefit from them. The main way in which this can be achieved is through the related goals of secondary prevention—the prevention of existing alcohol problems from getting worse—and early intervention—the attempt to modify hazardous or harmful drinking before the stage is reached where more intensive treatment for alcohol problems is needed. It is here that the two domains of brief intervention are linked, since, to the extent that OBIs are successful, the load on specialist treatment services will be lightened. In this particular respect, OBI and BT can be thought of as points along a continuum of intervention characterized by increasing intensity. There is no reason also why OBI should not be the starting point in a stepped care model of alcohol intervention (see above), bridging generalist and specialist services.

With regard to defining characteristics, we have already noted that the principal targets of OBIs are drinkers who are not explicitly complaining of, or overtly seeking help for, problems with alcohol. These interventions applied in routine practice are called "opportunistic" (Heather, 1998) because the opportunity created by attendance in settings where people are presenting for some other purpose is used to identify hazardous or harmful drinkers and offer them advice and counselling, e.g. primary health care, general medical wards, social work agencies, criminal justice settings, etc. For this reason, the over-riding task in delivering OBIs is in most cases motivational, since drinkers who may have recognized little or no harm from their drinking must be convinced that their drinking is actually or potentially harmful and persuaded to modify it. In the language of the stages of change model (Prochaska & DiClemente, 1992), the intervention aims to move them from the precontemplation or contemplation stages to the preparation and action stages.

It also follows from the opportunistic nature of OBIs that excessive drinkers must be identified as such before advice or counselling can be offered. This can be done by using questionnaires (see Chapter 2, this volume), laboratory markers, drinking history or simple enquiry, but these methods will not be described here. We may merely note that an instrument has been specially developed for this purpose [the Alcohol Use Disorders Identification Test (AUDIT): Saunders et al., 1993] and is being increasingly used in many parts of the world.

It has already been explained that OBIs are normally directed at a goal of reduced, moderate drinking rather than total abstinence. This is because an insistence on abstinence would be a major disincentive for behaviour change among the great majority of individuals who are the targets of OBIs. The evidence shows that the use of the moderation goal is highly effective in this population (Bien, Miller & Tonigan, 1993) and, indeed, that the abstinence goal is counterproductive (Sanchez-Craig & Lei, 1986). There is, however, no reason in principle why the abstinence goal cannot be employed in OBIs if the drinker prefers it or if it is advisable for some other reason.

Lastly, although the origins of OBIs in the primary health care setting were stressed above, they can be, and have been, applied in other settings, medical and non-medical, in various parts of the world. Medical settings include general hospital wards (Chick et al., 1985; Elvy, Wells & Baird, 1988; Heather et al., 1996), accident and emergency departments (Gentilello et al., 1999; Longabaugh et al., 2001), somatic outpatient clinics (Persson & Magnusson, 1989), facial injury outpatient clinics (Smith et al., 2003) hypertension clinics

(Maheswaran et al., 1992), obstetric clinics and practices (Chang et al., 1999) and health screening programmes (Kristenson et al., 1983; Romelsjö et al., 1989; Nilssen, 1991). Non-medical settings include social services (Gorman et al., 1990; Shawcross et al., 1996), the workplace (Babor & Grant, 1992; Higgins-Biddle & Babor, 1996; Richmond et al., 1999), educational institutions (Werch et al., 1999; Baer et al., 2001), the criminal justice system (Baldwin, 1990) and even taverns and bars (Reilly et al., 1998).

Effectiveness of Opportunistic Brief Interventions

The research literature on the effectiveness of brief interventions has been reviewed a number of times (Bien, Miller & Tonigan, 1993; Fremantle et al., 1993; Heather, 1995a; Kahan, Wilson & Becker, 1995; Wilk, Jensen & Havighurst, 1997; Poikolainen, 1999; Moyer et al., 2002). These reviews have included studies based on different definitions of brief intervention, have been concerned with somewhat different research questions and have used different review methods and meta-analytic techniques. Nevertheless, the overall con-clusion from these reviews strongly favours the effectiveness of OBI. In terms of effect size, Fremantle et al. (1992) estimated that OBIs consisting of assessment of alcohol consump-tion and the provision of information and advice are effective in reducing consumption by 20% compared with no intervention. Wilk et al. (1997) calculated that heavy drinkers who received an OBI were twice as likely to moderate their drinking 6–12 months after inter-vention as heavy drinkers who had received no intervention.

One of the above-mentioned reviews will be considered here in somewhat more detail. Poikolainen (1999) confined his meta-analysis to studies of OBI in primary health care and identified 14 data sets meeting his criteria. The main purpose of the review was to distin-guish and separately analyse studies of very brief intervention (5–20 minutes) and more extended (several visits) brief intervention. The somewhat surprising conclusion was that extended brief interventions were effective among women but that other brief interven-tions (very brief interventions among women and extended or very brief interventions among men) appeared effective is some studies but not in all. However, the average effect of OBIs could not be reliably estimated in these other studies because of statistical heterogeneity, due probably to methodological weaknesses, the use of different outcome measures and the varying components of the brief interventions themselves. The main conclusions from Poikolainen's review are that there is a need for increased methodolog-ical rigour and uniformity in future studies of OBI, and that, for the time being, we must rely on the results of individual studies to reach generalized conclusions regarding the effec-tiveness of OBI.

When individual studies are inspected, it appears that the largest and most rigorous trials (e.g. Wallace et al., 1988; Israel et al., 1996; Fleming et al., 1997) show beneficial effects of OBI for men as well as women. Perhaps the strongest body of evidence in favour of OBI comes from the WHO clinical trial of brief intervention (Babor & Grant, 1992), an inter-national collaboration involving 10 countries and 1655 heavy drinkers recruited from a combination of various, mostly medical settings. Either by a combined analysis of all the data or by confining attention to the larger and better designed studies (see Heather, 1994), it was clearly established that, among male excessive drinkers at least, an OBI delivered at the primary care level and consisting of 5 minutes' simple advice, based on 15 minutes of structured assessment, was effective in reducing alcohol consumption compared to non-intervention controls, with concomitant improvements in health. In the WHO study no additional benefit of more extended counselling was observed.

This positive verdict on OBI should not be taken to mean that its overall effectiveness can be accepted without qualification or that there are no outstanding matters that need clarification in research. As Poikolainen (1999) points out, it may well be that certain kinds of OBI are effective in certain contexts, while other kinds are not and, if so, we need to know what the characteristics of successful interventions are, especially with respect to the issue of the optimal length and intensity of intervention for different categories of excessive drinker. We also need more information on the longer-term effects of OBI beyond the conventional follow-up point of 1 year. Fleming et al. (2002) found continuing benefits of grief intervention after 4 years but Wutzke et al. (2002) in Australia reported that any such benefits had disappeared after 10 years, suggesting the need for regular follow-up and reinforcement of OBI.

Another crucial issue is the extent to which the findings of research apply to the implementation of OBI in regular, routine practice. The most prominent and positive trials of OBI in the literature (e.g. Wallace et al., 1988; Anderson & Scott, 1992; Fleming et al., 1997) are *efficacy* rather than *effectiveness* trials, i.e. they provided a test of brief interventions under optimum research conditions, rather than under real-world conditions of routine primary health care (Flay, 1986). For example, excessive drinkers entering the study were identified and recruited by the research team, rather than by the busy physician in the normal course of his/her practice, and this may have resulted in more motivated patients being selected for study (cf. Kahan et al., 1995). Edwards & Rollnick (1997) demonstrated that subjects lost to controlled trials of OBI, due to unavailability for study or drop-out from follow-up, differed systematically from those included in ways that would probably be associated with a poorer response to intervention. In a project in which OBI was investigated in naturalistic general practice settings (Richmond et al., 1995), far fewer patients returned for consultation following assessment, and the beneficial effects of brief intervention, although still arguably present, were weaker than those reported in efficacy studies. More effectiveness trials of OBI are clearly needed.

From a clinical perspective, Rollnick, Butler & Hodgson (1997) introduced several "concerns from the consulting room" into the discussion of OBI and were especially critical of a simple "advice-giving" framework for intervention. They argued that medical practitioners and nurses might not be satisfied with the evidence on which this framework is based, due to small effect sizes of intervention and to the disjunction in aims between a public health approach to alcohol problems and the practitioners' over-riding interest in the welfare of the individual patient. If true, this would create obvious barriers to the implementation of OBI in practice. So too, practitioners might experience difficulty in interpreting evidence about harmful consumption when counselling their patients, especially those who may be drinking above medically recommended levels but who have not experienced any significant alcohol-related harm. Lastly, Rollnick et al. maintain that advice giving, in the sense of direct persuasion and information, is likely to be ineffective or even counterproductive and is, in any case, bedevilled by practical problems and uncertainties about putative public health gains. The authors offer a number of solutions to the problems they describe, including incorporating into intervention programmes the guidance on what to do with more severely dependent drinkers that many practitioners demand and widening brief alcohol interventions to embrace other health behaviours and personal concerns in a "patient-centred approach". At the very least, the case for offering to practitioners a relatively more intensive, motivational approach to brief interventions is well made by Rollnick and his colleagues.

Cost–benefits

A theme of this chapter has been the need to include economic considerations in evaluations of the potential of brief interventions. For example, one of the best arguments in favour of implementing OBIs in practice must surely be that they can save money for the health care system, either by early intervention among drinkers who might eventually need expensive treatment for end-organ damage or simply by limiting the extent of current alcohol-related harm in the community. Fremantle et al. (1993) calculated that the direct cost of a brief intervention delivered to an excessive drinker was less than £20.

In terms of possible economic benefits, in the Malmö study in Sweden, Kristenson et al. (1983) found that, compared to a non-intervention control group, excessive drinkers who had received an OBI showed a 80% reduction in sick absenteeism from work in the 4 years following the intervention, a 60% reduction in hospital days over 5 years and a 50% reduction in mortality from all causes over 6 years following intervention. In Canada, Israel et al. (1996) reported that intervention group patients showed significantly reduced physician visits in the year following counselling compared to controls. In a review of evidence relevant to the introduction of the managed care system in the USA, Holder, Miller & Carina (1995) estimated that, for every US$10,000 dollars spent on brief alcohol or drug abuse intervention, US$13,500–US$25,000 would be saved in medical spending for the managed care provider.

A formal economic evaluation of OBI has now been reported by Fleming and his colleagues (2000, 2002) from Wisconsin, USA. They found substantial economic benefits of OBI, with a $43,000 reduction in health care costs for every $10,000 invested.

Implementing Opportunistic Brief Interventions

The effort to implement OBI in settings other than health care has hardly begun, and this discussion will therefore focus on medical and nursing practice. Partly inspired by the promising research findings that have been reviewed in this chapter, there has been a great deal of attention over the years to the implementation of OBI in routine medical practice in several countries of the world. Unfortunately, as in other fields of health care, many studies have documented a wide gap between actual and recommended good practice based on research evidence. As but one illustration of this, Kaner et al. (1999a) reported findings from a questionnaire survey of general medical practitioners (GPs) in the English Midlands. The results showed that GPs did not to make routine enquiries about alcohol, with 67% enquiring only "some of the time". The fact that 65% of GPs had managed only 1–6 patients for excessive drinking in the last year is striking in view of evidence that approximately 20% of patients presenting to primary health care are likely to be at least hazardous drinkers (Anderson, 1993). Given figures on GPs' average list size in the UK, this suggests that the majority of GPs may be missing as many as 98% of the excessive drinkers presenting to their practices. The situation regarding the detection of excessive drinkers among patients on general hospital wards is comparable. For example, in a study designed to establish whether housemen took an adequate drinking history from their patients, Barrison et al. (1980) noted a failure to record alcohol consumption in 39% of cases; furthermore, in only 37% of the medical notes studied was an accurate history of consumption obtained, while in the remainder only an inaccurate descriptive estimate was recorded. There is little reason to believe that the situation is better in countries other than the UK.

Thus, there is little evidence that medical practitioners have increased their levels of enquiry, identification and intervention regarding excessive drinking over the past 20 years. If the medical profession is too busy or otherwise unwilling to take on this work, the nursing profession represents an engine of great potential in this implementation process (Deehan et al., 1998). It may also be true that medical practitioners are now more likely than they were to see alcohol interventions as a legitimate part of their work, and that changes are taking place within the medical profession with respect to preventive work in general, although these changes will inevitably take time to be fully realized. Meanwhile, ways must be sought to ensure a more adequate response to alcohol problems in medical and nursing practice.

A great deal has been written on the barriers to greater involvement of medical practitioners in OBI and to possible incentives that might be helpful in this regard, but space does not permit a full examination of these ideas (but see Chapter 9 in Raistrick, Hodgson & Ritson, 1999). What can be said is that the best way to implement OBI among the medical and nursing professions is itself an empirical issue. Phase III of the *WHO International Collaborative Project on the Identification and Management of Alcohol-related Problems in Primary Health Care* included a randomized controlled trial of ways to encourage the uptake and utilization of a brief intervention package by GPs (Gomel et al., 1998). In the UK arm of this WHO project (Lock et al., 1999), a total of 729 GPs were randomly allocated to one of three strategies for marketing OBI: direct mail, telemarketing or a personal marketing interview. Personal marketing transpired to be the most effective dissemination strategy but telemarketing was the most cost-effective. In a second component of this study (Kaner et al., 1999b), 128 GPs who had agreed to take part in the trial were randomized to one of three groups: (a) training and support; (b) training and no support; (c) a control group that received the intervention programme with written guidelines only. Results showed that trained and supported GPs were significantly more likely to implement the OBI programme at no greater cost than incurred in the other groups. Results from other countries participating in this WHO collaborative project have been published (Gomel et al., 1998; Hansen et al., 1999; McCormick et al., 1999).

Following on from these findings and a large amount of other relevant research, Phase IV of the WHO collaborative project is concerned with the development of strategies for the widespread, routine and enduring implementation of screening and brief intervention in the primary health care systems of countries taking part. The WHO Phase IV study is an example of action research in which the overall objective is to make a significant difference to the "real-world" conditions under which OBI is disseminated and implemented. A total of 13 countries, mostly from Europe, are represented in the study.

Conclusions Regarding Opportunistic Brief Intervention

With regard to smoking cessation, Chapman (1993) has argued that the effects of brief interventions in medical practice are likely to be modest compared with whole population preventive strategies, like higher taxation on cigarettes, increased environmental restrictions on smoking and advertising restrictions; by analogy, the same argument could be applied to excessive drinking. However, this argument misses the point that there is no necessary competition between OBI strategies and preventive control measures; indeed, there are good reasons to believe they these strategies could reinforce each other and work to mutual benefit in the attempt to reduce harmful drinking. It is easy to see, for example, how the widespread implementation of alcohol OBI by the medical, nursing and other professions could facilitate the introduction of effective control measures, by helping to create a climate of opinion in which such measures become more politically acceptable. On the other hand, an environment that does not support and encourage excessive drinking would assist efforts to instigate lasting behaviour changes in OBIs.

In any case, if environmental and other control measures for alcohol continue to be resisted by governments, which is likely to be the case for some time yet, widespread implementation of OBI is probably the only alternative for impacting on alcohol-related public health. Given the barriers to this implementation that have been described in the literature, it is clear that this will be no easy task but it is nevertheless a task that should be started sooner rather than later. In the same way that it took over 30 years for brief advice against cigarette smoking to be fully accepted as an essential contribution to public health, it may take a similar period for OBI against excessive drinking to be widely accepted and implemented in practice.

KEY WORKS AND SUGGESTIONS FOR FURTHER READING

Bien, T.H., Miller, W.R. & Tonigan, J.S. (1993).   Brief interventions for alcohol problems: a review. *Addiction*, **88**, 315–336.

Despite being now somewhat out of date and tending to conflate brief treatment and opportunistic brief interventions, this is a very useful review of theory and practice regarding brief interventions.

Heather, N. (1995a).   Brief intervention strategies. In R.K. Hester & W.R. Miller (Eds), *Handbook of Alcoholism Treatment Approaches: Effective Alternatives*, 2nd edn. Needham Heights, MA: Allyn & Bacon.

A guide to brief interventions for practitioners plus a narrative review of the research literature.

Moyer, A., Finney, J., Swearingen, C. & Vergun, P. (2002).   Brief interventions for alcohol problems: a meta-analytic review of controlled investigations in treatment-seeking and non-treatment seeking populations. *Addiction*, **97**, 279–292.

The latest and best systematic review and meta-analysis in this area. It adopts the distinction recommended here between BT and OBI.

National Institute on Alcohol Abuse and Alcoholism (1995).   *The Physician's Guide to Helping Patients with Alcohol Problems*. Washington, DC: National Institutes of Health.

A how-to-do-it guide for medical practitioners in the USA.

Rollnick, S., Mason, P. & Butler, C. (1999).   *Health Behaviour Change: A Guide for Practitioners*. Edinburgh: Churchill Livingstone.

A recent and highly recommended guide to the negotiation of behaviour change, including drinking, in health care settings.

REFERENCES

Anderson, P. (1993).   Effectiveness of general practice interventions for patients with harmful alcohol consumption. *British Journal of General Practice*, **43**, 386–389.

Anderson, P. & Scott, E. (1992).   The effect of general practitioners' advice to heavy drinking men. *British Journal of Addiction*, **87**, 891–900.

Babor, T.F. & Grant, M. (Eds) (1992).   *Project on Identification and Management of Alcohol-related Problems. Report on Phase II: A Randomized Clinical Trial of Brief Interventions in Primary Health Care*. Geneva: World Health Organization.

Baer, J., Kivlahan, D.R., Blume, A., McKnight, P. & Marlatt, G.A. (2001).   Brief intervention for heavy-drinking college students: 4-year follow-up and natural history. *American Journal of Public Health*, **91**, 1310–1315.

Baldwin, S. (Ed.) (1990).   *Alcohol Education and Offenders*. London: Batsford.

Barrison, I.G., Viola, L. & Murray-Lyon, I.M. (1980). Do housemen take an adequate drinking history? *British Medical Journal*, **281**, 1040.

Bien, T.H., Miller, W.R. & Tonigan, J.S. (1993). Brief interventions for alcohol problems: a review. *Addiction*, **88**, 315–336.

Breslin, F.C., Sobell, M.B., Sobell, L.C., Buchan, G. & Cunningham, J.A. (1997). Toward a stepped care approach to treating problem drinkers: the predictive utility of within-treatment variables and therapist prognostic ratings. *Addiction*, **92**, 1479–1489.

Carpenter, R.A., Lyons, C.A. & Miller, W.R. (1985). Peer-managed self-control program for prevention of alcohol abuse in American Indian high school students: a pilot evaluation study. *International Journal of the Addictions*, **20**, 299–310.

Chaney, E.F., O'Leary, M.R. & Marlatt, G.A. (1978). Skill training with alcoholics. *Journal of Consulting & Clinical Psychology*, **48**, 419–426.

Chang, G., Wilkins-Haug, L., Berman, S. & Goetz, M.A. (1999). Brief intervention for alcohol use in pregnancy: a randomized trial. *Addiction*, **94**, 1499–1508.

Chapman, P.L.H. & Huygens, I. (1988). An evaluation of three treatment programmes for alcoholism: an experimental study with 6- and 18-month follow-ups. *British Journal of Addiction*, **83**, 67–81.

Chapman, S. (1993). The role of doctors in promoting smoking cessation. *British Medical Journal*, **307**, 518–519.

Chick, J., Lloyd, G. & Crombie, E. (1985). Counselling problem drinkers in medical wards: a controlled study. *British Medical Journal*, **290**, 965–967.

Chick, J., Ritson, B., Connaughton, J., Stewart, A. & Chick, J. (1988). Advice vs. extended treatment for alcoholism: a controlled study. *British Journal of Addiction*, **83**, 159–170.

Cisler, R., Holder, H.D., Longabaugh, R., Stout, R.L. & Zweben, A. (1998). Actual and estimated replication costs for alcohol treatment modalities: case study from Project MATCH. *Journal of Studies on Alcohol*, **50**, 503–512.

Deehan, A., Templeton, L., Taylor, C., Drummond, C. & Strang, J. (1998). Are practice nurses an unexplored resource in the identification and management of alcohol misuse? Results from a study of practice nurses in England and Wales in 1995. *Journal of Advanced Nursing*, **28**, 592–597.

Drummond, D.C., Thom, B., Brown, C., Edwards, E. & Mullan, M. (1990). Specialist vs. general practitioner treatment of problem drinkers. *Lancet*, **336**, 915–918.

Edwards, A.G.K. & Rollnick, S. (1997). Outcome studies of brief alcohol intervention in general practice: the problem of lost subjects. *Addiction*, **92**, 1699–1704.

Edwards, G. & Taylor, C. (1994). A test of the matching hypothesis: alcohol dependence, intensity of treatment and 12 month outcome. *Addiction*, **89**, 553–561.

Edwards, G., Duckitt, E., Oppenheimer, E., Sheehan, M. & Taylor, C. (1983). What happens to alcoholics? *Lancet*, **30**, 269–271.

Edwards, G., Orford, J., Egert, S., Guthrie, S., Hawker, A., Hensman, C., Mitcheson, M., Oppenheimer, E. & Taylor, C. (1977). Alcoholism: a controlled study of "treatment" and "advice". *Journal of Studies on Alcohol*, **38**, 1004–1031.

Elvy, G.A., Wells, J.E. & Baird, K.A. (1988). Counselling problem drinkers in medical wards: a controlled study. *British Journal of Addiction*, **83**, 83–89.

Finney, J.W. & Monahan, S.C. (1996). The cost-effectiveness of treatment for alcoholism: a second approximation. *Journal of Studies on Alcohol*, **57**, 229–243.

Flay, B.R. (1986). Efficacy and effectiveness trials (and other phases of research) in the development of health promotion programs. *Preventive Medicine*, **15**, 451–474.

Fleming, M.F., Barry, K.L., Manwell, L.B., Johnson, K. & London, R. (1997). Brief physician advice for problem alcohol drinkers: a randomized controlled trial in community-based primary care practices. *Journal of the American Medical Association*, **277**, 1039–1045.

Fleming, M.F., Mundt, M.P., French, M.T., Manwell, L.B., Stauffacher, E.A., & Barry, K.B. (2000). Benefit-cost analysis of brief physician advice with problem drinkers in primary care settings. *Medical Care*, **38**, 7–18.

Fleming, M.F., Mundt, M.P., French, M.T., Manwell, L.B., Stauffacher, E.A., & Barry, K.B. (2002). Brief physician advice for problem drinkers: long-term efficacy and benefit-cost analysis. *Alcoholism: Clinical and Experimental Research* **26**, 36–43.

Fremantle, N., Gill, P., Godfrey, C., Long, A., Richards, C., Sheldon, T. et al. (1993). *Brief interventions and Alcohol Use*. Effective Health Care Bulletin No. 7. Leeds, UK: Nuffield Institute for Health.

Galanter, M. (1993). *Network Therapy for Alcohol and Drug Abuse: A New Approach in Practice*. New York: Basic Books.

Gentilello, L.M., Rivara, F.P., Donovan, D.M., Jurkovich, G.J., Daranciang, E., Dunn, C.W. et al. (1999). Alcohol interventions in a trauma center as a means of reducing the risk of injury recurrence. *Annals of Surgery*, **230**, 473–480.

Gibbs, L. & Flanagan, J. (1977). Prognostic indicators of alcoholism treatment outcome. *International Journal of the Addictions*, **12**, 1097–1141.

Gomel, M.K., Wutzke, S.E., Hardcastle, D.M. et al. (1998). Cost-effectiveness of strategies to market and train primary health care physicians in brief intervention techniques for hazardous alcohol use. *Social Science & Medicine*, **47**, 203–211.

Gorman, D.M., Werner, J.M., Jacobs, L.M. & Duffy, S.W. (1990). Evaluation of an alcohol education package for non-specialist health care and social workers. *British Journal of Addiction*, **85**, 223–233.

Hansen, L.J., de Fine Olivarius, N., Beich, A. & Barfod, S. (1999). Encouraging GPs to undertake screening and brief intervention in order to reduce problem drinking: a randomized controlled trial. *Family Practice*, **16**, 551–557.

Heather, N. (1994). Brief interventions on the world map. Comments on WHO Project on Identification and Management of Alcohol-related Problems; Report on Phase II: a randomized clinical trial of brief interventions in primary health care. *Addiction*, **89**, 665–667.

Heather, N. (1995a). Brief intervention strategies. In R.K. Hester & W.R. Miller (Eds), *Handbook of Alcoholism Treatment Approaches: Effective Alternatives*, 2nd edn. Needham Heights, MA: Allyn & Bacon.

Heather, N. (1995b). Interpreting the evidence on brief interventions for excessive drinkers: the need for caution. *Alcohol & Alcoholism*, **30**, 287–296.

Heather, N. (1996). The public health and brief interventions for excessive alcohol consumption: the British experience. *Addictive Behaviors*, **21**, 857–868.

Heather, N. (1998). Using brief opportunities for change in medical settings. In W.R. Miller & N. Heather (Eds), *Treating Addictive Behaviors*, 2nd edn. New York: Plenum.

Heather, N. (1999). Some common methodological criticisms of Project MATCH: are they justified? *Addiction*, **94**, 36–39.

Heather, N., Campion, P., Neville, R. & MacCabe, D. (1987). Evaluation of a controlled drinking minimal intervention for problem drinkers in general practice (the DRAMS Scheme). *Journal of the Royal College of General Practitioners*, **37**, 358–363.

Heather, N., Robertson, I. & Davies, P. (1985). *The Misuse of Alcohol: Crucial Issues in Dependence, Treatment and Prevention*. London: Croom Helm.

Heather, N., Rollnick, S., Bell, A. & Richmond, R. (1996). Effects of brief counselling among male heavy drinkers identified on general hospital wards. *Drug & Alcohol Review*, **15**, 29–38.

Higgins-Biddle, J.C. & Babor, T.F. (1996). *Reducing Risky Drinking: A Report on the Early Identification and Management of Alcohol Problems through Screening and Brief Intervention*. Prepared for the Robert Wood Johnson Foundation. Farmington, CT: University of Connecticut Health Center.

Holder, H.D., Longabaugh, R., Miller, W.R. & Rubonis, A.V. (1991). The cost effectiveness of treatment for alcohol problems: a first approximation. *Journal of Studies on Alcohol*, **52**, 517–540.

Holder, H.D., Miller, T.R. & Carina, R.T. (1995). *Cost Savings of Substance Abuse Prevention in Managed Care*. Berkeley, CA: Center for Substance Abuse Prevention.

Institute of Medicine (1990). *Broadening the Base of Treatment for Alcohol Problems*. Washington, DC: National Academy Press.

Israel, Y., Hollander, O., Sanchez-Craig, M., Booker, S., Miller, V., Gingrich, R., & Rankin, J.G. (1996). Screening for problem drinking and counseling by the primary care physician-nurse team. *Alcoholism: Clinical & Experimental Research*, **20**, 1443–1450.

Kahan, M., Wilson, L., & Becker, L. (1995). Effectiveness of physician-based interventions with problem drinkers: a review. *Canadian Medical Association Journal*, **152**, 851–859.

Kaner, E., Heather, N., McAvoy, B., Haighton, C. & Gilvarry, E. (1999a). Intervention for excessive alcohol consumption in primary health care: attitudes and practices of English general practitioners. *Alcohol & Alcoholism*, **34**, 559–566.

Kaner, E.F.S., Haighton, C.A., McAvoy, B.R., Heather, N. & Gilvarry, E. (1999b). A RCT of three training and support strategies to encourage implementation of screening and brief alcohol intervention by general practitioners. *British Journal of General Practice*, **49**, 699–703.

Kissin, B. (1977). Comments on "Alcoholism: a controlled trial of 'treatment' and 'advice'." *Journal of Studies on Alcohol*, **38**, 1804–1808.

Kristenson, H., Ohlin, H., Hulten-Nosslin, M., Trell, E. & Hood, B. (1983). Identification and intervention of heavy drinking in middle-aged men: results and follow-up of 24:60 months of long-term study with randomized controls. *Alcoholism: Clinical & Experimental Research*, **20**, 203–209.

Lock, C.A., Kaner, E.F.S., Heather, N., McAvoy, B.R. & Gilvarry, E. (1999). A randomized trial of three marketing strategies to disseminate a screening and brief alcohol intervention programme to general practitioners. *British Journal of General Practice*, **49**, 695–698.

Longabaugh, R., Wirtz, P.W., Zweben, A. & Stout, R.L. (1998). Network support for drinking, Alcoholics Anonymous and long-term matching effects. *Addiction*, **93**, 1313–1333.

Longabaugh, R., Woolard, R.F., Nirenberg, T.D., Minugh, A.P., Becker, B., Clifford, P.R. et al. (2001). Evaluating the effects of a brief motivational intervention for injured drinkers in the emergency department. *Journal of Studies on Alcohol*, **62**, 806–816.

Maheswaran, R., Beevers, M. & Beever, D.G. (1992). Effectiveness of advice to reduce alcohol consumption in hypertensive patients. *Hypertension*, **19**, 79–84.

Mattick, R.P. & Jarvis, T. (Eds) (1993). *An Outline for the Management of Alcohol Problems: Quality Assurance Project*. National Drug Strategy Monograph Series No. 20. Canberra: Australian Government Publishing Service.

Mattick, R.P. & Jarvis, T. (1994). Brief or minimal intervention for "alcoholics"? The evidence suggests otherwise. *Drug & Alcohol Review*, **13**, 137–144.

McCormick, R., Adams, P., Powell, A., Bunbury, D., Paton-Simpson, G. & McAvoy, B. (1999). Encouraging general practitioners to take up screening and early intervention for problem use of alcohol: a marketing trial. *Drug and Alcohol Review*, **18**, 171–177.

McCrady, B.S., Stout, R.L., Noel, N.E., Abrams, D.B & Nelson, H.F. (1991). Comparative effectiveness of three types of spouse-involved behavioural alcoholism treatment: outcomes 18 months after treatment. *British Journal of Addiction*, **86**, 1415–1424.

McLellan, A.T., Luborsky, L., Woody, G.E., Druley, K.A. & O'Brien, C.A. (1983). Predicting response to alcohol and drug abuse treatments: role of psychiatric severity. *Archives of General Psychiatry*, **40**, 620–625.

Miller, W.R. & Baca, L.M. (1983). Two-year follow-up of bibliotherapy and therapist-directed controlled drinking training for problem drinkers. *Behavior Therapy*, **14**, 441–448.

Miller, W.R. & Taylor, C.A. (1980). Relative effectiveness of bibliotherapy, individual and group self-control training in the treatment of problem drinkers. *Addictive Behaviors*, **5**, 13–24.

Miller, W.R., Brown, J.M., Simpson, T.L. et al. (1995). What works? A methodological analysis of the alcohol treatment outcome literature. In R.K. Hester & W.R. Miller, (Eds), *Handbook of Alcoholism Treatment Approaches: Effective Alternatives*. Needham Heights, MA: Allyn & Bacon.

Miller, W.R., Gribskov, C.J. & Mortell, R.L. (1981). Effectiveness of a self-control manual for problem drinkers with and without therapist contact. *International Journal of the Addictions*, **16**, 1247–1254.

Miller, W.R., Sovereign, R.G. & Krege, B. (1988). Motivational interviewing with problem drinkers: II. The Drinker's Check-up as a preventive intervention. *Behavioural Psychotherapy*, **16**, 251–268.

Miller, W.R., Taylor, C.A. & West, J.C. (1980). Focused vs. broad-spectrum behavior therapy for problem drinkers. *Journal of Consulting & Clinical Psychology*, **48**, 590–601.

Miller, W.R., Zweben, A., DiClemente, C. & Rychtarik, R. (1992). *Motivational Enhancement Therapy: A Clinical Research Guide for Therapists Treating Individuals with Alcohol Abuse and Dependence*. Project MATCH Monograph Series, Vol. 2, DHHS Publication No. (ADM) 92–1894. Washington, DC, Department of Health & Human Services.

Moyer, A., Finney, J., Swearingen, C. & Vergun, P. (2002). Brief interventions for alcohol problems: a meta-analytic review of controlled investigations in treatment-seeking and non-treatment-seeking populations. *Addiction*, **97**, 279–292.

National Institute on Alcohol Abuse and Alcoholism (1995). *The Physician's Guide to Helping Patients with Alcohol Problems*. Washington, DC: National Institutes of Health.

Nilssen, O. (1991). The Tromsø Study: identification of and a controlled intervention on a population of early-stage risk drinkers. *Preventive Medicine*, **20**, 518–528.

Oei, T.P.S. & Jackson, P. (1980). Long-term effects of group and individual social skills training with alcoholics. *Addictive Behaviors*, **5**, 129–136.

Office of National Statistics (1998). *Living in Britain: Results from the 1996 General Household Survey*. London: The Stationery Office.

Orford, J. & Edwards, G. (1977). *Alcoholism: A Comparison of Treatment and Advice with a Study of the Influence of Marriage*. Maudsley Monographs No. 26. Oxford: Oxford University Press.

Persson, J. & Magnusson, P.-H. (1989). Early intervention in patients with excessive consumption of alcohol: a controlled study. *Alcohol*, **6**, 403–408.

Poikolainen, K. (1999). Effectiveness of brief interventions to reduce alcohol intake in primary health care populations: a meta-analysis. *Preventive Medicine*, **28**, 503–509.

Popper, K.R. (1959). *The Logic of Scientific Discovery*. London: Hutchinson.

Prochaska, J.O. & DiClemente, C.C. (1992). Stages of change in the modification of problem behaviors. In M. Hersen, R.M. Eisler & P.M. Miller (Eds), *Progress in Behavior Modification*. Newbury Park, CA: Sage.

Project MATCH Research Group (1997a). Matching alcoholism treatments to client heterogeneity: Project MATCH posttreatment drinking outcomes. *Journal of Studies on Alcohol*, **58**, 7–29.

Project MATCH Research Group (1997b). Project MATCH secondary *a priori* hypotheses. *Addiction*, **92**, 1655–1682.

Project MATCH Research Group (1998). Matching alcoholism treatments to client heterogeneity: Project MATCH three-year drinking outcomes. *Alcoholism: Experimental & Clinical Research*, **22**, 1300–1311.

Raistrick, D., Hodgson, R. & Ritson, B. (Eds) (1999). *Tackling Alcohol Together: the Evidence Base for UK Alcohol Policy*. London: Free Association Books.

Reilly, D., Van Beurden, E., Mitchell, E., Dight, R., Scott, C. & Beard, J. (1998). Alcohol education in licensed premises using brief intervention strategies. *Addiction*, **93**, 385–398.

Richmond, R., Heather, N., Wodak, A., Kehoe, L. & Webster, I. (1995). Controlled evaluation of a general practice-based brief intervention for excessive drinking. *Addiction*, **90**, 119–132.

Richmond, R.L., Kehoe, L., Hailstone, S., Wodak, A. & Uebel-Yan, M. (1999). Quantitative and qualitative evaluations of brief interventions to change excessive drinking, smoking and stress in the police force. *Addiction*, **94**, 1509–1521.

Romelsjö, A., Andersson, L., Barrner, H., Borg, S., Granstrand, C., Hultman, O. et al. (1989). A randomized study of secondary prevention of early stage problem drinkers in primary health care. *British Journal of Addiction*, **84**, 1319–1327.

Rollnick, S., Butler, C. & Hodgson, R. (1997). Brief alcohol interventions in medical settings: concerns from the consulting room. *Addiction Research*, **5**, 331–342.

Rollnick, S., Mason, P. & Butler, C. (1999). *Health Behaviour Change: A Guide for Practitioners*. Edinburgh: Churchill Livingstone.

Royal College of Physicians (1987). *A Great and Growing Evil: The Medical Consequences of Alcohol Abuse*. London: Tavistock.

Russell, M.A.H., Wilson, C., Taylor, C., & Baker, C.D. (1979). Effect of general practitioners' advice against smoking. *British Medical Journal*, **283**, 231–235.

Sannibale, C. (1988). The differential effect of a set of brief interventions on the functioning of a group of "early-stage" problem drinkers. *Australian Drug & Alcohol Review*, **7**, 147–155.

Sanchez-Craig, M. & Lei, H. (1986). Disadvantages of imposing the goal of abstinence on problem drinkers: an empirical study. *British Journal of Addiction*, **81**, 505–512.

Saunders, J.B., Aasland, O.G., Babor, T.F. et al. (1993). Development of the Alcohol Use Disorders Identification Test (AUDIT): WHO Collaborative Project on early detection of person with harmful alcohol consumption, II. *Addiction*, **88**, 791–804.

Shawcross, M., Robertson, S., Jones, A., Maciver, J. & de Souza, R. (1996). *Family and Alcohol Project: Report on a Pilot Project.* Edinburgh: Lothian Regional Council Social Work Department.

Sisson, R.W. & Azrin, N. (1989). Family members' involvement to initiate and promote the treatment of problem drinkers. *Journal of Behaviour Therapy & Experimental Psychiatry*, **17**, 15–21.

Skutle, A. & Berg, G. (1987). Training in controlled drinking for early-stage problem drinkers. *British Journal of Addiction*, **82**, 493–501.

Smith, A.J., Hodgson, R.J., Bridgeman, K. & Shepherd, J.P. (2003). A randomised controlled trial of a brief intervention after alcohol-related facial injury. *Addiction*, **98**, 43–52.

Sobell, M.B. & Sobell, L.C. (1993). Treatment for problem drinkers: a public health priority. In J.S. Baer, G.A. Marlatt & R.J. McMahon (Eds), *Addictive Behaviors Across the Lifespan: Prevention, Treatment and Policy Issues.* Newbury Park, CA: Sage.

Thom, B., Franey, C., Foster, R., Keaney, R. & Salazar, C. (1994). *Alcohol Treatment Since 1983: A Review of Research Literature.* Report to the Alcohol Education & Research Council. London: Centre for Research on Drugs and Health Behaviour.

Thomas, E.J. & Ager, R.D. (1993). Unilateral family therapy. In T.J. O'Farrell (Ed.), *Treating Alcohol Problems: Marital and Family Interventions.* New York: Guilford.

Tuchfeld, B.S. (1977). Comments on "Alcoholism: a controlled trial of 'treatment' and 'advice'", *Journal of Studies on Alcohol*, **38**, 1808–1813.

UKATT Research Team (2001). United Kingdom Alcohol Treatment Trial: hypotheses, design and methods. *Alcohol and Alcoholism*, **36**, 11–21.

Wallace, P., Cutler, S. & Haines, A. (1988). Randomised controlled trial of general practitioner intervention in patients with excessive alcohol consumption. *British Medical Journal*, **297**, 663–668.

Werch, C.E., Pappas, D.M., Carlson, J.M. & DiClemente, C.C. (1999). Six-month outcomes of an alcohol prevention program for inner-city youth. *American Journal of Health Promotion*, **13**, 237–240.

Wilk, A.I., Jensen, N.M. & Havighurst, T.C. (1997). Meta-analysis of randomized control trials addressing brief interventions in heavy alcohol drinkers. *Archives of Internal Medicine*, **12**, 274–283.

Wutzke, S., Conigrave, K., Saunders, J. & Hall, W. (2002). The long-term effectiveness of brief interventions for unsafe alcohol consumption. *Addiction*, **97**, 665–675.

Zweben, A., Pearlman, S. & Li, S. (1988). A comparison of brief advice and conjoint therapy in the treatment of alcohol abuse: the results of the Marital Systems study. *British Journal of Addiction*, **83**, 899–916.

Chapter 9

Treating Comorbidity of Alcohol Problems and Psychiatric Disorder

Kim T. Mueser
Dartmouth Medical School, Hanover, NH, USA
and
David Kavanagh
Department of Psychiatry, Royal Brisbane Hospital, Herston,
Queensland, Australia

Synopsis

Alcohol use disorders have an increased prevalence in persons with psychiatric disorders. The comorbidity between substance misuse and psychiatric disorders is highest for antisocial personality disorder, schizophrenia and bipolar disorder, followed by anxiety and affective disorders. Because anxiety and affective disorders are the most prevalent psychiatric illnesses, the large majority of people with comorbid psychiatric and alcohol use disorders have an anxiety or affective disorder.

    Treatment of alcohol and psychiatric comorbidity must be tailored to patients' insight and motivation to address their substance abuse, eschewing confrontational strategies that can threaten the therapeutic alliance and provoke symptom relapses. The concept of stages of treatment provides an overarching heuristic in treating comorbid disorders. According to this model, patients progress through a series of stages in the process of recovery from alcohol misuse problems, and are responsive to interventions appropriate to that stage. The different stages include engagement, persuasion, active treatment, *and* relapse prevention. *Awareness*

The Essential *Handbook of Treatment and Prevention of Alcohol Problems.* Edited by N. Heather and
T. Stockwell.
© 2004 John Wiley & Sons Ltd. ISBN 0-470-86296-3.

of patients' stage of treatment can improve outcomes by optimizing treatments appropriate to patients' motivational states.

In recent years there has been a movement towards treating alcohol misuse and psychiatric disorders in an integrated fashion, in which both disorders are treated simultaneously by the same clinicians. The necessity of integrated treatment stems from problems in non-integrated treatment approaches, in which patients either failed to receive one or both types of treatment, or treatment by different providers was not coordinated and was often contradictory. Integrated treatment is especially critical for patients with severe mental illness such as schizophrenia, who often receive little or no treatment for their substance use problems. Several other features of effective treatment for alcohol misuse in people with severe mental illness include assertive outreach, comprehensiveness, attention to safe and protective living environments and a long-term commitment.

The treatment of anxiety and affective disorders has also moved towards integrated models, although somewhat more slowly than in people with severe mental illness. Where the anxiety or affective disorder is unremitting or recurrent, we expect that treatment will be more effective if it teaches patients not only to manage each disorder but to maintain control of alcohol use during an exacerbation of their symptoms. However, the integrated treatment will rarely need to be as intensive or long-term as in severe mental disorders, and will usually rely heavily on patients' self-management skills.

Treatment of comorbidity of alcohol-related problems and antisocial personality disorder sometimes raises particular concern among therapists and often involves more severe alcohol abuse than in other comorbid disorders. However, current data suggest that once the severity of the alcohol-related problems is controlled, treatment for alcohol abuse or dependence in this population may be as effective as in the general community.

Optimal treatment of comorbidity with alcohol abuse or dependence requires clinicians with skills in the management of both disorders and full access to treatment resources required for each one. Problems with the management of comorbidity will not be addressed fully until clinician training and service structures allow a complete integration of patient management.

Psychiatric comorbidity in people with alcohol abuse or dependence presents multifaceted challenges for practitioners. One set of challenges involves accurate detection. Practitioners need to ensure that their primary focus of referral or treatment does not blind them to comorbidity. Psychiatric disorders can go undetected in a person with severe alcohol problems, due to the prominence of alcohol-related symptoms. Conversely, in psychiatric settings, alcohol problems can be overlooked in the context of severe psychiatric symptoms or functional impairment. There can also be uncertainty when diagnosing a psychiatric disorder in a person with alcohol misuse, due to the overlap in symptoms and the similar consequences of both disorders. A further set of challenges is posed by the selection and delivery of appropriate treatments for people with comorbid problems. Different or additional interventions for the psychiatric symptoms may be required, and the treatment of alcohol abuse or dependence may need to be tailored to the specific psychiatric disorder. This complexity underscores the importance of both recognizing and treating psychiatric comorbidity in people with an alcohol use disorder.

We begin with a review of the epidemiology of alcohol and psychiatric disorder comorbidity, in which we include both large community-based surveys of alcohol and psychiatric comorbidity and studies in treatment settings. Next, we describe the principles of treating patients with alcohol misuse and comorbid psychiatric disorders. As these principles differ according to the type of disorder, we discuss treatment strategies separately for three broad classes of disorders: severe mental disorders (such as schizophrenia), anxiety and affective disorders, and antisocial personality disorder.

EPIDEMIOLOGY OF ALCOHOL AND PSYCHIATRIC DISORDER COMORBIDITY

Studies examining substance misuse and psychiatric comorbidity generally fall into one of two types: community-based surveys and studies of patients in treatment settings (e.g. in a psychiatric hospital, or at an outpatient clinic for alcohol disorders). Each type of study has its own advantages and disadvantages. The primary advantage of community-based surveys is that they provide the most accurate estimate of comorbidity for the *population* of people with a particular disorder. If the population comorbidity is estimated from samples of patients in treatment rather than from a community survey, the true level of comorbidity will be overestimated because the psychiatric and the alcohol use disorders can independently propel the person into treatment (a phenomenon known as "Berkson's Fallacy"; Berkson, 1949). The major limitation of community surveys is that very large numbers of people must be sampled in order to assess enough people with disorders that occur at low base rates in the general population, such as bipolar disorder or schizophrenia.

The primary advantage of comorbidity studies that are conducted in treatment settings is that they provide the best estimates of comorbidity for patients who are receiving treatment for at least one of their disorders. Such information has practical value to clinicians who need to know about the extent and nature of comorbidity in their patients. A drawback to surveys of patients in treatment is that the observed comorbidity rates depend heavily on the specific treatment setting (e.g. inpatient, outpatient, emergency room) and the demographic characteristics of the patients receiving treatment (Galanter, Castaneda & Ferman, 1988; Mueser et al., 1990). Estimates of comorbidity from surveys in both community and treatment settings are also subject to geographical variations in substance use and changes in substance preferences and normative levels of use over time: both of these effects can be substantial (Becker, 1967; Johnson & Muffler, 1992; Kavanagh et al., in press; Mueser, Yarnold & Bellack, 1992).

Community-based Surveys

Two large community-based surveys of alcohol and psychiatric disorder comorbidity have been conducted over the past 15 years in the USA, the Epidemiologic Catchment Area (ECA) Study (Regier et al., 1990) and the National Comorbidity Survey (NCS; Kessler et al., 1996). Another large survey was recently completed in Australia (National Survey of Mental Health and Well-being; MHW; Teeson et al., 2000).

The ECA Study was a large survey that included over 20,000 people throughout the USA. This study oversampled people in different institutional settings, including state psychiatric hospitals, Veterans Administration Medical Centers, general hospitals, jails and nursing homes. This oversampling provided enough people with severe mental disorders to evaluate comorbidity with alcohol use disorders. For all participants, interviews were conducted to evaluate recent and lifetime substance misuse and psychiatric disorders. The NCS and MHW studies involved structured interviews with over 8000 and over 10,000 community residents, respectively. Oversampling of patients in institutional settings was not done, so few people with schizophrenia-spectrum and bipolar disorder were evaluated. However, the MHW survey was supplemented by a separate study of 980 people with psychotic disorders (Jeblensky et al., 1999).

In all of the community surveys, alcohol use disorders were often comorbid with drug use disorders. For example, in the ECA study the odds ratio (OR) for drug use disorder in people with an alcohol use disorder was 7.1; 21.5% of people with a lifetime alcohol use disorder also had a lifetime drug use disorder.

The three community samples also showed high rates of comorbidity between alcohol misuse and psychiatric disorders. The most common types of psychiatric disorders in the general population are anxiety disorders and affective disorders. Alcohol problems are associated with increased rates of both psychiatric disorders. For example, in the ECA study the lifetime rate of anxiety disorders for the general population was 14.6%, and 8.3% had an affective disorder. Among people with an alcohol disorder, the rate of anxiety disorders increased to 19.4% (OR = 1.5) and affective disorders rose to 13.4% (OR = 1.9). The combination of high population rates and increased risks with alcohol disorders means that anxiety and affective disorders are the most common comorbid problems in people with alcohol abuse or dependence.

Relatively low rates of some psychiatric disorders in the general population result in lower absolute rates of dual diagnosis in the general community, even though the proportional increase in risk is sometimes considerably higher. In the ECA study, the highest proportional increase was in antisocial personality disorder (ASPD; OR = 21.0), followed by bipolar disorder (OR = 5.1) and schizophrenia (OR = 3.3). As a result, the life-time incidence of alcohol misuse in people with schizophrenia was 33.7%, in bipolar disorder it was 43.6%, and in ASPD 73.6% had an alcohol disorder at some time in their lives.

Treatment-based Surveys

Most studies examining alcohol misuse and psychiatric comorbidity have been conducted in treatment settings. In general, these studies also show high rates of comorbidity, in some cases even higher rates than in the community-based studies, as expected from Berkson's Fallacy. Across numerous studies of people receiving treatment for severe mental disorders (including schizophrenia, schizoaffective disorder, bipolar disorder and major depression), the lifetime rate of alcohol misuse is often over 40% (Duke, Pantelis & Barnes, 1994; Fowler et al., 1998; Graham et al., 2001; Mueser et al., 1990, 1992, 2000; Rosenthal, Hellerstein & Miner, 1992b; Shaner et al., 1993; Stone et al., 1993). Although fewer treatment-based studies have been conducted of the prevalence of alcohol use disorders among people in treatment for anxiety disorders, the available evidence suggests similarly high rates (Kushner, Abrams & Borchardt, 2000; Stewart, 1996).

Just as research has documented high rates of alcohol misuse in treatment-seeking psychiatric patients, people in treatment for alcohol-related problems also have high rates of psychiatric comorbidity. For example, Ross et al. (1988) evaluated lifetime psychiatric disorders in 501 people who sought treatment for alcohol or drug misuse. Of these people, 84.2% also had a psychiatric disorder. The most common disorders were anxiety disorders (61.9%), ASPD (46.9%) and affective disorders (33.7%). Similar findings have been reported by Powell et al. (1982) and Hesselbrock et al. (1985).

Summary of Epidemiology of Alcohol Misuse–Psychiatric Comorbidity

Numerous studies show that alcohol use disorders have a high comorbidity with psychiatric disorders. Treated samples tend to have higher rates of comorbidity than community samples. Rates of alcohol misuse comorbidity tend to be highest for ASPD, followed by severe mental disorders such as schizophrenia and bipolar disorder, followed by other affective disorders and anxiety disorders. Because severe mental disorders and ASPD have a relatively low prevalence in the general population compared to anxiety and depression, the majority of patients with an alcohol misuse–psychiatric comorbidity have anxiety or affective disorders.

TREATMENT

In recent years there has been a growing recognition of the importance of providing treatment for alcoholism that is tailored to patients' level of insight and motivation to work on their substance misuse. Rather than emphasizing direct confrontation of patients who deny problems related to their substance misuse, social pressure to acknowledge the evils of alcohol abuse and immediate endorsement of abstinence as a treatment priority, motivational approaches initially focus on relationship formation and harm reduction. While motivational strategies have gained some ascendance in the treatment of primary substance misuse, their importance has been even more rapidly accepted in work with individuals with comorbid disorders, whose psychiatric disorders are often inextricably tied to their use of alcohol and drugs.

Stages of Treatment

A useful overarching heuristic in work with all comorbid disorders is provided by the concept of stagewise treatment. The *stages of treatment* are based on the observation that people with an alcohol misuse problem who change their behavior over the course of treatment typically progress through a series of stages, and that each stage is characterized by different attitudes, behaviors and goals. By understanding a patient's current stage of treatment, the clinician can optimize treatment so that it matches his/her current level of motivation, and avoid driving the person away from treatment by attempting interventions that are mismatched to his/her motivation. Four stages of treatment have been identified: engagement, persuasion, active treatment and relapse prevention (Mueser et al., 2003; Osher & Kofoed, 1989). We provide a brief description of each stage of treatment, including the goal of each stage, and examples of interventions appropriate to that stage.

Engagement Stage

Efforts to change another person's behavior are doomed to failure if a therapeutic alliance has not first been established. Therefore, at the engagement stage the primary goal of treatment is to establish a working alliance (or therapeutic relationship) between the patient and clinician. A working alliance can be operationally defined as regular contact (e.g. weekly) between the patient and clinician (McHugo et al., 1995). Until this relationship is established, no efforts are directed at changing the substance misuse. A wide range of strategies exist for engaging the patient in treatment, including assertive outreach, resolving a crisis, attending to basic needs (e.g. medical, housing), and legal constraints (e.g. outpatient commitment).

Persuasion Stage

At the persuasion stage, the clinician has a working alliance with the patient, but the focus of the relationship is not on addressing the patient's substance misuse. Therefore, at this stage the patient is still actively misusing substances, or has only recently begun to cut down on substance use. The goal of this stage is to convince the patient that his/her substance misuse is an important problem, and to marshal motivation to begin working on that problem.

Motivational interviewing (Miller & Rollnick, 2002) is one useful strategy for helping patients understand the negative impact of their substance use on their own personal goals. Persuasion groups (Mueser et al., 2003), in which patients are provided with an opportunity to share their experiences with substance use with a minimum of direct confrontation or social censure, can help patients develop motivation to address their substance misuse. Commitment to work on substance misuse can be operationally defined as an actual reduction in substance misuse (McHugo et al., 1995), or another change in behavior that is associated with a reduction in risk (e.g. ceasing intravenous administration of a drug). In many cases, the duration of these attempts may at first be inhibited by the self-control skills the patient can marshal: in these instances, re-engagement occurs in close conjunction with training in skills to deal with situations in which previous lapses occurred.

Miller & Rollnick (2002) emphasize that commitment to change is a function of both motivation and self-efficacy or confidence in being able to change. As Bandura (1986) noted, past achievements are much more powerful influences on self-efficacy than verbal persuasion that is unrelated to past performance. The attention of patients is drawn to successful aspects of past control attempts, rather than to their ultimate failure to deal with the substance-related problems up to now. While a sense of self-efficacy tends to have limited generalization across performance domains (Bandura, 1986), commitment to change may sometimes be aided by success in another domain, such as work-related skills that open up options for a viable substance-free life-style.

The current cognitive abilities of some patients are so limited that their behavior is governed primarily by currently salient stimuli, rather than by behavioral plans. Commitment to change then becomes a fleeting phenomenon that is restricted by an inability to sustain attention or recall information. The effects of skills training or even of persuasion groups may then be relatively small. A temporary reduction in substance intake or risk of harm may sometimes be achieved in these patients by cueing them to engage in activities that are inconsistent with substance use (e.g. helping the person buy groceries on the day they receive disability payments, or scheduling an outing at a time where they are at particular risk of misuse). In cases where the substance misuse is restricted to a narrow range of situations, or where an ongoing structured environment can be created, behavioral scheduling and reinforcement can have a significant impact. However, unless the cognitive deficit is reduced by the changes in substance intake, the impact of this supportive environmental intervention will necessarily be as ephemeral as the patient's attention and memory.

Active Treatment Stage

Once the patient has begun to reduce his/her substance use, the motivation to work on substance misuse is harnessed, and the goal of treatment shifts to further reduction of substance use or the maintenance of abstinence. Many of the strategies developed for people with a primary substance use disorder can be used with dually diagnosed patients once they reach the active treatment stage. Examples of interventions at this stage of treatment include cognitive-behavioral counseling to address "high-risk" situations, self-help groups, and social skills training to address substance use situations. Structured activities, such as work preparation or leisure pursuits that decrease opportunities for using substances and divert attention from substance use, can assist in development of substance control.

Relapse Prevention Stage

In relapse prevention, the patient has achieved substance control for a substantial period (e.g. at least 6 months). The goals are to both guard against a relapse of substance misuse and to extend the gains made to other areas of functioning, such as social relationships, work and housing. Awareness of vulnerability to relapse can be achieved through continued participation in self-help groups, or individual or group work with substance misuse as a focus. The focus in the relapse prevention stage on other areas of functioning, such as relationships, leisure activities and work, reflects the belief that the better a patient's life is, the less vulnerable he/she will be to a relapse of substance misuse.

Integrated Dual Diagnosis Treatment

Until recently, patients with substance misuse and mental disorders had their two disorders treated separately, when treated at all. These traditional treatment models followed a policy of either sequential or parallel treatment. In sequential treatment, patients first receive treatment for one disorder, followed by treatment for the other disorder. In the most extreme version of sequential treatment, a disorder that is considered "primary" is treated initially, and the second is only treated if it does not remit after treatment of the first. In parallel treatment, patients receive treatment for both disorders simultaneously from different groups of professionals, including specialists in the management of substance misuse and others who treat mental health problems. Both approaches assume that each disorder can be treated in isolation of the other. Sequential treatment assumes an absence of substantial reciprocal interaction between the disorders; parallel treatment assumes an absence of problematic interactions between treatments.

By the late 1980s, problems with traditional approaches to treating comorbid substance abuse and mental disorders were widely recognized and their ineffectiveness was broadly accepted—at least in the case of comorbidity with severe mental disorders (Polcin, 1992; Ridgely, Goldman & Willenbring, 1990). The separation of mental health and substance abuse treatment resulted in many patients never receiving services for one of their comorbid disorders, due to restrictive eligibility criteria or inadequate detection or management by the treatment provider. Sequential treatment approaches tend to be ineffective because significant comorbid disorders tend to have a web of reciprocal influence that makes the treatment of one disorder in isolation difficult. Parallel treatment approaches are problematic because different treatment providers usually fail to integrate their interventions, which can result in contradictory or incompatible treatments (e.g. the use of strong interpersonal confrontation is favored by some substance misuse professionals, but eschewed by most professionals who treat severe mental disorders). In addition, deficiencies in communication between the therapists who are involved in parallel treatment present substantial problems for patient management, especially when these therapists work in different agencies (Kavanagh et al., 2000).

The recognition of problems with traditional approaches to dual diagnosis treatment has led to the development of integrated treatment models for severe mental disorders and substance misuse (Drake et al., 1991; Kavanagh, 1995; Minkoff, 1989; Mueser et al., 2003; Rosenthal, Hellerstein & Miner, 1992a). At the core of integrated treatment models is the assumption that the same clinician or team of clinicians treats both the mental disorders and the substance misuse simultaneously. When deciding whether an intervention is appropriate at a particular stage, clinicians working within this approach take into account the total picture of symptoms, cognitive abilities and context, rather than focusing on progress within a single problem dimension.

Severe Mental Disorders

The evidence for integrated treatment is currently strongest in the context of severe mental disorders. A review of 36 studies of integrated treatment for dual disorders involving severe mental illness found many of the studies were limited by small sample sizes, lack of experimental design, short treatment and follow-up periods, and the use of assessments not validated for people with severe mental illness (Drake et al., 1998d). However, several trends in findings were apparent. First, the simple addition of substance abuse groups to standard mental health treatment had little effect on outcomes. Second, as reported in primary substance abuse treatment, successful engagement in treatment was associated with improved outcomes. Third, programs that provided integrated dual diagnosis treatment, in which both substance misuse and mental illness were treated simultaneously, tended to have superior outcomes to traditional parallel or sequential treatment approaches (Barrowclough et al., 2001; Carmichael et al., 1998; Drake et al., 1997, 1998b; Godley, Hoewing-Roberson & Godley, 1994).

Research on the critical ingredients of effective dual diagnosis treatment programs is sparse. However, in addition to the use of motivational enhancement strategies described above, most integrated programs share a number of common features, including assertive outreach, comprehensiveness, attention to stable housing and a long-term perspective (Mueser et al., 2003). We briefly describe these core components below.

Assertive Outreach

Patients with severe mental disorders and alcohol misuse frequently are in and out of treatment, and they often become non-compliant during exacerbations of their substance misuse. In order to involve them in treatment, assertive outreach in the community to engage patients in their natural living environments is often necessary. In the absence of assertive outreach, it is difficult or impossible to engage many patients in dual diagnosis treatment.

Outreach to patients with psychotic disorders requires special delicacy, as substance misuse often worsens these symptoms, clouding judgment and increasing social withdrawal. It is critical that outreach in the early stages of treatment is focused on establishing a relationship with the patient while avoiding confrontation, and persuasion work aimed at developing insight into the effects of substance use. Patients often stop taking prescribed medications for their psychiatric illness when they misuse substances, in part for fear of those medications interacting with the substance they use, and education about these interactions may be necessary to achieve psychiatric stabilization.

In addition to the importance of assertive outreach for engaging patients in treatment, outreach can also be helpful later in the course of treatment. Meeting with patients in the community can provide the clinician with valuable information about the possible effects of the patient's environment on his/her continued substance misuse or threats to relapse. In addition, assertive outreach can provide valuable information about patients' ongoing substance misuse and the availability of social supports.

The benefits of outreach are supported by the results of a study recently completed by Drake et al. (1998b). Dually diagnosed patients at seven different mental health centers were randomly assigned to either standard case management teams or assertive community treatment (ACT; Stein & Santos, 1998) teams, and provided with integrated treatment over 3 years. The primary difference between the ACT and standard case management teams was in the intensity of services and extent of outreach provided. While patients in both treatment groups improved, those who received ACT improved more in their alcohol misuse outcomes.

Comprehensiveness

People with severe mental disorders and substance misuse have multiple needs in addition to their substance misuse problems. Effective, integrated dual diagnosis treatment programs attend to these needs and provide services to address functioning in a wide range of areas other than substance misuse. Typically, impairments in other areas of functioning interact with substance abuse, requiring rehabilitation in order to successfully address the substance misuse.

One important area requiring attention is problems in social relationships. Impairments in social functioning are a core characteristic of schizophrenia, and are common in other disorders such as bipolar disorder (American Psychiatric Association, 1994). Substance abuse may facilitate social functioning in these individuals by providing opportunities for social interactions and shared leisure activities with others (Salyers & Mueser, 2001). However, with increased substance misuse and negative consequences, relationships with others often become strained, and social exclusion occurs (Drake, Brunette & Mueser, 1998a). Therefore, social skills training has been advocated to help dually diagnosed patients develop skills for dealing with substance use situations more effectively, and to establish relationships with people who do not misuse substances (Bellack & DiClemente, 1999; Bellack et al., 1997). Data from one quasi-controlled study has supported the effects of social skills training for dually diagnosed patients (Jerrell & Ridgely, 1995).

Another area in need of attention in a comprehensive program is family relationships. Substance abuse in patients with severe mental illness is associated with increased problems in family relationships (Dixon, McNary & Lehman, 1995; Salyers & Mueser, 2001), violence directed towards relatives (Steadman et al., 1998), and housing instability and homelessness (Susser, 1989). Family treatment aims at educating families about dual disorders, stress reduction, improved adherence to treatment, and harm reduction (and preferably abstinence) from substance use (Mueser & Fox, 2002). Without family intervention, many dually diagnosed patients eventually lose the support of their relatives and the benefits of the buffering role families play in shielding patients from stress, and consequently suffer a worse course of their disorders (Caton et al., 1994; 1995). Controlled research on family intervention has shown it to be effective for both substance use disorders (Stanton & Shadish, 1997) and severe mental illness (Baucom et al., 1998; Mueser & Glynn, 1999), and one study has shown family treatment to be effective for dually diagnosed patients (Barrowclough et al., 2001; Haddock et al., in press).

Comprehensive treatment also needs to attend to patients' involvement in meaningful, structured tasks, such as school or work. Ample evidence shows that supported employment models of vocational rehabilitation improve work outcomes of patients with severe mental illness (Bond et al., 1997; Drake et al., 1999). Competitive work can decrease the opportunity patients have for using substances and improve self-esteem through involvement in a socially approved activity.

Two other areas that require attention include teaching patients illness management skills and supported housing. Patients often report using substances to manage their symptoms (Addington & Duchak, 1997; Carey & Carey, 1995), and one study reported that trait negative affect in schizophrenia is associated with substance misuse (Blanchard et al., 1999). Many patients need help in developing more effective strategies for coping with their psychiatric symptoms, negative mood states and personal life stress in order to avoid resorting to substance use. Furthermore, they need assistance in learning how to recognize and respond to the early warning signs of psychotic relapse, which, if not attended to, may worsen substance misuse and increase vulnerability to full-blown relapses of either or both disorders. Programs have been designed and empirically validated for facilitating patient coping and preventing relapses (e.g. Perry et al., 1999). Although psychological strategies to manage symptoms often form an important part of integrated treatment for dual diagnosis (Kavanagh et al., 1998), their specific effects on dually diagnosed patients have not yet been evaluated in a controlled trial.

Safe and Protective Living Environments

Substance misuse does not occur in a vacuum, and dual diagnosis treatment must attend to the effects of the environment on patients' continued substance use. Indeed, evidence from one study shows that dually diagnosed patients with numerous substance users in their social networks have a poorer prognosis than similar patients with fewer users (Trumbetta et al., 1999). Although there is broad recognition of the importance of the environment to the treatment of dual disorders (Osher & Dixon, 1996), the solutions to the problem are varied, and depend heavily on the resources available to the treatment providers.

Short-term residential facilities appear to be ineffective because patients relapse immediately upon discharge (Bartels & Drake, 1996). Some evidence indicates that longer-term residential treatment, with a very gradual reintegration into the community, may be beneficial for dual disorder patients who fail to respond to community-based treatment (Brunette et al., 2001). In some settings, treatment agencies arrange for safe housing through contacts in the community (e.g. Drake et al., 1997). Family treatment or social network intervention, focused on engaging other people in the patients' social milieu and decreasing opportunities for substance use, may be helpful. Last, when a social environment appears refractory to change, endeavoring to either move the patient to another setting, or arrange for him/her to spend less time there (such as by going to work or training programs) may decrease some of the deleterious effects of the environment on substance misuse.

Long-term Commitment

Just as a psychotic disorder is a persistent problem for many patients, so is substance misuse. Research on integrated treatment programs for dually diagnosed patients suggests that the best outcomes are usually achieved by programs that provide longer-term treatment, rather than short-term intervention (Drake et al., 1998c). Therefore, patients with chronic dual diagnoses are most likely to benefit in programs that have a long-term commitment to their treatment.

It is possible that individuals who have recently developed a psychosis, and whose substance misuse is of a briefer duration, may benefit from shorter-term interventions focused on substance misuse (White et al., 1999). Pilot testing suggests that such interventions, which employ both motivational and educational strategies, have great promise (Kavanagh et al., 2003) and are in need of further evaluation in large-scale controlled trials.

Anxiety and Depression or Dysthymia

Despite the prevalence of anxiety or depression in alcohol misuse, there is remarkably little in the research literature to guide us on management of the comorbidity. Almost all of the existing treatment trials focus on pharmacotherapy for the anxiety or mood disorder (Cornelius et al., 1997; McGrath et al., 1996; Tollefson, Montague & Tollefson, 1992), rather than the efficacy or effectiveness of psychological interventions. At present there is no controlled trial to demonstrate a superiority for integrated treatment, and some commentators continue to advocate parallel (Oei & Loveday, 1997) or sequential treatment (Scott, Gilvarry & Farrell, 1998) in the absence of such a study.

It is perhaps less immediately obvious that the treatment of anxiety or depression should be integrated with alcohol intervention than is the case with a pervasive and severe disorder such as schizophrenia. However, we do know that both the psychological treatment of alcohol misuse (Lennox, Scott-Lennox & Bohlig, 1993; Project MATCH Research Group, 1997) and the pharmacological treatment of depression (Worthington et al., 1996) tend to be less effective when conducted in the presence of the other disorder than when the comorbidity is not present.

Treatment design in anxiety and depression has been strongly influenced by the notion of primacy or independence of the disorders. This has largely been because of the high rate of spontaneous recovery of anxiety or depressive symptoms during treatment for alcohol dependence. For example, Brown & Schuckit (1988) found that 42% of people entering inpatient alcohol dependence treatment had a depressive syndrome, but only 6% had clinical levels of depression after 4 weeks of abstinence. This has led a number of commentators to recommend either that treatment for the anxiety or depression should be delayed to provide an opportunity for remission (Oei & Loveday, 1997), or that a decision on the order of treatment should be made in response to assessment of which disorder is primary (Scott et al., 1998).

Schuckit et al. (1997) have argued that it is possible to distinguish depressive episodes that have clearly been independent of alcohol use by applying a retrospective time-line technique. "Independent" depression either precedes the development of alcohol dependence or occurs during at least one period of sustained abstinence. Depression that is not clearly independent is assumed to be secondary to the alcohol misuse. The notion is that assessment of independence may assist in determining whether treatment of the depression is necessary.

However, recent data suggests that even in "non-independent" depression, treatment with desipramine (Mason et al., 1996) or with cognitive-behavioral therapy (Brown et al., 1997) can improve the depression and the outcome of treatment for alcohol dependence. Indeed, the assumption that non-independent depression is truly secondary may often be unsound. Depression that occurs during alcohol misuse can be of independent origin. The terminology "independent" is also potentially misleading, since it suggests a lack of inter-relationship with the alcohol problem. Most often, the true situation is likely to be one of mutual influence, or of co-occurring problems whose primary or secondary status shifts over time (Hodgkins et al., 1999). A search for the single primary problem may in these cases be inappropriate.

Some of the issues are illustrated by a recent self-report study on post-traumatic stress disorder (PTSD) and concurrent substance misuse (Brown, Strout & Gannon-Rowley, 1998). Participants reported that their two disorders tended to be functionally related, so that as each worsened or improved, the other changed in parallel. When this relationship is present, whether one disorder is secondary or both are primary problems may be less important than their linkages and co-variation. If treatment of one disorder is successful, the other may well show an improvement or even a remission. But the delay of the second treatment is likely to impede the effectiveness of the first, especially if the person is attempting to reduce or stop his/her consumption in the community with limited support for the attempt. Furthermore, the opportunity to train the person in skills to deal with the comorbidity, should it recur, is lost if the second problem resolves before the comorbidity issue has been addressed in treatment.

A wide search of existing literature found only two controlled trials on the treatment of coexisting depressive symptoms and alcohol misuse (Brown et al., 1997; Turner & Wehl, 1984). Each of the studies attested to the effectiveness of cognitive-behavioral therapy

(CBT) for depression in parallel with treatment of the alcohol problems. In Turner & Wehl's (1984) study, CBT gave superior alcohol and mood outcomes to the standard alcohol treatment alone, but only in an individual rather than group format. In Brown et al.'s (1997) study of people receiving treatment for alcohol dependence, CBT for depression achieved better reductions in depressive symptoms during treatment and better alcohol outcomes from 3–6 months post-treatment than did relaxation training. Neither of the studies was restricted to people with major depression, and the cut-off on depressive symptoms was relatively low (e.g. Brown et al., 1997; a Beck Depression Inventory score $\geq$ 10). We still await a controlled trial consisting entirely of patients who are experiencing a major depressive episode or dysthymic disorder.

Research in clinical depression is available for pharmacotherapies. These studies suggest that, while the effectiveness of some antidepressants is reduced by the presence of alcohol problems (Worthington et al., 1996), drugs such as imipramine (McGrath et al., 1996) and fluoxetine (Cornelius et al., 1997) are more effective than placebos for the treatment of comorbid depression. Alcohol-related outcomes have tended to be better for dual-diagnosis patients whose depression responded to the pharmacological treatment.

Research into the treatment of comorbid anxiety is even less well advanced. Buspirone has shown better alcohol and anxiety outcomes than placebos in three out of four double-blind trials on people with comorbid anxiety and alcohol misuse (Kranzler et al., 1994; Malcolm et al., 1992; Tollefson, Lancaster & Montague-Clouse, 1991; Tollefson et al., 1992), and an open-label case series with sertraline produced promising symptomatic and alcohol-related outcomes in PTSD (Brady, Sonne & Roberts, 1995). Open clinical trials of integrated treatment of PTSD and substance abuse problems (Brady et al., 2001; Kuhne, Nohner & Baraga, 1986; Najavits et al., 1998) suggest that a combined approach may be effective, and one controlled study has supported this (Triffleman et al., 1999). One controlled study has been completed evaluating the effects of cognitive-behavior therapy for social phobia combined with alcoholism treatment compared to alcoholism treatment alone (Randall et al., 2001). Surprisingly, this study found no benefit for the cognitive-behavior treatment group over alcoholism treatment alone for social phobia and actually worse outcomes for some alcohol use measures. Since both groups in this study received the same amount of treatment, the results reflect the negative effects of diluting alcoholism treatment with social phobia treatment, rather than adding the latter to the former. On the other hand, a series of three case studies by Lehman, Brown & Barlow (1998) suggests that standard cognitive-behavioral treatment of panic disorder may sometimes result in improvements, not only of the panic symptoms but also of secondary alcohol misuse.

On theoretical grounds, we expect that an integrated treatment will be more effective in anxiety and depression, just as it is in severe mental disorder. Integration of treatment is likely to be most critical in cases where the anxiety or depression is either unresponsive to treatment or is prone to recurrence. In these cases, it may be especially important to train participants to maintain their self-management of alcohol use in the face of anxiety or dysphoria, and to prevent a lapse in alcohol control from precipitating a full relapse of both disorders.

However, there are likely to be important differences between the design of integrated interventions for alcohol disorders and anxiety and depression and the structure of treatments in psychosis. People with comorbid anxiety or depression tend to be more cognitively intact and have more functional abilities than people with psychotic disorders, including skills in self-monitoring and self-management of behavior. They are also more likely to have financial and other resources, such as social supports, and their comorbid disorder has a better chance of complete remission. As a result of these factors, the treatment may not always need to be as extensive as that described in the previous section. In some cases of low alcohol dependence, such as the single cases of panic disorder and alcohol abuse treated by Lehman et al. (1998), simply drawing attention to the alcohol misuse by initial assessment and ongoing alcohol monitoring may be sufficient to trigger self-management of the problem. In most cases, some skills training or support will be required to help them succeed at an attempt to control their alcohol intake.

In anxiety disorders, the disorder itself does not impede the development of motivation in the same way as in a disorder such as schizophrenia, and in some anxiety disorders such as phobias there is a relatively low chance of recurrence after treatment. In contrast, depression shares both of these problems with the severe mental disorders. Engagement needs to overcome the pessimism, lack of self-efficacy and lack of expected reward value that are associated with both dysphoria and negative symptoms. This may sometimes result in an extended engagement stage. Major depression, bipolar disorder and schizophrenia also share a high risk of relapse after resolution of an acute episode. However, we expect that treatment of alcohol–depression comorbidity will rarely need to be as extended as in the more severe disorders, and that it will typically focus less on assertive follow-up and more on self-monitoring and self-management.

An effective psychological intervention for the anxiety and depressive aspects of the comorbid problems should at this stage be guided by what we know about effective treatment of these disorders when alcohol misuse is not also present. That is, the treatment of anxiety is likely to be dominated by exposure-based procedures, with cognitive therapy for negative cognitions that are impeding treatment progress (Brown & Barlow, 1992). Treatment of depression is likely to focus on cognitive therapy (Beck et al., 1979) or interpersonal therapy (Klerman et al., 1984). In each case, the therapy will be modified to deal with the comorbidity (e.g. Beck et al., 1993; Scott et al., 1998), in terms of both the specific targets of the treatment and the timing of particular treatment components.

Full integration with a cognitive-behavioral alcohol intervention would not end with a minor modification of existing treatments that were essentially presented in parallel by the same therapist. Such an approach would not assist participants to make the conceptual links that were required, and could lead to excessive demands on them at some points of the intervention. Rather, the combined intervention would meld the treatments for the two disorders more fully. For example, engagement would focus on the combined disorder, self-monitoring would encompass both problems, and early success would be attempted in both problem areas. Skills training would routinely encompass both problems: e.g. in depression, increasing pleasurable activities that were inconsistent with alcohol use would help to boost mood and allow a test of pessimistic cognitions, but would also decrease periods of time when the person was at risk of alcohol misuse. Minimization of relapse risk would include training in early detection and prevention of recurrence of either problem, but would particularly focus on reduction in risk of recurrence of the comorbidity. Some examples of these integrated treatments already exist (Kuhne et al., 1986; Najavits et al., 1998); we expect to see a proliferation of these interventions and the further development of an empirical basis for their use over the coming years.

Antisocial Personality Disorder (ASPD)

Epidemiologic studies indicate that the highest psychiatric–substance misuse comorbidity is with ASPD. There is a large literature showing that ASPD is related to a more severe course of alcohol and drug use disorders, including an earlier age of misuse, more binge drinking and more physical and legal consequences (Cadoret, Troughton & Widmer, 1984; Epstein et al., 1994; Penick et al., 1984). Indeed, the importance of ASPD is illustrated by the fact that it has been at the backbone of all major typologies of alcoholism, ranging from the delta/gamma subtypes (Jellinek, 1960) to Cloninger's (1987) Type I/II distinction, to Babor's et al.'s (1992) Type A/B distinction (see Epstein, 2001).

Early studies of differential treatment response for substance misuse suggested that patients with comorbid ASPD had a worse prognosis (e.g. Kadden et al., 1989; Rounsaville et al., 1987; Woody et al., 1985). However, the conclusions reached by these studies may be incorrect because of the confounding effects of substance use severity on treatment outcomes. Patients with substance misuse and ASPD tend to have more severe substance disorders. Their poor prognosis may be a reflection of their more severe substance misuse, rather than their ASPD. In line with this interpretation, research does not indicate that patients with ASPD have a worse response to substance misuse treatment once the severity of their disorder has been statistically controlled (Alterman & Tarter, 1986; Cacciola et al., 1994; McKay et al., in press). In fact, one study suggested that patients with ASPD and substance misuse responded quite well to a highly structured cognitive-behavioral treatment program for substance use disorder (Brooner et al., 1998).

CONCLUSIONS

Surveys of both community and treatment samples show there is a high rate of substance misuse and psychiatric comorbidity. Co-occurring alcohol and drug use tend to be highest in people with antisocial personality disorder (ASPD), followed by patients with severe mental illnesses such as schizophrenia or bipolar disorder, followed by patients with affective or anxiety disorders, whose substance misuse nevertheless exceeds that of people in the general population. Recognition of the importance of comorbidity has developed recently, and consequently the research base upon which recommendations can be made is rather slim. Nevertheless, several points must be stressed that are supported by a broad consensus. Perhaps the most important step involves the recognition of both disorders. With rates of comorbidity so high, a careful evaluation should be conducted to ensure proper diagnosis. In alcohol and drug treatment settings, this involves an assessment of psychiatric disorders, of which the most common in those settings are affective and anxiety disorders. In psychiatric treatment settings, assessments should routinely screen for substance use disorders.

A second principle of treatment is that motivational strategies should be used in order to match the intervention to patients' motivational states. Dually diagnosed patients tend to be highly sensitive to interpersonal stress, and confrontational approaches risk increasing their psychiatric symptoms and driving them away from treatment. Awareness of the patient's level of motivation to work on substance misuse maximizes the chances of successfully engaging patients in treatment and ensuring that selected interventions are optimally timed.

Third, it is best if both substance misuse and psychiatric disorders are treated simultaneously, by the same treatment providers. Dually diagnosed patients often "fall between the cracks" of the substance misuse and psychiatric treatment systems, and fail to receive one or both needed treatments (Kavanagh et al., 1998). Furthermore, since both disorders tend to worsen the other, effective treatment of one disorder requires knowledge and coordination with treatment of the other. Concurrent treatment of both disorders avoids the common trap of attempting to distinguish which disorder is "primary" and which is "secondary" when such distinctions are often difficult or impossible to make.

Finally, effective treatment of substance misuse and psychiatric comorbidity requires that treatment for the psychiatric disorder be specialized for that disorder. Over the past several decades significant advances have been made in the treatment of different psychiatric disorders. Knowledge of empirically validated interventions, both pharmacological and psychological, is critical in order to effectively treat the psychiatric illness (and hence the substance misuse as well). In this regard, the nature of dual diagnosis treatment must be informed by the specific psychiatric disorder, as well the individual characteristics of the patients.

Recognition of the high comorbidity of substance misuse and psychiatric disorders has grown tremendously over the past decade and clinicians are now aware of the importance of assessing both disorders in their patients. Research on effective treatment of comorbidity is still in its infancy, but it has provided important guidelines for integrating the treatment of both disorders. As our knowledge of the treatment of dual disorders grows, traditional distinctions between the psychiatric and substance misuse fields, including training, requirements for the credentialing of professionals, administration and funding should hopefully break down. Ultimately this may lead to the integration of the service systems themselves. Whole systems are needed to treat whole people. The movement afoot towards providing integrated mental health and substance misuse treatment bodes well for the outcomes of patients with comorbid disorders.

KEY WORKS AND SUGGESTIONS FOR FURTHER READING

Daley, D.C., Moss, H.B. & Campbell, F. (1993). *Dual Disorders: Counseling Clients with Chemical Dependency and Mental Illness*, 2nd edn. Center City, MN: Hazeldon.

Provides a useful survey of the problem of dual diagnosis and describes a modified 12-step treatment to these disorders.

Drake, R.E., Mercer-McFadden, C., McHugo, G.J., Mueser, K.T., Rosenberg, S.D., Clark, R.E. & Brunette, M.F. (Eds) (1998). *Readings in Dual Diagnosis*. Columbia, MD: International Association of Psychosocial Rehabilitation Services.

A selection of previously published articles and book chapters on dual disorders, with sections including overview, etiology, assessment, clinical issues, treatment and special issues.

Graham, H.L. (1998). The role of dysfunctional beliefs in individuals who experience psychosis and use substances: implications for cognitive therapy and medication adherence. *Behavioural and Cognitive Psychotherapy*, **26**, 193–208.

Describes the application of cognitive therapy to clients with psychosis and substance use disorders.

Graham, H.L., Copello, A., Birchwood, M.J. & Mueser, K.T. (Eds) (2003). *Substance Misuse in Psychosis: Approaches to Treatment and Service Delivery*. Chichester, UK: Wiley.

Provides a useful compilation of chapters on treatment of dual disorders organized into the following sections: social and psychological perspectives of problem substance use among those with psychosis, integrated service delivery models, treatments for substance misuse in psychosis, special populations, and the evolving evidence base.

Kavanagh, D.J., Young, R., Boyce, L., Clair, A., Sitharthan, T., Clark, D. & Thompson, K. (1998). Substance Treatment Options in Psychosis (STOP): a new intervention for dual diagnosis. *Journal of Mental Health*, **7**, 135–143.

Mercer-McFadden, C., Drake, R.E., Clark, R.E., Verven, N., Noorsdy, D.L. & Fox, T.S. (1999). *Substance Abuse Treatment for People with Severe Mental Disorders: A*

Program Manager's Guide. Concord, NH: New Hampshire–Dartmouth Psychiatric Research Center.

Information for program planners on establishing and financing dual disorder services.

Mueser, K.T., Drake, R.E. & Wallach, M.A. (1998). Dual diagnosis: a review of etiological theories. *Addictive Behaviors*, **23**, 717–734.

Reviews different theories accounting for the high prevalence of substance use disorders in persons with schizophrenia and bipolar disorder.

Mueser, K.T., Noordsy, D.L., Drake, R.E. & Fox, L. (2003). *Integrated Treatment for Dual Disorders: A Guide to Effective Practice*. New York: Guilford Publications.

Provides a comprehensive clinical guide to the treatment of dual disorders, with chapters on background and organizational factors, assessment and treatment planning, individual treatment approaches (case management, motivational interviewing, cognitive-behavioural therapy), group approaches (stage-based groups, social skills training, self-help), family treatment and other treatment approaches (residential, coerced/involuntary, vocational, rehabilitation, psychopharmacology).

Najavits, L.M. (2002). *Seeking Safety: A Treatment Manual for PTSD and Substance Abuse*. New York: Guilford Publications.

Provides curriculum for addressing trauma and PTSD in persons with substance misuse problems.

Onken, L.S., Blaine, J.D., Genser, S. & Horton, A.M. Jr (1997). *Treatment of Drug-dependent Individuals with Comorbid Mental Disorders*. National Institute on Drug Abuse Research Monograph No. 172, NIH Publication No. 97–4172, Rockville, MD: National Institutes of Health.

Surveys the problem of alcohol and drug use disorders in persons with mental illness. Chapters cover a broad range of topics, including the effects of depression on substance misuse treatment, assessment problems, anxiety disorders and substance misuse comorbidity, cigarette smoking comorbidity, treatment of severe mental illness and substance misuse, and substance use and HIV risk in persons with severe mental illness.

Roberts, L.J., Shaner, A. & Eckman, T.A. (1999). *Overcoming Addictions: Skills Training for People with Schizophrenia*. New York: Norton.

Describes a social skills training program for persons with schizophrenia and substance use disorders.

REFERENCES

Addington, J. & Duchak, V. (1997). Reasons for substance use in schizophrenia. *Acta Psychiatrica Scandinavica*, **96**, 329–333.

Alterman, A.I. & Tarter, R.E. (1986). An examination of selected typologies: hyperactivity, familial, and antisocial alcoholism. In M. Galanter (Ed.), *Recent Developments in Alcoholism*, Vol. IV (pp. 169–189). New York: Plenum.

American Psychiatric Association (1994). *Diagnostic and Statistical Manual of Mental Disorders (DSM-IV)*, 4th edn, revised. Washington, DC: American Psychiatric Association.

Andrews, G., Hall, W., Teeson, M. & Henderson, S. (1999). *The Mental Health of Australians: National Survey of Mental Health and Well-being, Report 2*. Canberra: Mental Health Branch, Commonwealth Department of Health and Aged Care.

Babor, T.F., Hofmann, M., DelBoca, K., Hesselbrock, V., Meter, R.E., Dolinsky, Z.S. & Rounsaville, B.

(1992). Types of alcoholics, I. Evidence for an empirically derived typology based on indicators of vulnerability and severity. *Archives of General Psychiatry*, **49**, 599–608.

Bandura, A. (1986). *Social Foundations of Thought and Action: A Social Cognitive Theory.* Englewood Cliffs, NJ: Prentice-Hall.

Barrowclough, C., Haddock, G., Tarrier, N., Lewis, S., Moring, J., O'Brien, R., Schofield, N. & McGovern, J. (2001). Randomized controlled trial of motivational interviewing, cognitive behavior therapy, and family intervention for patients with comorbid schizophrenia and substance use disorders. *American Journal of Psychiatry*, **158**, 1706–1713.

Bartels, S.J. & Drake, R.E. (1996). A pilot study of residential treatment for dual diagnoses. *Journal of Nervous and Mental Disease*, **184**, 379–381.

Baucom, D.H., Shoham, V., Mueser, K.T., Daiuto, A.D. & Stickle, T.R. (1998). Empirically supported couple and family interventions for adult mental health problems. *Journal of Consulting and Clinical Psychology*, **66**, 53–88.

Beck, A.T., Rush, A.J., Shaw, B.F. & Emery, G. (1979). *Cognitive Therapy of Depression*. New York: Guilford.

Beck, A.T., Wright, F.D., Newman, C.F. & Liese, B.S. (1993). *Cognitive Therapy of Substance Abuse*. New York: Guilford.

Becker, H.S. (1967). History, culture, and subjective experience: an exploration of the social bases of drug-induced experiences. *Journal of Health and Social Behavior*, **8**, 163–176.

Bellack, A.S. & DiClemente, C.C. (1999). Treating substance abuse among patients with schizophrenia. *Psychiatric Services*, **50**, 75–79.

Bellack, A.S., Mueser, K.T., Gingerich, S. & Agresta, J. (1997). *Social Skills Training for Schizophrenia: A Step-by-step Guide*. New York: Guilford.

Berkson, J. (1949). Limitations of the application of four-fold tables to hospital data. *Biological Bulletin*, **2**, 47–53.

Blanchard, J.J., Squires, D., Henry, T., Horan, W.P., Bogenschutz, M., Lauriello, J. & Bustillo, J. (1999). Examining an affect regulation model of substance abuse in schizophrenia: the role of traits and coping. *Journal of Nervous and Mental Disease*, **187**, 72–79.

Bond, G.R., Drake, R.E., Mueser, K.T. & Becker, D.R. (1997). An update on supported employment for people with severe mental illness. *Psychiatric Services*, **48**(3), 335–346.

Brady, K.T., Dansky, B.S., Back, S.E., Foa, E.B. & Carroll, K.M. (2001). Exposure therapy in the treatment of PTSD among cocaine-dependent individuals: Preliminary findings. *Journal of Substance Abuse Treatment*, **21**, 47–54.

Brady, K.T., Sonne, S.C. & Roberts, J.M. (1995). Sertraline treatment of comorbid posttraumatic stress disorder and alcohol dependence. *Journal of Clinical Psychiatry*, **56**, 502–505.

Brooner, R.K., Kidorf, M., King, V.L. & Stoller, K. (1998). Preliminary evidence of good treatment response in antisocial drug abusers. *Drug and Alcohol Dependence*, **49**(3), 249–260.

Brown, P.J., Strout, R.L. & Gannon-Rowley, J. (1998). Substance use disorder PTSD comorbidity: patient's perceptions of symptom interplay and treatment issues. *Journal of Substance Abuse Treatment*, **15**, 445–448.

Brown, R.A., Evans, D.M., Miller, I.W., Burgess, E.S. & Mueller, T.I. (1997). Cognitive-behavioral treatment for depression in alcoholism. *Journal of Consulting and Clinical Psychology*, **65**, 715–726.

Brown, S.A. & Schuckit, M.A. (1988). Changes in depression among abstinent alcoholics. *Journal of Studies on Alcohol*, **49**, 412–417.

Brown, T.A. & Barlow, D.H. (1992). Comorbidity among anxiety disorders: implications for treatment and DSM-IV. *Journal of Consulting and Clinical Psychology*, **60**, 835–844.

Brunette, M.F., Drake, R.E., Woods, M. & Hartnett, T. (2001). A comparison of long-term and short-term residential treatment programs for dual diagnosis patients. *Psychiatric Services*, **52**, 526–528.

Cacciola, J.S., Rutherford, M.J., Alterman, A.I. & Snider, E.C. (1994). An examination of the diagnostic criteria for antisocial personality disorder in substance abusers. *Journal of Nervous and Mental Disease*, **182**, 517–523.

Cadoret, R., Troughton, E. & Widmer, R. (1984). Clinical differences between antisocial and primary alcoholics. *Comprehensive Psychiatry*, **25**, 1–8.

Carey, K.B. & Carey, M.P. (1995). Reasons for drinking among psychiatric outpatients: relationship to drinking patterns. *Psychology of Addictive Behaviors*, **9**, 251–257.

Carmichael, D., Tackett-Gibson, M., O'Dell, L., Jayasuria, B., Jordan, J. & Menon, R. (1998). *Texas Dual Diagnosis Project Evaluation Report 1997–1998*. College Station, TX: Public Policy Research Institute, Texas A&M University.

Caton, C.L., Shrout, P.E., Eagle, P.F., Opler, L.A., Felix, A.F. & Dominguez, B. (1994). Risk factors for homelessness among schizophrenic men: a case-control study. *American Journal of Public Health*, **84**(2), 265–270.

Caton, C.L.M., Shrout, P.E., Dominguez, B., Eagle, P.F., Opler, L.A. & Cournos, F. (1995). Risk factors for homelessness among women with schizophrenia. *American Journal of Public Health*, **85**, 1153–1156.

Cloninger, C.R. (1987). Neurogenetic adaptive mechanisms in alcoholism. *Science*, **236**, 410–416.

Cornelius, J.R., Salloum, I.M., Ehler, J.G., Jarret, P.J., Cornelius, M.D., Perel, J.M., Thase, M.E. & Black, A. (1997). Fluoxetine in depressed alcoholics. *Archives of General Psychiatry*, **54**, 700–705.

Dixon, L., McNary, S. & Lehman, A. (1995). Substance abuse and family relationships of persons with severe mental illness. *American Journal of Psychiatry*, **152**, 456–458.

Drake, R.E., Antosca, L.M., Noordsy, D.L., Bartels, S.J. & Osher, F.C. (1991). New Hampshire's specialized services for the dually diagnosed. In K. Minkoff & R.E. Drake (Eds), *New Directions for Mental Health Services*, Vol. 50 (pp. 57–67). San Francisco, CA: Jossey-Bass.

Drake, R.E., Brunette, M.F. & Mueser, K.T. (1998a). Substance use disorder and social functioning in schizophrenia. In K.T. Mueser & N. Tarrier (Eds), *Handbook of Social Functioning in Schizophrenia* (pp. 280–289). Boston, MA: Allyn & Bacon.

Drake, R.E., McHugo, G.J., Bebout, R.R., Becker, D.R., Harris, M., Bond, G.R. & Quimby, E. (1999). A randomized clinical trial of supported employment for inner-city patients with severe mental illness. *Archives of General Psychiatry*, **56**, 627–633.

Drake, R.E., McHugo, G.J., Clark, R.E., Teague, G.B., Xie, H., Miles, K. & Ackerson, T.H. (1998b). Assertive community treatment for patients with co-occurring severe mental illness and substance use disorder: a clinical trial. *American Journal of Orthopsychiatry*, **68**(2), 201–215.

Drake, R.E., Mercer-McFadden, C., McHugo, G.J., Mueser, K.T., Rosenberg, S.D., Clark, R.E. & Brunette, M.F. (Eds) (1998c). *Readings in Dual Diagnosis*. Columbia, MD: International Association of Psychosocial Rehabilitation Services.

Drake, R.E., Mercer-McFadden, C., Mueser, K.T., McHugo, G.J. & Bond, G.R. (1998d). Review of integrated mental health and substance abuse treatment for patients with dual disorders. *Schizophrenia Bulletin*, **24**(4), 589–608.

Drake, R.E., Yovetich, N.A., Bebout, R.R., Harris, M. & McHugo, G.J. (1997). Integrated treatment for dually diagnosed homeless adults. *Journal of Nervous and Mental Disease*, **185**(5), 298–305.

Duke, P.J., Pantelis, C. & Barnes, T.R.E. (1994). South Westminster schizophrenia survey: alcohol use and its relationship to symptoms, tardive dyskinesia and illness onset. *British Journal of Psychiatry*, **164**, 630–636.

Epstein, E.E. (2001). Classification of alcohol-related problems and dependence. In N. Heather, T.J. Peters & T. Stockwell (Eds), *International Handbook of Alcohol Dependence and Problems* (pp. 47–70). Chichester: John Wiley & Sons.

Epstein, E.E., Ginsburg, B.E., Hesselbrock, V.M. & Schwarz, J.C. (1994). Alcohol and drug abusers subtyped by antisocial personality and primary or secondary depressive disorder. In T.F. Babor, V. Hesselbrock, R.E. Meyer & W. Shoemaker (Eds), *Types of Alcoholics: Evidence from Clinical, Experimental and Genetic Research*, Vol. 708 (pp. 187–201). New York: New York Academy of Sciences.

Fowler, I.L., Carr, V.J., Carter, N.T. & Lewin, T.J. (1998). Patterns of current and lifetime substance use in schizophrenia. *Schizophrenia Bulletin*, **24**, 443–455.

Galanter, M., Castaneda, R. & Ferman, J. (1988). Substance abuse among general psychiatric patients: place of presentation, diagnosis and treatment. *American Journal of Drug and Alcohol Abuse*, **14**, 211–235.

Godley, S.H., Hoewing-Roberson, R. & Godley, M.D. (1994). *Final MISA Report*. Bloomington, IL: Lighthouse Institute.

Graham, H.L., Maslin, J., Copello, A., Birchwood, M., Mueser, K., McGovern, D. & Georgiou, G. (2001). Drug and alcohol problems amongst individuals with severe mental health problems in an inner city area of the UK. *Social Psychiatry and Psychiatric Epidemiology*, **36**, 448–455.

Haddock, G., Barrowclough, C., Tarrier, N., Moring, J., O'Brien, R., Schofield, N., Quinn, J., Palmer, S., Davies, L., Lowens, I., McGovern, J. & Lewis, S. (in press). Randomised controlled trial of cognitive-behaviour therapy and motivational intervention for schizophrenia and substance use: 18 month, carer and economic outcomes. *British Journal of Psychiatry*.

Hesselbrock, M.N., Meyer, R.E. & Keener, J.J. (1985). Psychopathology in hospitalized alcoholics. *Archives of General Psychiatry*, **42**(11), 1050–1055.

Hodgkins, D.C., el-Guebaly, N., Armstrong, S. & Dufour, M. (1999). Implications of depression on outcome from alcohol dependence: a three-year prospective follow-up. *Alcoholism: Clinical and Experimental Research*, **23**, 151–157.

Jeblensky, A., McGrath, J., Herrman, H., Castle, D., Gureje, O., Morgan, V. & Korten, A. (1999). People living with psychotic illness: an Australian study 1997–98. Banberra, Australia: Department of Health and Aged Care.

Jellinek, E.M. (1960). Alcoholism: a genus and some of it species. *Canadian Medical Association Journal*, **83**, 1341–1345.

Jerrell, J. & Ridgely, M. (1995). Evaluating changes in symptoms and functioning of dually diagnosed clients in specialized treatment. *Psychiatric Services*, **46**(3), 233–238.

Johnson, B.D. & Muffler, J. (1992). Sociocultural aspects of drug use and abuse in the 1990s. In J.H. Lowinson, P. Ruiz, R.B. Millman & J.G. Langrod (Eds), *Substance Abuse: A Comprehensive Textbook*, 2nd edn (pp. 118–137). Baltimore, MD: Williams and Wilkins.

Kadden, R., Cooney, N., Getter, H. & Litt, M. (1989). Matching alcoholics to coping skills or interactional therapies: posttreatment results. *Journal of Consulting and Clinical Psychology*, **57**(6), 698–704.

Kavanagh, D.J. (1995). An intervention for substance abuse in schizophrenia. *Behaviour Change*, **12**, 20–30.

Kavanagh, D.J., Greenaway, L., Jenner, L., Saunders, J., White, A., Sorban, J., Hamilton, G. and members of the Dual Diagnosis Consortium (2000). Contrasting views and experiences of health professionals on the management of comorbid substance abuse and mental disorders. *Australian and New Zealand Journal of Psychiatry*, **34**, 279–289.

Kavanagh, D.J., Waghorn, G., Jenner, L., Chant, D.C., Carr, V., Evans, M., Herrman, H., Jablensky, A. & McGrath, J.J. (in press). Demographic and clinical correlates of comorbid substance abuse disorders in psychosis: Multivariate analyses from an epidemiological sample. *Schizophrenia Research*.

Kavanagh, D.J., Young, R., White, A., Saunders, J.R., Wallis, J. & Ceait, A. (2003). SOS—a brief intervention for substance abuse in early psychosis. In H. Graham, A. Copello, M. Birchwood & K. Mueser (Eds), *Substance Misuse in Psychosis: A Handbook of Approaches to Treatment and Service Delivery* (pp. 244–258). Chichester: John Wiley.

Kavanagh, D.J., Young, R., Boyce, L., Clair, A., Sitharthan, T., Clark, D. & Thompson, K. (1998). Substance Treatment Options in Psychosis (STOP): a new intervention for dual diagnosis. *Journal of Mental Health*, **7**, 135–143.

Kessler, R.C., Nelson, C.B., McGonagle, K.A., Edlund, M.J., Frank, R.G. & Leaf, P.J. (1996). The epidemiology of co-occurring addictive and mental disorders: implications for prevention and service utilization. *American Journal of Orthopsychiatry*, **66**(1), 17–31.

Klerman, G.L., Weissman, M.M., Rounsaville, B.J. & Chevron, E.S. (1984). *Interpersonal Psychotherapy of Depression*. New York: Basic Books.

Kranzler, H., Burleson, J., DelBoca, F., Babor, T., Korner, P., Brown, J. & Bohn, M. (1994). Buspirone treatment of anxious alcoholics. *Archives of General Psychiatry*, **51**, 720–731.

Kuhne, A., Nohner, W. & Baraga, E. (1986). Efficacy of chemical dependency treatment as a function of combat in Vietnam. *Journal of Substance Abuse Treatment*, **3**, 191–194.

Kushner, M.G., Abrams, K. & Borchardt, C. (2000). The relationship between anxiety disorders and alcohol use disorders: A review of major perspectives and findings. *Clinical Psychology Review*, **20**, 149–171.

Lehman, C.L., Brown, T.A. & Barlow, D.H. (1998). Effects of cognitive-behavioral treatment for panic disorder with agoraphobia on concurrent alcohol abuse. *Behavior Therapy*, **29**, 423–433.

Lennox, R.D., Scott-Lennox, J.A. & Bohlig, E.M. (1993). The cost of depression-complicated alcoholism: health-care utilization and treatment effectiveness. *Journal of Mental Health Administration*, **20**, 138–152.

Malcolm, R., Anton, R.F., Randall, C.L., Johnston, A., Brady, K. & Thevos, A. (1992). A placebo-controlled trial of buspirone in anxious inpatient alcoholics. *Alcoholism: Clinical and Experimental Research*, **16**, 1007–1013.

Mason, B.J., Kocsis, J.H., Ritvo, E.C. & Cutler, R.B. (1996). A double-blind, placebo-controlled trial of desipramine for primary alcohol dependence stratified on the presence or absence of major depression. *Journal of the American Medical Association*, **275**, 761–767.

McGrath, P.J., Nunes, E.V., Stewart, J.W., Goldman, D., Agosti, V., Ocepek-Welikson, K. & Quitkin, F.M. (1996). Imipramine treatment of alcoholics with primary depression. *Archives of General Psychiatry*, **53**, 232–240.

McHugo, G.J., Drake, R.E., Burton, H.L. & Ackerson, T.H. (1995). A scale for assessing the stage of substance abuse treatment in persons with severe mental illness. *Journal of Nervous and Mental Disease*, **183**(12), 762–767.

McKay, J., Alterman, A.I., Cacciola, J.S. & Mulvaney, F. (2000). Prognostic significance of antisocial personality disorder in cocaine dependent patients entering continuing care. *Journal of Nervous and Mental Disease*, **188**, 287–296.

Miller, W. & Rollnick, S. (2002). *Motivational Interviewing: Preparing People to Change Addictive Behavior*, 2nd Edition. New York: Guilford.

Minkoff, K. (1989). An integrated treatment model for dual diagnosis of psychosis and addiction. *Hospital and Community Psychiatry*, **40**(10), 1031–1036.

Mueser, K.T., & Fox, L. (2002). A family intervention program for dual disorders. *Community Mental Health Journal*, **38**, 253–270.

Mueser, K.T. & Glynn, S.M. (1999). *Behavioral Family Therapy for Psychiatric Disorders*, 2nd edn. Oakland, CA: New Harbinger.

Mueser, K.T., Noordsy, D.L., Drake, R.E. & Fox, L. (2003). *Integrated Treatment for Dual Disorders: A Guide to Effective Practice*. New York: Guilford Press.

Mueser, K.T., Yarnold, P.R. & Bellack, A.S. (1992). Diagnostic and demographic correlates of substance abuse in schizophrenia and major affective disorder. *Acta Psychiatrica Scandinavica*, **85**, 48–55.

Mueser, K.T., Yarnold, P.R., Levinson, D.F., Singh, H., Bellack, A.S., Kee, K., Morrison, R.L. & Yadalam, K.G. (1990). Prevalence of substance abuse in schizophrenia: demographic and clinical correlates. *Schizophrenia Bulletin*, **16**, 31–56.

Mueser, K.T., Yarnold, P.R., Rosenberg, S.D., Swett, C., Miles, K.M. & Hill, D. (2000). Substance use disorder in hospitalized severely mentally ill psychiatric patients: prevalence, correlates, and subgroups. *Schizophrenia Bulletin*, **26**, 179–192.

Najavits, L.M., Weiss, R.D., Shaw, S.R. & Muenz, L.R. (1998). "Seeking safety": outcome of a new cognitive behavioral psychotherapy for women with posttraumatic stress disorder and substance dependence. *Journal of Traumatic Stress*, **11**, 437–456.

Oei, T.P.S. & Loveday, W.A.L. (1997). Lifetime diagnosis of major depression as a multivariate predictor of treatment outcome for inpatients with substance abuse. *Drug and Alcohol Review*, **16**, 261–274.

Osher, F.C. & Dixon, L.B. (1996). Housing for persons with co-occurring mental and addictive disorders. In R.E. Drake & K.T. Mueser (Eds), *Dual Diagnosis of Major Mental Illness and Substance Abuse Disorder II: Recent Research and Clinical Implications* (pp. 53–64). New Directions for Mental Health Services, Vol. 70. San Francisco, CA: Jossey-Bass.

Osher, F.C. & Kofoed, L.L. (1989). Treatment of patients with psychiatric and psychoactive substance use disorders. *Hospital and Community Psychiatry*, **40**, 1025–1030.

Penick, E.C., Powell, B.J., Othmer, E., Bingham, S.F., Rice, A.S. & Liese, B.S. (1984). Subtyping alcoholics by coexisting psychiatric syndromes: course, family history, outcome. In D.W. Goodwin, K. Teilman-Van Dusen & S.A. Mednick (Eds), *Longitudinal Research in Alcoholism* (pp. 167–196). Boston, MA: Kluwer-Nijhoff.

Perry, A., Tarrier, N., Morriss, R., McCarthy, E. & Limb, K. (1999). Randomised controlled trial of efficacy of teaching patients with bipolar disorder to identify early symptoms of relapse and obtain treatment. *British Medical Journal*, **318**, 149–153.

Polcin, D.L. (1992). Issues in the treatment of dual diagnosis clients who have chronic mental illness. *Professional Psychology: Research and Practice*, **23**(1), 30–37.

Powell, B.J., Penick, E.C., Othmer, E. et al. (1982). Prevalence of additional psychiatric syndromes among male alcoholics. *Journal of Clinical Psychiatry*, **43**, 404–407.

Project Match Research Group (1997). Matching alcoholism treatments to client heterogeneity: Project MATCH posttreatment drinking outcomes. *Journal of Studies on Alcohol*, **58**, 7–29.

Randall, C.L., Thomas, S. & Thevos, A.K. (2001). Concurrent alcoholism and social anxiety disorder: A first step toward developing effective treatments. *Alcoholism: Clinical and Experimental Research*, **25**, 210–220.

Regier, D.A., Farmer, M.E., Rae, D.S., Locke, B.Z., Keith, S.J., Judd, L.L. & Goodwin, F.K. (1990). Comorbidity of mental disorders with alcohol and other drug abuse: results from the Epidemiologic Catchment Area (ECA) study. *Journal of the American Medical Association*, **264**, 2511–2518.

Ridgely, M.S., Goldman, H.H. & Willenbring, M. (1990). Barriers to the care of persons with dual diagnoses: organizational and financing issues. *Schizophrenia Bulletin*, **16**(1), 123–132.

Rosenthal, R., Hellerstein, D. & Miner, C. (1992a). A model of integrated services for outpatient treatment of patients with comorbid schizophrenia and addictive disorders. *American Journal on Addictions*, **1**(4), 339–348.

Rosenthal, R.N., Hellerstein, D.J. & Miner, C.R. (1992b). Integrated services for treatment of schizophrenic substance abusers: demographics, symptoms, and substance abuse patterns. *Psychiatric Quarterly*, **63**, 3–26.

Ross, H.E., Glaser, F.B. & Germanson, T. (1988). The prevalence of psychiatric disorders in patients with alcohol and other drug problems. *Archives of General Psychiatry*, **45**, 1023–1031.

Rounsaville, B.J., Dolinsky, Z.S., Babor, T.F. & Meyer, R.E. (1987). Psychopathology as a predictor of treatment outcome in alcoholics. *Archives of General Psychiatry*, **44**, 505–513.

Salyers, M.P. & Mueser, K.T. (2001). Social functioning, psychopathology, and medication side effects in relation to substance use and abuse in schizophrenia. *Schizophrenia Research*, **48**, 109–123.

Schuckit, M.A., Tipp, J.E., Bergman, M., Reich, W., Hesselbrock, V.M. & Smith, T.L. (1997). Comparison of induced and independent major depressive disorders in 2945 alcoholics. *American Journal of Psychiatry*, **154**, 948–957.

Scott, J., Gilvarry, E. & Farrell, M. (1998). Managing anxiety and depression in alcohol and drug dependence. *Addictive Behaviors*, **23**, 919–931.

Shaner, A., Khalsa, M.A., Roberts, L., Wilkins, J., Anglin, D. & Hsieh, S.C. (1993). Unrecognized cocaine use among schizophrenic patients. *American Journal of Psychiatry*, **150**, 758–762.

Stanton, M.D. & Shadish, W.R. (1997). Outcome, attrition, and family-couples treatment for drug abuse: a meta-analysis and review of the controlled, comparative studies. *Psychological Bulletin*, **122**(2), 170–191.

Steadman, H.J., Mulvey, E.P., Monahan, J., Robbins, P.C., Appelbaum, P.S., Grisso, T., Roth, L.H. & Silver, E. (1998). Violence by people discharged from acute psychiatric inpatient facilities and by others in the same neighborhoods. *Archives of General Psychiatry*, **55**, 393–401.

Stein, L.I. & Santos, A.B. (1998). *Assertive Community Treatment of Persons with Severe Mental Illness*. New York: Norton.

Stewart, S.H. (1996). Alcohol abuse in individuals exposed to trauma: a critical review. *Psychological Bulletin*, **120**, 83–112.

Stone, A.M., Greenstein, R.A., Gamble, G. & McLellan, A.T. (1993). Cocaine use by schizophrenic outpatients who receive depot neuroleptic medication. *Hospital and Community Psychiatry*, **44**(2), 176–177.

Susser, E., Strvening, E.L. & Conover, S. (1989). Psychiatric problems in homeless men: lifetime psychosis, substance use, and current distress in new arrivals at New York City Shelters. *Archives of General Psychiatry*, **46**, 845–850.

Teeson, M., Hall, W., Lynskey, M. & Degenhardt, L. (2000). Alcohol and drug use disorders in Australia: implications of the National Survey of Mental Health and Well-being. *Australian and New Zealand Journal of Psychiatry*, **34**, 206–213.

Tollefson, G.D., Lancaster, S.P. & Montague-Clouse, J. (1991). The association of buspirone and its metabolite 1 pyrimidinylpiperazine in the remission of comorbid anxiety with depressive features and alcohol dependency. *Psychopharmacology Bulletin*, **27**, 163–170.

Tollefson, G.G., Montague, C.J. & Tollefson, S.L. (1992). Treatment of comorbid generalised anxiety in a recently detoxified alcoholic population with a selective serotonergic drug (buspirone). *Journal of Clinical Psychopharmacology*, **12**, 19–26.

Triffleman, E.G., Marmar, C.R., Delucchi, K.L. & Ronfeldt, H. (1995).   Childhood trauma and post-traumatic stress disorder in substance abuse inpatients. *Journal of Nervous and Mental Disease*, **183**, 172–176.

Trumbetta, S.L., Mueser, K., Quimby, E., Bebout, R. & Teague, G.B. (1999).   Social networks and clinical outcomes of dually diagnosed homeless persons. *Behavior Therapy*, **30**, 407–430.

Turner, R.W. & Wehl, C.K. (1984).   Treatment of unipolar depression in problem drinkers. *Advances in Behaviour Research and Therapy*, **6**, 115–125.

White, A., Kavanagh, D.J., Wallis, G., Young, R. & Saunders, J. (1999).   *Start Over and Survive (SOS) Treatment Manual: Brief Intervention for Substance Abuse in Early Psychosis*. Brisbane: University of Queensland.

Woody, G.E., McLellan, A.T., Luborsky, L. & O'Brien, C.P. (1985).   Sociopathy and psychotherapy outcome. *Archives of General Psychiatry*, **42**, 1081–1986.

Worthington, J., Fava, M., Agustin, C., Alpert, J., Nierenberg, A.A., Pava, J.A. & Rosenbaum, J.F. (1996).   Consumption of alcohol, nicotine, and caffeine among depressed outpatients. *Psychosomatics*, **37**, 518–522.

Chapter 10

Natural Recovery from Alcohol Problems

Harald K.-H. Klingemann
*University of Applied Sciences, School of
Social Work, Berne, Switzerland*

Synopsis

*Disputes regarding the dogma of abstinence or the claim that it is possible to revert to con-
trolled drinking illustrate a deep-seated lack of belief in the individual's chances of changing
without treatment. However, when people do change from substance misuse, most of them
change on their own. Features common to the successful quitting of alcohol, gambling,
overeating and drug taking are mostly ignored. In general, the hypothesis of "spontaneous
recovery" challenges the concept of addiction as a disease that is in principle irreversible and
progressive. At the same time, the spectrum of definitions of the different terms describing
this phenomenon is varied. In clinical usage, "spontaneous remission" simply means
"an improvement in the patient's condition without effective treatment"; psychological
working definitions emphasize the individual's own cognitive achievement; from a sociological viewpoint, the primary consideration is the exit from a deviant career without
formal intervention. Theoretically, the increasing adoption in the clinical domain of
Prochaska & DiClemente's (1983) stages of change model has been described as an important paradigm shift.*
    *The variety of theoretical aspects of self-change is also associated with numerous
practical problems of research methodology, which are outlined in this chapter after a
discussion of definitional issues. Studies in this area have been mostly conducted either
from a survey/cohort perspective or from a qualitative in-depth approach attempting to
"zoom in" on the change process. Canadian population surveys have suggested that about
78% of interviewees with alcohol problems had overcome them without professional*

The Essential *Handbook of Treatment and Prevention of Alcohol Problems.* Edited by N. Heather and
T. Stockwell.
© 2004 John Wiley & Sons Ltd. ISBN 0-470-86296-3.

treatment. A considerable proportion had reverted to moderate, controlled consumption. Intensive case studies in smaller samples highlight, among other things, the role of social support and control and the influence of life events or stress factors in the motivation to overcome problem use, and point to an impressively creative potential of individual coping strategies.

This chapter not only provides a review of self-change research but also outlines treatment and policy implications. Policy planners in the addiction field find themselves faced with growing criticism of the increasing and costly impact of professional therapy and the abstinence dogma in various spheres of life. Under-utilization of the resources of numerous treatment services also raises questions about the reasons for "treatment rejection" and supports the view that, from the study of clinical populations only it is not possible to understand the needs of the much more important hidden population of problem drinkers. In this context, the concept of "assisted natural remission" is introduced and illustrated by various forms of bibliotherapy. Finally, psychological models and perspectives on change need to be complemented by a sociological approach. This views the societal climate of opinion (discrimination, judgements of different types of deviance in the general population and in the media) and objective features of the treatment system (barriers to treatment and perceptions of available programs) as key parameters which can promote or impede individual chances for change.

"SELF-HEALING": TABOO IN RESEARCH AND THERAPY?

Michael Caine, his days of philandering and heavy drinking well and truly behind him, says that he is too old to mess around with women. The 65 year-old actor's film career has taken on a new life with his portrayal of a sleazy impresario in *Little Voice*, winning a Golden Globe award and sparking speculation that an Oscar might be next. "I used to do a bottle of vodka a day in the 1960s—no problem. You are just topping yourself up", Caine told *The Times* of London in an interview. Meeting the model Shakira Baksh changed all that. "I stopped when I met my wife", he said. "Romance took over and, of course, women do not like drunks" (*International Herald Tribune*, p. 20; "People", February 2, 1999).

The idea that alcoholics can overcome their dependence without extensive professional help has been, and to some extent still is, met with disbelief among many professionals in the treatment and social care field, as well as among the general public. The tenet, "once an alcoholic, always an alcoholic" is shared not just by adherents of Alcoholics Anonymous, and disputes regarding the dogma of abstinence or the claim that it is possible to revert to controlled drinking or drug-taking illustrate the deep-seated lack of belief in the individual's chances of change without treatment. As a rule, features common to the progression of individual drug and alcohol careers, on the one hand, and to "privately organized remission processes" in people with eating disorders and smokers, on the other (Tinker & Tucker, 1997), are mostly ignored. Although this *Handbook* is about alcohol problems, we will also address other problem areas, because there are many informative studies of natural remission covering a range of substances, and results point to similarities between various types of recovery, consequently supporting an underlying concept of addiction.

In general, the notion of "spontaneous recovery" contradicts the concept of addiction as a disease that is, in principle, irreversible and progressive. Similar attitudes are found in the sociological labelling approach, which for a long time focused one-sidedly on the progressive consolidation of deviant careers and viewed the individual as a victim of stigmatization by the agencies of social control (Sack, 1978).

DEFINITIONS

Concepts such as "spontaneous remission" and "natural recovery" are not in any way new, neither are they confined to specific types of addiction, such as alcoholism or drug consumption. The relative significance of attempts at self-change, as compared with success rates in treatment in the clinical domain, was the subject of early studies of the neuroses (Eysenck & Rachman, 1973). Coping strategies, creative avoidance and self-protection mechanisms in schizophrenics have also been treated in various ways in psychiatric research and related very broadly to psychological and behavioural approaches to coping behaviour (Böker et al., 1984). In addition to cognitive models of personality (see Miller, 1981), the sociology of life histories (Kohli, 1978), the principles of humanistic psychology (Hay, 1984) and psychoanalytical interpretations of self-destructive behaviour (Battegay, 1988) have been offered as primary theoretical concepts, irrespective of the specific problem area concerned.

The spectrum of definitions of the different terms related to the phenomenon is therefore equally varied. In clinical usage, "spontaneous remission" means simply "an improvement in the patient's condition without effective treatment" (Roizen, Cahalan & Shanks, 1978). Psychological working definitions emphasize the individual's own cognitive achievement ("self-initiated recovery or change in behaviour"; Marlatt & Gordon, 1985). From a sociological viewpoint, the primary consideration is the exit from a deviant career without formal intervention (Stall, 1983). "Natural" and "spontaneous" are increasingly being replaced as keywords by neutral terms, such as "untreated recovery". Nevertheless, common to all these conceptualizations is the assumption that an *unwanted* condition is overcome without professional help.

These approaches can be seen in perspective if self-destructive behaviour is viewed in functional terms as an, albeit unsuccessful, attempt at self-change. Thus, Lange (1981) concludes, again from observations of schizophrenics, that the development of a psychosis in many patients might be interpreted in wholly positive terms as a defensive reaction against a society which suppresses self-realization and thus is viewed as an attempt at self-change.

A variety of theoretical aspects are also associated with numerous practical problems of research methodology. Hidden or unregistered study populations cannot be recruited by means of conventional sampling techniques, while alternative "active case finding" strategies have also their limitations. Snowball procedures reflect local communication networks, while recruitment through the media generates other selective effects—responding to a media call is already a sign of a basic willingness to change and of a more severe problem at hand. Along these lines, a systematic comparison of media recruitment and survey sampling among natural remitters from problem alcohol use from a large-scale German study showed that media recruitment leads to biased samples, with more severely dependent subjects and fewer controlled drinking remitters; media-recruited individuals also believed more strongly than general population survey subjects that treatment would take too much time and effort (Rumpf et al., 2000). Both active case-finding and media calls only reach people who are or were *aware* of their addiction.

An ethical problem in this research area is the risk that successful "spontaneous remitters" will once again be destabilized or discriminated against *through the research contacts*. Finally, the recording and measurement of the processes of change in life histories or variations in addictive behaviour place heavy demands on study instruments or analytical methods, with little opportunity for using standardized procedures.

THE STATE OF RESEARCH

Major starting points for the discussion of self-change phenomena in addiction research are the literature reviews by Smart (1975) in the field of alcoholism, by Waldorf & Biernacki (1979) on overcoming heroin addiction, and the attempt at a comparative review of self-change in eating disorders, nicotine, alcohol and heroin addiction by Stall & Biernacki (1986). Overall, it can be seen that self-change is not a rare phenomenon and that success rates approximate to those of professional treatment (cf. Blomqvist, 1996). Figures for specific self-change rates naturally vary with the definitional criteria used. We end up with very different remission rates if we choose, for instance, life-long abstinence or return to moderate drinking as reference points, and if we compare subjects with a long drinking history with mildly dependent cases. Taking into account the fact that treatment provision reaches only a minority of those with problems, and bearing in mind the considerable variation in addictive behaviour according to numerous longitudinal studies (Fillmore et al., 1988), this finding is hardly surprising. Canadian population surveys have suggested that about 78% of interviewees with alcohol problems had overcome them without professional treatment. A considerable proportion (38–63%, depending on the survey) had reverted to moderately controlled consumption (Sobell, Cunningham & Sobell, 1996a). Even when eating disorders, medication misuse and gambling addiction were included, only 12% of those interviewed in a population sample by McCartney (1996) had resorted to professional treatment (mainly general practitioners and self-help groups).

Intensive case studies in smaller samples highlight, among other things, the role of social support and control and the influence of life events or stress factors on the motivation to overcome problem use, and point to the creative potential of individual control strategies (Blackwell, 1983). The analytical phase model of self-change, proposed by Stall & Biernacki (1986), has proved to be a useful framework for integrating numerous individual events. In this model, the first phase of remission involves the emergence of a motivation for change; the second phase, the public negotiation of a new, non-stigmatized identity; and the third phase, the stabilization of what has been achieved. According to Stall & Biernacki, in the decision phase, persistent financial and health problems may be considered a specific trigger for the motivation for change, but so can the stress from social sanctions. In the second phase, when sometimes far-reaching changes in lifestyle are instigated but are complicated by withdrawal reactions, the mobilization of social resources is important. In this context, Granfield & Cloud (1999) have introduced the concept of "recovery capital", which is used to refer to the total sum of one's resources (social, physical and human) that can be brought to bear in an effort to overcome alcohol and drug dependency—maintaining bridges with non-using family members and friends, relying on a supportive "safety net" and the commitments of other people, and relying on legal rights with respect to labour market employment, to mention just a few elements. This recovery capital tends to be distributed unevenly between social classes, an aspect that has been little studied (Granfield & Cloud, in press). These more sociologically-orientated approaches to individual life-history change processes correspond to the six-stage model of Prochaska & DiClemente in the clinical domain (see Prochaska, Norcross & DiClemente, 1994), which has to some extent been described as a paradigm shift (Burman, 1997) and has gained broad acceptance in research. It involves a more detailed analytical distinction between "precontemplation" (no change is considered), "contemplation" (medium-term intention to change), "preparation" (immediate intention to change and initial preparatory action), "action" (attempts at changing behaviour) and "maintenance" (continued efforts to change behaviour and continuous support of the new behaviour).

After a lengthy period of neglect of the whole area of spontaneous recovery, a change began during the 1990s which, once again, made discussion of the importance of self-change respectable. Policy planners in the addiction field found themselves faced with growing criticism of the increasing (and also costly) impact of professional therapy, and of the abstinence dogma, in various spheres of life (Peele, 1989). Economic considerations in the financing of treatment sparked interest in so-called minimal intervention, such as long-term, low-intensity case monitoring (Stout et al., 1999) and "assisted spontaneous remissions". The low acceptance or under-utilization of the resources of numerous treatment services also raised questions about the reasons for treatment rejection and supported the view that it was not possible to understand, from the study of clinical populations only, the needs and possibilities for change among the much more important "hidden problem group". A successful outreach for this group implied, also, the increasingly pragmatic recognition of the concept of harm reduction or low-threshold intervention which, on its part, was also based on a more realistic assessment of the possibilities and acceptance of professional forms of therapy. The idea of harm minimization is not in any way new in the alcohol area, but has gained increasing significance, particularly in view of interesting parallels with other drugs (Plant, Single & Stockwell, 1997).

These general developments have also stimulated research efforts, offered a wider framework for understanding addiction-related change processes or divorced them from a fixation on therapy (Miller, 1998), and encouraged discussion and re-assessment of research available so far. An example from the most recent past is the re-assessment of Vaillant's (1983, 1995) unique long-term study on the natural history of alcoholism.

Taken as a whole, these more recent studies largely confirm the stage model mentioned earlier, which stresses cognitive cost–benefit processes (Prochaska & DiClemente, 1983). This finding also appears to apply in cross-addiction and cross-cultural comparisons. Tinker & Tucker (1997), in their study of overcoming problems of obesity with and without treatment support, observed a combination of short- and long-term, predominantly negative, influences on motivation similar to self-remission processes from studies of addiction problems. In an interview study in Sweden, similar behaviour-orientated control strategies were found in alcohol, tobacco and drug spontaneous remitters (e.g. altered life conception, change in social contacts) (Mariezcurrena, 1996). In an English study which, for the first time, compared smoking, eating disorders, alcoholism and gambling addiction, the over-riding importance of subjective will-power and motivation for change (awareness of reasons for change, particularly social pressure and change in life circumstances, such as new job, etc.) was apparent (McCartney, 1996). Social-class-specific opportunities and forms of treatment-free remission were found in a small mixed sample of drug and alcohol addicts (Granfield & Cloud, 1996) and also in a large-scale analysis of problem drinkers (Humphreys, Moos & Finney, 1995). According to this, middle-class addicts with good social networks and, in particular, an intact feeling of self-worth developed into moderate/controlled alcohol consumers, whereas members of the lower social class, subscribing to a "hitting bottom" syndrome, became abstinent significantly more often (Humphreys et al., 1995). With regard to the "abstinence strategy" and "controlled drinking" types of self-change, interesting distinctions can be drawn in life-event profiles. According to King & Tucker (1998), a 4-year group comparison showed that abstaining spontaneous remitters exhibited a steady decrease in the number of reported negative life events, whereas controlled drinking spontaneous remitters (but also stabilized for many years) reported an increase in the fourth year. The authors postulate that:

> . . . as their drinking remained normalized and less central as a life problem, the moderation drinkers were increasingly able to tolerate some instability and change without resuming problem drinking . . . by comparison, the environments of abstainers were increasingly uneventful . . . (p. 541).

According to the only Swiss study available, it was possible to identify motivation, implementation and stabilization phases from an in-depth analysis of the life histories of heroin and alcohol spontaneous remitters, as well as the significance of cognitive decision and learning processes. As this is one of the few comparative prospective studies, main results from the first (1989) and second (1992/1993 and 1996) phases of the research will be highlighted in somewhat greater detail. The 30 heroin and 30 alcohol spontaneous remitters generally went through a conscious phase of preliminary deliberation, with an objectively high "loss stress" (i.e. the number of negatively experienced life events during the year preceding spontaneous recovery), which progressed to a serious motivation for change through additional, in most cases positive and social, triggers. Contrary to previous findings, support played *no* role in the decision implementation (although it probably did in medium-term stabilization). The spontaneous remitters tend to withdraw in this vulnerable phase and are unaware of informal and professional help provision or reject it as inappropriate. They apply an impressive repertoire of implementation techniques and everyday methods. Specifically, spontaneous remitters resort to distancing techniques (e.g. throwing away the contents of the bar; changing the journey home to avoid passing the pub, etc.), drug-related substitution ideas (e.g. instead of alcohol, new cosmo-organic nutrition, coffee consumption, etc.), the imagination of effects (e.g. anticipated effects of further consumption; a belief that one is specifically vulnerable to alcohol), and individual behaviour management (e.g. hobbies, reading) (Klingemann, 1992).

These concrete resources used in implementing change have generally received little attention in research; one exception is the extensive narrative material in the study by Burman (1997) of 38 male and female alcoholic spontaneous remitters. Burman's typology of self-change strategies, similar in many respects to the Swiss study, included: "bargaining with time—a trial commitment", "programmed self-talks and public announcements", "preserving painful memories" and "journalling".

Overall, the self-remission process in alcohol and heroin spontaneous remitters appeared to follow a *similar* basic pattern. However, differences were apparent which pointed to a more difficult course of self-remission, but also a more stable natural recovery, in heroin spontaneous remitters. According to the findings from the first study, heroin spontaneous remitters had a harder task in the first place to achieve control because, for example, of initial stress levels and persistent craving problems. However, the prognosis for this group was more favourable in terms of medium-term stabilization than that for alcohol spontaneous remitters; the self-assessment of their future progress, as well as that of others, was more positive than in the alcohol reference group. This was all the more surprising because the stress situation of heroin spontaneous remitters at the time of the interview always appeared relatively more precarious than in the reference group. This could be tentatively explained by the relatively more pronounced cognitive support and social orientation of the self-remission decision in the preliminary phase, as well as the establishment of primarily *non*-substance drug substitutes (e.g. religion, relationships) in the stabilization phase among heroin remitters. It is precisely the combination of the pressure from continuing public stigmatization, on the one hand, and perceived primary group support, on the other, which might be interpreted as an ideal basis for challenging the inner-directed remitter to pursue new goals in life.

A comparison of alcohol and heroin cases ($n = 30$ in each group, 100% retrieval) in a follow-up study 4 years later confirmed the tendency for a more positive outcome for self-change in the latter group. Only three out of 30 non-treated heroin remitters reported a fully-blown relapse (with an additional three cases indicating a lapse) compared to nine out of 30 non-treated alcohol remitters (with two additional lapses). Natural recovery from alcohol problems seems to be much more difficult than quitting illicit drug use. Alcohol

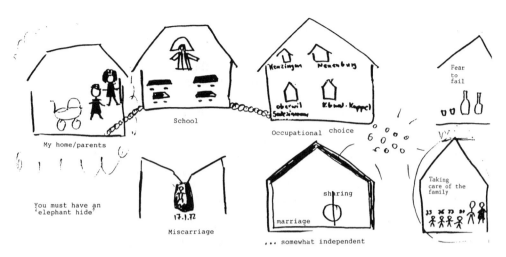

Figure 10.1 'Biographical drawing' of a spontaneous remitter from problem alcohol use (female 35 years old, works in a kindergarten). From Klingemann (1990), with permission

remitters continue to be confronted with risk situations and easy availability, whereas the drug world is far less culturally integrated.

Future Research Priorities

Having outlined some of the more important research findings in this area of work, we will now indicate where we think future research is especially needed.

1. *Prospective longitudinal studies*, which help answer questions of causal relationship, and a better integration of qualitative and quantitative approaches. A clear-cut survey approach falls short of the very complicated life histories of spontaneous remitters. The combined use of open-ended questions, narrative approaches, projective methods and standardized questionnaires seems to be promising. If one looks at the complicated ups and downs of the life-charts of spontaneous remitters, one realizes that one can never hope to capture these transitions, passages and career shifts with a series of simple questionnaire items. Figure 10.1, taken from the Swiss study mentioned above, illustrates this very clearly (see also the first use of this method by Alasuuntari, 1986, with a sample of blue-collar alcoholics in Finland).
2. *Improvements in methodological design*, such as the incorporation of control groups and validity tests by interviews with collaterals. Comparing different "true" stories of recovery helps to get a better understanding of how individuals managed to quit. Collaterals tend to be more distanced; quitters may exaggerate their problems of the past to see themselves as "heroes".
3. *Comparative studies*, which include various problem areas—particularly licit and illicit drugs, but also eating disorders, medication misuse and substance-unrelated addictions (e.g. gambling addiction)—in an integrated research design. Above all, increased attention should be paid to the question of multiple problem solutions.

Is it easier for people who quit drinking also to stop smoking? Does one success experience carry over to other types of addiction and encourage people to work on other problems as well?

4. *Increased attention to societal conditions*, which might promote or impede individual change. By way of example, mention may be made of the varying degrees of stigmatization of addiction and other social problems by the public and the different ways the media portray alcoholics, drug addicts and gamblers, which in turn will influence perceived chances of change and willingness to help such people.

5. *Investigation of change processes in different cultural contexts*. The few findings available so far do not point to distinct cultural differences but, on the contrary, underline the overriding dominant role of cognitive appraisal processes in very different countries such as the USA, Switzerland, Canada (Sobell et al., 1999) and Australia (Brady, 1995). It seems that health problems, life objectives, support and pressure from collaterals are *leitmotivs*, which show up almost universally. However, the different focus and development of alcohol (Klingemann, Takala & Hunt, 1992) and drug (Klingemann & Hunt, 1998) treatment systems already indicate significant influences on remission rates and individual control strategies. If little alcohol treatment is available in a specific country and access is difficult in terms of cost and admission criteria, natural recovery rates may be higher than in countries with elaborate treatment systems and guaranteed individual rights to proper treatment. Natural recovery from smoking is the rule, with no specific treatment offered in most cases (Steward, 1999).

CONCLUSIONS FOR TREATMENT AND FOR ALCOHOL POLICY

The provisional demonstration of effective self-change processes does not in any way make professional intervention superfluous. What is required, however, is harmonization of various treatment programmes and specific interventions tailored to the needs of groups targeted for spontaneous remissions at critical points. Finfgeld (1998) discusses how health care providers might promote the process of change and help people to "reinvest in themselves" by, for instance, teaching life management skills and providing accurate problem information.

Bibliotherapy can be regarded as the most prominent case of "assisted spontaneous remission". The basic idea is that written material can assist the individual in the recovery process. This material can be categorized according to the way it is administered, the underlying didactic impetus/content, the target group it is intended should use the manual, and the producer/source. More precisely, we can distinguish between self-help manuals, which are entirely self-administered, those that require minimal contact with a therapist, and manuals used in the context of regular therapeutic meetings. As to the last-named, drinking diaries have been developed to provide doctors with an interactive and cost-effective method of responding to low-dependence problem drinkers they encounter in their practice. In Scotland, the DRAMS scheme (Drinking Responsibly and Moderately with Self-Control) was tested (Heather, 1986) and subsequently adopted also in different cultural contexts (e.g. in Switzerland; Noschis, 1988).

Furthermore, self-help material may be based explicitly on the principles of self-management and stages of change theory to facilitate the transition to the action and maintenance stages. The material may simply help to monitor and structure personal observations of drinking occasions and quantities consumed, or the written material can be simply of a general informative nature, with no stepwise or didactic programme whatever.

Self-help manuals are available for both problem drinkers and their partners (Barber & Gilbertson, 1998). While all this material is produced by professionals for people ready to change, there are also cases of "natural bibliotherapy", when spontaneous remitters keep a diary themselves or use related books or materials not produced by professionals as a self-help manual in the strict sense.

> At the time we always drank a lot at Christmas, heavily, and so it wasn't that nice for the kids. I was always in a bad mood and it seemed that the whole world was against me—and then it struck me—I thought, "Now I've really got to do something about this". Anyway, on the 24th we were in a library with our daughter to take a book back—I still don't know exactly how it happened—there was this shelf—I still had a headache from the night before and I was a little unsteady on my feet but something drew—no idea how it happened—either way, something drew me to this shelf and at head height there were various books: "ways away from alcohol"— this book, that book, lots of books on drugs and such like—and then I simply picked up two books, took them home and started reading on Saturday night right through into Sunday—I was reading and crying and from then on I knew, as I had already known, "You've got to do something". And the book—incredibly well-written because—well there it was at the begin- ning—you should only read it when you haven't touched a drop. And so I waited another day (laughs) to get everything out of my system, and then I began to read. And there were so many things in the book that you know full well yourself—but that it takes the book to show you—that's how it is. And then you do the test and insert the points and at the end you add them up and see how many you have. And then you are shocked—5 points is critical and I had 22—it gave me courage (laughs) and then you want to flick back through the pages but when you read further—the very next paragraph—it says stop, don't do it: "why are you flicking back through the pages?". And you laugh because the book caught you out, and then you get to thinking, "How would it be if I stopped drinking altogether?" (Case No. 112, Klingemann, 1992).

Studies by Heather (1986), Heather, Kissoon-Singh and Fenton (1990) and others (e.g. Miller & Taylor 1980) clearly demonstrate the benefits of self-help manuals compared with other forms of brief low-threshold interventions, such as the use of telephone help-lines. However, as the short case description above illustrates, "it is necessary to establish whether it is the self-management ingredients of a self-help manual that make for effective biblio- therapy or the act of reading any reasonably relevant and well-intentioned material" (Heather, 1986, p. 338). Finally, cognitive impairment by alcohol diminishes the capability for self-regulation and monitoring of one's own behaviour and limits the use of these manuals mainly to low-dependence cases.

In this context, addicts' perceptions of treatment programmes are highly instructive and highlight corrections that are necessary to available help. Happel, Fischer & Wittfeld (1993) observed that self-activated forms of strategy and control to achieve remission frequently contradict concepts shared by official drug professionals. Thus, for example, a positive view of the period of addiction in one's own life history is instead depicted as "persistent think- ing about addiction", and everyday methods of coping with the problem are often not recognized or picked up by the professional treatment provider. As a result, demands for unconventional support of the individual's own efforts and greater utilization of the skills of those affected can be made. More recent research also points to the fact that cognitive appraisal processes may generally be considered as a basis of motivation for change, irre- spective of the specific remission strategy later chosen involving treatment or self-change. Often astonishing similarities between the everyday methods of spontaneous remitters and the methods of paid therapists (Tinker & Tucker, 1997) can be noted.

What can therapists learn from spontaneous remitters? Is it possible to replicate or inte- grate powerful motivators and facilitators of change in real life in treatment activities? Blomqvist (1996) shows the practical and political limits of such a transfer in practice by pointing out that: ". . . many such activities are most likely to lose their authenticity when explicitly used for therapeutic purposes, thereby creating a 'problem of imitation'", and warns, ". . . the same idea may be taken as an argument for restricting treatment offers to the most destitute cases, whose prospect of encountering in their 'natural environment' experiences that may promote change are extremely poor" (p. 1830).

Case material from a Swiss study illustrates this point nicely. Could Yvonne's bottle trick be used by others or copied by therapists?

"OK", I said, about 3 or 4 years ago, "I can't go on like this". I made up my mind I wanted to be a writer, a journalist, and you just can't do that on alcohol, I couldn't write like that. And then I got out a bottle of whisky and I said to myself, "There must be a way", and I looked at the bottle for a long time and I got the idea that you could dilute it. And then I started, on the first day I had a little drink, a small glass, just like I always had these little drinks, I poured it from the full bottle and then water, I poured a little glass of water in. And so on, every day I had a glass, two, three glasses till nothing was left in the bottle except water, but the taste of whisky, that was still in the bottle and every day I poured myself a drink or two, until there was only water left . . . I drank that, thinking that it was "whisky"—and so it was for me . . . And then I started drinking coffee—by the litre! (laughs) (subject aged 54, cutter, excerpts from the tape-recorded summary of the auto-remission; Klingemann, 1992).

People's perceptions of available treatment programmes and their own everyday methods are not the only factors that determine whether self-change or expert advice is sought. We also need to consider the physical and geographical problems of access, stigmatization/reputation of treatment, and costs and time demands for a potential patient. Copeland (1997) describes the gender-specific aspects of these limitations. The increasing acceptance of concepts such as "harm reduction" and "low-threshold inter-vention" is a reflection of the effort to improve general accessibility to treatment and overcome specific barriers, such as time schedules, costs, the possibility of bringing children along, and rigid admission criteria. Happel et al. (1993) urge greater individualization in the treatment system, and complaints about poor gender-specific provision are consistent with the conclusions from an analysis of remission processes (Lind-Krämer & Timper-Nittel, 1991).

Reflecting definitions of spontaneous remission discussed at the outset, basic questions are raised as to what should be considered to be "treatment" and what community reac-tions to alcohol and drug problems are legitimate and effective. Do material support and aids to survival or the use of complete treatment programmes smooth the path to success-ful self-change in the medium term, or do they undermine the potential for self-help and self-change (Blomqvist, 1996)? The provision of minimal intervention in conjunction with proactive alcohol prevention in the community context is a highly promising avenue (Sobell et al., 1996b). However, the decisive factor is the acceptance by populations that already have an initial impetus for change (spontaneous remitters in the contemplation/appraisal phase), and that would not benefit from costly outpatient or inpatient care to begin with.

In addition to these therapeutic perspectives, we need to consider the important role of the conditions for a *self-change-friendly societal climate* in the broader sense. More specifi-cally, the perception of possibilities for change by the addict as well as by others and willingness to talk about it interact closely with images of addictive behaviour held by the general public. The major discrepancy between the objective prevalence of self-change processes and their public visibility and evaluation is illustrated by a comparison between groups with different experiences of treatment and consumption behaviour in a Canadian study. Whereas 53% of interviewees who had overcome their dependence without treat-ment knew of similar cases, only 14% in one (admittedly non-representative) population group were aware of self-change cases. The other study groups (third parties in respect of spontaneous remitters, unsuccessful spontaneous remitters and treatment cases) fell between these two extremes (Cunningham, Sobell & Sobell, 1998).

What is the reason for a distortion of awareness to such an extent that even people whose sensitivity to self-change processes is heightened by their own experience still underestimate the phenomenon? An important factor is the problem-specific stigma. While only 5% of spontaneous remitters in the Canadian study had inhibitions about telling others they had stopped smoking, 24% of interviewees considered it inadvisable to declare publicly that they had abandoned an alcohol career (Cunningham et al., 1998). In his study, Klingemann (1992) showed how people react when they learn that someone has overcome a problem with alcohol or heroin. First, among both heroin and alcohol spontaneous remitters, it was primarily employers and colleagues, as well as neighbours—in other words, groups which can hand out "rewards" or "punishments" to the individual—who were not informed about the self-change. Second, successful heroin spontaneous remitters who "confessed" to self-change reported negative reactions far more frequently than alcohol spontaneous remitters, which again points to differing degrees of stigmatization.

A reduced potential for stigmatization and increased social support, together with an increased belief in self-efficacy on an individual level, can improve the chances of remission for addicts. They, too, are consumers of mass media messages (Elwood & Ataabadi, 1997), a circumstance which is used in research as a recruitment strategy, but which in public work and prevention is given too little consideration. Last, if these findings are seen at a macrosocial level, then undoubtedly the way in which social problems are presented in the public (media) arena (Widmer, Boller & Coray, 1997) can exert a considerable influence on collective stereotypes and the willingness to provide informal support and help.

National alcohol policy and prevention campaigns can have a definite effect at this level and promote a favourable climate for self-change. An interesting example is the prevention campaign "Handle with Care" run in 1999. This publicity campaign by the Swiss Federal Office of Public Health used slogans and TV advertisements focusing on binge drinking situations (bowling evening, birthday party, disco, etc.). An attempt was made here to induce a transition from the precontemplation to the contemplation phase. In addition, the situational reference does not require continuous monitoring of one's behaviour but it increases the individual awareness of the problem and reinforces relevant avoidance and control strategies. Close attention should, however, be paid to ensuring that the threshold of inhibition for seeking treatment in more serious cases is not *raised* as a result of the propagation of self-help potential among the public (Cunningham et al., 1998).

Finally, from a macrosocietal perspective, one might also assume that more general cultural values and societal belief systems will influence chances for self-change. One might plausibly assume that individually-centred, achievement-orientated Western societies in particular offer good preconditions for self-change philosophies, with active individuals believing in their abilities to resolve the problem situated at the centre. In contrast to this, the disease concept tends as a rule to imply a more passive patient role and expensive expert involvement or, as in the case of the AA movement, even demands an acknowledgement of powerlessness over alcohol and a life-long, ongoing recovery process. Welfare agencies, collective approaches, the belief in state intervention and expert knowledge place far less emphasis on the individual potential for remission and would probably tend more to impede self-change processes. Burman (1997) illustrates this point in her qualitative study in respect of the assessment of self-help groups by spontaneous remitters:

> Many respondents resisted the mandatory labelling, as well as the philosophy of powerlessness over alcohol and recovering as an endless process. As one man stated: "I can't keep seeing myself as an alcoholic if I'm ever going to close that door, *take control* and move on with my life" (p. 47, emphasis added).

ACKNOWLEDGEMENT

Work on this chapter was carried out while the author was affiliated to the Swiss Institute for the Prevention of Alcohol and Other Drug Problems (SIPA).

KEY WORKS AND SUGGESTION FOR FURTHER READING

Blomqvist, J. (1996).   Paths to recovery from substance misuse: change of lifestyle and the role of treatment. *Substance Use and Misuse*, **31**, 1807–1852.

This review article provides an excellent overview of natural recovery research. Blomqvist argues for the integration of outcome research and research on spontaneous recovery and raises the issue of the definition of "treatment".

Moos, R.H. (1994).   Treated or untreated, an addiction is not an island unto itself. *Addiction*, **89**, 507–509.

The title says it all. Best to be read after a comprehensive review article.

Vaillant, G.E. (1996).   A long-term follow-up of male alcohol abuse. *Archives of General Psychiatry*, **53**, 243–249.

For those who do not have time to read Vaillant's (1995) book, this article presents the complex study in a nutshell and raises core questions about the natural history of alcoholism from a clinical perspective.

Brady, M. (1995).   *Giving Away the Grog. Aboriginal Accounts of Drinking and Not Drinking*. Canberra: Commonwealth Department of Human Services and Health.

This is a fine collection of narratives of Australian aborigines, which illustrates change processes in an unfamiliar cultural context.

Peele, S. (1989).   *Diseasing of America—Addiction Treatment Out of Control*. Lexington, MA: Lexington Books.

A provocative book, especially for a North American readership used to the 12-step philosophy and the "war on drugs" rhetoric. More a policy book than a scientific reader, the book suggests why natural recovery research has sparked so much controversy.

Miller, W.R. (1998).   Why do people change addictive behavior? The 1996 H. David Archibald Lecture. *Addiction*, **93**, 163–172.

This article puts the influential transtheoretical model of change by Prochaska and his colleagues into perspective and focuses on the concept of "assisted natural recovery", touching upon principles of motivational interviewing, self-efficacy and brief intervention.

Klingemann, H., Sobell, L., Barker, J. et al. (2001).   *Promoting Self-change from Problem Substance Use: Practical Implications for Policy, Prevention and Treatment*. Dordrecht: Kluwer Academic.

This book offers an up-to-date review of self-change from problem use of licit and illicit drugs, and from gambling, and provides a "tool-box" for the practice-oriented reader.

REFERENCES

Alasuuntari, P. (1986). Alcoholism in its cultural context: the case of blue-collar men. *Contemporary Drug Problems*, **13**, 641–686.

Barber, J.G. & Gilbertson, R. (1998). Evaluation of a self-help manual for the female partners of heavy drinkers. *Research on Social Work Practice*, **8**(2), 141–151.

Battegay, R. (1988). *Autodestruktion*. Bern: Verlag Hans Huber.

Blackwell, J.St. (1983). Drifting, controlling and overcoming: opiate users who avoid becoming chronically dependent. *Journal of Drug Issues*, **13**, 219–236.

Blomqvist, J. (1996). Paths to recovery from substance misuse: change of lifestyle and the role of treatment. *Substance Use and Misuse*, **31**, 1807–1852.

Böker, W., Brenner, H., Gerstner, G., Keller, F., Müller, J. & Spichtig, L. (1984). Self-healing strategies among schizophrenics: attempts at compensation for basic disorders. *Acta Psychiatrica Scandinavia*, **69**, 373–378.

Brady, M. (1995). *Giving Away the Grog. Aboriginal Accounts of Drinking and Not Drinking*. Canberra: Commonwealth Department of Human Services and Health.

Burman, S. (1997). The challenge of sobriety: natural recovery without treatment and self-help groups. *Journal of Substance Abuse*, **9**, 41–61.

Copeland, J. (1997). A qualitative study of barriers to formal treatment among women who self-managed change in addictive behaviours. *Journal of Substance Abuse Treatment*, **14**, 183–190.

Cunningham, J.A., Sobell, L.C. & Sobell, M.B. (1998). Awareness of self-change as a pathway to recovery for alcohol abusers: results from five different groups. *Addictive Behaviors*, **23**, 399–404.

Elwood, W.N. & Ataabadi, A.N. (1997). Influence of interpersonal and mass-mediated interventions on injection drug and crack users: diffusion of innovations and HIV risk behaviors. *Substance Use and Misuse*, **32**, 635–651.

Eysenck, H.J. & Rachman, S.J. (1973). *Neurosen und Heilmethoden. Einführung in die moderne Verhaltensthetapie* [The Causes and Cures of Neurosis]. Berlin-Ost: Verlag der Wissenschaft.

Fillmore, K.M., Hartka, E., Johnstone, B.M., Speiglman, R. & Temple, M.T. (1988). Spontaneous remission from alcohol problems: a critical review. Unpublished manuscript, University of California at Berkeley, CA.

Finfgeld, D.L. (1998). Self-resolution of drinking problems as a process of reinvesting in self. *Perspectives in Psychiatric Care*, **34**, 5–15.

Granfield, R. & Cloud, W. (1996). The elephant that no one sees: natural recovery among middle-class addicts. *Journal of Drug Issues*, **26**, 45–61.

Granfield, R. & Cloud, W. (1999). *Overcoming Addiction without Treatment*. New York: New York University Press.

Happel, H.-V., Fischer, R. & Wittfeld, I. (1993). *Selbstorganisierter Ausstieg. Überwindung der Drogenabhängigkeit ohne professionelle Hilfe (Endbericht)*. Frankfurt: Integrative Drogenhilfe an der Fachhochschule Ffm L.V.

Hay, L.L. (1984). *You Can Heal Your Life*. London: Eden Grove Editions.

Heather, N. (1986). Change without therapists. The use of self-help manuals by problem drinkers. In W.R. Miller & N. Heather (Eds), *Treating Addictive Behaviors* (pp. 331–359). New York/London: Plenum.

Heather, N., Kissoon-Singh, J. & Fenton, G.W. (1990). Assisted natural recovery from alcohol problems: effects of a self-help manual with and without supplementary telephone contact. *British Journal of Addiction*, **85**, 1177–1185.

Humphreys, K., Moos, R.H. & Finney, J.W. (1995). Two pathways out of drinking problems without professional treatment. *Addictive Behaviors*, **20**, 427–441.

King, M.P. & Tucker, J.A. (1998). Natural resolution of alcohol problems without treatment: environmental contexts surrounding the initiation and maintenance of stable abstinence or moderation drinking. *Addictive Behaviors*, **23**, 537–541.

Klingemann, H. (1990). "Der Freitag, wo alles kaputt war" oder "Die Macht des Positiven"? Eine dimensionale Analyse "natürlicher Heilungen" bei kritischem Alkohol- und Heroinkonsum. *Zeitschrift für Soziologie*, **19**(6), 444–457.

Klingemann, H. (1992).   Coping and maintenance strategies of spontaneous remitters from problem use of alcohol and heroin in Switzerland. *International Journal of the Addictions*, **27**, 1359–1388.

Klingemann, H., Takala, J.-P. & Hunt, G. (Eds) (1992).   *Cure, Care, or Control—Alcoholism Treatment in Sixteen Countries*. New York: State University of New York Press.

Klingemann, H. & Hunt, G. (Eds) (1998).   *Drug Treatment Systems in an International Perspective: Drugs, Demons and Delinquents*. Thousand Oaks, CA: Sage.

Kohli, M. (1978).   *Soziologie des Lebenslaufs*. Soziologische Texte, Vol. 109: N.F. Darmstadt-Neuwied: Luchterhand.

Lange, H.U. (1981).   Anpassungsstrategien, Bewältigungsreaktionen und Selbstheilversuche bei Schizophrene. *Fortschritte der Neuroligie Psychiatrie*, **49**, 275–285.

Lind-Krämer, R. & Timper-Nittel, A. (1991).   *Geschlechtsspezifische Analyse von Drogenabhängigkeit*. Projektgruppe Rauschmittelfragen, Forschungsprojekt "Amsel", Abschlussbericht, Vol. 2. Frankfurt: Jugendberatung und Jugendhilfe e.V.

Mariezcurrena, R. (1996).   Recovery from addictions without treatment: an interview study. *Scandinavian Journal of Behaviour Therapy*, **25**, 57–84.

Marlatt, G.A. & Gordon, J.R. (Eds) (1985).   *Relapse Prevention: Maintenance Strategies in the Treatment of Addictive Behaviors*. New York: Guilford.

McCartney, J. (1996).   A community study of natural change across the addictions. *Addiction Research*, **4**, 65–83.

Miller, L. (1981).   Predicting relapse and recovery in alcoholism and addiction: neuropsychology, personality, and cognitive style. *Journal of Substance Abuse Treatment*, **8**, 277–291.

Miller, W.R. (1998).   Why do people change addictive behavior? The 1996 H. David Archibald Lecture. *Addiction*, **93**, 163–172.

Miller, W.R. & Taylor, C.A. (1980).   Focused vs. broad spectrum behavior therapy for problem drinkers. *Journal of Consulting and Clinical Psychology*, **48**, 590–601.

Noschis, K. (1988).   Testing a self-help instrument with early-risk alcohol consumers in general practice: a progress report. *Contemporary Drug Problems*, **15**(3), 365–382.

Peele, S. (1989).   *Diseasing of America—Addiction Treatment Out of Control*. Lexington, MA: Lexington Books.

Plant, M., Single, E. & Stockwell, T. (1997).   *Alcohol: Minimising the Harm*. London: Free Association Books.

Prochaska, J.O. & DiClemente, C.C. (1983).   Stages and processes of self-change of smoking: toward an integrative model of change. *Journal of Consulting and Clinical Psychology*, **51**, 390–395.

Prochaska, J.O., Norcross, J.C. & DiClemente, C.C. (1994).   Transtheoretical therapy: toward a more integrative model of change. *Psychotherapy: Theory, Research and Practice*, **19**, 276–288.

Roizen, R., Cahalan, D. & Shanks, P. (1978).   Spontaneous remission among untreated problem drinkers. In D.B. Kandel (Eds), *Longitudinal research on drug use* (pp. 197–221). New York: Wiley.

Rumpf, H.-J., Bischof, G., Hapke, U., Meyer, C. & John, U. (2000).   Studies on natural recovery from alcohol dependence: sample selection bias by media solicitation. *Addiction*, **2000**, 765–775.

Sack, F. (1978).   Probleme der Kriminalsoziologie. In R. König (Ed.), *Handbuch der empirischen Sozialforschung, Vol. 12. Wahlverhalten, Vorurteile, Kriminalität*. Stuttgart: Ferdinand Enke Verlag.

Smart, R.G. (1975).   Spontaneous recovery in alcoholics: a review and analysis of the available research. *Drug and Alcohol Dependence*, **1**, 277–285.

Sobell, L.C., Cunningham, J.A. & Sobell, M.B. (1996a).   Recovery from alcohol problems with and without treatment: prevalence in two population surveys. *American Journal of Public Health*, **86**(7), 966–972.

Sobell, L.C., Cunningham, J.C., Sobell, M.B., Agrawal, S., Gavin, D.R., Leo, G.I. & Singh, K.N. (1996b).   Fostering self-change among problem drinkers: a proactive community intervention. *Addictive Behaviors*, **21**, 817–833.

Sobell, L.C., Klingemann, H., Toneatto, T., Sobell, M.B., Agrawal, S. & Leo, G.I. (1999).   *Cross-cultural qualitative analysis of factors associated with natural recoveries from alcohol and drug problems*. Paper presented at the KBS thematic meeting, Les Diablerets, Switzerland, 7–12 March.

Stall, R. (1983).   An examination of spontaneous remission from problem drinking in the bluegrass region of Kentucky. *Journal of Drug Issues*, **13**, 191–206.

Stall, R. & Biernacki, P. (1986).   Spontaneous remission from the problematic use of substances:

an inductive model derived from a comparative analysis of the alcohol, opiate, tobacco and food/ obesity literatures. *International Journal of the Addictions*, **21**, 1–23.

Steward, C. (1999). Investigation of cigarette smokers who quit without treatment. *Journal of Drug Issues*, **29**, 167–186.

Stout, R.L., Rubin, A., Zwick, W., Zywiak, W. & Bellino, L. (1999). Optimizing the cost-effectiveness of alcohol treatment: a rationale for extended case monitoring. *Addictive Behaviors*, **24**, 17–35.

Tinker, J.E. & Tucker, J.A. (1997). Motivations for weight loss and behavior change strategies associated with natural recovery from obesity. *Psychology of Addictive Behaviors*, **11**, 98–106.

Vaillant, G.E. (1983). *The Natural History of Alcoholism: Cases, Patterns, and Paths to Recovery*. Cambridge, MA: Harvard University Press.

Vaillant, G.E. (1995). *The Natural History of Alcoholism Revisited*. Cambridge, MA: Harvard University Press.

Waldorf, D. & Biernacki, P. (1979). Natural recovery from heroin addiction: a review of the incidence literature. *Journal of Drug Issues*, **9**, 281–289.

Widmer, J., Boller, B. & Coray, R. (Eds) (1997). *Drogen im Spannungsfeld der Öffentlichkeit*. Basel: Helbing & Lichtenhan.

Chapter 11

Alcoholics Anonymous and Other Mutual Aid Groups

Chad Emrick
*University of Colorado Health Sciences Center, Denver,
CO, USA*

Synopsis

Alcoholics Anonymous was founded in the USA in 1935. Currently, there are an estimated nearly 2,000,000 active members worldwide in nearly 99,000 groups in over 140 countries. Since the mid-1940s, a number of other mutual aid groups for alcoholics developed outside of North America, including the Abstainer Clubs in Poland, Links in Sweden, Vie Libre and Croix d'Or in France, Clubs for Alcoholics in Treatment in Italy, Club of Treated Alcoholics in Croatia, Freundeskreise in Germany, 24-Hours Movements in Mexico, and Danshu-Tomo-no-Kai and the All Nippon Sobriety Association in Japan. More recently, alternatives to AA have emerged in North America: Women for Sobriety, Secular Organizations for Sobriety, Rational Recovery, and Moderation Management, for example.

The philosophy, structure, and therapeutic processes of AA are centered around the organization's Twelve Steps and Twelve Traditions. Alternative mutual-aid groups possess varied structures and processes, many of which differ from those of AA. This variability broadens the opportunity each individual has for finding a compatible mutual aid group.

Substantial cross-cultural variation is found in the demographic characteristics of AA members. Also, there is international variability in the degree to which alcohol-troubled individuals use mutual aid groups other than AA.

Treatment outcome studies have found that, compared to alcohol-troubled patients who do not go to AA within the context of professional treatment, those who go to AA during

The Essential *Handbook of Treatment and Prevention of Alcohol Problems.* Edited by N. Heather and T. Stockwell.
© 2004 John Wiley & Sons Ltd. ISBN 0-470-86296-3.

or after professional treatment are more likely to improve in drinking behavior and have improved psychological health. AA's effectiveness can be traced to members' learning to use therapeutic and adaptive processes to deal with life. Besides leading to improvements in the lives of its members, AA and other mutual-aid groups have the advantage of being considerably less costly than professional treatment.

Attendance at AA meetings may occur without a member becoming actively involved in the therapeutic processes of the organization. To facilitate effective involvement in AA and other mutual-aid groups, health care providers need to familiarize themselves with the philosophy, structure and therapeutic processes of each group. Knowledge needs to be acquired regarding: how to integrate mutual aid groups with professional treatment; how to direct individual clients to specific groups, given the heterogeneity of individual groups within a mutual aid organization; how to facilitate mutual aid group involvement with individuals who belong to special populations; and how to match individuals to mutual aid groups. With regard to the last item, AA-orientated treatment appears to be most useful for outpatients whose social interactional systems support drinking and for those who have relatively low levels of anger at the start of treatment. For inpatients who are relatively high in their dependence on alcohol, an AA-orientated aftercare treatment may be most suitable. For outpatients who have been involved in AA prior to professional treatment, encouraging them once again to go to AA offers an approach that is more compatible to the drinker than are methods that are not 12-step-group focused.

Alcoholics Anonymous and other mutual aid groups are not always helpful to alcohol-troubled individuals. Sometimes, people with alcohol problems need to be assisted in finding alternative treatments, either of a professional or mutual-aid sort.

Recent research has yielded a virtual explosion of new understanding concerning the therapeutic processes, effectiveness and suitable utilization of AA and, by extension, other mutual aid groups. Health care providers are now able to provide wiser counsel than ever about mutual aid groups when dealing with their patients who have alcohol problems.

The primary purpose of this chapter is to inform health care workers and other interested readers about Alcoholics Anonymous. Pertinent findings from recent quantitative research on AA are exploited in this effort and observations from relevant contemporary clinical writings are used to amplify these findings. This information is given application to care-givers for making maximum use of AA. Alternatives to AA are explored in order to broaden the perspective with regard to mutual aid groups for alcohol-troubled individuals.

HISTORICAL DEVELOPMENT OF AA AND OTHER MUTUAL AID GROUPS

AA was founded in the USA in 1935 by two chronic alcoholics, Bill W. and Dr Bob S. Several ideas stemming from the founders' contacts with Moral Rearmament (a Christian evangelical movement) helped shape the philosophy and structure of the organization. In 1938 and 1939, this philosophy was codified in the Twelve Steps. In 1950, AA's organizational structure was codified in the Twelve Traditions. Growth of the organization was very slow until around 1940, when several US articles were published about AA. Since then, this organization has enjoyed rapid development. It has grown into a worldwide organization with an estimated nearly 2,000,000 active members in nearly 99,000 groups in over 140 countries (personal communication, General Service Office of Alcoholics Anonymous, November 4, 1999).

Since the mid-1940s, a number of other mutual aid groups for alcohol-troubled individuals have been established outside of North America. While all of them differ in organization and functioning from AA, each was "influenced, positively or negatively, by the example of AA" (Room, 1998, p. 133). Abstainer Clubs were formed in Poland; Links emerged in Sweden; Vie Libre and Croix d'Or were established in France; Clubs for Alcoholics in Treatment (CATs) took root in Italy; Club of Treated Alcoholics emerged in Croatia; traditional temperance-based organizations, as well as Freundeskreise, found life in the state of Hesse in Germany; 24-Hours Movements were established in Mexico; and Danshu-Tomo-no-Kai and the All Nippon Sobriety Association came into existence in Japan.

In North America, the development of alternatives to AA is a relatively recent phenomenon. The pioneers of these alternatives defected from AA for a variety of reasons, "including dislike of the sexism, the powerlessness concept, rigidity, religiosity, the cult-like atmosphere, and the all powerful God approach" (Kasl, 1992, p. 163). Jean Kirkpatrick founded Women for Sobriety (WFS) in 1976 (see Kaskutus, 1996). This organization addresses the special needs of female problem drinkers by taking a holistic approach to health and fostering autonomy from men. In 1985, two organizations that promote a secular approach to alcohol problems were founded: James Christopher started Secular Organizations for Sobriety (SOS), also called Save our Selves (see Connors and Dermen, 1996); and Jack Trimpey established Rational Recovery (RR) (see Galanter, Egelko & Edwards, 1993; Trimpey, 1996). As with AA, all these alternatives view abstinence as the goal of recovery from alcohol problems. As a counterpoint to these groups, an organization that promotes harm reduction as its members' goal was formed by Audrey Kishline in the early 1990s (Kishline, 1994). This organization, Moderation Management®, provides group support for the establishment of moderate drinking practices.

AA'S PHILOSOPHY, STRUCTURE AND THERAPEUTIC PROCESSES

AA's philosophy, although rooted in the Judeo-Christian tradition, contains thought elements that are consonant with a variety of religious and philosophical traditions. Thus, people with a wide spectrum of beliefs can find a home in this organization. The organization itself is structured around the Twelve Steps and the Twelve Traditions (Alcoholics Anonymous World Services, 1986) (see Appendix). Therapeutic processes are played out in "working" the steps, having (for some members) one-to-one guidance and support from a senior member (identified as a "sponsor"), and participating in group meetings that possess therapeutic processes akin to those found in professionally led psychotherapy groups (Emrick, Lassen & Edwards, 1977).

The process of going through the Twelve Steps is adumbrated here for the reader who is unfamiliar with these steps. In Step One, members adopt the perspective that they cannot control their drinking behavior through conscious, deliberate effort. In Step Two, members incorporate the belief that only a Power greater than oneself can help them become free of alcohol dependence. In Step Three, members surrender to this Higher Power—and in so doing let go of their struggle with drinking behavior as well as with the thoughts, feelings, physical sensations, and behavioral predispositions that are associated with such behavior. In Step Four, members undertake a self-analysis of fear, guilt and resentment that are often major contextual factors in drinking behavior. One's resentments are given especial attention and members are guided through procedures for developing a less blaming, more self-responsible perspective with regard to resentments and associated actions. In Step Five, members share the product of their self-analysis with their Higher Power and another individual. In Steps Six and Seven, more letting go of an active struggle with one's inner life is prompted. Whatever behaviors are identified in Steps Four and Five as dysfunctional are viewed as beyond the scope of the individual to change directly. Rather, the individual lets go of a deliberate struggle, "turning over" these behaviors to a Higher Power to effect change. In Steps Eight and Nine, members extend the development of responsibility to their interpersonal relationships. Responsibility is taken for harm caused others (by omission and commission), and restitution to those one has harmed is undertaken, unless restitution efforts would bring harm either to the member or someone else. Because self-awareness is inevitably limited, members are encouraged, once they have made amends for the harmful actions of which they are aware, to look the harmed individual square in the face and ask him/her to identify harmful acts that the member has forgotten. Responsibility is then extended to these behaviors. In Steps Ten and Eleven, activities are engaged that serve to maintain the therapeutic gains achieved in taking the earlier steps. Finally, in Step Twelve, the healing gained through involvement in the program (referred to as a "spiritual awakening") is maintained by helping newcomers to the organization and by serving to sustain the organization itself. Increasing one's awareness of, acceptance of and enactment of the paradoxes of life is at the core of spiritual awakening within the context of active AA involvement. A member's philosophical perspective on life becomes infused with such paradoxical truths as "in order to win, one has to lose" and "in order to give, one has to receive". It is from this place of awareness that experienced members help new members and contribute through service activities to the maintenance of the organization.

The Twelve Traditions of AA are intended to preserve AA as an organization that is completely dedicated to helping individuals live life free of alcohol. Central to AA is an essentially anarchistic organizational structure. There are no permanent leaders, and leaders are instructed to "serve but never govern". Each group maintains autonomy, owns no property, and receives income only from voluntary contributions. Members are to avoid identifying themselves to the public media as members of AA. AA does not "give endorsements, make alliances, or enter public controversies" (Alcoholics Anonymous World Services, 1976, p. xix). AA is not to solicit new members through any promotional activity. By virtue of its organizational structure, AA has been able to avoid usurpation of power by any individual or faction of members. Such avoidance has been strongly contributive to AA's remarkable success as a social movement.

Although AA's essential organizational structure and therapeutic processes are notably consistent throughout its multinational operations, interesting variations are found across countries and within different regions of a country. The International Collaborative Study of Alcoholics Anonymous (Mäkelä et al., 1996) investigated AA in eight societies, offering fascinating facts concerning AA's international variation. For example, 30–50% of AA members in Iceland, Mexico, Poland and German-speaking Switzerland view the Higher Power referred to in the Twelve Steps as a Christian God, while only 13% perceive the Higher Power construct in this fashion in Sweden. The Higher Power construct is viewed as the "AA fellowship or the power of the group", not a metaphysical entity, by 59% of Swedish members and 47% of Icelandic members, whereas only 34% of Mexican members impute this quality to the construct. Recitation of the Lord's Prayer at the end of meetings is a common practice in many parts of the USA and in some Icelandic groups, but is rare or non-existent in Austria, Finland, France, Poland, Sweden and Switzerland. Even the practice of having a sponsor guide a member through the Twelve Steps has international variation. In the USA and Mexico, for example, more than 70% of the members have a sponsor, whereas in Poland, only 30% do.

STRUCTURE AND PROCESSES OF ALTERNATIVE MUTUAL AID GROUPS

Alternatives to AA differ in some remarkable ways from AA with respect to their organizational structure and therapeutic processes. These differences are so numerous that just a few of them can be identified in this chapter. The reader is guided to Room (1998) and Emrick et al. (1977) for a fuller treatment of these differences. Women for Sobriety groups, for example, discourage talk about one's drinking history. In stark contrast, story-telling in AA is to be limited to one's drinking and the effects drinking has had on the member's life. AA members are to avoid commenting directly on each other's statements (i.e. there is the rule of "no crosstalk"), while the Mexican 24-Hours Movements meetings encourage members to be directly aggressive with fellow members, believing that such confrontation is conducive to change. Only individuals with alcohol use problems can become a member of AA (with spouses and friends belonging to an auxiliary group: Al-Anon). In contrast, family members are invited to join Vie Libre in France and the Clubs movements in Croatia and Italy. In Japan, cultural beliefs lend to wives being *expected* to become members of Danshu-Tomo-no-Kai or the All Nippon Sobriety Association. Finally, in contrast to the emphasis AA places on developing a relationship with a Higher Power, the Swedish Links movement downplays any reference to a Higher Power; and SOS and RR are distinctly void of any reference to a Higher Power.

Differences in structure and function across mutual aid groups, such as those identified here, benefit individuals with alcohol problems by increasing the opportunity each has for finding a compatible mutual aid group.

WHAT ARE THE DEMOGRAPHIC CHARACTERISTICS OF THE CURRENT AA MEMBERSHIP?

The demography of AA membership varies considerably across nations, with "historical contingencies and internal differences in the national movements" shaping the membership (Mäkelä et al., 1996, p. 102). The International Collaborative Study of Alcoholics Anonymous (see Mäkelä et al., 1996) found, for example, that women comprise only 10% of the membership in Mexico, whereas 44% of the membership in Austria are female, with this disparity not being related directly to the prevalence of female problem drinkers in these countries. Demographic diversity is reflected in the fact that in Mexico and Iceland, around 30% of AA members are under the age of 30, compared to less than 10% of the membership in Austria, Finland, Sweden and German-speaking Switzerland. With respect to socioeconomic levels, AA members in Mexico include a number of urban workers and rural poor, and Japan draws in those who are "less well-off" (Room, 1998, p. 136). Similarly, in Finland, Iceland and Switzerland the membership is drawn significantly from the working class. In contrast, members in Austria and, to some degree, Sweden are typically from the higher socioeconomic levels (Mäkelä et al., 1996). Clearly, cultural factors help shape the demographics of AA's membership.

Besides at-large cultural variables, contextual variables more proximal to the individual impact the mutual aid group affiliation process. These more proximal contextual factors have such complex and inconsistent relationships with AA affiliation (see Emrick, 1999) that health care providers have little in the way of clear-cut guidelines for determining, in advance, who will be a good match for AA or other mutual aid groups. Nevertheless, there are a couple of trends within the AA data set that health care providers might wish to reflect upon when working with a patient toward the possibility of involvement in AA. These trends indicate that the more severe an individual's drinking or other identified problem, and the less that person has available in the way of interpersonal supports for abstinence in the "natural" environment (particularly for an outpatient), the more likely the individual is to join AA. These trends notwithstanding, health care practitioners would do well to hold to the position that any given patient *may* or *may not* be a suitable candidate for AA or other mutual aid group.

HOW OFTEN ARE AA AND OTHER MUTUAL AID GROUPS USED BY ALCOHOL ABUSERS?

Although AA appears to be increasingly utilized, the extension of AA into the population of individuals with alcohol use disorders may still be quite modest, with a penetration rate of perhaps less than 10% in the USA, for example (Hasin & Grant, 1995; Hasin, 1994). At the same time, of alcohol-troubled individuals who *do* seek the support of mutual help groups in the USA, the vast majority go to AA, inasmuch as this organization has an overwhelming hegemony among mutual help groups in North America. In fact, it is estimated that 95% of the groups that exist for problem drinkers in North America are AA (Room, 1998). The nearly total reliance on AA for mutual help among alcohol-dependent individuals extends to some other countries as well, such as Iceland, Australia and New Zealand. There are some countries, however, in which alternative mutual help groups are utilized as much or more so than AA. For example, in Austria, only about 50% of the mutual help groups are AA; and in Poland, 47% of individuals who go to mutual help groups attend AA. Still lower proportions of AA groups among all available mutual help groups are found in Sweden (24%), Germany (17%) and Italy (14%). In Japan, just 14% of individuals who go to mutual help groups go to AA, with the proportion among problem drinkers who seek the support of mutual help groups being even lower in France (11%).

HOW EFFECTIVE IS AA?

Even though AA is widely used by problem drinkers in some cultures to assist them in dealing with their alcohol problems, and although many health care providers, at least in North America, strongly endorse the effectiveness of AA, is such use and such endorsement warranted? Certainly humans are capable of engaging in widely shared behaviors that are not particularly the most constructive. Is this the case with AA?

By now, ample research data have accumulated that document the effectiveness of AA as a resource for helping individuals maintain an alcohol-free lifestyle. In effect, research evidence substantiates the experiential knowledge that AA members and health care providers possess concerning the effectiveness of 12-step groups.

Outcome Studies

A strong element in the expanding structure of positive AA findings consists of data that emerged from a meta-analysis of 107 studies on AA (Emrick et al., 1993). The results of this analysis suggest "that professionally treated patients who attend AA during or after treatment are more likely to improve in drinking behavior than are patients who do not attend AA, although the chances of drinking improvement are not overall a great deal higher" (Emrick et al., 1993, p. 57). Also, a positive relationship between AA affiliation and psychological health was observed.

Most salient among the recent original research findings on AA's effectiveness are the findings of investigators at the Center for Health Care Evaluation in Menlo Park, CA, USA. In one of these studies (Humphreys, Moos & Cohen, 1997), 515 subjects from an original sample of 631 individuals with previously untreated drinking problems were followed up at 1 year. Of those in the sample who attended AA meetings but did not receive inpatient or outpatient professional treatment, significant improvement was found on all measures of drinking problems, as well as on several other measures of functioning. A total of 395 subjects in this sample were followed up at 8 years, at which time it was found that the number of AA meetings attended during the first 3 years of follow-up was positively related to remission from alcohol problems 8 years after the beginning of the project. AA attendance in the first 3 years of the study also predicted, at 8-year follow-up, lower levels of depression as well as higher-quality relationships with friends and partners or spouses. Humphreys et al. (1997) concluded that, compared with professionally delivered inpatient or outpatient treatment, "AA probably helped more people more substantially in this sample" (p. 237).

This same research group evaluated the effects of different types of aftercare treatment 1 year after inpatient treatment in a large sample of veterans (Finney, Moos & Humphreys, 1999; Moos et al., 1999; Ouimette, Moos & Finney, 1998; Ouimette et al., 1999). Followed up were 3018 veterans who had been treated for substance abuse in an inpatient setting. The majority of patients, all of whom were male, were non-Caucasian; 83% of the sample were dependent on alcohol, with about 52% of those with alcohol problems being dependent on other substances. They were evaluated with regard to their outcome status approximately 1 year after being discharged from the inpatient program. Participation in AA or NA in the 3 months prior to the 1-year follow-up was associated with a greater likelihood of being abstinent, free of substance use problems, free of significant distress and psychiatric symptoms, and being employed. These findings held even when controlling for the influence of aftercare treatment, and they applied to dually diagnosed patients as much as to those with only substance use disorders (for the latter, see Ouimette et al., 1999). Statistical analyses suggested that 12-step involvement after inpatient treatment helped maintain the gains made during inpatient treatment (Finney et al., 1999). These results led the researchers to conclude that, "Overall, 12-step attendance and involvement were more strongly related to positive outcomes than was outpatient treatment attendance" (Ouimette et al., 1998, p. 519).

Treatment Cost

Humphreys & Moos (1996) took another angle toward assessing the effectiveness of AA. They compared the per-person treatment costs for problem drinkers who sought help from a professional outpatient alcoholism treatment provider with the costs of treatment for drinkers who initially chose to go to AA. Costs were assessed for a three-year period. Over the course of the study, some individuals within both groups required detoxification and inpatient/residential treatment. Furthermore, some drinkers who initially went to AA also had outpatient treatment and vice versa. When all cost factors were calculated, those individuals who initially attended AA incurred per-person treatment costs that were 45% lower than the costs for those who initially sought outpatient treatment. If nothing else, AA appears to be as effective as professional outpatient treatment, while being considerably less costly, in helping at least some individuals with alcohol problems.

Mechanisms of Effectiveness of AA

The mounting research evidence in support of the effectiveness of AA begs the question: what are the mechanisms which mediate the effectiveness of AA? Several recent research efforts provide fascinating and enlightening data pertaining to the operational ingredients in AA's effectiveness (see Emrick, 1999). These data indicate that the more present and active an individual's connection is with AA, the more the member uses a variety of therapeutic/adaptive processes including behavioral change processes, such as avoidance of high-risk situations and the use of active cognitive and behavioral coping strategies. AA's benefits can thereby be traced to the increased utilization of therapeutic/adaptive processes that occurs within the context of increased involvement in AA.

AA GROUP AFFILIATION VS. GROUP INVOLVEMENT

Given that AA's therapeutic benefits are awarded most to those individuals who become actively involved in the organization, reflecting the axiom that "you get out of it only what you put into it," researchers and health care providers need to take into account an individual's degree of participation in AA when assessing that person's responses to the organization. Practitioners and researchers may find it helpful to avail themselves of one or more instruments that have been developed for arriving at a quantitative determination of the degree to which their patients/subjects are actively involved in AA. A number of these instruments exist, most notably those developed by Tonigan, Connors & Miller (1996), and Humphreys, Kaskutas & Weisner (1998). Researchers are encouraged to develop similar instruments for determining the degree of involvement in other mutual aid groups.

FACILITATION OF INVOLVEMENT IN AA AND OTHER MUTUAL AID GROUPS

Since AA and other mutual aid groups can be a vital resource in the recovery of individuals from alcohol abuse and dependence, health care practitioners need to prepare their clients for participation in these organizations. Empirical support for this suggestion comes from two recent major research efforts, both of which show that 12-step-orientated treatment results in a higher percentage of patients involving themselves in 12-step groups and that this involvement, in turn, produces higher abstinence rates (Project MATCH Research Group, 1998; Humphreys et al., 1999).

To be successful in their efforts, professionals need to have an accurate understanding of the philosophy of each mutual aid group. If AA is the target of attention, for example, practitioners need to understand that AA is *not*, according to Miller & Kurtz (1994), an organization that asserts that:

> (1) There is only one form of alcoholism or alcohol problem; (2) moderate drinking is impossible for everyone with alcohol problems; (3) alcoholics should be labeled, confronted aggressively or coerced into treatment; (4) alcoholics are riddled with denial and other defense mechanisms; (5) alcoholism is purely a physical disorder; (6) alcoholism is hereditary; (7) there is only one way to recover; or (8) alcoholics are not responsible for their condition or actions (p. 165).

Practitioners can also assist their patients in becoming beneficially involved in AA and other mutual aid groups by offering basic instruction concerning the structure and therapeutic processes of the mutual aid group at issue. If AA is the focus of attention, health care professionals may facilitate involvement by having contact with their patients' sponsors, encouraging individuals to pick a home group, and encouraging clients to attend AA meetings frequently (particularly at the beginning of participation).

Learning How to Integrate AA, Other Mutual Aid Groups and Professional Treatment

Health care professionals can further enhance the effective use of AA and other mutual aid groups by acquiring knowledge about how best to integrate mutual aid groups and professional treatment (see e.g. Zweben, 1995). Integration is advised because alcohol-dependent individuals who combine these two systems of care appear to have better outcomes (at least with respect to alcohol abuse) than do those who utilize only one type of help. Professionals need to learn the language and culture of AA and other mutual aid groups in order to understand where the two systems differ and where the commonalities in concepts and processes exist. For example, both systems facilitate the development of cognitive and behavioral change processes; only the language used to foster this development differs. By possessing a working knowledge of the language and culture of both systems, health care providers can become more skilled in aiding their patients' use of both forms of help, simultaneously, alternately or sequentially. As recent research data suggest, the most effective way to promote use of both types of care is to fashion a professional treatment approach that is consonant with that found in the mutual aid group environment (Humphreys et al., 1999).

Even when focusing on mutual aid groups alone, health care professionals should keep in mind that patients may benefit from the language and culture of one mutual aid group more than another. Still other patients may find a combinatorial approach most helpful. That is, they may derive greatest benefit from attending AA along with another mutual aid group. Consistent with this consideration, Kaskutus (1996) found that about one-third of the members of Women for Sobriety attended AA concurrently with WFS involvement. Likewise, Connor & Dermen (1996) found that 35% of the members of SOS attended AA along with SOS.

Tailoring Facilitation Efforts to Specific Groups

Professionals may enhance their referral effectiveness by becoming familiar with the unique characteristics of specific groups within a mutual aid organization. This recommendation is based on the fact that heterogeneity has been found across different groups within AA (see, e.g. Montgomery, Miller & Tonigan, 1993). Because of such heterogeneity, a patient may find one particular group within a mutual aid organization to be compatible with individual needs, while other groups may be inappropriate. Helping patients understand the heterogeneity of groups and, therefore, the need to attend several groups before deciding which one(s) best fit(s), is a service health care providers are encouraged to offer.

Becoming Knowledgeable about Special Population Considerations

Recent reports identify points of consideration (as well as, in some case, guidelines) for facilitating AA involvement among individuals with special characteristics, viz. veterans with PTSD, lesbians, adolescents, persons with dual disorders, women, non-affiliative substance abusers, and individuals within a particular ethnic group (see Emrick, 1999). Health care providers need to become knowledgeable about, and sensitive to, these special population issues in order to be effective maximally in facilitating AA group involvement among their patients. Obviously, similar attention to special population considerations must be given with regard to other mutual aid groups as well.

Matching Patients to AA and Other Mutual Aid Groups

An intuitively appealing, although practically difficult, approach to facilitating the utilization and effectiveness of AA and other mutual aid groups is that of finding appropriate matches for these groups. Results from Project MATCH, a major, multi-site study conducted in the USA, suggest three matching strategies health care providers might keep in mind when considering a referral to AA:

1. For drinkers who have a social support system that is supportive of drinking (particularly by having frequent contact with frequent drinkers), facilitating participation in AA (through Twelve-Step Facilitation Therapy) appears to result in better drinking outcome than does trying to motivate the individual to give up drinking (through Motivational Enhancement Therapy) or providing treatment based on cognitive-behavioral theory (i.e. Cognitive Behavioral Coping Skills Therapy) (Project MATCH Research Group, 1998; Longabaugh et al., 1998; Zywiak et al., 2002).
2. Alcohol-dependent individuals who are angry at the start of treatment may benefit more from a non-confrontational approach to acquire motivation to change their drinking behavior (i.e. Motivational Enhancement Therapy) than from treatment that encourages them to attend AA (i.e. Twelve-Step Facilitation Therapy) or from cognitive-behavioral treatment (Project MATCH Research Group, 1998).
3. Those inpatients who have relatively high dependence on alcohol may benefit more from a 12-step-group orientated aftercare treatment than from treatment based on cognitive-behavioral theory (Project MATCH Research Group, 1997).

An intriguing addendum to these matching strategies is found in a publication by Winzelberg & Humphreys (1999). In their study of 3018 male substance abusing inpatients, clients who were low in religious behaviors were less likely to be referred to a 12-step mutual aid group. However, such individuals had a favorable response to 12-step-group referrals and subsequently experienced better substance abuse outcome. It appears, therefore, that health care providers should not be wary of encouraging their less religious clients to get involved in 12-step groups. As Winzelberg & Humphreys state, ". . . a non-religious patient may benefit from referral to AA or NA more than either the clinician or the patient expects" (p. 794).

Although not of the stature of a proposed matching strategy, another Project MATCH finding merits notation. Problem drinkers treated in residential settings who were strong in seeking meaning in life had better drinking outcome, at least for a period of time, when they were given aftercare treatment that was orientated toward AA participation rather than comparison aftercare treatments (Tonigan, Miller & Connors, 1997b). Because this finding is quite tentative, further research needs to be undertaken before the "meaning in life" variable can serve as a guide in making clinical decisions. Nonetheless, clinicians are encouraged to be sensitive to the interplay between a patient's search for meaning in life and the treatment that patient receives.

MATCHING AA MEMBERS TO
ROFESSIONAL TREATMENT

How are health care providers to approach their patients who have been involved previously in AA but who are now seeking the services of a professional? Does prior AA involvement affect what type of treatment will be most helpful? Again, Project MATCH data offer us a suggestion (Tonigan, Miller & Connors, 1997a). It appears that for outpatients who have been involved in AA prior to professional treatment, encouraging them through Twelve-Step Facilitation Therapy to resume or maintain involvement in AA offers a more compatible approach than does offering Motivational Enhancement Therapy or therapy based on cognitive-behavioral theory.

Matching strategies along these lines may be identified for other mutual aid groups should researchers and clinicians undertake collaborative efforts to mine these groups for relevant data.

AA AND OTHER MUTUAL AID GROUPS ARE NOT
ALWAYS HELPFUL

The health care practitioner must ever keep in mind that any intervention possesses the potential to harm people if it also holds the power to help some people. Should a health care provider assume that AA or another mutual aid organization "can't hurt", he/she may fail to intervene appropriately if a client/patient claims to be worsening through his/her involvement in a mutual aid community.

If health care practitioners assess that a mutual aid group is having iatrogenic effects for a patient, they need to work with that patient to reverse such effects. One obvious corrective course is to assist the patient in finding alternative treatments. To insist on a patient's continued attendance at a particular mutual aid group when the patient is being harmed by such attendance is equivalent to instructing a patient to stay on medication that is not only failing to improve that patient's condition but is also causing harmful side-effects. Good medical and other professional practice proscribes such behavior.

CONCLUSION

This chapter has covered a wide spectrum of issues concerning AA and other mutual aid groups. Information has been presented regarding the historical development of AA and other mutual aid groups: the philosophy, structure and therapeutic processes of AA and other mutual help groups; the demographics of mutual aid group membership; the degree to which AA and other mutual aid groups are being used; the effectiveness of AA; the distinction between mere attendance at mutual aid group meetings and active involvement in a mutual aid community; ways to enhance the utilization of mutual aid groups; referral of AA-involved patients to appropriate professional treatment; and the limits of AA and other mutual aid groups.

In this author's opinion, a virtual explosion of new understandings concerning AA and other mutual aid groups has arisen from the research reviewed in this chapter. Health care providers, armed with considerably greater knowledge than ever before about AA and other mutual aid groups, can now offer their patients even wiser counsel regarding such groups.

ACKNOWLEDGEMENTS

The author is very indebted to Nancy Moore, who not only brought her expert computer and editing skills to the preparation of the manuscript, but also provided invaluable support and encouragement throughout the project. Through Scott Tonigan PhD, I was guided to the most significant current research activity pertaining to AA. His scholarly, compassionate support is deeply valued.

KEY WORKS AND SUGGESTIONS FOR FURTHER READING

Alcoholics Anonymous World Services Inc. (1976). *Alcoholics Anonymous: The Story of How Many Thousands of Men and Women Have Recovered from Alcoholism*, 3rd edn. New York: Alcoholics Anonymous World Services, Inc.

This book is known in AA as "*The Big Book*". Functioning as "The Bible" of AA, it presents a conceptual model of alcoholism, details the method of recovery that AA members are to follow, offers advice to spouses and employers of alcoholics, gives guidance on how to re-establish family relationships after the cessation of drinking, and presents the stories of a number of individuals who have experienced recovery through the fellowship of AA.

Alcoholics Anonymous World Services (1986). *12 + 12: Twelve Steps and Twelve Traditions*. New York: Alcoholics Anonymous World Services.

This book, written by Bill Wilson, a co-founder of AA, presents a codification of the organizational principles and practices of AA. Anyone wishing to understand how AA operates and the principles underlying its activities must read this book.

Kurtz, E. (1979). *Not-God: A History of Alcoholics Anonymous*. Center City, MN: Hazelden Educational Materials.

Written by an historian of American civilization, this is an authoritative account of the philosophical and social development of AA within the contexts of American history and the history of religious ideas. This is a must read for anyone who wishes to acquire a profound understanding of the history and philosophy of AA.

Mäkelä, K. et al. (1996). *Alcoholics Anonymous as a Mutual-help Movement: A Study in Eight Societies*. Madison, WI: University of Wisconsin Press, 1996.

This book is a report of the International Collaborative Study of Alcoholics Anonymous that investigated AA in eight countries. The purpose of the investigation was to analyze AA as an international mutual aid movement that is adaptive to cultural context. A history of the organization, including its expansion internationally, precedes an analysis of AA from the conceptual frameworks of AA as a social movement and social network, AA as a belief system, and AA as a system of interaction. Also addressed are AA's relationship to professional treatment and other alcohol-focused mutual help movements, as well as the application of the Twelve Steps of AA to problems other than alcohol.

McCrady, B.S. & Miller, W.R. (1993). *Research on Alcoholics Anonymous: Opportunities and Alternatives*. New Brunswick, NJ: Rutgers Center of Alcohol Studies.

This volume contains the papers presented at a 1992 conference of scholars and scientists who focused on the current state of knowledge about AA and explored issues concerning future research on AA. Included in this book are papers on how change occurs in AA, the contexts of this change, how change among AA members can be measured, and how studies of AA can be designed. This books contains an extensive appendix that details the responses of conference participants to 10 questions concerning future research on AA.

Project MATCH Research Group (1998). Matching alcoholism treatments to client heterogeneity: Project MATCH three-year drinking outcomes. *Alcoholism: Clinical and Experimental Research*, **22**, 1300–1311.

This article reports data from Project MATCH, a monumental clinical trial conducted in the USA that sought to identify possible optimal matches between client intake characteristics and types of treatments. This particular paper presents the analysis of data collected at 3 year follow-up and can serve as a door to numerous other publications that have emerged from this clinical trial. Given that one of the treatments investigated in Project MATCH targets the facilitation of AA involvement as its main goal, this project is highly relevant to the issue of how professional treatment relates to AA attendance and affiliation.

Room, R. (1998). Mutual help movements for alcohol problems in an international perspective. *Addiction Research*, **6**, 131–145.

This article adumbrates the historical development of AA and other mutual aid groups for alcohol-troubled individuals throughout the world. Informative differentiations among the groups are made with respect to organizational structure, principles and practices; the philosophical underpinnings of the groups; and the basis of group membership.

Symposium (1999). A comparative evaluation of substance abuse treatment. *Alcoholism: Clinical and Experimental Research*, **23**, 528–572.

This series of papers reports the findings of a major prospective naturalistic study of US male veterans following inpatient treatment for substance abuse. The results of this investigation strongly demonstrate the effectiveness of AA participation during aftercare, at least for the sample studied. Also receiving empirical support is the contribution to good outcome made by the delivery of professional treatment that is conceptually consistent with AA.

REFERENCES

Alcoholics Anonymous World Services (1976). *Alcoholics Anonymous: The Story of How Many Thousands of Men and Women have Recovered from Alcoholism*, 3rd edn. New York: Alcoholics Anonymous World Services.

Alcoholics Anonymous World Services (1986). *12 + 12: Twelve Steps and Twelve Traditions*. New York: Alcoholics Anonymous World Services.

Connors, G.J. & Dermen, K.H. (1996). Characteristics of participants in Secular Organizations for Sobriety (SOS). *American Journal of Drug and Alcohol Abuse*, **22**, 281–295.

Emrick, C.D. (1999). Alcoholics Anonymous and other 12-step groups. In M. Galanter & H.D. Kleber (Eds), *Textbook of Substance Abuse Treatment*, 2nd edn (pp. 403–411). Washington, DC: American Psychiatric Press.

Emrick, C.D., Lassen, C.L. & Edwards, M.T. (1977). Non-professional peers as therapeutic agents. In A.S. Gurman & A.M. Razin (Eds), *Effective Psychotherapy: A Handbook of Research* (pp. 120–161). Oxford: Pergamon.

Emrick, C.D., Tonigan, J.S., Montgomery, H. & Little, L. (1993). Alcoholics Anonymous: what is currently known? In B.S. McCrady & W.R. Miller (Eds), *Research on Alcoholics Anonymous: Opportunities and Alternatives* (pp. 41–76). New Brunswick, NJ: Rutgers Center of Alcohol Studies.

Finney, J.W., Moos, R.H. & Humphreys, K. (1999). A comparative evaluation of substance abuse treatment. II. Linking proximal outcomes of 12-step and cognitive-behavioral treatment to substance use outcomes. *Alcoholism: Clinical and Experimental Research*, **23**, 537–544.

Galanter, M., Egelko, S. & Edwards, H. (1993). Rational recovery: alternative to AA for addiction? *American Journal of Drug and Alcohol Abuse*, **19**, 499–510.

Hasin, D.S. (1994). Treatment/self-help for alcohol-related problems: relationship to social pressure and alcohol dependence. *Journal of Studies on Alcohol*, **55**, 660–666.

Hasin, D.S. & Grant, B.F. (1995). AA and other help-seeking for alcohol problems: former drinkers in the US general population. *Journal of Substance Abuse*, **7**, 281–292.

Humphreys, K., Kaskutas, L.A. & Weisner, C. (1998). The Alcoholics Anonymous Affiliation Scale: development, reliability, and norms for diverse treated and untreated populations. *Alcoholism: Clinical and Experimental Research*, **22**, 974–978.

Humphreys, K. & Moos, R.H. (1996). Reduced substance-abuse-related health care costs among voluntary participants in Alcoholics Anonymous. *Psychiatric Services*, **47**, 709–713.

Humphreys, K., Moos, R.H. & Cohen, C. (1997). Social and community resources and long-term recovery from treated and untreated alcoholism. *Journal of Studies on Alcohol*, **58**, 231–238.

Humphreys, K., Huebsch, P.D., Finney, J.W. & Moos, R.H. (1999). A comparative evaluation of substance abuse treatment: V. Substance abuse treatment can enhance the effectiveness of self-help groups. *Alcoholism: Clinical and Experimental Research*, **23**, 558–563.

Kasl, C.D. (1992). *Many Roads, One Journey: Moving Beyond the Twelve Steps*. New York: HarperCollins.

Kaskutus, L.A. (1996). Pathways to self-help among Women for Sobriety. *American Journal of Drug Alcohol Abuse*, **22**, 259–280.

Kishline, A. (1994). *Moderate Drinking: The Moderation Management Guide for People Who Want to Reduce Their Drinking*. New York: Three Rivers Press.

Kurtz, E. (1979). *Not-God: A History of Alcoholics Anonymous*. Center City, MN: Hazelden Educational Materials.

Longabaugh, R., Wirtz, P.W., Zweben, A. & Stout, R.L. (1998). Network support for drinking, Alcoholics Anonymous and long-term matching effects. *Addiction*, **93**, 1313–1333.

Mäkelä, K., Arminen, I., Bloomfield, K. et al. (1996). *Alcoholics Anonymous as a Mutual Help Movement: A Study in Eight Societies*. Madison, WI: University of Wisconsin Press.

McCrady, B.S. & Miller, W.R. (Eds) (1993). *Research on Alcoholics Anonymous: Opportunities and Alternatives*. New Brunswick, NJ: Rutgers Center of Alcohol Studies.

Miller, W.R. & Kurtz, E. (1994). Models of alcoholism used in treatment: contrasting AA and other perspectives with which it is often confused. *Journal of Studies on Alcohol*, **55**, 159–166.

Montgomery, H.A., Miller, W.R. & Tonigan, J.S. (1993). Differences among AA groups: implications for research. *Journal of Studies on Alcohol*, **54**, 502–504.

Moos, R.H., Finney, J.W., Ouimette, P.C. & Suchinsky, R.T. (1999). A comparative evaluation of substance abuse treatment: I. Treatment orientation, amount of care, and 1-year outcomes. *Alcoholism: Clinical and Experimental Research*, **23**, 529–536.

Ouimette, P.C., Moos, R.H. & Finney, J.W. (1998). Influence of outpatient treatment and 12-step group involvement on one-year substance abuse treatment outcomes. *Journal of Studies on Alcohol*, **59**, 513–522.

Ouimette, P.C., Gima, K., Moos, R.H. & Finney, J.W. (1999). A comparative evaluation of substance abuse treatment. IV. The effect of comorbid psychiatric diagnoses on amount of treatment, continuing care, and 1-year outcomes. *Alcoholism: Clinical and Experimental Research*, **23**, 552–557.

Project MATCH Research Group (1997). Project MATCH secondary *a priori* hypotheses. *Addiction*, **92**, 1671–1698.

Project MATCH Research Group (1998). Matching alcoholism treatments to client heterogeneity: Project MATCH three-year drinking outcomes. *Alcoholism: Clinical and Experimental Research*, **22**, 1300–1311.

Room, R. (1998). Mutual help movements for alcohol problems in an international perspective. *Addiction Research*, **6**, 131–145.

Tonigan, J.S., Connors, G.J. & Miller, W.R. (1996). Alcoholics Anonymous Involvement (AAI) scale: reliability and norms. *Psychology of Addictive Behavior*, **10**, 75–80.

Tonigan, J.S., Miller. W.R. & Connors, G.J. (1997a). *Prior Alcoholics Anonymous Involvement and Treatment Outcome: Matching Findings and Causal Chain Analyses*, Vol. 8. Project MATCH Monograph. Bethesda, MD: NIAAA.

Tonigan, J.S., Miller, W.R. & Connors, G.J. (1997b). *The Search for Meaning in Life as a Predictor of Treatment Outcome*, Vol. 8. Project MATCH Monograph. Bethesda, MD: NIAAA.

Trimpey, J. (1996). *Rational Recovery: The New Cure for Substance Addiction*. New York: Pocket Books.

Winzelberg, A. & Humphreys, K. (1999). Should patients' religiosity influence clinicians' referral to 12-step self-help groups? Evidence from a study of 3018 male substance abuse patients. *Journal of Consulting and Clinical Psychology*, **67**, 790–794.

Zweben, J.E. (1995). Integrating psychotherapy and 12-step approaches. In A.M. Washton (Ed.), *Psychotherapy and Substance Abuse: A Practitioner's Handbook* (pp. 124–140). New York: Guilford.

Zywiak, W.H., Longabaugh, R. & Wirtz, P.W. (2002). Decomposing the relationships between pretreatment social network characteristics and alcohol treatment outcome. *Journal of Studies on Alcohol*, **63**, 114–121.

APPENDIX

The Twelve Steps of Alcoholics Anonymous

1.   We admitted we were powerless over alcohol—that our lives had become unmanageable.
2.   Came to believe that a Power greater than ourselves could restore us to sanity.
3.   Made a decision to turn our will and our lives over to the care of God *as we understood Him*.
4.   Made a searching and fearless moral inventory of ourselves.
5.   Admitted to God, to ourselves and to another human being the exact nature of our wrongs.
6.   Were entirely ready to have God remove all these defects of character.
7.   Humbly asked Him to remove our shortcomings.
8.   Made a list of all persons we had harmed, and became willing to make amends to them all.
9.   Made direct amends to such people wherever possible, except when to do so would injure them or others.
10. Continued to take personal inventory and when we were wrong promptly admitted it.
11. Sought through prayer and meditation to improve our conscious contact with God, *as we understood Him*, praying only for knowledge of His will for us and the power to carry that out.
12. Having had a spiritual awakening as the result of these steps, we tried to carry this message to alcoholics, and to practice these principles in all our affairs.

The Twelve Traditions of Alcoholics Anonymous

1.   Our common welfare should come first; personal recovery depends upon AA unity.
2.   For our group purpose, there is but one ultimate authority—a loving God as He may express Himself in our group conscience. Our leaders are but trusted servants; they do not govern.
3.   The only requirement for AA membership is a desire to stop drinking.
4.   Each group should be autonomous except in matters affecting other groups or AA as a whole.
5.   Each group has but one primary purpose—to carry its message to the alcoholic who still suffers.
6.   An AA group ought never endorse, finance or lend the AA name to any related facility or outside enterprise, lest problems of money, property and prestige divert us from our primary purpose.
7.   Every AA group ought to be fully self-supporting, declining outside contributions.
8.   Alcoholics Anonymous should remain forever non-professional, but our service centers may employ special workers.

9. AA, as such, ought never be organized; but we may create service boards or committees directly responsible to those they serve.
10. Alcoholics Anonymous has no opinion on outside issues; hence the AA name ought never be drawn into public controversy.
11. Our public relations policy is based on attraction rather than promotion; we need always maintain personal anonymity at the level of press, radio and films.
12. Anonymity is the spiritual foundation of all our traditions, ever reminding us to place principles before personalities.

The Twelve Steps and Twelve Traditions are reprinted with permission of Alcoholics Anonymous World Services Inc. Permission to reprint the Twelve Steps and Twelve Traditions does not mean that AA has reviewed or approved the contents of this publication, nor that AA agrees with the views expressed herein. AA is a program of recovery for alcoholism *only*—use of the Twelve Steps and Twelve Traditions in connection with programs and activities which are patterned after AA, but which address other problems, or in any other non-AA context, does not imply otherwise.

Part II

Prevention of Alcohol Problems

Edited by Tim Stockwell
National Drug Research Institute, Curtin
University of Technology, Perth, Australia

EDITOR'S INTRODUCTION

A significant development in the field of alcohol prevention towards the end of the twentieth century was the gradual emergence in some quarters of "harm minimization" as a guiding principle. This term has its origins in relation to the prevention of blood-borne viruses and overdoses associated with the illegal use of injectable drugs, mostly opiates (Midford & Lenton, 1996). It refers to the impact of a range of strategies that can reduce the risk of death and illness to injecting drug users. Harm minimization for illicit drugs is politically unacceptable in some countries, being associated, rightly or wrongly, with "going soft" on drug users and with attempts to legalize drugs. There is growing acceptance of the term in relation to the prevention of alcohol problems where, in most countries, there is no question other than that alcohol will continue to be widely available and used by the majority of the population (Plant, Single & Stockwell, 1997). Even as applied to alcohol, however, the term is still controversial and some of the contributors to the following chapters would probably distance themselves from it on the grounds that it may be mistaken for "going soft" on alcohol availability.

Harm minimization for alcohol problems is best characterized as the development of specific evidence-based strategies that reduce the occurrence of serious harms *without necessarily* requiring abstinence or reducing overall alcohol consumption. Examples of harm minimization strategies will be presented here which do not require a reduction in consumption to be effective, e.g. the introduction of non-breakable glassware at potentially violent drinking places. Most harm minimization strategies, however, do require a degree of reduction in alcohol consumption, at least in some high-risk situations, e.g. before driving a motor vehicle or operating machinery.

Harm minimization is sometimes seen as an alternative perspective to the total consumption approach, which has dominated alcohol policy for three decades (Bruun et al., 1975; Edwards et al., 1994). This refers to the policy goal of reducing the total consumption of a population as a means for reducing related problems. This position is discussed in detail in the first two chapters of this section and a number of practical and scientific difficulties are identified. For example, at what point does one stop reducing both availability and consumption? The total consumption approach alone gives no guidance regarding what are optimal levels, providing instead the somewhat open-ended principle that "less is best". Harm minimization principles can be applied alongside efforts to control population consumption, but the fundamental goal must remain as to whether harm is minimized and whether the means to achieve this are broadly acceptable and non-discriminatory.

Increasing the price of alcohol by raising taxes is the classic case of an effective but unpopular and even politically dangerous strategy. The opening chapter of this section (Österberg, Chapter 12) describes how studies from numerous countries using data from several decades have in almost every instance shown that alcohol behaves like most other commodities in that its consumption is negatively responsive to price. It is known that beer consumption is less responsive to price changes than is consumption of wine and spirits but, nonetheless, an increase in the price of beer is almost invariably associated with a decrease in its consumption. Naturally, the extent of this responsiveness (referred to by economists as "elasticity") varies across place and time, reflecting as it does the varying nature of both supply and demand for alcohol in different parts of the world. There is evidence for example that, when the physical availability of alcohol is tightly regulated, consumption is less responsive to price changes. It is known that price elasticities also vary for different types of drinker (e.g. people who drink less tend to be less affected by price changes) and for different types of beverage. As well as the net or average price of alcoholic drinks, it becomes critical also for public health and safety to consider the distribution of alcohol taxes across different beverages. Among the thousands of alcoholic beverages available in developed markets (e.g. Ponicki et al., 1995), there are usually a few that occupy the basement in terms of quality but not alcohol content. These can be preferentially selected by high-risk drinkers and greatly limit the benefits from across-the-board price increases (e.g. Stockwell et al., 1998). It is arguable, therefore, that redistributing alcohol taxes, rather than simply increasing them, can have public health benefits. It is also clear, however, that studies reviewed in this section show a direct link between changes in alcohol taxes and in serious alcohol-related harms without needing to invoke the idea of controlling total consumption.

The second chapter (Stockwell & Gruenewald, Chapter 13) in this section extends the concept of alcohol's availability beyond its economic accessibility. The "effective" price of alcohol includes such aspects of physical availability as convenience, e.g. in terms of distance travelled or time taken to purchase alcohol in a given locality. It is clear that while dramatic changes in both physical and economic availability can result in dramatic changes in national levels of harm, local factors can modify these consequences in important ways. If a drinker lives close by an area in which large numbers of premises compete for custom by offering heavily discounted drink at certain times ("happy hours"), then even a 20% increase in alcohol taxes may make little difference to their drinking patterns. The elucidation of the effects of changes in physical availability at the local level (principally the density of liquor outlets, the hours and days of trading) is a demanding analytic task. The places where people live, purchase alcohol, drink it and then (on occasion) experience serious alcohol-related harm are usually overlapping and often quite separate. Population-level studies to examine the impacts of changes in physical availability need to be mindful of the effects of such local factors as traffic flows and the socioeconomic profiles of adjoining neighbourhoods. Despite these complexities, a strong case can be made for utilizing local and regional controls on the physical availability of alcohol to limit alcohol-related harm. Other local factors though need to be taken into account if this knowledge is to be operationalized into effective local policy—and more research is required to facilitate that process.

It is easy to be lured into imagining a world in which wise, evidence-based and benevolent regulation of alcohol markets occurs so that price, outlet density, trading hours and serving practices are all arranged so that alcohol-related harm is minimized. This, of course, happens only in dreamland. Regulators have to be mindful of consumers' demands for reasonable access to alcohol, which plays an important part in the leisure time of a great part of the voting public in many societies. They must also be mindful of the livelihoods of the many people working in the different sectors of the manufacture and sale of alcohol. Dramatic changes in alcohol policies can even lose elections, may result in substantial job losses and usually result in an upsurge of illegal supplies. The issue then comes down to how best to develop an effective system of alcohol regulation at the national and local level that facilitates pleasurable low-risk use, minimizes harm to health and sustains a major industry. Chapter 14 (Homel, McIlwain & Carvolth) provides a penetrating analysis of the ways in which regulatory systems, local communities and alcohol suppliers can (but often fail to) create safer drinking environments. Numerous evidence-based strategies are outlined for creating lower-risk environments, ranging from safer glassware and more peaceable security staff to more proactive local police. The importance of local politics, as both the medium through which effective community action can occur and as an obstacle to its sustained implementation, is made starkly evident. The glare of public scrutiny on these matters is only intense when local people and businesses are being badly inconvenienced. Effective regulation of licensed premises to minimize violence is rarely a high priority for local regulators.

Drink–driving countermeasures are reviewed in Chapter 15 (McKnight & Voas). In alcohol prevention these stand out as rare examples where scientific evidence and popular opinion are as one. Measures such as rigorously implemented random breath testing and low blood-alcohol levels for drivers are demonstrably effective in saving lives and are highly publicly acceptable in those countries where they have been implemented. As a specific, evidence-based set of measures that reduce alcohol-related harm without reducing the availability or total consumption of alcohol, drink–driving prevention is an example *par excellence* of harm minimization in practice. The necessity of drink–driving countermeasures is usually well understood by communities; the potential harms are serious and can impact on all road users, while the intervention itself is applied without fear or favour in a way that only minimally inconveniences drivers with a legal blood alcohol limit. Other local prevention initiatives are not so readily accepted. Treno & Holder (Chapter 16) analyse six successful examples of community action to reduce alcohol-related problems in order to identify the ingredients of success. It is useful to consider this chapter in combination with the others from this section, where evidence for specific types of strategies (controls on price, availability, situational risk factors and so on) is summarized. Treno & Holder largely focus on the processes that seem to be successful in mobilizing a community to engage in evidence-based community action on alcohol. It is not enough to know what can work but also how to get it to happen (this simple truth also applies at the national policy level).

The last three chapters deal in different ways with the more subjective issues around the communication of alcohol's effects, both positive and negative. Midford & McBride (Chapter 17) provide a distinctly harm minimization-based analysis of school-based alcohol education. They overview the somewhat patchy results from alcohol education efforts in general and arrive at a set of well-documented principles to underpin more effective approaches in the future. In particular, they caution against an unrealistic goal of total abstinence in favour of providing advice to children on low-risk drinking—in terms of both how much to drink and coping strategies to reduce the risk of negative consequences, e.g. unwanted pregnancies, being driven by a drunk driver. Promising early results are outlined from a harm minimization approach to alcohol prevention in schools. Chapters 18 (Boots & Midford) and 19 (Hill & Casswell) deal with the issues of public communications about alcohol: the first from public health proponents intending to reduce consumption and/or harm, the second from the alcohol industry to increase sales through advertising and sponsorship. Boots & Midford identify media advocacy as a key strategy for public health activists to influence public and political debates about alcohol and its control. In a complementary way, Hill and Casswell review the evidence for a relationship between total and high-risk alcohol use and alcohol promotions. It is clear that associations can be shown such that young people who are more aware of alcohol promotions are more likely to go on to drink in a high-risk fashion. However, associations can always be explained away if one is determined to be sceptical. A safe and rational position at this point of time is to suppose that all public messages and information influence the overall context with alcohol is consumed, the effects of alcohol are understood and alcohol prevention policies are implemented—or neglected.

While good science must continue in the field of alcohol prevention, it is also clear that little progress in the implementation of effective strategies will be achieved unless public awareness of the issues is high and, in turn, impacts on the making of local, regional and public policy. Public health advocacy on alcohol-related harm is vital if prevention strategies are to happen. As recommended in Chapter 13, there is an important role to be played in the dissemination of accurate local, regional and national data on high-risk alcohol consumption and serious alcohol-related harms (see e.g. Chikritzhs et al., 1999). A range of mutually supportive strategies is outlined in this section, which can be understood within the framework of harm minimization. It is suggested here and elsewhere (e.g. Plant et al.,

1997) that harm minimization is an optimal stance for public health advocacy on the need for specific and effective strategies to reduce serious alcohol-related harms.

REFERENCES

Bruun, K., Edwards, G., Lumio, M., Mäkelä, K., Pan, L., Popham, R.E., Room, R., Schmidt, W., Skog, O.-J., Sulkunen, P. & Österberg, E. (1975). *Alcohol Control Policies in Public Health Perspective.* Helsinki: Finnish Foundation for Alcohol Studies.

Chikritzhs, T., Jonas, H., Heale, P., Dietze, P., Hanlin, K. & Stockwell, T. (1999). *Alcohol-caused Deaths and Hospitalisations in Australia, 1990–1997.* National Alcohol Indicators, Bulletin No. 1. Perth, Western Australia: National Drug Research Institute, Curtin University of Technology.

Edwards, G., Anderson, P., Babor, T.F., Casswell, S., Ferrence, R., Giesbrecht, N., Godfrey, C., Holder, H.D., Lemmens, P., Mäkelä, K., Midanik, L.T., Norström, T., Österberg, E., Romelsjö, A., Room, R., Simpura, J. & Skog, O.-J. (1994). *Alcohol Policy and the Public Good.* New York: Oxford University Press.

Midford, R. & Lenton, S. (1996). Clarifying "harm reduction"? *Drug & Alcohol Review,* **15**, 411–414.

Plant, M., Single, E. & Stockwell, T. (1997). *Alcohol: Minimising the Harm. What Works?* London: Free Association Books.

Ponicki, W., Holder, H., Gruenewald, P. & Romelsjo, A. (1995). Altering alcohol price by ethanol content: results from a Swedish tax policy in 1992. *Addiction,* **92**, 859–870.

Stockwell, T., Masters, L., Phillips, M., Daly, A., Gahegan, M., Midford, R. & Philp, A. (1998). Consumption of different alcoholic beverages as predictors of local rates of night-time assault and acute alcohol-related morbidity. *Australian & New Zealand Journal of Public Health,* **22**, 237–242.

Chapter 12

Effects of Price and Taxation

Esa Österberg
*National Research and Development Centre for Welfare and
Health, Helsinki, Finland*

Synopsis

This chapter starts with a general discussion of the role of alcohol taxation, on the one hand as a means of curbing total alcohol consumption and alcohol-related problems, and on the other hand as a means to collect revenues to the coffers of the state and/or local authorities.

Next, the effects of changes in alcohol prices on alcohol consumption and related problems are scrutinized. This means that econometric studies of effects in changes of alcohol prices on alcohol consumption are reviewed. In this connection, results of studies on both changes in alcohol prices on total alcohol consumption and the consumption of different categories of alcoholic beverages are summarized. Econometric studies looking at the relation between changes in alcohol prices and alcohol-related problems are also reviewed. In addition, studies dealing with the relationship between alcohol prices, on the one hand, and alcohol consumption and alcohol-related problems, on the other, are discussed.

Price elasticities are not inherent attributes of alcoholic beverages. Therefore, one should not expect studies relating to different regions, periods and categories of alcohol beverages to produce similar elasticity values. In the interpretation of elasticity values, the points of departure should be the social, cultural and economic circumstances affecting drinking alcohol in each country and period. This means that the factors producing certain kinds of elasticities and the factors behind the changes in elasticity values are discussed.

Alcohol taxation is one way to curb alcohol consumption and alcohol-related problems and/or to collect tax revenues. The state or local authorities can not, however, decide at will the tax burden of alcoholic beverages. Therefore this chapter also discusses the feasibility of alcohol taxation.

The sale of alcoholic beverages at prices higher than their production and distribution costs is a generally accepted custom. Quite often the purpose and rationale for special taxes on

The Essential *Handbook of Treatment and Prevention of Alcohol Problems.* Edited by N. Heather and T. Stockwell.
© 2004 John Wiley & Sons Ltd. ISBN 0-470-86296-3.

alcoholic beverages are not, however, explicitly stated. In practice, taxing alcoholic beverages has been a well-established means of raising government revenue. In some countries, alcoholic beverages have been susceptible to such taxation because of their status as luxury commodities, offering a credible justification to tax them. In some other countries, alcoholic beverages have been suitable objects for excise taxes because of their nature as an everyday commodity offering a wide tax basis, and in some countries they have been taxed because of their detrimental social and public health consequences, and the external costs they impose on the state and the society. The rationale for levying a special tax on alcoholic beverages is seldom questioned, and what discussion there is on the subject usually revolves around how expensive alcoholic beverages should be relative to other commodities, and whether taxes should vary according to the alcohol content of the beverages and to the different alcoholic beverage categories, i.e. distilled spirits, wines and beer (Bruun et al., 1972; see also Crooks, 1989; Baker & McKay, 1990; Cook & Moore, 1993a).

Taxation of alcoholic beverages has traditionally been an important source of state revenue in many countries. Between 1911 and 1917, for example, in the USA the federal revenues from alcoholic beverages each year amounted to over one-third of the total receipts from taxes levied by the government (Landis, 1952). Similar figures can also be found on the other side of the Atlantic Ocean, for instance from The Netherlands, the UK and the Nordic Countries, Denmark, Finland, Iceland, Norway and Sweden. The relative importance of alcohol taxation as a source of state income has declined in most countries during the twentieth century, particularly after the advent of modern income taxation. In many countries the share of alcohol taxes in state budgets has declined also because of decreases in alcohol tax rates both in nominal but especially in real terms. For instance, in recent decades Ireland, which amongst the Western countries has shown the highest shares of alcohol taxes of total state revenues, has experienced a clear decrease in its alcohol tax incomes in relation to total state incomes. In 1970 this share was still 16.5% but dropped to 10.4% in 1978 (Davies & Walsh, 1983). In 1996 the share was estimated to be 5.0% (Hurst et al., 1997). Despite these trends, alcohol tax revenues are still of considerable fiscal significance in many countries (Hurst et al., 1997, p. 562).

From the consumers' point of view, excise duties on alcoholic beverages are factors which are increasing prices of alcoholic beverages and sometimes putting an extra pressure on household budgets. If an increase in alcohol taxes and alcohol prices leads to a large decrease in alcohol consumption, then the share of alcohol expenditure in family budgets may also decrease. However, the dilemma for policy makers who view alcohol taxation as a means on preventing alcohol problems is worsened when higher prices on alcoholic beverages result in only a small drop in alcohol consumption and a substantial increase in household alcohol expenditure. In this case lowering the amount of alcohol that a heavy drinker consumes by increasing alcohol taxes will usually mean that his/her family will suffer greater financial hardships. This is not, however, necessarily the case. If higher alcohol taxes and prices mean people spend more money on alcoholic drinks, then the state will collect more alcohol tax revenue. And, in principle at least, this could mean that other forms of taxation will fall or, consequently, that more public services becomes available. The taxation question, then, is largely a matter of who pays excise taxes on alcohol and how these tax revenues are employed—if employed wisely, the outcome can be a greater measure of prosperity for all.

Raising prices of alcoholic beverages with special taxes or limiting alcohol availability in some other way will not only affect the drinker or the state; the alcohol industry and its employees will also be hit. Understandably, those engaged in the production and distribution of alcoholic beverages therefore feel that they must have as big a say in alcohol control policy as possible. This is particularly true in countries where the alcohol industry is fettered by stringent control measures. But even in such countries there exists a difference between the short term and the long term. Limiting the availability of alcoholic beverages may result in a number of brewery and distillery workers or wine growers losing their jobs in the short term. However, those displaced may find employment elsewhere and the long-term outcome may well be increased general prosperity (Österberg, 1982). On the other hand, there are also instances where alcoholic beverage taxes are used in support of agri-cultural, cultural or economic objectives in a country. For instance, in Australia the wine industry is exempt from excise taxes because it is considered to be a primary producing industry on which the livelihood of many small grape growers is dependent. In addition, in that country no excise tax is levied on spirits used for fortifying wine (Hurst et al., 1997). In the European Union there is a minimum excise tax rate on wine but this rate has been set to zero, because the wine industry makes a significant contribution to the domestic economy in many wine-growing EU member states.

On the other side of the coin, it can be concluded that alcohol has significant adverse effects on the physical, psychological and social health of individuals, families and com-munities throughout the world. Alcohol is a dependence-producing drug and this depend-ence is associated with an increased risk of morbidity and mortality. Moreover, alcohol is also an intoxicant and drunkenness is associated with an increased risk of injury and mor-tality, both to the drinker and to others. The adverse effects of drinking alcohol are diffuse and costly and are not confined to a minority of easily identified heavier drinkers. This is sometimes called the "preventive paradox", describing the fact that alcohol problems cannot be eliminated simply by getting rid of heavy alcohol consumers, because lighter drinkers also suffer from alcohol problems. And as the number of light drinkers is much larger than the number of heavy drinkers, their share or the total burden of alcohol prob-lems is important. The impact of alcohol on all-cause mortality is affected, amongst other things, by the prevalence of different diseases and injuries, the age structure of the popu-lation and the level of alcohol consumption at the societal level. The impact of alcohol is therefore culturally and temporally specific. At younger ages, for instance, deaths from traffic accidents and violence predominate (World Health Organization, 1995).

In research conducted at both the societal and individual level, alcohol has been found to increase the risk of death from a number of specific causes, including: injury from traffic accidents and other trauma; violence; suicide; poisonings; liver cirrhosis; cancers of the upper aerodigestive tract; cancer of the liver; breast cancer; haemorrhagic stroke; alcoholic psychosis; alcohol dependence; pancreatitis; malnutrition; neurological disorders; alco-holism; and fetal alcohol syndrome. On the other hand, alcohol consumption has been found to reduce the risk of coronary heart disease and ischaemic stroke. The reduced risk for coronary heart disease has been found at the level of one drink every second day, and there is little additional reduction of risk beyond consumption levels of about one to two drinks a day (World Health Organization, 1995).

Epidemiological data on the contribution of alcohol use to the prevalence of disease are mainly found in developed countries, with limited data available for developing countries. The best available estimates are found in *The Global Burden of Disease* (Murray & Lopez, 1996), which estimates that alcohol contributed to 3.5% of the global burden of disease and disability and 1.5% of total deaths in 1990. Alcohol is ranked fourth among the top 10 risk factors for disease and disability for men, following malnutrition, poor water supply and sanitation, and unsafe sex. The contribution of alcohol use to overall disease and disability varies greatly by region: it is highest in the established market economies (10.3%), Latin America (9.7%) and the former Soviet Union (8.3%). It is lowest in the Middle East (0.4%) and India (1.6%). Globally, alcohol is estimated to have caused about three-quarters of a million more deaths than it averted, with more than 80% of this excess mortality occurring in developing countries. The burden of social problems from drinking is mostly unmeasured, but qualitative evidence suggests it is large in the developing as well as the developed world.

Alcohol control policies, i.e. legal, economic and physical factors which bear on the availability of alcohol, seek to reduce the harmful effects of alcohol use whilst recognizing its real and perceived benefits. Across space and historical time and within the context of culturally determined value systems, administrative formulae and beliefs as to the fundamental nature of the target issues, these problems have provoked an extraordinary diversity of policy responses. A number of policies have also been demonstrated to be effective in the reduction of alcohol-related harm, amongst them excise taxes on alcoholic beverages.

ECONOMETRIC STUDIES

The effect of changes in prices of alcoholic beverages on alcohol consumption has been more extensively investigated than any other potential alcohol control measure. The most widely employed research approaches have relied on econometric methods. According to different reviews, econometric studies dealing with all alcoholic beverages or a certain category of alcoholic beverages are currently available in at least the following countries: Australia, Belgium, Canada, Denmark, Germany, Finland, France, Ireland, Italy, Kenya, The Netherlands, New Zealand, Norway, Poland, Portugal, Spain, Sweden, the UK and the USA (see Huitfeldt & Jorner, 1972; Lau, 1975; Ornstein, 1980; Ornstein & Levy, 1983; Godfrey, 1986; Olsson, 1991; Clements & Selvanathan, 1991; Yen, 1994, Edwards et al., 1994; Österberg, 1995). This list of countries also shows that our knowledge of the effects of changing alcohol prices on alcohol consumption chiefly derives from Western industrialized nations.

In econometric studies, the responsiveness or sensitivity of quantity demanded of the determinants of demand is measured by elasticity. The sensitivity of the quantity demanded to changes in prices, when other determinants remain unchanged, is called the price elasticity of demand, or own-price elasticity.

The values of price elasticities for alcoholic beverages estimated in different studies have consistently shown that when other factors remain unchanged, a rise in the price of alcoholic beverages has generally led to a drop in alcohol consumption, and that a decrease in price of alcoholic beverages has usually led to a rise in alcohol consumption. In other words, alcoholic beverages appear to behave on the market like most other commodities and in the way presupposed by the theory of consumer demand. On the other hand, in studies dealing with different geographical regions and periods, different values of income and price elasticities have been found with respect to both total alcohol consumption and the consumption of different categories of alcoholic beverages. These variations are partly due to the methods applied, the accuracy of the basic data, and the statistical factors of uncertainty relating to the elasticities. However, disparities in elasticity values also stem from differing social, cultural and economic circumstances prevailing in different regions and in different periods. Therefore, when looking at the results of different studies, it is not possible to find any general, typical or mean elasticity value for all alcoholic beverages, or even for beer, wines or spirits separately, because elasticities describing the reactions of the consumers to price increases are not inherent attributes of alcoholic beverages, but rather reflections of the prevailing drinking habits and culture.

On a very general level, it may be said that consumer preferences are linked to the benefits consumers derive from using different commodities, in this case, drinking alcoholic beverages, and consumer preferences are therefore reflected in elasticity values. When taking into account the many different uses of alcoholic beverages—as intoxicants, thirst quenchers, drinks with meals, medicines or means of recreation and enjoyment—it is not surprising that the demand for all alcoholic beverages or a certain category of alcoholic beverages may respond very differently to a certain change in price in different countries and in different periods. Therefore, the interpretation of elasticity values calls for a close examination of drinking habits and the uses to which alcoholic beverages are put in a certain society at a certain point in time.

If the demand for a given category of alcoholic beverages is price-elastic, that is, relatively sensitive to price changes, a rise in price will have a strong diminishing effect on its consumption, and decrease the share of personal disposable income allocated to that beverage category. Consequently, a decline in price will have a strong increasing effect on its consumption, and raise the share of personal disposable income allocated to that beverage category. Alcoholic beverages can also be price-inelastic, that is, relatively insensitive to price changes. In this case, a price increase would have only a small impact on the consumption of this beverage category, and increase the share of personal disposable income allocated to those beverages. A decline in price will have a relatively small positive effect on the consumption of this beverage category and decrease the share of personal disposable income allocated to those beverages. If the demand for alcoholic beverages is unit price-elastic, a rise in price will have a diminishing effect on alcohol consumption of equal proportion and keep the share of personal disposable income allocated to alcoholic beverages fairly constant. Consequently, a percentage reduction in prices increases the consumption of alcoholic beverages by the same percentage and keeps the share of personal disposable income allocated to alcoholic beverage constant.

So far, discussions of small or large effects of price on alcohol consumption in this chapter have concerend unit changes in the consumpiton of alcoholic beverages. Even in circumstances where the demand for alcoholic beverages is price-inelastic, a large absolute change in the price of alcoholic beverages will still have a larger effect on alcohol consumption than only a slight change in alcohol prices in situations where alcohol demand is price-elastic. Degree of price change as well as the value of the price elasticity must be jointly taken into account when predicting the impact of changing prices of alcoholic beverages on alcohol consumption.

The value of price elasticity denotes the way consumers have reacted to changes in prices during the study period. If alcohol prices have, for instance, fallen steadily during that period, the estimated price elasticity may not necessarily apply to a situation of increasing alcohol prices, because the assumption that elasticities are symmetrical may not be valid as far as alcoholic drinks are concerned. A symmetrical elasticity would mean that a given rise or fall in alcohol prices produces an equivalent effect in the opposite direction on consumption. However, since some people may become addicted to alcohol, it is quite possible that a rise in alcohol consumption introduced by a cut in prices would not be checked by an equivalent increase in alcohol prices (Bruun et al., 1975).

EFFECTS OF CHANGING PRICES ON CONSUMPTION

There are great differences between countries in the way alcohol consumers have reacted to changes in prices of alcoholic beverages (see Edwards et al., 1994, pp. 112–114). This is something that is to be expected because of the differences in drinking habits between countries. But, to make it more difficult, even the results of economic studies dealing with one and the same country do not present a very clear picture. For instance, in the USA estimated price elasticities for beer range from almost zero to −1.39, available estimates of price elasticities for wine range from −0.44 to −1.78, and the estimated price elasticities for distilled spirits range from 0.08 to −2.03 (Österberg, 1995, p. 149).

In a review of price elasticities for alcoholic beverages, Ornstein (1980) wanted to see whether the weight of the evidence indicated that beer, wine, and distilled spirits were price-elastic, price-inelastic or unit price-elastic, and whether they were substitutes, complements or unrelated in consumption. He also discussed the possibility of identifying a range of "true" elasticities for the USA (and Canada) by a comparison of diverse studies (Ornstein, 1980). In a later review, Ornstein & Levy (1983), using the same data as Ornstein (1980), reconsidered the range of price-elasticity estimates in the USA. After a detailed description, comparison, evaluation and discussion of 20 studies, they reported that their "summary estimates of own-price elasticities for beer, wine, and distilled spirits were −0.3, −1.0 and −1.5, respectively. These are crude at best, particularly for wines, but seem the best available" (Ornstein & Levy, 1983, p. 343; see also Leung & Phelps, 1993). In her reviews of demand models from 1989 and 1990, Godfrey (1989, 1990) discussed three alcohol demand studies in the UK as well as her own estimates and the elasticities used by the treasury in their alcohol tax revenue calculations. These figures show that in the UK the demand for beer has generally been price-inelastic (i.e. a given percentage change in the price of beer produces a smaller percentage change in demand for beer, not that demand is unresponsive to price changes) and the demand for wines and spirits has been more responsive to prices than beer (Godfrey, 1989). Later studies accord with this interpretation (see Österberg, 1995, p. 150).

It has been argued that alcohol control measures other than taxes and prices affect the values of price elasticities. This argument seems to be reasonable, since lifting of other alcohol control measures gives alcohol prices more regulative power. In Sweden, Huitfeldt & Jorner (1972) have shown that lifting the "motbok" connected with the Bratt rationing system—where the possibility of buying distilled spirits in Sweden was individually regulated until 1955—in fact led to a rise in the value of the price elasticity for distilled spirits. It can, therefore, be argued that the more restricted the availability of alcoholic beverages, the smaller is the influence of a unit change in prices of alcoholic beverages on alcohol consumption (Huitfeldt & Jorner, 1972).

In Finland, Ahtola, Ekholm & Somervuori (1986) studied the changes in the values of price elasticities for alcoholic beverages for the period 1955–1980. They found that the value of price elasticities was decreasing over time and interpreted this to show that alcoholic beverages have come to be seen more and more as an everyday commodity. In the mid-1950s, the total alcohol consumption per capita in Finland was under 2 litres in terms of 100% alcohol, while at the beginning of the 1980s it was over 6 litres. These figures could also be interpreted to show that the value of price elasticity has a tendency to decrease as incomes and the standard of living rise.

Econometric studies use as their material factual changes in alcohol prices, which are normally relatively small. It can therefore be asked if they have any predictive value in cases where changes in alcohol prices are dramatic. An unusual example of the effects of radical price changes on consumption comes from Denmark. Due to food shortages during World War I, the price of Danish *akvavit* was raised more than 10 times and the price of beer was almost doubled. These drastic price increases reduced per capita consumption of alcohol by 75% within 2 years. The decrease was mostly due to the diminished consumption of distilled spirits, especially *akvavit*, and only later did the consumption of beer increase to change Denmark from a spirit-drinking country to a beer-drinking country. Not only was the total alcohol consumption affected, but also the rate of registered cases of delirium tremens declined to one-thirteenth, and deaths due to chronic alcoholism to one-sixth of their previous rates (Bruun et al., 1975).

Other examples of great price changes are not as dramatic as the Danish one. They have, however, taken place more recently. For instance, a 10% increase in the real price of alcoholic beverages in Finland in 1975 put an end to the increase in alcohol consumption that had continued in the country since the early 1960s (Salo, 1987, 1990). In Sweden, the marked increase in consumption which followed the abolition of the Bratt system in 1955 was halted and eventually reversed by radical increases in prices. In 1957 and 1958, for instance, the real price of distilled spirits went up by more than 30%. This contributed to a decline in spirits consumption from 0.8 litres per capita per month in 1956 to 0.6 litres in 1958, i.e. a decrease of one-quarter (Huitfeldt & Jorner, 1972).

EFFECTS ON DIFFERENT POPULATION GROUPS

In econometric studies based on time series data, the values of price elasticities reflect in many ways the average reactions of consumers to changes in prices. It is particularly the treatment of alcohol consumers as a group that has raised doubts about the validity of the estimated elasticity values. Although it can be inferred from econometric studies that a rise in the price of alcoholic beverages reduces alcohol consumption, it cannot be determined who the people are that have reduced their alcohol consumption and by how much. However, the use of individual data can shed light on debates that cannot be solved by using aggregate data. One good example is the disagreement about whether or not heavy drinkers are responsive to changes in prices of alcoholic beverages. This is an important issue, because in both public discussions and in the alcohol literature it is often asserted that increases in prices of alcoholic beverages will only affect light or moderate drinkers and will have no effect on heavy drinkers or problem drinkers, because they are either addicted to or physically dependent on alcohol. Consequently, unwillingness to raise prices is likely to be provoked if the effect on pricing policy is felt mainly by moderate drinkers and leaves the heavy drinkers to carry out as before.

In the early 1970s many bars, taverns and restaurants in Western countries initiated a variety of sales programmes to attract more customers. These programmes, called "happy hours", included some kind of price reduction; it might be two beverages for the price of one, a 25% reduction for all beverages, free beverages for a particular type of patron, or "all-you-can-drink" specials. Consequently, happy hours offer one possibility to study the effect of decreasing prices on alcohol consumption. In the USA, Babor et al. (1978) conducted an observational study of the drinking habits of 16 regular bar patrons, in happy hour and non-happy-hour times. Happy-hour patrons drank 9.6 drinks per day, while non-happy-hour patrons drank only 3.7 drinks, despite the fairly small reduction in drink prices during the happy hour. Furthermore, happy hour patrons engaged in more drinking sessions, which also lasted longer (Babor et al., 1978). In another experimental study, 34 men who were admitted to McLean Hospital in Boston for 30 days were studied (Babor et al., 1980). Those 34 men consisted of 14 heavy drinkers and 20 fairly light drinkers. Their patterns of drinking were tested under happy-hour or non-happy-hour conditions. As expected, both light and heavy drinkers drank more when drinks were less expensive. In the happy hour condition, light drinkers drank about twice as much and heavy drinkers about 2.4 times as much as in the non-happy-hour condition. Both light and heavy drinkers had longer episodes of drinking under happy hour conditions, but heavy drinkers also increased their short drinking episodes.

Surveys have also been used to study the effects of changing alcohol prices on alcohol consumption. In 1981 the effect of price on consumption was studied in Scotland by means of two surveys, one before and one after a rise in the price of alcoholic beverages (Kendell et al., 1983). According to this study, the impact of the price increase was strongest among the heaviest drinkers, for both men and women. Heavy drinkers also experienced the largest reduction in the number of adverse effects related to alcohol consumption. In the USA, Grossman et al. (1987) and Coate & Grossman (1988) have studied the price sensitivity of young people's demand for alcohol, using data from the National Health and Nutrition Examination Surveys, cycles I and II. Both studies conclude that youth beer consumption is inversely related to the price of beer, and that the effects of higher prices are not limited to infrequent or light drinkers. Instead, the results provide weak evidence that heavy drinkers are more sensitive to price changes than moderate drinkers (Grossman, Coate & Arluck, 1987; Coate & Grossman, 1988). A similar kind of study by Laixuthai and Chaloupka (1993) found that higher beer excise taxes significantly reduce both the frequency of youth drinking and the probability of heavy drinking. This study, like the other studies mentioned above, also implies that a tax increase will result in larger reductions amongst frequent and fairly frequent young drinkers than amongst infrequent young drinkers. Furthermore, it is interesting to note that, like some studies based on time series data, this study shows that there is an interplay between price controls and other measures affecting alcohol availability. It was shown that the price sensitivity of youth drinking fell after the legal minimum drinking age of 21 years came into force in all states (Laixuthai & Chaloupka, 1993). More recently in the USA Chaloupka and Wechsler (1996) have studied the effects of beer prices on drinking and binge drinking among students in colleges and universities, using a nationally representative sample from the year 1993. They found that price had a statistically significant effect on underage drinking and binge drinking among female students but not among male students.

PRICE CHANGES AND ALCOHOL-RELATED PROBLEMS

Seeley (1960) wrote about the relationship between the price of alcoholic beverages and death by liver cirrhosis in Ontario. He used alcohol consumption as an intermediate variable and was able to conclude that deaths from liver cirrhosis rose and fell with average alcohol consumption, and that average alcohol consumption rose and fell inversely with the price of alcoholic beverages. One development in the field in later years has been to link changes in the price of alcoholic beverages directly to alcohol-related problems. In this way one is able to get indirect evidence of the effects of price policy on heavy consumers. The other benefit of this kind of study design is that it takes care of problems caused by the possible substitution of recorded and unrecorded alcohol consumption. Furthermore, in recent studies full price instead or monetary price is often used. In this context, the full price of alcoholic beverages includes not only the monetary price of alcoholic beverages but also a wide variety of other costs of drinking and heavy drinking, such as the time costs of obtaining alcoholic beverages.

In the USA Cook (1981) adopted Simon's (1966) approach, using as a quasi-experiment the changes in state liquor excise-tax rates legislated between 1960 and 1975 in licence states. A follow-up study by Cook & Tauchen (1982) sought to improve this method while still taking advantage of the underlying quasi-experiment. They considered not only the relationship between spirit consumption and tax changes but also cirrhosis and car accidents in relation to tax changes. The Cook (1981) study discovered that states which raised their liquor tax had a greater reduction or smaller increase in cirrhosis mortality than other states in the corresponding year. In the Cook & Tauchen (1982) study the median price elasticity for liquor was −1.8 and it was concluded that liquor consumption, including that of heavy drinkers as indicated by cirrhosis mortality, is quite responsive to price and that a liquor tax increase tends to reduce the fatality rate of car accidents (see also Chaloupka et al., 1992; Sloan, Reilly & Schenzler, 1994). In addition, Sloan and his colleagues (1994) also considered the effects of changing prices of alcoholic beverages on a variety of other death rates related to alcohol use, including deaths from diseases primarily related to alcohol, motor vehicle traffic accidents, homicides, suicides, diseases where alcohol is a contributing factor, and other accidental deaths. They found that higher alcoholic beverage prices do not lead to significant reductions in deaths primarily related to alcohol.

Schweitzer, Intriligator & Salehi (1983) developed an econometric model of alcoholism that could incorporate its causes, effects and possible control. According to them, such a model should give more complete and more direct insights into the problems of alcoholism than previous demand studies. They used cross-sectional data on 35 US states in 1975 to estimate a simultaneous model of beer and spirits consumption, alcoholism, and alcohol-related mortality. According to their results, a rise in the price of spirits lowers alcoholism, but a rise in the price of beer appears to increase it.

Saffer & Grossman (1987a, b) examined the impact of beer excise taxes on youth motor vehicle fatality rates. Both studies concluded that increases in beer taxes significantly reduce youth motor vehicle fatalities. Chaloupka, Saffer & Grossman (1993) continued this research tradition. They concluded that higher beer excise taxes are among the most effective means to reduce drinking and driving in all segments of the population. More recent studies using individual data also conclude that increases in beer taxes are effective in reducing drinking and driving and involvement in non-fatal traffic accidents. For example, Kenkel (1993), using the 1985 National Health Interview Survey, estimated that a 10% increase in the price of alcoholic beverages would reduce the probability of drinking and driving by about 7% for males and 8% for females, with even larger reductions among those 21 years and under.

Several recent studies have examined the impact of the price of alcoholic beverages on homicides and other crimes and family violence. Using annual state-level data on violent crime rates, Cook & Moore (1993b) were able to conclude that higher beer taxes would lead to significant reductions in rapes and robberies but would have little impact on homicides and assaults. In an analysis of the Uniform Crime Reports data, Chaloupka & Shaffer (1992) considered the impact of beer taxes on a variety of crime rates, including total crime, violent crime, property crime, homicide, rape, assault, robbery, burglary, larceny and motor vehicle theft rates. They concluded that increases in beer taxes led to statistically significant reductions in nearly every crime rate, with the exception of the assault rate. An analysis of vital statistics data on homicide rates resulted in that higher alcoholic beverage prices would lower homicide rates (Sloan, Reilly & Schenzler, 1994). More recently, the impact of beer taxes and other alcohol control policies on domestic violence directed at children has been studied. It was estimated that there is a significant inverse relationship between child abuse and other violence towards children and the price of beer (Markowitz & Grossman, 1998).

CROSS-ELASTICITIES

In econometric analyses of demand, the estimation of cross-elasticities—i.e. of the change in demand for one type of alcoholic beverage caused by a change in the price of some other type of alcoholic beverage—has proved to be an extremely difficult task. Although the price changes in the cases studied in the Nordic countries have mostly been within a modest range, they nevertheless seem to result in some substitution of one type of beverage for another (Nyberg 1967; Huitfeldt & Jorner 1972). When discussing cross-price elasticities in North America, Ornstein (1980) finds that reported elasticities are inconsistent both within and across different studies. His overall conclusion was that consumption of each beverage category is significantly related to its own price and little affected by changes in the price of substitute alcoholic beverages (Ornstein, 1980). According to Godfrey (1989), the UK estimates of demand models based upon time series data have in general been unsuccessful in identifying the cross-substitution effects with accuracy, even in the case of close substitutes, and all cross-price elasticities found have been very small.

The cross-elasticities estimated in econometric studies may also be of little use in actual alcohol policy-making. The estimated elasticities are derived from aggregate data using average price rates. However, it has been observed in many studies that heavy consumers usually prefer the cheaper beverages in each type of alcoholic beverage. Under such circumstances, the substitution between different types of alcoholic beverage is perhaps not so much determined by changes in the average price of each type as by changes in prices of the cheapest brands in each type (Bruun et al., 1975).

Because all alcoholic beverages include ethyl alcohol, they are potential substitutes for each other. A substitution between different classes of alcoholic beverages means that alcohol is substituted by alcohol, that is, with the same substance from the public health point of view. Alcoholic beverages also serve as substitutes for other commodities and thus they can be replaced by other commodities. This means that the level of alcohol consumption is related to the prices of alcoholic beverages relative to other commodities. When discussing other commodities as substitutes for alcoholic beverages, it should be noted that the substitution process may equally well lead to either unhealthier or healthier drinking habits. A rise in wine prices may result in a substitution of commercially produced wine by soft drinks, by self-produced wine, by "moonshine" or even by drugs. Although a rise in alcohol prices can lead to a shift in consumption to illegal alcohol or drugs, it should be remembered that these types of substitution processes are affected by restrictions and limitations of those beverages or drugs to which consumers are apt to move. In all probability, the more decisive factors in these substitutions are the control measures that bear upon the availability of those substitutes, and it is scarcely conceivable that illicit traffic of alcohol could be altogether eliminated by cutting the prices of legally produced alcohol. Furthermore, if prices of legally produced alcohol are kept constant or lowered because of the possible undesirable substitution for illegal alcoholic beverages, the harmful effects of the legitimate alcohol may exceed the socially acceptable level of alcohol problems.

OVERVIEW AND DISCUSSION

This chapter has reviewed the role of alcohol taxation as a means of curbing total alcohol consumption and alcohol-related problems. In this connection, the results of studies on both changes in alcohol prices on total alcohol consumption and on the consumption of different categories of alcoholic beverages have been summarized. Also econometric and other studies looking at the relation between changes in alcohol prices and alcohol-related problems have been examined. The evidence presented in this chapter suggests that alcohol price levels do have an independent effect on the level of alcohol consumption and alcohol-related problems. Consumers of alcoholic beverages seem to be responsible for the prices of these beverages, and heavy drinkers are no exceptions of this rule. On the contrary, in many studies the impact of the price increase was strongest among the heaviest drinkers. Price elasticities are not, however, inherent attributes of alcoholic beverages. Therefore, studies relating to different regions, periods and categories of alcoholic beverages do not produce similar elasticity values. In the interpretation of elasticity values, the points of departure should be the social, cultural and economic circumstances affecting drinking alcohol in each country and period.

The rationale for levying a special tax on alcoholic beverages is seldom questioned, and what discussion there is on the subject usually revolves around how expensive alcoholic beverages should be relative to other commodities. The level of taxation varies greatly in different countries (see e.g. Hurst et al., 1997). In most countries, however, the tax counted per litre of alcohol is higher in the form of distilled spirits than in the form of beer or wine. In this context, Japan seems to be one of the rare exceptions. Wine and beer taxes are nearer each other but, at least in the industrialized countries, beer seems to be taxed, on average, a little bit harder than wine. Because beer and wine are more expensive beverages to produce than distilled spirits in terms of the alcohol content, equal tax rates per litre of alcohol would mean that ethyl alcohol would be cheaper in the form of distilled spirits than in the form of wine or beer. From an economic perspective, the principle of taxing alcoholic beverages on the basis on alcohol strength, both within each beverage category and across different beverage categories, is often held as the most effective solution, because other solutions lead to a distortion of the allocation of resources within the alcohol sector (see e.g. Baker & McKay, 1990).

Even if increases in alcohol taxes mean lower alcohol consumption and lower problem rates, it is not always easy to use alcohol taxes as an instrument of public health. For instance, Edwards et al. (1994) mention four objections to this kind of policy. First, and particularly in a developing country, a price increase imposed on commercial beverages may stimulate illicit or home production. That danger should be heeded and monitored but, as noted in this chapter, allowing commercial production to go unfettered because of this fear also carries its own risks. Second, the budgetary authorities may view the tax obtained from beverage alcohol as a valuable and easily collectable revenue, and be reluctant to impose tax increases for fear of a consequent net loss in state incomes. Only a knowledge of the elasticities that pertain in particular circumstances can answer that question, but in most situations a price increase will swell rather than depress the tax take. The third objection to taxation as a control measure is that such an approach is not socially equitable, with tax increases imposing a proportionally greater burden on the poorer segment of the population. The evidence available does not, however, totally support this contention, since alcohol taxes will in many circumstances impose a lower relative burden on low-income groups than most other commodity taxes. The fourth point to be considered is that the efficacy of fiscal control may, in some circumstances, be eroded where borders are long or open. That speaks to the need for a strong voice to be given to health advocacy at the international level when trade and customs deals are being struck.

KEY WORKS AND SUGGESTIONS FOR FURTHER READING

Bruun, K., Edwards, G., Lumio, M., Mäkelä, K., Pan, L., Popham, R.E., Room, R., Schmidt, W., Skog, O.-J., Sulkunen, P. & Österberg, E. (1975). *Alcohol Control Policies in Public Health Perspective*, Vol. 25. Helsinki: Finnish Foundation for Alcohol Studies.

This monograph gives the basic evidence for alcohol taxes and prices as measures of controlling alcohol availability. It also places price control in the context of other measures affecting alcohol availability and sheds light on the whole idea of why alcohol consumption should be controlled.

Edwards, G.A.P., Babor, T.F., Casswell, S., Ferrence, R., Giesbrecht, N., Godfrey, C., Holder, H.D., Lemmens, P., Mäkelä, K., Midanik, L.T., Norström, T., Österberg, E., Romelsjö, A., Room, R., Simpura, J. & Skog, O.-J. (1994). *Alcohol Policy and the Public Good*. New York: Oxford University Press.

The chapter on alcohol prices in this monograph could be described as an updated version of the price chapter in Bruun et al. (1995). It summarizes the research evidence up to the early 1990s.

Hurst, W., Gregory, E. & Gussman, T. (1997). *Alcoholic Beverage Taxation and Control Policies. International Survey*. Ninth edition. Ottawa: Brewers' Association of Canada.

Brewers Association of Canada has surveyed alcohol taxation each third year since the beginning of the 1970s. A good source for those who wish to know how alcoholic beverages are taxed and what trends one can find in alcohol tax levels in industrialized countries.

Ornstein, S.I. & Levy, D. (1983). Price and income elasticities and the demant for alcohol beverages. In M. Galanter (Ed.). *Recent Developments in Alcoholism*, Vol. 1 (pp. 303–345). New York: Plenum.

A review of econometric studies in North America. It gives good descriptions of the studies conducted and is a quick way to become familiar with different kinds of practical solutions and problems in studies on the effects on alcohol consumption of changing alcohol prices.

Godfrey, C. (1989). Factors influencing the consumption of alcohol and tobacco: the use and abuse of economic models. *British Journal of Addiction*, **84**, 1123–1138.

Another review of demand models. A good discussion of economic theory, estimation techniques and statistical testing. Alcohol and tobacco receive special attention as commodities with dependence-inducing characteristics.

REFERENCES

Ahtola, J., Ekholm, A. & Somervuori, A. (1986). Bayes estimates for the price and income elasticities of alcoholic beverages in Finland from 1955 to 1980. *Journal of Business and Economic Statistics*, **4**, 199–208.

Babor, T.F., Mendelson, H., Greenberg, I. & Kuehnle, J. (1978). Experimental analysis of the "happy hour": effects of purchase price on alcohol consumption. *Psychopharmacology*, **58**, 34–41.

Babor, T.F., Mendelson, J.H., Uhly, B. & Souza, E. (1980). Drinking patterns in experimental and barroom settings. *Journal of Studies on Alcohol*, **41**, 635–651.

Baker, P. & MacKay, S. (1990). *The Structure of Alcohol Taxes: A Hangover from the Past?* London: Institute for Fiscal Studies.

Bruun, K., Edwards, G., Lumio, M., Mäkelä, K., Pan, L., Popham, R.E., Room, R., Schmidt, W., Skog, O.-J., Sulkunen, P. & Österberg, E. (1975). *Alcohol Control Policies in Public Health Perspective*, Vol. 25. Helsinki: Finnish Foundation for Alcohol Studies.

Chaloupka, F.J. & Saffer, H. (1992). Alcohol, illegal drugs, public policy and crime. Presented at Annual Meeting of Western Economic Association. San Francisco, CA, July.

Chaloupka, F.J., Saffer, H. & Grossman, M. (1993). Alcohol control policies and motor vehicle fatalities. *Journal of Legal Studies*, **22**, 161–186.

Chaloupka, F.J. & Wechsler, H. (1996). Binge drinking in college: the impact of price, availability, and alcohol control policies. *Contemporary Economic Policy*, **14**, 112–124.

Chaloupka, F.J., Grossman, M., Becker, G.S. & Murphy, K.M. (1992). Alcohol addiction: An econometric analysis. Presented at the Annual Meeting of the Allied Social Science Associations, Anaheim, CA, December.

Clements, K.W. & Selvanathan, S. (1991). The economic determinants of alcohol consumption. *Australian Journal of Agricultural Economics*, **35**, 209–231.

Coate, D. & Grossman, M. (1988). Effects of alcoholic beverage prices and legal drinking ages on youth alcohol use. *Journal of Law and Economics*, **31**, 145–171.

Cook, P.J. (1981). The effect of liquor taxes on drinking, cirrhosis, and auto fatalities. In M. Moore & D. Gerstein (Eds), *Alcohol and Public Policy: Beyond the Shadow of Prohibition* (pp. 255–285). Washington, DC: National Academy of Sciences.

Cook, P.J. & Moore, M.J. (1993a). Drinking and schooling. *Journal of Health Economics*, **12**, 411–430.

Cook, P.J. & Moore, M.J. (1993b). Economic perspectives on reducing alcohol-related violence. In S.E. Martin (Ed.), *Alcohol and Interpersonal Violence: Fostering Multidisciplinary Perspectives* (pp. 193–212). Washington, DC: US Government Printing Office.

Cook, P.J. & Tauchen, G. (1982). The effect of liquor taxes on heavy drinking. *Bell Journal of Economics*, **12**, 379–390.

Crooks, E. (1989). *Alcohol Consumption and Taxation*. London: Institute for Fiscal Studies.

Davies, P. & Walsh, D. (1983). *Alcohol Problems and Alcohol Control in Europe*. New York: Gardner.

Edwards, G.A.P., Babor, T.F., Casswell, S., Ferrence, R., Giesbrecht, N., Godfrey, C., Holder, H.D., Lemmens, P., Mäkelä, K., Midanik, L.T., Norström, T., Österberg, E., Romelsjö, A., Room, R., Simpura, J. & Skog, O.-J. (1994). *Alcohol Policy and the Public Good*. New York: Oxford University Press.

Godfrey, C. (1986). *Factors Influencing the Consumption of Alcohol and Tobacco—A Review of Demand Models*. York, UK: Addiction Research Centre for Health Economics.

Godfrey, C. (1989). Factors influencing the consumption of alcohol and tobacco: the use and abuse of economic models. *British Journal of Addiction*, **84**, 1123–1138.

Godfrey, C. (1990). Modelling demand. In A. Maynard & P. Tether (Eds), *Preventing Alcohol and Tobacco Problems*, Vol. 1 (pp. 35–53). Aldershot: Avebury.

Grossman, M., Coate, D. & Arluck, G.M. (1987). Price sensitivity of alcoholic beverages in the United States: Youth alcohol consumption. In H.D. Holder (Ed.), *Advances in Substance Abuse: Behavioral and Biological Research: Control Issues in Alcohol Abuse Prevention: Strategies for States and Communities* (pp. 169–198). Greenwich, CT: JAI.

Huitfeldt, B. & Jorner, U. (1972). *Efterfrågan på rusdrycker i Sverige* (The Demand for Alcoholic Beverages in Sweden). Rapport från Alkoholpolitiska utredningen (Report from the Alcohol Policy Commission). Stockholm: Government Official Reports.

Hurst, W., Gregory, E. & Gussman, T. (1997). *Alcoholic Beverage Taxation and Control Policies*. *International Survey*. Ninth edition. Ottawa: Brewers Association of Canada.

Kendell, R.E., de Roumanie, M. & Ritson, E.B. (1983). Effect of economic changes on Scottish drinking habits, 1978–82. *British Journal of Addiction*, **78**, 365–379.

Kenkel, D.S. (1993). Driving, driving and deterrence: the effectiveness and social costs of alternative policies. *Journal of Law and Economics*, **36**, 877–913.

Laixuthai, A. & Chaloupka, F.J. (1993). Youth alcohol use and public policy. *Contemporary Policy Issues*, **11**, 70–81.

Landis, B.Y. (1952). Some economic aspects of inebriety. In *Alcohol, Science and Society*. New Haven, CT: Quarterly Journal of Studies on Alcohol.

Lau, H.-H. (1975). Cost of alcoholic beverages as a determinant of alcohol consumption. In R.J. Gibbins, Y. Israel & H. Kalant (Eds), *Research Advances in Alcohol and Drug Problems*, Vol. 22 (pp. 211–245). New York: Wiley.

Leung, S.F. & Phelps, C.E. (1993). "My kingdom for a drink . . . ?" A review of estimates of the price sensitivity of demand for alcoholic beverages. In M.E. Hilton & G. Bloss (Eds), *Economics and the Prevention of Alcohol-related Problems*. Research Monograph No. 25, NIH Pub. No. 93–513 (pp. 1–32). Rockville, MD: National Institute on Alcohol Abuse and Alcoholism.

Markowitz, S. & Grossman, M. (1998). *Alcohol Regulation and Violence towards Children*. Working Paper No. 6359. Cambridge, MA: National Bureau of Economic Research.

Murray, C.J.L. & Lopez, A.D. (Eds) (1996). *The Global Burden of Disease. A Comprehensive Assessment of Mortality and Disability from Diseases, Injuries, and Risk Factors in 1990 and Projected to 2020*. Global Burden of Disease and Injury Series, Vol. 1. Cambridge, MA: Harvard School of Public Health.

Nyberg, A. (1967). *Alkoholijuomien kulutus ja hinnat* (Consumption and Prices of Alcoholic Beverages), Vol. 15. Helsinki: Finnish Foundation for Alcohol Studies.

Olsson, O. (1991). *Prisets och inkomstens betydelse för alkoholbruk, missbruk och skador* (The Effect of Prices and Income on Alcohol Consumption and Related Problems). Stockholm: Swedish Council for Information on Alcohol and other Drugs (CAN).

Ornstein, S.I. (1980). Control of alcohol consumption through price increases. *Journal of Studies on Alcohol*, **41**, 807–818.

Ornstein, S.I. & Levy, D. (1983). Price and income elasticities and the demant for alcohol beverages. In M. Galanter (Ed.), *Recent Developments in Alcoholism*, Vol. 1 (pp. 303–345). New York: Plenum.

Österberg, E. (1982). Alcohol and Economics. In E.M. Pattison & E. Kaupfman (Eds), *Encyclopedic Handbook of Alcoholism* (pp. 415–425). New York: Gardner.

Österberg, E. (1995). Do alcohol prices affect consumption and related problems? In H. Holder &

G. Edwards (Eds), *Alcohol and Public Policy: Evidence and Issues* (pp. 145–163). Oxford: Oxford University Press.

Saffer, H. & Grossman, M. (1987a).   Beer taxes, the legal drinking age, and youth motor vehicle fatalities. *Journal of Legal Studies*, **16**, 351–374.

Saffer, H. & Grossman, M. (1987b).   Drinking age laws and highway mortality rates: cause and effect. *Economic Inquire*, **25**, 403–417.

Salo, M. (1987).   *Alkoholijuomien anniskelukulutuksen määrän kehitys vuosina 1969–1986 ja eräitä anniskelua koskevia kysyntämalleja* (Developments on On-premises Retail Sales of Alcoholic Beverages, 1968–1986, and Some Demand Models for On-premises Retail Sales). Research Report No. 9, Alko, Helsinki: Economic Research and Planning.

Salo, M. (1990).   *Alkoholijuomien vähittäiskulutuksen analyysi vuosilta 1969–1988* (An Analysis of Off-premises Retail Sales of Alcoholic Beverages, 1969–1988). Research Report No. 15. Alko, Helsinki: Economic Research and Planning.

Schweitzer, S.O., Intriligator, M.D. & Salehi, J. (1983).   Alcoholism: an econometric model of its causes, its effects and its control. In M. Grant, M. Plant & A. Williams (Eds), *Economics and Alcohol* (pp. 107–127). London: Croom Helm.

Seeley, J.R. (1960).   Death by liver cirrhosis and the price of beverage alcohol. *Canadian Medical Association Journal*, **83**, 1361–1366.

Simon, J.L. (1966).   The price elasticity of liquor in the US and a simple method of determination. *Econometrica*, **34**, 193–205.

Sloan, F.A., Reilly, B.A. & Schenzler, C. (1994).   Effects of prices, civil and criminal sanctions, and law enforcement on alcohol-retaled mortality. *Journal of Studies on Alcohol*, **55**, 454–465.

World Health Organization (1995).   *Alcohol and Health—Implications for Public Health Policy.* Report of a WHO Working Group, Oslo, 9–13 October. Oslo: World Health Organization.

Yen, S.T. (1994).   Cross-section estimation of US demand for alcoholic beverage. *Applied Economics*, **26**, 381–392.

Chapter 13

Controls on the Physical Availability of Alcohol

Tim Stockwell
*National Drug Research Institute, Curtin University of Technology,
Perth, Western Australia*
and
Paul Gruenewald
Prevention Research Center, Berkeley, CA, USA

Synopsis

This chapter reviews the evidence regarding the circumstances under which changes in the physical availability of alcohol achieved through changes in the legal drinking age, outlet densities and trading hours can affect high-risk drinking and alcohol-related harm. With the growing reluctance of governments to use controls on alcohol's physical availability to reduce problems, this form of availability has tended to increase in both developed and developing countries over the past two decades. In developed countries this has not always been associated with an obvious increase in alcohol-related problems. Such markets are often "saturated". Alcohol is available to broad segments of society, from a great number of places and at all hours of the day and night. In these contexts, availability is but one of a complex array of influences on drinking behaviour and is expressed in different problems in different contexts. In developing countries this level of market "saturation" has not yet been achieved. Given the limited research currently available, the likely consequences of greatly increased physical availability of alcohol in these markets can only be inferred from studies of markets in developed countries.

In general terms, the research evidence suggests that each of the main forms of physical availability have powerful impacts on local levels of serious harm. However, in each case there

The Essential *Handbook of Treatment and Prevention of Alcohol Problems.* Edited by N. Heather and T. Stockwell.
© 2004 John Wiley & Sons Ltd. ISBN 0-470-86296-3.

are important contingencies that condition the development of such problems. This leads to substantial possibilities for local variation in problems related to the use of alcohol in different contexts. This is less true in relation to legal drinking ages. Increases in the legal drinking age have been consistently found to reduce levels of serious harm associated with the affected age groups (teenagers and young adults). These laws, however, are controversial and often difficult to change. It appears that significant and readily achievable benefits may be obtained from a more vigorous enforcement of existing laws.

The effects of greater densities of alcohol outlets on levels of local problems, on the other hand, appear to be strongly dependent on context. This dependence poses difficult methodological problems for alcohol researchers. Current evidence suggests that different relationships of outlet densities to problems may be observed across different sized areas of analysis, for different types of problems and for different types of licensed outlets. With this in mind, it appears that the regulation of licensed premises will move towards the use of local data to determine the risks associated with decisions that affect license density.

The effects of hours and days of sale on alcohol related problems are also found to be important from a harm reduction perspective. Large changes in the times at which alcohol is available (e.g. days of sale) are consistently related to expected changes in problem levels. Smaller changes (e.g. hours of sale) have only recently been found to have significant local impacts. It is suggested that local planners take special notice of the potential for late night trading to affect the local alcohol environment from a public health and safety point of view.

Future research should develop and refine models that can be applied at the local, state and national levels at which critical decisions about alcohol availability are made. Regulatory mechanisms are required which enable levels of problem consumption and harm to be monitored and incorporated into planning and policy formation. These steps will move the field towards effective approaches for the reduction of serious alcohol-related harm.

One of the most significant powers at the disposal of government to limit alcohol-related problems is the ability to control both the physical and economic availability of alcohol. There are many ways in which alcohol can be made less available through government intervention, whether at the local, state or national levels. These powers, however, are often controversial and may cut across the perceived interests of a number of important stakeholders. The manufacturing and retail arms of the alcohol industry attempt to maximize profits from sales of alcohol, state and national governments become dependent on alcohol tax revenues as part of their tax base, and many members of the voting public in Western-style democracies prefer to have ready access to affordable alcohol. Of course, stakeholders who advocate the minimization of the adverse consequences of alcohol consumption on public health, safety and order are also members of this community. These stakeholders may advocate for greater government controls on the physical and economic availability of alcohol; however, active expression of this public interest in a form that is politically potent, readily understood and supported by ordinary citizens is relatively rare.

Alcohol's availability varies markedly across the globe and it is still possible to find countries where alcohol is either completely prohibited or in which there are discrete localities or regions where the sale of alcohol is prohibited. However, while the evidence has mounted regarding the public health significance of alcohol, the 1990s in particular have witnessed a global expansion of alcohol's availability. This expansion has been marked by a growth in both the nature of availability within traditional alcohol consuming countries and the sheer number of countries in which alcohol is now readily available. Jernigan (1997) has documented strategies used by some alcohol companies to create new markets in the developing world. The rapid globalization of world trade, supported by major international treaties such as the General Agreement on Tariffs and Trade, has effectively restricted the extent to which individual governments can heavily tax alcohol or otherwise restrict access (see Österberg, Chapter 12, this volume). In most Western countries there has been an increase in the number and type of outlets at which alcohol can be sold, in the number and range of alcohol products and in the days and hours of sale. In many countries without a long tradition of public access to alcohol, availability has been introduced and expanded with little in the way of regulatory control on the manner of its sale and promotion. Unrestricted sales of alcohol in street-corner kiosks in Estonia and the ubiquitous street vending machines in Japan are but two examples of this trend (Jernigan, 1997).

Opponents of controls on availability of alcohol are quick to point out that the pattern of deregulation established in the latter half of the twentieth century has, at least in some instances, been accompanied by declining levels of per capita consumption in some developed countries. For example, Duffy & Plant (1986) report that the substantial relaxation of Scotland's liquor licensing laws in 1976 were not associated with increased alcohol consumption in comparison with neighbouring England (these laws permitted trading on Sundays and later trading hours during the week). Deregulation of liquor licensing in Victoria, Australia, in the late 1980s resulted in a dramatic increase in the number of liquor licenses issued but was associated with a decline in overall alcohol consumption (Storey et al., 1998). So are reductions in alcohol availability a potent weapon for achieving reductions in alcohol-related harm? We believe they are. However, we also believe that research endeavours to elucidate the relationships between availability and use are highly complex, demand a great deal of the alcohol researcher and are unlikely to provide simple answers to the question, "Do reductions in availability reduce alcohol-related problems?" While the answer to this question is usually "yes" it is also sometimes "no", depending on the local context. Consideration of local context is often missing from much of the research literature. Thus, reported failures to obtain "significant" effects of changes in availability on use or problems often border on scientific anecdote; attempts to support a null finding in the absence of adequate theory or experimental control. The studies cited above are cases in point. There is no *a priori* reason to believe that Sunday sales should affect use unless one argues that such sales uniquely contribute to alcohol access (e.g. by permitting sales that would not otherwise take place on other days). Similarly, deregulation of licenses may or may not affect access to alcohol, depending upon the geographic distribution of outlets, their locations with respect to consumers and the current "saturation" of the markets themselves (i.e. the degree to which demand is already met by current availability). Sunday sales, and greater numbers of alcohol outlets, may sometimes be irrelevant to access (individuals being so able to purchase alcohol at other times and places).

The evidence in relation to specific types of controls will be discussed here and it will be noted that there are multiple influences on levels of alcohol consumption and harm at the population level, so that simplistic conclusions from single examples can frequently be misleading. We will indicate how both theory and research must be enriched to deal with the contingent relationships of alcohol availability, use and problems.

AVAILABILITY THEORY

Historically, efforts to control alcohol's availability so as to reduce alcohol-related harms have been based on the view that "less is best", i.e. the less that alcohol is available the better for public health and safety. The idea that level of alcohol-related harm in a society is closely associated with degree of alcohol availability is sometimes referred to as the "Availability Theory". The theory was first articulated on the basis of a growing body of epidemiological research in 1975 (Bruun et al., 1975). The major conclusion of this World

Health Organization report was that population levels of alcohol-related harm are directly related to the levels of per capita alcohol consumption and, hence, the control of alcohol consumption through restrictions on alcohol availability becomes legitimate and a pressing public health concern. To paraphrase Single (1988), there are three separate but linked propositions contained within Availability Theory:

1. The greater the availability of alcohol in a society, the higher the average consumption of its population.
2. The higher the average consumption of a population, then the greater number there will be of excessive drinkers.
3. The greater the number of excessive drinkers in a population, the greater the extent of adverse health and social problems stemming from alcohol use.

From a modern perspective, these propositions present a deterministic view that runs counter to many of our experiences as alcohol researchers. In general, the research does not seem to support the notions that greater availability *invariably* leads to greater levels of drinking, and that changes in average drinking levels *invariably* lead to greater "excessive" drinking and problems, even if in practice they usually do. There remain significant empirical questions regarding these assertions. The relationships between availability and drinking problems are complex and multifaceted. Greater availability may and may not be related to greater use, and may be related to problems independent of use. Increases in average drinking levels may and may not be related to greater "excessive" drinking. "Excessive" drinking itself may and may not be related to greater problems. What we suggest is that, when viewed from the perspective of contemporary research, each proposition of the theory needs qualification and should be understood as a conditional, not absolute, description of the relationship between drinking and harm.

Contemporary research into the relationships of alcohol availability to use and problems has placed the three basic propositions of Availability Theory in a new context. The basic questions asked with regard to these propositions are:

- What are the mechanisms that relate decreases in availability to decreases in use?
- Are the effects of changes in availability restricted to "excessive" consumers?
- Are the greatest health consequences always incurred by "excessive" drinkers?

Contemporary answers to these questions are:

- The "full price" of alcohol consists of both its real price and the convenience costs of obtaining this good, and these "full prices" affect levels of use (Grossman, 1988).
- Changes in availability affect both drinking patterns and routine drinking activities of all consumers (Gruenewald, Millar & Treno, 1993).
- Traditional definitions of "excessive drinkers" as persons who on average, over all days, drink significant amounts of alcohol (e.g. more than 60 g) in fact exclude the many people who experience alcohol-related harm as a consequence of occasional "binges"— the so-called "prevention paradox" (Kreitman, 1986; Gmel et al., 2001).

While some of the important implications of these observations will be discussed below, it is essential to recognize that this work has altered the entire context in which these scientific issues are discussed. The deterministic sense displayed by the original propositions of Availability Theory has been altered by contingent views of availability's effects. Changes in availability affect drinking only to the degree that they affect the "full price" of alcohol; this need not always be the case for all consumers (Abbey et al., 1993). Changes in availability may not affect use, but may still affect routine drinking activities related to problems; reducing availability at bars and restaurants reduces crashes independent of drinking levels (Gruenewald et al., 1996a, 1999). Changes in availability may not effect the overall volume of alcohol defined on external criteria as "excessive" but may influence the frequency of high risk or "excessive" drinking occasions. This leads us to the following expansion of the basic propositions of Availability Theory:

1. Greater availability of alcohol in a society will increase the average consumption of its population when such changes reduce the "full price" of alcohol, i.e. the real price of beverages at retail markets plus the convenience costs of obtaining them.
2. Greater availability of alcohol in a society will directly affect alcohol-related harm when such changes affect the distribution of "routine drinking activities"; behaviours drinkers engage in when consuming alcohol (e.g. drinking at bars vs. at home; drinking socially vs. alone).
3. Greater average consumption in a population will be related to increases in drinking among some segments of the population along one or more of the several basic dimensions of drinking; rates of abstention, frequencies of use, quantities consumed and variances in drinking levels.
4. Greater adverse health and social problems stemming from alcohol use will appear across the drinking population, focused in those subpopulations most exposed to risk. These risks will be distributed differently across population subgroups, depending upon differences in routine drinking activities (2, above) and drinking patterns (3, above).

In this chapter evidence will be outlined for the view that some restrictions on alcohol's availability do indeed usually reduce alcohol consumption and related harm. However, the limitations of the original propositions of Availability Theory will also be discussed including the idea that extreme forms of restriction sometimes produce adverse outcomes. Future directions will then be provided for developing an optimal regulatory system for alcohol's local availability, in which consumer demand for alcohol is balanced against public health and safety concerns.

FORMS OF ALCOHOL AVAILABILITY

The means for controlling alcohol's availability can be usefully divided into those that reduce economic availability and those that reduce physical availability.

Economic availability is essentially the price of alcoholic drinks as a proportion of disposable income among potential consumers. The retail price of alcohol is directly influenced by levels of taxation, formal and informal controls on drink prices, the costs of production, levels of consumer demand and the cost of any related services supplied along with alcoholic beverages (e.g. live entertainment on licensed premises). As discussed in Chapter 12 (Österberg), the price of alcohol appears to have an influence on level and pattern of consumption and, beyond noting that this relationship is mediated by a complex array of other factors, it will not be discussed further here.

Physical availability is essentially the availability of alcohol in one's physical environment mediated by the likelihood that one will come into contact with these sources of drink. Thus, the physical availability of alcohol is principally determined by local liquor licensing laws and the nature of their enforcement, but may be strongly modified by other aspects of human behavior. Licensing laws may govern permitted hours of sale, persons who may be licensed, numbers and types of outlets, persons to whom alcohol may be sold, types and strengths of alcohol beverages sold, permitted locations of alcohol outlets, the physical characteristics of premises, and the range of other services or products that may be provided. In many instances, how these laws are enforced in practice falls short of both the intention and the letter of the law. In particular, laws regarding service to underage and intoxicated customers are frequently ignored (Lang et al., 1996; Rydon et al., 1996; Grube, 1997) and local outlet densities grow disproportionately large as outlets concentrate along geographic boundaries between wealthy and poor areas (Gruenewald et al., 1999) and are "grand-fathered" into urban planning areas (LaScala, Gerber & Gruenewald, 2000). It is vital, therefore, to understand regulatory systems and strategies as well as the legal context when considering the extent of alcohol's availability.

It is also vital to understand that the effects of physical availability are, unlike beverage prices, local rather than global. Alcohol beverage prices are relatively homogenous with respect to the physical geography of nations, states, provinces, counties, communities and neighbourhoods (e.g. varying by a factor of 83 within markets and less than 1.1 between neighbourhoods in a recent community-based study in the USA; Gruenewald et al., 1999). Beverage availability, on the other hand, is typically quite homogenous on large scales (e.g. at the state level in the USA) but heterogeneous at the smaller scales of communities and neighbourhoods (in the same study, varying by a factor of 300). Hence, while it is a simple matter of beverage choice that enables consumers to off-set price increases (by selecting less expensive beverages; Gruenewald & Treno, 2000), it is a more complicated matter to off-set the effects of reduced availability (by selecting alternative establishments, taking on additional travel time, altering travel schedules, and so on). Of course, it becomes a very difficult matter to overcome sparse levels of availability when they are encountered (e.g. in the more remote regions of Western Australia). For these reasons, the impacts of availability policy on the use of alcohol may be as heterogeneous as patterns of availability themselves. The reduction of one outlet in an urban area has significantly different meaning and implications than the reduction of one outlet in a rural outpost. Similarly, the reduction of one outlet on one side of town has different meaning and implications than the reduction of one outlet on another. The outlet in the rural outpost may be the only one for 300 miles. The bar closed at the end of the street may be frequented by most of the neighbourhood, the bar across town rarely used.

For these reasons, although the formulation of economic policies (e.g. beverage taxes, mark-ups, etc.) tend to take place on a more global level (at the levels of states and nations), the formulation of policies to influence physical availability of alcohol can and often does occur at all levels of governance. Thus, it is rarely the case that the price of alcoholic drinks may be influenced at the local level (in Australia this does occasionally occur, often through informal agreements). On the other hand, outlet licensing laws and regulations typically allow input from local communities who wish to restrict the hours and days of sale of alcohol. In the USA, planning and zoning regulations may be used to restrict the distribution of alcohol outlets in community areas and, at the urban level, are the primary determinants of local distributions of availability. At the other extreme, international agreements may restrict labelling and taxation of alcoholic products or ban sales of alcohol altogether. For all these reasons, it is important to be clear about the geographic parameters of a particular alcohol control measure.

AVAILABILITY, DRINKING AND HARM: A SUMMARY AND DISCUSSION OF THE RESEARCH EVIDENCE

Three key areas of research into the physical availability of alcohol will be discussed in turn; the legal drinking age, outlet densities and hours and days of sale. Research in these areas is most well developed and deserving of thorough review. Other major methods for influencing economic availability (e.g. price controls; Österberg, Chapter 12, this volume) and otherwise intervening in the drinking process itself (e.g. responsible beverage service practices; Homel et al., Chapter 14, this volume) have been discussed in other chapters and will not be taken up again here.

Before discussing these three key areas of research, however, it is important at the outset to consider the general arguments that have been used historically to link population levels of drinking (i.e. per capita measures of consumption) to high-risk drinking and alcohol-related harm. Along with Availability Theory, these general arguments serve as a backdrop to all contemporary discussions of alcohol availability, use and harm.

General Considerations: Availability Theory vs. the Single Distribution Theory

After some decades of work, there is now a large and impressive literature which establishes that, with very few exceptions, per capita alcohol consumption and alcohol-related harm are associated at the national, regional and, sometimes, local levels. The major review *Alcohol Policy and the Public Good* (Edwards et al., 1994) was a collaborative exercise in which the scientific literature available at that time was carefully examined. A major conclusion was that average level of consumption is associated with levels of harmful social and health consequences. At the population level it was observed that per capita alcohol consumption was related to levels of cirrhosis mortality, suicide and alcohol-related traffic crashes. Since that review, other studies have found these relationships to vary according to the specific types of beverage and alcohol-related harm considered. For example, it appears that beer sales are more closely related to drinking and driving, while spirits sales are more closely related to suicide and cirrhosis mortality rates (Kerr, 2000; Gruenewald & Ponicki, 1995a, b; Gruenewald, Ponicki & Mitchell, 1995). These findings, however, do not detract from the central point that alcohol sales, in total or beverage specific, remain correlated with specific problems. As such, relationships between beverage specific sales and problems are also contingent upon and qualified by drinking behaviours of consumers that link consumption of some beverages in some contexts to specific problems. Thus, Gruenewald et al. (1999) show that even greater levels of specificity apply within local community areas where, as in Perth, Western Australia, sales of high-alcohol beers are uniquely associated with drinking and driving (among all beer sold).

These scientific findings, relatively uncontroversial in and of themselves, and based on the rather reasonable tenets of Availability Theory, are nevertheless politically contentious because of their serious implications for the alcohol beverage industry. If these findings were used to inform government policy (e.g. through higher taxes, fewer retail outlets, restricted hours and days of sale), profits of the beverage industry would no doubt suffer. Thus, critics of these observations, and Availability Theory in general, frequently cite scientific criticisms that have been successfully levelled at a related theory, sometimes referred to as the Single Distribution Theory or, alternatively, the Ledermann Model (1956) after the French epidemiologist who originated it. The latter asserts there is a simple mathematical relationship between the level of per capita consumption and the number of excessive drinkers in any given population, increases in the former directly leading to increases in the latter (and, not surprisingly, increases in related problems). Subsequent analyses have demonstrated that there is no such consistent and precise relationship (e.g. Skög, 1985), and these demonstrations are sometimes cited as a failure of Availability Theory. However, it should be noted that. Availability Theory, as usually represented, suggests that an overall relationship does exist between alcohol sales and problem levels, but does *not* suggest that this relationship is a simple one. Rather, as noted above, it is argued here that a set of contingent mechanisms exist relating overall measures of consumption to patterns of use and problems, relating to a variety of social, economic, political and psychological conditions that bear upon the use of alcohol.

In conjunction with this point, more recent research points to the quite reasonable possibility that changes in availability do not have to affect alcohol sales *per se* in order to affect a change in both patterns and rates of alcohol problems. The archetypal example here is a law that effectively closes all on-premise alcohol outlets, but otherwise preserves the availability of alcohol. Would rates of alcohol-related traffic crashes then change? All evidence appears to point to the affirmative; reducing on-premise outlet densities will lead to reductions in alcohol-related crashes (Scribner et al., 1994; Gruenewald et al., 1996). On the other hand, would such a change alter beverage use? The evidence on this point is ambiguous. At the largest scales (e.g. states in the USA), reductions in availability affect use (Gruenewald, Ponicki & Holder, 1993). At smaller scales (e.g. neighbourhoods within communities in the USA), there is little evidence that availability affects use (Gruenewald et al., 2000), but considerable changes in the distribution of availability effect substantial changes in the distribution of alcohol-related crashes (Gruenewald et al., 1996). Thus, moving well beyond the Lederman model and its detractors, contemporary approaches to Availability Theory suggest a much more diversified and precise picture of the contingent relationships among these aspects of access to and use of alcohol.

Clearly, a more sophisticated view of alcohol availability, patterns of use and harm is required. These patterns of use should include not only traditional measures of drinking, but also more contemporary measures of routine drinking behaviours. One need not change drinking levels *per se* to alter the characteristics and rates of drinking problems. The contingent nature of drinking and problems assures that this is the case. One need only successfully argue that changes in availability affect aspects of drinking behavior that bear upon harm. Availability Theory, developed along these lines, will enable researchers to explore these aspects of human drinking behaviors and develop rational policy based on a deeper understanding of the contingent causes of drinking problems.

The Legal Drinking Age

Policies to restrict the minimum drinking age at which licensed sales to underage youth are permitted are intended to restrict youth access to alcohol and prevent the early onset and rapid development of drinking problems among youth and young adults. To date the research focus has been upon the determination of the extent to which raising the minimum drinking age results in reduction in use and problems among young adults. It is of some interest in this regard to also determine the effects of lower minimum drinking ages on later alcohol problems and the development of alcohol dependence. This is a rather limited area of current study and one that deserves considerable further investigation. A related issue of some importance concerns the effectiveness of laws concerning the age at which it is legal to allow a child to drink alcohol in private settings (e.g. it is an offence in the UK to give alcohol to a child less than 5 years of age). There is some cross-sectional evidence indicating that early onset of alcohol use is related to alcohol dependence (Grant, 1996). Some longitudinal evidence (Reifman et al., 1998) also indicates that the age at which a child first consumes alcohol predicts whether he/she will drink above low risk levels later in life. However, the extent to which laws governing such private behaviour can ever be enforced other than in the most extreme cases is probably small and this issue has not been a major focus of research or policy.

By contrast, there is now a strong and consistent body of knowledge in relation to the impact of drinking age laws for public drinking and making legal purchases of alcohol. This was influential in assisting community advocacy groups such as Mothers Against Drink Driving (MADD) to push successfully for the drinking age to be raised to 20 or 21 in many US States in the 1980s, following experiences with earlier periods of relaxation (Wagenaar, 1993). These drinking age laws stand as the highest in the world, being shared with Malaysia, South Korea and Ukraine (International Center on Alcohol Policy, 1998). Most countries for which information is available have 18 as the legal drinking age and a handful of European countries have adopted 16 (Austria, Belgium, France, Italy and Spain).

There is persuasive evidence that changes to the minimum legal drinking age directly result in corresponding changes in levels of a variety of problems relating to alcohol intoxication, including road traffic fatalities, juvenile crime, serious assault and drunkenness convictions for the affected age groups (Wagenaar, 1993). The US General Accounting Office (1987) conducted a systematic review of this topic and, on the basis of 14 studies judged to be methodologically sound, estimated reductions in fatal road crashes among young drivers to be 5–28%. In one study of changes in drinking age laws across four Australian states, reductions were significantly associated with increases in assaults. Following the drop in drinking age from 21 to 18 in Western Australia in 1970, rates of serious assault increased by 231% for juveniles in comparison with Queensland (Smith, 1988).

Changes to drinking age laws are often controversial, with strongly divided opinions in the community. In 1999 the government of New Zealand introduced a Bill to lower the legal drinking age from 19 to 18, despite public opinion polls indicating a majority of opinion was against this change. Analyses of public opinion from various countries indicate divided views on this issue (Lang et al., 1995). An alternative strategy that enjoys strong public support is to enforce existing underage drinking laws more effectively. A number of studies have employed young people who either are underage or appear underage to attempt to purchase alcohol on licensed premises. In both the USA (Grube, 1997) and Australia (Lang et al., 1996), these studies indicate that the first attempt to purchase alcohol is successful on about 50% of occasions, suggesting that after four tries the chance of at least one success rises above 90%. The Community Trials Project in California included a successful component to reduce underage drinking. The evaluation of this component found that law enforcement, rather than server training, was the most effective ingredient. Police-operated underage stings were most effective in reducing underage access to alcohol (Grube, 1997).

An additional strategy to reduce alcohol-related harm for young drivers is to have a 2 or 3 year probationary license period for new drivers, during which not only are there stricter speeding restrictions but a zero permitted blood alcohol level. As reviewed in Chapter 15 (McKnight & Voas), there is some evidence in support of the effectiveness of the enforcement of drinking and driving laws when this is based upon principles of deterrence specific to drinking and driving in a particular locality.

In summary, worldwide drinking age laws vary between 16 and 21 years. Public opinion regarding these laws is usually divided, so they are difficult and controversial to change. Raising and lowering the age limits are clearly associated with, respectively, increases and decreases in levels of serious alcohol-related harm for young people. Similar effects can be achieved through enforcement and regulation strategies, although it should be noted that this requires concerted local effort and commitment, which may not always be forthcoming.

Outlet Density

Although associations between densities of licensed premises, alcohol consumption and harm are widely reported, it is a complex statistical task to establish causal relationships between changes in the density of licensed premises and these outcomes. The multifaceted determinants of drinking and problems in local settings are such that observed statistical associations (or failures to obtain such associations) may be due to a host of unmeasured characteristics relating human activities to drinking places and problems. Notwithstanding this, controls on numbers of licensed premises are a common feature of many licensing systems.

Evidence for an association between outlet density, drinking and harm comes from two major sources: (i) cross-sectional studies that compare cities, counties or other geographic areas at one point in time; (ii) longitudinal studies which examine the relationships between trends in outlet density, consumption and harm. A few studies have managed, in effect, to combine the power of both approaches and conduct cross-sectional time series analyses of trends across both time and place.

Cross-sectional Studies

Many cross-sectional studies have found associations between density of licensed outlets, levels of alcohol consumption and harm. Several North American studies have examined data from defined geographical areas and shown that outlet density is related to levels of some alcohol problems. For example, Watts & Rabow (1983) examined alcohol availability, alcohol sales and problems across the 213 cities of California. They found that cities with high problem rates were those with the greatest availability of alcohol, as measured by outlet density per head of population. In particular, there was a strong association between the density of taverns or "beer parlours" with rates of public drunkenness arrests, on the one hand, and between liquor stores and liver cirrhosis rates, on the other.

A few state-level studies of increasing rigour were conducted in the 1990s, including Nelson's (1990) detailed study of cross-sectional relationships between beverage prices, outlet densities and alcohol use and Gruenewald, Madden & Janes's (1992) study of beverage specific availability, beverage prices and use. The findings were relatively consistent; greater beverage prices and lower outlet densities were related to lower sales of alcohol. It is noteworthy that Gruenewald et al. (1992) were able to show that both beer prices and densities of beer outlets significantly affected beer sales. However, these studies need to be interpreted with caution, since they failed to account for spatial autocorrelation among geographic units, a factor that can strongly bias statistical estimates from cross-sectional models. The tendency of data from one unit to resemble (or contrast) data from adjacent areas violates the assumption of unit independence underlying classical statistical models used to analyse these data. Failure to adjust for significant autocorrelation can result in false conclusions. The degree of spatial autocorrelation appears to increase on smaller spatial scales (e.g. community-level vs. state-level analyses; Chou, 1991). For example, Stevenson et al. (1999) did not find significant autocorrelations in a study of alcohol consumption and assaults at the postcode level for New South Wales, Australia, while Gruenewald et al. (1996) have found significant autocorrelation at the neighbourhood level of analysis within communities in California.

Scribner, MacKinnon & Dwyer (1994) and Jewell & Brown (1995) demonstrated significant cross-sectional relationships between outlet densities and alcohol-related motor vehicle accidents. Parker & Rebhun (1995), Scribner, MacKinnon & Dwyer (1995), and Speer et al. (1998) demonstrate significant cross-sectional relationships between outlet densities, homicide and assaults. All these studies are noteworthy for their control of variation in sociodemographic characteristics across geographic areas. Thus, in a pairing of studies unique to this area, Gorman et al. (1998) reported that the geographic distribution of assaults is unrelated to the distribution of outlets (at the city level within states). By contrast, Speer et al. (1998) found that the geographic distribution of assaults was related to the distribution of outlets, although at the neighborhood level within cities. The geographic scale of analysis would appear to be central to the different results in these two studies. It is to be noted, however, that these studies did not control for the effects of spatial auto-correlation and should also be treated with caution.

An important direction in recent years has been towards small area analysis of patterns of consumption and harm in local neighbourhoods. This kind of work is of great potential value to local policy makers in relation to critical local licensing decisions, e.g. the issuing of new licenses, extensions of trading hours and zoning. Several recent studies have employed sophisticated spatial techniques, not only to control for spatial auto-correlation but also to examine whether problems that occur in neighbourhoods are a function of adjoining areas with high densities of liquor outlets (so-called "spatial lag effects"). Gruenewald et al. (1996) studied the geographic patterning of alcohol-related crashes across four communities in California. It was found that alcohol-related crashes most often took place in neighbourhoods containing the largest densities of restaurants (not bars). In addition, the analysis of spatial lag effects revealed that rates of alcohol-related crashes in target neighborhoods were directly related to outlet densities in adjacent neighbourhoods.

Three other studies have used similar geostatistical techniques to examine the relationships between outlet densities and violence. It appears that rates of youth violence in minority neighbourhoods are related to greater off-premise outlet densities (Alaniz, Cartmill & Parker, 1998), rates of alcohol-related pedestrian injuries are greater in neighbourhoods near on-premise outlets (LaScala, Gerber & Gruenewald, 2000), and rates of violent assaults are greater in high-density outlet areas selling greater proportions of specific beverage types (i.e. high-alcohol beer and spirits; Stevenson, Lind & Weatherburn, 1999). A more recent fourth study (Gorman et al., 2001) has replicated the observation that outlet densities are related to violence in neighbourhood areas, but added to this is the observation that rates of violence are also related to the sociodemographic characteristics of adjacent neighborhoods. Thus, not only is the level of impoverishment of target neighbourhoods relevant to rates of violence, but the impoverishment of other adjacent nearby neighbourhoods is also important. Finally, using a related technique (generalized potentials), a fifth study by Wieczorek & Coyle (1998) has begun to identify the types of community neighbourhoods in the USA that are more likely to produce drunken drivers (i.e. areas with larger populations of youthful, lower educated, White males with unskilled jobs).

Going beyond the dichotomous characterization of outlets as on- or off-premises, specific types of on-premises drinking environments are another important contextual factor. Stockwell et al. (1992a) examined a unique set of data regarding alcohol-related harm (assaults, road crashes and drink–driving offences) and consumption (alcohol sales recorded for taxation purposes) at the level of individual licensed premises. Comparing on the basis of units of alcohol sold per premises, it was found that among on-premises establishments, nightclubs, taverns and "hotels" (large venues devoted almost entirely to drinking in Australia) were at high risk for having customers involved in drinking and driving offences, crashes and assaults. That is, drink-for-drink, these outlets were more likely to sell to consumers who became involved in problem outcomes. A further study demonstrated that the highest risk premises were those whose patrons were more likely to have high blood alcohol levels on exiting (Stockwell et al., 1992b). Gruenewald et al. (1999) also conducted analyses on these data and detected significant relationships between the types of beverages sold at individual premises and patterns of drink–driving offences—increases over time in sales of lower strength beers from these premises were associated with reductions in drinking and driving offences.

The above studies begin to form the basis for providing empirical evidence upon which to base licensing decisions, both in terms of general principles and also of specific situations on a particular locality. For example, in Australia, a more relaxed approach might be taken by licensing authorities to the issuing of licenses for "low-risk" premises and tighter controls on hotels and nightclubs. Communities might act to site new premises in "low-risk" rather than "high-risk" locations. It is interesting to note that in the example of deregulation of licensing in Victoria, Australia, discussed above, the great increase in licensed venues was in a low-risk category—small restaurants and wine bars (Storey et al., 1998).

The future of policy applications from this approach, of course, awaits much further research. Much needs to be learned regarding the types of specific local factors that may either protect against or facilitate the occurrence of harm. For example, in a recent study by Gruenewald & Treno (2000), it is demonstrated that the effects of outlet densities on alcohol-related crash rates are strongly contingent upon local traffic flow and the available pool of drinking drivers. Effects of outlets are strongest in areas of communities where there is considerable traffic flow and which are near to larger populations of drinking drivers (spatial lags). Thus, the contextual dependence of these effects on local conditions again supports the view presented here of the contingent nature of availability. It also provides the first indications of an effective direction for local outlet policy. One could imagine a future in which local communities assess specific neighbourhood characteristics before licensing alcohol outlets, placing new outlets in low-risk areas.

Longitudinal Studies

One problem with cross-sectional studies is that the demonstrated associations cannot tell us whether increases in outlet density stimulate demand for alcohol or whether they are merely responsive to a higher level of demand from consumers. Other problems include a failure to take into account the density of outlets in geographical as well as population terms, biases due to alcohol consumption by non-resident visitors to community neighbourhoods, difficulties in obtaining sufficient observations for statistically powerful analyses of geographic data, and the problem of ignoring correlated changes in the real price of alcohol. Some longitudinal studies have been conducted that overcome some of these methodological difficulties.

Within the USA Gruenewald, Ponicki & Holder (1993) collectively analysed a 10 year panel of data available from 38 states, employing cross-sectional time series analyses. The results of the study demonstrated a significant effect of outlet densities upon alcohol sales. Elasticities related to outlet densities (on a per-person basis) were 0.411 for spirits and 0.378 for wine. Importantly, the study also showed that the geographic spread between outlets and people was similarly and independently significant, with greater distances being related to reductions in alcohol use. The time series approach was consistent with the notion that increases in outlet density frequently preceded increases in per capita alcohol consumption. The converse of consumption stimulating increases in densities was not confirmed. In other words the number of licensed premises per unit population appears to drive consumption more than the converse. A major limitation still of this study was the lack of sales data for beer—only sales of spirits and wine were available for analysis. It should be noted, however, that a number of earlier, less sophisticated, studies that examined outlet density and beer sales also found positive relationships (see Gruenewald, Madden & Janes, 1992).

Gruenewald et al. (2000) replicated this study at the neighbourhood level in analyses of six communities over 5 years and found quite different results. At this geographic level, neither outlet densities nor beverage prices were related to rates of self-reported abstention, or frequencies and quantities consumed. As these authors suggest, the scale of the spatial processes underlying access to alcohol (e.g. how far one typically drives when shopping) interacts with the effects of changing outlet densities (i.e. for a change in local outlet density to "matter", it must either increase or decrease the convenience of obtaining alcohol for a significant number of people). It appears that very local planning and zoning activities can have substantive effects on problems proximally related to outlets (e.g. crashes and violence). More global interventions are required to attack problems (e.g. heavy drinking) less closely related to the local distribution of outlets.

Outlet Density: Summary

These studies strongly suggest that limits on outlet density may be an effective means of controlling alcohol problems and need to be taken more seriously as an effective policy tool for the reduction of alcohol-related harm. Clearly, further research into the effectiveness of these policies needs to be conducted. In future, research on this topic will need to be better informed by theoretical models of the manner in which availability, consumption and harm interact across different harm domains. It would seem that each problem studied at the community and neighbourhood level will require its own theoretical analysis. For example, models of alcohol-related crashes, in which the relationships between sources of drinkers, sources of drink and driving patterns are the focus of attention (Gruenewald et al., 1996), cannot be directly extended to studies of alcohol-related violence. There the dynamics of aggressive interactions within alcohol environments matter a great deal (Parker & Auerhahn, 1998) and the relationships between locations of violent acts, residences of victims and offenders, and alcohol outlets are critical. Further development, empirical testing and refinement of these different models hold the promise of providing a rational basis for decisions about outlet densities at the local area level.

HOURS AND DAYS OF SALE

It is important to make a distinction between the related issues of the hours of trading and the number of days of trading. It will be argued here that the evidence for an effect of the number of drinking days is stronger than an effect of trading hours, although recent evidence suggests even the latter represents an important issue to be considered in the local regulation of licensed premises.

A number of Scandinavian studies have focused on natural experiments involving the introduction of the closure of liquor stores for a whole day, usually Saturday or Sunday. In Sweden, Olsson & Wikström (1982) found reductions in levels of drunkenness, domestic and public violence following the Saturday closure of stores, although not, interestingly, any reduction in the total consumption of alcohol. Similar experiments in Norway (Nordlund, 1985) and Finland (Österberg and Säilä, 1991) also yielded evidence of significant reductions in problems associated with alcohol intoxication, with either small or non-existent effects on overall consumption. More recently, the effects of closures of liquor stores and bars on social security pay-days in Aboriginal communities and other restrictions have been studied in Australia (Gray, 2000). In most instances there have been parallel reductions observed in alcohol consumption and alcohol-related harm, although in one case, as in the Scandinavian examples, only harm indicators were affected and not consumption *per se*. It should also be noted that other restrictions were also introduced in these communities, such as the rationing of cask wine sales. Collectively, these studies point to the need for a better understanding of the unique local contexts in which such experiments in alcohol availability occur. It is interesting that overall consumption throughout the whole week is not always reduced by closures on a single day, while problem incidents are. As noted in the introduction, this represents an important variation on traditional Availability Theory and prompts the additional investigation of the key contextual variables that contribute to the reductions in problems.

In relation to variations in trading hours, a significant contribution has been made to this literature by the Australian researcher Ian Smith in the late 1980s. He published a series of studies which documented changes in alcohol-related harm in different states before and after a relaxation in pub trading or liquor store trading hours. His analyses clearly show that small alterations in trading hours shift the pattern of road traffic accidents, so that a peak occurs shortly after the new closing time. In some instances they show a significant increase in accidents in comparison with a control state on the day when extended trading hours occur (Smith, 1988). What they do not show, however, is an overall increase in total numbers of accidents across all times. This means that it is impossible to rule out the explanation that peoples' drinking and driving habits have simply shifted or been redistributed across the whole week. Much research in this area, as with that concerned with outlet densities, has failed to take into account a number of variables. The absence of a dramatic increase in alcohol problems in Scotland following a substantial deregulation of trading hours in 1976 was highly influential in persuading the Clayson Committee (1984) to recommend similar deregulation in England and Wales. During the period after the deregulation, Scotland experienced a particularly severe recession that was greater in severity than that of its neighbours. An independent study conducted in Edinburgh in 1978 (Kendell et al., 1983), found that there was a substantial drop in alcohol consumption in accord with a rise in the real price of alcohol. As noted earlier in this chapter, these are additional cases of scientific anecdote driving policy decisions. None of the original studies was sufficiently well performed to justify the confirmation of "null effects" used to defend the policy change. None of the original studies considered alternative impacts of the change under consideration (e.g. drinking levels), or examined mechanisms suspected to mediate the outcomes of the studies, or took into account the geographic bases and likely geostatistical problems (e.g. process scale and map resolution) that could affect observed outcomes.

A detailed study of the impact of extended trading hours in the city of Fremantle, Western Australia, during the 1987 Americas Cup failed to demonstrate any significant changes in rates of alcohol problems or consumption levels for local residents, although it did suffer from some inherent weaknesses in design (McLaughlin & Harrison-Stewart, 1992). Due to the enormous influx of visitors to the area it was not, of course, possible to examine overall rates of drink–driving and assault offences in any meaningful way. In fact, it appeared that the local residents made very little use of the extended hours. The only exception here was that those residents who reported the heaviest typical levels of consumption were more likely to take advantage of the opportunity to drink in hotels after midnight. This finding parallels that of another of Ian Smith's studies, in which it was determined that persons who frequented hotels and taverns in Perth with early morning opening tended to have higher rates of problem drinking (Smith, 1986).

More recent Australian studies have examined in finer detail the impacts of experimental extensions of trading hours of nightclubs in Darwin (D'Abbs, 1993) and of "hotels" (i.e. bars or pubs) in Perth, Western Australia (Chikritzhs et al., 1997; Chikritzhs and Stockwell, 2002). The former study found significant evidence of an increase in late night and early morning violence and public drunkenness, which resulted in the permitted hours being reduced once more. In the Perth study, specific data were obtained on drink–driving offences, assaults and alcohol sales associated with specific premises before and during the granting of permits for individual premises to trade until 1 p.m. instead of midnight. In comparison with premises that did not apply for these permits, those granted extended trading evidence substantial increases in alcohol sales, assaults on or near their premises and

alcohol-related road crashes involving customers who had last drunk there. While the partially controlled design of this study limits the extent to which economic confounding will
have affected the results, the findings still leave open the possibility that the later trading
hours for some premises simply shifted across time and place and the overall impact was
not great. However, it should also be considered that, at the local community and planning
levels, it is highly significant information that trading hours have these impacts. It is likely
that local communities will wish to shift serious alcohol-related problems elsewhere.
Furthermore, in many locations emergency services and public transport are thinner on the
ground and more expensive in the early hours of the morning; another consideration for
local planners.

In summary, the international experience with trading hours and days appears to demonstrate that modifications in these have some impacts on the patterning of problems of
alcohol intoxication, across both time and place. In both instances, this fact should be considered in the local regulation of alcohol availability and the planning of public transport
and emergency services. In the case of large changes in temporal availability of alcohol (i.e.
whole days), there is evidence of parallel changes in problem occurrences, although not
always in overall weekly alcohol consumption. In relation to small variations in late night
trading hours, there is suggestive but not conclusive evidence that later trading hours may
increase problem rates and consumption. Local contextual factors are likely to be critical
in this respect and warrant further attention from researchers.

REGULATORY APPROACHES TO THE MINIMIZATION OF ALCOHOL-RELATED HARM

A common compromise response to the Temperance Movement in many parts of the world
in the early twentieth century was for governments to assume ownership of alcohol supply
and retail outlets. In both North America and Scandinavia, many state and national governments established government alcohol monopolies, with the intention of curbing the
worst excesses of commercial alcohol sales and related harms. Over the past 50 or so years,
a number of these monopolies have been converted to enable private licensed sales of
alcohol. In response, a substantial evaluation literature has sprung up regarding the impact
of privatization on per capita consumption and harm. A recent review of this literature
(Her et al., 1999) noted that there was substantial blurring between the nature of the operation of private and government-owned alcohol retail systems. Some private systems were
heavily regulated and some government monopolies were highly commercially orientated
in their operation (see also Janes & Gruenewald, 1991). In addition, in nearly all instances
privatization promoted a long-term increase in per capita consumption. It was recommended that further studies also examine more systematically the impacts of such major
changes in regulatory style on indices of alcohol-related harm.

In the discussions of the importance of the major means of influencing the physical availability of alcohol, among the themes that have emerged is the importance of local contextual factors in determining the net outcome of a particular change in alcohol's availability.
It follows that if general principles from the international literature cannot always be
applied to every specific context, systems should be established at the local level for monitoring the occurrence of alcohol-related harm across key domains, such as violent crime,
drink–driving, injury, death and illness. The application of Geographic Information System
technology to this area (Midford et al., 1998; Wieczorek and Hansen, 1997) and the
utilization of local level indicators (Stockwell et al., 1998) could facilitate a rational and
empirically-based approach to minimizing harm at the local level. An encouraging trend in

this area has been for liquor licensing laws in some English-speaking countries, such as Canada, New Zealand and Australia, to adopt the minimization of alcohol-related harm as the principle objective. The existence of strategies that can be targeted successfully at high-risk drinking environments to make them safer places (see Homel et al., Chapter 14) suggests the need for strong local information bases on serious harm which can target these strategies and assist in their evaluation. Health, police and liquor-licensing authorities could be assisted to apply this information in the regulation of the conduct of liquor licensees (see Rydon & Stockwell, 1997). In fact, when this strategy is pursued at the local level, it has been shown to be successful in forming policy in community areas (Reynolds, Holder & Gruenewald, 1997; Gruenewald, Roeper & Millar, 1996b). Examples of local harm indicators that appear to be most relevant here are rates of assaults, road crashes and hospital injury presentations between the hours of 9 p.m. and 4 a.m. (Brinkman et al., 2000).

There has been increasing interest in the 1990s in the development and application of community-based indicators for monitoring alcohol-related harm and the effectiveness of responses at the local level (see Gruenewald et al., 1997; Holder, 1998). An important reason for the need to develop local monitoring systems is that with the increasing emphasis in some countries on harm minimization as a primary objective of liquor licensing laws, local licensing issues are increasingly contested and defended against this principle. As an example, in one Australian jurisdiction (Gull Petroleum vs. Health Department of Western Australia, 1999) it has been ruled that applications of general principles from the research literature in relation to alcohol's commercial availability do not constitute expert testimony, and that local factors and research are the sole determining legitimate sources of evidence.

CONCLUSIONS

Some important lessons can be learned from a review of the literature on the macro relationships between alcohol availability, alcohol consumption and alcohol-related harm. While the relationships under study still require further study, in most instances it has been found that changes in the physical availability of alcohol affect local, regional and state levels of alcohol-related use and problems. There are many challenges to be addressed by researchers and policy makers in the future, principally to examine the specific impacts of different types of change to alcohol's availability on different patterns and levels of drinking with attendant problems. It will be important to examine the moderating effects of different drinking settings, the routine activities of the actors in these settings and to develop the technology for monitoring local, state and national harm indicators.

The major scientific challenges will be: (a) to determine what are the primary processes in communities that influence the production of alcohol-related harm; and (b) to develop models that can be used to estimate the amount of alcohol-related harm associated with different types and distributions of alcohol outlets. Although simple direct relationships between alcohol availability and harm are unlikely to be uncovered in community settings, in-depth scientific investigations into the community systems underlying alcohol-related problems will reveal the contingent relationships that result in alcohol-related harm.

An important challenge for the development of evidence-based alcohol policy will be to determine a means to establish optimum geographic distributions of different types of alcohol outlets for a range of different community contexts. In this regard it should be noted that the local effects of distributions of alcohol outlets on one problem (e.g. traffic crashes) may be quite different from the local effects on another (e.g. violence). Thus, over-concentrations of outlets in downtown retail areas may contribute relatively little to alcohol-related crashes (Gruenewald & Treno, 2000) but very much to increased rates of violence

(Gorman et al., 2001). The dispersion of these same outlets into areas of greater traffic flow may aggravate alcohol-related crash rates while mitigating violent events. Although it is much too early for the scientific research evidence to speak comprehensively to these issues, that they can be broached in current scientific discourse represents a major step forward in the field. Next steps will require much more detailed understanding of the genesis and distribution of alcohol-related problems across community areas.

A fundamental challenge for policy in the area of regulating alcohol availability will be to determine effective mechanisms whereby local distributions of outlets can be regulated to minimize alcohol-related harm while within the context of "fair" competitive practices (balancing retail access against secondary costs of distribution and use). Even with the best scientific evidence in hand, policy makers must balance the needs for sensible community growth (e.g. in retail and residential sectors) against the secondary costs related to availability in the context of local community values. These values may tend toward the reduction of alcohol-related problems along one or another dimensions important to community residents. Thus, one community could balance the costs of drunken driving events against the benefits of the substantial tax base created through greater retail growth; another could balance local rates of pedestrian injury relative to efficient traffic flow through dense retail areas; still another may consider violence related to outlet over-concentration to be so problematic as to require the implementation of severe distance requirements (spreading out outlets relative to one another). Regardless of the concern of community residents, students of this area should be prepared to build the scientific foundations upon which such decisions can be made.

KEY WORKS AND SUGGESTIONS FOR FURTHER READING

Edwards, G., Anderson, P., Babor, T.F. et al. (1994). *Alcohol Policy and the Public Good.* Oxford: Oxford University Press.

> To date, the major review of studies relating to alcohol availability and harm. An international group of scientists under the auspices of WHO each contribute chapters on a wide range of alcohol policy issues, summarizing the available evidence.

Gruenewald, P.J., Treno, A.J., Taff, G. & Klitzner, M. (1997). *Measuring Community Indicators: A Systems Approach to Drug and Alcohol Problems.* Thousand Oaks, CA: Sage.

> An introduction and guide for researchers interested in measuring local levels of alcohol use and harm for the purpose of evaluating prevention strategies and policies.

Stockwell, T. (Ed.) (1995). *Alcohol Misuse and Violence, 5. An Examination of the Appropriateness and Efficacy of Liquor Licensing Laws across Australia.* Canberra: Australian Government Publishing Service.

> While the focus of this multi-authored book is on recommendations for Australian policy, it contains several reviews of key literatures on alcohol availablity and harm, not only in relation to violence. It also summarizes surveys of public opinion regarding policy options on alcohol availability.

Holder, H.D. (1998). *Alcohol and the Community: Systems Approach to Prevention.* London: Cambridge University Press.

> An overview of the design, implementation and outcomes from the most comprehensively evaluated community alcohol intervention trial ever conducted. Efforts to reduce alcohol's availability were one of four major strategies adopted. Offers a systems view

of how control policies might be integrated with other regulatory and education strategies.

REFERENCES

Abbey, A., Scott, R.O. & Smith, M.J. (1993). Physical, subjective, and social availability: their relationship to alcohol consumption in rural and urban areas. *Addiction*, **88**, 489–499.

Alaniz, M.L., Cartmill, R.S. & Parker, R.N. (1998). Immigrants and violence: the importance of neighborhood context. *Hispanic Journal of Behavioral Sciences*, **20**, 155–174.

Brinkman, S., Stockwell, T., Chikritzhs, T. & Mathewson, P. (2000). An indicator approach to the measurement of alcohol related violence. In P. Williams (Ed.), *Alcohol, Young People and Violence*. Canberra: Australian Institute of Criminology, Research and Public Policy.

Bruun, K., Edwards, G., Lumio, M., Makela, K., Pan, L., Popham, R. et al. (1975). *Alcohol Control Policies in Public Health Perspective*. The Finnish Foundation for Alcohol Studies, Vol. 25. Helsinki: Forssa.

Chikritzhs, T., Stockwell, T. & Masters, L. (1997). *Evaluation of the Public Health and Safety Impact of Extended Trading Permits for Perth Hotels*. Technical Report, National Centre for Research into the Prevention of Drug Abuse, Division of Health Sciences. Perth: Curtin University of Technology.

Chikritzhs, T. & Stockwell, T. (2002). Impact of later trading hours for Australian public houses (hotels) on levels of violence. *Journal of Studies on Alcohol*, **63**, 591–599.

Chou, Y.H. (1991). Map resolution and spatial autocorrelation. *Geographical Analysis*, **23**, 228–246.

Clayson, C. (1984). Licensing law and health: the Scottish experience. Action on Alcohol Abuse Policy Forum: Licensing Law and Health, 4 December, London.

D'Abbs, P., Forner, J. & Thomsen, P. (1993). *Darwin Nightclubs: A Review of Trading Hours and Related Issues*. Darwin: Menzies School of Public Health.

Duffy, J.C. & Plant, M.A. (1986). Scotland's liquor licensing changes; an assessment. *British Medical Journal*, **292**, 36–39.

Edwards, G., Anderson, P., Babor, T.F. et al. (1994). *Alcohol Policy and the Public Good*. Oxford: Oxford University Press.

Gmel, G., Klingemann, S., Müller, R. & Brenner, D. (2001). Revising the preventive paradox: the Swiss case. *Addiction*, **96**(2), 273–284.

Gorman, D.M., Speer, P.W., Labouvie, E.W. & Subaiya, A.P. (1998). Risk of assaultive violence and alcohol availability in New Jersey. *American Journal of Public Health*, **88**, 97–100.

Gorman, D.M., Speer, P.W., Gruenewald, P.J. & Labouvie, E.W. (2001). Spatial dynamics of alcohol availability, neighbourhood structures and violent crime. *Journal of Studies on Alcohol*, **62**, 628–636.

Grant, B.F. (1996). Prevalence and correlates of drug use and DSM-IV drug dependence in the United States: results of the National Longitudinal Alcohol Epidemiologic Survey. *Journal of Substance Abuse*, **8**, 195–210.

Gray, D. (2000). Indigenous Australians and liquor licensing restrictions. *Addiction*, **95**, 1469–1472.

Grossman, M. (1998). Health economics of prevention of alcohol-related problems. Paper presented at the Workshop on Health Economics of Prevention and Treatment of Alcohol-Related Problems, National Institute on Alcohol Abuse and Alcoholism, Washington, DC.

Grube, J.W. (1997). Preventing sales of alcohol to minors: results from a community trial. *Addiction*, **92**, S251–S260.

Gruenewald, P.J. (2000). The epiphenomena of beverage specific effects. *Addiction*, **95**, 347–358.

Gruenewald, P.J., Madden, P. & Janes, K. (1992). Alcohol availability and the formal power and resources of state alcohol beverage control agencies. *Alcoholism: Clinical and Experimental Research*, **16**, 591–597.

Gruenewald, P.J., Millar, A.B. & Treno, A.J. (1993). Alcohol availability and the ecology of drinking behavior. *Alcohol Health & Research World*, **17**, 39–45.

Gruenewald, P.J., Ponicki, W.R. & Holder, H.D. (1993). The relationship of outlet densities to alcohol consumption: a time series cross-sectional analysis. *Alcoholism: Clinical and Experimental Research*, **17**, 38–47.

Gruenewald, P.J. & Ponicki, W.R. (1995a).   The relationship of the retail availability of alcohol and alcohol sales to alcohol-related traffic crashes. *Accident Analysis and Prevention*, **27**, 249–259.

Gruenewald, P.J. & Ponicki, W.R. (1995b).   The relationship of alcohol sales to cirrhosis mortality. *Journal of Studies on Alcohol*, **56**, 635–641.

Gruenewald, P.J., Ponicki, W.R. & Mitchell, P.R. (1995).   Suicide rates and alcohol consumption in the United States: 1970–1989. *Addiction*, **90**, 1063–1075.

Gruenewald, P.J., Millar, A.B., Treno, A.J., Yang, Z., Ponicki, W.R. & Roeper, P. (1996a).   The geography of availability and driving after drinking. *Addiction*, **91**, 967–983.

Gruenewald, P.J., Roeper, P. & Millar, A. (1996b).   Access to alcohol: geography and prevention for local communities. *Alcohol Health & Research World*, **20**, 244–251.

Gruenewald, P.J. & Treno, A.J. (2000).   Local and global alcohol supply: economic and geographic models of community systems. *Addiction*, **95**, 5537–5550.

Gruenewald, P.J., Treno, A.J., Taff, G. & Klitzner, M. (1997).   *Measuring Community Indicators: A Systems Approach to Drug and Alcohol Problems*. Thousand Oaks, CA: Sage.

Gruenewald, P.J., Millar, A.B., Ponicki, W.R. & Brinkley, G. (2000).   Physical and economic access to alcohol: the application of geostatistical methods to small area analysis in community settings. In R. Wilson & M. DuFour (Eds), *Small Area Analysis and the Epidemiology of Alcohol Problems*. NIAAA Monograph, Rockville, MD: NIAAA.

Gruenewald, P.J., Stockwell, T., Beel, A. & Dyskin, E.V. (1999).   Beverage sales and drinking and driving: The role of on-premise drinking places. *Journal of Studies on Alcohol*, **60**, 47–53.

Gull Petroleum v. Health Department of WA, Liquor Licensing Court of Western Australia, April, 1999.

Her, M., Giesbrecht, N., Room, R. & Rehm, J. (1999).   Privatizing alcohol sales and alcohol consumption: evidence and implications. *Addiction*, **94**(8), 1125–1139.

Holder, H.D. (1998).   *Alcohol and the Community: A Systems Approach to Prevention*. London: Cambridge University Press.

International Center for Alcohol Policies (1998).   *Drinking Age Limits*. ICAP Reports 4, March. Washington, DC: International Center for Alcohol Policies.

Janes, K. & Gruenewald, P.J. (1991).   The role of formal law in alcohol control systems: a comparison among states. *The American Journal of Drug and Alcohol Abuse*, **17**, 2.

Jernigan, D. (1997).   *Thirsting for Markets—The Global Impact of Corporate Alcohol*. San Rafael, CA: The Marin Institute for the Prevention of Alcohol and Other Drug Problems.

Jewell, R.T. & Brown, R.W. (1995).   Alcohol availability and alcohol-related motor vehicle accidents. *Applied Economics*, **27**, 759–765.

Kendell, R.E., De Roumanie, M. & Ritson, E.B. (1983).   Effect of economic changes on Scottish drinking habits, 1978–82. *British Journal of Addiction*, **78**(4), 365–379.

Kerr, W.C. (in press).   Beverage-specific alcohol consumption and cirrhosis mortality in a group of English-speaking beer drinking countries. *Addiction*.

Kreitman, N. (1986).   Alcohol consumption and the Preventive Paradox. *British Journal of Addiction*, **81**(3), 353–364.

Lang, E., Stockwell, T. & Whitehead, M. (1995).   In T. Stockwell (Ed.), *Alcohol Misuse and Violence Report No 5: A Review of the Appropriateness and Efficacy of Liquor Licensing Laws across Australia*. Canberra: Australian Government Publishing Service.

Lang, E., Stockwell, T., Rydon, P. & Beel, A. (1996).   The use of pseudo patrons to assess compliance with licensing regarding underage drinking. *Australian Journal of Public Health*, **20**(3), 296–300.

LaScala, E.A., Gerber, D. & Gruenewald, P.J. (2000).   Demographic and environmental correlates of pedestrian injury collisions: a spatial analysis. *Accident Analysis and Prevention*, **32**, 651–658.

Ledermann, S. (1956).   *Alcohol, Alcoholism, Alcoholisation*, Vol 1. Connees scientifiques de caractere physiologique, economique et social. Institute National d'Etudes Demographique, Travaus et Documents, Cah. No. 29. Paris: Presses Universitaires de France.

Mclaughlin, K.L. & Harrison-Stewart, A.J. (1992).   The effect of a temporary period of relaxed licensing laws on the alcohol consumption of young male drinkers. *International Journal of the Addictions*, **27**(4), 409–423.

Midford, R., Masters, L., Phillips, M., Daly, A., Stockwell, T., Gahegan, M. & Philp, A. (1998).   Alcohol consumption and injury in Western Australia: a spatial correlation analysis using geographic information systems. *Australian and New Zealand Journal of Public Health*, **22**(1), 80–85.

Nelson, J.P. (1990). State monopolies and alcoholic beverage consumption. *Journal of Regulatory Economics*, **2**, 83–98.

Nordlund, S. (1985). Effects of Saturday closing of wine and spirits shops in Norway. Presented at the 31st International Institute on the Prevention and Treatment of Alcoholism, Rome, June 2–7.

Olsson, O. & Wikström, P.H. (1982). Effects of the experimental Saturday closing of liquor retail stores in Sweden. *Contemporary Drug Problems*, **11**(3), 325–353.

Österberg, E. & Säilä, S. (Eds) (1991). *Natural experiments with decreased availability of alcoholic beverages: Finnish alcohol strikes in 1972 and 1985.* Helsinki: Finnish Foundation for Alcohol Studies.

Parker, R.N. & Rebhun, L.A. (1995). *Alcohol and Homicide: A Deadly Combination of Two American Traditions.* Albany, NY: State University of New York Press.

Parker, R.N. & Auerhahn, K. (1998). Alcohol, drugs, and violence. *Annual Reviews of Sociology*, **24**, 291–311.

Rabow, J., Watts, R.K. & Hernandez, A.C.R. (1993). Alcoholic beverage licensing practices in California: a study of a regulatory agency. *Alcoholism: Clinical and Experimental Research*, **17**, 241–245.

Reifman, A., Barnes, G.M., Dintcheff, B.A., Farrell, M.P. & Uhteg, L. (1998). Parental and peer influences on the onset of heavier drinking among adolescents. *Journal of Studies on Alcohol*, **59**(3), 311–317.

Reynolds, R.I., Holder, D. & Gruenewald, P.J. (1997). Community prevention and alcohol retail access. *Addiction*, **92**(2), S155–S171.

Rydon, P., Stockwell, T., Lang, E. & Beel, A. (1996). "Pseudo-drunk" patron evaluation of bar-staff compliance with Western Australian liquor law. *Australian Journal of Public Health*, **20**(3), 290–295.

Rydon, P. & Stockwell, T. (1997). Local regulation and enforcement strategies for licensed premises. In M. Plant, E. Single & T. Stockwell (Eds), *Alcohol: Minimizing the Harm—What Works?*, New York: Free Association Books.

Scribner, R.A., MacKinnon, D.P. & Dwyer, J.H. (1994). Alcohol outlet density and motor vehicle crashes in Los Angeles County cities. *Journal of Studies on Alcohol*, **55**, 447–453.

Scribner, R.A., MacKinnon, D.P. & Dwyer, J.H. (1995). The risk of assaultive violence and alcohol availability in Los Angeles County. *American Journal of Public Health*, **85**, 335–340.

Single, E.W. (1988). The availability theory of alcohol related problems. In C.D. Chaudron & D.A. Wilkinson (Eds), *Theories on Alcoholism* (pp. 325–351). Toronto: Addiction Research Foundation.

Skög, O.-J. (1985). *The distribution of Alcohol Consumption. Part III: Evidence of a Collective Drinking Culture.* Oslo: National Institute for Alcohol Research.

Smart, R. & Mann, R. (1992). Alcohol and the epidemiology of liver cirrhosis. *Alcohol Health and Research World*, **16**, 217–222.

Smith, D.I. (1988). Effect on traffic accidents of introducing Sunday alcohol sales in Brisbane, Australia. *International Journal of the Addictions*, **23**(10), 1091–1099.

Smith, D.I. (1986). Comparison of patrons of hotels with early opening and standard hours. *International Journal of the Addictions*, **21**, 155–163.

Speer, P.W., Gorman, D.M., Labouvie, E.W. & Ontkush, M.J. (1998). Violent crime and alcohol availability: relationship in an urban community. *Journal of Public Health Policy*, **19**, 175–190.

Stevenson, R.J., Lind, B. & Weatherburn, D. (1999). The relationship between alcohol sales and assault in New South Wales, Australia. *Addiction*, **94**(3), 397–410.

Stockwell, T., Somerford, P. & Lang, E. (1992a). The relationship between license type and alcohol related problems attributed to licensed premises in Perth, Western Australia. *Journal of Studies on Alcohol*, **53**(5), 495–498.

Stockwell, T., Rydon, P., Gianatti, S., Jenkins, E., Ovenden, C. & Syed, D. (1992b). Levels of drunkenness of customers leaving licensed premises in Perth, Western Australia: a comparison of high and low "risk" premises. *British Journal of Addiction*, **87**, 873–881.

Stockwell, T., Masters, L., Phillips, M., Daly, A., Midford, R., Gahegan, M. & Philp, A. (1998). Consumption of different alcoholic beverages as predictors of local rates of assault, road crash and hospital admission. *Australian and New Zealand Journal of Public Health*, **22**(2), 237–242.

Storey, H., Broderick, G. & Hamilton, M. (1998). *Control Act 1987: Review.* Melbourne: State Government of Victoria.

US General Accounting Office (1987).   *Drinking Age Laws: An Evaluation Synthesis of Their Impact on Highway Safety.* Washington, DC: US Superintendant of Documents.

Wagenaar, A. (1993).   Research effects public policy: the case of the legal drinking age in the United States. *Addiction*, **88**(Suppl.), 75s–81s.

Watts, R.K. & Rabow, J. (1983).   Alcohol availability and alcohol-related problems in 213 California cities. *Alcoholism: Clinical and Experimental Research*, **7**, 47–58.

Wieczorek, W.F. & Coyle, J.J. (1998).   Targeting DWI prevention. *Journal of Prevention & Intervention in the Community*, **17**, 15–30.

Wieczorek, W.F. & Hansen, C.E. (1997).   New modeling methods: geographic information systems and spatial analysis. *Alcohol Health & Research World*, **21**, 331–339.

Chapter 14

Creating Safer Drinking Environments

Ross Homel
Gillian McIlwain
School of Criminology and Criminal Justice, Griffith University,
Brisbane, Queensland, Australia
and
Russell Carvolth
Alcohol, Tobacco and Other Drug Services, Queensland Health,
Brisbane, Queensland, Australia

Synopsis

The focus of the chapter is violence and crime in the licensed drinking environment. The central argument is that creating safer licensed environments is primarily a regulatory problem, not just an "alcohol problem", and that formal enforcement is a necessary but not sufficient tool for creating a culture of compliance. A system of regulation that is responsive to industry conditions will rely on the interaction of formal regulation, which is the political domain; informal regulation; mobilizing civil society; and self-regulation, taming the market.

To be effective, regulatory systems must reduce situationally specific risk factors in the licensed environment that are related primarily to management practices and to "hidden deals" between licensees and regulators. Effective regulation will ensure that the physical environment is attractive and sends a message to patrons about appropriate behaviour; that it does not irritate or frustrate people by being crowded, excessively noisy, hot or smoky; that provocation related to forms of entertainment is minimized; and that non-salty food is freely available. The social environment will not be permissive, having clear limits concerning sexual

The Essential *Handbook of Treatment and Prevention of Alcohol Problems.* Edited by N. Heather and T. Stockwell.
© 2004 John Wiley & Sons Ltd. ISBN 0-470-86296-3.

and other behaviours; drinking to intoxication, especially by large numbers simultaneously, will be discouraged; trained, peace-loving security and bar staff will be employed; and people identified as regularly aggressive will be kept out.

There is limited evidence that formal enforcement through visible, random checks on licensees can be effective, as can undercover policing combined with warnings to managers. There is consistent evidence that mobilizing local community groups and agencies through organized community action can bring about major reductions in aggression and violence in and around venues, although the effects have not been demonstrated to be permanent in any locality. Critical ingredients of community action include: strong directive leadership during the establishment period; the mobilization of community groups concerned about violence and disorder; the implementation of a multi-agency approach involving licensees, local government, police, health and other groups; the use of safety audits to engage the local community and identify risks; a focus on the way licensed venues are managed (particularly those that cater to large numbers of young people); the "re-education" of patrons concerning their role as consumers of "quality hospitality", and attention to situational factors, including serving practices, that promote intoxication and violent confrontations.

Approaches available to regulators include licensing provisions; policy development; cooperation with the industry to develop standards; developing formal and informal codes of practice; education, publicity and information campaigns (especially at the local level); incentives for responsible operators; and working with the community. These approaches can usefully be arranged in an enforcement pyramid, the broad base representing frequently used approaches based on suasion, cooperation and negotiation, the sharp end representing the ultimate but infrequently used sanctions, such as the closure of an establishment. In addition, to ensure transparency and accountability in this most difficult of regulatory arenas, a system of responsive regulation will accord a central place to community empowerment and to the role of public interest groups.

Fights are known to occur in or around pubs and taverns, and sometimes people get hurt. Usually young men are involved, and usually they're drunk—or so people assume. Fights like this are a problem, of course, especially if one's son or daughter is involved, but unless the injuries are really serious, it seems no one worries too much—least of all the police, who dislike the messy business of trying to get statements from people who can't stand up straight and are frequently uncooperative, incoherent or violently ill (Homel & Tomsen, 1991).

However, the enforcement problem can take on a new dimension if lots of fights and incidents of disorderly conduct occur in a local "hot spot" on a regular basis. Downtown entertainment areas in many towns and cities often take on this character, becoming notorious for law-and-order and public safety problems that make extra attention from regulatory authorities and local government politically unavoidable. But then the response is often purely political: sweeping the streets clean of the human riff-raff in a series of well publicized blitzes for public relations purposes, rather than attending to the underlying problems of how venues and the surrounding public space are managed and regulated.

Despite the often blasé attitudes of the regulators, there is an emerging awareness in the research literature that a serious public health issue is at stake (e.g. Stockwell et al., 1995). One feature of assault victimization found in all crime victim surveys, including those analysed by Homel & Mirrlees-Black (1997) in Queensland, is the extremely high rates of victimization of teenagers and young adults. The survey data also highlight the importance of environmental or situational factors as risk factors for young people. In general, those who go out for entertainment at night, particularly to hotels and nightclubs, have a higher than average risk of assault. The same pattern applies to teenagers: about half of male and female teenage victims are assaulted in places they go to regularly (away from a home environment) which provide leisure or entertainment. Many of these places, especially for those aged 18 years or over, are licensed venues. It follows that one important strategy for reducing violence is to increase the safety of leisure and entertainment venues, including hotels and nightclubs, especially for young patrons.

We argue in this chapter that creating safer licensed environments is primarily a regulatory problem, not just an "alcohol problem". A fundamental assumption is that whatever the effects of alcohol, its role is mediated by cultural, personal and contextual factors that are still the subject of active research. To quote Homel, Tomsen & Thommeny (1992: 681), who conducted observational studies of aggression and violence in licensed venues in Sydney:

> A key assumption was that there is a complex (but nevertheless real) relation between violence and public drinking (not the mere ingestion of ethanol) which is imbedded in Australian history and culture and reproduced in institutional arrangements and regulatory and police practices regarding drinking. In our research we aimed to transcend the narrow debate about the effects of ethanol *the substance* by focusing on the *total environment* of drinking and its regulation (or lack of regulation) by management, police and other public officials. Thus, we considered features of the external regulation of licensed premises as well as more directly observable characteristics such as physical layout, patron mix and social atmosphere.

If safety in licensed environments is a regulatory problem, it is a problem not much different in its essential nature from, say, persuading small businesses to comply with environmental laws or nursing home proprietors to maintain minimum prescribed standards of care. There are of course specific features of drinking environments that might make them problematic for the safety of their patrons (or staff), and it is very important that these be understood if wise regulations are to be devised. Nursing home regulations will not suffice for nightclubs.

One difficulty historically is that licensing and other laws relevant to the licensed environment have often not been very wise, in the sense that the known risk factors, such as simultaneous binge drinking by a large number of patrons, have not influenced the legal provisions (Stockwell, 1997). An even greater difficulty is that in many countries the laws, inadequate as they might be, have not been enforced very well. These difficulties have led in other fields both to extensive law reform and to the creation of complex mechanisms for persuading the target population if they cannot be coerced. In the licensed environments arena, the trend has been partly to new laws but even more to alternative regulatory models that rely in some way on new forms of "non-legal" persuasion or on legal measures that fall short of prosecution (Stockwell, 1995). In recent years an important element in the search for new kinds of regulatory "levers" to effect change has been the use of community action techniques.

This chapter is mainly about this search for new forms of regulation through community action. The focus is the licensed environment, especially hotels, taverns and nightclubs that provide entertainment for young people, since these are more likely to be sites of alcohol-related harm (Casswell, Zhang & Wyllie, 1993; Stockwell, Somerford & Lang, 1992). The perspective is Australian, although we draw on all the published international research of which we are aware. We begin with a brief review of what is known about risk and protective factors in the licensed environment, and then examine the literature from North America and Australia on community initiatives. We conclude that although promising new regulatory forms are emerging, no-one has yet succeeded in demonstrating a permanent reduction in disorder, crime and violence through community action. This may reflect failures of implementation or, in other cases, the failure of the formal apparatus of state control—police and liquor licensing authorities—to "follow through" with consistent enforcement in the aftermath of a community initiative.

The search for a satisfactory system of regulation requires "praxis in concrete institutional arenas" (Ayres & Braithwaite, 1992). Slogans like "zero tolerance" will not suffice, neither will any rigid adherence to a single doctrine, regardless of context. It is clear that community action *can* reduce aggressive incidents and injuries. The challenge is to institutionalize the critical ingredients, especially the power of community groups to act as credible watchdogs, in forms that are sensitive to the political environment and to local conditions.

RISK AND PROTECTIVE FACTORS

While methods of preventing alcohol-related crime at large "one-off" or irregular public events have some relevance to the present discussion, the primary focus of this chapter is on the slightly different issue of the prevention of violence that may occur routinely in and around licensed venues.[1] Consequently, the discussion in this section is based on the review chapter on "safer bars" by Graham & Homel (1997) (a more recent review by Graham & West, 2001), and the earlier studies by Graham et al. (1980) and by Homel and his colleagues (Homel, Tomsen & Thommeny, 1992; Homel & Clark, 1994; Tomsen, Homel & Thommeny, 1991).

The Physical Environment

Using the Environment to Create Expectations about Behaviour

Attractive, nicely furnished, well-maintained premises give a message to the patron that the managers do not anticipate physical violence and associated damage to furnishings. Graham et al. (1980) found in their study of bars in Vancouver that aggression was significantly correlated with poorly maintained, unclean, unattractive bar environments. In Sydney (Homel & Clark, 1994), a relationship was found between bar cleanliness and aggression.

Avoiding Physical Environment Features that Irritate or Frustrate People

Aggression in bars has been found to be associated with poor ventilation and smoky air, inconvenient bar access and inadequate seating, high noise level and crowding (Graham et al., 1980; Graham, 1985; Homel & Clark, 1994). A plausible link between these aspects of the environment and aggressive behaviour is the role of these factors in irritating, frustrating or otherwise provoking bar patrons, particularly highly intoxicated bar patrons.

In a study of crowding, Macintyre & Homel (1997) concluded that, for any given level of patron density (people per square metre), some venues exhibited higher levels of crowding (unintended low-level physical contacts) than others. The more crowded venues tended to be the more violent, and in these high-risk establishments crowding increased more rapidly with patron density than in low-risk venues. Crowding appeared to arise partly from inappropriate pedestrian flow patterns caused by poor location of entry and exit doors, dance floors, bars and toilets.

---

[1] For research and guidelines on the maintenance of order at large public events and in public places, see: Alcoholic Liquor Advisory Council (1996); Bjor, Knutsson & Kuhlhorn (1992); Department of Tourism, Sport & Racing (1999); Dunstan & McDonald (1996); Ramsay (1989, 1990, 1991); Magnificent Events Company (1996).

Minimizing Provocation Related to Games and Entertainment

Graham et al. (1980) found that aggression was more likely in bars where there was dancing and pool playing (no relationship with aggression was found for other games such as darts and shuffleboard). Gibbs (1986) in his review article used the example of pool playing to demonstrate how formal and informal rules can be used to structure bar environments in order to reduce both frequency and severity of aggression. His suggestions included limits on betting, establishing protocols regarding appropriate behaviour around pool games, and keeping observers of the game out of any disputes that arise.

Safer Glassware and Other Harm Reduction Strategies

Shepherd (1994) observed that some of the more severe injuries resulting from bar fights were caused by using broken glasses or bottles as weapons, and suggested the substitution of tempered glass. Many venues do use plastic glasses on a routine basis.

Encouraging Eating with Drinking

The availability of food (especially full meals) has been associated with reduced risk of aggression in bars (Graham, 1985; Homel & Clark, 1994). This may be because the types of bars that serve food are less likely to have aggressive patrons; they are more likely to have a positive social atmosphere; and because eating while drinking slows absorption of alcohol, reducing the blood alcohol level the drinker reaches (Wedel et al., 1991).

The Social Environment and Social Control

Creating a Social Atmosphere with Clear Limits

The "permissiveness" of the environment has been shown to be associated with aggressive behaviour (Graham et al., 1980; Homel & Clark, 1994; Hauritz et al., 1998). This includes overall decorum expectations, abusive swearing, sexual activity among patrons, sexual competition, prostitution, drug use and dealing, male rowdiness, and male roughness and bumping. Management and staff behaviour is also important: there is greater aggression where bar staff are very permissive and do not engage in responsible serving practices (e.g. serving underage patrons) (Homel & Clark, 1994), or where staff exercise little control over patrons' behaviour (Graham et al., 1980). Aggression has also been found to be more likely in bars where drunkenness is frequent (Graham et al., 1980; Homel & Clark, 1994) and where there are discount drinks and other drink promotions (Homel et al., 1992).

Discouraging Drinking to Intoxication

A high proportion of intoxicated patrons is associated (in complex ways) with aggression. High levels of intoxication signal a generally permissive environment, but there is also a consistent relationship between drunkenness and aggression in a number of studies (Graham & West, 2001) that suggests a variety of causal paths. In addition, the *severity* of aggression is related to levels of drunkenness (Graves et al., 1981).

Fostering a Positive Social Atmosphere

Positive atmospheres that are friendly rather than tense and hostile, that include quiet laughter and small talk rather than hostile talk, and where patron boredom is low, are associated with a lower risk of aggression (Graham et al., 1980; Homel & Clark, 1994).

Employing Trained Peace-loving Staff

Aggression has been found to occur in response to venue staff exercising social control such as refusing service and otherwise intervening with intoxicated patrons (Felson, Baccaglini & Gmelch, 1986; Graves et al., 1981; Homel & Clark, 1994). Bouncers, in particular, have been identified as sometimes *increasing* the harm associated with bar-room aggression (Homel et al., 1992; Marsh & Kibby, 1992).

Keeping out Aggressive People

Certain bars are violent because they are frequented by aggressive people (Graham & West, 2001; Tomsen et al., 1991). Therefore, a necessary feature of safer bars is the capability to recognize and ban, if necessary, persistent trouble-makers.

PREVENTION PROGRAMS

To be effective, prevention programs must reduce multiple risk factors in the licensed environment. It may not much matter which particular risk factors are manipulated, provided that several of the features discussed in the previous section are covered. However, whatever else is done, controls on the incidence of intoxication, particularly mass intoxication, must probably be implemented for violence to decline substantially (Hauritz et al., 1998; Homel & Clark, 1994).

Responsible Server Programs

These programs employ a variety of techniques to prevent intoxication, including observing patrons and being able to recognize intoxication; promoting non-alcoholic and low-alcohol drinks; serving well-priced, attractive and well-marketed food low in salt content; and training staff in techniques for monitoring patrons and adjusting service as necessary. Training is also provided in refusal of service to patrons who are intoxicated or who show signs of becoming intoxicated. Bar staff are trained in offering positive alternatives, such as soft drinks or food at discounted prices, and both management and staff are trained in negotiation techniques with patrons who are becoming difficult or aggressive. The importance of a well-publicized "house policy" to provide a positive context for responsible serving practices and for negotiation with patrons is emphasized (Simpson et al., 1987).

The small number of rigorous evaluations of responsible serving programs that have been published have reported mixed results. On the positive side, Saltz (1987), in an evaluation of an experimental 18 hour training programme in a USA Navy base, reported that the likelihood of a customer being intoxicated was cut in half, although for the establishment as a whole absolute consumption and the rate of consumption were not affected. Graham and her colleagues (2003) showed in a randomised experiment involving 500 staff from 18 of the 26 large capacity (300+) Toronto bars that the combination of a risk assessment completed by the owner/manager and a 3-hour training program for bar staff and managers in managing problem behaviours improved knowledge and attitudes and reduced incidents of severe aggression as documented by trained observers. On the other hand, Lang et al. (1998b) studied a responsible serving training program of 1–2 hours duration in seven sites. They found that there was no significant reduction in patrons with blood alcohol levels greater than 0.15% (i.e. those who were "very drunk"), or in the number of drinking and driving offences from the intervention sites. Researchers who pretended to be drunk were rarely refused service, and identification was rarely checked.

Lang et al. (1998b) attribute the disappointing results to poor implementation of the training and a lack of support among managers. They argue that server training should be mandatory, and that licensing laws must be routinely enforced if the goals of responsible service are to be met. It is noteworthy that in most of the programmes in the USA, responsible serving programmes are supported by legal sanctions or are embedded in broader community interventions. The crucial role of enforcement is highlighted by Jeffs & Saunders (1983), who reported the positive impact in an English seaside resort of the impact of uniformed police dropping in at random intervals two or three times a week and very conspicuously checking (in an amiable way) for under-age drinkers or intoxicated patrons. McKnight & Streff (1994) in the USA show that intensive undercover police operations, preceded by education of licensees about the enforcement activities, after-visit reports to licensees not cited, and media publicity, resulted (in comparison with a control county) in greatly increased refusals of service to "pseudopatrons" simulating intoxication and a marked decline in drunk drivers who had been served at the target establishments.

The great problem that is faced in most countries is that enforcement of licensing laws is not a high priority and therefore is not well resourced. Moreover, in some countries, such as Australia, the licensing area has been a seedbed for the corruption of police and other officials (Homel, 1996). For these and other reasons, "enforcement" approaches that do not depend solely on agencies of the state have become attractive in recent years.

Community Action Projects

Community approaches emphasize regulation of alcohol-related disorder and violence through procedures that empower residents, business people and citizen groups to resolve problems with licensed establishments and to take effective action at the local level. Resources and reports that are available to understand and implement this approach include: Alcohol Advisory Council of Western Australia (1989); Braun & Graham (1997); Eastern Sydney Area Health Service (1995); Gilling (1993); Lakeland & Durham (1991); Lang, Keenan & Brooke (1998a); Marsdon & James (1992); Parkdale Focus Community (1995); Robinson & Tether (1990); Robinson, Tether & Teller (1989); Shane & Cherry (1987); Standing Conference on Crime Prevention, (1986); Tether & Robinson (1986); the St Kilda Project (1997); Victorian Community Council Against Violence (1990); Welsh (1996).

There is a theoretical literature on community action, mainly from the USA and Canada, that emphasizes its complexity and difficulty (e.g. Giesbrecht et al., 1990; Giesbrecht and Ferris, 1993; Giesbrecht, Krempulec and West, 1993; Holder, 1992). Giesbrecht, Krempulec & West (1993) argue that the complexity arises from the "unstable mix" of processes such as research, community action, evaluation, and the type and level of intervention. The authors argue that by tackling the four main sources of problems faced by community projects, this unstable mix may be overcome. The four problems are: the ideologies and agendas of main parties; the difficulties faced by evaluators when the dynamics of implementation are beyond their control; the failure to train community members in "how-to-do" community-based interventions; and meeting goals because of funding problems, ill-defined timelines, political interference, poor methodology, and conflict among project participants (Lang, Keenan & Brooke, 1998a).

Giesbrecht et al. (1993) argue that problems might be overcome by locating the research agenda within a health promotion framework, which is seen as relevant to a wide range of agencies, programs and services at a community level. The bottom line, according to the authors, is the ability of such projects to facilitate manageable partnerships; to ensure scientific rigor in a dynamic context; and to impart skills and resources to community members so that they can realize worthy and realistic goals.

Despite the difficulties, community action can be demonstrated to work. Putnam,

Rockett & Campbell (1993) report the results of a very comprehensive community intervention on Rhode Island which resulted in a 21% reduction in Emergency Room assault injury rates in the intervention site compared with a 4% increase for the comparison communities. Motor vehicle crash injuries were also reduced. The community intervention involved server training as well as publicity campaigns, local task force activities, and community forums, and was supported by training of police and increased levels of enforcement with respect to alcohol-related accidents and crimes.

Undoubtedly the most wide-ranging and well-resourced attempt to date to reduce alcohol-related accidental injuries and deaths through community-based methods has been the work of Harold Holder and his colleagues in the USA (Holder et al., 1997a,b). This 5-year project carried out in three experimental communities consisted of five mutually reinforcing components: community mobilization; promotion of responsible beverage service for bar staff and managers/licensees of on-premises alcohol outlets; deterrence of drinking and driving through local enforcement; reduction in retail availability of alcohol to minors; and reductions in the number and density of alcohol outlets to limit general access to alcohol. The project did not target particular groups, but was based on the assumption that changes in the social and structural contexts of alcohol use can alter individual behaviour.

The community mobilization process involved working as much as possible with existing community coalitions, tailoring programme materials for each site, generating as far as possible resources from within the communities, and channelling existing community resources, skills and interests, rather than only introducing them from the outside. As Treno & Holder (1997, p. S176) observe, ". . . the Community Trials Project was composed of three independent replications of a generic prevention design . . . in which implementation approaches were designed within each community . . .".

The project brought about a 10% reduction in alcohol-involved traffic crashes, a significant reduction in underage sales of alcohol, and increased adoption of local ordinances and regulations to reduce concentrations of alcohol outlets. The specific aspect of the project of most relevance to the present chapter was the responsible beverage service (RBS) component:

> The general operating principle of this component was to create a combination of incentives and disincentives that would strongly encourage on-premise licensees to provide server training in responsible beverage serving practices and to strengthen their policies related to preventing intoxication and keeping intoxicated patrons from driving (Holder et al., 1997b, p. S162).

Saltz & Stanghetta (1997) conclude that this component achieved modest success as measured by the number of businesses trained, by the introduction of limited law enforcement around service to intoxicated patrons where none had existed previously, and by increases in levels of community debate about RBS policies. However, these program elements did not produce significant changes in serving practices. Saltz & Stanghetta argue that to achieve any impact, it is essential to involve the hospitality industry; to avoid voluntary RBS training; and (once again) to reinforce mandatory training with enforcement of the law around service to intoxicated patrons.

The Australian Experience

Perhaps as a response to the vacuum created by an inadequate regime of legal regulation, community action projects targeting licensed premises have proliferated in recent years in Australia. Examples include the Westend Forum in Melbourne (Melbourne City Council,

1991); Eastside Sydney Project (Lander, 1995); the St Kilda Project (1997); the Tennant Creek Project (a community collaboration against striptease shows; Boffa et al; 1994); the Kings Cross Licensing Accord (New South Wales Health Department, 1997); the Armidale Community Alcohol Strategy Committee (Cope, 1995); the Halls Creek initiative (Douglas, 1995), and several projects in South Australia (Fisher, 1993; Walsh, 1993). Limited evaluation data are available for these projects, although most show at least qualitative signs of impact, and some (like the Halls Creek project) suggest falls in alcohol consumption and reductions in crime and alcohol-related presentations at hospital.

Stockwell (1997), Boots et al. (1995) and Felson et al. (1997) report three recent Australian initiatives that have been evaluated: the "Freo Respects You" project in Fremantle, Western Australia, the COMPARI (Community Mobilization for the Prevention of Alcohol-Related Injury) project in Geraldton, Western Australia, and the "Geelong Accord" in Victoria. Recent work that colleagues and I have conducted in Queensland is summarized in the next section.

"Freo Respects You" was a collaborative project involving the hospitality industry, police, and liquor licensing and health authorities. The project was designed to increase levels of responsible service of alcohol in participating premises by providing incentives for drinkers to avoid excessive intake (e.g. offering competitively priced, reduced alcohol-drinks and good food); avoiding incentives for intoxication (e.g. very cheap, high-strength drinks); instituting policies to minimize the harm of being intoxicated (e.g. transport schemes) and establishing policies to minimize intoxication by refusing service to intoxicated customers. The other major component of the intervention was a series of training programs for licensees, managers and bar staff covering liquor licensing laws, strategies for dealing with drunk customers and the development of responsible house policies.

An evaluation of the project revealed that there was a significant increase in the awareness of bar staff's obligations under the Liquor Act and an increase in the rate at which bar staff at participating premises requested age ID. There were small improvements in the responsible house policies of some of the participating premises, including the provision of free non-alcoholic drinks for drivers and lower-priced reduced-alcohol beers. However, discounting of full-strength drinks continued and bar staff reported that they were serving obviously drunk customers. Stockwell (1997) suggests that the Fremantle Project was hindered by the fact that there was insufficient "ownership" of the project by licensed operators and that only medium- to high-risk premises participated.

The COMPARI project in Geraldton commenced in 1991. A local community taskforce was established in 1992, involving police, local government, health and education officers and the local public. The taskforce was encouraged to develop a sense of ownership through actively seeking alternative funding from local government and the regional health authority (Midford et al., 1994). Unfortunately, the evaluation found that, with regard to measures of alcohol-related harm, there was no evidence of a positive impact from the COMPARI project. Key informant interviews indicated that community awareness of alcohol issues had increased, along with improved knowledge about associated harm. There was, however, only minimal impact among young people. In line with experience with similar projects undertaken elsewhere, community participation was found to be highest during the early part of the project, following which numbers gradually reduced. Community leadership and organization, however, were judged to have improved as the project developed. The survey of community attitudes found a statistically significant increase in support for local council having a role in alcohol issues. There was an increased level of awareness of the project and the various activities, especially the "skipper" campaign, alcohol-free concerts and the campaign around the establishment of a new tavern.

The "Geelong Local Industry Accord," was a cooperative effort beginning in 1991, involving police, the Liquor Licensing Commission, hotel and nightclub licensees, and local government, although in practice police appear to have taken on the main leadership role (Felson et al., 1997; Kelly, 1993; Rumbold et al., 1998). Essentially the Accord is a code of practice that facilitates self-regulation by licensees throughout the region. "Best practice" provisions included specified types of photo-identification, minimum $5 cover charges after 11.00 p.m., no passouts from venues with an entry charge, no underage patrons and responsible service of alcohol (including elimination of gimmicks that promote rapid and excessive consumption of alcohol). A key strategy of the Accord was to stop "pub-hopping" by means of entry and exit controls.

No before–after measures of alcohol and drug related harm were available but police records suggest that reported assault and property damage rates reduced after the Accord was implemented (Rumbold et al., 1998). Moreover, in comparison with two other regional centres, practices in Geelong venues were significantly better in terms of responsible drinking promotions, amenities and responsible serving practices, although no differences were found with respect to crowding or overall levels of intoxication. In comparison with other community-based initiatives, the Geelong Accord seems to have maintained a positive impact over a period of several years. Rumbold et al. (1998) attribute this "longevity" to several factors, particularly the fact that the Accord was developed and resourced entirely within the local community, and the levels of stability in the local liquor industry and amongst police, local government and liquor licensing personnel.

It seems that the Fremantle, Geraldton and Geelong initiatives were mostly "top-down" rather than community-initiated interventions, despite the levels of cooperation achieved at the local level. In fact, most "community" projects seem to require at least some external resources or initiative to get them going, even if the level of community involvement and empowerment eventually achieved is quite high. As Midford et al. (1994) conclude, the "top-down" and "bottom-up" approaches both have strengths and weaknesses, and in practice should be seen as complementary rather than mutually exclusive.

The Queensland Safety Action Projects

The Surfers' Paradise Safety Action Project was a community-based initiative in 1993, designed to reduce violence in and around licensed venues in the central business district of the main tourist area on Queensland's Gold Coast. (Homel et al., 1997). Key features of the implementation included channelling funding through local government; creating a representative steering committee and community forum; forming task groups to address safety of public spaces, management of venues and security and policing; encouraging nightclub managers to introduce a Code of Practice, regulating serving and security staff, advertising, alcohol use and entertainment; and regulating managers through "risk assessments" and through a community-based monitoring committee. More subtle but equally important aspects of the implementation included: rehabilitating the image of nightclub managers and integrating them into the local business community; using managers committed to the reform process from another city to encourage and bring pressure to bear on local licensees; employing a Project Officer who was female and who had considerable interpersonal skills; and balancing the conflicting political agendas of participating agencies.

The evaluation showed a marked initial impact of the project, with reductions in practices that promote the irresponsible use of alcohol (such as binge-drinking incentives) and improvements in security practices, entertainment, handling of patrons and transport policies. Physical and verbal aggression inside and outside venues, based on structured observations pre- and post-implementation and on police and security data, showed substantial declines. Male and female drinking rates and drunkenness declined markedly, but there was no change in prices for drinks or admission. There were dramatic improvements in publicity to patrons about house policies and associated improvements in server practices, the physical environment (e.g. clean toilets and accessible bars) and security practices (e.g. ID checks at door).

However, there are indications that displacement of problem patrons may have been at least partly responsible for the impact of the project. In addition, observational data collected 2 years after completion of the project indicated that violence and drunkenness levels had returned to pre-project levels, and that compliance with the Code of Practice had almost ceased (Homel et al. 1997). Licensees attributed the deterioration to a failure on the part of regulators to deal with "cowboy operators" who flouted the Code of Practice and engaged in dangerous but (at least in the short term) profitable practices.

In 1995 the Surfers' Paradise Safety Action Project was replicated in Cairns, Townsville and Mackay in North Queensland (Hauritz et al., 1998). Many of the features of the Surfers' Paradise project were incorporated in the replications, but not all features were present at all sites, while others that seemed important in Surfers' (such as a community monitoring committee) were introduced quite late in some of the projects.

Using structured observational methods in 1994 and 1996, big reductions were observed in each city on overall physical and non-physical aggression. Paralleling this, there were marked improvements on most indicators of host responsibility practices, especially practices to control consumption. Publicity to patrons improved, with an increase in the use of underage drinking warnings, Patron Care signs and other forms of publicity. Presumably as a result of these initiatives, some drinking measures showed marked changes. Male and female drinking rates were not judged to have changed significantly, and neither did the estimated levels of female drunkenness, but male drunkenness appeared to decline sharply. These results imply that staff intervened in a firm way when serving men in order to prevent intoxication.

The fact that the situation in Surfers' Paradise was badly deteriorating in the 1994–1996 period suggests that the improvements observed in the replication projects were not part of a more general trend.

GUIDELINES FOR SOCIAL POLICY AND BEST PRACTICE

From the Queensland safety action research, features that characterize successful community interventions include: strong directive leadership during the establishment period; the mobilization of community groups concerned about violence and disorder; the implementation of a multi-agency approach involving licensees, local government, police, health and other groups; the use of safety audits to engage the local community and identify risks; a focus on the way licensed venues are managed (particularly those that cater to large numbers of young people); the "re-education" of patrons concerning their role as consumers of "quality hospitality"; and attention to situational factors, including serving practices, that promote intoxication and violent confrontations.

In a review of the experience of many communities with action on alcohol and drug issues, Lang et al. (1998a) emphasize the importance of ownership and control of programmes by the communities themselves, in contrast to control by outside "experts". They propose guidelines for community action based on a philosophy of: harm reduction; using community diversity as an asset (providing a wealth of social resources to address issues of concern); encouraging broad community and organizational collaboration allowing the sharing of resources to achieve common goals; and accommodating the dynamic nature of community action, emphasizing ongoing reassessment.

The themes of "grass roots" action and interagency collaboration also emerged from the UK Home Office working group on violence associated with licensed premises (Standing Conference on Crime Prevention, 1986), together with a number of other practical management strategies. The working group recommended the development of local interagency liaison groups, such as "Pub Watch" (see below); an investigation of the relationship between licensing hours and violence; that premises should be encouraged to become more family-orientated to help reduce age segregation; that "difficult" pubs should be run as community ventures with a local community management structure; and that attempts be made to involve the liquor industry in identifying and disseminating good practices among members.

The authors identified a number of good practices that came to their attention during the course of the research. One example was communication and cooperation between police, industry, local government, tenant associations and local resident action groups, evolving into local Licensing Forums or Committees. This process has resulted in some pubs becoming seen as part of the community and to a great extent self-policing. The report notes that problem premises are well known to industry, police, local authorities and local residents, so a cooperative approach at the grass roots level to monitor and deal with such premises is required.

A comprehensive summary of possible prevention strategies that builds on recent literature is provided by Braun & Graham (1997). These authors also provide examples of specific measures and a summary of the evidence for their impacts. Their overall emphasis is on ways of mobilizing and empowering the community. Consequently, they focus on creating coalitions linking community groups with representatives from key commercial and government agencies, including the police, liquor licensing authority, taxi/bus services and retail associations. The role of these coalitions includes auditing licensed venues and the surrounding neighbourhood to identify problems and develop measures to reduce risks to personal safety. The authors emphasize that community mobilization needs to be supported by legal, regulatory and enforcement methods.

Many of Braun & Graham's principles encourage licensees to lift their horizons and accept responsibility for behaviour within community settings beyond their own establishments. With support from external organizations such as the police, they need to assume responsibility for monitoring their customers and ensuring that bar staff serve in a responsible manner. Thus, bar staff should be trained in responsible practices and door staff should also be registered and trained. The authors observe that strict enforcement of the liquor laws is necessary to increase perceptions that there will be adverse consequences from serving underage or intoxicated customers.

Braun & Graham document several valuable techniques for effective harm reduction. One key proposal concerns the formation of a town planning committee aiming to limit harm through effective environmental design. The committee's role would be to consider appropriate locations for services, such as fast food outlets and transportation, in relation to licensed venues. Other proposals involve mobilizing licensees to monitor and report violent offences by their customers. One such measure is Pub Watch, which is a communication system for licensees to warn each other about any disorderly incidents in their area via a "ring-around" arrangement. Pub Watch is closely linked to Pub Ban schemes, which involve banning known offenders. Pub Ban can be supported by the creation of an incidence register of bar fights, which would fully document the occurrence of fights in or near licensed establishments.

CONCLUSION: TOWARD BETTER REGULATORY MODELS FOR CREATING AND MAINTAINING SAFE DRINKING ENVIRONMENTS

There are many signs from the emerging literature on community action and formal enforcement that disorder and violence in the licensed environment can indeed be reduced.

There is less compelling evidence that anyone has yet succeeded in effecting a permanent reduction in these problems. So the challenge is to build on the successes and learn from the failures, in order to devise systems of regulation that continue to work over time. There is certainly no shortage of good ideas with which to experiment.

The most important lessons from the literature concern *systems* of regulation. The importance of consistent and vigorous enforcement from police and liquor licensing authorities is clear, from the examples of both success and failure in achieving and maintaining reductions in violence. However, there are lessons as well for other forms of regulation: those deriving from the persuasive powers of agency and citizen partnerships at the local community level, and those relating to the practices that are best implemented by licensees and managers themselves. Getting the balance right between these three levels—formal regulation, which is the *political* domain; informal regulation, mobilizing *civil society*; and self-regulation, taming the *market*—is one of the primary challenges for those interested in the prevention of violence and associated problems in and around licensed venues.

On the basis of their experience with safety action projects, Hauritz et al. (1998) developed a model of the change process that posited parallel but interacting processes at the three levels of regulation. This model, perhaps in modified form, is proposed as a tool for any person or group concerned with reducing violence and crime in the licensed environment.

Hauritz and her colleagues assumed that certain *antecedent conditions*, such as a political environment emphasizing deregulation of liquor licensing or a lack of faith by licensees in the formal system of regulation, lead to a range of *problem behaviours*. These behaviours could include cut-throat competition between venues and irresponsible drinks promotions, a police crack-down on symptoms (arresting drunks in the streets), rather than dealing with problem venues, and a fragmented local response. These conditions and problems create a climate conducive to the development of a range of *intervention strategies* at each of the three levels of regulation. Strategies could include interagency cooperation, community mobilization and the formation of a licensed venues association to promote compliance with a code of practice and to "legitimize" the role of licensees as part of the local business community. These interventions produce certain positive *outcomes*, such as reduced violence or legislative reform, which can be *reinforced* if key players and organizations are rewarded through career enhancement or positive publicity. The reinforcers of positive change are more likely to have a continuing effect if key reforms are institutionalized through legislation or community-based monitoring systems. They referred to this process of institutionalization as *mechanisms to safeguard change*.

A crucial philosophy that guided Hauritz and her colleagues and which, in the light of the failed projects in the literature, may be an important guideline for future interventions, was the need to be *situationally specific* in the analysis of problems and the formulation of solutions. The theoretical basis is "situational crime prevention" (Clarke, 1997, p. 4), which involves a shift from thinking in terms of offenders and their motivations to offences and their settings. In the case of licensed premises this implies a focus on all the management practices that give rise to unsafe environments. As previously emphasized, alcohol-serving practices are only one aspect of unsafe environments. Other aspects include such things as physical design, selection and training of security staff, the permissiveness of the social climate in venues, and the hidden "deals" between managers and regulators. The relevance of situational theory to these kinds of issues can be illustrated not only by the traditional typology that was focused on the physical environment, but by Clarke & Homel's (1997) recent extension of situational methods to include techniques for removing excuses, or inducing guilt or shame. These include: *rule setting* (e.g. through codes of practice); *stimulating conscience* (e.g. by encouraging managers to regard themselves as responsible businessmen); *controlling disinhibitors* (e.g. by controlling alcohol through server intervention); and *facilitating compliance* (e.g. by creating a regulatory environment in which it is financially worthwhile for licensees to adhere to the code of practice).

A focus on venue management leads not only "inward" to specific contexts, but "outward" to the local community and to the larger arena in which laws and regulations are created and enforced (or not). The concept of "responsive regulation" (Ayres & Braithwaite, 1992) is particularly useful in this context. Ayres & Braithwaite propose regulatory approaches that are responsive to industry context and structure, regulatory culture, and history, and which incorporate, as key ideas, "tit-for-tat" strategies that combine punishment and persuasion in an optimum mix; "tripartism" (empowering citizen associations) as a way of solving the dilemma of regulatory capture and corruption; and "enforced self-regulation", in which private sets of rules written by business (such as codes of practice), are publicly ratified and, when there is a failure of private regulation, are publicly enforced.

Central to their model is an "enforcement pyramid" of penalties, from the frequently used techniques of persuasion and warning letters through to the infrequently used techniques of license suspension and revocation ("capital punishment" of alcohol outlets). The ideological basis of their ideas is ". . . a replacement of the liberal conception of the atomized free individual with a republican conception of community empowerment" (p. 17). Tripartism fosters the participation of community associations by giving them full access to all the information available to the regulator; by giving them a seat at the negotiating table; and by giving them the same standing to sue or prosecute as the regulator. Thus, they propose a model in which no one element, whether it be self-regulation, formal enforcement or citizen involvement, can operate effectively without the others.

There are many questions that must be addressed in each community as new forms of regulation are developed. An excellent general reference, whether or not readers are Australian, is the extensive report prepared by Stockwell et al. (1995), focusing on the appropriateness and efficacy of liquor licensing laws across Australia. This report particularly contrasts the complex and fragmentary nature of the Australian regulations with the Canadian situation. However, no jurisdiction has a monopoly on best practice, so to conclude this chapter some questions are raised and ideas proposed that may assist in the "praxis" of responsive regulation (Ayres & Braithwaite, 1992, p. 99).

A fundamental question is whether any form of regulation beyond effective police or licensing authority enforcement is really required. Why not just devise clearer and more comprehensive laws, and ensure that the authorities have the resources and motivation to enforce them (Solomon & Prout, 1994)? Is it really necessary to complicate the regulatory problem by emphasizing the community and self-regulation layers?

The critical role of formal enforcement has already been noted, although the evidentiary base is still thin. The paper by Jeffs & Saunders (1983) suggests that some form of visible, random enforcement in licensed venues can be quite effective, while the research of McKnight & Streff (1994) suggests that an undercover police presence, combined with warnings to managers, can be a potent deterrent. More evidence on the effects of enforcement in a variety of settings is urgently required, addressed particularly to the appropriate balance between visible and covert methods. But, as Solomon & Prout observe (p. 79), when it comes to law enforcement, "resources and priorities" are the problem. This reflects the fact that in many jurisdictions it is just not politically feasible to expect that police or licensing officers will be particularly zealous in law enforcement. The industry is too important economically to jeopardize good relations, so probably the most that can be expected of formal enforcement is that it will be used to support and reinforce other regulatory measures.

The overall aim of regulation should not be to "catch crooks," but to develop *a culture of compliance.* Of course a few heads on stakes might be essential occasionally to get the attention of unruly and anarchistic operators, but generally less savage techniques will be appropriate. The options, apart from prosecution, include persuasion and non-prosecution enforcement measures. Approaches available to regulators include: *licensing provisions* (e.g. imposing conditions in specific cases); *policy development* (e.g. advocating for change in licensing authority priorities); *cooperation with the industry to develop standards* (e.g. what exactly are the maximum acceptable degrees of "permissiveness" in a nightclub?); *developing formal and informal codes of practice* (working with a representative industry body if possible); *education, publicity and information campaigns* (especially at the local level, and designed and implemented with full industry cooperation); *incentives for responsible operators* (lower license fees for exemplary performance?); and, of course, *working with the community.*[2]

These approaches can usefully be arranged in an enforcement pyramid, the broad base representing frequently used approaches based on suasion, cooperation and negotiation, the sharp end representing the ultimate but infrequently-used sanctions, such as the closure of an establishment (the business equivalent of capital punishment). Many specific techniques that are used, at least occasionally, in some jurisdictions have already been noted. Others that are used in allied fields, such as environmental regulation, include: *abatement notices* (to control "nuisance practices"); *show-cause notices* (an operator is given time to make written representations why further action should not be taken); *enforcement notices* (setting out the grounds on which it is issued and the action required to comply); and *on-the-spot fines.* An increasingly common practice in environmental regulation is the *environmental management plan*, which can be issued by the regulator or voluntarily by the operator. The issuer devises objectives and strategies for compliance, stipulates a timetable and proposes performance indicators and monitoring and reporting mechanisms. Some of these techniques are already used by liquor licensing authorities but all could be used more frequently, with a greater emphasis on experimentation and evaluation.

But "head office" busyness will never be enough. All regulatory arenas are littered with the putrescent remains of cost cutting, shady deals and blatant corruption. The liquor licensing field, for obvious historical and cultural reasons, is particularly prone to regulatory capture and to official misconduct. For this reason, more than any other, a system of responsive regulation will give a central place to community empowerment and to the role of public interest groups. It does seem however, as Ayres & Braithwaite (1992) sadly observe, that the ideal of a full partnership role at the negotiating table with industry and government for such interest groups is as yet too remote to be promoted as a realistic goal. But the literature on community action *has* taught us that in the present political environment in at least some countries, local groups can be credible watchdogs, if not full partners, and can also bark loud enough to be effective "terriers for reform".

KEY WORKS AND SUGGESTIONS FOR FURTHER READING

Ayres, I. & Braithwaite, J. (1992).   *Responsive Regulation: Transcending the Deregulation Debate.* New York: Oxford University Press.

This is essential reading for anyone interested in grappling with the theoretical and practical issues involved in effective regulation of any industry.

---

[2] I am indebted to my wife, Beverley, for valuable insights into the world of environmental regulation.

Braun, K. & Graham, K. (1997). *Community Action for Safer Bars: Summary of Relevant Literature and Examples of Strategies Aimed at Reducing Violence in Licensed Establishments.* Toronto: Addiction Research Foundation.

A valuable document that sets out in detail what we can learn from the research literature about strategies to reduce violence.

Homel, R. (1997). *Policing for Prevention: Reducing Crime, Public Intoxication and Injury.* Crime Prevention Studies No. 7. Monsey, NY: Criminal Justice Press.

This edited volume has several chapters on policing licensed venues (especially the chapters by Stockwell, Felson, Homel and Macintyre).

Graham, K. & Homel, R. (1997). Creating safer bars. In M. Plant, E. Single & T. Stockwell (Eds), *Alcohol: Minimizing the Harm* (pp. 171–192). London: Free Association Press.

This chapter summarizes the evidence on risk and protective factors for violence in licensed venues.

Hauritz, M., Homel, R., McIlwain, G., Burrows, T. & Townsley, M. (1998). Reducing violence in licensed venues through community safety action projects: the Queensland experience. *Contemporary Drug Problems, 25,* 511–551.

A recent paper that presents evidence that reductions in violence through community action are achievable. It includes a model of the community change process.

Lang, E., Keenan, M. & Brooke, T. (1998). *Guidelines for Community Action on Alcohol and Drug Issues, and Annotated Bibliography.* Melbourne: Turning Point Drug and Alcohol Centre.

This document combines community action guidelines with a comprehensive annotated bibliography.

Stockwell, T. (Ed.) (1995). *Alcohol Misuse and Violence: An Examination of the Appropriateness and Efficacy of Liquor Licensing Laws across Australia.* Report No. 5, Commonwealth Department of Health, Housing, Local Government and Community Services. Canberra: Australian Government Publishing Service.

The most comprehensive document available on the many facets of liquor licensing regulation as it relates to violence. Although Australian, it is relevant to problems faced in many countries.

REFERENCES

Alcohol Advisory Council of Western Australia (1989). *Licensed Premises: Your Right to Object.* Perth, WA: Alcohol Advisory Council of Western Australia.

Alcoholic Liquor Advisory Council (1996). *Good Times: Managing a Successful Public Event.* Auckland: Alcoholic Liquor Advisory Council.

Ayres, I. & Braithwaite, J. (1992). *Responsive Regulation: Transcending the Deregulation Debate.* New York: Oxford University Press.

Bjor, J., Knutsson, J. & Kuhlhorn, E. (1992). The celebration of Midsummer Eve in Sweden—a study in the art of preventing collective disorder. *Security Journal,* **3**(3), 169–174.

Boffa, J., George, C. & Tsey, K. (1994). Sex, alcohol and violence: a community collaborative action against striptease shows. *Australian Journal of Public Health,* **18**(4), 359–366.

Boots, K., Cutmore, T., Midford, R., Harrison, D. & Laughlin, D. (1995). *Community Mobilisation for the Prevention of Alcohol-related Injury. Project Evaluation Report. Reducing Alcohol-related*

Harm: What Can Be Achieved by a Three Year Community Mobilisation Project. Bentley WA: National Centre for Research into the Prevention of Drug Abuse, Curtin University of Technology.

Braun, K. & Graham, K. (1997). *Community Action for Safer Bars: Summary of Relevant Literature and Examples of Strategies Aimed at Reducing Violence in Licensed Establishments.* Toronto: Addiction Research Foundation.

Casswell, S., Zhang, J.F. & Wyllie, A. (1993). The importance of amount and location of drinking for the experience of alcohol-related problems. *Addiction*, **88**, 1527–1534.

Clarke, R. (1997). *Situational Crime Prevention: Successful Case Studies*, 2nd edn. Guilderland, NY: Harrow and Heston.

Clarke, R. & Homel, R. (1997). A revised classification of situational crime prevention techniques. In S.P. Lab (Ed.), *Crime Prevention at a Crossroads* (pp. 17–30). Cincinnati, OH: Anderson Publishing Co. and Academy of Criminal Justice Sciences.

Cope, K. (1995). Developing an alcohol strategy from the grassroots up—the Armidale Community Alcohol Strategy Committee. In R. Midford (Ed.), *National Workshop on Community-based Alcohol Harm Prevention.* Bentley WA: National Centre for Research into the Prevention of Drug Abuse, Curtin University of Technology.

Department of Tourism, Sport and Racing: Liquor Licensing Division and Queensland Police (1999). *A Planning Guide for Event Managers: Alcohol Safety and Event Management.* Brisbane, Queensland: Queensland Government.

Douglas, M. (1995). Alcohol abuse in Halls Creek: the process of change. In R. Midford (Ed.), *National Workshop on Community-based Alcohol Harm Prevention.* Bentley WA: National Centre for Research into the Prevention of Drug Abuse, Curtin University of Technology.

Dunstan, G. & McDonald, R. (1996). Situational crime prevention and the art of celebration. Paper presented at the Last Night First Light Conference, Byron Bay, Australia.

Eastern Sydney Area Health Service (1995). *Preventing Alcohol-related Violence: A Community Action Manual.* Sydney: St Vincent's Hospital.

Felson, R.B., Baccaglini, W. & Gmelch, G. (1986). Bar-room brawls: aggression and violence in Irish and American bars. In A. Campbell & J.J. Gibbs (Eds), *Violent Transactions: The Limits of Personality.* Oxford: Basil Blackwell.

Felson, M., Berends, R., Richardson, B. & Veno, A. (1997). Reducing pub hopping and related crime. In R. Homel (Ed.), *Policing for Prevention: Reducing Crime, Public Intoxication and Injury* (pp. 115–132). Crime Prevention Studies, No. 7. Monsey, NY: Criminal Justice Press.

Fisher, J. (1993). Partnership for personal safety: preventing violent crime in and around licensed premises. Presented at the National Conference on Crime Prevention, Griffith University, Brisbane.

Gibbs, J. (1986). Overview. In A. Campbell & J. Gibbs (Eds), *Violent Transactions: The Limits of Personality.* Oxford: Basil Blackwell.

Giesbrecht, N., Conley, P., Denniston, R., Glicksman, L., Holder, H., Pederson, A., Room, R. & Shain, M. (Eds) (1990). *Research, Action, and the Community: Experiences in the Prevention of Alcohol and Other Drug Problems.* OSAP Prevention Monograph No. 4. Rockville, MD: US Department of Health and Human Services.

Giesbrecht, N. & Ferris, J. (1993). Community-based research initiatives in prevention. *Addiction*, **88**(Suppl.), 83–93.

Giesbrecht, N., Krempulec, L. & West, P. (1993). Community-based prevention research to reduce alcohol-related problems. *Alcohol Health & Research World*, **17**(1), 84–88.

Gilling, D. (1993). The multi-agency approach to crime prevention: the British experience. Presented at the National Conference on Crime Prevention, Griffith University, Brisbane.

Graham, K. (1985). Determinants of heavy drinking and drinking problems: the contribution of the bar environment. In E. Single & T. Storm (Eds), *Public Drinking and Public Policy.* Toronto: Addiction Research Foundation.

Graham, K. & Homel, R. (1997). Creating safer bars. In M. Plant, E. Single & T. Stockwell (Eds), *Alcohol: Minimizing the Harm* (pp. 171–192). London: Free Association Press.

Graham, K., LaRoque, L., Yetman, R., Ross, T.J. & Guistra, E. (1980). Aggression and barroom environments. *Journal of Studies on Alcohol*, **41**, 277–292.

Graham, K., Osgood, D.W., Zibrowski, E., Purcell, J., Gliksman, L., Leonard, K., Pernanen, K., Saltz,

R.F. & Toomey, T.L. (2003).   The effect of the *Safer Bars* Program on physical aggression in bars: Results of a randomized control trial. Paper presented at *Preventing Substance Use, Risky Use and Harm: What is Evidence-Based Policy?* (A Kettil Bruun Society Thematic Meeting). Perth, Australia, February 24–27, 2003.

Graham, K. & West, P. (2001).   Alcohol and crime: Examining the link. In N. Heather, T.J. Peters & T. Stockwell (Eds), *International Handbook of Alcohol Dependence and Problems* (pp. 439–470). Chichester: John Wiley & Sons Ltd.

Graves, T.D., Graves, N.B., Semu, V.N. & Sam, I.A. (1981).   The social context of drinking and violence in New Zealand's multi-ethnic pub settings. In T.C. Harford & L.S. Gaines (Eds), *Social Drinking Contexts.* Research Monograph No. 7. Rockville, MD: NIAAA.

Hauritz, M., Homel, R., McIlwain, G., Burrows, T. & Townsley, M. (1998).   Reducing violence in licensed venues through community safety action projects: the Queensland experience. *Contemporary Drug Problems*, **25**, 511–551.

Holder, H.D. (1992).   Undertaking a community prevention trial to reduce alcohol problems: translating theoretical models into action. In H.D. Holder & J.M. Howard (Eds), *Community Prevention Trials for Alcohol Problems* (pp. 227–243). Westport, CT: Praeger.

Holder, H.D., Saltz, R.F., Grube, J.W., Treno, A.J., Reynolds, R.I., Voas, R.B. & Gruenewald, P.J. (1997a).   Summing up: lessons from a comprehensive community prevention trial. *Addiction*, **92**(2), S293–S301.

Holder, H.D., Saltz, R.F., Grube, J.W., Voas, R.B., Gruenewald, P.J. and Treno, A.J. (1997b).   A community prevention trial to reduce alcohol-involved accidental injury and death: overview. *Addiction*, **92**(2), S155–S171.

Homel, R. (1996).   Review of T. Stockwell (Ed.), *An Examination of the Appropriateness and Efficacy of Liquor-Licensing Laws across Australia.* Canberra: AGPS. *Addiction*, **91**(8), 1231–1233.

Homel, R. & Clark, J. (1994).   The prediction and prevention of violence in pubs and clubs. *Crime Prevention Studies*, **3**, 1–46.

Homel, R., Hauritz, M., Wortley, R., McIlwain, G. & Carvolth, R. (1997).   Preventing alcohol-related crime through community action: the Surfers Paradise Safety Action Project. In R. Homel (Ed.), *Policing for Prevention: Reducing Crime, Public Intoxication, and Injury* (pp. 35–90). Crime Prevention Studies No. 7. Monsey, NY: Criminal Justice Press.

Homel, R. & Mirrlees-Black, C. (1997).   *Assault in Queensland.* Brisbane: Queensland Criminal Justice Commission.

Homel, R. & Tomsen, S. (1991).   Pubs and violence: violence, public drinking, and public policy. *Current Affairs Bulletin*, **68**(7), 20–27.

Homel, R., Tomsen, S. & Thommeny, J. (1992).   Public drinking and violence: not just an alcohol problem. *Journal of Drug Issues*, **22**, 679–697.

Jeffs, B.W. & Saunders, W.M. (1983).   Minimizing alcohol related offences by enforcement of the existing licensing legislation. *British Journal of Addiction*, **78**, 67–77.

Kelly, W. (1993).   *Geelong "Local Industry Accord": A Partnership in Crime Prevention.* Geelong Local Industry Accord, Best Practices Committee. Geelong: Australia.

Lakeland, G. & Durham, G. (1991).   AHB and community organisation: building a coalition in preventing alcohol problems. A paper prepared for the Perspectives for Change Conference, Wellington, New Zealand.

Lander, A. (1995).   *Preventing Alcohol-related Violence: A Community Action Manual.* Sydney: Eastern Sydney Area Health Service and St Vincent's Alcohol & Drug Service.

Lang, E., Keenan, M. & Brooke, T. (1998a).   *Guidelines for Community Action on Alcohol and Drug Issues, and Annotated Bibliography.* Melbourne: Turning Point Drug and Alcohol Centre.

Lang, E., Stockwell, T., Rydon, P. & Beel, A. (1998b).   Can training bar staff in responsible serving practices reduce alcohol-related harm? *Drug and Alcohol Review*, **17**, 39–50.

Macintyre, S. & Homel, R. (1997).   Danger on the dance floor: a study of interior design, crowding and aggression in nightclubs. In R. Homel (Ed.), *Policing for Prevention: Reducing Crime, Public Intoxication, and Injury* (pp. 91–113). Crime Prevention Studies No. 7. Monsey, NY: Criminal Justice Press.

Magnificent Events Company (1996).   *Concept Plans for Managing Dysfunctional Events at Bondi Beach on Christmas Day and New Year's Day.* Bond University, Queensland: Australian Institute of Dramatic Arts.

Marsdon, G. & James, R. (1992). *From Pain to Power: Resident Action for the Prevention of Alcohol-related Problems.* Perth: National Centre for Research into the Prevention of Drug Abuse, Curtin University of Technology.

Marsh, P. & Kibby, K. (1992). *Drinking and Public Disorder.* A report of research conducted for the Portman Group by MCM research. London: Portman Group.

McKnight, A.J. & Streff, F. M (1994). The effect of enforcement upon service of alcohol to intoxicated patrons of bars and restaurants. *Accident Analysis and Prevention,* 26(1), 79–88.

Melbourne City Council (1991). *Westend Forum Project—1990/91. Final Report.* Melbourne, Victoria: Melbourne City Council.

Midford, R., Laughlin, D., Boots, K. & Cutmore, T. (1994). *Top down or bottom up: is one approach better for developing a community response to alcohol harm?* Paper presented at the APSAD Conference, *Alcohol, Drugs and the Family.* Melbourne, VIC: October 11–13.

New South Wales Health Department (1997). *Kings Cross Licensing Accord.* Sydney: New South Wales Health Department.

Parkdale Focus Community (1995). *Liquor Licensing and the Community: Resolving Problems with Licensed Establishments.* Toronto: Parkdale Focus Community.

Putnam, S.L., Rockett, I.R. & Campbell, M.K. (1993). Methodological issues in community-based alcohol-related injury prevention projects: attribution of program effects. In T.K. Greenfield & R. Zimmerman (Eds), *Experience with Community Action Projects: New Research in the Prevention of Alcohol and Other Drug Problems.* Center for Substance Abuse Prevention Monograph 14. Rockville, MD: US Department of Health and Human Services.

Ramsay, M. (1989). *Downtown Drinkers: The Perceptions and Fears off the Public in a City Centre.* Crime Prevention Unit Paper 19. London: Home Office.

Ramsay, M. (1990). *Lagerland Lost: An Experiment in Keeping Drinkers off the Streets in Central Coventry and Elsewhere.* Crime Prevention Unit Paper 22. London: Home Office.

Ramsay, M. (1991). A British experiment in curbing incivilities and fear of crime. *Security Journal,* 2(2), 120–125.

Robinson, D. & Tether, P. (1990). *Preventing Alcohol Problems: Local Prevention Activity and the Compilation of "Guides to Local Action".* Geneva: World Health Organization.

Robinson, D., Tether, P. & Teller, J. (Eds) (1989). *Local Action on Alcohol Problems.* London: Tavistock/Routledge.

Rumbold, G., Malpass, A., Lang, E., Cvetkovski, S. & Kelly, W. (1998). *An Evaluation of the Geelong Local Industry Accord: Final Report.* Melbourne: Turning Point Alcohol and Drug Centre.

St Kilda Project (1997). *Tool Kit. A Resource Guide for Community Groups Wishing to Develop a Harm Reduction Response to Alcohol and Other Drug Use.* St Kilda, Victoria: St Kilda Project & City of Port Phillip.

Saltz, R. (1987). The roles of bars and restaurants in preventing alcohol-impaired driving: an evaluation of server education. *Evaluation in Health Professions,* 10(1), 5–27.

Saltz, R.F. & Stanghetta, P. (1997). A community-wide Responsible Beverage Service program in three communities: early findings. *Addiction,* 92(2), S237–S249.

Shane, P. & Cherry, L. (1987). *Alcohol Problem Prevention through Community Empowerment: A Review and Summary of the Castro Valley Prevention Planning Project.* Alameda, CA: Alameda County Health Care Services Agency.

Shepherd, J. (1994). Violent crime: the role of alcohol and new approaches to the prevention of injury. *Alcohol and Alcoholism,* 29(1), 5–10.

Simpson, R., Brunet, S., Solomon, R., Stanghetta, P., Single, E. & Armstrong, R. (1987). *A Guide to the Responsible Service of Alcohol: Manual for Owners and Managers.* Toronto: Addiction Research Foundation.

Solomon, R. & Prout, L. (1994). A summary of provisions contained in Australian liquor laws of possible relevance to violence. In T. Stockwell (Ed.), *Alcohol Misuse and Violence: An Examination of the Appropriateness and Efficacy of Liquor Licensing Laws across Australia* (pp. 57–84). (Report No. 5: Presented at the National Symposium on Alcohol Misuse and Violence.) Prepared for the Commonwealth Department of Health, Housing, Local Government and Community Services. Canberra, Australia: Australian Government Publishing Service.

Standing Conference on Crime Prevention (1986). *Report of the Working Group on the Prevention of Violence Associated with Licensed Premises.* London: Home Office.

Stockwell, T. (Ed.) (1995). *Alcohol Misuse and Violence: An Examination of the Appropriateness and Efficacy of Liquor Licensing Laws across Australia.* Report No. 5, Commonwealth Department of Health, Housing, Local Government and Community Services. Canberra: Australian Government Publishing Service.

Stockwell, T. (1997). Regulation of the licensed drinking environment: a major opportunity for crime prevention. In R. Homel (Ed.), *Policing for Prevention: Reducing Crime, Public Intoxication and Injury* (pp. 7–34). Crime Prevention Studies No. 7. Monsey, NY: Criminal Justice Press.

Stockwell, T., Norberry, J. & Solomon, R. (1995). Proposed directions for future reforms of licensing laws. In T. Stockwell (Ed.), *Alcohol Misuse and Violence: An Examination of the Appropriateness and Efficacy of Liquor Licensing Laws across Australia* (pp. 287–308). (Report No. 5: presented at the National Symposium on Alcohol Misuse and Violence.) Prepared for the Commonwealth Department of Health, Housing, Local Government and Community Services. Canberra: Australian Government Publishing Service.

Stockwell, T., Somerford, P. & Lang, E. (1992). The relationship between license type and alcohol-related problems attributed to licensed premises in Perth, Western Australia. *Journal of Studies on Alcohol*, **53**, 495–498.

Tether, P. & Robinson, D. (1986). *Preventing Alcohol Problems. A Guide to Local Action.* London: Tavistock.

Tomsen, S., Homel, R. & Thommeny, J. (1991). The causes of public violence: situational vs. other factors in drinking related assaults. In D. Chappell, P. Grabosky & H. Strang (Eds), *Australian Violence: Contemporary Perspectives.* Canberra: Australian Institute of Criminology.

Treno, A.J. & Holder, H.D. (1997). Community mobilization: evaluation of an environmental approach to local action. *Addiction*, **92**(2), S173–S187.

Victorian Community Council Against Violence (1990). *Inquiry into Violence in and Around Licensed Premises.* Melbourne: Victorian Community Council Against Violence.

Walsh, B. (1993). Communities working together side by side to create safe seaside suburbs. Presented at Australian Institute of Criminology Conference, Melbourne.

Wedel, M., Pieters, J.E., Pikaar, N.A. & Ockhuizen, T. (1991). Application of a three-compartment model to a study of the effects of sex, alcohol dose and concentration, exercise and food consumption on the pharmacokinetics of ethanol in healthy volunteers. *Alcohol and Alcoholism*, **26**(3), 329–336.

Welsh, M. (1996). *The St. Kilda Project. A Community Response to Alcohol and Other Drug Issues.* Final Report, December 1996. St. Kilda: City of Port Phillip.

Chapter 15

Prevention of Alcohol-related Road Crashes

A. James McKnight
Transportation Research Associates, Annapolis, MD, USA
and
Robert B. Voas
Pacific Institute for Research and Evaluation, Calverton, MD, USA

Synopsis

Countermeasures to alcohol-related road crashes are considered within four categories: reducing alcohol consumption by reducing alcohol availability; separating drinking from driving; apprehending and removing the drinking driver from the road; and preventing the recurrence of drinking and driving among drink–driving offenders. This chapter is organized around those four elements of the impaired driving problem.

Traditional efforts to reduce drinking and driving have centered on the enforcement of impaired driving laws. Over the last two decades, however, the science of alcohol safety has expanded to include efforts to limit drinking as well as driving after drinking. This has occurred as research has demonstrated the effectiveness of making alcohol less available, particularly to youth, in reducing alcohol-related crashes. Efforts to reduce consumption have taken three forms: (a) limiting total consumption by regulating sales through prohibition of sales to minors in certain locations or jurisdictions and through the manipulation of price through excise taxes; (b) controlling the conditions of service (e.g. limiting "happy hours"); and (c) designing information campaigns to discourage heavy drinking.

It is possible for individuals to drink heavily and not be exposed to causing alcohol-related crashes if they do not have access to a vehicle. Programs to achieve this outcome include: public education efforts to persuade the drinkers themselves to take steps to avoid driving

The Essential Handbook of Treatment and Prevention of Alcohol Problems. Edited by N. Heather and T. Stockwell.
© 2004 John Wiley & Sons Ltd. ISBN 0-470-86296-3.

after drinking; programs to encourage servers, peers and hosts to prevent intoxicated individuals from driving; and organized efforts by alcohol outlets and community organizations to make provisions for alternative transportation. Public education efforts are most effective where they publicize other strategies that depend upon public awareness for their effectiveness.

Action to reduce alcohol-related crashes has been the enforcement by the police of impaired driving laws which, as traffic volumes have grown and laws more complex, has become a specialized task in many jurisdictions. A new enforcement science has developed that focuses on (a) identifying vehicles driven by impaired drivers, (b) detecting signs of drinking, (c) measuring impairment, and (d) measuring BAC levels. There is now compelling evidence for the effectiveness of reduced BAC levels and their enforcement through highly visible means.

Many strategies have been developed to prevent a drink–driver from re-offending. Three general areas of action can be distinguished: (a) applying traditional penalties, such as jail and fines directed at causing sufficient discomfort to deter the individual from repeating the offense; (b) suspending the driver's license to prevent future drinking and driving; and (c) requiring attendance at treatment or educational programs directed at assisting the offender to avoid future impaired driving and promoting recovery from dependence on alcohol. Unfortunately, most current remedial programs have shown limited success, as one-third to one-half of the drivers convicted of impaired driving repeat the offense.

Preventive efforts directed toward previous offenders can use sanctions to limit driving, including license suspension and revocation, vehicle impoundment and jail. Although the immediate effect of these sanctions is to reduce driving, they are also expected to create an unpleasant condition that deters future alcohol-impaired driving. Ignition interlocks are a promising technical development that has been found to be more effective than license suspension. Once the interlock is removed, however, there is little reduction in recidivism. There is limited take-up of this option by drivers in the USA unless the only alternative given is jail.

This chapter identifies a range of effective and less effective strategies for the reduction of serious injury and death on the roads caused by alcohol-impaired driving.

The contribution of alcohol impairment to death and injury on the highway has been well established through comparisons of blood alcohol levels among drivers in fatal crashes and non-crash-involved drivers using the roads at the same times and places. The first risk curve based on such comparisons, showing the increase in crash probability associated with increased BAC, produced by Borkenstein et al. (1974), has generally been confirmed by several investigators since that time (Hurst, 1973). The relationship of blood alcohol and risk of death in road crashes is exponential, with risk increasing sharply at blood alcohol levels between 0.08% and 10%. The most recent estimates for the USA (Zador, 1991) indicated that the relative risk of involvement in a single-vehicle fatal crash increased nine times in the BAC range from 0.05 to 0.09. In this BAC range, the corresponding risk curve for drivers 16–20 years old rises even more sharply. The relationships found in fatal crash accident data are reinforced by the results of laboratory research showing performance in a wide range of tasks, evidencing a marked decline at the same blood alcohol levels (Moskowitz & Robinson, 1988). In the USA, this increased risk results in a comprehensive cost to society of $115 billion or approximately 95 cents per 1-ounce drink. Forty cents of that cost is borne by non-drinking drivers (Miller, Lestina & Spicer, 1998).

Countermeasures to alcohol-related road crashes have fallen into four categories (Table 15.1) representing separate phases: reducing alcohol consumption by reducing alcohol availability; separating drinking from driving; apprehending and removing the drinking

Table 15.1 Countermeasures to alcohol-related road crashes

Reducing consumption	Separating drinking from driving	Removing the impaired driver from the road	Preventing recurrence of drinking and driving
Reduce availability MLDA	Information and education Public information School-based programs	Enforcement methods Identifying vehicles Sobriety checkpoints Detecting impairment	Specific deterrence Jail sentences Fines
Conditions of sale Civil liability Alcohol control laws	Individual interventions Individual intervention Host intervention Peer intervention Server intervention	Chemical Testing Evidential sensors Preliminary sensors Passive sensors BAC limits	Offender remediation Assessment Education and counseling Treatment
	Alternative transportation programs Designated driver programs Safe ride programs	Media advocacy	Incapacitation License actions Vehicle actions

driver from the road; and preventing the recurrence of drinking and driving among drink–driving offenders. This chapter is organized around those four elements of the impaired driving problem.

REDUCING CONSUMPTION

Traditional efforts to reduce drinking and driving have centered on the enforcement of impaired driving laws. Over the last two decades, however, the science of alcohol safety has expanded to include efforts to limit drinking as well as driving after drinking. This has occurred as research has demonstrated the effectiveness of making alcohol less available, particularly to youth, in reducing alcohol-related crashes. This has brought traffic safety into the broader public health arena. Efforts to reduce consumption have taken three forms: (a) limiting total consumption by regulating sales through prohibition of sales to minors in certain locations or jurisdictions and through the manipulation of price through excise taxes; (b) controlling the conditions of service (e.g. limiting "happy hours"); and (c) designing information campaigns to discourage heavy drinking.

Reducing Availability

The general availability of alcohol and its price (discussed elsewhere in this volume) is a factor in all alcohol abuse problems including impaired driving. However, perhaps the best evidence for the relationship of availability to alcohol-related crash involvement is provided by the minimum legal drinking age (MLDA) law in the United States. Though almost all developed nations set a minimum age below which it is illegal to purchase, possess, or consume alcoholic beverages, the USA's age limit of 21 is the highest in the world. The relationship of age to the effects of alcohol-impaired crash risk evident in crash–risk curves shows a relatively steeper rise in the likelihood of fatality for teenage drivers than for adults (Beirness, Simpson & Mayhew, 1993; Zador, 1991). The relationship reflects a combination of lowered tolerance to alcohol, as observed in laboratory studies relating blood alcohol to performance for various age groups (Moscowitz & Burns, 1976), and the relation of inexperience and immaturity to crash risk in general (Mercer, 1986).

Enactment of the MLDA law by the 50 states was stimulated by federal legislation withholding highway funds from states failing to lower the limits for drivers under age 21. Although the purchase of alcohol by underage individuals occurs in on- and off-premises settings, the enforcement of alcohol control laws has taken place primarily in the latter. Over-the-counter sale of alcohol to underage customers in the USA appears to be widespread (Preusser & Williams, 1991). Enforcement is lax, with many more actions against underage drinkers than against outlets (Wagenaar & Wolfson, 1995). It principally takes the form of infrequent "stings", in which purchases are attempted by underage customers working with the police—often underage police. When such enforcement results in well-publicized action against stores, the result has been a decline in illegal sales (McKnight, 1991). Although not strongly enforced, prohibitions against sales to those under age 21 and sanctions for possession by the underage individuals have appeared to combine to reduce significantly underage alcohol-related highway deaths. The National Highway Traffic Safety Administration (NHTSA) reports that the MLDA laws saved 17,000 lives between 1982 and 1997.

Conditions of Sale

Several programs have been introduced to prevent impairment by limiting the locations and times or the methods by which alcohol may be sold or served to prospective drivers. McKnight & Streff (1994) found intoxication of patrons to be associated with risky practices, such as selling doubles, triples, and beer by the pitcher. These risky practices include the hours when alcohol may be sold, the amount of alcohol served (e.g. beer pitchers), the alcohol content (e.g. doubles and triples), the reduced price promotions (e.g. "happy hours"), and the price discounts (e.g. two for one). Some measures are introduced at the discretion of the establishment; others are legislated, generally at the community level. In the USA, sports facilities have been examined as sources of alcohol-impaired driving. Voas et al. (1998d) found that 10% of the drivers came from some sporting events, although they made up only 2% of all over-the-limit drivers. Efforts undertaken at a national level have succeeded in limiting the sale of alcoholic beverages during sports events, particularly toward the end, just before patrons drive home. Although formal evaluation has been lacking, some reduction in beer sales when accompanied by an increase in food and non-alcoholic beverage sales has been reported (NHTSA, 1986). Other measures that have been taken to restrict the availability of alcohol more generally, such as limiting the density of outlets, have been concerned more with the overall consumption of alcohol than with individual episodes of drinking. Although there is general agreement that availability effects consumption and, by extension, alcohol problems, it has been difficult to assess the effect of laws and practices that lower availability (for a review of available studies, see Gruenewald, 1993.)

Research discloses that a leading source of intoxicated drivers are licensed on-premises drinking establishments, such as bars and restaurants, with the proportion of arrested drivers ranging from one-third to half (Wolfe, 1975; Damkot, 1979; Ontario Ministry of Transport and Communications, 1980; Palmer, 1986; Foss et al., 1990). Rydon, Lang & Stockwell (1993) studied risk factors associated with drinking leading to a wide range of harmful incidents (violence, injury, illness) and concluded that "the most significant risk factors were the amount of alcohol consumed and whether obviously intoxicated customers continued to be served". What makes a licensed establishment a highly attractive target for alcohol-impaired driving countermeasures is that the dispensing of alcohol is under the control of servers who are sober and, therefore, in a position to identify seriously impaired drivers.

The early 1980s saw the widespread introduction of programs intended to enable and encourage those who sell alcohol to withhold it from patrons who are, or might become, impaired by alcohol. Efforts to gain intervention by sellers have taken two general forms: legal sanctions against sellers who dispense alcohol irresponsibly, and training programs that teach sellers how to behave responsibly.

Sanctions against the irresponsible sale of alcoholic beverages has itself taken two forms: (a) civil liability laws that allow victims of irresponsible service of alcohol to collect financial damages from sellers; and (b) alcohol control laws imposing administrative and criminal penalties for the illegal sale of alcohol to the underaged and intoxicated. Alcohol prevention measures involving licensed establishments have been summarized by Mosher (1991).

Civil Liability

Laws allowing victims of irresponsible service to collect damages date back to the 1800s and were enacted primarily to protect wives and children from abuse and neglect resulting from the sale or service of alcohol to an establishment's patrons. As the arrival of the automobile shifted the primary locus of harm from the home to the highway, these "dram shop" laws were increasingly applied to the victims of road accidents. Some jurisdictions have passed laws specifically addressing the service of alcohol; other jurisdictions allow suits to be brought under common liability laws. Yet, still other jurisdictions specifically exempt alcohol sellers from liability for damages resulting from the sale of alcohol.

Beyond providing financial compensation to the victims of irresponsible alcohol service, dram shop laws are expected to deter such service and the harm it causes. However, the potential deterrent effect of dram shop laws has been compromised by the extremely low likelihood of a successful suit being brought and by the protection offered to offending establishments by liability insurance. Holder et al. (1990) pointed out that, "the pooling of risk can dilute incentives to adopt preventive serving practices". They noted no relationship between dram shop law and server training, age checking, or refusal of service. Attempts to evaluate the effect of dram shop law upon accidents are thwarted by the antiquity if the law, which prevents pre- and post-comparisons, and fundamental differ-ences among jurisdictions in other alcohol-related measures, which complicate cross-sectional comparisons.

Alcohol Control Laws

In many jurisdictions, it is illegal to sell an alcoholic beverage to purchasers, including the *underage* and the *intoxicated*, considered to be at risk of injury. Violations can result in criminal actions and fines against sellers and administrative action, such as fines and license suspensions, against the establishments.

Service of alcohol to already-intoxicated customers occurs almost entirely in on-premises bars and restaurants. Enforcement of laws prohibiting service to an intoxicated customer is even more rare than enforcement of laws prohibiting sales to an underage customer. Unpublished data collected by Mothers Against Drunk Driving show only one case of the former for every 15 of the latter. Most actions against servers appear to occur when the illegal service resulted in some form of harm, rather than from routine enforcement activity. Effective enforcement requires observing actual service to intoxicated patrons, an activity that demands more time than mounting a sting. Yet, the impact upon service to the intoxicated and the incidence of drink–driving can be highly cost-beneficial. An enforcement activity in which plain clothes officers cited licensed establishments that were serving visibly intoxicated patrons showed a three-fold increase in refusals of service to pseudopatrons simulating signs of intoxication and a one-fourth drop in the percentage of arrested drivers coming from bars and restaurants (McKnight & Streff, 1994). The savings in accident costs were estimated at $90 for each enforcement dollar.

The efficiency of alcohol-control efforts can be enhanced by focusing enforcement on establishments that are the most persistent violators. Arrested drivers queried for the sources of their last drinks can identify the greatest sources of trouble. As early as 1977, the California Department of Beverage Control undertook a program targeting establishments identified by motorists convicted of alcohol-impaired driving as sources of their last drink (Mosher & Wallack, 1979). Presently, several communities, as part of their alcohol-control efforts, target establishments that are the last-drink source in information collected by police or other agencies processing alcohol-impaired drivers.

SEPARATING DRIVING FROM DRINKING

It is possible for individuals to drink heavily and not be exposed to causing alcohol-related crashes if they do not have access to a vehicle. This reduces the proportion of fatal crashes that are alcohol-involved in Third World countries where per capita ownership of motor vehicles is low. In industrialized nations such as the USA, where most drinkers own vehicles, programs directed at separating drinking and drinking and driving offer significant potential for reducing the harm associated with heavy drinking. Such programs generally fall into three categories: public education efforts to persuade the drinkers themselves to take steps to avoid driving after drinking; programs to encourage servers, peers and hosts to prevent intoxicated individuals from driving; and organized efforts by alcohol outlets and community organizations to make provisions for alternative transportation.

Information and Education

The most direct way of getting drivers to avoid alcohol-impaired driving may be through the dissemination of information. From the earliest recognition of an alcohol-impaired driving problem, messages exhorting drivers not to drink before driving or not to drive after drinking have been delivered through many programs in different forms. The method of delivery ranges from public information announcements warning, "if you drink, don't drive", to lengthy educational programs addressing all aspects of the issue.

Public Information

Public information about drinking and driving has been distributed to the driving public through a variety of media including posters; mail-outs; and messages transmitted through the radio, television and print media as paid advertisements and public service announcements (PSAs), which can be widely distributed at low cost. Although messages crafted through formative research (Atkin, 1989) influence knowledge and attitudes, the challenge is getting the media to disseminate them in places and at times where they will reach the public. Gaining sponsorship for paid advertisements and the cooperation of news media seem to offer greater chances of reaching the intended audience. Public information programs disseminating information about drinking and driving have not evidenced a beneficial effect upon alcohol-related crashes (Wilde et al., 1971; Haskins, 1985; Atkin, 1989).

Detecting the small effect that can be anticipated from the relatively small amount of information would require a tightly controlled experiment involving many thousands of drivers—requirements that are largely incompatible.

Where public information has proved most valuable is publicizing alcohol safety efforts that depend upon public awareness for their implementation. These include: (a) enactment and heightened enforcement of laws and regulations for which the general deterrence value obviously depends on public awareness; (b) the availability of alternatives to driving while alcohol-impaired, including designated driver and safe-ride programs; and (c) the means by which drivers can check on their level of sobriety–impairment as they drink. In this context, the role of public information is that of a delivery mechanism for other countermeasures that are themselves effective in reducing alcohol-related crashes and violations.

School-based Programs

Most of the educational efforts to prevent alcohol-impaired driving have been within secondary education programs. Few adults enroll in alcohol- or driving-related courses except when required, doing so because of a traffic offense (see Preventing Recurrence of Drinking and Driving). Driver education courses have devoted up to several classroom hours to the prevention of drinking–driving among licensed teenagers. Improvements in measures of knowledge, attitude and self-reported behavior (KAB) have been covered in several studies summarized by Mann et al. (1986). The use of alcohol-involved crashes or citations as evaluative criteria is precluded by the small samples involved. One area in which education has been particularly effective among teenagers is intervention in the drinking or driving of other teenagers at events where alcohol is available. As previously noted, teenagers, as a group, tend to be more willing to intervene in the drinking of their peers than are adults, who are typically more reluctant to intrude in the behavior of other adults. Programs giving instruction and role-playing practice in intervention skills have also shown KAB improvement.

Much of the development, implementation, and evaluation of educational programs has taken place in the USA, as an element of secondary school driver education. Two developments over the past decade have diminished the treatment of alcohol-impaired driving in secondary schools. One is the elimination of driver education from many school systems, which is the result of a tightened economy. Although alcohol-impaired driving is often taught in health education courses, it is less extensively treated than in driver education courses. The second development reducing treatment of alcohol-impaired driving has been an increase of the legal drinking age from 18 to 21. The fact that secondary school students cannot drink legally and will not be allowed to for some time has led many to believe that education in the use of alcohol is unnecessary.

Individual Intervention

Attempts to encourage direct intervention in further drinking or in driving by the alcohol-impaired have been directed toward social hosts, peers and servers of alcohol.

Host Intervention

The 1996 National Roadside Survey (Voas et al., 1998d) revealed that US drivers coming from the homes of friends accounted for 45% of those with BACs greater than 0.01, although making up only 27% of the drivers surveyed. Drinking in private parties is characteristic of drivers who are under age 25, male, unemployed and drinking with others (Chang & Lapham, 1996). Private gatherings rank second behind licensed establishments as sources of drivers arrested for drinking, which accounts for about a quarter of all those arrested for driving while intoxicated (DWI). However, DWIs from unlicensed drinking locations are relatively more likely to be involved in accidents than those from licensed establishments (Lang & Stockwell, 1991).

Efforts to ensure responsible service of alcohol by social hosts have lagged behind those directed at servers in licensed establishments. First, their wide dispersion leaves efforts to encourage intervention largely to mass media communications. Second, social hosts are not subject to the same legal sanctions as licensed establishments; service to intoxicated guests is not a criminal offense. In the USA, 27 states have statutory or case laws making social hosts liable for injury to third parties, although in more than half the law applies only to service of minors. However, social host liability suits are rare, and, the public does not appear to support social host liability.

The literature reveals little effort to develop, conduct or evaluate prevention programs for social hosts. One program was administered to 271 adults in 18 locations around the USA and evaluated through pre- and post-measures KAB (McKnight, 1987). The pattern of behavior change observed was similar to that found among servers; that is, significant gains were being reported in alcohol service practices but not in preparation for or subsequent dealing with intoxicated guests. The analysis of attitudes disclosed a general disinclination of hosts to interfere with the drinking of adult guests. Two influences were of concern: appearing to be inhospitable and the belief that interference would lead to resentment and loss of friendship.

Peer Intervention

Efforts to enlist the associates of the alcohol-impaired driver in preventing harm from overdrinking are epitomized by the phase, "friends don't let friends drive drunk". The idea of peer intervention includes both keeping drivers from getting drunk and keeping drunks from getting behind the wheel. In most drinking contexts, peers are able to observe drinkers more closely, and thus can recognize the signs of impaired behavior more quickly than servers or hosts.

Although the concept of peer intervention applies to all drinkers, it has been most frequently advanced and studied within the underage population, whose drinking tends to occur surreptitiously in automobiles, remote outdoor locations or homes lacking adult supervision. Lee et al. (1997) found that, of teenagers who drank, 83% did so in someone else's home, 46% outdoors, 41% in a moving vehicle, 38% in their own home and only 22% in a bar or restaurant. Jones-Webb et al. (1997) found that adolescents drinking in homes consumed fewer drinks than those drinking in public places, even after controlling for demographic differences. Wagenaar et al. (1996) found that young people obtained alcohol primarily through purchases by persons of legal age; purchases by those under the legal age and home supplies accounted for most of the rest.

The disinclination of adult hosts to intervene in the drinking of other adults does not appear to be as true of the youths. An evaluation of a secondary school alcohol program found that those completing the program reported no less drinking-and-driving behavior than those taking a standard driver education program and a no-treatment control. However, they appeared to be more likely to intervene in the drinking and driving of their peers (McKnight et al., 1979). Collins & Frey (1992) surveyed college students and found that 87% had intervened with someone. The most frequent form of intervention was driving others home, followed by preventing them from driving, telling them not to drive, having someone else drive, offering to follow them, and threatening to prevent them from driving. Attempts to intervene were successful 80–89% of the time; success did not vary as a function of gender (same or opposite) or the relationship to an intervener. Similar results were reported by Monto et al. (1992), who found that two-thirds of the college students had intervened with others; the incidence of intervention was unrelated to gender, age or race.

Peer intervention instruction has been evaluated through a random experiment. The treatment group was given an alcohol segment containing the peer intervention program, and the control group was given an alcohol program of equal length but without intervention instruction (McKnight et al., 1984). Although pre-post knowledge gains were found for both groups, attitude and enduring intervention behavior change were found only among students receiving intervention training.

Server Intervention

The 1980s saw the rise of server training as a way to reduce the harm resulting from irresponsible service of alcohol. Typically, training programs for wait-persons and bartenders take only a few hours and address: (a) the safety, health, and economic problems of irresponsible service; (b) the laws and regulations governing service; (c) the prevention of alcohol problems through better serving practices, age identification and alternative beverages; and (d) the prevention of impaired driving by identifying impairment, refusing service and providing transportation. Programs for managers also included instruction in promotion, service and transportation policies. By 1990, server training had become something of a cottage industry. The early history and development of programs has been extensively reviewed by Christy (1989).

The effectiveness of server training has been evaluated by Russ & Geller (1986); Gliksman & Single (1988); Mosher et al. (1989); McKnight (1991); Howard-Pitney et al. (1991); Rydon, Lang & Stockwell (1993); Rydon et al. (1996); and Saltz & Stanghetta (1997). Most programs have led to significant improvement in server knowledge and attitude, as well as intervention in the form of discouraging overconsumption and encouraging alternative beverages. Improved management practices have included not permitting multiple drink orders, requiring individual drink requests rather than "rounds", and limiting the number of drinks available at last call. However, success in reducing the risk of drink–driving has not been forthcoming. Service to intoxicated patrons and "pseudopatrons" simulating signs of intoxication has not been significantly reduced. These outcomes contrast markedly with those achieved through enforcement of alcohol control laws.

Obstacles to intervention by servers are formidable, including difficulty in observing signs of intoxication while busily engaged in talking and delivering (McKnight, 1991), conflict with a service orientation and possible loss of patron gratuities, patron persistence in seeking service and the "customer is always right" tradition, and frequent lack of management support. Countering these disincentives to intervention requires strict enforcement of alcohol control laws. One of the few programs to evidence a beneficial effect was carried out by a Navy NCO club where tight management control could be exercised (Saltz, 1986).

Despite the lack of demonstrated effectiveness, a number of jurisdictions have mandated the training of servers as a condition of licensing. The results have been no more encouraging than those of optional training. Molof & Kimball (1994) found no apparent change in the rate of drinking or the mean BAC or percentage of patrons with BACs greater than 0.10 associated with the Oregon mandatory training law. However, legislation mandating

server training has generally been tied to a reduction in licensee liability for damages resulting from illegal service by trained servers. To the extent that it relieves management of
liability for harm resulting from illegal and harmful service, it cannot be viewed as a step
toward the responsible sale of alcohol.

Alternative Transportation Programs

Drivers who are too impaired to operate a motor vehicle safely must find another way to
get home or to another destination. Two forms of alternative transportation are designated
driver programs and ride programs.

Designated Driver Programs

Any vehicle driven to a drinking event is a potential source of alcohol-impaired driving.
McKnight et al. (1995) conducted in-depth interviews of 600 individuals convicted of
drink–driving and retraced the decisions involving the event leading to their arrest. They
found that once the individuals left home, impaired driving became almost inevitable. This
finding indicates the importance of having a designated driver available when the possibility of heavy drinking exists. National surveys reveal that most Americans are aware of
the designated driver concept and that 93% reported that using a designated driver is good
or excellent idea (Winsten, 1994). Roadside surveys conducted in 1986 and 1996 found that
the proportion of drivers acting as designated drivers had increased from 5% to 25% (Fell,
Voas & Lange, 1997). In a telephone survey, Lange, Voas & O'Rourke (1998) found that
only 15.3% of their respondents were unfamiliar with the "designated driver" term.
However, the definition offered by 25.9% of those familiar with the term did not require
a designated driver to be identified before the planned drinking event or to avoid consuming alcohol during the event. Apsler, Harding & Goldfein (1987) conducted a national
study of commercial establishments that claimed to have designated driver programs that
offered free soft drinks to the designated drivers and found participation by drivers to be
low. The study of decisions leading to alcohol-impaired driving by McKnight et al. (1995)
showed that many who agree to serve as designated drivers renege after drinking, even
though it means riding with a drunk driver.

Some have expressed concern that the presence of a designated driver might encourage
the owner-drivers to drink more than they would otherwise, making them a greater danger
if either they or the designated drivers change their minds. Apsler et al. (1987) could not
determine if the presence of a designated driver resulted in increased drinking by peers
or if the reported designated drivers actually did the driving. In a later study, Harding &
Caudill (1997) found drinkers reporting small, but significant, increases in consumption
when drinking outside the home when with a designated driver. Therefore, it would appear
that a designated driver program is not as effective as a countermeasure for preventing
alcohol-impaired driving as originally envisioned. It seems to work best when designated
drivers are non-drinkers and drive their own cars to drinking events, thus helping to ensure
that they will indeed do the driving.

Safe Ride Programs

Several communities have organizations that provide free rides largely to individuals who
drive while being alcohol impaired. Harding, Apsler & Goldfein (1988) surveyed 335 ride

services in response to calls from their passengers or the drinking establishments serving them. They found the biggest obstacle to be the inability of more than 15% of these programs to transport the driver's vehicle. Drivers were reluctant to leave their vehicles behind or return to the drinking location to collect their vehicles. The literature failed to assess their value in reducing alcohol-impaired driving, including whether or not their availability increased consumption among potential clients. Ross (1992b) has suggested that one approach to individuals could be to provide them with free taxi rides to drinking establishments. This would ensure their inability to drive away and, consequently, a heavy drinker would be forced to find alternative transportation to return home, as the vehicle would not be at the drinking location.

REMOVING THE IMPAIRED DRIVER FROM THE ROAD

The historic area for action to reduce alcohol-related crashes has been the enforcement by the police of impaired driving laws. British laws against driving horse-drawn carriages existed in the nineteenth century. US laws against drink–driving were enacted at the end of the first decade of the twentieth century. Initially, enforcement duty fell on all police officers. As the number of vehicles on the roadways increased and the traffic laws multiplied, however, the larger urban departments began to establish traffic divisions with specific responsibilities to supervise driver compliance with traffic regulations. In the 1950s and 1960s, as the role of alcohol in the most serious crashes came to be recognized, some departments formed special drink–driving enforcement units. This specialization became more necessary as the impaired driving laws became more complex and the technology of detection and blood alcohol concentration testing became more intricate.

Enforcement Methods

The immediate goal of enforcing alcohol-impaired driving laws is to remove dangerous drivers from the road. However, the ultimate objective is to deter potentially impaired drivers from driving after heavy drinking. Deterrence depends upon both an effective enforcement system and sufficient media coverage to make the public aware of the enforcement effort, which is discussed below. A new enforcement science has developed that focuses on: (a) identifying vehicles driven by impaired drivers; (b) detecting signs of drinking; (c) measuring impairment; and (d) measuring BAC levels.

Identifying Vehicles Driven by Impaired Operators

Current roadside breath-test surveys indicate that approximately 17% of drivers on weekend evenings in the USA have been drinking and 8% have BACs greater than 0.05, making them potentially liable to arrest for impaired driving (Voas et al., 1998d). The first problem for enforcement is to identify the vehicles driven by the over-the-limit drivers. Traditionally, traffic patrol officers come across drinking drivers in the course of enforcing speeding and other traffic regulations. However, without specialized training, they generally miss half or more of the high-BAC drivers with whom they come in contact (Taubenslag & Taubenslag, 1975). Consequently, apprehension rates are low. Borkenstein (1975) estimated that drivers with BAC greater than 0.10 were apprehended only once in 2000 trips by officers trained to detect the special impaired driving cues developed by the NHTSA.

Where high-intensity DUI enforcement operations involving special patrols of specially trained officers are implemented, the apprehension rate rises to about 1 in 300 trips (Voas & Hause, 1987; Beitel, Sharp & Glauz, 1975).

Sobriety Checkpoints

Another approach to contacting impaired drivers is random stopping and assessment of every driver using the road at times and locations where drinking and driving is common. In this procedure, drivers are stopped at random and the officer conducts a brief interview at the driver's window to determine whether there is evidence of drinking. If such evidence is detected, the driver is invited out of the vehicle for further observation. In Australia and Sweden, this random-stopping procedure is coupled with an immediate screening breath test that all motorists are required to provide. In the state of Victoria, large bus-like mobile units are stationed at checkpoints. These units provide facilities in which breath tests can be administered to two or more suspects at a time, and initial paperwork can be done on those drivers who are over the limit. This Australian random-testing procedure has been shown to be effective in reducing alcohol-related crashes (Homel, 1988; Homel, McKay & Henstridge, 1995; Span & Stanislaw, 1995).

In the USA, the Fourth Amendment to the US Constitution precludes random stopping except in structured checkpoint operations. However, even in such operations, the Fourth Amendment is currently interpreted as precluding mandatory breath testing of all individuals stopped. Therefore, a behavioral element is a part of the decision-making process at American checkpoint operations. By surveying drivers passing through checkpoints, Lund & Jones (1987), Ferguson, Wells & Lund (1993) and Wells et al. (1997) have found that officers miss as many of 50% of the drivers who have BACs higher than the 0.10 limit, partially because of the relatively brief 30–60 second interview permitted at the checkpoint. Despite this limitation, research has clearly demonstrated that, in the USA, checkpoints are effective in reducing alcohol-impaired driving crashes (Ross, 1992a; Levy, Shea & Asch, 1989; Foss et al., 1997; Lacey, Jones & Fell, 1997; Voas, Rhodenizer & Lynn, 1985; Stuster & Blowers, 1995).

The impact of this checkpoint technique on drinking-and-driving accidents throughout the USA has been generally limited because sobriety checkpoints are viewed by enforcement agencies as expensive and complex to mount (Ross, 1992a). However, Stuster & Blowers (1995) have demonstrated that checkpoints employing relatively few officers (four to six) can be as effective as the much larger checkpoints that are normally mounted. Most communities should be able to use small checkpoints at least once or twice a month. Currently, however, checkpoints are primarily mounted three or four times a year during national holidays. In states such as California, Tennessee and North Carolina, where the state police assist communities in operating several checkpoints each month throughout the year, there is considerable evidence of their effectiveness (Lacey et al., 1997; Foss et al., 1997; Stuster & Blowers, 1995).

Detecting Impairment

In Australia and Sweden, any driver stopped can be tested for alcohol (Homel, 1988). In Britain, drivers can be tested under three conditions: when in a crash, when committing a traffic offense, or when an officer suspects drinking. Ross (1973), in a detailed study of the British Road Safety Act, indicated that this procedure was highly effective in reducing nighttime crashes. In the USA, whatever the reason for stopping the vehicle, the officer must have probable cause to believe the driver is impaired before requiring a BAC test. This is a three-step process: (a) assessment for visible signs of drinking; (b) a sobriety test; and (c) a chemical test.

Visible Signs

The first step in the measurement process involves a brief interview of the driver in his/her vehicle, during which an officer makes an initial determination as to whether the driver is likely to be impaired. The research literature does not encourage confidence in the ability of people to correctly estimate alcohol impairment in relation to legal BAC limits. Physicians examining suspected drinking drivers in Scandinavia identified as impaired only about 50% of those with BACs greater than 0.10. Studies by Langenbucher & Nathan (1983) and Pisoni & Martin (1989) showed only police officers to be reasonably accurate in classifying drinkers in terms of impairment. Work by Pagano & Taylor (1980), Taubenslag & Taubenslag (1975), Vingilis, Adlaf & Chung (1982), Jones & Lund (1985) & Compton (1985), by contrast, found that even the police were highly inaccurate.

Teplin & Lutz (1985) developed a scale for using observable signs to enable hospital staff to judge the presence of alcohol in accident victims arriving at emergency rooms. They found a correlation of 0.83 between the *number* of signs observed and BAC level. Use of prescribed cut-off points yielded probabilities of correctly identifying impaired victims ranging between 0.72 and 0.87. Much of the correlation reported came from accuracy identifying victims with very high blood alcohol levels. McKnight et al. (1997) undertook a study in which 1250 drinkers with 0.08–0.12% BAC were judged by casual observers in social situations. Observers correctly identified alcohol-impaired drinkers (>0.04), true positives, over half the time, and misidentified the unimpaired as impaired, false positives, about a quarter of the time. Those trained in using cues and observing only a few drinkers at a time were the most accurate. In judging intoxication (BAC > 0.08%), observers were as accurate, but more conservative, with true positives at slightly more than 50% and false positives less than 10%. Cues of intoxication were slurring of speech, fumbling objects, sloppy appearance and clothing, rudeness, hostility and stumbling, in order of increasing impairment.

Sobriety Tests

Once an initial determination has been made that the driver may be impaired through an interview at the driver's window, the officer invites the driver out of the vehicle to conduct a set of "sobriety tests". For decades, police have used a variety of performance tests to assess the degree of impairment for drivers suspected of alcohol-impaired driving. The admissibility of these tests as evidence relied entirely upon court acceptance of their validity as indices of inability to drive safely. A set of Standardized Field Sobriety Tests (SFSTs) was developed in the NHTSA by Tharp, Burns & Moskowitz (1981), based upon measured relationships between performance on various tasks and measured blood alcohol level. The three tests showing the most reliable relationships are: (a) the *horizontal gaze nystagmus (HGN)* test, a method for observing the irregularities in pupillary motion of the eye tracking a stimulus moving horizontally across a field of view; (b) the *walk-and-turn (WAT)* test, which determines the ability of an individual to remember directions, walk a straight line and execute a turn in place; (c) the *one-leg-stand (OLS)* test, which determines the ability of an individual to count in a prescribed manner while maintaining balance on one foot.

The US government funded the training of officers throughout the country in using these standardized tests. Several studies have indicated that they are useful to the police in apprehending impaired drivers (Burns & Dioquino, 1997; Anderson, Schweitz & Snyder, 1983). These tests play two roles in drink-driving enforcement. First, they provide probable cause to require a breath test, which is considered more intrusive than a sobriety test. Second, they provide evidence of impairment when suspects refuse to take a breath test, results of the breath test are challenged, or the defense claims that the results of the breath test do not provide a true indication of impairment.

Of the three SFST measures, HGN is by far the most reliable indicator of blood alcohol level and the only one that can identify drivers just above the statutory limits of 0.08% and 0.10% (Perrine et al., 1992). Moreover, it is the primary measure with any validity in identifying drivers at the low BACs, including the 0.04% level imposed on drivers of commercial vehicles and the even lower levels called for under "zero tolerance" laws (McKnight et al., 1997).

Chemical Testing

For the first half of the twentieth century, the primary basis for convicting operators of driving while impaired was through the testimony of the arresting officers regarding their appearance and behavior. However, since World War II, a movement has grown based on the work earlier in the century of Widmark (1932) to define the offense in terms of blood alcohol concentration. The first country to do so was Norway in 1936, which defined the impaired driver offense as operating a vehicle with a 0.05 BAC (Voas, 1982). This *per se* definition of the impaired driving offense has gradually been adopted by European nations, the USA and Austria over the last 30 years. The ability to use a particular BAC limit as a definition of impaired driving depended upon the development of accurate and inexpensive methods to measure blood alcohol levels. Initially, BACs were measured either in blood or in urine. However, the development of an inexpensive breath test device, the "Breathalyzer", by Borkenstein & Smith (1961) in the 1950s (which could be operated by police officers with minimal training) increased the availability and ease of BAC measurement and extended the utility of the *per se* definition of impaired driving. Initially, the breath test was primarily used in the USA, with Europe continuing to use blood samples.

A significant advance occurred in the mid-1960s, with the development of disposable breath-test devices that could be used by the police in the field. This permitted Sweden to initiate its innovative program of sobriety checkpoints, where drivers were stopped at random and tested using these disposal devices. Field units using either a semiconductor or a fuel cell sensor were developed in the early 1970s. These permitted an even more convenient and accurate method of breath testing, using small hand-held units about the size of a cigarette package, which police could use in the field (Moulden & Voas, 1975). The availability of these devices made programs such as the Random Testing in Australia possible.

A final technological development in the breath-testing field was the production of passive breath test units, which could be integrated with police flash lights to allow officers to rapidly screen motorists at the roadside (Voas, 1983; Lund & Jones, 1987). Thus, in current enforcement, three types of breath-test devices can be distinguished: (a) evidential test used to collect data for presentation in court; (b) preliminary breath tests used by officers in the field to confirm that drivers are over the limit before taking them to the police station for an evidential test; and (c) passive sensors used by officers early in their investigation to determine whether there is evidence of heavy drinking.

Evidentiary Breath Testers (EVTs)

If there is probable cause to suspect that a driver is over the limit, the individual may be taken to the police station for an evidential breath test. These semi-automatic test devices are generally set to perform a calibration, take two breath samples and print the result. In the USA, the NHTSA has established model specifications for these devices (NHTSA, 1992). The operator must ensure that the suspect takes nothing into his/her mouth for 20 minutes before the test. The operator must also inform the suspect before the test that refusal will result in license suspension.

Preliminary Breath Testers (PBTs)

PBTs are small hand-held units that can be carried in the field by police officers and used to measure BACs. These devices assist the police in determining whether there is probable cause to arrest a potential offender to then be arrested and taken to the police station for an evidential test. These devices have proved to be accurate evidential breath-test machines used for collecting court data (Frank & Flores, 1989). Distribution of preliminary breath testers to police officers has been shown to increase the number of arrests of alcohol-impaired driving offenders. An econometrics study by Saffer & Chaloupka (1989) showed that states with PBT had lower alcohol-related fatality rates than did states without these laws.

Passive Alcohol Sensors (PASs)

Since evidential and preliminary breath testers insert a small tube into the mouth to collect the sample, their use is generally viewed as a "search" under the US Constitution and, therefore, must be "reasonable". This means that the officer must suspect drinking and have probable cause to arrest the offender before requiring either an EVT or a PBT. The PAS, on the other hand, collects expired air from 2–6 inches in front of the driver's face. This expired air is mixed with ambient air, so the measurement lacks precision; however, it is reasonably sensitive to the presence of alcohol (Voas, 1983). The ability of police officers to detect drinking through their sense of smell is limited by the fact that ethanol, the active impairing drug, is essentially odorless. What the nose detects is the additional substances in different types of drinks (e.g. Bourbon, Scotch, vodka), their special tastes. Further, olfactory sensitivity varies considerably among officers. As a result, passive sensing can be useful for detecting drinking when officers have limited contact with the driver, such as at checkpoints, or when enforcing zero tolerance laws where low BACs must be detected. Farmer et al. (1999), in the 1996 National Roadside Survey, demonstrated that using a passive sensor on randomly stopped nighttime drivers detected 37% of the drivers with BACs between 0.05 and 0.08, 63% of the drivers with BACs between 0.08 and 0.10, and 73% of the drivers with BACs of at least 0.10. Since, as noted above, officers typically miss 50% of the drivers with BACs greater than 0.10 at checkpoints, passive sensors offer the possibility of increasing significantly the detection rates in such operations.

BAC Limits

In most countries, the police have the right to require the driver to take a breath test if they have stopped the vehicle legally. In the USA, however, the Fourth Amendment requires that "searches be reasonable". Therefore, an officer can require a driver to provide a breath sample for a BAC test only if he/she has probable cause to make an arrest. If there is probable cause, the US Supreme Court in the Smerber vs. California case determined that a chemical test involved the collection of physical evidence and, therefore, could be forced on the driver. However, most police departments did not want to get involved in restricting offenders and forcibly taking blood samples. Therefore, "implied consent" legislation was passed by the states under which drivers implicitly agreed to submit to a measure of their blood alcohol when they accept a license to drive. This allows the Department of Motor Vehicles to suspend that driver's permit if he/she refuses to take the test. The significance of the EVT was further enhanced when 40 states adopted the administrative license revocation (ALR) laws. The ALR laws provide that, if a breath test is taken and found to be higher than the state BAC limit, the offender will also have his/her license administratively suspended.

The specific levels that define the maximum BAC at which one may legally drive vary considerably from one country to another, as well as between jurisdictions within some countries. For example, in North America and some European countries, the legal limit is relatively high, 0.08–0.10%. In Australia, New Zealand and some Scandinavian countries, 0.05% is the legal limit. A review by Moskowitz, Burns & Williams (1985) revealed that alcohol impairment begins at as little as a 0.02 BAC. Analyses of roadside survey and crash data by Zador (1991) and Hurst (1973) have shown that at a BAC of 0.05 or greater, there is a significant increase in the risk of involvement in an alcohol-related fatal crash. However, only about 10% of fatal crashes in the USA involve BACs of less than 0.10 (NHTSA, 1998). Blood alcohol concentrations above this level account for most of those at a highly elevated relative risk and also the largest numbers of alcohol-related fatalities.

A recent trend in the USA has been to establish lower BAC limits for youthful drivers. These so-called "zero tolerance" laws make it illegal for those under age 21 to operate a vehicle with any alcohol in their systems. Reductions in nighttime single-vehicle accidents following passage of zero tolerance laws have been reported (Blomberg, 1992; Hingson, Heeren & Winter, 1994; Hingson, Heeren & Morelock, 1986; Hingson et al., 1991; Voas, Tippetts & Fell, under review). However, the extent to which the laws are actually enforced is open to question. Very low BACs rarely evidence themselves in observable driving behavior; therefore, few arrests appear to occur at low levels. Voas, Lange & Tippetts (1998a) found that police principally used the zero tolerance law in the state of California to cite young drivers over the adult limit. Thus, the total number of drinking and driving arrests showed only a small increase. Further, there was little evidence that young drivers targeted by the law perceived a significant increase in risk of apprehension. Still, the California zero tolerance law was associated with a decline in the number of underage drinking drivers in fatal crashes—possibly because the law changed peer attitudes regarding drinking and driving.

Media Advocacy

It is generally accepted that new laws and enforcement programs must be publicized to be effective. If the public is unaware of a change in the law or an increase in its enforcement, it is unlikely that it will effect their drinking and driving.

Studies such as that by Blomberg (1992) and Voas & Hause (1987) in Stockton, California, demonstrated that publicity doubled the impact of new laws and new enforcement efforts. Two types of approaches have been used to publicize special programs or laws.

The traditional approach to publicizing new laws has been to create public service announcements (PSAs) through a series of steps: (a) identifying the target group at which the law or program is aimed; (b) identifying the media that reaches that target group; (c) developing an appeal that will gain the attention of the target group (such as well-known athletic figures); and (d) creating a message that is to be conveyed. The strength of this approach is it provides relatively professional, high-quality messages. Its weakness is that the station manager must be persuaded to run the PSAs at times when the target audience is likely to be watching. This may require considerable effort by community public relations personnel.

A more recent alternative is to apply "media advocacy" procedures, which begin with the collection of data relevant to a community, such as the number of drivers killed in the last year. Community spokespersons announce the information at news conferences. This interesting new information is released to the media through community leaders. The appearance of these leaders on local television or in local newspapers serves to persuade the public that the issue is important in their community and that action is supported by the local leadership. Appearing on television and in local papers serves to commit the participating leaders to the prevention program and facilitates recruiting them into the community coalition dealing with the problem. This process is also designed to motivate action organizations, such as the police, by featuring officers and police chiefs in news events and having community spokespersons praise the department, indicating the importance of the department's enforcement actions. Thus, although the media advocacy effort ultimately delivers a message to the drinking driver target group, in the process it also helps to organize and empower community leaders to take action to support the program. A community-wide media program described by Holder & Treno (1997) provided a demonstration of this process.

PREVENTING RECURRENCE OF DRINKING AND DRIVING

Once impaired drivers have been identified and removed from the road, it is possible to move from the general deterrence aimed at all operators on the highway to specific deterrence, using remedies frequently tailored to the characteristics of an individual driver and his/her offense. Three general areas of action can be distinguished: (a) applying traditional penalties such as jail and fines, directed at causing sufficient discomfort to deter the individual from repeating the offense; (b) suspending the driver's license to prevent future drinking and driving; and (c) requiring attendance at treatment or educational programs directed at assisting the offender to avoid future impaired driving and promoting recovery from dependence on alcohol. Because a drinking–driving conviction allows the state to identify high-risk drivers, and because it brings these drivers under the control of the courts, communities are presented with a special opportunity to attack the impaired-driving problem. Unfortunately, in the USA, most current remedial programs have shown limited success, as one-third to one-half of the drivers convicted of impaired driving repeat the offense.

Specific Deterrence

Traditional penalties, such as jails and fines, have generally been justified on two bases: (a) a *general deterrent* effect on those not yet convicted of impaired driving; and (b) a *specific deterrent* effect on offenders currently suffering the penalties by promoting avoidance of future offenses. Because of these two bases for justifying traditional penalties, arguments over sanctions are often confused by the conflicting opinions of those focusing on general, as compared to specific, deterrence. A further confusion is presented by the interests of the government and the courts in using fines to promote "self-sufficiency" in the criminal justice effort by paying for such activities such as breath tests, police patrols and court expenses.

Jail Sentences

There is limited evidence for the general deterrent effectiveness of jail sentences for reducing impaired driving by the public as a whole (Nichols & Ross, 1989; Zador et al., 1988; Jones et al., 1988). However, there is little evidence that this sanction has a specific deterrent effect on the offenders who are actually incarcerated (Voas, 1986; Simpson, Mayhew & Beirness, 1996). Moreover, its use for DWI offenders is limited by the cost of incarceration and overcrowded jails (Voas, 1985). Nevertheless, the availability of jail sanctions is an important motivational tool for the courts. It provides a penalty for failure to conform to the probation requirements established by the court (Voas et al., 1999). Lower cost, alternative confinement procedures, such as electronic house arrest, have been shown as ineffective in reducing recidivism (Jones et al., 1996). Finally, the authority to impose a jail sanction may provide the legal basis for referring offenders to residential treatment programs. Programs such as the DWI Center in Prince Georges County, Maryland, have significantly reduced DWI recidivism in first and multiple offenders (Voas & Tippetts, 1990).

Fines

Other than an early report by Homel (1988) in Australia, there is no reliable evidence that fines have any general or specific deterrent effect on impaired driving. However, they can play an important role in helping to finance some essential enforcement activities such as breath testing. Yet, many fines are either uncollected or paid over a long time as courts tend to accept defendant pleads that they are either indigent or do not have the funds to pay the fines. Further, fines are frequently waived to allow the offender to pay for the required treatment program.

Offender Remediation

A variety of programs have been developed and administered to cope with alcohol-impaired driving. For the lack of a better term, "remedial" will be applied to the educational, counseling and treatment programs designed to deal the population of drivers found guilty of alcohol-impaired driving.

Assessment

Convicted drinking drivers in the USA represent a heterogeneous group (Perrine, Peck & Fell, 1989). Some offenders can be classified as high-risk drivers who drink; others might be classified as problem drinkers who drive. It has been hypothesized that some first offenders are apprehended for drink–driving because they lack an understanding of the effect of alcohol on performance and they lack knowledge of the law. Other offenders are apprehended principally because they are addicted to alcohol and have little or no control over their drinking. Because of wide variations in the characteristics of first offenders, courts have established the capability to conduct presentencing investigations, using interviews and brief questionnaires to separate first offenders into two broad classes: *social drinkers* and *problem drinkers*. Those identified through this assessment process as *social drinkers* are assigned by the courts to a relatively brief educational program involving 10–12 hours of instructions over 3–4 weeks. Offenders assessed to be *problem drinkers* are assumed to have limited conscious control of their drinking; therefore, they require intensive treatment to overcome their alcohol abuse or dependence problem (Wells-Parker & Popkin, 1994). Several reviews of the assessment instruments used in this process have demonstrated that they are reasonably accurate in discriminating between *social* and *problem* drinkers (Popkin et al., 1988; Lapham, Skipper & Simpson, 1997).

Education and Counseling

Drivers not previously found guilty of an alcohol offense are generally given the opportunity to participate in programs involving some combination of education or counseling to avoid or shorten the period of license suspension. Perhaps the first well-documented remedial effort designed to deal specifically with alcohol-impaired driving was that reported by Steward & Malfetti (1970). Although the substance of education and counseling programs varies from one program to another, the most common focal points are: (a) the effects of alcohol—from its general effect upon health and everyday functioning to its specific effects upon safe operation of motor vehicles; (b) the relationship between amount and rate of consumption to the blood alcohol level and impairment; (c) the laws governing drinking and driving and the sanctions for which violators are at risk; and (d) the influences that lead to heavy drinking and ways of neutralizing them.

The effectiveness of various court-mandated remedial programs in reducing drink–driving recidivism among DUI offenders has been extensively studied. The results of these studies have been reviewed and synthesized (Voas, 1972; Struckman-Johnson & Mushill, 1976; Swenson & Clay, 1977; Mann et al., 1983). These reviewers found that, although most of the studies faced serious methodological problems that undermined their conclusiveness, certain programs evidenced some small impact upon recidivism when compared with the absence of any program.

The alternative to education and counseling programs is generally suspension of licenses. McKnight & Voas (1991) found that without some form of education, counseling or treatment program, the effects of suspension upon alcohol-impaired driving lasted only as long as the driver was incapacitated by the license suspension. Further, this could be attributed to a reduction in driving exposure rather than any selective effect upon drink–driving itself. An extensive meta-analysis of 215 independent evaluations of remedial programs by Wells-Parker et al. (1995) found remedial programs yielding an average reduction of 8–9%, both in recidivism for alcohol-impaired driving offenses and in alcohol-related accidents. Alternatively, licensing sanctions alone "tended to be associated with reduction in occurrence of non-alcohol . . . crashes". The effects of the individual interventions could not be readily differentiated because the evaluations addressed varying combinations of remediation. Moreover, the populations addressed varied considerably from one intervention to another. However, educational programs for first offenders predominated.

Treatment

Historically, first offenders were considered candidates for education and counseling, with treatment being considered only after two or more convictions. More recently, however, many jurisdictions are providing assessment programs in which drivers are screened at the outset to determine the nature and extent of their drinking problem. The requirements of effective treatment for alcohol dependency goes beyond drink–driving and is addressed separately in another chapter of this volume.

For many, alcohol-impaired driving is a symptom of a more fundamental alcohol dependency. Recognition that many convicted drink–drivers exhibit drinking problems and are alcohol-dependent dates back to the late 1960s (Waller et al., 1967; Selzer et al., 1967). Successful treatment of alcohol-dependent drivers requires a more intensive and extensive form of remediation than education or counseling. Where education and counseling generally focuses upon separating drinking from driving, treatment addresses the use of alcohol itself. Indeed, a large segment of the patient population being treated for alcohol dependency has entered treatment because of an alcohol-impaired driving conviction.

Incapacitation

Although most drivers in fatal crashes do not have records of alcohol-impaired driving, being convicted of a prior offense raises the risk of being involved in an alcohol-related fatal crash (Simpson et al., 1996; Hedlund & Fell, 1995). Preventive efforts directed toward previous offenders can use sanctions to limit driving, including license suspension and revocation, vehicle impoundment and jail. Although the immediate effect of these sanctions is to reduce driving, they are also expected to create an unpleasant condition that deters future alcohol-impaired driving. In addition, participation in the remedial programs discussed earlier is often motivated almost entirely by the requirement to complete such programs as a condition for relief from sanctions.

License Actions

Research supports for the effectiveness of license suspension as a way to reduce DWI recidivism and alcohol-related crashes among individuals convicted of impaired driving (Peck, Sadler & Perrine, 1985; Nichols & Ross, 1989; McKnight & Voas, 1991; Ross, 1992a). This action is, however, only partially effective because the effects of suspension are generally confined to the period of the suspension itself, and for first offenders these periods are usually relatively short. A second offense is considered indicative of a fundamental alcohol problem and is typically accompanied by a much longer suspension. Further, multiple offenses can result in revocation of the driver's license, thus requiring drivers to seek licenses as new drivers. Yet even the longer suspension and revocation periods may not be sufficient to provide an opportunity for treatment interventions to have an impact on impaired driving.

Driving on a suspended license is common because it cannot be detected by the police unless drivers are apprehended for another infraction. It estimated that up to 75% of US drivers suspended for DWI continue to drive to some extent (Nichols & Ross, 1989; Ross & Gonzales, 1988). Where special insurance coverage is required for license reinstatement, it is common for drivers to continue operating on a suspended license rather than seek reinstatement (Voas & Tippetts, 1996b). However, a combination of reduced and/or more careful driving leads to lower accident and recidivism rates for drivers on suspension (Blomberg, Preusser & Ulmer, 1987; Voas, Tippetts & Taylor, 1998c; Voas & Tippetts, 1996a).

Many states offer drivers the opportunity to regain licenses before the end of a suspension period where the suspension would cause a hardship. Popkin et al. (1983) found that, as might be expected, drivers receiving hardship licenses had a higher incidence of accidents and violations than those not legally permitted to drive. Voas & McKnight (1991) found that the availability of a hardship license had little effect in reducing the general deterrent value of the license suspension penalty. A study by Wells-Parker & Cosby (1987) revealed that the hardship imposed by suspension rarely involved loss of employment. However, the net effect of hardship licensing depends upon the balance between the costs of higher accident rates and the benefits of increased mobility, a trade-off not yet calculated.

Administrative License Suspension

It is well established that the deterrent effect of any penalty is benefited by certainty and immediacy (Ross, 1984). License suspension through the court system often involves extensive delay of, and frequently escape from, adverse consequences. To overcome this problem, many jurisdictions have passed laws allowing the drivers' licensing agency to suspend licenses administratively for drivers showing blood alcohol levels greater than the legal limit. Forty of the 50 states in the USA have enacted what has come to be known as Administrative License Revocation (ALR) laws, although licenses are typically suspended rather than revoked. Some jurisdictions allow police to confiscate licenses on the spot and others require an action by the Department of Motor Vehicles. In some jurisdictions, the suspension is immediate; in others, the drivers are permitted to continue driving for a short period. Based on a decision of the US Supreme Court, all ALR laws require that offenders have the opportunity to request a hearing.

Zador et al. (1988) and Klein (1989) have demonstrated that the ALR law has a general deterrent effect, as evidenced by a reduction in alcohol-impaired driving offenses among the general driving public following passage of laws. Voas et al. (1998c) and Beirness et al. (1997) have shown that ALR laws have also reduced recidivism among convicted alcohol-impaired driving offenders. Zobeck & Williams (1994) reviewed 46 studies on administrative license suspension as part of a meta-analysis of literature on the effects of alcohol-impaired driving control efforts, and found an average reduction of 5% in alcohol-related crashes and a reduction in fatal crashes of 26%.

Vehicle Actions

There is considerable evidence that, in the USA, efforts to prevent high-risk, impaired driving offenders from driving on public roads by suspending their driving privileges are failing. Evidence of this is shown by the large number of suspended drivers who are apprehended while operating a vehicle illegally and who do not reinstate their licenses when eligible to do so. The Department of Motor Vehicles in California estimates that there are close to 1 million suspended drivers in that state and that only 16% of the suspended drivers attempt to reinstate their licenses when eligible (Tashima & Helander, 1999). Voas & Tippetts (1994) found that half of the first offenders suspended for 90 days in the state of Washington were still suspended 4 years later. To deal with this illicit driving problem, states are beginning to pass legislation aimed at depriving the DUI offenders who are caught driving a vehicle while suspended (Voas, 1992).

Ignition Interlocks

The most permissive vehicle action for preventing DUI offenders from driving while impaired is placing interlocks in the ignition to prevent an impaired driver from operating the vehicle. Before the engine can be started, the driver must provide an alcohol-free breath sample. After the initial test to start the vehicle, the system is designed to require tests every few minutes, thus preventing a confederate from starting the engine for an alcohol-impaired driver (Voas & Marques, 1992). Unlike license suspension or other forms of immobilization, interlocks permit cars to be driven if the operator is not at a BAC < 0.03.

Eight studies of interlock programs conducted under the authority of a local court or a motor vehicle department has found them to be more effective than full license suspension in preventing recidivism among alcohol-impaired drivers (Voas et al., 1999). However, seven of the studies found that, once the interlock is removed, offenders have the same recidivism rate as suspended offenders. A major problem for the implementation of alcohol interlocks in the USA is that only a small proportion (generally less than 10%) of DUI offenders are willing to install them in order to drive legally. Only when the court is willing to make the alternative incarceration are the majority of drink–driving offenders motivated to accept an interlock (Voas et al., 1998a).

Vehicle Impoundment

A more severe form of vehicle action is impounding the vehicle of an offender so that it cannot be operated by either the offender or anyone else. Vehicle impoundment laws are generally applied to multiple alcohol-impaired driving offenders or to those convicted of driving while suspended. Studies of these laws in California (DeYoung, 1997), Ohio (Voas, Tippetts & Taylor, 1997, 1998b), and the province of Manitoba, Canada (Beirness et al., 1997), have demonstrated that impounding a vehicle for 1–6 months at the time of arrest reduces recidivism of multiple DUI offenders.

One problem of using vehicle impoundment or forfeiture is that it involves taking private property. In many cases, it is the property of someone other than the offender, because approximately half of those apprehended for unlicensed driving are operating vehicles owned by others. The vehicle license plate, on the other hand, is state property. A law enacted in Minnesota permits the police officer to seize the vehicle license plate when an individual is apprehended for their third alcohol-impaired driving offense, immobilizing the car without actually taking possession of it. The plate is destroyed and offenders cannot register another vehicle or obtain a plate until they can demonstrate that their drivers' licenses have been reinstated. A study by Rodgers (1994) indicated that this law reduced recidivism among third-time offenders.

KEY WORKS AND SUGGESTIONS FOR FURTHER READING

U.S. Government Accounting Office (1989). *Surgeon General's Workshop on Drunk Driving: Background Papers, December 14–16, 1988*. Washington, DC: Office of the Surgeon General, US Department of Health and Human Services, Public Health Service.

This collection of papers provides authoritative summaries of the key issues: causes of drink driving, prevalence, effectiveness of different prevention strategies and discussions of legal issues.

National Institutes of Health (Public Health Service) (1996). *Alcohol Health & Research World. Vol. 20(4)*. Springfield, VA: National Technical Information Service, US Department of Commerce.

Another set of authoritative reviews.

Ross, H.L. (1981). *Deterring the Drinking Driver: Legal Policy and Social Control*, 2nd edn. Lexington, MA: Lexington Books.

A classic text that provides theories that have guided policing practices in this area for the past three decades.

Ross, H.L. (1992). *Confronting Drunk Driving: Social Policy for Saving Lives.* New Haven, CT: Yale University Press.

This book in many ways updates the previous one in light of accumulated evidence regarding what works in the prevention of drink–driving.

REFERENCES

Anderson, T.E., Schweitz, R.M. & Snyder, M.B. (1983). *Field Evaluation of a Behavioral Test Battery for DWI.* Technical Report DOT-HS-806-475. Washington, DC: National Highway Traffic Safety Administration.

Apsler, R., Harding, W. & Goldfein, J. (1987). *The review and assessment of designated driver programs as an alcohol countermeasure approach.* Final Report HS 807 108, February). Washington, DC: US Department of Transportation, National Highway Traffic Administration.

Atkin, C.K. (1989). Advertising and marketing: mass communication effects on drinking and driving. In *Surgeon General's Workshop on Drunk Driving: Background Papers. Washington, DC, December 14–16, 1988* (pp. 15–34). Rockville, MD: US Department of Health and Human Services, Public Health Service, Office of the Surgeon General.

Beirness, D.J., Simpson, H.M. & Mayhew, D.R. (1993). Predicting crash involvement among young drivers. In H.-D. Utzelmann, G. Berghaus & G. Kroj (Eds), *Alcohol, Drugs and Traffic Safety— T92. Proceedings of the 12th International Conference* (pp. 885–890). Cologne: Verlag TUV Rhineland.

Beirness, D.J., Simpson, H.M., Mayhew, D.R. & Jonah, B.J. (1997). The impact of administrative license suspension and vehicle impoundment for DWI in Manitoba. In C. Mercier-Guyon (Ed.), *Proceedings of the 14th International Conference on Alcohol, Drugs and Traffic Safety* (pp. 919–925). Annecy, France: Centre d'Etudes et de Recherches en Medecine du Trafic.

Beitel, G.A., Sharp, M.C. & Glauz, W.D. (1975). Probability of arrest while driving under the influence of alcohol. *Journal of Studies on Alcohol,* **36**, 109–115.

Blomberg, R. (1992). *Lower BAC Limits for Youth: Evaluation of the Maryland 0.02 Law.* DOT HS 806 807. Washington, DC: US Department of Transportation.

Blomberg, R., Preusser, D. & Ulmer, R. (1987). *Deterrent Effects of Mandatory License Suspension for DWI Convictions.* DOT-HS-807-138. Washington, DC: National Highway Traffic Safety Administration.

Borkenstein, R.F. (1975). Problems of enforcement, adjudication and sanctioning. In S. Israelstam & S. Lambert (Eds), *Alcohol, Drugs and Traffic Safety* (pp. 655–662). Toronto: Addiction Research Foundation of Ontario.

Borkenstein, R.F., Crowther, R.F., Shumate, R.P., Ziel, W.B. & Zylman, R. (1974). The role of the drinking driver in traffic accidents (The Grand Rapids study). *Blutalkohol,* **II**(1), 1–132.

Borkenstein, R.F. & Smith, H.W. (1961). The breathalyzer and its application. *Medicine, Science and the Law,* **1**, 13.

Burns, M. & Dioquino, T. (1997). *Florida Validation Study of the Standardized Field Sobriety Test (SFST) Battery.* Project No. AL-97-05-14-01. State Safety Office, Department of Transportation, State of Florida.

Chang, I. & Lapham, S.C. (1996). Validity of self-reported criminal offenses and traffic violations in screening of driving-while-intoxicated offenders. *Alcohol and Alcoholism,* **31**, 583–590.

Christy, C.C. (1989). Server Intervention/Responsible Beverage Service (SI/RBS): A Source Document Addressing Related Literature. Unpublished doctoral thesis, George Peabody College for Teachers, Vanderbilt University, Nashville, TN.

Collins, M.D. & Frey, J.H. (1991). Drunken driving and informal social control: the case of peer intervention. *Deviant Behavior,* **13**, 73–87.

Compton, R.P. (1985). *Pilot Test of Selected DWI Procedures for Use at Sobriety Checkpoints.* Technical Report DOT-HS-806-724. Washington, DC: National Highway Traffic Safety Administration.

Damkot, D.K. (1979). Alcohol and the rural driver. In *Incurrence in Alcoholism*. Vol. VI (pp. 319–325). New York: Grune and Stratton.

DeYoung, D.J. (1997). *An Evaluation of the Specific Deterrent Effect on Vehicle Impoundment on Suspended, Revoked and Unlicensed Drivers in California*. Final Report No. DOT HS 808 727. Washington, DC: Department of Transportation, National Highway Traffic Safety Administration (NHTSA).

Farmer, C.M., Wells, J.K., Ferguson, S.A. & Voas, R.B. (1999). Field evaluation of the PAS III passive alcohol sensor. *Journal of Crash Prevention and Injury Control*, **1**(1), 55–61.

Fell, J., Voas, R.B. & Lange, J.E. (1997). Designated driver concept: extent of use in the USA. *Journal of Traffic Medicine*, **25**(3–4), 109–114.

Ferguson, S.A., Wells, J.K. & Lund, A.K. (1993). The role of passive alcohol sensors in detecting alcohol-impaired drivers at sobriety checkpoints. Paper presented at the Insurance Institute for Highway Safety, Arlington, VA.

Foss, R.D., Beirness, D.J., Tolbert, W.G., Wells, J.K. & Williams, A.F. (1997). Effect of an intensive sobriety checkpoint program on driving–driving in North Carolina. In C. Mercier-Guyon (Ed.), *Proceedings of the 14th International Conference on Alcohol, Drugs and Traffic Safety* (pp. 943–948). Annecy, France: Centre d'Études et de Recherches en Medecine du Trafic.

Foss, R.D., Voas, R.B., Beirness, D.J. & Wolfe, A.C. (1990). *Minnesota 1990 State-wide Drinking and Driving Roadside Survey*. Contract No. 525493. St. Paul, MN: Minnesota Department of Public Safety, Office of Traffic Safety.

Frank, J.F. & Flores, A.L. (1989). *The Accuracy of Evidential Breath Testers at Low BACs*. Report No. DOT HS 807 415. Washington, DC: National Highway Traffic Safety Administration.

Gliksman, L. & Single, E. (1988). A field evaluation of server intervention programs: accommodating reality. Paper presented at the Canadian Evaluation Society Meetings, Montreal.

Gruenewald, P.J. (1993). Alcohol problems and the control of availability: theoretical and empirical issues. In M.E. Hilton & G. Bloss (Eds), *Economics and the Prevention of Alcohol-related Problems*. Research Monograph No. 25, NIH Pub. No. 93-3513 (pp. 59–90). Bethesda, MD: National Institute on Alcohol Abuse and Alcoholism.

Harding, W.M., Apsler, R. & Goldfein, J. (1998). *A Directory of Ride Service Programs*. Final Technical Report, DOT HS 807 290. Washington, DC: US Department of Transportation, National Highway Traffic Safety Administration.

Harding, W.M. & Caudill, B.D. (1997). Does the use of designated drivers promote excessive alcohol consumption? In C. Mercier-Guyon (Ed.), *Proceedings of the 14th Annual Conference on Alcohol, Drugs and Traffic Safety, Volume 3. Annecy, France, 21–26 September 1997* (pp. 1359–1364). Annecy, France: Centre d'Études et de Recherches en Médecine du Traffic.

Haskins, J.B. (1985). The role of mass media in alcohol and highway safety campaigns. *Journal of Studies on Alcohol*, **10**, 184–191.

Hedlund, J. & Fell, J. (1995). Persistent drinking drivers in the US. In *39th Annual Proceedings of the Association for the Advancement of Automotive Medicine*. (pp. 1–12). Chicago, IL: Association for the Advancement of Automotive Medicine.

Hingson, R., Heeren, T. & Morelock, S. (Eds) (1986). *Preliminary Effects of Maine's 1982 0.02 Laws to Reduce Teenage Driving after Drinking*. London: Royal Society of Medicine Services.

Hingson, R., Heeren, T. & Winter, M. (1994). Lower legal blood alcohol limits for young drivers. *Public Health Reports*, **109**(6), 739–744.

Hingson, R., Howland, J., Heeren, T. & Winter, M. (1991). Reduced BAC limits for young people (impact on night fatal) crashes. *Alcohol, Drugs and Driving*, **7**(2), 117–127.

Holder, H.D., Janes, K., Mosher, A.M., Musty, R.E. & Voas, R.B. (1990). *Alcoholic Beverage Server Liability and the Reduction of Alcohol-involved Problems*. Berkeley, CA: Prevention Research Center.

Holder, H.D. & Treno, A.J. (1997). Media advocacy in community prevention: news as a means to advance policy change. *Addiction*, **92**(2), S189–S199.

Homel, R. (1988). *Policing and Punishing the Drinking Driver. A Study of General and Specific Deterrence*. New York: Springer-Verlag.

Homel, R., McKay, P. & Henstridge, J. (1995). The impact on accidents of random breath testing in New South Wales, 1982–1992. In C.N. Kloeden & A.J. Mclean (Eds), *Proceedings of the 13th International Conference on Alcohol, Drugs and Traffic Safety, Adelaide, 13 August–19 August 1995*,

Vol. 2 (pp. 849–855). Adelaide: NHMRC Road Accident Research Unit, University of Adelaide 5005.

Howard-Pitney, B., Johnson, M.D., Altman, D.G., Hopkins, R. & Hammond, N. (1991). Responsible alcohol service: a study of server, manager, and environmental impact. *American Journal of Public Health*, **81**(2), pp 197–198.

Hurst, P.M. (1973). Epidemiological aspects of alcohol in driver crashes and citations. *Journal of Safety Research*, **5**(3), 130–148.

Jones, I.S. & Lund, A.K. (1985). Detection of alcohol-impaired drivers using passive alcohol sensor. *Journal of Police Science and Administration*, **145**(2), 153–160.

Jones, R.K., Joksch, H.C., Lacey, J.H. & Schmidt, H.J. (1988). *Field Evaluation of Jail Sanctions for DWI*. Final Report No. DOT HS 807 325. Washington, DC: Department of Transportation, National Highway Traffic Safety Administration (NHTSA).

Jones, R.K., Lacey, J.H., Berning, A. & Fell, J.C. (1996). Alternative sanctions for repeat DWI offenders. In *40th Annual Proceedings of the Association for the Advancement of Automotive Medicine* (pp. 307–315). Des Plaines, IL: Association for the Advancement of Automotive Medicine.

Jones-Webb, R., Toomey, T., Miner, K., Wagenaar, A.C., Wolfson, M. & Poon, R. (1997a). Why and in what context adolescents obtain alcohol from adults: a pilot study. *Substance Use & Misuse*, **32**(2), 219–228.

Jones-Webb, R., Short, B.J., Wagenaar, A.C., Toomey, T.L., Murray, D.M., Wolfson, M. & Forster, J.L. (1997b). Environmental predictors of drinking and drinking-related problems in young adults. *Journal of Drug Education*, **27**(1), 67–82.

Klein, T. (1989). *Changes in Alcohol-involved Fatal Crashes Associated with Tougher State Alcohol Legislation*. Final Report under Contract No. DTNH-122-88-C-07045. Washington, DC: National Highway Traffic Safety Administration.

Lacey, J.H., Jones, R.K. & Fell, J.C. (1997). The effectiveness of the "Checkpoint Tennessee" program. In C. Mercier–Guyon (Ed.), *Alcohol, Drugs and Traffic Safety*, Vol. 2 (pp. 969–975). Annecy, France: Centre d'Etudes et de Recherches en Médecine du Trafic.

Lang, E. & Stockwell, T. (1991). Drinking locations of drink-drivers: a comparative analysis of accident and non-accident cases. *Accident Analysis & Prevention*, **23**(6), 573–584.

Lange, J.E., Voas, R.B. & O'Rourke, P. (1998). What is a designated driver anyway? Results of a California survey on definitions and use of designated drivers. *Journal of Traffic Medicine*, **26**(3–4), 101–108.

Langenbucher, J.W. & Nathan, P.E. (1983). Psychology, public policy, and the evidence for alcohol intoxication. *American Psychologist*, 1070–1077.

Lapham, S.C., Skipper, B.J. & Simpson, G.L. (1997). A prospective study of the utility of standardized instruments in predicting recidivism among first DWI offenders. *Journal of Studies on Alcohol*, **58**, 524–530.

Lee, J.A., Jones-Webb, R., Short, B. & Wagenaar, A.C. (1997). Drinking location and risk of alcohol-impaired driving among high school seniors. *Addictive Behaviors*, **22**(3), 387–393.

Levy, D., Shea, D. & Asch, P. (1989). Traffic safety effects of sobriety checkpoints and other local DWI programs in New Jersey. *American Journal of Public Health*, **79**(3), 291–293.

Lund, A.F. & Jones, I.S. (1987). Detection of impaired drivers with a passive alcohol sensor. In P.C. Noordzij & R. Roszbach (Eds), *Alcohol, Drugs and Traffic Safety '86* (pp. 379–382). New York: Excerpta Medica.

Mann, R.E., Vingilis, E.R., Leigh, G., Anglin, L. & Blefgen, H. (1986). School-based programmes for the prevention of drinking and driving: issues and results. *Accident Analysis and Prevention*, **18**(4).

Mann, R.E., Vingilis, E.R., Leigh, G. & deGenova, K. (1983). A critical review on the effectiveness of drinking-driving rehabilitation programs. *Accident Analysis and Prevention*, **15**, 441–461.

McKnight, A.J. (1987). *An Evaluation of a Host Responsibility Program*. Washington, DC: National Highway Traffic Safety Administration.

McKnight, A.J. (1991). Factors influencing the effectiveness of server-intervention education. *Journal of Studies on Alcohol*, **52**(5), 389–397.

McKnight, A.J., Langston, E.A., McKnight, A.S., Resnick, J.A. & Lange, J.E. (1995). *Why People Drink and Drive: The Bases of Drinking-and-driving Decisions*. Publication No. DOT HS 808 251. Washington, DC: US Department of Transportation, National Highway Traffic Safety Administration.

McKnight, A.J., Marques, P.R., Langston, E.A. & Tippetts, A.S. (1997). Estimating blood alcohol level from observable signs. *Accident Analysis and Prevention*, **29**(2), 247–255.

McKnight, A.J., Mason, R.W., McPherson, L. & Oates, J.F. Jr. (1984). *Evaluation of Peer Intervention Training for High School Alcohol Safety Education*. Washington DC: National Highway Traffic Safety. Administration.

McKnight, A.J., Preusser, D.F., Psotka, J., Katz, D.B. & Edwards, J.M. (1979). *Youth Alcohol Safety Education Criteria Development*. NTIS Publication No. PB80-17894-0. Washington, DC: US Department of Transportation.

McKnight, A.J. & Streff, F.M. (1994). The effect of enforcement upon service of alcohol to intoxicated patrons of bars and restaurants. *Accident Analysis and Prevention*, **26**(1), 79–88.

McKnight, A.J. & Voas, R.B. (1991). The effect of license suspension upon DWI recidivism. *Alcohol, Drugs and Driving*, **7**(1), 43–54.

Mercer, G.W. (1986). *Age vs. Driving Experience as Predictors of Young Drivers' Traffic Accident Involvement*. Vancouver: Ministry of the Attorney General.

Miller, T.R., Lestina, D.C. & Spicer, R.S. (1998). Highway crash costs in the United States by driver age, blood, alcohol level, victim age, and restraint use. *Accident Analysis and Prevention*, **30**(2), 137–150.

Molof, M.J. & Kimball, C. (1994). *A Study of the Implementation and Effects of Oregon's Mandatory Alcohol Server Training Program*. Eugene, OR: Oregon Research Services Inc.

Monto, M.A., Newcomb, M.D., Rabow, J.E. & Hernandez, A.C.R. (1992). Social status and drunk driving intervention. *Journal of Studies on Alcohol*, **53**(1), 63–68.

Mosher, J.F. (1991). *Responsible Beverage Service: An Implementation Handbook for Communities*. Palo Alto, CA: Health Promotion Resource Center.

Mosher, J.F., Delewski, C., Saltz, R.F. & Hennessey, M. (1989). *Monterey/Santa Cruz Responsible Beverage Project: Final Report*. San Rafael, CA: Marin Institute for the Prevention of Alcohol and other Drug Problems.

Mosher, J.F. & Wallack, L.M. (1979). *The DUI Project: A Description of an Experimental Program to Address Drinking–Driving Problems*. Sacramento, CA: California Department of Alcoholic Beverage Control.

Moskowitz, H., Burns, M.M. & Williams, A.F. (1985). Skills performance at low blood alcohol levels. *Journal of Studies on Alcohol*, **46**(2), 482–485.

Moskowitz, H. & Robinson, C. (1988). *Effects of Low Doses of Alcohol on Driving-related Skills: A Review of the Evidence*. Report No. DOT HS 807 280. Washington, DC: National Highway Traffic Safety Administration.

Moulden, J.V. & Voas, R.B. (1975). *Breath Measurement Instrumentation in the US*. Technical Report DOT-HS-801-621. Washington, DC: National Highway Traffic Safety Administration.

National Highway Traffic Safety Administration (1986). *Techniques of Effective Alcohol Management: Findings from the First Year*. Washington, DC: National Highway Traffic Safety Administration.

National Highway Traffic Safety Administration (1992). Model specifications for breath alcohol ignition interlock devices (BAIIDs). *57 Federal Register*, **67**, 11772–11787.

National Highway Traffic Safety Administration (NHTSA) (1998). *Fatality Analysis Reporting System data files, 1982–1997*. Washington, DC: National Highway Traffic Safety Administration, National Center for Statistics and Analysis.

Nichols, J.L. & Ross, H.L. (1989). The effectiveness of legal sanctions in dealing with drinking drivers. In *Surgeon General's Workshop on Drunk Driving: Background Papers* (pp. 93–112). Washington, DC: US Department of Health and Human Services, Public Health Service, Office of the Surgeon General.

Ontario Ministry of Transport and Communications (1980). *The 1979 Ontario roadside BAC survey: Summary report, Interministerial Committee on Drinking and Driving*. Toronto: Ontario Ministry of Transport and Communications.

Pagano, M.R. & Taylor, S.P. (1980). Police perceptions of alcohol intoxication. *Journal of Applied Social Psychology*, **10**(2), 166–177.

Palmer, J.W. (1986). *Minnesota Roadside Survey: Alcohol-positive Drivers*. Saint Cloud, MN: Saint Cloud University.

Peck, R.C., Sadler, D.D. & Perrine, M.W. (1985). The comparative effectiveness of alcohol rehabilitation and licensing control actions for drunk driving offenders: a review of the literature. *Alcohol, Drugs and Driving: Abstracts and Reviews*, **1**(4), 15–40.

Perrine, M.W., Foss, R.D., Vélez, C., Voas, R.B. & Meyers, A.R. (1992). Validity and inter-rater reliability of the field sobriety test. *Alcoholism: Clinical & Experimental Research*, **16**(2), 417 (Abstr. 377).

Perrine, M.W., Peck, R.C. & Fell, J.C. (1989). Epidemiologic perspectives on drunk driving. In USPHS, Office of the Surgeon General (Ed.) *Surgeon General's Workshop on Drunk Driving: Background Papers* (pp. 35–76). Washington, DC: US Department of Health and Human Services.

Pisoni, D.B. & Martin, C.S. (1989). Effects of alcohol on the acoustic-phonetic properties of speech: perceptual and acoustic analyses. *Alcoholism: Clinical and Experimental Research*, **13**(4), 577–587.

Popkin, C., Li, L., Lacey, J., Stewart, R. & Waller, P. (1983). *An Initial Evaluation of the North Carolina Alcohol and Drug Education Traffic Schools*, Vol. 1. Chapel Hill, NC: Highway Safety Research Center, University of North Carolina.

Popkin, C.L., Kannenberg, C.H., Lacey, J.H. & Waller, P.F. (1988). *Assessment of Classification Instruments Designed to Detect Alcohol Abuse*. Washington, DC: National Highway Traffic Safety Administration.

Preusser, D.F. & Williams, A.F. (1991). *Sales of Alcohol to Underage Purchasers in Three New York Counties and Washington, DC*. Washington, DC: Insurance Institute for Highway Safety.

Rodgers, A. (1994). Effect of Minnesota's license plate impoundment law on recidivism of multiple DWI violators. *Alcohol, Drugs and Driving*, **10**(2).

Ross, H. & Gonzales, P. (1988). The effect of license revocation on drunk-driving offenders. *Accident Analysis and Prevention*, **20**(5), 379–391.

Ross, H.L. (1973). Law, science and accidents: the British Road Safety Act of 1967. *Journal of Legal Studies*, **2**, 1–78.

Ross, H.L. (1984). *Deterring the Drinking Driver: Legal Policy and Social Control*, 2nd edn. Lexington, MA: Lexington Books.

Ross, H.L. (1992a). Are DWI sanctions effective? *Alcohol, Drugs and Driving*, **8**(1), 61–69.

Ross, H.L. (1992b). *Confronting Drunk Driving: Social Policy for Saving Lives*. New Haven, CT: Yale University Press.

Russ, N.W. & Geller, E.S. (1986). *Evaluation of a Server Intervention Program for Preventing Drunk Driving*. Blacksburg, VA: Virginia Polytechnic Institute and State University, Department of Psychology.

Rydon, P., Lang, E. & Stockwell, T. (1993). High risk drinking settings: the association of serving and promotional practices with harmful drinking. *Addiction*, **88**, 1519–1526.

Rydon, P., Stockwell, T., Lang, E. & Beel, A. (1996). Pseudo-drunk-patron evaluation of bar-staff compliance with Western Australian liquor law. *Australian and New Zealand Journal of Public Health*, **20**, 31–34.

Saffer, H. & Chaloupka, F. (1989). Breath testing and highway fatality rates. *Applied Economics*, **21**, 901–912.

Saltz, R.F. (1986). Server intervention: will it work? *Alcohol Health & Research World*, **10**(4), 12–19.

Saltz, R.F. & Stanghetta, P. (1997). A community-wide responsible beverage service program in three communities: early findings. *Addiction*, **92**(2), S237–S249.

Selzer, M.L., Payne, C.E., Westervelt, F.H. & Quinn, J. (1967). Automobile accidents as an expression of psychopathology in an alcoholic population. *Quarterly Journal of Studies in Alcoholism*, **28**, 517–528.

Simpson, H.M., Mayhew, D.R. & Beirness, D.J. (1996). *Dealing with Hard Core Drinking Driver* (107 pp.). Ottawa: Traffic Injury Research Foundation.

Span, D. & Stanislaw, H. (1995). Evaluation of the long-term impact of a deterrence-based random breath testing program in New South Wales. In C.N. Kloeden & A.J. Mclean (Eds), (1995). *Proceedings of the 13th International Conference on Alcohol, Drugs and Traffic Safety, Adelaide, 13 August–19 August 1995*, Vol. 2 (pp. 840–844). Adelaide: NHMRC Road Accident Research Unit, University of Adelaide 5005.

Steward, E.I. & Malfetti, J.L. (1970). *Rehabilitation of the Drunken Driver*. New York: Teachers College Press.

Struckman-Johnson, D.L. & Mushill, E.F. (1976). *Program Level Evaluation of A.S.A.P. Diagnosis,*

Referral and Rehabilitation efforts. Vol. II: Analysis of A.S.A.P. Diagnosis and Referral Activity. Washington, DC: US Department of Transportation.

Stuster, J.W. & Blowers, M.A. (1995). *Experimental Evaluation of Sobriety Checkpoint Programs.* DTNH22-91-C-07204. Washington, DC: National Highway Safety Administration.

Swenson, P.R. & Clay, T.R. (1977). *An Analysis of Drinker Diagnosis, Referral and Rehabilitation Activity, ASAP Phoenix, Arizona.* Washington, DC: National Highway Traffic Safety Administration.

Tashima, H.N. & Helander, C.J. (1999). *1999 Annual Report of the California DUI Management Information System.* CAL-DMV-RSS-99-179. Sacramento, CA: California Department of Motor Vehicles, Research and Development Section.

Taubenslag, W.N. & Taubenslag, M.J. (1975). *Selective Traffic Enforcement Program (STEP).* Washington, DC: National Highway Traffic Safety Administration.

Teplin, L.A. & Lutz, G.W. (1985). Measuring alcohol intoxication: the development, reliability and validity of an observational instrument. *Journal of Studies on Alcohol*, **46**(6).

Tharp, V.K., Burns, M. & Moskowitz, H. (1981). *Development and Field Test of Psychophysical Tests for DWI Arrests.* Final Report No. DOT-HS-805-864. Washington, DC: Department of Transportation, National Highway Traffic Safety Administration.

Vingilis, E.R., Adlaf, E.M. & Chung, L. (1982). Comparison of age and sex characteristics of police-suspected impaired drivers and roadside-surveyed impaired drivers. *Accident Analysis and Prevention*, **14**, 425–430.

Voas, R.B. (1972). *ASAP Program Evaluation Methodology and Overall Program Impact.* Technical Report DOT-HS-880-874. Washington, DC: National Highway Traffic Safety Administration.

Voas, R.B. (1982). *Drinking and Driving: Scandinavian Tough Penalties and United States Alternatives.* Final Report on NHTSA Contract DTNH22-82-P-05079. Washington, DC: National Highway Traffic Safety Administration.

Voas, R.B. (1983). Laboratory and field tests of a passive alcohol sensing system. *Abstracts & Reviews in Alcohol & Driving*, **4**(3), 3–21.

Voas, R.B. (1985). *The Drunk Driver and Jail.* Technical Report DOT-HS-806-761. Washington, DC: National Highway Traffic Safety Administration.

Voas, R.B. (1986). Evaluation of jail as a penalty for drunken driving. *Alcohol, Drugs and Driving: Abstracts and Reviews*, **2**(2), 47–70.

Voas, R.B. (1992). *Final Report on Assessment of Impoundment and Forfeiture Laws for Drivers Convicted of DWI.* NHTSA Contract No. DTNH22-89-4-07026. Washington, DC: National Highway Traffic Safety Administration.

Voas, R.B. & Hause, J.M. (1987). Deterring the drinking driver: the Stockton experience. *Accident Analysis and Prevention*, **19**(2), 81–90.

Voas, R.B., Lange, J.E. & Tippetts, A.S. (1998a). Enforcement of the zero tolerance law in California: a missed opportunity? In *Association for the Advancement of Automotive Medicine, 42nd Annual Proceedings, Charlottesville, VA, October 5–7, 1998* (pp. 369–383). Des Plaines, IL: Association for the Advancement of Automotive Medicine.

Voas, R.B. & Marques, P.R. (1992). Model specifications for breath alcohol ignition interlock devices (BAIIDs). *Federal Register*, **57**(67), 11772–11787.

Voas, R.B., Marques, P.R., Tippetts, A.S. & Beirness, D.J. (1999). The Alberta Interlock Program: the evaluation of a province-wide program. *Addiction*, **94**, 1857–1867.

Voas, R.B. & McKnight, A.J. (1991). *An Evaluation on Hardship Licensing for DWIs. Volume II: Effect on General and Specific Deterrence.* Final Report under NHTSA Contract No. DTNH22-84-C-07292. Landover, MD: National Public Services Research Institute.

Voas, R.B., Rhodenizer, A.E. & Lynn, C. (1985). *Evaluation of Charlottesville Checkpoint Operations.* Final Report under DOT Contract DTNH-22-83-C-05088. Washington, DC: National Traffic Safety Administration.

Voas, R.B. & Tippetts, A.S. (1990). Evaluation of treatment and monitoring programs for drunken drivers. *Journal of Traffic Medicine*, **18**, 15–26.

Voas, R.B. & Tippetts, A.S. (1994). Unlicensed driving by DUIs—a major safety problem? TRB ID No. CR077. Paper presented at the 73rd Annual Meeting, Transportation Research Board, Landover, MD.

Voas, R.B. & Tippetts, A.S. (1996a). Are licensing sanctions effective at reducing impaired driving?

In *Transportation Research Circular: Progress and Promise in Alcohol, Other Drugs and Transportation* (pp. 16–18). Washington, DC: Transportation Research Board.

Voas, R.B. & Tippetts, A.S. (1996b). Unlicensed driving by DUIs—A major safety problem. In *Transportation Research Circular; Progress and Promise in Alcohol, Other Drugs and Transportation* (pp. 38–39). Washington, DC: Transportation Research Board, National Transportation Safety Board.

Voas, R.B., Tippetts, A.S. & Taylor, E. (1997). Temporary vehicle immobilization: evaluation of a program in Ohio. *Accident Analysis and Prevention*, 29(5), 635–642.

Voas, R.B., Tippetts, A.S. & Taylor, E. (1998b). Temporary vehicle impoundment in Ohio: a replication and confirmation. *Accident Analysis and Prevention*, 30(5), 651–655.

Voas, R.B., Tippetts, A.S. & Taylor, E.P. (1998c). Impact of Ohio administrative license suspension. In *Association for the Advancement of Automotive Medicine, 42nd Annual Proceedings, Charlottesville, VA, October 5–7, 1998* (pp. 401–415). Des Plaines, IL: Association for the Advancement of Automotive Medicine.

Voas, R.B., Wells, J., Lestina, D., Williams, A. & Greene, M. (1998d). Drinking and driving in the United States: the 1996 National Roadside Survey. *Accident Analysis and Prevention*, 30(2), 267–275.

Wagenaar, A.C. & Wolfson, M. (1995). Deterring sales and provision of alcohol to minors: a study of enforcement in 295 countries in four states. *Public Health Reports*, 110(4), 419–427.

Wagenaar, A.C., Toomey, T.L., Murray, D.L., Short, B.J., Wolfson, M. & Jones-Webb, R. (1996). Sources of alcohol for underage drinkers. *Journal of Studies on Alcohol*, 57(3), 325–333.

Waller, J.A., King, E.M., Nielson, G. & Turkel, H.W. (1967). Alcohol and other factors in California highway fatalities. Paper presented at the Eleventh Annual Meeting of the American Association of Automotive Medicine, Springfield, IL.

Wells, J.K., Greene, M.A., Foss, R.D., Ferguson, S.A. & Williams, A.F. (1997). Drinking drivers missed at sobriety checkpoints. *Journal of Studies on Alcohol*, 58(5), 513–517.

Wells-Parker, E., Bangert-Drowns, R., McMillen, R. & Williams, M. (1995). Final results from a meta-analysis of remedial interventions with DUI offenders. *Addiction*, 90(7), 907–926.

Wells-Parker, E. & Cosby, P.J. (1987). *Impact of Driver's License Suspension on Employment Stability of Drunken Drivers*. Social Research Report Series 87-3. Mississippi State University, Social Science Research Center.

Wells-Parker, E. & Popkin, C. (1994). Deterrence and rehabilitation: Rehabilitation and screening—research needs for the next decade. *Journal of Traffic Medicine*, 23, 71–78.

Widmark, E.M.P. (1932). *Die theoretischen Grundlagen und die praktsch Verwendbarkeit der gerichlich-medizinischen Alkoholbetimmung*. Berlin: Urban und Schwarzenberg.

Wilde, C.J.S., Hoste, J.L., Sheppard, D. & Wind, G. (1971). Road safety campaigns: design and evaluation. In *Organization for Economic Cooperation and Development* (p. 75). Paris.

Winsten, J.A. (1994). Promoting designated drivers: the Harvard Alcohol Project. *American Journal of Preventive Medicine*, 10(Suppl. 1), 11–14.

Wolfe, A.C. (1975). Characteristics of late-night, weekend drivers: results of the US national roadside breath-testing survey and several local surveys. In S. Israelstam & S. Lambert (Eds), *Proceedings of the 6th International Conference on Alcohol, Drugs, and Traffic Safety* (pp. 411–449). Toronto: Addiction Research Foundation of Ontario.

Zador, P.K., Lund, A.K., Field, M. & Weinberg, K. (1988). *Alcohol-impaired Driving Laws and Fatal Crash Involvement*. Washington, DC: Insurance Institute for Highway Safety.

Zador, P.L. (1991). Alcohol-related relative risk of fatal driver injuries in relation to driver age and sex. *Journal of Studies on Alcohol*, 52(4), 302–310.

Zobeck, T.S. & Williams, G.D. (1994). *Evaluation Synthesis of the Impacts of DWI Laws and Enforcement Methods: Final Report*. Contract No. ADM-281-89-0002. Rockville, MD: Office of Policy Analysis, National Institute on Alcohol Abuse and Alcoholism (NIAAA).

Chapter 16

Prevention at the Local Level

Andrew J. Treno
and
Harold D. Holder
Prevention Research Center, Berkeley, CA, USA

Synopsis

The prevention of alcohol problems at the local level has a relatively short but rich history compared to the community efforts to reduce other health problems. For example, health professionals concerned with the prevention of chronic diseases have accumulated over 20 years of experience in local programs designed to reduce cardiovascular disease (CVD). Typically, these have been directed toward either high-risk subsets of the population, carried out in clinical settings or in worksites, or directed at the entire populations in communities. Based upon the successes of studies, similar programs have been developed over the past 10 years or so to address problem drinking and alcohol-related problems. However, few of these have been characterized by: (a) the development of a careful baseline planning and pre-intervention period; (b) well-defined community-level alcohol-involved problems as targets; (c) a long-term implementation and monitoring period; (d) a follow-up or final scientific evaluation of changes in target problems; and (e) an empirically documented successful result in the target that can be attributed to the intervention. Thus it is difficult to say with certainty whether these programs have been effective.

This chapter presents the project designs and findings of programs designed to address problem drinking and alcohol-related problems and include all five of the above characteristics. Specifically, for each study we consider the presence of a baseline measurement period, the specific problem targeted and its operationalization, the implementation and monitoring period, the structure of scientific evaluation of expected program effects, and the extent to which such effects were found to be attributable to program efforts.

The chapter is organized in the following manner. It begins by presenting a brief discussion of the pre-history of local alcohol programs. Here we note the success of local efforts addressing other chronic health problems, such as heart disease, smoking and adolescent pregnancy, and note that the success of such programs provided optimism

The Essential *Handbook of Treatment and Prevention of Alcohol Problems.* Edited by N. Heather and T. Stockwell.
© 2004 John Wiley & Sons Ltd. ISBN 0-470-86296-3.

concerning the potential for local efforts to combat problem drinking and alcohol-related problems. The chapter then notes that alcohol programs designed to alter individual use of alcohol, either through school-based education or the media campaigns following the chronic health problem model, have found only limited success. As an alternative approach, the chapter then discusses a number of alcohol programs designed around environmental approaches. The chapter concludes with a summary of what is currently known about the efficacy of local alcohol programs and a discussion of potential areas for future research.

The reduction of alcohol problems in the community through local efforts has had a rich but brief history and shares a common heritage with community prevention concerning other health problems. Thus, these efforts have attracted increased interest among researchers, community organizers and funding agencies. However, this flurry of interest should not detract from important differences in philosophies and strategies motivating these diverse programs or important characteristics of target problems. Most of these studies have been directed toward either high-risk subsets of the population, carried out in clinical settings or in worksites, or directed at the entire populations in communities, and involve some combination of community organization and health education. Moreover, most have addressed chronic health problems, such as cardiovascular disease.

Based upon the successes of studies evaluating chronic health problems, similar programs were developed to address problem drinking and alcohol-related problems. However, there is reason to believe that such strategies are unlikely to be effective in the prevention of alcohol-related problems. First, these interventions involve high-risk medical conditions. Second, they assume that individuals have the power to rationally control their behavior. Clearly, a number of factors make the case of alcohol different from that of CVD. For example, there are both greater needs and greater opportunities for regulating behaviors associated with alcohol-related problems than behavior associated with CVD. Moreover, the acute effects of alcohol in producing alcohol problems are more closely linked in time and space to the consumption of alcohol than are the dietary patterns associated with CVD, the chronic disease expression. Finally, norms associated with drinking differ dramatically from those associated with problematic dietary patterns.

Here we review community prevention efforts that address the entire community and which use strategies and approaches that go beyond educational programs to attempt changes in the local social, economic or physical environment related to risky drinking. Thus, we do not review school-based programs that are located within the community, which address drinking and related problems in the schools using only informational approaches. As noted elsewhere in this *Handbook*, education-only strategies have produced modest results (see Chapter 17). Of course, a number of reasons likely underlie these less-than-impressive results, including high rates of absenteeism, drop-outs among high-risk youth, limited time to devote to such problems, and social rootedness of drinking in US culture in general and among youth in particular (Grube, 1997).

As an alternative to such traditional approaches, local communities have developed community-wide programs to address alcohol problems. Adopting broader environmental approaches, such programs have differed from more traditional approaches in that they attempt to seek policy change, seek to bring about system-level community level change, use the media to target policy makers, and seek to mobilize the broader community to pursue desired changed. While such alternative approaches appear promising, only recently have there been systematic attempts to evaluate such efforts (Holder et al., 1997). For this reason local policy makers find themselves attempting to implement policy changes in the absence of a scientific basis supporting such changes. This chapter presents a summary of what is currently known about the effectiveness of such local prevention programs. In discussing the findings of such program evaluations, we consider the presence of a baseline measurement period, the specific problem targeted and its operationalization, the implementation and monitoring period, the structure of scientific evaluation of expected program effects, and the extent to which such effects were found to be attributable to program efforts (see Table 16.1 for summary). The studies considered here generally meet a number of criteria to qualify for inclusion. First, they are community-wide in their focus, as opposed to being targeted at high-risk groups. Second, they seek to bring about community-level system change. Third, to the extent that they use media strategically, such use is targeted at key community leaders in the pursuit of policy change. Fourth, they seek to mobilize the entire community in the pursuit of such change. In keeping with the international orientation of this collection, we discuss selected projects conducted in the USA, Scandinavia, Australia and New Zealand. Specifically, we discuss the Lahti Project, the Compari Project, the Saving Lives Project, the CMCA Project, the New Zealand CAP Project and the Community Trials Project. These projects, representative of a variety of cultural differences, illustrate various environmental approaches to the reduction of alcohol-related problems. For evaluation of programs that are more focused on bringing about individual-level change through the use of persuasion targeted at high-risk groups, the reader is directed toward other chapters included in this volume.

The logic behind targeting communities, as opposed to individuals, is compelling. First, substance use occurs largely within community contexts. That is, particularly in the case of alcohol, communities provide structures (e.g. zoning of alcohol establishments) through which alcohol is typically obtained. Second, many of the costs associated with alcohol are born collectively at the community level in the form of car crashes and alcohol-related violence.

A fundamental distinction may be made between the manner in which traditional and environmental approaches conceptualize communities. Specifically, traditional approaches view communities as catchment areas, while environmental approaches view communities as systems. From the catchment area perspective, the community is viewed largely as a collection of target groups with adverse behaviors and associated risks. Prevention operates largely through educational efforts to reduce the demand for alcohol. The strategy is thus to find, and treat or serve, those most at risk. No particular structural change is proposed and those outside the targeted groups are left unaffected. As an alternative, Holder (1997) has proposed a systems approach to the reduction of alcohol problems that operates by changing the community structures that provide the context in which alcohol consumption occurs. Such supply-orientated approaches may provide advantages over demand approaches, in that they do not require the identification of at-risk individuals or even their active cooperation. Moreover, since most alcohol-related problems do not involve alcoholics, this approach may be particularly effective in the case of alcohol. Here the view is that the problem is created by the system, rather than by problem individuals. Thus, rather than attempt to reduce alcohol-related problems through the education and treatment of problem drinkers, efforts may be directed toward affecting policy makers in positions to implement zoning restrictions governing outlet densities. More broadly, collective risk is thus reduced through interventions affecting community processes that influence alcohol use. In our review of community alcohol projects, the distinction between demand-orientated catchment area approaches and supply-orientated systems approaches will be a major point of reference.

THE COMMUNITY ACTION PROJECT

The Community Action Project (CAP), conducted between October 1982 and March 1985 in six New Zealand (four experimental, two control) communities, was targeted at increasing support among the general public for public policies, as well as attitudes and behavior, supportive of moderate alcohol use through the use of print media (Casswell & Gilmore, 1989).

Table 16.1 Effectiveness of local prevention programs

Project	Baseline	Target Problem	Implementation	Evaluation	Result
CAP	Data collected pre- and post-intervention	Public support for alcohol policy Attitudes supportive of moderate alcohol use	Two sites media only, two sites media and community organization, two sites control	Quasi-experimental design Analyzed project history community survey, key informant interviews	Declining public support for alcohol policy relative to advertising, availability, and price in comparison communities Increased support for restrictions on sales and age limits in media and community organization sites
Lahti	Data collected pre- and post-intervention	Prevention of alcohol-related harm	Experimental site, two comparison sites Experimental site exposed to modular activities corresponding to problem construction, key person interviews, education and information, heavy drinking, social support, alcohol supply, and evaluation	Local newspapers and community survey	Changes in community perceptions relative to alcohol Increased program awareness
COMPARI	Time series data collected pre- and post-intervention	Alcohol problem reduction through changes in context of use	Project activities in one site corresponded to networking and support, community development, alternative options health education, health marketing and policy institutionalization	ARIMA modeling of alcohol sales, assaults, traffic crashes and alcohol-related morbidity	No significant differences found

Table 16.1   (*continued*)

Project	Baseline	Target Problem	Implementation	Evaluation	Result
Saving Lives	Data collected pre- and post-intervention	Reductions in alcohol-impaired driving and related problems	Project designed locally in six experimental communities matched to five comparison sites. Included a host of program activities	Quasi-experimental design modeling fatal and injury crashes, seatbelt use and traffic sitations	25% Reduction in fatal crashes relative to rest of state
CMCA	Data collected at baseline and at 2.5 years after intervention implementation	Reduction in youth access	Randomized 15-community trial (7 experimental and 8 control) collected at baseline and at follow-up after a 2.5 year intervention. Included decoy operations, keg regi stration, restrictions on hours of sale, responsible beverage service programs, education programs, etc.	Quasi-experimental design examined youth telephone surveys, merchant surveys, apparent minor surveys, and media and process data	Increased ID checking Decreased provision of alcohol to minors Decreased consumption
Community Trials	Data collected pre-intervention and throughout the project	Reductions in alcohol-related injuries and death	Interventions inplemented in three sites matched to three comparison sites, targeted at community mobilization, reduction of drink–driving, youth access, availability and responsible beverage service	Quasi-experimental design examined community survey, youth survey, roadside survey, local media, intoxicated patron, apparent minor, and project history data	10% reduction in alcohol involved car crashes 43% Reduction in violence, lower alcohol sales to youth

The project design was quasi-experimental. Cities were matched in terms of size and overall ethnic breakdown and economic composition. Of six cities selected, four were exposed to the mass media campaign. Two of these were also exposed to the community organization campaign. Two served as controls. In the four experimental communities, the mass media campaign was utilized to influence drinking behavior at the individual level among young males. In the two experimental sites, which included the community organization program, a full-time project organizer was employed. These project organizers worked with local community organizations in support of project goals. Additionally, social service personnel were used to establish task-orientated work groups. This project attempted to operate at the individual level by supporting healthy behaviors, at the community level by increasing support for policy change, and at the policy level by affecting both advertising and alcohol availability. Efforts were made to affect access by influencing licensing. Beverage service practices were influenced by contact with both the police and the alcohol service industry. Community organizers attempted to influence policy through the city government process.

The project evaluation was conducted using process data, documenting the project's history, survey data, key informant interviews, analysis of local print media and surveys with independent random samples from each of the six participating surveys. Data were collected pre- and post-intervention for all six communities.

Results of the survey analysis of attitudes toward three policy areas (alcohol advertising, availability and price) were somewhat equivocal. While no change could be found in the two experimental conditions, declining support for these policies were found in the comparison sites. A significant difference was, however, found for support for restrictions dealing with alcohol sales in supermarkets and age limits in the intensive intervention site. These findings have generally been interpreted as suggesting that the project efforts prevented further liberalization of attitudes toward alcohol, as found in the comparison communities. A number of non-policy related items were also considered. In general, these results suggested a shift toward predicted change in the intensive intervention sites.

THE LAHTI PROJECT

The Lahti Project was conducted in Lahti, Finland and was aimed at the prevention of alcohol-related harm. The project started in the autumn of 1992 and continued until 1995 (Homila, 1995, 1997). The project involved members of most sectors of the community and was coordinated through the city's health bureau. The work was organized into modules corresponding to the following activities: constructing alcohol problems in the community; group interviews of key persons; education and information; health care intervention for heavy drinkers; social support; influencing the supply of alcohol; and evaluation. The core of the project consisted of seven researchers, information experts and the local coordinator, who met approximately every 2 months. Project coordinators maintained a minimum of weekly contact.

Baseline project measures consisted primarily of pre-intervention surveys of drinking surveys conducted in Lahti and two comparison communities, which were repeated during the post-intervention period. Additionally, the content of alcohol-related newspaper articles was examined.

The project's program evaluation showed some community-level effects. These were primarily in community perceptions and attitudes relative to alcohol, as well as overall awareness of the program. The results were less conclusive in terms of behavioral outcomes, as no statistically significant change in drinking levels could be found (Homila, 1997). Thus, while the project demonstrated efficacy in mobilizing community level efforts, less could be said about program outcomes.

THE COMPARI PROJECT

The Community Mobilization for the Prevention of Alcohol Related Injury (COMPARI) project was conducted in the Western Australian regional city of Geraldton between

January 1992 and February 1995. Based on the view that most alcohol problems are not the results of actions of alcoholics, the project was designed to reduce alcohol injury by focusing not on heavy drinkers or alcoholics, but rather on the general context of use in the community. After completion of the university-managed demonstration project, the project was transferred to local control. It currently operates under a contract awarded by the government and is the only non-metropolitan alcohol and drug program undertaking community-wide activities in Western Australia (Midford et al., 1998).

COMPARI project activities may be broadly classed into five areas: (a) networking and support (e.g. coordinating local committee on domestic violence); (b) community development (e.g. giving project presentations to community service groups); (c) alternative options health education (e.g. underage youth disco); (d) health marketing (e.g. media campaign presenting safe partying tips); and (e) policy institutionalization (e.g. implementation of guidelines to license applications to serve liquor on council property and the development and delivery of a training package in the responsible serving of alcohol).

The project was evaluated using ARIMA modeling techniques. Several time series were analyzed. These included wholesale alcohol sales, assaults, traffic crashes and hospital morbidity, weighted to reflect likely association with alcohol. These analyses failed, however, to demonstrate an impact. Specifically, alcohol consumption remained relatively flat, as did most harm indicators. One harm indicator approached but did not attain significance, possibly due to the short length of the series. Whether more post-intervention data will demonstrate an effect is not known.

THE SAVING LIVES PROJECT

The Saving Lives Project was conducted in six communities in Massachusetts and was designed to reduced alcohol-impaired driving and related problems such as speeding. In each community a full-time coordinator from within city government organized a task force representing various city departments. Each project was funded at $1 per inhabitant annually, with half of the funds paying the coordinator, police enforcement, program activities and educational materials. Programs were designed locally and involved a host of activities, media campaigns, business information programs, speeding and drink–driving awareness days, speed watch telephone hotlines, police training, high-school peer-led education, Students Against Drunk Driving chapters, college prevention programs, etc. The program evaluation involved a quasi-experimental design and utilized five comparison communities as controls, which, while slightly more affluent that experimental sites, had similar demographic characteristics, rates of traffic citations and fatal crashes. Project monitoring considered, as measures, fatal and injury crashes, seat belt use, telephone surveys and traffic citations. While some baseline differences were found, comparison communities roughly reflected the characteristics of the experimental sites. Evaluation indicated that during the 5 program years, Saving Lives cities experienced a 25% greater decline in fatal crashes than the rest of Massachusetts.

THE CMCA PROJECT

The Communities Mobilizing for Change on Alcohol (CMCA) was designed to reduce the flow of alcohol to youth under age 21. In simplified form, the project identified five core components: (a) influences on community policies and practices; (b) community policies; (c) youth alcohol access; (d) "youth alcohol consumption", and subsequently; (e) "youth alcohol problems". Although the project was clearly community-wide in terms of the community institutions involved, the project was thus focused on one particular target group, youth.

The CMCA project recruited 15 communities (defined by school districts with at least 200 students in the ninth grade and who drew students from no more than three municipalities) in Minnesota and western Wisconsin before using randomization to determine which would be the intervention communities and which would form the comparison group. Pairs of communities (along with one group of three, due to there being an odd number of communities) were created by matching on their size, state, proximity to a college or university, and baseline data from an alcohol purchase survey. One member community of each pair was then selected to be the intervention site when the time came to begin the community organizing. In the end, there were seven intervention sites and eight comparisons, ranging in size from approximately 8000 to 65,000 people with an average of about 20,000.

The project involved activating the communities that could, in turn, select interventions designed to influence underage access to alcohol. Such interventions could include decoy operations with alcohol outlets, citizen monitoring of outlets selling to youth, keg registration, developing alcohol-free events for youth, shortening hours of sale for alcohol, responsible beverage service training, and developing educational programs for youth and adults. The CMCA project hired a part-time local organizer from within each community who was trained and supervised by project staff.

Evaluation data were collected at baseline, and again about 2.5 years after beginning the intervention. These data included surveys of 9th and 12th grade students at baseline, 12th graders at follow-up, telephone surveys of 18–20 year-olds, surveys of alcoholic beverage merchants, and a survey of outlets using 21 year-old women who appeared to be younger, to see if they would be sold or served alcohol without having identification. Other data sources included monitoring of mass media and process-orientated data, both qualitative and quantitative, to capture how the intervention moved ahead and the obstacles staff and communities faced in reaching their objectives.

Merchant survey data revealed that they increased checking for age identification, reduced their likelihood of sales to minors, and reported more care in controlling sales to youth (Wagenaar et al., 1996). The telephone survey of 18–20 year-olds showed a lower frequency of providing alcohol to other minors, and lower likelihood of buying and consuming alcoholic beverages themselves (Wagenaar et al., 2000).

PREVENTION RESEARCH CENTER'S COMMUNITY TRIALS PROJECT

The Community Trials Project (Holder et al., 1997) was a five-component community-level intervention conducted in three experimental communities matched to three comparisons. The five interacting components included: (1) a "community knowledge, values, and mobilization" component, to develop community organization and support for the goals and strategies of the project; (2) a "responsible beverage service practices" component, to reduce the risk of intoxicated and/or underage customers in bars and restaurants; (3) a "reduction of underage drinking" component, to reduce underage access; (4) a "risk of drinking and driving" component, to increase local driving while intoxicated (DWI) enforcement efficiency and reduce drink–driving; and (5) an "access to alcohol" component, to reduce the availability of alcohol. Each component of the project was successfully implemented in each of three experimental communities.

In all three experimental communities, indigenous local program staff were hired during the first project year. A project coordinator (a trained and experienced community organizer) provided regular on-site technical assistance with community mobilization. An orientation early in the first year of the project presented overall project goals in detail, along with the five prevention components and their rationale. During the second project year, training in media advocacy was given to local staff. Additional assistance was provided by a professional advisor on political/legislative action, alcohol problem prevention and community organization and activism. In each community, active coalitions were in place at the onset of the project. During the second year, accompanying local staff training, a series of coalition trainings on project research rationales and component designs was given by PRC scientific staff.

While broad-based community coalitions provided general support for environmental approaches, component-specific strategies were developed and intervention plans formulated by designated task forces for each component. For example, in the Northern California site, policy implementation took the form of increased DUI enforcement, mandatory training for Conditional Use Permit (CUP) holders,[1] implementation of responsible beverage service (RBS) standards at community events, incorporation of coalition recommendations regarding zoning amendments (e.g. distance requirements), and enforcement efforts in support of the California Zero-Tolerance law.[2] In another site, implementation included increased arrests for DUI, introduction and use of passive DUI breathalyzers, DUI sweeps, establishment of clerk training, and both on-site and off-site police stings. In the third site, implementation included strengthened DUI enforcement, clerk trainings, adoption of density regulations (i.e. distance requirements), and the establishment of underage stings that involve police use of underage buyers to determine whether retail outlets were in compliance with underage drinking laws.

Project effects were measured in terms of both component-specific intermediary effects and project outcomes. Due to the project's design, project outcomes could not be linked to specific project interventions. Intermediary effects, however, could. The goal of the RBS component was to reduce the likelihood of customer intoxication at licensed on-premises establishments. Thus, the component's potential contribution to lowering intoxication and injuries was evaluated using trained associates, who entered a sample of on-premises establishments and ordered a number of drinks sufficient to require intervention on the part of the server. In preliminary analyses, however, no significant differences in server intervention were observed between experimental and comparison sites (Saltz & Stanghetta, 1997). Similarly, the evaluation of the youth access component was accomplished through the use of underage purchase surveys, involving the use of adults judged by a panel to look underage, in purchase attempts. The evaluation of the effects of these activities showed that randomly selected outlets in the experimental sites were about equally likely as those in comparison sites to sell alcohol to an apparent minor on pre-test. On post-test, experimental community outlets were about half as likely to sell alcohol to an apparent minor as those in comparison sites.

The activities of the risk of drink–driving component were evaluated by considering changes in alcohol-involved traffic crashes. Evaluation results indicated that this component's activities were associated with a statistically significant impact corresponding to an overall reduction in alcohol-involved crashes, i.e. 78 crashes over a 28-month intervention period, representing an annual reduction of 10%. The activities of the alcohol access

---

[1] Sales of alcohol are licensed as a Conditional Use by municipal governments in California. Conditional User Permits (CUPs) are given conditional upon outlets remaining in conformity with planning and zoning regulations and other license conditions.
[2] "Zero Tolerance" is maintained by law in California toward any underage driver having any detectable blood alcohol level. In this circumstance the law requires license revocation until age 21.

component were evaluated in terms of the response of communities to density issues. The range of local responses to these efforts included the reconsideration of alcohol policies by city councils, the adoption of new ordinances regulating outlets (i.e. distance requirements), changes in state administrative policies regarding license review (allowing greater local input), and citizen participation in licensing hearings. The impacts of these responses included alterations of regulations regarding special event permits (e.g. banning alcohol at some public activities), successful protests of licenses (eliminating sales of alcohol from some premises), and reductions in outlet densities. Overall, the project demonstrated decreases in self-reported DUI and a 43% decrease in emergency room assault injuries in intervention communities relative to comparison communities (Holder et al., 2000).

In sum, relative to the three comparison communities, it was shown that component 1 (community mobilization) affected media coverage of alcohol-related stories and provided support for other program developments; component 2 led to the training of a substantial number of managers and servers; component 3 led to pressure on retailers to reduce sales to underage youth and the implementation of police stings; component 4 led to significant increases in police enforcement activity against drink–driving; and component 5 led to community action directed at regulating alcohol outlets (Holder et al., 1997). Additionally, in a summary article, Holder and his colleagues (1997) characterize the preliminary overall findings of their project as follows: (a) community mobilization was able to accomplish the implementation of the planned interventions; (b) there was significant community support for those interventions, especially when there were research results to support them; (c) there were increases in media coverage of alcohol-related trauma and control policies as a result of training of community members; and (d) there were reductions in sales of alcoholic beverages to underage decoys. The primary outcome of interest, alcohol-involved traffic crashes, was estimated (via time-series analysis with matched comparison communities) to have dropped by about 10% annually over the 28 months intervention period for which data were available.

As a summary of these experiences, the researchers highlighted six points as being essential to mobilizing communities to support preventive interventions:

1. Explaining the research base for interventions is important to community actors.
2. Existing community coalitions may take their own lead and require project staff to guide them to reconsider specific interventions.
3. Pre-existing community support for project interventions is key to rapidly developing intervention programs.
4. Existing support for project interventions among community leaders may be used to focus mobilization efforts.
5. Community conditions may provide unforeseen opportunities for intervention and to galvanize public support (e.g. local festivals).
6. Media events may generate project enthusiasm.

These experiences were seen to parallel those of other international (Midford et al., 1995; Gorman & Speer, 1996) and US (Hingson et al., 1996; Wagenaar & Perry, 1994) community interventions.

CONCLUSIONS

This review of community approaches to the prevention of alcohol problems at the local level can draw important conclusions. First, the case studies reviewed here demonstrate the potential of a well-defined, theory-driven community action approach to reduce local alcohol problems. Each of these examples, and other local efforts not discussed here, show that local initiatives can be efficacious.

Second, community action projects are just that, projects that seek to address the total community system and are not naturally limited to a specific target group or service group. These are not projects in which a local program to provide services to a specific target group happens to be located in a community. These are efforts to involve community leadership in designing, implementing and supporting approaches to reduce problems across the community in total.

Third, community projects can effectively involve leaders and citizens, i.e. they encourage local participation. Thus, in each of the community projects, mobilization as an effort to engage the community in an action project to actually reduce alcohol problems is an essential element. These programs are designed to increase a sense of and actual local ownership.

Fourth, each of these community projects described involved a partnership between the community and researchers. As Holder & Reynolds (1998) have observed, such partnerships work best when each of the participants receives the respect and appreciation of the other, i.e. there is a recognition of what each partner brings to the relationship. Each of these projects represented instances in which researchers participated in the design, supported the implementation of program activities, and conducted the process and quantitative evaluation for the local program. Such evaluations not only contribute to increasing the scientific basis of community action projects designed to reduce alcohol problems, but also increase the level of solid information that can be shared with the community about the results of their own effort.

Fifth, local programs are designed or implemented uniformly. These projects reflect unique and important cultural differences. However, as shown in this review, they all share in common the five elements described in the introduction.

Sixth, community projects confirm the research evidence that changes in attitudes and beliefs are easier to attain than changes in either individual behavior (e.g. rates of problem drinking) or outcome measures (e.g. alcohol-related car crashes). A number of factors may account for this. Traditional attempts to treat and serve isolated high-risk groups have ignored the fact that most alcohol problems are not produced by members of such groups. Members of high-risk groups may be hard to find or resistant to change and the cost associated with the treatment/service approach may be prohibitive.

Recommendations based upon local prevention efforts suggest that alcohol problems are best considered in terms of the community systems that produce them. Local prevention strategies have the greatest potential to be effective when prior scientific evidence is utilized. Many of the local projects described here implemented a series of interventions that prior research had indicated were likely to reduce alcohol-related problems. Thus, complementary system strategies that seek to restructure to total alcohol environment are more likely to be effective than single intervention strategies. Finally, prevention strategies with the natural capacity for long-term institutionalization are to be favored over interventions that are only in place for the life of the project.

ACKNOWLEDGEMENTS

Research and preparation for this article were supported by the Center for Substance Abuse Prevention (CSAP) and the National Institute on Alcohol Abuse and Alcoholism (NIAAA) under Grant No. AA09146.

KEY WORKS AND SUGGESTIONS FOR FURTHER READING

Allamani, A., Casswell, S., Graham, K., Holder, H., Holmila, M., Larsson, S. & Nygaard, P. (Eds) (2000).   Community Action and the Prevention of Alcohol-Related Problems at the Local Level. *Substance Use and Misuse*, **35** (Special Issue, 1, 2) 1–202.

A good summary of community action programs from around the world, as well as a description of the history of local efforts to reduce alcohol problems at the total community level.

Casswell, S. & Gilmore, L. (1989).   An evaluated community action project. *Journal of Studies on Alcohol*, **50**, 339–346.

Paper that demonstrates the essential steps in developing local prevention initiatives, based upon experiences in New Zealand.

Hawks, D., Stockwell, T. & Casswell, S. (1993).   Helping research and policy meet, *Addiction*, **88** (Suppl.), 5S–7S.

An description of how public policy becomes implemented in practice and the partnership of policy advocates with researchers.

Hingson, R., McGovern, T., Howland, J., Heeren, T., Winter., M. & Zakocs, R. (1996). Reducing alcohol-impaired driving in Massachusetts: the Saving Lives program. *Ameican Journal of Public Heath*, **86**, 791–797.

Paper describing the interventions and results of a series of local efforts to reduce traffic problems in communities in the USA.

Holder, H.D. (1997).   *A Community Systems Approach to Alcohol Problem Prevention*. Cambridge: Cambridge University Press.

Book which describes a systems approach to community prevention of alcohol problems. The book can be used by researchers and local prevention professionals in planning effective prevention strategies in the community.

Homila, M. (Ed.) (1997).   *Community Prevention of Alcohol Problems*. London: Macmillan.

Describes the design and results of a community prevention project in Finland. Excellent illustration of the use of qualitative and quantitative information in evaluation.

REFERENCES

Casswell, S. & Gilmore, L. (1989).   An evaluated community action project. *Journal of Studies on Alcohol*, **50**, 339–346.
Gorman, D.W. & Speer, P.W. (1996).   Preventing alcohol abuse and alcohol-related problems through community interventions: a review of evaluation studies. *Psychology and Health*, **11**, 95–131.
Grube, J.W. (1997).   Preventing alcohol sales to minors: results from a community trial. *Addiction*, **92**, S251–S260.
Hingson, R., McGovern, T., Howland, J., Heeren, T., Winter., M. & Zakocs, R. (1996).   Reducing alcohol-impaired driving in Massachusetts: the Saving Lives program. *American Journal of Public Heath*, **86**, 791–797.
Holder, H.D. (1997).   *A Community Systems Approach to Alcohol Problem Prevention*. Cambridge: Cambridge University Press.

Holder, H.D. & Reynolds, R. (1998). Science and alcohol policy at the local level: a respectful partnership. *Addiction*, **93**(10), 1467–1473.

Holder, H.D., Gruenewald, P.J., Ponicki, W.R. et al. (2000). Effect of community-based interventions on high-risk drinking and alcohol-related injuries. *Journal of the American Medical Association*, **284**, 2341–2347.

Holder, H.D., Saltz, R.F., Grube, J.W., Voas, R.B., Gruenewald, P.J. & Treno, A.J. (1997). A community prevention trial to reduce alcohol-involved accidental death and injury: overview. *Addiction*, **92** (Suppl. 2), S155–S171.

Homila, M. (1995). Community action on alcohol: experiences of the Lahti Project in Finland. *Health Promotion International*, **10**(4), 283–291.

Homila, M. (Ed.) (1997). *Community Prevention of Alcohol Problems*. Geneva: World Health Organization.

Midford, R., Boots, K., Masters, L. & Chikritzhs, T. (1998). Time series analysis of outcome measures from a community alcohol harm reduction project in Australia. Presented at the 1998 Kettil Brun Society's Fourth Symposium on Community Action, Research and the Prevention of Alcohol and Other Drug Problems, Russell, New Zealand, February 8–13.

Saltz, R.F. & Stanghetta, P. (1997). A community-wide responsible beverage service program in three communities: early findings. *Addiction*, **92**, S237–S249.

Wagenaar, A.C. & Perry, C.L. (1994). Community strategies of the reduction of youth drinking: theory and application. *Journal of Research on Adolescence*, **4**(2), 319–345.

Wagenaar, A.C., Murray, D.M., Gehan, J.P. et al. (2000). Communities mobilizing for change on alcohol: outcomes from a randomized community trial. *Journal of Studies on Alcohol*, **61**, 85–94.

Wagenaar, A., Toomey, T.L., Murray, D.M., Short, B.J., Wolfson, M. & Jones-Webb, R. (1996). Sources of alcohol for underage drinkers. *Journal of Studies on Alcohol*, **57**, 325–333.

Chapter 17

Alcohol Education in Schools

Richard Midford
and
Nyanda McBride
*National Drug Research Institute, Curtin University of Technology,
Perth, Western Australia*

Synopsis

Young people typically initiate alcohol use while at school and their drinking is the cause of major social and public health problems. As a consequence, there is obvious appeal to school-based alcohol education. However, to date, success has been limited.

School alcohol education dates from the late nineteenth century, but drug education as a whole expanded considerably during the 1950s and 1960s. Programmes of that era emphasized abstinence and drew on behaviour theory as the basis for their change strategies. So-called "scare tactics" paired fear arousal with use, in an attempt to establish negative attitudes to alcohol and other drugs. Another approach involved providing "factual" information on the negative consequences of use. Evaluations of these programmes indicated that they were largely ineffective in changing behaviour. This spurred two developments during the 1970s, affective programmes and abuse prevention. The former sought to reduce alcohol and other drug use by enhancing personal development, but again research evidence indicated little impact. The latter sought to prevent the problematic consequences associated with use and could be considered harm reduction. In America, official support for abuse prevention was short-lived and abstinence-focused programmes resurfaced during the 1980s. However, this time interventions drew on social influence approaches, which sought to boost resistance to use through social skills training. Harm-reduction education tended to be adopted more in Europe and Australasia. Here there is greater acceptance of the logic of using such an approach with alcohol, because the drug is legally available and use by young people is prevalent.

The Essential *Handbook of Treatment and Prevention of Alcohol Problems.* Edited by N. Heather and T. Stockwell.
© 2004 John Wiley & Sons Ltd. ISBN 0-470-86296-3.

The evolution of alcohol education has in the main been driven by failure to achieve the desired behaviour change. In part, this failure was due to an unrealistic emphasis on abstinence, further compounded by poor science. There are, however, indications that recent alcohol education programmes are more rigorous, have goals other than abstinence and have achieved behaviour change. Reviews and meta-analyses of recent alcohol and other drug education programmes indicate that successful programmes tend to include interactive social skills training and normative belief components, whereas programmes that do not have a sustained effect tend to rely on didactic resistance training.

Most alcohol education for young people is classroom-based. However, a number of studies have involved the community in drug education programmes, on the basis that the cues from the social environment are critical in establishing adolescent patterns of alcohol use and strategies to reduce adolescent access to alcohol can only be enacted at a community level. The benefits of such a community-wide approach are promising, but need to be seen in the context of the resources involved.

Alcohol education has developed considerably in the last decade, but particular programmes are often adopted because they are aggressively marketed, rather than because they are demonstrably effective. Alcohol education in the future needs to be more realistic about its goals and accountable for its achievements. An approach that is broadly useful has to acknowledge that the majority of young people will drink and that education should equip them to handle drinking situations in a way that reduces harm.

THE ATTRACTION OF SCHOOL-BASED ALCOHOL EDUCATION

In Western industrialized societies, young people typically start drinking alcohol in their early teenage years, well before they reach legal drinking age (Johnston et al., 1989). The 1996 American National Household Survey on Drug Abuse (Substance Abuse and Mental Health Services Administration, 1997) estimated that 38.3% of males and 39.4% of females in the 12–17 year-old age group had tried alcohol. The prevalence of use is much higher in other countries. A survey conducted in 1997 estimated that 73% of Norwegian 15–16 year-olds had drunk alcohol (Grytten, 1997). The National Drug Household Survey in Australia indicated that not only have most teenagers tried alcohol, but the age at which they first started drinking has progressively decreased over the past 30 years (Jones, 1993). In the UK, a survey of 15 and 16 year-old students found that 77.9% reported that they had been intoxicated from drinking and that 48.3% had been intoxicated within the last 30 days (Miller & Plant, 1996). On their last occasion of drinking, the average number of standard drinks consumed by the male English students in this study was 8.5 (Miller & Plant, 1996). Such worldwide research consistently indicates that the majority of young people not only drink, but also that they are starting to drink at a younger age, that they drink in a risky manner and that they disproportionately experience acute health and social problems because of drinking (McBride, Midford & Farringdon, 1998). As a consequence, there is obvious appeal to school-based alcohol education. Schools are places of learning. The great majority of youth are attending school when they start drinking and, as Hansen (1993) comments, are a captive audience. Accordingly, if schools educate young people about alcohol, they will make better decisions, which in turn will prevent problems. Such logic has led to the development of numerous school-based prevention programmes, but to date the success of these programmes has been limited.

WHAT MAKES ALCOHOL EDUCATION DIFFERENT?

Alcohol education is inextricably a part of drug education, because alcohol is a drug and many of the education issues are common across the spectrum of drug use. However, alcohol is a drug with unique status, which influences what will be effective education for young people. Alcohol is widely available, is socially acceptable and consumption by adults is both legal and prevalent, whereas it is axiomatic that illicit drug use is illegal and societal norms prohibiting use are much stronger. This means that young people face a more salient range of choices about drinking. Should I drink? When should I start drinking? How much should I drink? In what circumstances should I drink? Given this different set of decisional demands, alcohol education is arguably a more complex task than general drug education. This can be taxing for educators, because young people are likely to want education that is immediately useful in making these decisions and be more discerning of the information they receive, because of their own experiences with alcohol. Alcohol's status as a legal drug makes it easier to talk openly about use and prevention. However, it can also make it more difficult to bring about behaviour change. Educators have to contend with an environment in which adult drinking is prevalent and there are strong and pervasive media images that portray drinking as an attractive, even necessary, adult behaviour (Perry & Kelder, 1992; Petosa, 1992). Given such desirable associations, it is not surprising that so many young people are attracted to drinking.

The social influence approach, based on resisting the social pressures to use drugs, seems to have been quite effective in preventing cannabis use among young people (Perry & Kelder, 1992), yet this approach has been less successful in reducing alcohol use. Perry & Kelder attribute this lack of success to the perception by young people that alcohol use is normative. Support for this hypothesis is provided by a study by Hansen & Graham (1991). These researchers found that students who received social influence education that corrected misperceptions as to the amount of alcohol consumed by young people, consumed significantly less alcohol than those who received no such education. These results indicate that students were basing their own drinking behaviour on an inflated judgement of what was usual consumption by others in their age group. Given the difficulties for alcohol education in a permissive context, Perry & Kelder (1992) suggest that one way to curtail use in young people may be to establish conservative norms. This would seem beyond the scope of alcohol education programmes in pluralistic societies, as the influences that establish normative drinking behaviour go well beyond what is taught in the classroom. Education may be a useful way to impart skills to young people, but those skills will be used in a social context and policy makers and educators really have to grapple with what can be achieved by alcohol education within this broader context. Is abstinence a realistic or even a desirable goal for most young people, given that in Western industrialized societies most will drink as adults? Alternatively, should alcohol education aim to better prepare young people to make responsible decisions about drinking, as advocated by Beck (1998) and Milgram (1996), so that harmful consequences are reduced or eliminated?

THE HISTORICAL DEVELOPMENT OF ALCOHOL EDUCATION

Beck (1998) reported that, in America, provision of formal school-based alcohol education dates from the 1880s, when the temperance movement sought to take preventative action against alcohol, tobacco and other drugs, by teaching youth about their dangers. Leaders of this movement were very successful in gaining support for compulsory temperance education in schools and by 1901 every American state and territory had mandated compulsory temperance education (Mezvinsky, 1961). These programmes focused strongly on abstinence and taught that alcohol was both dangerous and seductive. Any amount of use amounted to abuse, because it led to physical harm and moral degeneration.

During this same period, approaches to alcohol education on the other side of the Atlantic varied considerably and reflected the values and norms of the society in which they occurred. The development of alcohol education in Norway, for example, echoed what occurred in America to a remarkable degree. Education started in primary schools in the late nineteenth century and was strongly linked to the temperance movement (Waahlberg, 1988). However, dissatisfaction with the narrow focus of such education led to progressively greater involvement of teachers and a broadening of the information provided. The French provided compulsory alcohol education in schools, but students were encouraged only to abstain from drinking spirits. The message in relation to fermented beverages such as wine and beer was "drink in moderation". Beck (1998) considered that this early French approach to alcohol education constituted the first harm reduction approach by a government in this area.

The temperance movement, and the school alcohol education programmes it supported, probably reached their peak of influence in America during the Prohibition years of the 1920s and early 1930s. The repeal of Prohibition in 1933 signalled the failure of a solely abstinence-orientated approach to alcohol, and prohibitionist approaches to alcohol education were rapidly abandoned. Where some form of education continued, there was increased emphasis on responsible decision making and informed choice. However, two factors led to an overall decline in alcohol education over the next three decades. Lender & Martin (1987) indicated that the societal backlash against prohibition approaches meant that many schools provided little or no education on alcohol. Coupled with this, the post-prohibition drug bureaucrats, led by Harry Anslinger, considered that illicit drugs, particularly cannabis, constituted the greater problem (Beck, 1998). Anslinger asserted, in a series of public appearances and radio broadcasts, that cannabis use led to killings, sex crimes and insanity and this use of sensationalism and scare tactics, coupled with disregard for contrary scientific evidence, characterized drug education campaigns for several decades (Schlosser, 1994; Wallack, 1980). Drug education based on information was discouraged in this climate, as knowledge was considered to encourage experimentation (Anslinger & Tomkins, 1953).

In the early 1960s, the previously dominant view, that no education was good prevention, was increasingly challenged. As a consequence, drug education as a whole expanded considerably during the decade. Programmes during this period drew on behaviour theory in developing their change strategies. Typically, so-called factual information was provided on the harmful effects of drug use in order to establish negative attitudes and a fear of use. Some of these programmes emphasized the provision of objective information. However, others continued to use scare tactics in the belief that such an approach would maximize fear arousal. Fear arousal approaches have generally lacked credibility with their target group when the images and messages they presented were extreme and inconsistent with that groups' personal experiences of drug use (Coggans & Watson, 1995). However, even without the hyperbole, information-only approaches have made little impact and, in a review of drug education from this period, Kinder et al. (1980) indicated that there was:

> . . . little to support the notion that presenting factual information is an appropriate and effective method of changing attitudes and behaviours (p. 1044).

This acknowledged failure spurred two developments during the 1970s, affective programmes and abuse prevention (Gorman, 1996; Beck, 1998). Affective programmes sought to reduce alcohol and other drug use by enhancing personal development. Many programmes were not drug-specific but rather focused on personal development, with the objective of ensuring that young people were properly equipped to make positive, healthy choices (Sharp, undated). Programmes typically included training in self-esteem, decision-making, values clarification, stress management and goal setting. Again, the evidence indicated that these programmes did not demonstrably succeed in changing behaviour (Hansen, 1993). This was not surprising, according to Dielman (1994), because, like the information programmes that preceded them, these affective programmes had use or abuse reduction as their stated goal, but were evaluated against a completely different dependent variable, such as increase in self-esteem. In addition, this model makes assumptions that alcohol and drug use by young people is driven by individual deficiency and that the problem can be addressed by enhancing self-esteem or improving decision-making skills. In the case of alcohol, this is a difficult position to defend. Use by adults must be considered normative and this sets up the expectation in young people that drinking alcohol is part of becoming an adult. In such a social context, alcohol consumption is actually conformist. The other major drug education development at this time, abuse prevention programmes, were based on the premise that drinking by young people would occur and that pragmatic programmes should seek to prevent or minimize the problematic consequences of such use. Such an approach today would be considered harm reduction, although it was not called that at the time.

Harm-reduction approaches have tended to be adopted more in Europe, Canada and Australasia, where they gained credibility initially because of their success in combating the spread of HIV among intravenous drug users. In America, there was a short period during the late 1970s when official support was given to harm reduction as a guiding principle in drug education, primarily because of the well-documented failure of previous abstinence-only approaches (Beck, 1998). However, abstinence re-emerged strongly within a few years, as a result of the influence of the "parent power movement" (Beck, 1998). This grass-roots movement convinced governments to only support non-use or "zero tolerance" education programmes, and US federal guidelines mandate that prevention programmes emphasize such an approach (Office for Substance Use Prevention, Alcohol, Drug Abuse, and Mental Health Administration, 1989).

The education programmes that were developed in the 1980s generally reflected this abstinence goal, but were more sophisticated in their methodology. The social influence model, developed from Bandura's (1977) social modelling theory and McGuire's (1964) work on resistance training, has dominated this most recent phase of alcohol and drug education. The approach is based on the belief that young people begin to smoke, drink and use other drugs because of social pressure to do so from a variety of sources, such as the mass media, their peers and even the image they have of themselves. In order to successfully resist the adoption of undesirable behaviour, young people need to be inoculated by prior exposure to counter-arguments and have the opportunity to practise the desired coping behaviour.

The social influence model was initially used to prevent young people taking up smoking, and its success in this area led to the approach being used to reduce the uptake of other drugs, including alcohol (Perry & Kelder, 1992). Duryea et al. (1984) used an inoculation approach with ninth grade students in an American mid-west school and achieved significant gains in knowledge and responsible attitudes, but no assessment of actual drinking behaviour was included in the study. Other studies in which drinking behaviour was measured indicate that social influence or inoculation interventions have a limited impact on drinking behaviour. Gorman (1996) conducted a comprehensive review of alcohol education programmes based on this approach and found that only three of the 12 reviewed programmes reported consistently lower alcohol use, following intervention. However, there were methodological difficulties with each of these studies. He concluded that while social influence has become the pre-eminent model for drug education programmes, the evidence supporting the effectiveness of such an approach is sparse. In fact, he suggested there is little reason to indicate that such an approach would be effective, because many of the components of social influence programmes are the same as those that comprised the failed affective programmes of the 1970s. He also made the point that prevention education has, to date, been driven by the idea that alcohol use by young people is primarily caused by interpersonal factors. This is too simplistic, given the considerable literature on the role of environment in alcohol use and harm (Holder, 1992; Lang, 1994; Wittman, 1990). Other education approaches need to be trialled that take into consideration those environmental factors that are particularly salient to young people's choices about drinking.

THE CURRENT STATE OF KNOWLEDGE

Early reviews of drug education programmes were consistently damning of their methodology and achievements (Goodstadt, 1980; Kinder et al., 1980; Schaps et al., 1981). However, Dielman (1994) indicated that these programmes and the accompanying research were useful as both a foundation and an impetus for the development of better interventions. A number of reviews and meta-analyses of contemporary drug education programmes, were conducted during the 1980s and 1990s, which identified the programme approaches most likely to make a difference. Tobler (1986) conducted a meta-analysis of 143 drug prevention programmes designed for young people and concluded that programmes that combined peer influence with specific skills training were the most effective, although programmes offering alternatives to drug use, such as sporting or social activities, were particularly useful for "at-risk" students. Bangert-Drowns (1988) conducted a meta-analysis of 33 school-based prevention programmes, which in the main focused on alcohol and emphasized education strategies. The evaluation examined changes in drug-related knowledge, attitudes towards drugs and drug use behaviour. He found that education increased drug-related knowledge and changed attitudes, but drug use behaviour only changed in students who had volunteered to participate in the education. He also found that mode of delivery was important. Programmes that used lectures as their only intervention had less influence on attitudes than those that used discussion. The importance of interactive delivery style was reinforced by a more recent meta-analysis of 120 school-based drug education programs undertaken by Tobler & Stratton (1997). These researchers found that the most important factor in effective programs was interactive process, whereby students were actively engaged in discussions, role-plays and games. Only the interactive programs produced significant change in attitudes and drug use. The interactive programs were equally successful with alcohol, tobacco and cannabis. However, ideal group process cannot stand alone. Certain knowledge content as to the effects of drug use and skills training in making and implementing decisions about use were also essential (Tobler & Stratton, 1997).

Meta-analyses have also identified the contribution of peer leadership. Bangert-Drowns (1988) found that use of peer leaders was associated with greater attitude change and Tobler and her colleagues in a comparison of teacher-led and peer-led interventions found that peer-led programs reduced drug use by nine percent as compared with a five percent reduction achieved by teacher-led programs (Tobler et al., 2000). Cuijpers (2002) however, was less convinced. In his meta-analysis of 12 studies he found that while peer-led programs were somewhat more effective, leadership type is not critical in isolation, it is part of a complicated mix of elements that determine program effectiveness. Coggans & Watson (1995) considered that peer-led approaches could take advantage of factors such as peer modelling and normative attitudes and values. However, they recommended that peer leaders be selected very carefully. Students considered good role models by adults are not necessarily well regarded by the target group. Botvin (1990) considers that, ideally, peer leaders should be credible with high-risk adolescents, have good communication skills, show responsible attitudes, but at the same time be somewhat unconventional. Botvin (1990) considered that even ideal peer leaders are likely to lack the organizational and management skills possessed by effective professional teachers, and accordingly he has recommended that the best of both worlds could be achieved by using teachers and peer leaders in combination. The timing of drug education is likely to be critical, according to a number of researchers (Dielman, 1994; Duncan et al., 1994). Kelder et al. (1994) commented that primary prevention is most effective if instituted before behavioural patterns are established and more resistant to change. Dielman (1994) considered that alcohol education programmes should be undertaken when they are particularly salient to young people's life experiences, such as when they are starting to drink. The general consensus in the literature (Johnston, O'Malley & Bachman, 1989; Dielman, 1994; Duncan et al., 1994) is that the optimal time for initiating youth alcohol interventions is during the late primary/early high school years, as this is when experimentation starts. However, onset of use can vary in different populations and Dielman (1994) has suggested that the timing of programmes can be optimized for a particular population, by reference to the appropriate prevalence data.

Dusenbury & Falco (1995) considered that the research literature indicates that certain types of school-based education, "can achieve at least modest reductions in adolescent drug use" (p. 420). In order to identify the key elements of effective drug education, they reviewed school-based programmes conducted between 1989 and 1994 and interviewed 15 leading researchers in the area. From this process they identified 11 critical components for an effective programme. Ballard et al. (1994) undertook a similar process of consultation and review in developing their 15 principles for drug education in schools. They considered that these principles offer a framework for policy makers, school administrators, teachers, parents and other stakeholders to use when making decisions about the selection, design and implementation of drug education programmes. They are remarkably similar to Dusenbury & Falco's key elements and these two sets of critical components have provided the basis for the summary of effective drug education elements, contained in Table 17.1. In addition, three features of successful drug education programmes not mentioned in these two reviews, but consistently identified in other research, have been included in this table. These features are: appropriate timing of the intervention, to ensure that prevention programmes are initiated when prevalence of use by young people is still very low (Kelder et al., 1994); use of peer leaders to focus on the social factors that influence drug use (Coggans & Watson, 1995); fidelity of implementation to ensure that programmes are delivered as intended (Dielman, 1994). This set of critical components was derived from the broader drug education literature, but it clearly should be considered when undertaking alcohol education.

THE IMPORTANCE OF PARENTS

The major influence that parents have on the drinking behaviour of their children is consistently identified in the literature. Drinking usually begins within the family, and Foxcroft & Lowe (1997) considered that good family function and positive family associations with alcohol fostered responsible drinking by young people. They found that higher consumption was associated with low family support, low family control, regular parental drinking and indifference to drinking by their children. McCallum (1990), in a review of the literature, indicated that parents have a major influence on their children's drug use behaviour through modelling, attitudes and family relationships, although she noted that many parents were unaware of their degree of influence and how this could be used to bring about better

Table 17.1   Summary of critical elements in effective school-based drug education and prevention

Theme	Component	Source	Comment
Context	Drug education is best taught in the context of broader health skills	Ballard et al. (1994) Dusenbury & Falco (1995)	Ongoing, comprehensive, developmentally appropriate health programmes promote general competence and provide a context for understanding drug-related behaviour
Consistency	Drug education messages across the school environment should be consistent and coherent	Ballard et al. (1994)	School policies and practices should reinforce the objectives of drug education programmes
Basis in evidence	Drug education needs to be based on research as to effective curriculum practice and the needs of students	Ballard et al. (1994) Dusenbury & Falco (1995)	Effective programmes are based on an understanding of contemporary theory and research evidence as to what causes drug use and what factors provide protection
	Drug education programmes should be evaluated	Ballard et al. (1994) Dusenbury & Falco (1995)	Evaluation will provide formal evidence of the worth of the programme in contributing to short- and long-term goals, as well as improving the design of future programmes. The quality of evaluation studies should also be assessed
Timing of education	Prevention education is best delivered before behavioural patterns are established	Kelder et al. (1994)	Drug education programmes should start when prevalence of use by young people is still very low
	Drug education programmes should be immediately relevant, developmentally appropriate and have sequence, progression and continuity	Ballard et al. (1994) Dusenbury & Falco (1995)	Programmes must be credible and useful to students, which means they need to be provided regularly at different stages of schooling
Education goals	Drug education strategies should relate to programme objectives	Ballard et al. (1994)	Strategies should be selected because they are expected to achieve the objectives of the programme
	Objectives for drug education should be linked to the overall goal of harm minimization	Ballard et al. (1994)	The concept of harm minimization encompasses a range of strategies, including non-use, which aim to reduce harmful consequences of drug use
Education strategies	Social resistance skills training	Dusenbury & Falco (1995)	Such an approach helps young people to identify pressures to use drugs and gives them the skills to make alternative responses
	Normative education	Dusenbury & Falco (1995)	This gives young people an accurate indication as to the extent of drug use in their peer group, which is typically lower than expected

Table 17.1 (*continued*)

Theme	Component	Source	Comment
	Interactive teaching techniques	Dusenbury & Falco (1995)	Techniques such as role play, group discussion and joint activities promote active involvement in the learning process
	Approaches to drug education should address the values, attitudes and behaviours of the community and the individual	Ballard et al. (1994)	Responsible decisions by students about drugs are more likely where peer and community groups demonstrate responsible attitudes and practices
	Drug education programmes should reflect an understanding of the interrelationship between individual, social context and drug in determining drug use	Ballard et al. (1994)	The drug experience is influenced by these three components and effective education programmes need to deal with these influences in an integrated manner
	Drug education programmes should focus on drug use that is most likely and most harmful	Ballard et al. (1994)	Generally, school-based drug education should concentrate on lawfully available drugs, because their use by young people is more likely. While illicit drug use disproportionately attracts media attention and public concern, it should be addressed in particular contexts or subgroups, where it is particularly prevalent and harmful
	Peer-led education	Coggans & Watson (1995)	Peers leaders are credible and effective in presenting the social factors that influence drug use
Collaborative approaches	Mechanisms should be developed to involve students, parents and the wider community in school-based drug education	Ballard et al. (1994) Dusenbury & Falco (1995)	Broadening school-based education by including family, community and media components will reinforce desired behaviours by providing a supportive environment
Sensitivity to different needs	Drug education should be responsive to developmental, gender, cultural, language, socioeconomic, and life-style differences	Ballard et al. (1994) Dusenbury & Falco (1995)	Drug education programmes that are sensitive to the different backgrounds of the young people they target will be more relevant and effective
Teachers	Teachers should be trained and supported to conduct drug education	Ballard et al. (1994) Dusenbury & Falco (1995)	The classroom teacher, with specific knowledge of students and the learning context, is best placed to provide contextual drug education. Programmes are most successful when teachers receive training and support, particularly in undertaking interactive teaching activities

continued overleaf

Table 17.1 *(continued)*

Theme	Component	Source	Comment
	Drug education programmes and resources should be selected to complement the role of the classroom teacher	Ballard et al. (1994)	The classroom teacher is central to the delivery of effective drug education and should not be compromised by external programmes
Programme implementation	Drug education programmes should demonstrate adequate coverage, sufficient follow-up and ability to achieve long-term change	Ballard et al. (1994) Dusenbury & Falco (1995)	An adequate intervention, complemented by follow-up, is needed to counter effect decay and the ongoing influences to use drugs. Stand-alone and one-off interventions are not likely to be effective
	Fidelity of implementation	Dielman (1994)	Monitoring should be undertaken to ensure that programmes are delivered in the intended manner, as failure may occur because of inadequate implementation, rather than as a result of any deficiency in the design of the programme

choices (McCallum, 1996). Mallick, Evans & Stein (1998) suggested that the first step in getting parents involved in drug education is to make them more aware of their influence, and McCallum (1990) considered that parents would have more impact if they were confident about their contribution. Many parents feel ill-equipped to discuss drug matters with their children, or make representations about drug education policy, because of a lack of knowledge. Accordingly, programmes that inform, engage and support parents are a useful start in tapping their potential to contribute to the drug education process.

Mallick, Evans & Stein (1998) reported that parents see drugs as their greatest issue of concern in relation to their children. However, the basis for this predominantly stems from sensationalist media reporting, with all its attendant myths, exaggerations and simplistic prescriptions. As a consequence, parents' dealings with their children tend to be directive and based on the premise that "Just say no" is the only safe message, even though there is some acknowledgment that this may not be heeded. These researchers concluded that parents needed drug education themselves, so that they could assist effectively in the drug education of their children. Many in their study were receptive to this idea but the views and motivation of hard-to-reach parents were not gauged, even though the involvement of this group may be particularly beneficial. McCallum (1990) reported that the most promising prevention programmes involved parents learning communication skills, setting limits and providing consistent support. This is reflected in the work of Spoth and his colleagues. These researchers have consistently found that brief family skills training interventions increased parenting skills, strengthened the parent–child relationship and reduced use of alcohol and other drugs by the young people who attended. Reduction in use was maintained over time, which indicates that the skills learned provided the basis for a sustained change in family functioning (Spoth et al., 1996a; Spoth, Redmond & Shin, 2001).

Recruitment to intensive, on-site programs is likely to be difficult and experience from

Spoth's "Strengthening Families Program" indicates that incentives such as meals, child-care and coupons that can be exchanged for small treats boost participation (Spoth et al., 1996b). French & South (1998) looked at a number of ways of involving parents in supporting school based drug education and found that initially there was resistance to finding out more about drug use, because what they already knew was worrying enough. French & South considered that a useful way of dealing with the barriers presented by these parental anxieties was to facilitate peer-led education among parents, as this was more interactive and less intimidating than being talked to by experts. Quinn (1996) has suggested that the media may be an effective way of reaching parents who would otherwise have little contact with the school, but such a mass communication approach has difficulty conveying the complexity of drug use issues. Parents in Mallick, Evans & Stein's (1998) study have reinforced this view, with suggestions that if the media reduced its sensational reporting of drug use and provided more balanced and accurate information, parents would be better informed, less fearful and more capable of addressing their children's drug issues in a balanced and effective manner.

WHOLE-OF-SCHOOL AND COMMUNITY-WIDE APPROACHES

An important recent trend in alcohol and other drug education is the increased emphasis given to whole-of-school and community approaches (Midford & McBride, 1999; Perry et al., 1996; Ballard, Gillespie & Irwin, 1994). This acknowledges that drug education occurs within a broader social setting and that greater benefit is likely to occur if there is contextual support for the formal curriculum programmes. McBride, Midford & Farringdon, (1998) suggested that whole-of-school approaches should ensure that the school policy and practices complement the education message; that services are provided for at-risk students and that the local school community, particularly parents, are involved in the education process. However, these authors also acknowledged that getting schools to adopt a comprehensive approach to drug education is difficult. There are an increasing number of educational issues vying for a place on the school agenda, and attracting broad support for an issue that is generally not seen as core business for a school is difficult, particularly if additional resources and training are not provided. Any effect achieved by intense whole-of-school programmes will also be more vulnerable to withdrawal of resources. A curriculum approach, however, is more achievable in terms of existing resources, more easily integrated into and maintained within existing teaching structures and offers greater coverage per unit cost. Evaluation of a national drug education programme in Australia (Midford & McBride, 1999) indicated that comprehensive and intense drug education in selected schools achieved a greater level of drug education activity than system-wide teacher training. However, this change only occurred in a few schools, whereas the global approach achieved less change, but in a greater number of schools. Midford & McBride (1999) suggested that the emphasis of a programme should be determined by its objectives, whether that be reach or intensity. Schools that have had little drug education will probably be best served by broad-based teacher training, which will create the skill base and motivation for further development. In contrast, those schools that have reached a certain level of accomplishment in drug education are more likely to have the capacity to undertake a more intense, whole-of-school approach.

Perry and her colleagues (Perry et al., 1996, Perry and Kelder, 1992, Perry and Murray, 1985) recognized the importance of the social environment in determining drug use by young people and suggested that, if schools are to be effective in achieving sustained change, their programmes have to be reinforced at the broader community level. They offered several reasons for undertaking community-wide prevention efforts in support of school drug education. Those students with a high risk of alcohol and drug use are likely to be alienated from the education process and thus may not be receptive to school-based programmes. They are also more likely to drop out of school early and thus not receive school-based education. Major social influences that affect alcohol and drug use by young people include parents, peers, significant adults in the community and the media. Most of these groups are not associated with the school and prevention messages may best come directly from these sources. The community also formally and informally regulates alcohol consumption by young people. There are laws that regulate access to alcohol and there are social norms as to acceptable drinking practices. These contribute in a major way to the patterns of consumption by young people and changes here may complement education programmes.

A good example of a broad community approach to alcohol education for young people is provided by Project Northland. This is a large, long-term, community-wide programme, conducted in six north-eastern counties of Minnesota. The project sought to prevent or reduce alcohol use among younger adolescents and has achieved a measure of success (Perry et al., 1996). At the end of 3 years, students in the school districts who received the intervention, reported lower onset of use and lower levels of use than students in the control districts. However, this must be seen in context. The achievements of a well-funded project implemented by highly motivated and capable researchers are not likely to be replicated in schools that do not receive this extra support. Follow-up of these students in high school also indicated that the initial positive results attenuated. Perry et al. (1998) reported that by the end of the 10th grade, there was no significant difference in alcohol consumption between students in the intervention and control districts. It would seem that although a number of normative and interpersonal factors were influenced by the initial 3 year intervention, these changes were not sufficient to maintain lower levels of use when the students reached high school. These results indicate that alcohol use may be particularly resistant to long-term change, which Perry et al. (1993) attribute to society not providing consistent, clear and compelling messages about adolescent alcohol use. However, the relevance, for older adolescents, of an abstinence-focused alcohol education approach also seems a factor, whether or not such a goal is reinforced at the local community level. Education programmes, no matter how comprehensive or well-resourced, cannot control all messages on alcohol. The perception gained by many young people via media images and personal experience is that alcohol is an integral part of adult life and learning how to drink is a part of becoming an adult (Petosa, 1992). It seems logical, therefore, to assume that as young people approach adulthood, an increasing number will drink alcohol.

Flay (2000) indicates that the effects of drug education with a community component appear to be larger, occur in more domains and are less likely to diminish over time. However, success tends to occur with drugs other than alcohol and limitations in research design and lack of replication mean that existing studies provide little information on the differential effectiveness of programme components. Whole-of-school or community approaches do offer promise, but have to resist making the same mistake of the early curriculum-based approaches. If the goal is unrealistic, adding extra components to the intervention will not make it any more likely that the goal will be achieved. Abstinence is clearly unrealistic as the only goal, and alcohol prevalence data clearly indicates it is not supported by broader community norms in Western industrialized societies (Grytten, 1997; Jones, 1993; Miller & Plant, 1996; Substance Abuse & Mental Health Services Administration, 1997). As a consequence, not only is the legitimacy of such a goal questionable, but programmes based on such a goal may actually be counterproductive. They provide the appearance that prevention education is being undertaken, while offering little to the large proportion of young people who are already drinking or who may be experiencing consequences from drinking by others.

PERSISTENCE WITH INEFFECTIVE APPROACHES

An example of a drug education programme with a long history of acceptance in schools, but a poor evaluation record in terms of achieving behaviour change, is DARE (Drug Abuse Resistance Education). The programme was developed in 1983 by the Los Angeles Police Department and the Los Angeles Unified School District, with the intention of teaching students the skills to resist drug use. It essentially uses a didactic approach to deliver a strong abstention message, although its distinguishing feature is that community police officers, rather than teachers, provide the education. Ennett et al. (1994) reported that DARE has been adopted by over 50% of school districts in America and the programme also has a significant international presence, with representation in almost 20 countries (Rogers, 1993). DARE has a high profile in the community and is relatively expensive to implement, because of the use of police officers to conduct the extracurricular education. This has meant that a number of evaluations of the programme have been conducted. Some have indicated that the programme is well regarded, such as the study by Donnermeyer & Wurschmidt (1997), which found that 97% of educators in a sample of mid-western schools conducting the DARE programme endorsed the programme. Other evaluations of the programme's impact in particular locations, such as that conducted by Dukes, Ullman & Stein (1995) with students in Colorado Springs, have indicated that the programme does influence students. In the Colorado Springs study, DARE improved self-esteem and institutional bonding and decreased endorsement of risky behaviours, although drug-using behaviour was not measured. A meta-analysis of eight methodologically rigorous DARE outcome evaluations, however, concluded that the programme's short-term effect on drug-using behaviour was small (Ennett et al., 1994). The authors noted the disparity between the programme's popularity and prevalence and its effectiveness, and indicated that this could mean that it was taking the place of other more beneficial drug education interventions. Lindstrom & Svensson (1998) reported similar findings in their evaluation of the Swedish equivalent of DARE, the VAGA programme. They found that students who had undertaken the programme were no different in their attitudes to drugs or actual drug-using behaviour than students who had not participated. On the basis of their findings, they questioned the emphasis of the programme and the use of limited police resources for this task. Australia is another country that has funded drug education programmes that have a high public profile but no proven efficacy. The Life Education programme receives several million dollars a year from government, business and service groups and has a high profile in the community, yet an evaluation of students exposed to the programme found no evidence that it reduced use of alcohol, analgesics or tobacco. Rather, the Life Education students were slightly more likely to use these substances (Hawthorne, Garrard & Dunt, 1995). In a later evaluation of the social impact of the programme in the Australian state of Victoria, Hawthorne (1996) reported that because the programme was institutionalized and reached a wide student audience, estimates could be made of its impact at the population level. In relation to alcohol use, Hawthorne (1996) reported that 22% of all Victorian boys' recent drinking could be attributed to participation in Life Education.

Well-publicized programmes such as DARE and Life Education seem to build up a momentum that is difficult to stop, even though the empirical evidence attests to their ineffectiveness. DARE continues to be the drug education programme of choice in America, despite over a decade of predominantly negative evaluations and a recent review commissioned by the American Department of Education, which concluded that it was among the least effective programmes in use (Silvia & Thorne, 1997). Past experience indicates that ineffective drug education programmes are eventually superseded, but this takes considerable time and is inherently wasteful of resources. Hawthorne's (1996) suggestion for preventing the institutionalization of ineffective programmes is to conduct a thorough evaluation prior to widespread implementation.

THE PROMISE OF HARM REDUCTION APPROACHES

Dielman (1994) considered that the early drug prevention programmes were not able to demonstrate an impact on behaviour, because they tended to adopt unrealistic goals, such as the prevention of any drug use. However, it is arguable that this aspect of drug education has changed much in recent times. Drug education research still tends to be framed in terms of abstinence outcomes, because the great majority of studies have taken place in the USA (Foxcroft et al., 1997), where federal guidelines mandate that prevention programmes emphasize "zero tolerance" and abstinence (Office for Substance Use Prevention, Alcohol, Drug Abuse and Mental Health Administration, 1989). While the research on harm reduction as a goal for drug education has had little support in the past, there is a particularly compelling logic for the use of such an approach with alcohol. The drug is legal, socially acceptable, readily available and problems tend to be associated with binge-drinking occasions (Single, 1996). Given these parameters, abstinence is unlikely and greater benefit should accrue from education to reduce binge-drinking and equip people with the skills to deal better with the risks associated with settings where such drinking occurs. Such an approach is even more applicable to young people, because of their lack of knowledge about alcohol, their inexperience with drinking and their greater propensity to binge-drink in high-risk settings.

McBride et al. (1998) and the Australian Drug Foundation (undated) found that alcohol education was more meaningful for students if it acknowledged their experiences with alcohol. In this regard, a harm reduction approach was received positively by students, because it was not judgemental about their experiences and offered something useful to all students, whether they had started drinking or not. Midford & McBride (1999) found that in Australia, teachers generally understood and were very supportive of the concept, because it permitted them to be more open in their discussions of drug use. Parents in Australia were also supportive of the approach in relation to alcohol, because they typically introduced their own children to alcohol at home and did not expect schools to impose a moralistic view of alcohol use (Australian Drug Foundation, undated). In a study of alcohol and other drug use in Nova Scotia, Canada, Poulin & Elliot (1997) indicated that for the 27% of students who reported at least one alcohol-related problem, a harm-reduction approach would be more relevant than trying to prevent use. Yet these researchers acknowledged that there was little evidence as to the effectiveness of school-based harm reduction programmes.

An alcohol education study by Shope et al. (1994) is one of the first to explore the harm-reduction benefits they may derive from education. These researchers found that while there was no difference in the level of alcohol use between intervention and control groups, the harms deriving from alcohol use did not increase as rapidly in an intervention subgroup with a prior history of unsupervised drinking, as they did in comparable controls. While curriculum materials used in the study contained a strong abstinence message and there was criticism of the small numbers in the subgroup that demonstrated change (Gorman, 1996), it does seem to indicate that harm reduction can be achieved by school drug education and that this is not necessarily linked to reduced consumption. A recent alcohol education research study in Australia, designed to teach harm-reduction skills

(McBride et al., 2000) found that the intervention students were significantly more knowledgeable about alcohol after the first phase of the intervention than the control group. They also held attitudes that were significantly more supportive of safe alcohol use and harm reduction and consumed significantly less alcohol than the control group. Change in the level of alcohol harm experienced was not as dramatic, which was to be expected, given a retrospective reporting period longer than the interval between surveys and the gradual nature of behaviour change. However, one subgroup of intervention students, those who reported drinking with adult supervision, did experience significantly less harm than their non-intervention counterparts, subsequent to the intervention. These early findings are promising, and such evidence is very necessary if objective support is to be provided for what Duncan et al. (1994) considered to be a major paradigm shift in drug education, away from use-prevention to abuse prevention or harm reduction. They saw this as a rational response to the failure of efforts aimed at preventing drug use and a coherent organization of prevention resources, so as potentially to yield the greatest benefit to society. Demonstrable behaviour change lends further weight of argument to the benefit of this shift.

The essence of harm reduction is that it acknowledges that people will use drugs and gives priority to preventing harms rather than preventing use. Lenton & Midford (1996) define a harm reduction programme or policy as:

> . . . one in which (1) the primary goal is to reduce net health, social and/or economic harm without necessarily seeking to reduce use, and (2) it can be directly demonstrated against broadly agreed criteria, that net harm across these dimensions has been reduced, rather than claiming or inferring that harm has been reduced from changes in other indices (p. 412).

Some jurisdictions have accepted the logic of harm reduction, such as Canada and Australia, where harm reduction forms the basis of each country's respective national drug policy (Single, 1996; National Drug Strategy Committee, 1993). The approach was initially associated with reducing the harms associated with illicit drug use, which was resistant to traditional prevention and treatment methods. It has only more recently been seen as an appropriate goal for drug education (Duncan et al., 1994; Resnicow & Botvin, 1993). However, while the approach was successful in reducing the spread of HIV among the injecting drug population, there has been insufficient research carried out to determine whether it delivers more effective drug education than traditional abstinence or delayed onset approaches. Duncan et al. (1994) considered that preventing drug abuse or harmful drug use is a different task from preventing all drug use and, according to Resnicow & Botvin (1993) may make drug education more credible and more realistic. This also means that harm reduction may make drug education more effective in terms of achieving stated outcomes, as outcomes can be measured in terms of the amount of harm reduced, rather than in absolutist terms of whether or not abstention was achieved.

CONCLUSION

Drug education as a whole has developed considerably in the last decade and, as a part of this, there is greater understanding of the various influences involved. This is not to say that drug or alcohol education has become demonstrably more effective in changing behaviour. Rather, it seems that there is greater understanding at a component level of the forces that foster drinking and the programme elements that need to be included if a programme is to deal comprehensively and effectively with these forces.

In a recent meta-analysis of 55 school- or college-based drug education programme evaluations that met minimum methodological criteria, White & Pitts (1998) considered that 18 were methodologically sound studies and that 10 of these "sound" studies evidenced some impact on drug-using behaviour. Meta-analysis of 11 "sound" studies, with 1 year follow-up, indicated that the mean effect size was 0.037. This means that over a period of a year the best-researched drug education interventions were able to delay the onset of drug use or stop use in 3.7% of young people who would otherwise have used. Such a study has not been done separately with alcohol education programmes, but the effect size is likely to be even smaller, because both abstinence and use onset have proved more difficult to achieve in relation to alcohol. While this recent meta-analysis demonstrates that drug education programmes still have difficulty in changing behaviour, the authors identified promising individual approaches that produced slightly larger effects. The effective interventions were a mix of focused and generic training, although some elements that worked as part of one programme were also present in unsuccessful programmes. The great majority of programmes that had a longer-term impact were intense in their own right and supported by reinforcing messages. They also usually included booster sessions at a later stage of the programme. White & Pitts (1998), however, found that programmes rarely identified the separate contribution of each component element, which makes it difficult to tease apart why programmes work and optimize the composition of new initiatives.

The more recent drug education studies and reviews of the area indicate that sound school-based interventions do change behaviour and, while the change is small, it occurs at a population level, so the aggregate benefit of good programmes can be large if widely implemented. (McBride et al., 2000; Shope et al., 1994; White & Pitts, 1998). These findings reinforce the importance of assessing alcohol education in terms of utility. In this way there is some objective criterion to differentiate between those programmes that are simply well known or palatable and those that bring about meaningful change. This may seem self-evident, but the political and moral dimensions to drug education mean that certain approaches are more acceptable to the community. The American experience is that a great deal of money is spent on aggressively marketing programmes that either have not been evaluated or have been shown to be ineffective, rather than implementing proven programmes (Dusenbury, Falco & Lake, 1997; Hansen, Rose & Dyfoos, 1993).

Alcohol education will probably always be considered something that schools should provide, but in the past an emphasis on abstinence may have blinded educators to the inadequacies of the programmes chosen and, in the process, discredited the merit of education as a prevention measure. In the future, programmes need to be more realistic about their goals and accountable for their achievements. The benefit would be that schools spend time and money on education that has greater potential for bringing about useful change, and students are more likely to be provided with knowledge, values and skills that equip them to make better decisions about alcohol. In order to achieve these ends, there needs to be a broader range of research on alcohol education and this research must come to terms with the objectives of harm reduction. Beck (1998) pointed out that, because of historical movements aimed at prohibiting alcohol use, most research has evaluated how successful programmes have been at maintaining abstinence or delaying onset. As a consequence, evaluations may have assessed programmes as being ineffective because they did not achieve this. Such programmes may have actually achieved other benefits but typically these would not have been considered relevant. An even more concerning implication of this emphasis on abstinence is that other worthwhile goals, such as practising responsible decision making in relation to alcohol, or even just possessing the practical knowledge to be capable of making better decisions, have not been part of the research agenda. Within such a framework, they are not considered the legitimate business of alcohol education for young people. This continuing repetition of past mistakes suggests that it is timely for researchers to investigate less absolutist alternatives, on the basis that achieving some beneficial change is better than failing comprehensively to persuade young people that they should not drink at all. Alcohol consumption is an established aspect of Western industrialized societies. Accordingly, these societies have an obligation to educate and support their young people, so that they have the conceptual framework to be able to make responsible decisions about drinking as they grow older and the practical skills to implement those decisions.

KEY WORKS AND SUGGESTIONS FOR FURTHER READING

Beck, J. (1998).   100 years of "Just say no" vs. "Just say know". *Evaluation Review*, **22**(1), 15–45.

This article comprehensively reviews the history of American school-based drug education. Its particular contribution is that it provides an insight into how current approaches have been shaped by a long sequence of previous interventions and how future decisions need to be informed by past mistakes.

Dielman, T.E. (1994).   School-based research on the prevention of adolescent alcohol use and misuse: methodological issues and advances. *Journal of Research on Adolescence*, **4**(2), 271–293.

Dielman looks at why early school-based alcohol education approaches failed to achieve abstinence. He suggests that alcohol education programs need to be more realistic about what they can achieve and presents findings from his research, indicating that education can reduce alcohol harm.

Dusenbury, L. & Falco, M. (1995).   Eleven components of effective drug abuse prevention curricula. *Journal of School Health*, **63**(10), 420–425.

These two researchers comprehensively review recent school-based drug education programs and interview leading experts in prevention research to identify the key elements of effective drug education curricula. On the basis of their findings, they identify 11 critical components that contribute to effective programs.

Perry, C.C. & Kelder, S.H. (1992).   Prevention. *Annual Review of Addictions Research and Treatment*, 463–472.

This is a review of primary prevention strategies used with youth. The paper is broad-ranging and explores how the effectiveness of school based programs can be enhanced by parallel media, community and public policy interventions.

White, D. & Pitts, M. (1998).   Educating young people about drugs: a systematic review. *Addiction*, **93**(10), 1475–1487.

This is a very comprehensive meta-analysis of methodologically sound drug education studies. It provides a very useful summary as to the impact of drug education on drug using behaviour and identifies those components that consistently feature in the more successful programs.

REFERENCES

Anslinger, H.J. & Tompkins, W.F. (1953).   *The Traffic in Narcotics.* New York: Funk and Wagnalls.
Australian Drug Foundation (undated).   *Reducing the Risk 1. The Risk Reduction Approach to Alcohol Education.* Melbourne: Australian Drug Foundation.

Ballard, R., Gillespie, A. & Irwin, R. (1994). *Principles for Drug Education in Schools*. Belconnen, ACT: University of Canberra.

Bandura, A. (1977). *Social Learning Theory*. Englewood Cliffs, NJ: Prentice-Hall.

Bangert-Drowns, R.L. (1988). The effects of school-based substance abuse education—a meta-analysis. *Journal of Drug Education*, **18**(3), 243–264.

Beck, J. (1998). 100 years of "Just Say No" versus "Just Say Know". *Evaluation Review*, **22**(1), 15–45.

Botvin, G.J. (1990). Substance abuse prevention: theory, practice and effectiveness. In M. Tonry & J.Q. Wilson (Eds), *Drugs and Crime*, Vol. 13. Series: Crime and Justice: A Review of Research. Chicago, IL: University of Chicago Press.

Coggans, N. & Watson, J. (1995). Drug education: approaches, effectiveness and delivery. *Drugs: Education, Prevention and Policy*, **2**(3), 211–224.

Cuijpers, P. (2002). Peer-led and adult-led school drug prevention: A meta-analytic comparison. *Journal of Drug Education*, **32**(2), 107–119.

Dielman, T.E. (1994). School-based research on the prevention of adolescent alcohol use and misuse: methodological issues and Advances. *Journal of Research on Adolescence*, **4**(2), 271–293.

Donnermeyer, J.F. & Wurschmidt, T.D. (1997). Educators perceptions of the DARE program. *Journal of Drug Education*, **27**(33), 259–276.

Dukes, R.L. Ullman, J.B. & Stein, J.A. (1995). An evaluation of DARE (Drug Abuse Resistance Education), using a Solomon four-groups design with latent variables. *Evaluation Review*, **19**(4), 409–435.

Duncan, D.F., Nicholson, T., Clifford, P., Hawkins, W. & Petosa, R. (1994). Harm reduction: an emerging new paradigm for drug education. *Journal of Drug Education*, **24**(4), 281–290.

Duryea, E., Mohr, P., Newman, I., Martin, G. & Egwaoje, E. (1984). Six-month follow-up results of a preventative alcohol intervention. *Journal of Drug Education*, **14**, 97–104.

Dusenbury, L. & Falco, M. (1995). Eleven components of effective drug abuse prevention curricula. *Journal of School Health*, **65**(10), 420–425.

Dusenbury, L., Falco, M. & Lake, A. (1997). A review of the evaluation of 47 drug abuse prevention curricula available nationally. *Journal of School Health*, **67**(4), 127–133.

Ennett, S.T., Tobler, N.S., Ringwalt, C.L. & Flewelling, R.L. (1994). How effective is Drug Abuse Resistance Education? A meta-analysis of Project DARE Outcome Evaluations. *American Journal of Public Health*, **84**(9), 1394–1401.

Flay, B.R. (2000). Approaches to substance use prevention utilizing school curriculum plus social environment change. *Addictive Behaviours*, **25**(6), 861–885.

Foxcroft, D.R., Lister-Sharp, D. & Lowe, G. (1997). Alcohol misuse prevention for young people: a systematic review reveals methodological concerns and lack of reliable evidence of effectiveness. *Addiction*, **92**(5), 531–537.

Foxcroft, D.R. & Lowe, G. (1997). Adolescents' alcohol use and misuse: the socializing influence of perceived family life. *Drugs: Education, Prevention and Policy*, **4**(3), 215–229.

Goodstadt, M. (1980). School-based drug education in North America: what is wrong? What can be done? *Journal of School Health*, **56**, 278–281.

Gorman, D.M. (1996). Do school-based social skills training programs prevent alcohol use among young people? *Addiction Research*, **4**(2), 191–210.

Grytten, L. (1997). *Rusmidler I Norge Alcohol and Drugs in Norway 1997*. Oslo: The Norwegian Directorate for the Prevention of Alcohol and Drug Problems and the National Institute for Alcohol and Drug Research.

Hansen, W.B. (1993). School-based alcohol prevention programs. *Alcohol Health & Research World*, **17**(1), 54–60.

Hansen, W.B. & Graham, J.W. (1991). Preventing alcohol, marijuana, and cigarette use among adolescents: peer pressure resistance training vs. establishing conservative norms. *Preventive Medicine*, **20**, 414–430.

Hansen, W.B., Rose, L.A. & Dyfoos, J.G. (1993). *Causal Factors. Interventions and Policy Considerations in School Based Substance Abuse Prevention*, Washington, DC: US Congress, Office of Technology Assessment.

Hawthorne, G. (1996). The social impact of Life Education: estimating drug use prevalence among Victorian primary school students and the statewide effect of the Life Education programme. *Addiction*, **91**(8), 1151–1159.

Hawthorne, G., Garrard, J. & Dunt, D. (1995). Does Life Education's programme have a public health benefit? *Addiction*, **90**(2), 205–215.

Holder, H.D. (1992). What is a community and what are implications for prevention trials for reducing alcohol problems? In H.D. Holder & J.M. Howard (Eds), *Community Prevention Trials for Alcohol Problems*. Westport, CT: Praeger.

Kelder, S.H., Perry, C.L., Klepp, K.I. & Lytle, L.L. (1994). Longitudinal tracking of adolescent smoking, physical activity and food choice behaviour. *American Journal of Public Health*, **84**(7), 1121–1126.

Kinder, B., Pape, N. & Walfish, S. (1980). Drug and alcohol education. A review of outcome studies. *International Journal of the Addictions*, **15**, 1035–1054.

Jones, R. (1993). *Drug Use and Exposure in the Australian Community*. Canberra: Australian Government Publishing Service.

Johnston, L.D., O'Malley, P.M. & Bachman, J.G. (1989). *Drug Use, Drinking and Smoking: National Survey Results from High School, College, and Young Adult Populations, 1975–1988*. National Institute on Drug Abuse, DHHS Publication No.(ADM) 89-1638. Washington, DC: Superintendant of Documents, US Government Printing Office.

Lang, E. (1994). Community action regarding licensing issues. In T. Stockwell (Ed.), *Alcohol Misuse and Violence 5, An Examination of the Appropriateness and Efficacy of Liquor-Licensing Laws Across Australia*. Canberra: Australian Government Publishing Service.

Lender, M.E. & Martin, J.K. (1987). *Drinking in America: A History*. New York: Free Press.

Lenton, S. & Midford, R. (1996). Clarifying harm reduction? *Drug and Alcohol Review*, **15**, 411–413.

Lindstrom, P. & Svensson, R. (1998). Attitudes towards drugs among youths: an evaluation of the Swedish DARE programme. *Nordisk Alkohol & Narkotikatidskrift*, **15**(English Suppl.).

McBride, N. & Midford, R. (1996). Assessing organizational support for school health promotion. *Health Education Research Theory and Practice*, **11**(4), 509–518.

McBride, N., Midford, R. & Farringdon, F. (1998). Alcohol harm reduction education in schools: An Australian efficacy study. In T. Stockwell (Ed.), *Drug Trials and Tribulations: Lessons for Australian Drug Policy*. Perth: National Centre for Research into the Prevention of Drug Abuse, Curtin University of Technology, Perth.

McBride, N., Midford, R., Farringdon, F. & Phillips, M. (2000). Early results from a school alcohol harm minimisation intervention: the School Health and Alcohol Harm Reduction Project. *Addiction*, **95**(7), 1021–1042.

McBride, N., Midford, R., Woolmer, J. & Philp, A. (1998). *Youth Alcohol Forum: Evaluation Report*. Perth: National Centre for Research into the Prevention of Drug Abuse, Curtin University of Technology.

McCallum, T. (1990). Educating parents as drug educators. *Drug Education Journal of Australia*, **4**(3), 243–249.

McCallum, T. (1996). Who influences. *Youth Studies Australia*, **Spring**, 36–41.

McGuire, W.J. (1964). Inducing resistance to persuasion: some contemporary approaches. In L. Berkowitz (Ed.), *Advances in Experimental Social Psychology*. New York: Academic Press.

Mallick, J., Evans, R. & Stein, G. (1998). Parents and drug education: parents' concerns, attitudes and needs. *Drugs: Education, Prevention and Policy*, **5**(2), 169–176.

Mezvinsky, N. (1961). Scientific temperance instruction in the schools. *History of Education Quarterly*, **1**, 48–56.

Midford, R. & McBride, N. (1999). Evaluation of a national school drug education program in Australia. *International Journal of Drug Policy*, **10**(3), 177–193.

Milgram, G.G. (1996). Responsible decision making regarding alcohol: a re-emerging prevention/education strategy for the 1990s. *Journal of Drug Education*, **26**(4), 357–365.

Miller, P. M. & Plant, M. (1996). Drinking, smoking, and illicit drug use among 15 and 16 year-olds in the United Kingdom. *British Medical Journal*, **313**, 394–397.

National Drug Strategy Committee (1993). *National Drug Strategic Plan, 1993–97. Commonwealth Department of Health, Housing Local Government and Community Services*. Canberra: Australian Government Publishing Service.

Office for Substance Use Prevention, Alcohol, Drug Abuse and Mental Health Administration (1989). *Message and Material Review Process*, RPO726, Washington, DC: US Government Printing Office.

Perry, C.L. & Kelder, S.H. (1992). Prevention. *Annual Review of Addictions Research and Treatment*, 453–472.

Perry, C.L. & Murray, D.M. (1985). The prevention of adolescent drug abuse: implications from etiological, developmental, behavioural, and environmental models. *Journal of Primary Prevention*, **6**, 31–52.

Perry, C.L., Williams, C.L., Komro, K.A., Veblen-Mortenson, S., Forster, J.L., Bernstein-Lachter, R., Pratt, L.K., Munson, K.A. & Farbakhsh, K. (1998). Project Northland—Phase II: community action to reduce adolescent alcohol use. Paper presented at the Kettil Bruun Society's Fourth Symposium on Community Action Research, Russell, New Zealand, 8–13 February.

Perry, C.L., Williams, C.L., Veblen-Mortenson, S., Toomey, T.L., Komro, K.A., Anstine, P.S., McGovern, P.G., Finnegan, J.R., Forster, J.L., Wagenaar, A.C. & Wolfson, M. (1996). Project Northland: outcomes of a community-wide alcohol use prevention program during early adolescence. *American Journal of Public Health*, **86**(7), 956–965.

Perry, C.L., Williams, C.L., Forster, J.L., Wolfson, M., Wagenaar, A.C., Finnegan, J.R., McGovern, P.G., Veblen-Mortenson, S., Komro, K.A. & Anstine, P.S. (1993). Background, conceptualization, and design of a community-wide research program on adolescent alcohol use: Project Northland. *Health Education Research: Theory & Practice*, **8**(1), 125–136.

Petosa, R. (1992). Developing a comprehensive health promotion program to prevent adolescent drug abuse. In G. Lawson & A. Lawson (Eds), *The Prevention and Treatment of Adolescent Drug Abuse*. Gaithersburg, MD: Aspen.

Poulin, C. & Elliot, D. (1997). Alcohol, tobacco and cannabis use among Nova Scotia adolescents: implications for prevention and harm reduction. *Canadian Medical Association Journal*, **156**(10), 1387–1393.

Quinn, L. (1996). Mobilising parents. *Druglink*, **11**, 9–10.

Resnicow, K. & Botvin, G. (1993). School-based substance use prevention programs: why do effects decay? *Preventive Medicine*, **22**, 481–490.

Rogers, E.M. (1993). Diffusion and re-invention of project DARE. In T.E. Backer & E.M. Rogers (Eds), *Organizational Aspects of Health Communication Campaigns: What Works?* Newbury Park, CA: Sage.

Schaps, E., DiBartolo, R., Moskowitz, J., Palley, C.S. & Churgin, S. (1981). A review of 127 drug abuse prevention program evaluations. *Journal of Drug Issues*, **11**, 17–43.

Schlosser, E. (1994). Reefer madness. *Atlantic Monthly*, **274**(2), 45–63.

Sharp, C. (undated). *Alcohol Education for Young People: A Review of the Literature, 1983–1992. A report for the Alcohol Education and Research Council and the Portman Group*. London: National Foundation for Educational Research.

Shope, J.T., Kloska, D.D., Dielman, T.E. & Maharg, R. (1994). Longitudinal evaluation of an enhanced Alcohol Misuse Prevention Study (AMPS) curriculum for grades six–eight. *Journal of School Health*, **64**, 160–166.

Silvia, E.S. & Thorne, J. (1997). *School-based Drug Prevention Programs: A Longitudinal Study in Selected School Districts*. Research Triangle Park, NC: Research Triangle Park.

Single, E. (1996). Harm reduction as an alcohol-prevention strategy. *Alcohol Health and Research World*, **20**(4), 239–243.

Spoth, R., Redmond, C. & Shin, C. (2001). Randomized trial of brief family interventions for general populations: Adolescent substance use outcomes four years following baseline. *Journal of Consulting and Clinical Psychology*, **69**(4), 627–642.

Spoth, R., Redmond, C., Hockaday, C. & Shin, C. (1996b). Barriers to participation in family skills preventive interventions and their evaluations: A replication and extension. *Family Relations*, **45**, 247–254.

Spoth, R., Yoo, S., Kahn, J. & Redmond, C. (1996a). A model of the effects of protective parent and peer factors on young adolescent alcohol refusal skills. *Journal of Primary Prevention*, **16**, 373–394.

Substance Abuse and Mental Health Services Administration (1997). *National Household Survey on Drug Abuse: Population Estimates 1996*. DHHS Pub. No.(SMA)97-3137. Rockville, MD: US Department of Health and Human Services.

Tobler, N.S. (1986). Meta-analysis of 143 adolescent drug prevention programs: quantitative outcome results of program participants compared to a control or comparison group. *Journal of Drug Issues*, **16**, 537–567.

Tobler, N.S., Roona, M.R., Ochshorn, P., Marshall, D.G., Streke, A.V. & Stackpole, K.M. (2000). School-based adolescent drug prevention programs: 1998 meta-analysis. *The Journal of Primary Prevention*, **20**(4), 275–336.

Tobler, N.S. & Stratton, H.H. (1997). Effectiveness of school-based drug prevention programs: A meta-analysis of the research. *The Journal of Primary Prevention,* **18**(1), 71–128.

Waahlberg, R.B. (1988). Alcohol and drug education. In O.J. Skog & R.B. Waahlberg (Eds), *Alcohol and Drugs: The Norwegian Experience*, Oslo: National Directorate for the prevention of Alcohol and Drug Problems.

Wallack, L. (1980). Mass media and drinking, smoking and drug taking. *Contemporary Drug Problems*, **Spring**, 49–83.

White, D. & Pitts, M. (1998). Educating young people about drugs: a systematic review. *Addiction*, **93**(10), 1475–1487.

Wittman, F.D. (1990). Environmental design to prevent problems of alcohol availability: concepts and prospects. In N. Giesbrecht, P. Conley, R.W. Denniston et al. (Eds), *Research, Action, and the Community: Experiences in the Prevention of Alcohol and Other Drug Problems*. OSAP Prevention Monograph No. 4, Rockville, MD: Office for Substance Abuse Prevention.

Chapter 18

Mass Media Marketing and Advocacy to Reduce Alcohol-related Harm

Kevin Boots
Health Department of Western Australia, Perth, Western Australia
and
Richard Midford
National Drug Research Institute, Curtin University of Technology,
Perth, Western Australia

Synopsis

The alcohol industry has for many years used large advertising and public relations budgets to implement sophisticated mass media marketing and advocacy campaigns to further the sale of alcohol. Public health agents are also increasingly advocating and marketing messages about alcohol: those that seek to encourage responsible drinking behaviour and reduce alcohol-related harm. Over time, mass media marketing and advocacy to reduce alcohol-related harm has begun to match the sophistication achieved by the purveyors of alcohol advertising. In the process, much has been learned by public health agents about both marketing and advocacy.

Marketing campaigns that use social marketing strategies, and that seek to reduce alcohol-related harm, compete for advertising space with other advertisers. Sometimes these campaigns also aim to increase the social pressure upon consumers to modify their behaviour by highlighting or seeking to create opposing social norms. More recent campaigns have benefited from the application of new social science theories (such as theories of individual behaviour change and of social marketing), from the use of formative evaluation and from the setting of realistic campaign objectives. The first part of this chapter provides an overview of mass media marketing and examines the current theories of individual behaviour change that

The Essential *Handbook of Treatment and Prevention of Alcohol Problems.* Edited by N. Heather and T. Stockwell.
© 2004 John Wiley & Sons Ltd. ISBN 0-470-86296-3.

underpin the social marketing approach. The two main methods of mass media marketing, advertising and "edutainment", are described, and their application to two recent mass media marketing campaigns are detailed.

Unfortunately, an implicit tenet of the market-based, individual-focused health system is that those consumers who do not maintain health, or access health care services, are responsible for the consequences. Such an approach in its pure form does not acknowledge the structural determinants of health behaviour. In contrast to the marketing approach, mass media advocacy seeks to create change to the structural determinants of health. Mass media advocacy is a political activity that, along with coalition building and political lobbying, is used to influence decision-makers in order to achieve public health goals. It emphasizes the promotion of healthy behaviours and healthy public policy by influencing decision makers to accept the merit of health-promoting or -protecting policies or structures. The second part of this chapter illustrates the breadth of mass media advocacy activities undertaken by health advocates and provides a detailed example of successful advocacy to reduce alcohol-related harm.

Mass media marketing is most suited to issues that seek incremental change rather than those that directly challenge institutions such as the alcohol industry. Mass media advocacy, on the other hand, is a strategy well suited to challenging institutional practices and creating systemic change. However, in practice, both activities are often undertaken simultaneously. This is because the careful use of advertising can assist in advocating for structural change, and advocacy activity can reinforce or play a part in modifying individual behaviour. The apparent increase in success of these strategies can be attributed partly to improved implementation, partly to the new theories upon which they are now developed, and partly to improved evaluation methodology. Most importantly, however, has been the recognition that mass media marketing and mass media advocacy are more effective when they are only two of many elements within a broader change strategy.

In market-based societies the mass media has for many years been a fertile vehicle for the development and dissemination of alcohol advertising, and for political lobbying by the alcohol industry. Large advertising and public relations budgets, coupled with considerable expertise, have allowed the industry to refine its mass media marketing and advocacy activities with considerable precision. This means that the general public is receiving more sophisticated messages encouraging greater use of alcohol. However, public health agents have increasingly entered the fray by advocating and marketing different messages about alcohol; those that seek to encourage responsible drinking behaviour and reduce alcohol-related harm. Over time, mass media marketing and advocacy to reduce alcohol-related harm has begun to match the sophistication achieved by the purveyors of alcohol advertising. In the process, much has been learned about marketing and advocacy by public health agents in their attempts to have their messages heard in the mass media marketplace.

Mass media marketing and mass media advocacy are similar, in that they are both activities that use the mass media as a vehicle to achieve the same primary goal; that of creating change within the community. However, while change is central to both activities, the type of change targeted and the methods employed are quite different.

This difference in the target of change can be illustrated by reference to a model of change, such as that described by Thompson & Kinne (1990). In their "synthesis of change theories" model, Thompson & Kinne consider that the individual operates within a hierarchical community system. The community comprises component subsystems (such as health and police services) and functions within a broader contextual environment, influenced by such things as prevailing economic conditions. In Thompson & Kinne's model, the individual's behaviour is the end product of the successive influence of each of these components. They suggest that direct change to individual behaviour is brought about by a change in one or more of the subsystem levels within the community system. The reverse, however, also needs to be considered. The collective impact of individual behaviour can itself create change within community structures and the external environment. The target of mass media marketing is squarely on individual behaviour change, while the target of mass media advocacy is on the external environment and other structural determinants of the behaviour targeted.

The relative merit of these and other activities in reducing alcohol-related harm has been the subject of much empirical research over the years (Edwards et al., 1994). Andreasson and colleagues of the Stockholm North Centre for Addiction recently postulated that "if we were to construct a list of effective methods [to prevent alcohol problems], availability measures would be at the top and mass media campaigns at the bottom" (Andreasson et al., 1999). Although their ranking of 10 "prevention methods in the alcohol field according to effectiveness" did not consider the role of media advocacy, the targets of media advocacy (i.e. policies and economic conditions) were rated well above mass media campaigns in terms of influence on alcohol problems.

The worldwide dominance of market-based economies with associated values of "rugged individualism, self-determination, strong individual control and responsibility, and limited government involvement in social activity" (Wallack et al., 1993, p. 7) fosters a parallel approach to health care delivery. Within such a market framework, governments see their role as assisting individuals to make their own health-care choices. There is an expectation that the market-based health care system, when utilized in association with wise, thoughtful and prudent consumerism, rewards individuals by giving them personal control over their health and health-care needs. With equal services available to all, it is assumed that consumers will act in their own best interests; they will identify risks to their health and select health-care products that reduce risk to the extent that they would like.

This focus on the individual has been harnessed by public health practitioners through community interventions that use social marketing strategies. Marketing campaigns that seek to reduce alcohol-related harm compete for advertising space with other advertisers in the marketplace. One example from Australia of such competitive marketing occurred when a national football club promoting an anti-drink–drive message on their uniforms played a game of football against another sponsored by a brewery, within a competition named after a brand of beer. The purpose of social marketing is to compete in the marketplace against forces that have opposing aims, so as to modify consumer behaviour to promote health rather than illness. Sometimes these campaigns also aim to increase the social pressure upon consumers to modify their behaviour by highlighting or actually seeking to create opposing social norms.

The first part of this chapter provides a broad overview of mass media marketing and examines the current theories of individual behaviour change that underpin the social marketing approach. The two main methods of mass media marketing are then described and illustrated. These are advertising and the more recent strategy of "edutainment", which involves the placement of public health themes within popular entertainment.

Unfortunately, an implicit tenet of the market-based, individual-focused health system is that those consumers who do not maintain health, or access health care services, are responsible for the consequences. Such an approach in its pure form does not acknowledge the structural determinants of health behaviour and, as a consequence, there is a real danger of "blaming the victim" (Howat & Fisher, 1986). Social marketing campaigns that change social norms contribute to this by highlighting unhealthy behaviour as both preventable and deviant. A further danger associated with the social marketing of health is that such approaches may become the modern equivalent of the moralistic health crusades of yesteryear, which produced such legislation as the British "Act to Repress the Odious and Loathsome Sin of Drunkenness" in 1606 (Powell, 1988, p. 4).

The structural determinants of health behaviour not accounted for in social marketing campaigns include the impact of key events, secular trends, policies, economic conditions and technology on health outcomes (Thompson & Kinne, 1990). In contrast to the marketing approach, mass media advocacy seeks to create change to these systemic determinants. The importance of this aim is highlighted by Wallack et al. (1993), who noted that:

> For many communities, individual change is linked to social change and social change means addressing the power inequity that contributes to the problem. If power is defined as fundamental to improving health status, getting a message will not be a sufficient intervention. In this case, getting a voice will be the strategy. Unfortunately many of the populations that have the least power, the greatest health problems and the least resources for change are also the least visible to those who have the power to have an impact on disease-generating social conditions (p. 24).

The second part of this chapter examines the role and nature of mass media advocacy to reduce alcohol-related harm. Mass media advocacy is a political activity that, along with coalition building and political lobbying, is used to influence decision-makers in order to achieve public health goals. All three activities challenge the notion that health is a good or service that can be purchased or acquired by individuals according to personal choice. Rather, they emphasize the promotion of healthy behaviours and healthy public policy by influencing decision makers to accept the merit of health-promoting or -protecting policies or structures. This emphasis on the structural determinants of health makes mass media advocacy a potentially powerful tool. There are many reasons to use this tool, scores of different avenues to maximize the benefits of mass media advocacy and many examples of successful advocacy that has achieved the aim of reducing alcohol-related harm.

MASS MEDIA MARKETING

The mass media marketing of messages that aim to reduce alcohol-related harm is an activity that inherently supports and seeks to replicate product-marketing strategies that are associated with the free market economy and its focus on choice, on consumerism and on individuals. The methods used include those of advertising, "edutainment" and publicity.

Advertising is the major method used in the mass media marketing of messages that seek to reduce alcohol-related harm. Advertising may be paid or unpaid (such as public or community service announcements). It has frequently been used to: orientate the public to an issue, such as drink–driving; to teach new concepts or skills, such as how to pour a "standard drink" or to know what a "unit measure" is; to address specific problems, such as remaining under the legal blood alcohol limit; or to highlight the difference between hazardous consumption and safe consumption.

"Edutainment" refers to the deliberate placement of educational messages in media entertainment vehicles, such as television and radio soap operas, films, popular music, comics or novels, in order to achieve defined objectives (Egger, Donovan & Spark, 1993, p. 139). The main intention of edutainment is to have characters in mass media entertainment, particularly television soap opera characters with whom viewers identify, model certain behaviour that social marketers want replicated.

A third strategy used within mass media marketing is that of making publicity. Publicity is frequently used to supplement advertising or advocacy campaigns, but is seldom a strategy used in isolation. This strategy usually uses news networks and therefore, by definition, must present "new" (or at least "renewed") information. As a supplement to an advertising campaign, publicity will often result from an official "launch" of the campaign (frequently using a well-known identity or some form of gimmick) or from some controversy surrounding the campaign.

While edutainment is a new term, neither it nor advertising or publicity are recent phenomena. Groups such as temperance unions have been creating news and even sponsoring mass media advertising since the late nineteenth century, and popular entertainment, such as theatre, has been used as a vehicle to disseminate health-related wisdom since its inception. However, despite their long history, evidence of the effectiveness of early mass media marketing campaigns is difficult to find. According to Backer, Rogers & Sopory (1992, p. xiv), pre-1971 mass media health campaign evaluations mostly showed that the campaigns had failed. Montagne & Scott (1993) indicated that such old-style mass media campaigns in isolation mostly influenced knowledge and had little impact on behaviour. They also tended to target broad audiences, which reduced their ability to focus on specific issues. This meant that old-style campaigns were limited to reinforcing existing social attitudes and norms, such as not drinking and driving. In recent years, mass media marketing has been used as part of larger community-based drug prevention programmes (Pentz et al., 1989; Holder & Treno, 1997). These multi-component programmes have achieved a degree of success, although within such programmes it has been difficult to identify the specific contribution of mass media marketing. The strength of mass media marketing may be to reinforce community awareness of the problems created by alcohol use and prepare the ground for specific interventions (Holder & Treno, 1997). After investigating the efficacy of alcohol-related mass media marketing campaigns, Edwards et al. (1994) concluded that, "there is no present research evidence which can . . . justify expenditure of major resources on . . . mass media public education campaigns, unless these are placed in a broader context of community action" (p. 208). Consequently, it is within the context of broader community action that most examples of successful mass media marketing to reduce alcohol-related problems are found.

As components of such broader action, recent mass media marketing campaigns have, according to Backer et al. (1992, p. xiv), benefited from the application of new social science theories (such as theories of individual behaviour change and of social marketing), from the use of formative evaluation and from the setting of realistic campaign objectives. Each of these elements is described below, before examples of successful mass media advertising and edutainment campaigns are described.

Individual Behaviour Change

Two of the theories of individual behaviour change to have impacted on the development of mass media marketing campaigns are Bandura's (1986) social learning theory and Prochaska & DiClemente's (1992) "transtheoretical approach". Bandura (1986) was dissatisfied with the explanatory powers of the traditional deterministic theories of individual behaviour, which made no allowance for cognition and could not account for learning independently of behaviour. In his social learning theory, the individual is acknowledged as a thinking organism who makes conscious choices about how to interact with the environment. Some learning and change occurs through direct experience, but most occurs vicariously through observation and through modelling the actions of others. The individual can also be an agent for change and an object of change. This concept is known as reciprocal determinism (Nutbeam & Harris, 1998, p. 30) and is important in the understanding of the complex interplay between the individual and the environment and the development of social norms. Social norms are central to the ability of this theory to explain why some behaviours are acquired and others are not. An extension of this is that a change in norms will influence what behaviour people consider attractive and rewarding to learn. Bandura's (1986) insights into the complex relationship between people and their environment have provided the theoretical foundations for advertising campaigns in recent years, while his recognition of the importance of "modelling" has been fundamental to the development of health-promoting edutainment.

A second model of change that is particularly relevant to mass media marketing, due to its usefulness in identifying and segmenting target groups, is the "transtheoretical approach" (Prochaska, Redding & Evers, 1997). This model suggests that people can be divided into population subgroups according to their stage of progression toward adopting a desired behaviour. The stages of change originally postulated by Prochaska and DiClemente (1992) are pre-contemplation, contemplation, preparation, action, maintenance and termination. The stages are sequential, moving from when an individual is not yet considering modifying his/her unhealthy behaviour, to when the problem behaviour is completely eliminated and the individual is not able to be tempted to return to the unhealthy behaviour. People in one stage will respond to different messages from those in another stage. For example, a marketing campaign teaching people the skills of controlled drinking will be useful to problem drinkers who have recognized that change in their drinking is needed and are thus in the preparation or action stages. It will not, however, be appropriate for problem drinkers in the pre-contemplation phase who are not aware that such skills could be useful to them.

Social Marketing

Another body of knowledge that has had a significant impact upon the mass media marketing of alcohol harm issues is that of "social marketing". Social marketing is derived from "commercial marketing", which has the three basic tenants of "consumer orientation, an integrated approach, and the pursuit of profitability or other predetermined objectives" (Hastings & Haywood, 1991). The interplay between product, price, place and promotion, the "marketing mix", is considered fundamental to the success or failure of the marketing strategy.

Social marketing theory has provided a model of the process involved in developing mass media campaigns. Three elements of this process are the accurate identification of the target group, the creation of the most effective message, and the selection of the most appropriate method and media (Egger, Donovan & Spark, 1993).

Social marketing recognizes that knowledge of the target audience is paramount to successful mass media marketing. While media campaigns are popularly thought to be able to achieve "mass reach", it is a myth that a message disseminated amongst an entire population will reach everyone in that population. As a consequence, if public health agents want to reach specific groups, such as binge drinkers, they need to know about this group. Information that they should collect includes the target group demographics, needs, attitudes, beliefs and knowledge of the media channels they access. To be effective, it is important to understand that there is rarely one universal market for a single message, but a variety of different target groups that require different programmes and messages. Segmentation is a useful strategy to help define a market and target a message to ensure best use of resources. Market segmentation involves breaking down the total market into various subgroups. Each group is defined in a way that implies some differences in their response to various marketing activities. For example the subgroups may have different needs requiring different product variations; different media channels may reach them; or they may respond to different advertising appeals. The basis for target audience segmentation may be demographic, geographic, psychographic, sociodemographic, epidemiological, behavioural, attitudinal, related to the benefits sought, or related directly to the stages of change identified by the "transtheoretical approach" of Prochaska & DiClemente (Egger, Donovan & Spark, 1993).

Social marketing theory also focuses on "getting the message right". Language, style and tone must be consistent, not only with the campaign objectives, but also to the background and life-style of the target audience. The message must be understood, accepted and suitably motivating to the target audience. An approach must be developed that differentiates the message from others and that presents the message in a fresh and timely manner.

Another area in which social marketing theory has supported the development of mass media campaigns has been through its identification and critique of the array of marketing methods and media. As well as choosing between advertising, edutainment and publicity mass media, marketers must choose between a variety of media, such as television, the Internet, print media such as newspapers and magazines, and outdoor media such as billboards and signs. The choices between the forms of media are generally made according to cost and ability of the medium to target the selected audience, while the choices between method are made in relationship to the change outcome sought.

Formative Evaluations

Recent mass media marketing campaigns also benefit from the widespread use of evaluation. Specific formative evaluation is now recognized as critical to campaign development (Simons-Morton, Donohew & Davis Crump, 1997), and the increasing use of process, output and outcome evaluation further contributes to the refinement of campaigns as they proceed. Formative evaluation is about undertaking research and product testing before campaign implementation in order to identify the best message, medium and method available within the existing resource constraints. After the creation of the marketing objectives, the translation of these objectives into the campaign is of critical importance. Formative evaluation should involve testing of the marketing mix (i.e. price, product, place and promotion) with the intended target audience, and will often be undertaken using focus groups, surveys or in-depth interviews. The social science theories described above provide insights into how campaigns should be developed, but without formative evaluation mass media marketing campaigns run the risk of missing their target. Likewise, process, output and outcome evaluation has allowed public health promoters to modify and improve their campaigns in line with their intended goals.

Achievable Objectives

Backer, Rogers & Sopory (1992, p. xiv) also suggest mass media campaigns have benefited by setting more modest achievable campaign objectives and recent projects, such as the New Zealand Community Alcohol Project, have benefited by setting "realistic objectives" (Casswell, Ransom & Gilmore, 1990). Early campaigns that sought to create individual behaviour change focused their outcome evaluations on identifying significant community-wide changes in behaviour. This simplistic approach did not acknowledge the complex nature of the process of change or the complexities involved in the communication of information. More often than not, there are a range of intermediary steps that can be identified between campaign implementation and large-scale community change. For example, a campaign targeting binge drinkers, who are unaware that their drinking behaviour is defined as "binge-drinking", will not engage the target group. Such a campaign, targeting a group of people in a "precontemplation" stage, should have problem awareness as the primary objective, not behaviour change. In this example, the outcome measures used to identify campaign "success" would vary according to the primary objective. Should the objective be behaviour change and the relevant outcome measures applied, the campaign will almost certainly be deemed a "failure" (even if the campaign resulted in 100% of the target group contemplating whether they are binge-drinkers).

The triad of modest achievable objectives, formative research and a basis in valid social science theory has been the foundation of numerous recent mass media marketing campaigns. One example that primarily used the method of advertising and one that primarily used edutainment are described below. They constitute examples of the "best practice" use of mass media marketing to reduce alcohol-related harm.

Mass Media Advertising and Edutainment to Reduce Alcohol-related Harm: Case Studies

An evaluation of the Danish National Campaigns on Alcohol presented in the mass media since 1990 provides an example of what can be achieved by a mass media campaign based on many of the principles outlined above. The campaign had three overall goals related to "sensible" alcohol consumption and an overall goal of reduction in total consumption. These goals were operationalized into four objectives that included increasing knowledge of, and the number of, people who followed the national recommended guidelines for consumption, and of increasing the number of local organizations active in support of the campaign.

Strunge (1998) reported the evaluation results for the years 1990–1996, during which annual mass media campaigns were developed and implemented. Awareness of the campaigns was high (around 70%) in each year except 1991, and was particularly high in 1990. This latter result was probably related to the provocative nature of the 1990 campaign, which resulted in additional publicity in the news media. Correspondingly, the lower 1991 result was seen to be the result of the lack of a provocative message, a smaller campaign budget (50% of the 1990 budget), lack of television advertising, and a longer time-lag (5 weeks) between the campaign closure and the evaluation.

The campaign was shown to have reached its knowledge objectives. Knowledge of the weekly unit guidelines was shown to increase steadily over the period from absolute zero in 1990 to 52% of the population in 1997. Knowledge of the unit contents of beer and wine (which is essential to know in order to calculate the weekly amounts consumed) was low for wine (35–42%), but high for beer (60–70%), with an annual but less marked increase during the period surveyed.

A small percentage of survey respondents indicated that the campaigns had directly influenced their behaviour (4–5%), and 12% of people surveyed in 1997 stated that they had reduced their alcohol consumption, with the majority reporting that health concerns were the motivation for this reduction.

In his description of the campaign, Strunge (1998) reveals that realistic goals were established, that the media campaign was supported by community action, that evaluation was an integral part of the campaign strategy, and that careful consideration was given to identifying the target group, the best advertising medium and an appropriate message. He concluded that "it is possible to generate positive awareness of alcohol information", and that "a continuous effort is necessary to maintain and increase the effects of the campaigns".

The Harvard Alcohol Project is an important alcohol harm-reduction project that has attempted to use edutainment to reduce alcohol-related problems. Beginning in 1988, the project sought to introduce the concept of a "designated driver" as a new social norm in the USA. A significant aspect of the project was the use of entertainment television to promote the designated driver concept. The slogan, "The Designated Driver is the Life of the Party" was used because:

1. It promotes a new social norm that the driver does not drink any alcohol.
2. It lends social legitimacy to the non-drinker's role.
3. It encourages people to plan ahead for transportation if they intend to drink.
4. It asks for only a modest shift in behaviour (Winsten, 1994).

By 1994, more than 160 prime-time television programmes had included the notion of the designated driver in a television episode, sometimes as a sub-plot, sometimes casually within the dialogue, and, on over 25 occasions, as the entire theme of the television show. In order to achieve this coverage, the project staff spoke with more than 250 producers and writers associated with all the leading prime time television entertainment shows and convinced them to support the project objectives.

Evaluation of the impact of the concept has been undertaken by using opinion polls that ask respondents about their use of designated drivers. DeJong (1997) reported that in 1993 64% of adults reported that "they and their friends assign a designated driver when they go out for social events where alcoholic beverages are consumed". Of those who assign a designated driver, two-thirds said that they always designate a driver.

DeJong & Winsten (1990) describe the Harvard Alcohol Project as "a mix of state-of-the-art advertising and public relations strategies". It is a product of social science research, such as social marketing theory, of thorough formative evaluation and of ongoing process, output and outcome evaluation, and of a comprehensive programme that included community organization and advocacy strategies.

Obstacles to "Successful" Mass Media Marketing

A range of obstacles to successful mass media marketing of alcohol-related messages can also be identified from the literature. These include, first, the complexity of changing individual behaviour through marketing, particularly in the substance use area; second, the suitability of the mass media as a means of prevention and the related fundamental differences between non-profit mass media marketing and commercial mass media marketing; and third, the power that the liquor industry has over the media through its considerable financial investment in advertising.

The complexity involved in changing individual behaviour through mass media marketing reduces the power of this strategy to reduce alcohol-related harm. The mass media, by its nature, has difficulty in targeting individuals whose behaviour social marketeers want to change. Even the very best population targeting strategy, with careful audience segmentation, still results in a scatter-gun approach, where many of the audience are not the target. Furthermore, the delay between uptake of the behaviour change sought and most of the health benefits to be received is often considerable. As Backer, Rogers & Sopory (1992) note:

> Preventive behaviour is a particularly difficult goal to achieve through mass media campaigns. An individual must change behaviour now to lower the probability of some unwanted future event that may not happen anyway (p. xiv).

The solution frequently used to address this delay, that of focusing marketing efforts on immediate benefits, will often result in campaigns to sell lesser, easy-to-gain benefits in favour of more significant longer-term benefits.

A second obstacle to the successful mass media marketing of alcohol harm-reduction messages is related to medium of the mass media itself. As a tool for educational purposes, the medium has significant constraints because most mass media outlets are privately owned and exist for the purposes of providing entertainment to its audience, with the sponsorship of its advertisers. Perry and Kelder (1992) suggest that:

> The mass media is primarily a private commercial entertainment medium which, as most research to date confirms, substantially limits its potential as a primary prevention method.

Related to this is the fundamental difference between non-profit mass media marketing and commercial mass media marketing. While commercial marketing principles have been useful in improving mass media marketing of alcohol health-related messages, the flexibility that commercial marketers have to change their product, price, promotion and/or place is simply not available to the public health field, which "cannot abandon its product and diversify its main interests just because its main product may not be very popular" (Tones, 1996). The need to reduce complex issues into the simple format demanded by the medium (such as the 30-second advertisement) is a third obstacle of the medium itself. However, one way to reduce the potential of this obstacle to nullify such mass media campaigns is to ensure that the campaign is part of a broader educational strategy, that utilizes a range of educational tools and methods to build on the attention created by mass media exposure.

Third, in most countries the liquor industry is one of the major advertisers within the mass media. Consequently, there is likely to be a level of self-censorship within the mass media against messages which could impact upon liquor sales. This censorship will affect paid advertising less than unpaid public or community service announcements, but will impact upon attempts to introduce "edutainment" to soap opera-style media. For example, Perry & Kelder (1992) suggest that:

> Even the Harvard project, while a model of cooperation, sponsored a message consistent with the alcohol industry of reducing liability rather than reducing the quantity consumed.

It is likely that anticonsumption messages will receive more hostile treatment from the mass media than those that do not directly challenge the consumption of alcohol.

Each of these obstacles indicate that mass media marketing is most suited to mainstream issues that seek incremental change, rather than those that directly challenge institutions such as the alcohol industry. Mass media advocacy, on the other hand, is a strategy well-suited to challenging institutional practices and creating systemic change.

MASS MEDIA ADVOCACY

The term "advocacy" has many connotations and has been defined in a number of ways, including:

> Advocacy is a catch-all word for the set of skills used to create a shift in public opinion and mobilize the necessary resources and forces to support an issue, policy or constituency (Wallack et al., 1993, p. 27).

> Public health advocacy—sometimes called public health lobbying—is an expression used most often to refer to the process of overcoming major structural (as opposed to individual or behavioural) barriers to public health goals (Chapman & Lupton, 1994, p. 6).

In this chapter, "advocacy" refers to the promotion of healthy behaviours and healthy public policy by influencing decision makers to accept the merit of processes, policies or structures that bestow a health advantage. A major tool used in this process is political lobbying, which is the presenting of arguments in favour of a particular policy course to those making the policy decision. Another is coalition building, which involves the development of groups and individuals in a community which have a common policy objective. A third is the use of mass media, typically the news media, to highlight and advance a particular public health issue. This approach has been promoted by Wallack (1990a) and is commonly referred to as "media advocacy".

A major challenge for health advocates is to move the debate from individually focused, simple definitions of problems to a level of complex sociopolitical conceptualization, where the targeted health problem is seen as a product of the interaction between the individual and the environment. According to Wallack et al. (1993):

> Advocacy is necessary to steer public attention away from disease as a personal problem to health as a social issue . . . (and) . . . advocacy is a strategy for blending science and politics with a social justice value orientation to make the system work better, particularly for those with the least resources (p. 5).

The most successful public health policy reformers have based their advocacy on sound research data and have utilized all three approaches to achieve their objectives. The approach has been successfully applied in the areas of smoking control (Erickson et al., 1990), workplace health promotion (Chapman & Lupton, 1994) and the alcohol, AIDS and nutrition areas (Wallack, 1990b).

The History and Politics of Advocacy

Advocacy is by no means a new process, as those involved in promoting prohibition on alcohol in the 1890s were engaged in just the same practices (Lewis, 1992). Advocacy was, however, generally confined to issues of patients' rights. In these issues, the role of advocates was to represent victims or sufferers of injustice by speaking on their behalf to the authority that controlled their circumstances. The definitions provided above reveal that the modern use of the term "advocacy" is much broader than that of patients' rights and less moralistic than temperance movement campaigns of the 1800s.

Advocacy is a political activity, because it encourages social change via a political route. Such change is likely to challenge the status quo and therefore the concept and practice of advocacy is often described in negative terms by those in government. Advocacy can target the laws of federal, state or local government, policies of governments or private institutions, or the actions of groups or industries that seek to oppose public health goals. However, the hostility provoked by any attempt to change the status quo is a significant barrier to advocacy goals.

Advocacy Strategies

While media advocacy is a subject of this chapter, there is increasing recognition that successful media advocacy is dependent upon the implementation of coalition building and political advocacy. As Wallack et al. (1993) note:

The reality is that mass media, whether public information campaigns, social marketing approaches, or media advocacy initiatives, are simply not sufficient to stimulate significant and lasting change on public health issues. The power for change comes from a broader advocacy that has widespread community support. Coalition building, leadership development, and extensive public participation form the foundation from which successful advocacy and media initiatives can make a difference (p. 27).

Media advocacy has been defined by a number of people. Some examples are:

Media advocacy refers to the strategic use of news media by those seeking to advance a social or public policy initiative (Holder & Treno, 1997, p. S190).

Media advocacy is the process of overcoming major structural (as opposed to individual or behavioural) barriers to public health goals (Chapman & Lupton, 1994, p. 6).

Media advocacy seeks to influence the selection of topics by the mass media and shape the debate about these topics. Media advocacy's purpose is to contribute to the development and implementation of social and policy initiatives that promote health and well-being and are based on the principles of social justice (Wallack et al., 1993, p. 73).

Media advocacy to reduce alcohol-related harm may be used for many different purposes. For example, it can be used to set a public agenda by heightening the profile of an alcohol-related problem through the presentation of research findings; it can be used to espouse the benefits or success of a programme or intervention in order to support its refunding; it can be used to publicly oppose or question the actions of members of the alcohol industry when those actions are likely to increase alcohol-related harm; it can support the call for increased resource allocation to address alcohol-related problems; or it can highlight the inadequacies of government action to address alcohol-related problems.

In practice, media advocacy can involve many different actions, from covert action such as releasing confidential information to the media, to overt actions such as issuing a media release related to concerns about an alcohol product like alcoholic ice-blocks. Chapman & Lupton (1994) provide a list of 66 advocacy issues, tips and discussion points, and illustrate these with numerous examples that provide public health workers with a comprehensive picture of media advocacy in practice. Examples include:

Advertising in advocacy. Careful use of advertising can support or even initiate news or current affairs coverage, as well as being an advocacy tool in its own right. For example, a large paid advertisement in the Australian newspapers called on state health ministers to introduce standard drinks labelling on alcohol containers (see example below). This advertisement was used to generate media releases in each state with local organizations available for interview, and consequently significant media coverage was gained.

Anniversaries. Health promoters can often create a "new" newsworthy story out of a story that occurred in the past by advertising an anniversary of an event or instituting a day of remembrance. Such events will probably be significant public events, such as gun massacres, notorious chemical spills or nuclear accidents, or the death of a famous person from a particular disease/condition. This is similar to "*piggy-backing*" which is the act of adding your issue to a similar current issue being run in the media. For example, in the event of a large chemical spill somewhere in the world, a local advocacy group may choose to parallel their concerns about a chemical warehouse in their area with this event. This act of "piggy-backing" will often be supported by the media and receive media coverage.

Creative epidemiology. This is a term used to describe the process of translating complex epidemiological data into media-friendly terms. For example, if 18,000 people per year die in Australia as a result of smoking (on average), 10 people die every day in Perth as a result of smoking. Large numbers can lose their impact and therefore it is often useful to localize and humanize statistics.

Letters to the editor. Like advertising, the writing of a letter to the editor of a newspaper is another form of undertaking media advocacy. It may also result in further public debate and media interest. Such letters, however, must fit within the guidelines issued by the newspaper and are more likely to be published if well written and topical.

Opinion polls. Opinion polls can be a very effective part of media advocacy, because they can form the basis of a media release. The use of polls to support your view is of course a standard ploy used by people for many years. Such polls are often treated sceptically by the public, but nevertheless they can be invaluable if used carefully. Even "quick and dirty" polls of small sample sizes, which ask questions that produce the "right" answers, when released before a decision making process is to begin, and when released by a respected organization, can prove effective. Polls by opponents of your view, or those of related issues, can also be valuable as an opportunity to present your case. A prompt response will be required to "piggy-back" on someone else's research.

Mass Media Advocacy to Reduce Alcohol-Related Harm: Case Study

An example of the role that media advocacy can play to reduce alcohol-related harm is described by Hawks (1996) and by Stockwell & Single (1997). They record the process, outputs and outcome of attempts to introduce compulsory "standard drinks" labelling on all Australian alcohol containers. Ultimately successful and the first such regulation in the world, this process was nevertheless complex and required considerable expertise, time and effort, as well as a mix of advocacy strategies, to effect the desired change.

In Australia the process of introducing the "standard drink" began in 1989 with a proposal for such labelling to the Ministerial Council on Drug Strategy. The initial proposal was followed by a lengthy period of consultation, during which research into the need for public education, and into identifying the amount of public support of the concept, was undertaken. Further submissions were developed and debated and considerable advocacy for change eventually resulted in the government decision to act, and the creation of a National Food Authority regulation that enshrined standard drink labelling on all alcohol containers. The latter and final event occurred in December 1995, 6 years after the first action was initiated. A single year during this period a single year (1994), included extensive media advocacy from public health advocates.

By 1994 public health advocates had established a formidable coalition that included a research organization, the National Centre for Research into the Prevention of Drug Abuse, and an advocacy agency, the Alcohol Advisory Council of Western Australia, and had the support of an industry group, the Winemakers Federation. The coalition undertook extensive "behind-the-scenes" political lobbying, using the research data collected to support the submissions that had been developed. Likewise, two large industry groups representing brewers and distillers also undertook considerable lobbying activity, producing a glossy brochure supporting their case and sending a delegation of representatives to meet with all relevant government ministers throughout Australia. To counter industry lobbying, and to support the other advocacy strategies, a concerted media advocacy strategy was implemented in 1994 in the lead-up to, and following, a meeting of the Ministerial Council on Drug Strategy (who were responsible for recommending such action to the government). A half-page advertisement supporting legislation of "standard drinks" was placed in Australia's major national newspaper by 19 individuals and organizations, and a series of press releases were issued during September and October 1994 that resulted in widespread media coverage. Public confirmation of government support for standard drink labelling occurred on 30 September 1994 and the regulation was created in December 1995.

Hawks (1996) and Stockwell & Single (1997) identify a number of factors that worked against, and a number of factors that worked for, the legislation of standard drink labelling. The key factors that worked against the development of the legislation were the lobbying and media advocacy activities of the liquor industry, which sought to discredit arguments for change, and that the Minister of Health at the time the campaign started was personally not in support of standard drink labelling. The key factors that encouraged the adoption of the legislation included, first, the existence of a national alcohol policy that, even in draft form in 1986, recommended the provision of information on alcohol content for consumers; second, the usefulness of the research in highlighting the need for standard drink labelling and of public support for it; third, the existence of two separate agencies that were able to finance relevant research and coordinate the advocacy strategy, respectively; and fourth, the impact of key individuals who linked the coalition through their roles and activities.

The experience of these authors provides important lessons about media advocacy. The first of these is that advocacy for major change usually requires considerable time and commitment. This is so even when health advocates hold "the high moral ground" (as in this example, where the opposition was identified by the public as tainted by the motive of financial profit). Furthermore, media advocacy and other advocacy strategies are essential to achieve change when change is likely to have powerful and financial opponents. Such opponents will almost certainly undertake advocacy of their own. Nevertheless, media advocacy requires extreme care during both its planning and its implementation. This was highlighted when the coalition used media advocacy to attack the liquor industry position, inadvertently criticizing the Winemakers' Federation, who subsequently threatened legal action against a coalition that it supported. Finally, key individuals can be critical to the success or failure of advocacy strategies, especially when they are at the centre of the flow of information and advocacy activity or have decision-making power.

Using Media Advocacy

The use of media advocacy should, therefore, be conditional on the fulfilment of two criteria. First, in using this strategy, consideration must be given to ensure that media advocacy is applied only in appropriate circumstances, i.e. those circumstances in which goals are likely to be achieved and in which the advocacy agency can withstand the inevitable opposition to their activities. The use of media advocacy can be, and has been, counterproductive to achieving the aims sought (see e.g. DeJong, 1996).

The second criterion, is to ensure that media advocacy is supported by other public health strategies wherever possible. The two other advocacy strategies noted earlier (coalition building and political lobbying) should not be seen to be less valuable than media advocacy, and all should be undertaken within the framework of a comprehensive public health strategy. The timely and skilled use of media advocacy within the framework of a comprehensive advocacy strategy is more likely to achieve the desired results than a stand-alone, opportunistic approach, even when it results in wide exposure.

COMBINING MASS MEDIA MARKETING AND ADVOCACY

While in this chapter we have sought to dissect the elements of mass media marketing independently of those of mass media advocacy, frequently both activities are undertaken simultaneously. It has already been noted that the careful use of advertising can assist in advocating for structural change. Similarly, advocacy activity can reinforce or play a part in modifying individual behaviour. This interplay is most transparent in the act of creating and disseminating publicity. Publicity is both a marketing method and an advocacy tool because the efforts to increase publicity about a topic are in themselves acts of advocacy, and the public display of activities aimed at creating structural change can reinforce an individual's thoughts or actions about a specific issue or behaviour.

The media advocacy activity undertaken in the Community Prevention Trial project by Holder and colleagues, and in the New Zealand Community Action Project of Casswell and colleagues, demonstrate the potential inter-relationship between mass media advocacy and mass media marketing.

Holder & Treno (1997) described how media publicity was used as part of a larger multi-community prevention project to highlight and support the specific prevention components that targeted drink–driving, underage drinking, responsible beverage service and alcohol availability. As part of the drink–driving component, local police departments were provided with additional breath-testing equipment and new passive sensor devices, which provided an additional aid in the detection of over-the-limit drivers with no observable symptoms of heavy drinking. Use of this equipment represented a new approach to the detection of drink–driving and was newsworthy within the affected communities because of its novelty, and because what was being done in each community had national practice ramifications. Holder & Treno (1997) considered that the news coverage encouraged increased enforcement efforts by police, because it indicated community support. In this respect the initiative should be considered media advocacy, because it sought a change in institutional practice. There is, however, also a marketing aspect to this example, because the media coverage was designed to increase the perceived risk of drink–driving detection at an individual level. Three conclusions were drawn from this media strategy:

1. Mass communication in itself is not enough to reduce alcohol-related trauma, but can be effectively used to reinforce specific environmental efforts to reduce high-risk alcohol-related activities, such as drink–driving.
2. Local communication is best presented through local news media and can focus public attention on alcohol-related problems without having to use professionally produced material.
3. Media advocacy can be taken up by community members if appropriate training is provided, which means that the capacity to use this prevention measure is capable of being institutionalized within the community.

The Community Action Project undertaken in New Zealand between 1982 and 1985 aimed to create change at both the individual and the community level (Casswell, Ranson & Gilmore, 1990). Utilizing an experimental design, it compared the impact of two levels of intervention, mass media campaigns only and mass media campaigns with parallel community action, against non-intervention control sites. The mass media intervention in the intervention sites consisted originally of advertisements focused at individuals, but subsequently, and with much controversy and publicity, was focused at the policy level. The

project staff used the controversy associated with the original marketing campaign to stimulate debate, and as a result created even more publicity around the individual behaviour
change sought. When the advertising agency was unwilling to support the development of
policy-focused, advocacy-related advertising, further controversy developed. As a result of
both the advertising and the associated controversy, the mass media campaign was identified as having a beneficial effect on the public support of a range of alcohol polices. In
summary, Casswell et al. (1990) concluded that:

> The results suggest that the mass media campaign, despite having a focus on individual drink-
> ing behaviour, served the function of keeping alcohol problems on the public agenda and main-
> taining support for healthy public policies (p. 9).

CONCLUSION

The examples described in this chapter reveal the increasing sophistication with which mass
media marketing and mass media advocacy are being applied to attempts to reduce alcohol-
related harm. The activities described reveal that mass media marketing can be a significant element in changing individual behaviour, and that mass media advocacy can be a
significant element in creating change to social structures that impact upon behaviour.
Indeed, each strategy can be used to reinforce the impact of the other.

The increasing success of these strategies can be attributed partly to new theories upon
which they are now developed, partly to implementation of improved techniques and practices, and partly to greater reflection upon past mistakes and successes. Most importantly,
however, has been the recognition that mass media marketing and mass media advocacy
are most effective when they are only two of many elements within a broader change strategy. Such a strategy also includes a range of other activities, such as community development and community mobilization, school and community education, health promotion,
policy development and institutionalization, coalition building and political lobbying. In
this context, mass media marketing and mass media advocacy have already proved themselves to be important elements of alcohol harm reduction research projects in the USA
(Holder & Treno, 1997), Australia (Midford, Boots & Cutmore, 1999) and New Zealand
(Stewart & Casswell, 1993). It is also the context within which "best practice" forms of mass
media marketing and advocacy have been, and will continue to be, successfully employed
to reduce alcohol-related harm.

KEY WORKS AND SUGGESTIONS FOR
FURTHER READING

Atkin, C. & Wallack, L. (Eds) (1990). *Mass Communication and Public Health: Complexities and Conflicts*. Newbury Park, CA: Sage.

The product of a conference convened in the USA to "explore how the mass media
could become a more potent weapon to improve public health", this book is a collation
of ideas and issues identified by a range of high-profile speakers. The subtitle, "Complexities and Conflicts", adequately describes the best aspect of this book: that is, it highlights the problems and difficulties (as well as positing solutions) experienced in the
process of creating change through mass media marketing and advocacy.

Chapman, S. & Lupton, D. (1994). *The Fight for Public Health—Principles and Practice
of Media Advocacy*. London: British Medical Journal Publishing Group.

If you want to know "how to do" media advocacy, read this book. An excellent book from experienced and successful practitioners, *The Fight for Public Health* is full of innovative ideas to advocate public health issues. In the words of another critic, "I only hope Chapman hasn't given away too many secrets for his own good".

Egger, G., Donovan, R. & Spark, R. (1993). *Health and the Media: Principles and Practices for Health Promotion.* Sydney: McGraw-Hill.

Originally conceived as material for a postgraduate distance-learning programme, this book is a comprehensive volume targeted at health professionals. It integrates the theories behind, and the knowledge gained from, many years of commercial marketing with a public health approach. It is an easy to read, practical and well-illustrated book that gives readers a step-by-step understanding of mass media marketing.

Wallack, L., Dorfman, L., Jernigan, D. & Themba, M. (1993). *Media Advocacy and Public Health—Power for Prevention.* Newbury Park, CA: Sage.

Wallack and colleagues understand the relationship between politics and health. Their book challenges the view that the role of public health practitioners is to facilitate change in individual behaviour. This thorough sociopolitical analysis provides readers with a framework within which to comprehend and implement advocacy activities that are also described and illustrated. This is a book that advocates advocacy with all the skill and determination that it encourages of its readers.

REFERENCES

Andréasson, S., Lindewald, B., Hjalmarsson, K., Larsson, J., Wallin, E. & Rehnman, L. (1999). Exploring new roads to prevention of alcohol and other drug problems in Sweden: the STAD project. In S. Casswell et al. (Eds), Kettil Bruun Society Thematic Meeting: Fourth Symposium on Community Action Research and the Prevention of Alcohol and other Drug Problems. Auckland, NZ: Alcohol and Public Health Research Unit.

Backer, T.E., Rogers, E.M. & Sopory, P. (1992). *Designing Health Communication Campaigns: What Works?* Newbury Park, CA: Sage.

Bandura, A. (1986). *Social Foundations of Thought and Action: A Cognitive Theory.* Englewood Cliffs, NJ: Prentice Hall.

Casswell, S., Ranson, R. & Gilmore, L. (1990). Evaluation of a mass-media campaign for the primary prevention of alcohol-related problem. *Health Promotion International*, **5**(1), 9–17.

Chapman, S. & Lupton, D. (1994). *The Fight for Public Health—Principles and Practice of Media Advocacy.* London: British Medical Journal Publishing Group.

DeJong, W. (1996). MADD Massachusetts vs. Senator Bourke: a media advocacy case study. *Health Education Quarterly*, **23**(3), 318–329.

DeJong, W. (1997). College students' use of designated drivers: the data are in. *Prevention Pipeline*, **Nov/Dec**, 25–27.

DeJong, W. & Atkin, C. (1995). A review of national television PSA campaigns for preventing alcohol-impaired driving, 1987–1992. *Journal of Public Health Policy*, **16**(1), 59–79.

DeJong, W. & Winsten, J.A. (1990). The use of mass media in substance abuse prevention. *Health Affairs*, **Summer**, 30–46.

Edwards, G. et al. (1994). *Alcohol Policy and the Public Good.* Oxford: World Health Organization.

Egger, G., Donovan, R. & Spark, R. (1993). *Health and the Media: Principles and Practices for Health Promotion.* Sydney: McGraw-Hill.

Erickson, A., Ricks, A., McKenna, J. & Romano, R. (1990). Past lessons and new uses of the media in reducing tobacco consumption. *Public Health Reports*, **105**, 244–257.

Hastings, G. & Haywood, A. (1991). Social marketing and communication in health promotion. *Health Promotion International*, **6**(2), 135–145.

Hawks, D. (1996). *Not Much to Ask for, Really! The Introduction to Standard Drink Labelling in Australia.* Unpublished report.

Holder, H.D. & Treno, A.J. (1997). Media advocacy in community prevention: news as a means to advance policy change. *Addiction,* **92**(2), S189–S199.

Howat, P. & Fisher, J. (1986). Should health education focus only on self-responsibility? *New Zealand Journal of Health, Physical Education and Recreation,* **19**(1), 10–15.

Lewis, M. (1992). *A Rum State: Alcohol and State Policy in Australia.* Canberra: Australian Government Publishing Service.

Midford, R., Boots, K. & Cutmore, T. (1999). COMPARI. In *Community Action to Prevent Alcohol Problems.* Copenhagen: World Health Organization.

Montagne, M. & Scott, D.M. (1993). Prevention of substance use problems: models, factors, and processes. *International Journal of the Addictions,* **28**(12), 1177–1208.

Nutbeam, D. & Harris, E. (1998). *Theory in a Nutshell: A Practitioner's Guide to Commonly Used Theories and Models in Health Promotion.* Sydney: University of Sydney.

Pentz, M.A., Dwyer, J.H., MacKinnon, D.P., Flay, B.R., Hansen, W.B., Wang, E.Y.I. & Johnson, C.A. (1989). A multicommunity trial for primary prevention of adolescent drug abuse: effects on drug prevention. *Journal of the American Medical Association,* **261**, 3259–3266.

Perry, C.L. & Kelder, S.H. (1992). Prevention. *Annual Review of Addictions Research and Treatment,* 453–472.

Powell, K.C. (1988). *Drinking and Alcohol in Colonial Australia, 1788–1901 for the Eastern Colonies.* National Campaign Against Drug Abuse Monograph Series, No 3. Canberra: Australian Government Publishing Service.

Prochaska, J.O. & DiClemente, C.C. (1992). Stages of change in the modification of problem behaviors. In M. Hersen, R.M. Eisler & P.M. Miller (Eds), *Progress in Behavior Modification.* Newbury Park, CA: Sage.

Prochaska, J.O., Redding, C.A. & Evers, K.E. (1997). The transtheoretical model and stages of change. In K. Glanz et al. (Eds), *Health Behaviour and Health Education: Theory, Research and Practice.* San Francisco, CA: Jossey-Bass.

Simons-Morton, B., Donohew, L. & Davis Crump, A. (1997). Health Communication in prevention of alcohol, tobacco, and drug use. *Health Education and Behaviour,* **October**, 544–554.

Stewart, L. & Casswell, S. (1993). Media advocacy for alcohol policy support: results from the New Zealand Community Action Project. *Health Promotion International,* **8**(3), 167–175.

Stockwell, T. & Single, E. (1997). Standard unit labelling of alcohol containers. In M. Plant, E. Single & T. Stockwell (Eds), *Alcohol: Minimising the Harm. What Works?* London: Free Association Books.

Strunge, H. (1998). Danish experiences of national campaigns on alcohol, 1990–1996. *Drugs: Education Prevention and Policy,* **5**(1), 73–79.

Thompson, B. & Kinne, S. (1990). Change theory: applications to community health. In N. Bracht (Ed.), *Health Promotion at the Community Level.* Newbury Park, CA: Sage.

Tones, K. (1996). Models of mass media: hypodermic, aerosol or agent provocateur? *Drugs: Education, Prevention and Policy,* **3**(1), 29–37.

Wallack, L. (1990a). Improving health promotion: media advocacy and social marketing approaches. In C. Atkin and L. Wallack (Eds), *Mass Communication and Public Health: Complexities and Conflicts.* Newbury Park, CA: Sage.

Wallack, L. (1990b). Two approaches to health promotion in the mass media. *World Health Forum,* **11**, 143–164.

Wallack, L., Dorfman, L., Jernigan, D. & Themba, M. (1993). *Media Advocacy and Public Health—Power for Prevention.* Newbury Park, CA: Sage.

Winsten, J.A. (1994). Promoting designated drivers: the Harvard Alcohol Project. *American Journal of Preventive Medicine,* **10**(Suppl. 1), 11–14.

Chapter 19

Alcohol Advertising and Sponsorship: Commercial Freedom or Control in the Public Interest?

Linda Hill
and
Sally Casswell
*Alcohol and Public Health Research Unit, University of Auckland,
Auckland, New Zealand*

Synopsis

Alcohol is marketed through an integrated mix of strategies: television, radio and print advertisements, point-of-sale promotions, the Internet, and the association of brands with a variety of sports and cultural events.

In all Western countries, the use of alcohol is promoted, despite policies to restrict alcohol sales through licensing and other laws. The question for policy makers is whether the active promotion of alcohol should be permitted, or to what extent it should be constrained in the public interest to reduce alcohol-related harm and health-care costs.

Policy decisions on laws banning broadcast alcohol advertising or industry self-regulation of advertising standards continue to be contested by vested industries and public health advocates, but this examination of national policy differences shows how outcomes are shaped by politico-legal contexts. Where permitted, the content of broadcast and other alcohol advertisements is often governed by industry codes of practice. However, it is argued that these are largely irrelevant to the way alcohol advertising and other promotional strategies work. The codes do not address the way modern marketing embeds alcohol brands and drinking in young people's lived experience through sports and other activities and in portrayals of the life-styles to which they aspire.

The Essential *Handbook of Treatment and Prevention of Alcohol Problems.* Edited by N. Heather and T. Stockwell.
© 2004 John Wiley & Sons Ltd. ISBN 0-470-86296-3.

A review of a growing body of research concludes that alcohol advertising has a small but contributory effect to individual drinking behaviour and levels of alcohol-related harm, such as road fatalities. Of particular interest are studies of the responses of children and young people, since industry profitability logically requires the continual recruitment of a new generation of young heavy drinkers. Research also shows the cumulative way that advertising helps to shape perceptions about alcohol, contributing to the climate in which policy decisions are made.

This research evidence supports policy action against the promotion of alcohol and its negative effects on health choices and on the social and physical environments in which those choices are made. The authors call for an internationally coordinated response to some alcohol marketing practices, while recognizing that politico-legal contexts will continue to shape effective local strategies.

In all countries in which alcohol is sold, its use is promoted through advertising and other marketing practices. Arguments in support of alcohol advertising are often based on the legality of drinking by adults and on their freedom to receive information about a legal product (DISCUS, 1998; O'Neil, 1997; Starek, 1997; Pedlowe, 1998; Buchanan & Lev, 1989). An alternative view is that advertising and marketing is inherent to the *sale* of alcohol, which is regulated. This latter view underlies perspectives on alcohol advertising policy from countries traditionally more focused on a collective responsibility to protect the public interest, than on the pursuit of individual rights and freedoms.

In all Western countries, the sale of alcohol and the management of drinking venues and outlets are routinely restricted and licensed by law. Alcohol may therefore best be described as a regulated product, rather than a legal one. Advertising and other promotions are also constrained by forms of state regulation or self-regulation by the advertising, media, hospitality and alcohol industries involved. This chapter reviews marketing practices in different countries as outcomes of policy struggles over whether or what aspects of alcohol promotion should be regulated by the state or left to voluntary industry codes.

This chapter locates alcohol marketing practices within the political economy through the strategies and interests of the producing, retailing, advertising and media industries involved. Available research on how children, young people and others respond to alcohol advertisements on television, the most powerful of marketing media, is reviewed. Through the mass media and through promotions that embed alcohol into lived experience, new generations are recruited to drinking by linking alcohol brands to various adult life-styles that young people aspire to. In considering restrictions on the promotion of alcohol in the interest of public health, attention is given to politico-legal contexts underlying differing policy approaches adopted in different countries.

REACHING NEW MARKETS AND NEW GENERATIONS

The globalization of alcohol ownership and production (Jernigan, 1997; Walsh, 1997) contributes to coherence between marketing strategies in particular countries, and to international organization to influence policy frameworks that constrain sales and marketing (Marin Institute, 1998; Babor et al., 1996). A trend towards convergent patterns of drinking in European countries with traditionally different cultures around alcohol has been attributed to beer and distilled spirits advertising that transcends national boundaries (Gual & Colum, 1997). The promotion of alcohol and the softening of policy constraints are no less important in the "emerging markets" now being targeted in developing countries (Jernigan, 1997).

In English-speaking countries, about 10% of drinkers drink about half of the total alcohol consumed; it is this sector that contributes most to the alcohol producers' markets

(Casswell, 1997). Young males are most likely to be recruited to be these heavy drinkers and are disproportionately represented in statistics on alcohol-related harm, such as drink-driving, injury and premature mortality (Shanahan & Hewitt, 1999; Wyllie, Millard & Zhang, 1996; Fillmore et al., 1998; Leino et al., 1998). This drinking distribution is maintained over time, despite drinking levels abating among most men as they reach their 30s. The logical implication is that the alcohol industry continually needs to recruit new generations of young heavy drinkers in order to maintain profitability.

The question for policy makers in all countries is whether the active promotion of alcohol should be permitted, or to what extent it should be constrained in the public interest to help reduce alcohol-related harm and health-care costs (van Iwaarden, 1985; Mosher & Jernigan, 1989).

SHAPING THE SOCIAL CLIMATES AROUND ALCOHOL

Running counter to greater public awareness of risks and health-care costs associated with drinking have been pressures to deregulate the sale of alcohol. This is partly an effect of a wider politics of deregulation, but also of efforts to promote a public discourse in which alcohol is "normalized" as part of everyday life and drinking is seen as a matter of individual choice and responsibility. This choice is informed and created by direct and indirect means: not only advertisements and promotions but the unproblematic portrayal of drinking in entertainment and editorializing on television, radio, film and print. In these ways the alcohol industry acts as a "drug educator" (Stewart & Casswell, 1990), reaffirming drinking cultures, inculcating new generations and creating an environment supportive of industry when policy decisions are taken on alcohol regulation and public health strategies (Casswell, 1997, 1995a,b).

The impact of marketing on beliefs about the benefits of alcohol (Synder & Blood, 1992; Slater & Domenech, 1995) impairs the efforts of health promotion by creating what Wallack (1983) has described as a "hostile environment". Such an effect occurs not only through the impact directly on the beliefs of the younger drinker but may be shown in the attitudes of parents, family, the creators of health promotion communications and all those who might be expected to bring social influence to bear on the drinking culture. Such an effect is also likely on the decisions of policy makers. Print and broadcast media act as an indirect link between policy makers and the public, and decisions by policy makers to allow marketing of alcohol send a meta-message about the social climate surrounding alcohol to the public. Reciprocal effects are also likely and there may be influence on policy makers' subsequent decisions about other public policies which have a direct impact on drinking and related harm (McCombs & Shaw, 1972; Partanen & Montonen, 1988; Postman et al., 1988; van Iwaarden, 1985).

Content analyses of advertising show little portrayal of harmful consequences of drinking (Breed & DeFoe, 1979; Atkin & Block, 1981; Thomson et al., 1994) and Mosher & Wallack (1979) concluded that alcohol advertising was misleading, given the absence of accurate health information. Health promotion campaigns in the absence of broadcast advertising have been found to influence the social climate around alcohol (Casswell et al., 1990) but there is often a marked imbalance between the extent of commercial marketing and of health promotion material (Wallack, 1983; Thomson et al., 1994).

COMMERCIALIZED BROADCAST MEDIA

The alcohol industry promotes brands known world-wide alongside others that symbolize local loyalties, using an integrated mix of marketing strategies and media.

Television now reaches into most homes in Western countries and is rapidly increasing its audiences in developing countries. In many countries the broadcast media were established by the state, allowing early technical development to be funded by taxpayers. In the deregulatory 1980s and 1990s there has been pressure to move broadcasting to private ownership, with increased licensing of private stations and channels and increased commercialization of much state broadcasting. The resulting competition increases commercial pressures to liberalize alcohol advertising constraints.

In the New Zealand example, the stages in the restructuring and commercialization of broadcasting were paralleled by policy changes to permit first broadcast advertising for alcohol outlets, then corporate or sponsorship advertisements by alcohol producers and, from 1992, advertisements for alcohol brands were permitted in exchange for free air time for alcohol health promotion advertisements (Thomson et al., 1994; Casswell et al., 1993; Casswell, 1995a). Television alcohol ads quadrupled between 1991 and 1993 (Wyllie et al., 1996). In 1997 alcohol industry exposure in all media was around 10 times alcohol health promotion exposure (Hunter, 1997). The two companies that dominate the New Zealand alcohol market are large accounts for the media and advertising industries, who therefore have a strong investment in supporting their clients' lobby for alcohol advertising to continue under a voluntary code.

Radio, with its lower costs, attracts advertising by local drinking venues and alcohol outlets, as well as by major brands. In a New Zealand study, the four most common categories of advertisement were discounts for bulk purchase at bottle stores, discounted drinks in drinking venues, free drinks with meals, and bar tabs as prizes (Maskill & Hodges, 1997)—all promotions that may be considered to encourage hazardous drinking. None are covered by the current code on alcohol advertising. Moreover, the line between programme content, commentary and advertising messages is less clear-cut on radio than for television or print—sometimes deliberately so.

POINT-OF-SALE PROMOTIONS

The point-of-sale promotions featured in radio advertising are also of concern to inspectors and health promoters encouraging responsible management of licensed premises (Hill & Stewart, 1996). Price has been shown to be an effective mechanism for curbing consumption levels and intoxication, particularly among young and lower-income drinkers (Edwards et al., 1994). Discounting and price wars, "happy hours", "free drinks for females", "shooters", "yard glasses", "all-you-can-drink" evenings and some pub entertainments will have the contrary effect. The most problematic of these practices are usually in hotels, pubs and clubs, where young men do much of their heavy drinking and experience most alcohol-related problems (Casswell, Zhang & Wyllie, 1993; Stockwell et al., 1992). Since such promotions are advertised to attract customers, it may be a question of strategy whether these should be banned as irresponsible advertising or as irresponsible management reflecting on suitability to hold a licence to sell alcohol.

PROMOTING ALCOHOL THROUGH SPORTS AND CULTURE

Where alcohol advertising is banned, or partially banned, on the broadcast media, other marketing practices take on greater importance—as has been noted with the international tobacco industry (Deeks, 1992), from which alcohol borrows many of its strategies. Much research focuses on broadcast advertising, but by the early 1990s more than half of all advertising expenditure was other forms of promotion (Stewart & Rice, 1995). Most effective among these is marketing through sporting activities that attract young males, the group most likely to be—or to learn to be—heavier drinkers.

In New Zealand and Australia, there is a long-standing association between beer and those "old signifiers of masculine potency" and national pride, rugby players (Star, 1993; Hill, 1999; Phillips, 1984). The problem of "lager louts" at home and away games shows similar British linkages between football, nationalism and alcohol. Sports clubs are the social centre of many small communities in which youngsters learn about sports but also about drinking (Rekve, 1997). In Australasia, problematic and underage drinking in clubs and at sports events has become a focus of public health and regulatory concern, and of new cross-sectoral initiatives for alcohol health promotion.

In the USA, deals between beer sellers and baseball parks date back to the 1870s, but modern sports marketing of alcohol took off in 1970, the year tobacco advertising on television was restricted and Philip Morris took over Miller Breweries, sponsors of The Braves. High-powered sales techniques from the cigarette brand wars were applied to marketing alcohol as well as cigarettes through sports. These included market segmentation and targeting, image-orientated life-style marketing and an integrated mix of promotion types for each brand. The phenomenal growth of Miller led Anheuser-Busch and Coors to follow suit (Buchanan & Lev, 1989) in strategies now adopted world-wide.

Alcohol sponsorship deals for sports events, teams and clubs now routinely involve naming rights ("Smirnoff League", "Coors Extra Gold Motor Spectacular") and mentions in sports commentaries; signage on clothing, sports grounds and products retailed to fans; and opportunities for direct marketing through product donations and exclusive "pourage rights". Packages worth millions of dollars are concluded between sports federations and alcohol corporates to be the official beer of the World Cup or the Olympics (Baird, 1998). Sponsorship money is the price of entry to an event and its marketing opportunities, but high "leverage" spending on related media and retail promotions ensures maximum exposure and maximum sales.

A study of motor racing highlights promotional opportunities that move beyond passive absorption of images to embed the product in the lived experience and everyday activities of consumers and potential consumers, tapping into social processes that establish and reinforce cultural identity (Buchanan & Lev, 1989). Television commercials increasingly meet inattention, saturation or resistance (Clark, 1989), but sports sponsorship accesses audiences when they are most receptive to "experiential learning" about a product—while having a good time at an exciting branded event. Sports events attract large numbers of the right kind of audience—the young men likely to be heavier drinkers. Sponsorship agreements detail promotional opportunities evaluated by the number of carefully crafted "impressions" bombarding potential customers, together with on-site opportunities to try the product (Buchanan and Lev, 1989). Many events are family affairs, and alcohol "impressions" are also made on young people well below the drinking age, helping form in adolescence the attitudes and preferences that are taken on into later life (Kelder et al., 1994).

> It is one thing that adult fans are being exposed to it, but it is something completely different that 5 year-olds are walking around with a Liverpool T-shirt with Carlsberg written on it. . . . Building up a loyalty to label commodities among children and young people can be an investment that will provide an income for several decades (Rekve, 1997).

Global communications technology takes live and recorded sport into the homes of millions of potential customers. This makes sports, particular those signifying manhood and national pride, into a revenue-generating vehicle that delivers mass audiences for product promotions, as corporate, sporting and commercial broadcasting interests meet. Collaborations between the industries involved have included filming for best inclusion of alcohol signage, sometimes by the advertiser's agencies for supply to minor broadcasters. Home audiences, like event participants, see sponsorship brand logos and signage on sports fields and clothing in a different light from regular advertisements (Buchanan & Lev, 1989).

Football and motor sports are traditional routes to mass beer markets among young working-class males, but premium beers and spirits-based products seek niche markets by targeting diverse consumer identities through other sports, such as athletics, ice hockey, basketball, skiing, snowboarding. Specialist sport marketers now research and select sports to sponsor that will deliver particular target markets (Taylor, 1999). For those to whom there is more to life than sport, alcohol producers are also targeting rock music. Ballantine's follow up snowboarding events with live concerts, noting that young people are inspired by music, sport and modern technology (Rekve, forthcoming). Wine industries target older drinkers, including women, through a range of cultural events, and by promoting a sophisticated "culture" around wine itself.

WORLD WIDE WEB MARKETING

Alcohol is being embedded in virtual lives, as well as sporting ones. A German website for Ballantine's offers free animation software, allowing web surfers to socialize in an interactive bar. Surfers are asked to respect local drinking age laws in entering the bar. US beer websites also make a virtual game out of age identification. Carlberg's website provides Top 10 listings for various pop genres, next to hyperlinks to on-line supermarkets for beer supplies. All these features are devices of mass customization designed to attract high and repeat usage by browsers in the targeted audience group (Watson et al., 1998). A 1997 study concluded that the visual and interactive nature of the Internet puts unprecedented power in the hands of alcohol marketers, especially in reaching and influencing the young (Montgomery, 1997).

The US ban on broadcast tobacco advertising is interpreted as applying to *all* electronic media, meaning the absence of major tobacco producers on the Internet, in contrast with the growing presence of major alcohol producers.

SELLING LIFE-STYLES AND FANTASIES

Modern advertising targets mass and niche markets by associating brands with consumer identities and desired life-styles, sometimes through devices as simple as placing a brand logo at the end of life-style images.

> A beer is a beer is a beer . . . So therefore it is all about brands . . . We are not selling beer, we are selling image (Asia Pacific Breweries CEO, in Jernigan, 1997, pp. 9–10).

Dominant images in beer advertising are masculinity and national pride, presented through different models of male identity (Hill, 1999; Law 1997; Thomson et al., 1994; Postman et al., 1988). Adulthood is marked by new patterns of socializing, and alcohol is a powerful symbol of this—and of masculinity itself. This is explicit in a recent New Zealand beer slogan: "Lion Red—what it means to be a man" (Hill, 1999).

Some beer ads use subtle and acceptable imagery that nevertheless evokes known stereotypes of masculinity. Others use humour to present extreme stereotypes in ways that allow the drinker to claim the brand while distancing himself psychologically from his own drinking (Abrahamson, 1998; Law, 1997). The effectiveness of linking masculinity with sports was demonstrated in a US study of male teenagers who consistently preferred televized beer advertisements with sports content, compared with those without (Slater et al., 1995). Themes of masculinity and regionalism are also evoked in some spirits ads, particularly for whisky. Others employ less gendered messages about partying, and increasingly adopt swirling, magical imagery conveying the "mind-altering" qualities of alcohol (Hill, 1999).

Image advertising is responded to positively, especially by younger recipients (Covell, 1992; Kelly & Edwards, 1998). Research has shown that advertising becomes increasingly salient to young people over the age-span 10–14 years (Aitken et al., 1988) and 10–13 year-old males were more likely than older teenagers to say that alcohol advertising was an important source of information about drinking, and did encourage teenagers to drink (Wyllie et al., 1998b). Effective advertising operates at the symbolic, intuitive level of consciousness (Lannon & Cooper, 1983) and by linking attractive people with aspirational life-styles (Breed & DeFoe, 1979; Atkin & Block, 1981; Madden & Grube, 1994). This includes social camaraderie or "mateship" (Lieberman & Orlandi, 1987; Wyllie et al., 1997), so important for young people, which provides vicarious reinforcement for alcohol use (Bandura, 1977).

RELATIONSHIP BETWEEN ADVERTISING, CONSUMPTION AND HARM

A considerable body of research has attempted, using a variety of methodologies, to investigate whether there is a discernible link between advertising and consumption at either the aggregate or the individual level. These research data have played an important part in the policy debate around alcohol advertising and several analyses have been funded by industry sources (e.g. Strickland, 1982; Calfee & Scherega, 1994). Mosher & Jernigan (1989) have, however, described proof of the direct impact of advertising on drinking practices and problems as tangential from the standpoint of a public health model that stresses the need for consistency throughout the environment.

In the 1970s and early 1980s, much of the research on effects centred on econometric analysis of expenditure on advertising in relation to aggregate consumption data. This body of research produced some conflicting results, although the analyses from Britain covering the period from the mid-1950s to the late 1970s showed positive relationships for some beverages (McGuiness, 1980, 1983; Duffy, 1981). Other studies showed no effects (Bourgeois & Barnes, 1979; Ornstein & Hanssens, 1985; Grabowski, 1976), including a recent analysis of four European countries in the 1970s and 1980s (Calfee & Scherega, 1994). This approach is limited by the degree to which advertising expenditure varies, and Saffer (1993) suggested that, in many countries in which analyses have been carried out, advertising was already at high levels. He has instead looked at countries in which advertising bans have been implemented, compared with those in which they have not, carrying out cross-country time series analysis (Saffer, 1991). This showed an impact on both consumption and motor vehicle fatalities. The comparison of 17 countries for the period 1970–1983 found, for example, that the countries with a ban on spirits advertising had 16% lower consumption and 10% lower motor vehicle fatalities than countries with no such ban. The most recent study of the impact of advertising bans updated Saffer (1991) adding additional years and countries and correcting for serial correlation and endogeneity of advertising bans. It utilised a pooled time series data set from 20 countries over 26 years. This study concluded that alcohol advertising bans decreased alcohol consumption (Saffer and Daue, 2002). These studies contrasted with earlier investigations that found no effect of more partial and short-term bans (Smart

& Cutler, 1976; Makowsky & Whitehead, 1991; Schweitzer et al., 1983; Ogborne & Smart, 1980). A later regression analysis by Saffer (1997), comparing different regions of the USA using quarterly data from 1986–1989 and controlling numerous other relevant variables, found an impact of advertising on motor vehicle fatalities which was significant (although smaller than that of price).

Other research has looked for effects at the individual level. Experimental studies in which consumption behaviour was measured following exposure to alcohol advertising showed mixed results, but those showing more sophistication in design, with participants unaware of the purpose of the study and naturalistic settings (Atkin, 1995), have shown some positive effects. Some effect was shown on blood alcohol levels after viewing print advertisements for alcohol, but only if the advertisements were viewed while the people were already drinking (McCarty & Ewing, 1983). Other studies of print advertisements showed no effect on later consumption (Kohn et al., 1984). Television advertising, which might be expected to be more powerful in its effects, has been investigated in a number of studies with mixed results. For example, male college students shown advertising embedded in television programmes in relatively naturalistic settings were more likely to choose alcohol rather than soft drink (Kohn & Smart, 1984) and were likely to drink more (Wilks et al., 1992). However, the effects differed, depending on the timing and the number of ads shown, and a study using a less naturalistic situation showed no effect (Sobell et al., 1986).

An immediate impact of advertising on drinking, as measured in the previous studies, would not be expected if a more cumulative effect of advertising is assumed (Gerbner et al., 1986). In this perspective, which assumes a gradual effect over many thousands of exposures, it is more likely that an impact would be measured on the cognitions which arise when processing the advertising messages (Petty & Caccioppo, 1981). Two recent studies have measured such an effect on beliefs. Following repeated exposure to beer advertising, college students rated alcohol as more beneficial and less risky (Synder & Blood, 1992) and reported more positive assessments of the benefits of beer (Slater & Domenech, 1995). Such positive beliefs were predictive of plans about future alcohol use (Slater et al., 1995), although exposure of school children to advertisements did not effect expectancies of drinking (Lipsitz et al., 1993).

The effect of repeated exposure to advertising is also measured in the many surveys that compare participants who have been highly exposed and who report greater awareness or more positive responses to advertisements, with those who do not. This has been a very popular approach since the late 1970s, beginning with a large research programme funded by the US Bureau of Alcohol, Tobacco and Firearms (Atkin & Block, 1981, 1984). All of the many cross-sectional analyses of such survey data have found evidence of a positive relationship between self-reported exposure and/or response to advertising and positive beliefs and reports of consumption. In Atkin & Block's work, those who reported seeing the most advertisements tended to perceive the typical drinker as somewhat more fun-loving, happy and good-looking, and in turn this was associated with more favourable values regarding the amounts, situations and benefits of drinking (Atkin & Block, 1981, 1984). There were also differences in the levels of drinking reported by those who were more exposed and recalled advertising more. An analysis of 1227 people, mostly aged 12–22 years, found 33% of the half who were more exposed were drinking at least 5–6 drinks per week, compared with 16% of the less exposed (Atkin et al., 1983). Other studies have demonstrated an association between positive beliefs, expectancies of future drinking and/or current drinking behaviour (Strickland, 1982; Atkin et al., 1983; Grube & Wallack, 1994; Wyllie et al., 1998a,b). The likelihood that these associations reflect a causal effect of advertising on drinking has been strengthened by the use of structural equation modelling (Bentler, 1993) to analyse the more recent surveys. This found that the data are good fits to models assuming a causal pathway between advertising and expectations of future drinking (Grube & Wallack, 1994) and positive beliefs and consumption levels (Wyllie et al., 1998a,b).

Two published analyses of longitudinal data have similarly found an impact of response to advertising on consumption. In the first, the numbers of alcohol advertisements recalled at age 15 in response to a question about the portrayal of alcohol in the media significantly predicted heavier drinking among males aged 18 (Connolly et al., 1994). In the second analysis, liking for advertising measured at age 18 predicted heavier drinking and experience of more alcohol-related problems at age 21 (Casswell & Zhang, 1998). A follow up study when the longitudinal study members were 26 showed a small impact of liking for advertising on frequency of drinking (Casswell et al., 2002).

A review of the evidence of the effects of advertising published in 1994 suggested that alcohol advertising had a small but contributory effect on drinking behaviour (Edwards et al., 1994). The evidence published since that review further strengthens that conclusion.

LAWS RESTRICTING ADVERTISING

In many but not all Western countries, alcohol is being promoted on a falling market. A decline in aggregate consumption since the 1970s in part reflects the impact of preventative interventions to reduce alcohol-related harm (WHO, 1998; Stockwell et al., 1997; Moskowitz, 1989). These include excise taxes affecting price, drink–driving laws, responsible server training, mass media alcohol awareness campaigns and health promotion in schools and communities (Holder, 1994; Holder & Edwards, 1995; Stewart, 1997). Contributing market factors may include competition from soft drinks and a wider choice of items attractive to the youth market.

The alcohol industry has adopted marketing strategies developed by the tobacco industry, particularly in regard to attracting the young (Vaidya et al., 1996; Pollay et al., 1996; Meier, 1991). Research evidence led to widespread bans on broadcast advertising of tobacco on the logic that "any other measures . . . would not work as well if they had to compete with stylish and powerful tobacco advertising" (Secretary of State for Health, 1998). Similar policy conclusions can be reached from the growing body of research showing the contribution of alcohol advertising to alcohol-related harm.

All Western countries, to a greater or lesser extent, place constraints on alcohol advertising, using a mixture of state legislation and industry self-regulation (see Appendix). Outcomes reflect policy struggles in specific political and cultural contexts, and systems remain in flux as decisions continue to be contested. Restrictions by law are most common for banning alcohol advertisements from the broadcast media. Despite commercial pressures and the wider deregulatory climate, the trend is towards seeking stricter rather than more lenient controls in both regulatory or self-regulatory systems (Montonen, 1996).

Norway permits no alcohol advertising at all; France does not permit television advertising. Belgium has no advertising on state television, bans spirits advertising on commercial channels and all alcohol advertising on radio. Other countries, such as Austria and Ireland, ban broadcast advertising of spirits, or of beverages above a particular alcohol content, which may exclude just spirits, as in Spain and Finland, or all beverages except lower-alcohol beers, as in Denmark and Sweden. New Zealand, Italy and Portugal restrict alcohol advertising to later hours of viewing, and this has also been proposed by the German Minister of Health. Behind some of these outcomes are unsuccessful efforts to secure more restrictive legislation.

Until recently, the major spirits producers in the UK, the US and Germany maintained voluntary bans against advertising on television. The UK 30 year voluntary ban on advertising "dark spirits" on radio or television was abandoned in 1995 because of falling sales, particularly for whisky. The US spirits ban in 1948 (following a radio ban from 1936) was a closed-door commitment by industry to avert Senate proposals to ban all alcohol advertising on television. The ban was breached in 1996 by the Canadian company Seagram, following a sharp decline in its Asian markets. It was then lifted by the Distilled Spirits Council on the argument that other alcoholic beverages had an "unfair" advantage (DISCUS, 1996). Spirits advertisements were accepted by local and cable channels but by only one national network, Black Entertainment Television. This continuing situation represents an informal response by the networks to a high level of public controversy and political opposition (Center for Science in the Public Interest, 1998).

However, all efforts to formally restrict spirits advertising on US television have foundered. President Clinton, Rep. Joseph Kennedy and 16 state administrations applied for action by the Federal Communications Commission, the body that banned tobacco broadcast advertising. This was declined (Quello, 1997; Hundt, 1997). A 1997 bill asking Congress to "just say no" to advertising spirits on "any medium of electronic communication" failed to achieve sufficient support. A further bill was tacitly premised on a view of drinking as a "legal" adult activity; it argued for a ban on all alcohol advertising because of its harmful impact on children. Finally, in 1998 the Federal Trade Commission (FTC) was directed by Congress to investigate whether advertising practices by eight major alcohol producers targeted those under the legal drinking age.

The argument undermining these efforts to achieve a ban was that the First Amendment to the Constitution provides some, if lesser, protection for commercial speech. Restriction by government must pass three tests: the government interest must be substantial, the restriction must directly advance that interest, and it must not be more extensive than necessary to do so (Starek, 1997). The onus that this puts on government agencies to prove causal relationships undermines any "threat" of regulation by law. However, US courts may consider state restrictions constitutional if they relate to unlawful behaviour—such as sales to under-age drinkers (Starek, 1997). Hence the shift in tactical direction to a more limited inquiry into advertising standards.

This lack of success in countering alcohol advertising contrasts with strong state-level regulation of alcohol sales, reflecting contemporary societial concerns about drinking as well as a strong temperance tradition (Room, 1989). It is attributable in part to a particular US constitutional protection and related politico-legal discourse, which makes particular arguments available while limiting others. It has meant, for example, that warning labels on alcohol containers have been an achievable strategy, whereas television advertising bans have not. Warning labels, implemented first for tobacco products, then for alcohol in 1988, are consistent with discourses on freedom of commercial speech and on information requirements for efficient markets. However, this discourse also enabled the labelling of wine bottles with messages about health benefits of moderate alcohol consumption.

Research shows that alcohol container warning labels have had some success in increasing awareness, reaching target audiences and, to a more limited extent, influencing individual behaviour (Greenfield, 1997). Health warnings on television alcohol advertising could also influence beliefs regarding the risks and benefits of alcohol use in the long term (Slater & Domenech, 1995). This has several times been included in bills, without success, as has removing tax deductibility for company expenditure on alcohol advertising (Mosher, 1982). In 1992 the Advertising Tax Coalition and the State Advertising Coalition helped defeat an amendment in the US House of Representatives and 14 state initiatives to tax advertising (Saffer, 1997). Saffer estimated that such a move on advertising would reduce motor vehicle fatalities by about 1300 per year in the USA.

Across the border, Canada has a very different regulatory tradition. The sale of alcohol is strongly regulated by each province; drinking venues are licensed and sales by the bottle are a state monopoly. The Canadian Radio and Television Commission (CRTC) bans spirits advertising on television, although this is under pressure following Seagram's actions in the USA. Radio and television advertising are permitted for beer and wine and come under a CRTC code (Canadian Radio and Television Commission, 1996). However, the content of all alcohol advertisements is also regulated by each provincial Act. A distinctive issue is the prohibition of prizes, gifts or premiums with the purchase of alcohol (ASC, 1999).

France also has a strong stand against the promotion of alcohol, although its regulation of alcohol sales is light. Despite challenges under European treaties, the Loi Evin has banned alcohol advertising on television, ads directed at the young or on sports fields, most alcohol sports sponsorship, and also restricts radio advertising. To obtain change in the "simplistic and seductive discourse" that underlay earlier alcohol advertising images of leisure, sun, sex and success (Craplet, 1997), alcohol advertisement content is restricted to product characteristics and facts about consumption, production and region of origin. In most countries, however, the content of alcohol advertisements comes under voluntary codes, not state regulation.

INDUSTRY SELF-REGULATION OF ADVERTISING STANDARDS

In Australia, New Zealand, Ireland and some other countries where alcohol advertising is permitted on broadcast media, self-regulation through voluntary codes variously involves the media, advertising and alcohol industries (ASA, 1998; ASB, 1998; ASAI, 1999), and stands alongside more general rules on advertising standards.

Self-regulation in the USA is weakly organized in comparison with other countries, which regulatory theory would attribute to lack of a credible threat of state regulation (Ayres & Braithwaite, 1992). Advertising and media industry codes do not mention alcohol; separate voluntary codes cover beer, wine and most recently spirits, with complaints going to the industry organization that wrote the code. The only independent body to have considered alcohol advertising is the Federal Trade Commission (FTC), responsible for market competition and consumer choice but also for complaints about "unfair or deceptive" practices and "conduct injurious to consumers". In investigating advertising practices by eight large beer and spirits companies, it found that half the companies were not in compliance with their code, and two companies targeted those under the legal drinking age in a quarter of their advertisements. Nevertheless, the FTC recommended continuance of self-regulation, but with third-party review of complaints (FTC, 1999; Wiecking, 1999).

In theory, a voluntary code can be monitored by the public, but the effectiveness of this will depend on widespread knowledge of the code and a sufficiently independent complaints body with powers of sanction. Only Ireland's current code fits this description, although its sanctions are seldom used. Most advertising campaigns are designed as short bursts to avoid saturation effects, so complaints decisions must be fast. "Pre-vetting" may increase effectiveness, but industry self-regulation against its vested interests not infrequently leads to under-regulation and under-enforcement (Baggott, 1989). In Australia, self-regulation of alcohol advertising collapsed following strong criticism (Saunders & Yap, 1991; Rearck Research, 1991), and it was 2 years before a new code was negotiated. These problems are inherent, since the essence of self-regulation is that compliance with codes is voluntary (Montonen, 1996). Legislation may provide a formal framework that requires self-regulation, but no existing code of alcohol advertising standards is supported by state monitoring or sanctions, as for some other areas of business activity (Boddewyn, 1995; Baggott, 1989; Grabosky, 1995).

Recommendations to strengthen self-regulatory systems still do not address the content of industry codes, or the demonstrated "creativity" by which advertisement design continually outwits any restrictions (Clark, 1989).

CONTESTED CONTENT AND SCOPE OF VOLUNTARY CODES

Most voluntary codes on alcohol advertising fail to address the full range of promotional activities, and pay little attention to sports. Codes typically prohibit the portrayal of excessive drinking, underage drinkers, promises of social or sexual success and similar matters. However, the scope and the content of industry codes remain hotly contested ground between industry and public health advocates. Additions and refinements result from complaints, reviews and controversial advertisements.

The use of frog cartoons and Halloween imagery by major beer brands has been controversial in the USA (Leiber, 1998; Center for Alcohol Advertising, 1998), leading to recent changes in the Beer Institute's code (1999). In Britain there has been a similar outcry over cartoon characters on "alcopop" containers. But alcopops themselves are considered by many to be a product designed to attract children (Board of Science and Education, 1999; *The Globe*, 1997). Soft drinks mixed with colourless, tasteless spirits or liqueurs have long acted as a "bridge" drink (Clark, 1989). Alcopops are made attractive to teenage tastes by similar packaging to soft drinks and by being instantly ready.

In the USA, as efforts at the national level met frustration, resistance to local advertising developed in communities. In Baltimore, Chicago and Los Angeles, neighbourhood campaigns resulted in city ordinances banning alcohol billboards in inappropriate locations, such as near school playgrounds. These were contested in court. Once again, a policy struggle over alcohol advertising and responsible practices turned on what grounds and what level of power was required to restrict constitutional freedoms. In April 1999, however, a federal bill was passed allowing cities to adopt more restrictive regulation of billboards than under previous state law.

Sport has become another "arena in which the alcohol industry tests the limits of alcohol regulations and the elasticity of ethical rubberbands" (Rekve, forthcoming). In Europe and Scandinavia, national television channels can be viewed from neighbouring countries and language presents little barrier to basic marketing messages. Alcohol advertising at major sporting events frequently circumvents alcohol advertising bans or codes of practice in different countries. In countries that permit broadcast alcohol advertisements and those that do not, the association between alcohol and sports is pursued through the mass media in ways that most codes do little to restrain.

These controversies highlight questions about exactly what marketing practices a code should cover. What is "alcohol advertising", as opposed to programme content (Casswell, 1995b), or drinking venue management, or packaging and delivery, or corporate sponsorship of community activities? Although television commands the widest attention, it is by no means the only medium used to market alcohol, neither are formal advertisements always considered by advertisers as the most effective means (Casswell, 1995b; Clark, 1989). The wider the range of activities and the greater the number of players, however, the less effective self-regulation is likely to be (Ayres & Braithwaite, 1992).

CODES IRRELEVANT TO HOW ADVERTISING AND PROMOTION WORKS

An effect of industry self-regulation through voluntary codes is that the struggle over policy is diverted from the essential question of whether it serves the public interest to allow promotion of products that have considerable adverse impact on public health. Instead, energy is focused on continually refining the letter of codes, the detail of what does or does not constitute responsible advertising and what forms of marketing should be covered, in constant reaction to unacceptable practices. However, most codes are irrelevant to the way successful advertising actually works to reinforce current behaviour and the wider culture around drinking, and to recruit new generations of drinkers.

For example, codes on advertising standards commonly state that actors in alcohol ads must be adults. This restriction has little meaning, since studies of advertising for other products show that children generally desire what they see being enjoyed by a child a couple of years older (Clark, 1989). The young consume more television and more advertising than adults, like it more and are more influenced by it (Craplet, 1997; Eigen, 1996). To attract alcohol brand allegiance in the key market of young adult males, many advertisements simply depict the young adult life-styles that adolescents aspire to and associate them with the brand. Alcohol advertising has no need to show underage drinkers, sexual or other success—or even the product—when what it is selling is desired life-styles and fantasies.

Similarly, while codes explicitly prohibit the portrayal of intoxication, research suggests that advertisements do communicate the concept of intoxication (Rantila, 1993) and young recipients perceive intoxication and heavy consumption (Wyllie et al., 1997).

Moreover, the alcohol industry finds ample opportunities to associate its products positively with desired life-styles, of young people and others, as they are actually being lived. It is no longer appropriate to consider the effects of mass media advertising in isolation from other marketing tools (Stewart & Rice, 1995).

CONCLUSIONS

In the alcohol research field it is recognized that public health is a collective activity. Health goals for populations require ensuring that all public policies take health effects and health economics into account in setting priorities and in shaping social and physical environments, so that the healthy choice is the easy choice (Milio, 1988; Lehto, 1997). Marketing of alcohol, the research suggests, has a negative effect on the environment which helps shape individuals' choices.

Control strategies adopted at the level of the state face the increasing globalization of the alcohol industry and its marketing strategies. Policy and forms of regulation dictate the forms of promotion and circumventory tactics adopted by alcohol advertisers, but discussion about which marketing strategy, or which policy intervention or health promotion strategy, is more effective misses a key point. Modern marketing delivers through integrated packages of promotions, in which one type complements and "leverages" another. Regulatory practices and health promotion need similarly to consider and cover all the bases.

The ground contested between public health advocates and the alcohol industry can shift from the detail of legislation or codes of practices to the ideological climate in which policy decisions are made, or to shaping public opinion in ways that can affect the political acceptability of certain strategies to protect the public health. Such efforts on the part of the liquor and hospitality industries are no less important to the promotion of alcohol and the profitability of the industries than the marketing strategies themselves.

The need to develop an internationally coordinated response is increasingly clear (Eurocare, 1998), particularly with regard to broadcasting and to Internet promotions. Research evidence in this chapter supports policy action against the promotion of alcohol on the powerful broadcast media. In many countries, cultural linkages between sport, alcohol, masculinity and nationalism need to be targeted by health promoters and policy-makers.

One possible strategy is Norway's current promotion of sport as an "alcohol-free zone", with a local club focus on young players, family involvement and safety.

Nevertheless, at the national level, one strategy does not fit all. Different responses adopted by comparable countries provide valuable opportunities to learn from the experiences of others. However, responses are necessarily embedded in local contexts, and these will shape choices of national strategy that are both politically possible and likely to be effective.

NOTE

The focus of this chapter does not include fair trading and product description laws (both general and specific to alcohol) that impact on advertising and labelling, which are often elaborate in regard to wine. Neither does it cover—but readers may interested to note—a US trade law limiting vertical integration of alcohol and hospitality industries through restrictions on producers contributing financially to advertising by alcohol retail outlets and venues.

ACKNOWLEDGEMENT

This work was supported by programme funding from the Health Research Council of New Zealand and the Alcohol Advisory Council.

KEY WORKS AND SUGGESTIONS FOR FURTHER READING

Casswell, S. (1995a).   Does alcohol advertising have an impact on the public health? *Drug and Alcohol Review*, **14**, 395–404.

Draws on recent New Zealand and international research to examine a number of questions about the possible public health impact of policy which allows alcohol to be advertising on the broadcast media. The 1994 Leonard Ball Oration.

Casswell, S. & Zhang, J.F. (1998).   Impact of liking for advertising and brand allegiance on drinking and alcohol-related aggression: a longitudinal study. *Addiction*, **93**, 1209–1217.

Analysis of alcohol data from a longitudinal study of childhood development showed a measurable impact of advertising during a time of decline in aggregate alcohol consumption in New Zealand.

Buchanan, D.R. & Lev, J. (1989).   *Beer and Fast Cars: How Brewers Target Blue-collar Youth through Motor Sport Sponsorships*. Washington, DC: AAA Foundation for Traffic Safety.

Uncovers the many ways in which the association of alcohol with sport embeds drinking and brands to enjoyable lived experiences. Readers will readily recognize these strategies being used in relation to other sports and cultural events. For a general audience.

Clark, E. (1989).   *The Want Makers. Lifting the Lid of the World Advertising Industry*. London: Hodder and Stoughton.

A classic analysis of advertising strategies, for a general audience, with case studies of US alcohol and tobacco advertising.

Internet web-sites.

Readers are recommended to explore Internet addresses for various industry websites and advertising standards codes. Examples of campaigns against alcohol advertising can be found at: http://www.cspinet.org/booze/index.html (Centre for Science in the Public Interest, Washington); and http://www.apolnet.web.net/index.html (Alcohol Policy Network, Toronto); or check out how alcohol advertising appeals to kids by searching "Budweiser frog".

REFERENCES

Abrahamson, M. (1998).   Humour and mundane reason about alcohol drinking. Paper presented to the 24th Annual Alcohol Epidemiology Symposium of the Kettil Bruun Society, Florence, 1–5 June.

Advertising Standards Authority Inc. (ASA) (1998).   *Advertising Codes of Practice.* Wellington, New Zealand: ASA.

Advertising Standards Authority of Ireland (ASAI) (1999).   *Code of Advertising Standards for Ireland: Alcoholic Drinks.* http://www.asai.ie/ (as at May 1999).

Advertising Standards Authority. (1999).   *The British Codes of Advertising and Sales Promotion.* http://www.asa.org.uk (as at May 1999).

Advertising Standards Board (ASB) (1998, July).   *The Alcohol Beverages Advertising Code (ABAC) and Complaints Management System.* Sydney: ASB.

Advertising Standards Canada (ASC) (1999).   *Les Normes Canadienne de la Publicité.* http://www.canad.com/ (as at May 1999).

Aitken, P.P., Eadie, D.R., Leathar, D.S., McNeill, R.E. & Scott, A.C. (1988).   Television advertisements for alcoholic drinks do reinforce under-age drinking. *British Journal of Addiction*, **83**, 1399–1419.

Atkin, C. (1995).   Survey and experimental research on alcohol advertising. In S.E. Martin (Ed.), *Effects of the Mass Media on the Use and Abuse of Alcohol.* NIAAA Research Monograph 28. Bethesda, MD: US Department of Health and Human Services.

Atkin, C. & Block, N. (1981).   *Content and Effects of Alcohol Advertising.* US National Technical Information Service.

Atkin, C. & Block, N. (1984).   The effects of alcohol advertising. In T.C. Kinnear (Ed.), *Advances in Consumer Research* (pp. 688–693). Provo, UT: Association for Consumer Research.

Atkin, C., Neuendorf, K. & McDermott, S. (1983).   The role of alcohol advertising in excessive and hazardous drinking. *Journal of Drug Education*, **13**, 313–323.

Ayres, I. & Braithwaite, J. (1992).   *Responsive Regulation: Transcending the Deregulation Debate.* New York: Oxford University Press.

Babor, T.E., Edwards, G. & Stockwell, T. (1996).   Science and the drinks industry: cause for concern. *Addiction*, **91**, 5–9.

Baggott, R. (1989).   Regulatory reform in Britain: the changing face of self-regulation. *Public Administration*, **67**, 435–454.

Baird, R. (1998).   Big brands join £60 m FA package. *Marketing Week*, **21**(16), 9.

Bandura, A. (1977).   *Social Learning Theory.* Englewood Cliffs, NJ: Prentice-Hall.

Beer Institute. (1999).   *Advertising and Marketing Code, Washington, DC.* http://www.-beerinst.org/education/advert.html (as at 25.10.99).

Bentler, P.M. (1993).   *EQS: Structural Equations Program Manual.* Los Angeles, CA: BMDP Statistical Software.

Board of Science and Education (1999).   *Alcohol and Young People.* London: British Medical Association.

Boddewyn, J.J. (1995).   Advertising self-regulation: organization structures in Belgium, Canada, France and the United Kingdom. In W. Streeck & P.C. Schmitter (Eds), *Private Interest Government: Beyond State and Market.* London: Sage.

Bourgeois, J.C. & Barnes, J.G. (1979). Does advertising increase consumption? *Journal of Advertising Research*, **19**, 19–29.

Breed, W.A. & DeFoe, J.R. (1979). Themes in magazine alcohol advertisements. *Journal of Drug Issues*, **9**, 511–522.

Buchanan, D.R. & Lev, J. (1989). *Beer and Fast Cars: How Brewers Target Blue-collar Youth through Motor Sport Sponsorships*. Washington, DC: AAA Foundation for Traffic Safety.

Calfee, J.E. & Scheraga, C. (1994). The influence of advertising on alcohol consumption: a literature review and an econometric analysis of four European nations. *International Journal of Advertising*, **13**, 287–310.

Canadian Radio and Television Commission (CRTC) (1996). *Code for Broadcasting Advertising of Alcoholic Beverages.* http://www.crtc.gc.ca/ENG/general/codes/alcohole.htm (CRTC, 1998).

Casswell, S. (1995a). Does alcohol advertising have an impact on the public health? *Drug and Alcohol Review*, **14**, 395–404.

Casswell, S. (1995b). Public discourse on alcohol: implications for public policy. In H.D. Holder & G. Edwards (Eds), *Alcohol and Public Policy: Evidence and Issues*. Oxford: Oxford University Press.

Casswell, S. (1997). Public discourse on alcohol. *Health Promotion International*, **12**, 251–257.

Casswell, S. & Zhang, J.F. (1998). Impact of liking for advertising and brand allegiance on drinking and alcohol-related aggression: a longitudinal study. *Addiction*, **93**, 1209–1217.

Casswell, S., Pledger, M. & Pratap, S. (2002). Trajectories of drinking from 18 to 26: Identification and prediction. *Addiction*, **97**, 1427–1437.

Casswell, S., Ransom, R. & Gilmore, L. (1990). Evaluation of a mass-media campaign for the primary prevention of alcohol-related problems. *Health Promotion International*, **5**, 9–17.

Casswell, S., Stewart, L. & Duignan, P. (1993a). The negotiation of New Zealand alcohol policy in a decade of stabilised consumption and political change: The role of research. *Addiction*, **88**(Suppl.), 9S–17S.

Casswell, S., Zhang, J.F. & Wyllie, A. (1993b). The importance of amount and location of drinking for the experience of alcohol related problems. *Addiction*, **88**, 1527–1534.

Center for Alcohol Advertising (1998). *Hands off Halloween, 1998: History of Hands off Halloween and the Responsible Merchants Campaign*. Berkeley, CA: Center for Alcohol Advertising.

Center for Science in the Public Interest (1998). *A Rough Chronology of Broadcast Liquor Advertising Controversy, 1996–1998*. http://www.cspinet.org/booze/chronolo.htm

Clark, E. (1989). *The Want Makers. Lifting the Lid of the World Advertising Industry*. London: Hodder and Stoughton.

Connolly, G., Casswell, S., Zhang, J.F. & Silva, P.A. (1994). Alcohol in the mass media and drinking by adolescents: a longitudinal study. *Addiction*, **89**, 1255–1263.

Covell, K. (1992). The appeal of image advertisements: age, gender, and product differences. *Journal of Early Adolescence*, **12**, 46–60.

Craplet, M. (1997). Alcohol advertising: the need for European regulation. *Commercial Communications: The Journal of Advertising and Marketing Policy and Practice in the European Community*, **9**, 1–3.

Deeks, J. (1992). Who's choking smoking? Advertising, sponsorship and government regulation of the tobacco industry. In J. Deeks & N. Perry (Eds), *Controlling Interests: Business, the State and Society in New Zealand*. Auckland: Auckland University Press.

Distilled Spirits Council of the US (DISCUS) (1996). *Fact Sheet: Beverage Alcohol Advertising: A Constitutionally Protected Right*. http://www.discus.health.org (dated 25.10.96, sighted 13.5.99).

Distilled Spirits Council of the US (DISCUS) (1998). *A Code of Good Practice for Distilled Spirits Advertising and Marketing*. http://www.discus.health.org/newcode.htm (dated 4.3.1998, sighted 13.5.99).

Duffy, M. (1981). The influence of prices, consumer incomes and advertising upon the demand for alcoholic drink in the United Kingdom: an econometric study. *British Journal on Alcohol and Alcoholism*, **16**, 200–208.

Edwards, G., Anderson, P., Babor, T. et al. (1994). *Alcohol Policy and the Public Good*. Oxford: Oxford University Press.

Eigen, L.D. (1996). The young and restless: Generation X and alcohol policy. Paper presented to Alcohol Policy X Conference, Toronto, 5 May.

Eurocare (1998). *Counterbalancing the drinks industry: a summary of the Eurocare report on alcohol policy in the European Union.* http://www.eurocare.org/counterbalancing/ (November 1998).

Federal Trade Commission (FTC) (1999). *Self-regulation in the Alcohol Industry: A Review of Industry Efforts to Avoid Promoting Alcohol to Underage Consumers.* http://www.ftc.gov/reports/alchol/alcholreport.htm (September).

Fillmore, K.M., Golding, J.M., Graves, K.L., Kniep, S., Leino, E.V., Romelsjo, A., Shoemaker, C., Ager, C.R., Allebeck, P. & Ferrer, H.P. (1998). Alcohol consumption and mortality. III. Studies of female populations. *Addiction*, **93**, 219–230.

Gerbner, G., Gross, L. & Morgan, M. (1986). Living with television: the dynamics of the cultivation process. In J. Bryant & D. Zillman (Eds), *Perspectives on Media Effects* (pp. 17–40). Hillsdale, NJ: Erlbaum.

Grabosky, P.N. (1995). Using non-governmental resources to foster regulatory compliance. *Governance*, **8**, 527–550.

Grabowski, H. (1976). The effects of advertising on inter-industry distribution of demand. *Explorations in Economic Research*, **3**, 21–75.

Greenfield, T.K. (1997). Warning labels: evidence on harm-reduction from long-term American surveys. In M. Plant, E. Single & T. Stockwell (Eds), *Alcohol: Minimising the Harm*. London: Free Association Books.

Grube, J.W. & Wallack, L. (1994). The effects of television beer advertising on children. *American Journal of Public Health*, **84**, 254–259.

Gual, A. & Colom, J. (1997). Why has alcohol consumption declined in countries of southern Europe? *Addiction*, **92**(1), S21–S32.

Hill, L. (1999). What it means to be a Lion Red man: alcohol advertising and Kiwi masculinity. *Women's Studies Journal*, **1**, 65–85.

Hill, L. & Stewart, L. (1996). The Sale of Liquor Act, 1989: reviewing regulatory practices. *Social Policy Journal of New Zealand*, **7**, 174–190.

Holder, H.D. (1994). Public health approaches to the reduction of alcohol problems. *Substance Abuse*, **15**, 123–138.

Holder, H.D. & Edwards, G. (1995). *Alcohol and Public Policy*. Oxford: Oxford University Press.

Hundt, R. (1997). *Statement of FCC Chairman Reed Hundt on Broadcast Advertisements of Hard Liquor*. Washington: Federal Communications Commission, 9 July.

Hunter Monthly Media Expenditure Analysis (1997). *Estimated Industry Alcohol Advertising Expenditure and Alcohol Health Promotion Expenditure*. All media, December.

Jernigan, D. (1997). *Thirsting for Markets*. San Rafael, CA: Marin Institute.

Kelder, S.H., Perry, C.L. & Klepp, K.-I. (1994). Longitudinal tracing of adolescent smoking, physical activity and food choice behaviours. *American Journal of Public Health*, **84**, 1121–1126.

Kelly, K.J. & Edwards, R.W. (1998). Image advertisements for alcohol products: is their appeal associated with adolescents' intention to consume alcohol? *Adolescence*, **33**(129), 47–59.

Kohn, P.M. & Smart, R.G. (1984). The impact of television advertising on alcohol consumption: an experiment. *Journal of Studies on Alcohol*, **45**, 295–301.

Kohn, P.M., Smart, R.G. & Ogborne, A.C. (1984). Effects of two kinds of alcohol advertising on subsequent consumption. *Journal of Advertising*, **13**, 34–48.

Lannon, J. & Cooper, P. (1983). Humanistic advertising: a holistic cultural perspective. *International Journal of Advertising*, **2**, 195–213.

Law, R. (1997). Masculinity, place and beer advertising in New Zealand: the Southern Man campaign. *New Zealand Geographer*, **53**(2), 22–28.

Lehto, J. (1997). The economics of alcohol. *Addiction*, **92**(Suppl.), S55–S60.

Leiber, L. (1998). *Commercial and Character Slogan Recall by Children Aged 9–11 Years: Budweiser Frogs versus Bugs Bunny*. Berkeley, CA: Center on Alcohol Advertising.

Leino, E.V., Romelsjo, A., Shoemaker, C., Ager, C.R., Allebeck, P., Ferrer, H.P., Fillmore, K.M., Golding, J.M., Graves K.L. & Kneip, S. (1998). Alcohol consumption and mortality: studies of male populations. *Addiction*, **93**, 205–218.

Lieberman, L.R. & Orlandi, M.A. (1987). Alcohol advertising and adolescent drinking. *Alcohol Health and Research World*, **12**, 30–33, 43.

Lipsitz, A., Brake, G., Vincent, E.J. & Winters, M. (1993). Another round for the brewers: television ads and children's alcohol expectancies. *Journal of Applied Social Psychology*, **23**, 439–450.

Madden, P.A. & Grube, J.W. (1994). The frequency and nature of alcohol and tobacco advertising in televised sports, 1990–1992. *American Journal of Public Health*, **84**, 297–299.

Makowsky, C.R. & Whitehead, P.C. (1991). Advertising and alcohol studies: a legal impact study. *Journal of Studies on Alcohol*, **52**, 555–567.

Marin Institute for the Prevention of Alcohol and Other Drug Problems (1998). Big alcohol's smokescreen. *Newsletter*, **Winter**, 1–6.

Maskill, C. & Hodges, I. (1997). *Alcohol Messages on New Zealand Radio, 1995/96*. Wellington: Alcohol Advisory Council.

McCarty, D. & Ewing, J.A. (1983). Alcohol consumption while viewing alcoholic beverage advertising. *International Journal of the Addictions*, **18**, 1011–1018.

McCombs, M.E. & Shaw, D.L. (1972). The agenda-setting function of the mass media. *Public Opinion Quarterly*, **36**, 176–187.

McGuiness, T. (1980). An econometric analysis of total demand for alcoholic beverages in the UK, 1956–1975. *Journal of Industrial Economics*, **29**, 85–109.

McGuiness, T. (1983). The demand for beer, wine and spirits in the UK, 1956–1979. In M. Grant, M. Plant & A. Williams (Eds), *Economics and Alcohol: Consumption and Controls*. London: Croom Helm.

Meier, K. (1991). Tobacco truths: the impact of role models on children's attitudes towards smoking. *Health Education Quarterly*, **18**, 173–182.

Milio, N. (1988). Masking healthy public policy: developing the science by learning the art; an ecological framework for policy studies. *Health Promotion*, **2**, 263–274.

Montgomery, K. (1997). *Alcohol and Tobacco on the Web: New Threats to Young. Executive Summary*. Washington, DC: Center for Media Education (March).

Montonen, M. (1996). *Alcohol and the Media*. WHO Regional Publications, European series No. 62. Genera: World Health Organization.

Mosher, J.F. (1982). Federal tax law and public health policy: the case of alcohol-related tax expenditures. *Journal of Public Health Policy*, **34**(23), 260–283.

Mosher, J.F. & Jernigan, D.H. (1989). New directions in alcohol policy. *Annual Review of Public Health*, **10**, 245–279.

Mosher, J.F. & Wallack, L.M. (1979). Proposed reforms in the regulation of alcoholic beverage advertising. *Contemporary Drug Problems*, **Summer**, 87–106.

Moskowitz, J.M. (1989). The primary prevention of alcohol problems: a critical review of the research literature. *Journal of Studies on Alcohol*, **50**, 54–88.

Ogborne, A.C. & Smart, R.G. (1980). Will restrictions on alcohol advertising reduce alcohol consumption? *British Journal of Addiction*, **75**, 293–229.

O'Neil, R.M. (1997). Mr Jefferson, distilled spirits and TV ads. *Commercial Speech Digest*, Washington DC: The Media Institute (Spring).

Ornstein, S. & Hanssens, D. (1985). Alcohol control laws and the consumption of distilled spirits and beer. *Journal of Consumer Research*, **12**, 200–213.

Partanen, J. & Montonen, M. (1988). *Alcohol and the Mass Media*. EURO Reports and Studies No. 108. Copenhagen: World Health Organization Regional Office for Europe.

Pedlowe, G. (1998). Alcohol in emerging markets: identifying the most appropriate role for the alcohol industry. In M. Grant (Ed.), *Alcohol and Emerging Markets: Patterns, Problems and Responses*. Washington, DC: ICAP.

Petty, R. & Cacioppo, J. (1981). *Attitudes and Persuasion: Classic and Contemporary Approaches*. Dubrique, IA: William C. Brown.

Phillips, J. (1984). Rugby, war and the mythology of the NZ male. *New Zealand Journal of History*, **18**.

Pollay, R.W., Siddarth, S., Siegel, M., Haddix, A. et al. (1996). The last straw? Cigarette advertising and realized market shares among youths and adults, 1979–1993. *Journal of Marketing*, **60**(2), 1–16.

Postman, N., Nystrom, C., Strate, L. & Weingartner, C. (1988). *Myths, Men and Beer: An Analysis of Beer Commercials on Broadcast Television, 1987*. Falls Church: AAA Foundation for Traffic Safety.

Quello, R. (1997). *Statement of Commissioner James H. Quello re: Proposed Notice of Inquiry on Broadcast Advertisement of Distilled Spirits*. Washington, DC: Federal Communications Commission (9 July).

Rantila, K. (1993). Greimas och olreklamens magi [Greimas and the magic of beer commercials]. *Nordisk Alkoholtidskrift*, **10**, 70–80.

Rearck Research (1991). *A Study of Attitudes towards Alcohol Consumption, Labelling and Advertising.* A report prepared for the Dept of Community Services and Health, Canberra.

Rekve, D. (1997). *Status Report from a Joint Project between Alkokutt and the Norwegian Football Association.* Oslo: Alkokutt (March). http://www.alkokutt.no/english/

Rekve, D. (forthcoming). *Foul! Sports Sponsorship and the Drinks Industry: The Big Mis-Match.* Oslo: Alkokutt.

Room, R. (1989). Cultural changes in drinking and trends in alcohol problems indicators: Recent US experience. *Alcologia,* **1,** 83–89.

Saffer, H. (1991). Alcohol advertising bans and alcohol abuse: an international perspective. *Journal of Health Economics,* **10,** 65–79.

Saffer, H. (1993). Alcohol advertising bans and alcohol abuse: reply. *Journal of Health Economics,* **12,** 229–234.

Saffer, H. (1997). Alcohol advertising and motor vehicle fatalities. *Review of Economics and Statistics,* **79,** 431–442.

Saffer, H. & Daue, D. (2002). Alcohol consumption and alcohol advertising bans. *Applied Economics,* **30,** 1325–1334.

Saunders, B. & Yap, E. (1991). Do our guardians need guarding? An examination of the Australian system of self-regulation of alcohol advertising. *Drug and Alcohol Review,* **10,** 15–17.

Schweitzer, S.O., Intriligator, M.D. & Salehi, H. (1983). Alcoholism: an econometric model of its causes, its effects and its control. In M. Grant, M. Plant & A. Williams (Eds), *Economics and Alcohol: Consumption and Controls.* London: Croom Helm.

Secretary of State for Health. With Secretaries of State for Scotland, Wales and Northern Ireland *Smoking kills: A White Paper on Tobacco.* (1998). London: The Stationary Office (30 November).

Shanahan, P. & Hewitt, N. (1999). *Developmental Research for a National Alcohol Campaign.* Canberra: Summary report to the Commonwealth Department of Health and Aged Care.

Slater, M.D. & Domenech, M.M. (1995). Alcohol warnings in TV beer advertisements. *Journal of Studies on Alcohol,* **56,** 361–367.

Slater, M.D., Murphy, K., Beauvais, F., Rouner, D., van Leuven, J. & Domenech Rodriguez, M.M. (1995). *Modeling Predictors of Alcohol Use and Use Intentions among Adolescent Anglo Males: Social, Psychological, and Advertising Influences.* Annual Conference of the Research Society on Alcoholism, Steamboat Springs, CO, June.

Smart, R.G. & Cutler, R.E. (1976). The alcohol advertising ban in British Colombia: problems and effects on beverage consumption. *British Journal of Addiction,* **71,** 13–21.

Synder, L.B. & Blood, D.J. (1992). Caution: alcohol advertising and the Surgeon General's alcohol warnings may have adverse effects on young adults. *Journal of Applied Communication Research,* **20,** 37–53.

Sobell, L.C., Sobell, M.B., Riley, D.M., Klajner, F., Leo, G.I., Pavan, D. & Cancilla, A. (1986). Effect of television programming and advertising on alcohol consumption in normal drinkers. *Journal of Studies on Alcohol,* **47,** 333–339.

Star, L. (1993). Macho and his brothers: passion and resistance in sports discourse. *Sites,* **26,** 54–78.

Starek, R.B. (1997). *Advertising Alcohol and the First Amendment Address to the American Bar Association Section of Administrative Law and Regulatory Practice Committee on Beverage Alcohol Practice,* San Francisco, CA, 4 August.

Stewart, D.W. & Rice, R. (1995). Non-traditional media and promotions in the marketing of alcoholic beverages. In S.E. Martin (Ed.), *The Effects of the Mass Media on the Use and Abuse of Alcohol.* Bethesda, MD: US Dept of Health and Human Services.

Stewart, L. (1997). Approaches to preventing alcohol-related problems: the experience of New Zealand and Australia. *Drug and Alcohol Review,* **16,** 391–399.

Stewart, L. & Casswell, S. (1990). Creating a supportive environment for drinking: the alcohol industry as a drug educator. *Drug Education Journal of Australia,* **4**(3), 225–231.

Stockwell, T., Single, E. Hawkes, D. & Rehm, J. (1997). Sharpening the focus of alcohol policy from aggregate consumption to harm and risk reduction. *Addiction Research,* **5,** 1–9.

Stockwell, T., Somerford, P. & Lang, E. (1992). The relationship between licence type and alcohol related problems attributed to licensed premises in Perth, Western Australia. *Journal of Studies on Alcohol,* **53,** 495–498.

Strickland, D.E. (1982). Alcohol advertising: orientations and influence. *International Journal of Advertising,* **1,** 307–319.

Taylor, T. (1999).   Audience info the key to sports marketers. *Marketing News*, **33**(2), 10.

The Globe (1997).   *Alcopops under Fire in the European Union, 1* (pp. 10–11). London: Institute for Alcohol Studies.

Thomson, A., Casswell, S. & Stewart, L. (1994).   Communication experts' opinions on alcohol advertising in the electronic media. *Health Promotion International*, **9**, 145–152.

Vaidya, S.G., Naik, U.C. & Vaidya, J.S. (1996).   Effect of sports sponsorship by tobacco companies on children's experimentation with tobacco. *British Medical Journal*, **17 August**, 313.

van Iwaarden, M.J. (1985).   Public health aspects of the marketing of alcoholic drinks. In M. Grant (Ed.), *Alcohol Policies* (pp. 45–55). European Series No. 18. Copenhagen: WHO Regional Publications.

Wallack, L. (1983).   Mass media campaigns in a hostile environment: advertising as anti-health education. *Journal of Alcohol and Drug Education*, **28**, 51–63.

Walsh, B. (1997).   Trends in alcohol production, trade and consumption. *Addiction*, **92**(1), S61–S66.

Watson, R.T., Akselsen, S. & Pitt, L.F. (1998).   Attractors: building mountains in the flat landscape of the World Wide Web. *California Management Review*, **40**(2), 36–56.

Wiecking, F. (1999).   *FTC Report Downplays Failure of Alcoholic-beverage Advertisers to Comply with Their Own Advertising Standards.* Statement by Manager for Federal Affairs, Center for Science in the Public Interest, 10 September.

Wilks, J., Vardenega, A.T. & Callan, V.J. (1992).   Effect of television advertising on alcohol consumption and intentions to drive. *Drug and Alcohol Review*, **11**, 15–21.

Wine Institute (1999).   *Code of advertising standards, San Francisco.* http://www.wineinstitute.org/adcodewi.htm (as at 25.10.99).

World Health Organization (1998).   *Health 21: An Introduction to the Health for All Policy Framework for the WHO European Region.* Copenhagen: WHO.

Wyllie, A., Millard, M. & Zhang, J.F. (1996a).   *Drinking in New Zealand: A National Survey, 1995.* Auckland: Alcohol & Public Health Research Unit.

Wyllie, A., Holibar, F., Casswell, S., Fuamatu, N., Aioluputea, K., Moewaka Barnes, H. & Panapa, A. (1997).   A qualitative investigation of responses to televised alcohol advertisements. *Contemporary Drug Problems*, **24**, 103–132.

Wyllie, A., Waa, A. & Zhang, J.F. (1996b).   *Alcohol and Moderation Advertising Expenditure and Exposure.* Auckland: Alcohol & Public Health Research Unit.

Wyllie, A., Zhang, J.F. & Casswell, S. (1998a).   Positive responses to televised beer advertisements associated with drinking and problems reported by 18–29 year-olds. *Addiction*, **93**, 749–760.

Wyllie, A., Zhang, J.F. & Casswell, S. (1998b).   Responses to televised alcohol advertisements associated with drinking behaviour of 10–17 year-olds. *Addiction*, **93**, 361–371.

APPENDIX: RESTRICTIONS ON ALCOHOL ADVERTISING: EXAMPLES SHOWING INTERNATIONAL DIVERSITY

Australia

The Australian Association of National Advertisers has set up an Advertising Standards Board and an Advertising Claims Board, and established a new code of ethics. It has no powers of enforcement; however, relying on "the willingness of advertisers to adhere voluntarily to ethical standards". A new code on liquor advertising was adopted in 1998 after a 2 year hiatus, during which only a general Commercial Television Industry Code of Practice applied. An earlier code collapsed in 1996 when the Competition and Consumers Commission revoked authorizations to the Media Council of Australia following public criticism.

Austria

Legal ban on spirits advertising on radio; otherwise a voluntary code.

Belgium

No commercial advertising on state television, and legal ban on spirits advertising on commercial television. No alcohol advertising on radio. In other media, voluntary guidelines prohibit the encouragement of "drinking to excess" and advertisements targeted at the under-21s.

Canada

A statutory body, the Canadian Radio and Television Commission, code governs alcohol ads. Also provincial codes on all alcohol advertising as part of regulations and guidelines under provincial Acts covering state monopoly over distribution and off-sales and state licensing of drinking venues. Detailed rules on giving out samples of alcohol. Restrictions on gifts, prizes and premiums.

Denmark

Television and radio advertisements are not permitted for alcohol over 2.25% alcohol by volume (i.e. low-alcohol beer may be advertised). Other media must not aim alcohol advertisements at minors. In 1999 negotiations for guidelines allowing corporate logos and light beer ads on sports clothes failed.

Finland

Formerly, legal ban on alcohol advertising. Now, advertising permitted of beer and wine up to 22% alcohol by volume.

France

A legal ban since 1987 on television ads. The Loi Evin bans ads for alcohol over 1% alcohol by volume on television and in publications for young people and in places where sports events are held. Ad content is also controlled by law, not a voluntary code. In other media, alcohol advertisements must focus on product characteristics only, advise that alcohol abuse is bad for your health, and be pre-approved.

Greece

There are no specific restrictions other than limitations on the number of ads per day for each brand on television and radio.

Germany

By voluntary agreement, most spirits are not advertised on television. On other media, a voluntary code is in operation, similar to that in the UK.

Italy

Alcohol advertisements on television may be shown only after 8 p.m. A voluntary code similar to that in the UK governs content.

Ireland

A legal ban on spirits advertising on television and radio, and alcohol advertisements may not be shown before sports programmes. The same ad may not appear more than twice per night on any one channel. On other media a voluntary code on alcohol is one of a set of codes of the Advertising Standards Authority of Ireland.

Luxembourg

Television and radio advertisements must not show alcohol being consumed "in excess or feature young people, or sportsmen or drivers consuming alcohol". Otherwise no restrictions.

New Zealand

Advertising standards shifted to self-regulation with commercialization of the broadcasting media, under an Advertising Standards Authority (ASA) set up by statute. Outlet ads, then sponsorship ads, then brand advertising in 1992, were permitted without reference to Parliament. A Broadcasting Standards Authority is responsible for "saturation" and alcohol in programme content. The ASA's Code on Liquor Advertising now covers all brand and sponsorship advertising. Ads are pre-vetted. The Complaints Board and review committees have some non-industry members.

Norway

Advertising of alcoholic beverages or alcoholic beverage products is prohibited, including in advertisements for other goods and services. This has limited alcohol marketing opportunities on sports grounds and on sports team clothing. Visiting international teams have been required to comply with this.

Portugal

No alcohol advertising on television before 10 p.m. and advertisements must not show alcohol being consumed.

Spain

A ban on television and radio advertising of spirits and alcohol over 23% alcohol by volume. Other alcohol advertisements may be shown only after 9.30 p.m. A ban on all television spirits advertising in the Basque country.

Sweden

Since July 1979, there has been a ban on beer, wine and spirits, except for beer under 2.25% alcohol, with restrictions on ad content on showing intoxication, etc. Some advertising of beer up to 3.5% showing only bottle and manufacturer. New proposals following a 1999 review are likely to tighten these regulations in 1999.

Switzerland

Law prohibits comparing or publishing alcohol prices and restricts advertising, especially at sports meetings or events for young people. Alcohol ads are restricted to information and descriptions directly related to the product. But this policy is undermined by ads, particularly on television, coming from neighbouring countries.

The Netherlands

In 1987 a bill to prohibit all alcohol advertising on broadcast media was defeated. Since 1990 the liquor industry, including retail, follows a voluntary code developed by the Stichting Zelfregulering Alcoholbranche. Its complaints committee can fine up to 50,000 guilders. Ads can be for individual brands but no corporate ads; sports sponsorship is limited. A moderation message must be included in 40% of audio-visual ads. Ads should not encourage minors to drink.

UK

The BBC does not carry advertising. Alcohol advertising on other television and radio stations is the responsibility of statutory bodies, the Independent Broadcasting Authority and the Cable Authority, whose codes of practice cover alcohol advertising. A 1965 voluntary agreement between manufacturers and TV companies not to advertise spirits was abandoned in 1995.

Alcohol advertising in other media comes under a voluntary code, the Advertising Standards Authority's British Code of Advertising and Sales Promotion, which now limits advertising where more than a quarter of the audience is like to be under 18. It also governs the way alcohol or people drinking is presented in ads for other products.

Under all codes, advertisements should not encourage excessive drinking, market to audiences under 18 or depict drinkers under 25, characters likely to appeal to those under 18, activities or location where alcohol would be unsafe, or suggest that alcohol enhances mental, physical or sexual capabilities, popularity, masculinity, femininity or sporting achievement.

In 1996, complaints about "alcopops", containing 5% alcohol and being marketed to young people alongside soft drinks, led the Portman Group to promote its own limited industry code. This averted a proposed ban on the words "lemonade" or "cola" on mixed drink containers.

USA

Beer and wine ads are permitted on radio and television, with alcohol industry codes for each. In California it is illegal to offer inducements to encourage drinking, such as give-aways recently offered in Budweiser ads.

Ads for spirits were kept off radio from 1936 and television from 1948 by a voluntary industry ban, broken in 1996 by Seagrams. Spirits ads now appear on local and cable channels, but are still refused by nearly all national networks. DISCUS wrote a code of conduct; its directors will consider any complaints.

A series of city ordinances restricting alcohol billboards met challenges in the Supreme Court but has now led to recent federal legislation allow greater city control over content and location.

South Africa

An Advertising Standards Authority of South Africa code of conduct governs advertising of alcohol. All forms of alcohol may be advertised freely on radio, television and in print. Sports sponsorship by the alcohol industry is very high, especially for cricket, rugby and soccer. In 1997 the Department of Health established a committee to look at counter-advertising and warning labels, and another to look at possible restrictions on broadcast advertising and sports sponsorships.

Sources: Institute for Alcohol Studies, London; Alcohol and Public Health Research Unit, New Zealand.

Author Index

Subject Index